Mac® Security Bible

Mac® Security Bible

Joe Kissell

WILEY

Wiley Publishing, Inc.

Mac® Security Bible

Published by
Wiley Publishing, Inc.
10475 Crosspoint Blvd.
Indianapolis, IN 46256
www.wiley.com

Copyright © 2010 by Wiley Publishing, Inc., Indianapolis, Indiana

Published by Wiley Publishing, Inc., Indianapolis, Indiana

Published simultaneously in Canada

ISBN: 978-0-470-47419-8

Manufactured in the United States of America

10 9 8 7 6 5 4 3 2 1

For general information on our other products and services or to obtain technical support, please contact our Customer Care Department within the U.S. at (877) 762-2974, outside the U.S. at (317) 572-3993 or fax (317) 572-4002.

Library of Congress Control Number: 2009941350

About the Author

Joe Kissell is the senior editor of *TidBITS*, a website and email newsletter about the Mac and the Internet, and the author of numerous print and electronic books about Mac software, including *Take Control of Mac OS X Backups* and *Take Control of Upgrading to Snow Leopard*. He's also a senior contributor to *Macworld* and was the winner of a 2009 Neal Award for Best How-To Article.

Joe has worked in the Mac software industry since the early 1990s and previously managed software development for Nisus Software and Kensington Technology Group. He was named one of MacTech's 25 most influential people in the Mac community for 2007.

When not writing about Macs, Joe likes to cook, travel, watch movies, and practice tai chi. He also runs a number of websites, including `JoeKissell.com` and the popular Interesting Thing of the Day (`itotd.com`). Joe lives in Paris with his wife, Morgen Jahnke, and their cat, Zora.

Credits

Acquisitions Editor
Aaron Black

Project Editor
Christopher Stolle

Technical Editor
Paul Sihvonen-Binder

Copy Editor
Scott Tullis

Editorial Director
Robyn Siesky

Editorial Manager
Cricket Krengel

Business Manager
Amy Knies

Senior Marketing Manager
Sandy Smith

Vice President and Executive Group Publisher
Richard Swadley

Vice President and Executive Publisher
Barry Pruett

Project Coordinator
Patrick Redmond

Graphics and Production Specialists
Jennifer Henry
Andrea Hornberger
Jennifer Mayberry

Quality Control Technician
John Greenough

Proofreading
Laura L. Bowman

Indexing
Broccoli Information Management

Acknowledgments

Of the many security researchers and experts whose work influenced and informed this book, I'd like to give special credit to Rich Mogull (http://securosis.com), Charles Edge (http://krypted.com), and Bruce Schneier (www.schneier.com). I hope I've done justice to their excellent insights; any errors or misinterpretations are my own. Even more credit is due to my wife, Morgen Jahnke, who was unfailingly supportive and encouraging during the long months I spent glued to my computer while writing this book.

Introduction

For years, one of the most compelling selling points of Macs has been their apparent freedom from many of the security problems that have long plagued Windows users. Countless people have switched to Macs because they want to stop worrying about viruses, spyware, and other threats so common to PC users. According to conventional wisdom (and even some Apple marketing), Macs are inherently much safer than Windows PCs — and, sure enough, millions of people use Macs every day without incident, having never given a moment's thought to security.

And yet, curiously, some guy seems to have come up with enough to say about Mac security to fill a rather thick and heavy book. How can that be? Are Macs really as insecure as other computers — and are Mac users a bunch of blissfully ignorant folks on the fast track to digital oblivion? Or are the supposed security risks to Mac users nothing more than fear-mongering on the part of an over-zealous publisher?

Although Macs have many effective security features and are, in my humble opinion, vastly superior to PCs for a long list of reasons, the truth of the matter is that a computer running Mac OS X isn't inherently more secure than a computer running Windows (at least if it's a recent version of Windows). Fabulous user interface and industrial design notwithstanding, Macs are still computers, and they're still vulnerable to the kinds of risks that can affect any other computer.

The main reason Mac users have largely escaped the threats of viruses and other malware is that most of the people creating such nasty software simply want the most bang for their buck — so they choose the platform with the biggest base of users. There's no technical reason devastating Mac viruses couldn't exist — and perhaps some day they will.

Be that as it may, malware is just one tiny piece of the security puzzle. Another piece is physical security — preventing theft and unauthorized access or tracking a stolen Mac. There's also the matter of keeping confidential data private, whether it's on disk, in an email message, or typed in a form on a web page. And let's not forget network security. Macs use the same public Internet as other computers and are just as prone to attacks from people sniffing network traffic, creating fraudulent websites, and stealing (or guessing) passwords. The list goes on and on — just take a look at the Table of Contents!

Mac users need to learn about security for the same reasons other computer users do. The fact that you have a better computer doesn't make you immune to the ever-expanding array of potential threats. If you've never had your data stolen or your password hacked, you may simply be lucky. I'm sorry to say that these kinds of things happen to Mac users every day.

Fortunately, Mac users are a smart bunch, and the aim of this book is to make you even smarter by educating you about the ins and outs of a topic that's received far too little attention. If you apply what you learn in this book, you'll be much less likely to suffer the kinds of damage and loss that are becoming so common among computer users of all kinds.

Unlike most books on computer security, this one is written for mere mortals. As often as possible, I've approached the subjects in this book from the perspective of an ordinary Mac user rather than a computer geek. Although a few topics do inevitably get a bit complex, I've done my best to present the information in a way that presupposes no particular technical knowledge. Even if you don't know the meaning of TCP, AES, VPN, and other TLAs (three-letter abbreviations), you should be able to jump right in and learn how to compute more safely — and without sacrificing convenience.

On the other hand, if you're an IT pro, there's also plenty of detailed information here for you, and you can feel free to explore some of the more advanced concepts and techniques that may be a bit daunting for the average user. Whether you have a single Mac at home or manage a whole network at your place of business, you should find enough information in this book to understand your risks and the measures necessary to address them.

How This Book Is Organized

This book is divided into five major sections, each corresponding to a different aspect of Mac security. Here's a quick overview of what you find in each part.

Part I: Mac Security Basics

In this part, I describe the variety of threats you may encounter, and I explain how to make informed decisions about how to balance your need for security with other priorities. This part of the book discusses anti-theft measures, introduces you to the major security features built into Mac OS X, and shows you how to configure user accounts and various other settings for best results. It also discusses in detail the many issues involving passwords in general and the Mac OS X Keychain in particular, how to share resources on your Mac securely, and how to back up your Mac's data.

Part II: Protecting Your Privacy

This part explains how to prevent others from seeing or hearing confidential data you create, send, receive, or store using your Mac. This part also discusses how to communicate securely by using instant messaging, voice over IP, email, and the web as well as the more general topic of how to encrypt all your network communications by using a virtual private network (VPN). It also covers a variety of ways to encrypt the data on your Mac's disk to prevent it from being read by a thief or hacker.

Part III: Network Security Fundamentals

This part focuses primarily on how to prevent an attacker from breaking into or snooping on your Mac over a network. It begins with a candid discussion of malware — and whether or to what extent you should use software to prevent it from causing damage. It then discusses the ways you can secure both wired and wireless networks against intrusions, how a firewall can protect your Mac from certain kinds of network traffic, and what special measures you should take if you use your Mac as a web server. It concludes with a discussion of how to use logs to track down certain problems after the fact and to discover potential security issues you may never have noticed otherwise.

Part IV: Advanced Security Measures

This part covers techniques that enable someone with better-than-average technical skills to delve deeper into Mac security. As such, it's directed primarily at people who must manage a number of Macs in a professional setting of some kind. If you're an individual Mac user without a lot of spare time on your hands, you can skip both Part IV and Part V or use them to solve other sorts of problems, such as insomnia. However, if you have a bit of geek mojo — you're comfortable using the command line, you know a few things about networking protocols, and you enjoy experimenting — you can use the information in this part to probe the Macs on your network for potential security problems, watch individual Macs for unauthorized file changes, and examine a Mac that's been compromised by malware or a hacker to find out what went wrong.

Part V: Securing Mac OS X Server

This part covers security considerations specific to Leopard Server and Snow Leopard Server. The server version of Mac OS X is identical in most respects to the standard version but includes additional software and configuration tools that enable a Mac (most often an Xserve or Mac Pro) to provide a wide range of services to other devices, whether on the local network or around the world. The extra features of Mac OS X Server, such as Open Directory and NFS file sharing, bring tremendous advantages to workgroups of nearly any size, but they also provide more potential avenues of attack and require additional steps to keep secure.

As enterprise servers go, Mac OS X Server is easy to configure and run, but even so, Apple provides thousands of pages of documentation in the form of PDF files available at `www.apple. com/server/macosx/resources/documentation.html`. One of these files, *Mac OS X Server Security Configuration*, contains nearly 500 pages of instruction and advice from Apple on keeping your server and your network secure. I mention it to emphasize that this book can address only a small portion of that subject matter. If you're new to Mac OS X Server or if you're a nontechnical person entrusted with maintaining a server for a small organization, I hope the information I offer in this section will put you on the right track and help you to make smart decisions about how to use the operating system safely. It may also provide some helpful background to better make sense of Apple's documentation.

Note

This book also contains a glossary, which defines many of the important terms used throughout this book, and an appendix that lists other sources of information on Mac OS X security. ∎

Cross-Ref

See *Snow Leopard Server (Developer Series)* **by Daniel Eran Dilger (Wiley, 2010) for more on Mac OS X Snow Leopard Server.** ∎

What This Book Doesn't Cover

This may be the *Mac Security Bible*, but the topic of Mac security is broad enough to fill a whole shelf of holy books. Because this book was intended for laypeople rather than technical experts, I've deliberately skipped certain topics and have given others only cursory treatment.

For example, I only briefly discuss enterprise security — the complex issues one must contend with in a large corporation or government office. Those charged with securing Macs on a corporate network will surely find plenty of useful information here, but I don't pretend to address every potential aspect of Mac security for an enterprise. I also say nothing at all about the important subject of how to go about developing secure software. If you're a programmer trying to avoid security holes in your application, you should look elsewhere for guidance. And this isn't a book for hackers of any stripe. I do mention certain methods of attacking or exploiting Mac security weaknesses, but if you're looking for the nitty-gritty details of how to break into a Mac or Mac network (even for the virtuous reason of improving your own security), this isn't the ideal book for you.

In short, this book is neither written for security pros nor intended to turn you into one. Rather, it's intended to help ordinary Mac users understand the risks they may face and develop a sensible plan to keep their computers and their data safe.

I should also mention that this book is intended exclusively for users of Mac OS X 10.5 Leopard and Mac OS X 10.6 Snow Leopard (including Mac OS X Server 10.5 and 10.6). Although much of this book is also applicable in a general way to earlier versions of Mac OS X, the specific details and instructions may differ considerably, and I can't guarantee that any of the procedures discussed here will work as described with versions of Mac OS X prior to 10.5.

Tips for Readers

I wouldn't expect anyone to read this book straight through, but because it's organized roughly in order of increasing complexity, I suggest reading at least Chapter 1 first, to get an idea of this book's assumptions and learn some important background information. If you decide to dip randomly into any other chapter, keep in mind that most chapters also build from simpler to more complex concepts, so if you find yourself scratching your head at any point, try backing up and starting from the beginning of the current chapter. I've provided plentiful cross-references to help you pinpoint the spots elsewhere in this book where you can learn more about each topic.

There are numerous ways to do almost anything on a Mac, and in this book, I've generally selected the one or two methods for each activity that are easiest to explain. For example, many of the steps in this book require you to make changes in System Preferences. To open this application, you could click its icon in the Dock (if you haven't removed it from there), navigate manually to your Applications folder and double-click its icon, or choose System Preferences from the Apple menu. Once you've done that, you can click an icon to open its preferences pane or choose the name of the pane from the View menu. You might even use a third-party launcher such as LaunchBar to jump directly to a particular preferences pane. So, when you see a step such as Choose ➪ System Preferences and then click Accounts, feel free to use a different method to get to the same spot if it's more convenient for you.

I frequently direct you to files and programs stored in various locations on your Mac's hard disk. The slash (/) character by itself refers to the top level of your disk, and if a slash occurs at the beginning of a path, it means you start from the top and work your way down. For example, if I tell you to open /Applications/Utilities/Network Utility, that means to start at the top level of your disk (for example, by double-clicking your hard disk icon) and then find the Applications folder. Inside that, find the Utilities folder, and inside the Utilities folder, find Network Utility. The tilde (~) character is a shorthand way of referring to your home folder — that is, /Users/your-username. But you may want to use any of the many available shortcuts in Mac OS X to get to your destination in another way.

Finally, several chapters of this book contain steps that must be performed in Mac OS X's Terminal utility, which provides a command-line interface. When working in Terminal, as in any command-line environment, you type a command and then press Return or Enter to execute it.

Contents at a Glance

Contents

Contents

Contents

Contents

Contents

Part II: Protecting Your Privacy   257

Chapter 9: Securing Email, Chat, and Voice over IP 259

Contents

Contents

Contents

Contents

Contents

Contents

Contents

Contents

Contents

Part I

Mac Security Basics

Mac Security Overview

When someone asks me what could possibly fill a book on Mac security, I begin by mentioning that thieves find Macs quite attractive (for both their looks and their resale value) — which is clearly a security concern. Macs have no trouble receiving email, which can contain spam, phishing attempts, and malware. They can also easily send email, which often contains private information and could be intercepted in transit. I also point out that Mac users type their passwords and credit card information in forms on web pages, and bad guys sniffing network traffic don't care what operating system their victims are using. Even something as innocuous as the Bluetooth radio your Mac uses to communicate with mice, keyboards, headsets, and the like could be the means by which someone takes over your computer or installs malicious software.

At this point, as my interlocutor checks his watch, coughs politely, and begins backing away, I signal my willingness to continue listing the dozens of potential security concerns a Mac user may face. But I've made my point: Security is every bit as much of an issue for Mac users as for anyone else.

In this chapter, I describe some of the Mac's security strengths and weaknesses, discuss the risks and trade-offs involved in making decisions about security, and outline important initial steps to secure your Mac.

Mac Security: Myth versus Fact

"Macs don't get viruses."

This belief, along with countless other notions about Mac security, has found its way into popular thinking in recent years. But it sounds too good to be true, and smart users are rightly circumspect about such claims.

In fact, statements like this contain kernels of truth. But make no mistake about it: Macs are nothing more or less than powerful, complex computers; thus, they're subject to all the same security concerns as other computers, regardless of what operating system they run.

Let's look at a few areas in which the Mac is reputed to have particularly good security and see how perception compares to reality, beginning with what is perhaps the most commonly heard question.

Is it true that Macs don't get viruses?

As of late 2009, the total number of viruses that run natively on Mac OS X and are known to have propagated in the wild is zero. You read that right: zero.

However, this seemingly miraculous number requires considerable qualification.

First, when I say *virus*, I mean something quite specific: a self-replicating, self-propagating program that's generally invisible and intended to cause mischief of some sort. In ordinary conversation, all sorts of other *malware* — malicious software, such as worms, Trojan horses, keystroke loggers, and root kits — are lumped under the virus heading, even though technically such programs are nothing of the sort. Some of this other malware does indeed infect computers running Mac OS X. There's not a lot of it, and its exposure has so far been limited, but it's there.

Second, there's a particular kind of malware known as a *macro virus* that can be embedded in a Microsoft Office file and can both run and do damage on a Mac equipped with versions of Office other than Office 2008. This type of malware isn't truly a virus in the strictest sense, but it's still real and still dangerous.

Third, a small but significant number of genuine viruses exist that are capable of infecting a computer running Mac OS 9 or earlier versions — but not Mac OS X. So, you may well see these on lists of Mac viruses, but that's highly misleading in that they pose absolutely no danger to modern Macs.

Fourth, Mac OS X viruses have been created by security researchers as proofs of concept or to test antivirus software. Because these haven't been released into the wild and weren't intended to cause actual damage, they don't count, but they do illustrate the fact that a potential threat exists.

And finally, if you use Boot Camp or a virtualization program such as Parallels Desktop or VMware Fusion to run Windows on your Mac, you also have the capability of running thousands of Windows viruses! So, in a sense, any such virus would be running on a Mac, although it wouldn't be running natively under Mac OS X.

So, does malware exist on Mac OS X? Yes, it does. Do viruses exist? Not yet, according to the strict definition of the term — but that's not to say they never will.

Macs aren't in any way inherently immune to viruses. They're pretty resistant to viruses, but there's no logical reason a virus couldn't be created that would cause Mac users lots of headaches, and odds are that sooner or later, that will happen.

Even so, one can't be blamed for noticing the striking proportion of malware on Windows (an enormous amount) to the amount on Mac OS X (hardly any). Why is that? Here are a few reasons:

- **Windows is a bigger (and easier) target.** Although the Mac is quickly gaining market share, the number of Windows PCs is still vastly larger. So, statistically speaking, malware writers can achieve more success (if you can call it that) by writing programs that run on Windows. In addition, Windows users are more likely than Mac users to continue running long-outdated versions of their operating system, and because older versions are more prone to security problems, they make the bad guys' jobs easier.

- **Macs have historically had more safeguards against running unwanted software.** Windows 7 and Windows Vista are better in this regard than Windows XP, and later revisions of Windows XP are better than earlier ones. Even so, it has never been possible to run a program on your Mac merely by opening an email message to which that program was attached. You also can't insert a CD or DVD and have a program run automatically (although at one time you could). These are just two examples of differences in design that have enabled many nasty programs to spread on Windows that never would have had a chance on a Mac.

- **Macs use Unix-type access permissions.** Every file and folder on your Mac has permissions that specify how it can be used and by whom. In order to install any low-level software on your Mac, you (or someone) must type an administrator's password. This mechanism makes it difficult — although not impossible — for malicious software to install itself unnoticed.

In short, Macs do indeed have far less malware than Windows PCs, and that situation is likely to be true far into the future. But users who assume they'll never be at risk do so at their own peril.

Cross-Ref

For more on viruses and malware, including how to protect your Mac against them, see Chapter 14. ■

Can Macs spread viruses to Windows computers?

Suppose you get a virus in an email attachment, but because it's designed to run on Windows, it can't do any damage on your Mac. Now you forward that email message to a friend who's running Windows, perhaps without even realizing the attachment is there. Can that virus damage your friend's computer?

Absolutely. Macs can certainly act as carriers for malware, even when it does no damage to the Mac itself. Most anti-spam software filters out viruses and other malware attached to email messages. In fact, one of the main benefits of running antivirus software on your Mac is that you help prevent the spread of Windows viruses.

Is web browsing safe on a Mac?

Because most Mac web browsers have effective built-in safeguards against pop-up windows and other common irritations, it's easy to get the impression that web browsing is magically safe on a Mac. But in fact, it's no more or less safe than browsing on any other computer.

Once information — such as passwords or account numbers you type into a web form — leaves your computer, it travels over the Internet and to its destination in exactly the same way regardless of what browser or platform you use. Therefore, anyone with access to your network, to the computer on the other end, or to any segment of the Internet in between could conceivably figure out what websites you visit, what confidential information you type, and other facts you'd rather keep private.

Websites that use SSL (Secure Sockets Layer, a cryptographic protocol) to secure the connection between your browser and the server (as signified by a padlock icon in your browser) address a large part of this problem. You can address other parts of the problem by practicing safe browsing habits, by using a virtual private network (VPN), or both.

Cross-Ref

For more on safe browsing, see Chapter 10. For more on using a VPN, see Chapter 12. ■

Can someone eavesdrop on my network if I use a Mac?

If you're using a wireless network that doesn't require a password, someone can certainly eavesdrop on your network. In fact, the chances of this happening in an urban area are rather high. (A way to prevent this is presented later in this chapter.)

On a wired network or when using WPA security (discussed later in this chapter) on your wireless network, the answer is still yes, but it becomes so much harder for a hacker to accomplish that, in many cases, the threat isn't worth worrying about. Some people, however, do need to worry about it — namely, those with extremely sensitive information on their computers or who work in industries such as banking, where the threat of attack is especially high.

Cross-Ref

For more on the extent of wireless threats and how to address them, see Chapter 16. ■

Either way, the general principle holds: On the Internet, your Mac is just a computer, and if someone can eavesdrop on your network connection, the type of computer you're using doesn't, by itself, change anything.

Are Mac servers more secure than Windows servers?

Apart from the numerous specific security features built in to Mac OS X Server, the platform has the advantage of being built on an open-source base, giving it about the same level of intrinsic security for applications such as web and email services that any other Unix server has. Unfortunately, the flip side of that statement is also true: Mac servers inherit many of the limitations and problems common to all Unix servers. Because Unix platforms have traditionally made up a rather large percentage of web servers, risks such as PHP code injection exploits and distributed denial-of-service (DDoS) attacks are ever present, and nothing about Mac OS X makes it inherently immune to such vulnerabilities.

Cross-Ref

For more on Mac OS X Server security features, see Chapter 25. ■

Note

In a PHP code injection exploit, a hacker writes malicious code in the PHP language and injects it into an existing PHP script running on a website; for example, by way of a contact form or a specially crafted URL. In a denial-of-service (DoS) attack, many computers send a flood of specially crafted queries to a computer or router in an attempt to overwhelm it and prevent it from responding to normal traffic. ■

What's the biggest threat to Mac security?

Although this book describes threats from hackers to malicious software and from spies to faulty network equipment, by far the biggest threat to Mac security is you! The vast majority of people who use any computer, Mac or not, can preserve their privacy, avoid network attacks and data loss, and generally enjoy trouble-free computing simply by using common sense.

Conversely, the lack of common sense is the biggest contributor to security problems. Every day, people click links in spam messages, download and run software from sites they know nothing about, type passwords into insecure web forms, and do many other activities that are the computing equivalent of leaving one's wallet on a park bench with a sign that says "Steal Me."

Therefore, although this book covers a great many products and procedures that can increase your security, the most important thing I hope to teach you is how to be a smart and savvy Mac user when it comes to security. If you can tame the biggest security threat you face, the rest is easy.

Major Mac OS X Security Features

Macs aren't necessarily as safe as some people may think. Nevertheless, Apple has worked very hard to make Mac OS X as secure a computing environment as possible, and each major release of Mac OS X has included significant security improvements.

Some ways of securing your Mac require that you add third-party software or hardware. But right out of the box, a Mac running Leopard, Snow Leopard, or the server version of either has quite a few security features built in. Some of these work invisibly, behind the scenes, whereas others have an overt user interface.

Most security features work only when you turn them on or explicitly use them, and the Mac OS X default settings aren't nearly as secure as they could be. (I return to this matter later in this chapter.) But at least the capabilities themselves are there.

A comprehensive list would be quite long, and the remaining chapters of this book delve into many security features not mentioned here. But the following are some of the most important and useful security features of Mac OS X.

Open-source infrastructure

Unlike Windows, which is built largely from proprietary code that only Microsoft engineers can see, the Unix underpinnings of Mac OS X are open source. Thousands of engineers from around the world have examined, prodded, and tried to break it over the years — which is a good thing! Having large portions of the Mac OS X code open to public scrutiny greatly increases the chances that potential security issues can be noticed and repaired (perhaps even by people outside Apple) before they make their way into shipping versions of the operating system.

Access permissions

As in all varieties of Unix, every file, folder, and application in Mac OS X is marked with a series of indicators that specify which users can read, modify, and execute them. In Leopard and Snow Leopard, *access control lists* (ACLs) provide even greater granularity in determining access for shared files and folders. Access permissions can prevent one person from reading files belonging to another person who uses the same computer, but even more powerfully, they can prevent unauthorized people and programs (including viruses and other malware) from installing potentially dangerous software, changing critical system settings, and inflicting other kinds of damage.

Keychain

Mac OS X includes a system-wide mechanism for securely storing and accessing usernames, passwords, and other private data. Not all third-party applications make use of the Keychain, but many do, as do numerous Apple applications and services. Using a keychain ensures that your passwords are strongly encrypted when you're not logged in (and at any other time you lock your keychain); it also encourages users to create more — and more complex — passwords because the computer can do all the hard work of remembering them and typing them. You merely have to remember the single password that unlocks your keychain.

Firewalls

Leopard and Snow Leopard contain not one but two separate firewalls to protect Mac OS X against network attacks. Some have argued that this design decision amounts to a step backward in security because the firewall (IPFW) originally included with Mac OS X Tiger and present — but hidden — in Leopard and Snow Leopard is more powerful than the new default, application-based firewall. On the other hand, users are more likely to turn on a firewall that's easy to use and configure, so perhaps the design change was felicitous after all. In any case, both tools are there, ready to be put to use by anyone who's willing to learn a few firewall basics.

Encrypted disk images

Disk Utility, included as part of Mac OS X, can create strongly encrypted *disk images* that appear as single files when not in use but behave as a disk when opened. When you store a file in an encrypted disk image, it's extraordinarily safe from anyone who doesn't have the password.

FileVault

FileVault builds on the concept of encrypted disk images to protect everything in a user's home folder, including documents, preferences, and even media, such as photos, music, and movies. Although you may choose not to use FileVault for any of numerous reasons, the fact remains that it's a powerful security mechanism that has no counterpart in Windows.

VPN client

VPNs let you encrypt all your network traffic — even over an unsecure public Wi-Fi connection — so that no one can eavesdrop on the data you send and receive over the Internet. Leopard and Snow Leopard contain built-in client software for the two most popular VPN varieties — L2TP over IPsec and PPTP — and Snow Leopard also supports Cisco IPsec VPNs. This means you can connect to most corporate and public VPNs without having to purchase or install any additional software.

Firmware password protection

Mac *firmware* — the special low-level software built into the hardware itself that loads before your hard disk even spins up — can be protected with a password. (So, strictly speaking, this is a feature of your Mac rather than a feature of Mac OS X.) With this password set, a would-be snoop can't boot your Mac from an external hard disk, an optical disc, or a flash drive or do any of several other things that could bypass your login password in order to gain access to your personal files. Although firmware passwords aren't bulletproof, they add another layer of security that can help defuse certain threats.

Download tagging

When you download a file using the Leopard or Snow Leopard versions of Safari, Mail, or iChat, Mac OS X tags it with a time stamp and the URL it came from. The first time you try to open the file (or one of its constituent files, in the case of disk images and compressed archives of other sorts), Mac OS X displays a first-run alert, which shows you this metadata and asks you to confirm that you want to open the file. This mechanism can help you identify and avoid running software from untrusted sources, including Trojan horses and other malware.

Application signing

Mac OS X uses digital signatures to verify the identity and integrity of all Apple applications and participating third-party applications. This means many attempts to work around security features by covertly modifying applications fail because the signature no longer matches. Application signatures are used by parental controls and managed preferences, the application firewall, and the Keychain, among other parts of Mac OS X.

Other chapters in this book discuss these features in more detail.

Privacy versus Security

In discussions of computer hardware, software, and networking, the terms *privacy* and *security* tend to come up quite often in the same context, and some people assume they mean the same thing. In fact, they're quite different but are closely related.

Privacy is what you have when other people can't find out personal information you want to keep to yourself. When you close a curtain, lower your voice, or cover your hand while typing your PIN at an ATM, you're doing so to preserve your privacy — to keep others from seeing, hearing, or learning things about you that are none of their business. Likewise, on your Mac, your digital information is private when other people can't get at it without your knowledge and permission.

Security is a broader concept. You're secure when there are effective barriers (physical, electronic, psychological, or otherwise) protecting you, your property, or your information in some way. You might put your money in a safe to keep it secure, which means that it's protected from theft. Or you might lock the door of your hotel room to keep yourself secure, which means you're protected from contact with unwanted visitors. Barriers can protect a person from being injured or an object from being stolen — or information from being revealed. In terms of your computer, security encompasses measures you can take to protect your privacy (such as encrypting files and network connections) as well as things you can do to prevent your computer from being stolen, vandalized, or used for illicit purposes, such as sending out spam.

You can have security without privacy. Think of a house that's pretty secure: It has strong doors, solid locks, a working burglar alarm, and other features that make it hard to break into. It's secure in that it can help keep its occupants safe from intrusion and harm. However, if everyone in the house lives in a single room, they have no privacy from each other. If the curtains are open and people can see in, the occupants have little privacy from the outside. On a computer, as in a house, you can have terrific security without any privacy. For example, no matter how well your computer is locked down physically or your files are encrypted, if someone can read your personal email messages or bank balances over your shoulder, you have no privacy.

The opposite is also true: You can have privacy without security. If you're alone in a house in the country, with unlocked doors and no Internet connection, you, your Mac, and your data may have complete privacy. No one can see or hear you, read your files, or remotely take control of your computer. You and your equipment aren't secure in that there are no real barriers between you and the outside world, other than mere distance and isolation. But then, in such a situation, security may be irrelevant to you because there are no apparent threats to protect against. You have privacy without having used security measures to achieve it.

Practically speaking, most computer security measures exist in order to protect one's privacy in some way. They prevent other people from knowing your passwords, reading your files, and eavesdropping on your online conversations. By extension, they can protect your money, your business, and other important assets by preventing other people from accessing information about bank accounts, confidential legal documents, and so on.

Because privacy is the ultimate goal of so much computer security, this book covers both topics, even in cases where they don't necessarily overlap. What counts as security here is anything that helps keep your computer and its information strictly under your control.

Weighing Convenience against Security

Imagine a man who's paranoid about the security of his home and, as a result, installs six deadbolt locks on his front door, each with a different key. All those locks can increase his security in that they provide additional barriers to a would-be intruder. However, they come with a trade-off: The owner himself must also go through the bother of carrying all those keys and spending the time required to unlock all those deadbolts every time he comes home. He has traded a certain amount of convenience in exchange for a certain amount of security.

On your Mac, you must often — although not always — give up some convenience to get security. If you protect a sensitive file by encrypting it with a password, you make extra work for yourself (typing in the password whenever you want to access the file) in order to get the benefit of preventing anyone else from being able to read it. Although it may take you just a few seconds to unlock the file, it could take someone else hours (or much longer) to guess or crack your password. So, at least the inconvenience you create for yourself is quite small compared to the inconvenience you create for a potential intruder!

Sometimes, the inconvenience of security is so small as to be insignificant, whereas the benefit is great. It's no more difficult to set up a WPA (Wi-Fi Protected Access) password than a WEP (Wired Equivalent Privacy) password when configuring your wireless network, but the former provides vastly better security. You can even save the password for your wireless network in your keychain in such a way that you must type it only once — and forever thereafter, it protects you without any additional effort on your part. I further discuss WPA and WEP passwords later in this chapter.

Cross-Ref

For more on wireless networks, including WEP and WPA security, see Chapter 16. ■

The reverse is also true: Some security measures create significant inconvenience while offering comparatively little benefit. You can configure some web browsers to pop up a window every time a site you visit tries to write a cookie to store information on your Mac. In ordinary day-to-day browsing, you could easily see that alert and have to respond to it several times an hour. The aggravation of having to manually click a button every time you visit a web page arguably outweighs the rather small potential risk that a site could use a cookie to track your browsing behavior in a way that compromises your privacy.

Cross-Ref

For more on browser security settings and cookies, see Chapter 10. ■

The importance of weighing potential benefit against potential inconvenience — of judging risk against cost — is a recurring theme in this book. If you installed every available security application, turned on every security feature, used the longest possible passwords, and took every other potential measure to protect your Mac, you'd spend many thousands of dollars, slow your computer to a crawl, and put yourself through so much annoyance that you'd never want to use your computer. It would be extremely secure but at a price that's unreasonably high. The fact that you can do something to increase your security doesn't mean you should.

I can't overstate this: You need not — and should not — take every single security precaution in this book. A healthy awareness of your risks and a judicious use of appropriate security measures are good things; paranoia and excessive security measures aren't. The trick is figuring out which types and degrees of security are right for your particular situation. Your goal should be to provide yourself with the necessary protection without causing more inconvenience than that protection is worth.

How do you find that sweet spot? Here are some general guidelines to follow:

- **Take the no-brainer security steps.** You wouldn't intentionally leave your car keys in the ignition when you park at the mall, and you wouldn't leave your front door hanging open when you go on vacation. On your Mac, there are comparable actions you should get in the habit of taking — things that are pretty easy but which, were you to avoid doing them, would clearly be asking for trouble. See a section later in this chapter for some examples in this category.

- **Do what the law requires.** Depending on where you live or work and the nature of your business, you may be subject to certain laws about computer security, particularly ones involving privacy. For example, the laws governing medical records typically require multiple safeguards to prevent confidential patient data from being publicized. Government agencies and contractors, financial institutions, law firms, news outlets, and various other businesses must also comply with legal constraints about how data is stored, backed up, archived, transmitted over networks, and so on. I can't provide specific legal advice, except to recommend that you consult with a legal professional in your field to ensure that you know all the rules you must follow, regardless of the level of inconvenience they may entail.

- **Do what your employer requires.** After reading Chapter 14, you might conclude that in your specific situation, the risk of infection by malware is so low that it's not worth the cost or aggravation of installing antivirus software. Be that as it may, many businesses have company-wide policies mandating such software on all computers used by employees, regardless of operating system, perceived threat, or other considerations. Similarly, if your employer has policies about backups, firewalls, VPNs, or other security considerations — and you value your job — I urge you to abide by the rules even when they seem excessive or unnecessary.

- **Consider the value of your data.** All things being equal, the effort you put into protecting your data should correlate at least roughly to its value to someone else, should that information fall into the wrong hands. If your hard drive contains state secrets, the password to a bank account holding millions of dollars, or the plans for Apple's next iProduct, you've obviously got something that would be worth a great deal to a thief, hacker, or spy — and you should be prepared to endure some inconvenience to protect that information. However, if the most valuable piece of information you have is your secret recipe for chocolate chip cookies, it's probably not worth much inconvenience on your part to keep it safe.

- **Consider the consequences of loss.** Related to the value of your data is the consequence of losing it (or of having a security breach of some other kind). If someone hacks into your server and steals your customers' credit card information, what will that cost your company — in lost time and business, legal fees, and possibly even lawsuits? It would be worth considerable expense and inconvenience to prevent such a breach. On the other hand, if a hard drive contains no sensitive information and the only consequence of its loss would be spending $100 to replace it, then it's worth far less money and effort to protect it. Potential consequences of a loss are hard to calculate and can often be more serious than they appear at first glance. But they're important to think about when deciding how much effort to put into protecting your computer.

- **Ask yourself whether higher security really costs more.** Suppose your encryption software can use either a lower-security algorithm or a higher-security algorithm, and the only downside to the better algorithm is that your files take one second longer to open. For all practical purposes, there's no difference in inconvenience, so it makes sense to go with the higher-security option. Or if you're using a password manager to remember all your passwords, it's no harder for the program to remember a ten-character password than a four-character password, so you can and should use a more secure password without incurring extra inconvenience. When the cost (in time, money, or effort) of extra security is small or zero, it's always logical to go with the more secure option.

Cross-Ref

For more on password management tools to generate, remember, and fill in passwords for you, see Chapter 6. ■

- **Ask yourself whether greater inconvenience really gets you more security.** The flip side of the last point is that greater security is sometimes illusory or irrelevant. You can set your Mac to require that you type your password every time you turn it on or wake it up, which is a minor inconvenience for most of us. If you work in a busy office, the security you get in exchange is almost certainly worth it, but if your Mac is in a location where no one else can get to it — or if you have no sensitive data on it in the first place — you've given up convenience but achieved no real security benefit.

In an ideal world, perhaps every security product and setting would come with an objective rating of how much protection it provides and how much effort it requires. You could then look for options with a high ratio of security to effort. Although it's not quite that easy, that general principle is good to keep in mind as you review the numerous ways to keep your Mac secure.

Understanding Your Risks

Whether you're talking about the theft of a laptop or someone hijacking your Mac to serve as a chat server, the vast majority of security threats any computer user faces are random. Someone might happen to be looking for a guy walking down this block with a computer carrying case or probing every IP address on a network looking for a vulnerability. Generally speaking, an attacker goes through less effort to obtain a computer or its data if it's not known to contain something of particular value (per the previous point). Even so, it's clear that your risk of randomly having your laptop stolen is higher if you're walking down a crowded city street than if you're walking down a quiet country road, if only because the number of people you come in contact with is higher.

Judging one's level of risk is a bit of a guessing game; no matter how carefully you assess statistical risks, there's always a chance that you, your computer, or the packets you send across the Internet may be in the wrong place at the wrong time. Nevertheless, some general principles apply that can serve as a rough guide while you consider the security procedures in this book. All things being equal, it makes sense to put more effort into security if your situation puts you at a higher risk.

Keep the following factors in mind:

- **Proximity to potential attackers.** In terms of physical security — particularly the threat of theft or physical vandalism — your environment is of course the main consideration. For example, Macs in public places, such as schools, libraries, and cafés, are less safe than those in secluded home offices. But the same goes for network security. If you frequent websites where unsavory activities go on, your chances of encountering security problems are much greater than if you restrict your browsing to pbs.org and disney.com.

- **Business versus home use.** Business users and home users may face different sorts of threats. A business computer may be targeted for the data it contains, but because most corporate networks have reasonably good defenses, they make poor targets for hacking tools, such as *botnets*, which are large networks of computers that have been hijacked for some mischievous purpose. Computers on home networks, on the other hand, are much less likely to contain specific information of value to thieves, but because they aren't protected by such strong barriers, they're more likely to be turned into zombie robots and infected with consumer-oriented adware.

- **Type of network connection.** Wired networks are harder to snoop into than wireless networks. On the other hand, an always-on connection (like the one used by your desktop Mac at home) gives an attacker much more time to break into than a sporadic connection, such as a laptop you frequently move from one network to another as you go about town. Likewise, a Mac directly connected to the Internet with a publicly routable IP address has a greater risk of attack because it's reachable without going through or around any barriers; a Mac behind a router or gateway that assigns it a private IP address and uses NAT (network address translation) to connect to the outside world has a much lower risk.

Cross-Ref

For more on NAT, see Chapter 15. ■

- **Who you are.** Fame (or notoriety) comes at a price. If you're a well-known person, and if in particular you're known to have money, secrets, power, or merely fame, your security risk automatically increases. We've all read stories about a celebrity whose computer or phone was hacked into — private photos stolen, incriminating emails found, money extorted. If you expect people to recognize you when you walk down the street, take extra precautions with your Mac.

Needless to say, other factors can also affect your risk, and I mention some of these in conjunction with specific security factors later in this book.

The Theory and Practice of Best Practices

In many publications about computer security, the term *best practice* appears prominently and repeatedly. It's a way a developer, analyst, or other expert can succinctly say, "This is what I recommend to keep yourself out of trouble or what's generally recommended in the industry." More often than not, the best practice is simply the most secure option — which is to say the most restrictive.

The problem with best practices is that they usually presume a single course of action is best for everyone. As this chapter shows, that isn't the case. What's best for an individual user at home, an executive traveling with a laptop, and a system administrator managing a rack full of Xserves in a corporate data center may be very different. And what I consider a fair balance between security and convenience may seem too weak or too burdensome to someone else.

That's not to say you should disregard best practices. Far from it. You should certainly know what experts recommend, what companies consider safe behavior, and what the consequences of ignoring that advice may be. But blindly following best practices doesn't ensure security, and the choices you face are too complex to be distilled into tidy proclamations. You're far better off understanding your range of options and the pros and cons of each and then making your own decisions.

Granted, you may not always have a choice. If you're required (by your employer, a client, or industry rules) to follow a codified set of best practices, such as Common Criteria, far be it from me to subvert that policy. Even so, it pays to understand the reasoning behind the recommended practices and the way Mac OS X tools work because even strict security policies include some flexibility — and the more you know, the better you can balance convenience and security within the guidelines you must follow.

Cross-Ref
For more on Common Criteria, see Chapter 4. ■

This book largely avoids talking about best practices in so many words because I consider that an unhelpful way to approach security decisions. Instead, I typically describe the range of available options, point out the benefits and risks of each, and, where appropriate, suggest reasonable courses of action for various kinds of users. To be sure, in some cases, one option is so obviously good or bad or so universally true that a blanket statement is in order. But I find that best practices, as such, are better in theory than in practice.

Seven Things You Should Do Right Now

Learning the ins and outs of every security issue and tweaking every setting for the optimal combination of security and convenience can take quite some time. A good way to get started is to spend a few minutes performing the following seven tasks, which address some of the most common and egregious security problems with a default installation of Mac OS X. I provide only basic instructions here; future chapters include more detailed background information and additional options.

Note
These steps apply primarily to users of the standard client version of Mac OS X; users of Mac OS X Server must follow somewhat different procedures (as described in Chapters 25–31). ■

Update your software

As security vulnerabilities and other bugs are discovered in Mac OS X, Apple releases software updates to fix them. Using the very latest software is no guarantee of safety, but it significantly improves your odds. The same goes for third-party software, of course, but the software that makes up Mac OS X itself is the most crucial.

Cross-Ref
For more on software updates, see Chapter 4. ■

Even if you're not prepared to install Apple's latest major (paid) upgrade, you should at least download and install all the free updates available for the version of Mac OS X you're running. Of those, the most important by far are the Mac OS X updates (that is, Mac OS X 10.5.x or 10.6.x) and security updates, but updates to other software that uses the network extensively (including Safari and QuickTime) can also patch dangerous security holes. Updates to other individual programs, such as iPhoto or Pages, are less critical.

To update your Apple software, follow these steps:

1. **Choose ➪ Software Update to open Software Update.** Wait a few moments while Software Update checks for new software.

2. **Click to deselect the check box next to any update you don't want and then click Install X Items, as shown in Figure 1.1.** If no updates are available, simply click Quit.

3. **When prompted, type your administrator name and password in the appropriate fields and then click OK.** Software Update downloads and installs the software you selected.

4. Choose Software Update ⇨ Quit after installations occur or, if prompted to restart your Mac, click Restart.

FIGURE 1.1

In the Software Update window, click to deselect the check box for any update you don't want. Mac OS X updates and security updates should be your top priorities.

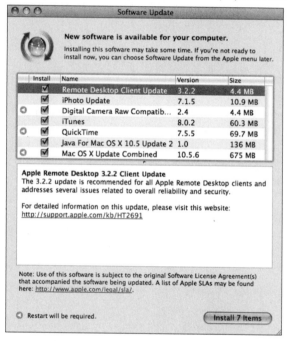

Set up a standard user account

The user account you create when you set up a new Mac or install a new version of Mac OS X is an administrator account, which gives you nearly unlimited power to change or delete files and install or run software. You need at least one administrator account on any Mac, but logging in as an administrator for ordinary, day-to-day computing can expose your computer to extra risks. For example, any malware you might encounter can do considerably more damage when run from an administrator account, and you can also make accidental changes to your Mac that would prevent it from running properly. Those risks may be acceptable for power users who are the sole operators of a given Mac, but most people should use non-administrator accounts except when specifically needed.

Cross-Ref

For more on administrator accounts, see Chapter 3. ∎

You can set up a new, non-administrator user account easily enough, but then the process of moving all your preferences, files, and other data from your existing account to the new account would be unnecessarily cumbersome. Instead, I suggest setting up a new administrator account, logging in as that administrator, and removing administrator privileges from your former account. You can then continue logging in under the account you've been accustomed to, using your new administrator account only when you need to install software or perform other special tasks.

To configure your existing user account as a standard user, follow these steps:

1. Choose ▲ ⇨ System Preferences to open System Preferences and then click Accounts to open the Accounts pane.

2. If the lock icon in the lower-left corner of the pane is in the locked state, click it, type your existing administrator username and password, and then click OK.

3. Click the Add (+) button below the list of accounts and then choose Administrator from the New Account pop-up menu to open a dialog box in which you can specify account details.

4. For the new administrator account, type a name and short name, type and verify a password, and then click Create Account.

Cross-Ref

For more on password creation, see Chapter 6. ∎

5. Select the name of your original administrator account in the list on the left in the Accounts pane.

6. Click the Allow user to administer this computer check box to deselect it and then close System Preferences.

You've now removed administrative privileges for your main account. If you ever want to log in as an administrator in the future (although that should seldom if ever be necessary, because you can use an administrator's password for authentication while logged in as another user), follow these steps:

1. Choose ▲ ⇨ Log Out *Your Name* to log out from your current account.

2. When the Login window opens, select or type the name of the new administrator account you created in step 4, type that account's password (as shown in Figure 1.2), and then click Log In.

3. When you're finished with your administrative activities, choose ▲ ⇨ Log Out *Your Name* to log out from your new administrator account.

FIGURE 1.2

In the Login window, after choosing or typing your username, type your password and then click Log In.

For the most part, you can do everything in your account that you could do before, but when you're prompted to type an administrator password (for example, to install software), you need to type the username and password for your new administrator account rather than for the standard account you're now using.

Change your keychain password

The Mac OS X Keychain securely stores usernames and passwords for things such as AirPort networks, shared network volumes, and websites you visit in Safari. The benefit of a keychain is that you can avoid having to remember all those passwords individually; just type a master password to unlock your keychain, and all the passwords inside are unlocked too. But by default, your primary keychain shares the same password as your user account, which means logging in (or, if you've turned on automatic login, simply turning on your Mac) unlocks your keychain. That eliminates the need to unlock your keychain manually, but it also means that anyone else who accesses your Mac could also use all the resources for which you've saved passwords. A safer approach is to use a separate password for your keychain, which prevents it from being unlocked without your explicit permission.

Cross-Ref

For more on Keychain, see Chapter 5. ■

To change your keychain password, follow these steps:

1. Open Keychain Access, which is located in /Applications/Utilities.

2. If the Keychain list isn't visible in the upper-left corner of the window, choose View ⇨ Show Keychains to show it.

3. Select your default keychain (shown in bold) from the Keychain list. Ordinarily, this has the name login, but it may have the same name as your short username.

4. Choose Edit ⇨ Change Password for Keychain *"Keychain Name"*. A dialog box opens.

5. In the fields provided, as shown in Figure 1.3, type your existing password, type and verify a new password, and then click OK.

FIGURE 1.3

Type a new password for your keychain in this dialog box to make it different from your user account's login password.

Turn off all unneeded sharing features

Mac OS X makes it easy to share files, printers, and other system resources with users on your local network and across the Internet. Sharing is useful and can usually be done safely. However, if you turn on sharing features you don't need or if you use certain settings that make files and other resources freely available, you expose yourself to unnecessary security risks. As a general principle, therefore, turn on only those sharing features you know you actively need, and for those sharing features you do activate, limit access to trusted users.

Cross-Ref

For more on sharing files and other system resources, see Chapter 7. ■

To configure your sharing features, follow these steps:

1. **Choose ⌥ System Preferences to open System Preferences and then click Sharing to open the Sharing pane.**

2. **Look at the list of services on the left, and if nothing is selected, you're done —** move on to the next topic — **but if you do see a check in one or more of the check boxes, move on to the next step.**

3. **Click the check box next to any service that you aren't sure you're using to deselect it.** If you later find that something isn't working properly, you can always come back and turn a service back on.

4. **For each service that you're actively using, click its check box and then make sure you've limited access to just the essential resources and users.** For example, if you turn on File Sharing (as shown in Figure 1.4) but don't configure any other options, you can log in to your own Mac from another computer to get at all your files, but no other user can have access. If you need other users to be able to access some of your data, share only the specific folder(s) they need (rather than your entire disk) and add only the users who need access to the Users list.

5. **Close System Preferences.**

FIGURE 1.4

This shows the Sharing pane as it appears in Leopard; the Snow Leopard version is slightly different.

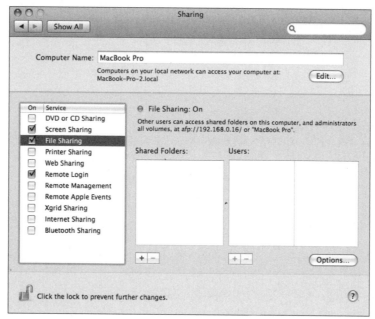

Turn on your firewall

The Mac OS X firewall protects your computer from some kinds of network attacks, whether they originate on the Internet or come from a computer on your local network. Leopard and Snow Leopard actually come with two firewalls, of which the one most visible to users has a simplified interface (see Figure 1.5) that lets you adjust access rights by application rather than by *port* (or network channel).

Cross-Ref

For more on firewalls, see Chapters 4 and 17. ■

For now, the wisest course of action is to set the firewall to one of two options that restrict some incoming connections. Either way, you can still make outgoing network connections (for example, with a web browser or email program), and essential network services such as DHCP (which lets your Mac obtain an IP address) and VPNs still work, but most other ways in which someone could remotely connect to your computer are blocked.

FIGURE 1.5

The most restrictive but safest firewall setting is Allow only essential services (in Leopard) or Block all incoming connections (in Snow Leopard, whose Advanced dialog box is shown here). If you want to access this Mac from another computer, however, click the Set access for specific services and applications radio button (in Leopard) or click the Block all incoming connections check box to deselect it, if necessary (in Snow Leopard).

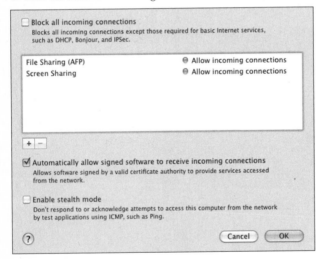

To turn on your firewall, follow these steps:

1. Choose System Preferences to open System Preferences and then click Security to open the Security pane.

2. Click the Firewall tab.

3. **In Snow Leopard, if the tab doesn't say "Firewall: On," click the Start button to turn it on.** (In Leopard, the firewall is always on, although it may be set to allow all connections, which means it's effectively off.)

4. **If you need to access this Mac from another computer (using File Sharing or Screen Sharing, for example), do one of the following:**

   • In Leopard, click the Set access for specific services and applications radio button.

   • In Snow Leopard, click the Advanced button; then, in the dialog box that opens, if the Block all incoming connections check box is selected, click it to deselect it. Click OK.

   If you don't need to access this Mac from another computer, then instead do this:

   • In Leopard, click the Allow only essential services radio button.

   • In Snow Leopard, click the Advanced button; then, in the dialog box that opens, click the Block all incoming connections check box. Click OK.

5. Close System Preferences.

Switch from WEP or nothing to WPA

If you use a Wi-Fi network to connect to the Internet wirelessly, you should be aware that someone else in your building, across the street, or parked in a car outside could be monitoring everything you send and receive: your email messages, passwords, chat sessions, and other private information. In fact, when you connect to an open Wi-Fi network (one that requires no password at all), monitoring your Internet traffic is so trivially easy that you should assume someone else is reading everything you type, at least if you're in an urban area. If you connect to a Wi-Fi network that uses WEP encryption, an old and insecure standard, it's only slightly harder for someone to sniff your traffic. It's like the difference between reading the back of a postcard and opening an envelope.

Luckily, a newer and highly secure wireless encryption standard called WPA has been widely available for years, and as long as you're using a reasonably modern Mac, switching to WPA is extremely easy.

Cross-Ref
For more on WPA and how to set up wireless routers, see Chapter 16. ■

If you're using an Apple AirPort base station to access the Internet, you can turn on WPA by following these steps:

1. **Open AirPort Utility, which is located in** `/Applications/Utilities`.

2. **Select your base station in the list on the left and then choose Base Station ⇨ Manual Setup to show your configuration options.**

3. Click the AirPort button on the toolbar and then click the Wireless tab, as shown in Figure 1.6.

4. **If the Wireless Security pop-up menu says None or WEP (Transitional Security Network), you need to change it by choosing either WPA2 Personal or WPA/WPA2 Personal.** The None or WEP options means you've got a highly insecure wireless network.

Cross-Ref

For more on WPA2 Personal and WPA/WPA2 Personal, see Chapter 16. ■

5. Type and verify a password for your wireless network.

6. Click Update and then wait for your base station to restart.

7. **From the AirPort menu in your main menu bar (the one that looks like a striped wedge), select your wireless network and then type the password you just set.** You can also click the Remember this network check box if you want to store the password in your keychain.

8. Click OK.

FIGURE 1.6

The Wireless pane in the AirPort Utility dialog box

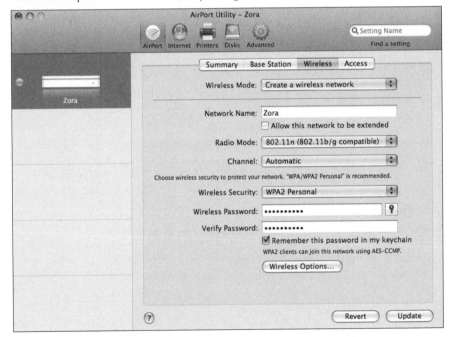

Back up your Mac

If someone were to steal your computer or if malware were to damage or delete your files, your best chance of recovering your data would be restoring it from a recent backup. In fact, there are many good reasons to back up your Mac — and many good ways of doing so. One way or another, I strongly recommend making a backup of all your data as soon as possible; you can always switch methods later if need be. If you don't already have a backup system of some kind set up, don't lose any time making it happen.

Cross-Ref

For more on backing up and restoring your data, see Chapter 8. ■

The easiest way to get started with backups is to use Time Machine, which Apple built into Leopard and Snow Leopard. To set up Time Machine quickly, follow these steps:

1. **Obtain an external hard drive — ideally one with a capacity at least as large as your Mac's internal drive — and then plug it into a USB or FireWire port, as appropriate.**

2. **Assuming you haven't already configured Time Machine, an alert like the one shown in Figure 1.7 opens.** If you've already configured Time Machine, no alert appears when you plug in a new drive.

3. **Click Use as Backup Disk.**

FIGURE 1.7

The easiest way to back up your Mac is to plug in an external hard drive, and if and when this alert appears, click Use as Backup Disk.

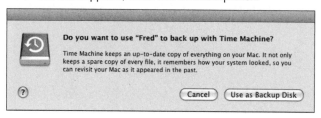

Within a few hours, Time Machine completes its first full backup of your hard disk, and it updates that backup with any new or changed files once an hour. You can continue using your computer normally while the backup runs.

Cross-Ref

For more on Time Machine and other backup options, see Chapter 8. ■

Summary

In this chapter, I described some of the myths and misconceptions about Mac security but also pointed out a number of Mac OS X features that do a splendid job of making computing safer. I described how privacy is one of the main goals of security, although not the only one.

Because security sometimes comes at the cost of convenience, you must balance the two carefully when making decisions about how to protect your Mac. You should also consider any particular risks that may increase your need for security, regardless of convenience.

I also explained how a goal of this book is to help you make good decisions about security that are customized to your specific needs. And I showed you some easy steps you can follow to increase your security right away.

Securing Your Mac against Theft

IN THIS CHAPTER

Physically locking down your Mac

Using an anti-theft alarm

Helping police (or a good Samaritan) return a lost or stolen Mac to you

Using software to track a wayward Mac

Mac OS X contains all sorts of tools you can use to protect your Mac against having its data accessed without permission — either in person or over a network. However, these are of little use to you if your Mac itself is stolen. So, your first order of business in thinking about Mac security should be to consider the physical security of your computer.

Numerous gadgets exist to reduce the chances of a Mac moving from a designated spot or at least to alert you if someone tries to take it. But despite your best efforts, a thief could still potentially make off with your computer. Even if that happens, though, all is not lost: If you've planned ahead, you can still take steps to recover a stolen Mac, ranging from the mundane (marking it so that police can identify it and its owner more easily) to the innovative (using a sticker that offers a unique tracking code and offers a reward for its return) to the high-tech (using tracking software to figure out where a thief has taken it).

In this chapter, I cover a variety of ways you can prevent your Mac from being stolen or get it back if someone does steal it.

Security Cables and Locks

Most Mac models — and numerous peripherals, such as monitors, AirPort base stations, and external hard drives — include a small oval slot designed to accept a special lock at the end of a flexible steel cable. Kensington, a prominent manufacturer of computer accessories, holds the patent to this slot (making them the only company I'm aware of that has patented a hole), and some other companies, such as Targus, sell cables made for use with the Kensington Security Slot under license.

In most cases, the cables have a loop at one end. You wrap the cable around an immovable object, slide the lock end through the loop, and then attach it to your computer. (Some cables are designed to be bolted to a special bracket or attached in some other way.) The locks at the ends come in several styles. Some take flat keys, some take round keys, and others use a combination.

In addition to preventing someone from walking off with your equipment, the security cables serve a secondary purpose on most desktop Mac models. With the lock inserted, the case can't be opened, which means that internal components (hard drives, RAM, video cards, and the like) are also protected, and certain security risks that require an attacker to have access to the inside of the computer are reduced.

Cross-Ref

For more on preventing a hacker from having access to the inside of your Mac, see Chapter 6. ■

Security cables serve as a modest deterrent to casual theft. For example, they make sense for locking down your laptop in your hotel room or at a coffee shop — or locking down desktop Macs in a library or computer lab that's monitored in some other way. However, they weren't designed to withstand bolt cutters, crowbars, and other heavy-duty tools. A determined thief won't be put off by these cables, particularly if keeping the case intact isn't a priority.

In addition, not all Mac models have a Kensington Security Slot. The MacBook Air was the first Mac in many years to lack a security slot, which is a pity given that its design and size probably make it especially attractive to thieves.

If your computer doesn't have a security slot, if you feel that a security cable provides inadequate theft protection, or if you want to keep a Mac entirely immobile, you have several other options:

- **Mounting brackets.** Several companies, including Noble Enterprises (www.applelocks.com) and D&D Security Resources (www.ddsecurity.com), make heavy-duty mounting brackets that affix to a Mac in some other way, such as being screwed into its base, and can then be bolted down to a desktop.

- **Secure enclosures.** Companies such as LapSafe (www.lapsafe.com) and D&D Security Resources sell padlocked enclosures that wrap around four sides of a Mac Pro or PowerMac and are then secured to a floor or another surface.

- **MacBook Air locks.** At least two companies have locks that work with a MacBook Air. The MacBook Air Lock Bracket by Turn Around Technologies (http://stores.ebay.com/Turn-Around-Technologies) is a heavy bracket that slides into the hinge on most laptop models, including the MacBook Air. It can then be attached to a standard cable lock. The laptop's lid is prevented from closing, which provides an additional theft deterrent. Noble Enterprises also has a MacBook Air lock designed around a special plate that affixes to the bottom of the computer with screws.

- **Video port locks.** Targus (www.targus.com) sells a cable lock called the DEFCON VPKL, which locks a cable to a VGA display port rather than to a Kensington Security Slot (while offering a pass-through connector for the video output). Although no recent Macs have built-in VGA ports, such a lock could be useful for older models.

Laptop Lockers

It goes without saying that most computer thefts occur when a computer is unattended. In the case of laptops, cable-based security systems are relatively easy to defeat, whereas heavier-duty locks that prevent the computer from moving at all can hinder usability. So, an alternative is simply to lock a laptop away securely when it's not in use, relying on a cable lock or human supervision to keep it from walking away when it's being used.

Laptop lockers come in a dizzying array of shapes, sizes, and configurations. Some are designed to hold an individual laptop — at home or in a dorm room, for example — and be bolted to a secure surface. Examples include Datum's LapTop Locker (www.datumfiling.com) and models from Data-Link Associates (www.datalinksales.com) and Tryten (www.tryten.com).

For classrooms and other environments with a large number of laptops, fixed and rolling lockers are available that hold anywhere from a handful to dozens of laptops. They're typically designed to enable charging while the laptops are being stored. Manufacturers of such products include American Locker (www.americanlocker.com), Data-Link, Datum, and Loxit (www.loxit.com), among many others.

Other Theft Deterrents

Locking down your computer isn't the only way of protecting it. If you're worried about someone making off with your laptop while you make a phone call or walk up to the counter for a coffee refill, a laptop alarm may give you some peace of mind. Like car alarms, these shouldn't be thought of as real protection but rather as a way of alerting you, the owner, and perhaps scaring off less-determined thieves. You can also add text to the login screen that might give a thief pause.

Laptop alarms (hardware)

One approach is to attach a device to your computer's carrying case that sounds an alarm if the case is moved. For example, the Targus DEFCON 1 Ultra Laptop Computer Security System is a combination lock with a motion sensor. When the lock is engaged and it undergoes any vibration, the alarm goes off.

A different way of dealing with the problem is to attach a specially designed RFID tag to your laptop itself and carry a keychain-sized monitor with you that detects when the device is separated beyond a certain range (for example, 30 or 100 feet) from the monitor. This can not only alert you to theft but let you know if you've accidentally left your laptop behind. Examples of this type of product are the TagAlert series of alarms manufactured by Remote Play (www.remoteplay.com).

Laptop alarms (software)

Yet another way of setting off an alarm is to use software that runs on your Mac itself. SlappingTurtle Software's free iAlertU (www.slappingturtle.com) uses the Sudden Motion Sensor built into most recent Mac laptops. The sensor is designed to notice if the computer is dropped and to instantly park the hard drive's heads to protect the disk from damage, but iAlertU puts it to a different use. When activated, any motion from the computer sets off an audible and visual alarm (as well as optionally emailing you an image from the laptop's iSight camera). You turn it off and on using an Apple Remote. As shown in Figure 2.1, you can also set iAlertU to respond to other triggers, such as someone closing the lid or using the keyboard or trackpad. Orbicule's TheftSensor (`www.orbicule.com/theftsensor`) is similar but currently works only with MacBooks (and not, for example, MacBook Pros — although the company reports that other models may be supported in the future).

FIGURE 2.1

iAlertU lets you set a variety of options for events — such as moving your laptop or closing its lid — that will trigger an alarm.

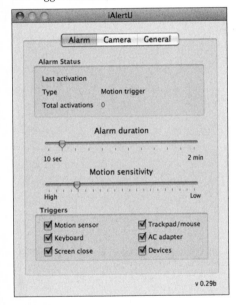

Login banners

The login window that opens when you turn on your Mac or log out normally displays a password field along with a list of users or an empty username field. With a little benign hacking, you can add text to this window. For example, the text could include:

- Your name and contact information

- A brief notice about your company's security policy

- A warning that the computer is protected by anti-theft products or that its contents are encrypted

Note

You can disable the login window (see Chapter 4), although I recommend against it. ∎

In the event that your computer is lost or stolen, contact information on this screen could aid in recovery, and it might dissuade some people from snooping or stealing your data.

To add a login banner, you must edit the file /Library/Preferences/com.apple. loginwindow.plist. Because this file is owned by root, you must either use the sudo command in Terminal to open it (for example, type **sudo open /Library/Preferences/com.apple.loginwindow.plist** to open it in your default GUI (graphical user interface) text editor or in the Apple Property List Editor if you've installed the Xcode Developer Tools) or use a text editor such as BBEdit that prompts you to authenticate with an administrator password when editing root-owned files.

Cross-Ref

For more on the root user, how file ownership works, and how to use the sudo command, see Chapter 3. ∎

In either case, once the file is open, find the first (and probably only) <dict> tag. Beneath that, add a new key and string:

```
<key>LoginwindowText</key>
<string>The text of your login banner goes here.</string>
```

Privacy Screens

Physical theft and electronic eavesdropping aren't the only ways someone can steal data from your computer. Someone looking over your shoulder can also see whatever's on your screen. This may not be a concern at home or in a private office, but if you work in a crowded office environment, on a plane, or in a public space (such as a café), you run the risk of someone nearby seeing your private information.

To address this concern, you can buy a variety of products that shield your screen from prying eyes, reducing the viewing angle so that only someone directly in front of the computer can read the screen. Privacy screens fall into two main categories: visors (or hoods) and filters.

A visor in this context is a tent-like structure (often made of fabric or lightweight plastic) that shields your screen from the top, sides, and sometimes bottom, giving you a tunnel of sorts to look through but making it extremely difficult for anyone nearby to see. As a bonus, it also reduces glare and shades the screen, making it easier to see in bright sunlight. Examples include the CompuShade (www.compushade.com), the Laptop Visor (www.laptopvisors.com), and the accordion-like Laptop Privacy Hood (www.canhamcameras.com/laptop.html).

The higher-tech and less-bulky approach is to use a 3M Privacy Filter, a thin film that applies to the screen of a laptop (or attaches to the front of a desktop monitor). The Privacy Filter reduces your screen's field of view, so you can see it at nearly full brightness when viewing it head-on, but it fades rapidly as the angle to the left or right increases, and someone sitting next to you would see only a dark screen. Be aware that the Privacy Filter only affects the side-to-side viewing angle; someone standing directly behind and above you could still read what's on your screen.

Close and save the file. The next time you log out or restart your Mac, the text you added appears in your login window.

Marking a Mac for Recovery

Even if you secure your Mac with a security cable or other lock, it could be stolen. In the case of a portable Mac, you could also simply lose it — as surprising as it may sound, thousands of people every year leave their computers in restaurants, airports, and other public places, forget them in rental car trunks, or otherwise misplace them. Whether your computer is deliberately stolen or not, it can inadvertently fall into someone else's hands, and if it does, your chances of getting it back are considerably better if your computer is physically marked in some way to show that it's yours.

Years ago, I frequently heard advice that a good way to identify objects you own was to engrave your name and social security number into them. Although your social security number does uniquely identify you, it can also be used to facilitate identity theft, so that's not a good option — and your name could help a thief more than it helps you. As for engraving, its benefit (permanence) can also be a detriment if you ever decide to sell or give away your computer, although it may be appropriate for other types of objects.

Marking valuable objects is still a good idea, but today, better options exist for doing so.

Tracking labels

Several companies sell labels that you can affix to your computer (or other valuables) featuring a tracking code and contact information. The idea is that if you were to lose the item, the person who finds it would notice the label, contact the company responsible for product tracking (using a toll-free number or a web URL), and make arrangements to return it to you, perhaps with the promise of receiving a small reward from you.

Tracking labels can also serve as a theft deterrent, at least to the extent that removing them could mar your computer's case and make it harder to resell. In addition, if your computer were to be stolen and later recovered by police, the presence of one of these labels would improve the chances that your Mac would find its way back to you.

Here are some companies that sell such labels:

- **BoomerangIt.** BoomerangIt (`www.boomerangit.com`) sells tamper-proof adhesive labels as well as luggage tags. Each tag has a unique ID and the words "Return for Reward" as an added incentive to return the item.

- **ReuniteIT.** A service of LoJack, ReuniteIT (`www.reuniteit.com`) sells similar tamper-resistant tags and labels designed to be used with all sorts of products, including cameras, computers, and luggage.

- **StuffBak.** Similar to BoomerangIt, StuffBak (`www.stuffbak.com`) sells individual labels and tags in a wide variety of sizes and shapes, including heavy-duty aluminum tags.

With optional enhanced service plans, you can have found items returned to you with no recovery fee or shipping cost.

- **Targus.** The Targus DEFCON A.R.T. Security Plate (www.targus.com) affixes to a computer with a powerful adhesive. It has a barcode that uniquely identifies the device it's attached to and contact information to arrange for the device's return if found. What makes these plates different from the other labels, though, is that when they're affixed, a special chemical on the adhesive side etches an indelible mark onto the device such that even if the plate were removed, the device would still have a trackable identifier.

- **TrackItBack.** TrackItBack (www.trackitback.com) sells permanent "Return for Reward" tracking labels in a variety of shapes and sizes, each with a URL and U.S. toll-free number to contact when an attached item is found.

- **Yellowtag.** This company, based in the United Kingdom (www.yellowtag.com), sells tags and labels similar to those made by the other providers in this list. But they also sell something called Microdots, which are tiny plastic dots — normally difficult to see except under ultraviolet light — containing your unique tracking code and a telephone number. The police can use Microdots to track and recover your items, although a thief would probably not notice them.

Operation Identification

For more than 30 years, a nationwide program called Operation Identification (www.opid.org) has existed to encourage the marking of valuables — preferably in a standardized way — as a deterrent to theft and as an aid to law enforcement when items are stolen. The program suggests that you do the following:

- Mark items with something that uniquely identifies you, such as your driver's license number. (If you do this, be sure to include the state that issued your license.) Don't, however, include your name. If you don't want to use an electric engraver — understandable for those who don't want to mar their beautiful Macs — consider using an invisible marker whose ink appears only when exposed to ultraviolet light.

- Keep a record of all the items you've marked, including their model, serial number, and any other descriptive information. Make sure you note where on the item the identifying mark was placed.

- Put an Operation I.D. sticker (often available from your local police) in your window to discourage would-be thieves.

Tracking and Recovering Stolen Macs

If your Mac is ever stolen, your first step should be to call your local police and file a report. Be sure to tell them about any labels or marks you've applied as well as the device's model and serial number.

You can give the police considerable help in finding your Mac by applying one or more technological tricks. All the products and procedures in this section require some setup to occur before your Mac is stolen. But having done that, you (or a company whose services you buy) may be able to provide the police with such useful information as the IP address of the stolen Mac, the computer's location (often to within a few hundred feet or less), and even photographs of the thief!

Caution

The information you obtain with these techniques could potentially lead you directly to the thief too, so I strongly recommend resisting the temptation to go after your Mac on your own. Give the information to the police and let them handle it for you. ■

Using tracking software and services

The first category of recovery tools involves software that runs on your Mac, usually combined with a tracking service run by the software's developer, that may enable you to discover the whereabouts of your Mac once it's in someone else's hands.

All these programs are based on the premise that a thief or the person to buy your stolen Mac is likely to let it connect to the Internet soon — at least before wiping its hard disk. This is a reasonable expectation because most thieves wouldn't go to the time and bother to isolate it from all networks, erase the disk completely, and reinstall Mac OS X from scratch before selling it or putting it to use.

Once your stolen Mac is connected to the Internet, it can send out a covert distress signal of sorts, which may contain various pieces of information but most notably includes its IP address. With the cooperation of the ISP to which that IP address is assigned, police should, in most cases, be able to discover the street address at which the computer is currently located — or at least that of the wireless hotspot it's connecting to, which should be within about 300 feet of the computer. Some of these programs provide other useful details too, and the methods they use to report them vary considerably.

Before I describe a selection of tracking programs in more detail, I should mention a few important caveats.

First, if you think tracking software sounds suspiciously like spyware, you're right — it's essentially benevolent software you can use to spy on your own Mac. Some of these programs send reports directly to you, whereas others send them to the developer's central tracking station. Although every developer of tracking software may assure you that they'd never use this data — or any back doors the software may contain — without your express permission, you must decide for yourself whether you're willing to entrust this sort of data to a third party.

Second, keep in mind that most tracking programs take pains to hide themselves to avoid detection by thieves, thus making removal difficult. However, they all become inactive if your stolen Mac is started up from another volume, such as an external hard drive or a Mac OS X Install DVD, and they can all be removed if the disk on which they were installed is completely reformatted. To make it harder for the thief to defeat the tracking program in one of these ways, most developers recommend that you enable firmware protection. However, firmware passwords aren't foolproof. An attacker who knows what to do and who has access to the computer's interior can get around it in minutes.

Cross-Ref

For more on firmware protection, see Chapter 6. ■

Also be aware that tracking software does no good if it can't actually run. For example, if you protect your boot disk with whole-disk encryption, your Mac can never boot without your password and the software can't run. Depending on the way the software is designed and installed, even less-extreme measures (such as requiring an administrator password when you turn on or wake up your Mac) could in some cases prevent tracking software from running. Therefore, if you're considering using software of this sort, you should carefully investigate how and when it runs and whether it may conflict with other security measures you use. You may need to decide whether protecting your confidential data or increasing your chances of recovering a stolen computer is the higher priority.

Cross-Ref

For more on whole-disk encryption and other ways of encrypting your files, see Chapter 13. ■

Adeona

Adeona (adeona.cs.washington.edu) is a free, open-source package with versions for Mac OS X, Windows, and Linux. It delivers your computer's IP address and other network information — as well as photos from a built-in iSight camera, if any — to a secure website. The information is encrypted with a key you provide, so only you (or a person you designate) can view it. The time between reports varies randomly but on average is about half an hour. The server Adeona uses stores a week's worth of reports at any given time.

If your Mac is stolen, you download and install software (on another computer) that lets you retrieve your encrypted location data. You can then deliver this information to the police or use a national tracking site, such as juststolen.net, to report the theft. Because Adeona is open source, there's no company behind it that can work directly with police on your behalf to help recover your computer.

BAK2u

BAK2u for Mac (www.bak2u.com) uses a $40 program called Verey that takes a more active approach than the other types of tracking software described here. Every time your Mac connects to a (wired or wireless) network, a dialog box opens asking for a password. If the user doesn't type the correct password within the time allowed, the program records video using the computer's iSight camera and sends it to you via email along with the computer's IP address, serial number, and other identifying information. (You can also opt to receive these alerts via Twitter.) Then, for good measure, BAK2u causes your computer's screen to freeze, preventing further use, and displays information about how to contact the machine's owner.

This isn't the program to use if you want to catch a thief by surprise. The alert that appears may prompt someone to return your computer, perhaps in exchange for a reward, rather than risk being arrested — but it also lets this person know you're on to him or her, which could lead the thief and your computer to disappear in a hurry. The password prompt may also be a turnoff for some users who would rather not have yet another series of intrusive barriers to ordinary use.

LoJack for Laptops

If you're familiar with the LoJack system, which uses a hidden tracking device to help police locate stolen cars, you have the general idea behind Computrace LoJack for Laptops, distributed by Absolute Software (www.lojackforlaptops.com). You purchase a subscription to the service (in increments of one year), install their special software on your Mac, and register on the company's website. During ordinary use, the software checks in with the Computrace monitoring center once a day. If your computer is lost or stolen, you must first file a police report and then contact Computrace to report the theft. When the computer checks in the next time, Computrace tells the LoJack software to increase its frequency of reports to once every 15 minutes. The company's staff then reports the information it gathers about the computer's whereabouts directly to the police and works with them to recover the computer. An optional premium subscription adds a service guarantee and the capability to remotely delete files on your computer when it's flagged as stolen.

LoJack's system offers a highly hands-off approach to recovering a stolen Mac. After filing the initial reports with the police and the company, you need not be involved in the process any further. This can be reassuring to those who would simply like the professionals to handle everything or who worry that the police may not accept evidence gathered by other means. On the other hand, because all the information captured by the LoJack software goes directly to a third party — without so much as the option for you to see it yourself — you must have a certain amount of faith in the company's privacy policy and procedures. In addition, because the LoJack software has at least one back door (the remote deletion capability), you must trust that it doesn't have others that might endanger your privacy.

Mac PhoneHome

Mac PhoneHome from Brigadoon (the makers of PC PhoneHome, www.pcphonehome.com) is a $30 program that silently sends an email message with location information to the address of your choice every time your Mac connects to the Internet. If your Mac is stolen, you must (as always) file a police report and then contact Brigadoon, whose agents work together with you and the police to recover the computer. In any case, the location information is sent only to you, which you may consider good (more privacy) or bad (more effort in the event of a theft).

MacTrak

Like Mac PhoneHome, the $60 MacTrak software from GadgetTrak (www.gadgettrak.com/products/mac) gathers information about your Mac's location and emails it directly to you — without putting any third party or server in the loop. But instead of sending out these messages all the time, the software does so only after you've activated it via a web-based form. Once you've done so, you receive email messages with your Mac's location — and a picture of whoever's sitting in front of its iSight camera — every 30 minutes.

MacTrak goes beyond providing the computer's IP address and uses Skyhook Wireless's international database of Wi-Fi base station locations to provide a physical location of your stolen Mac, often to within 20 yards or less, provided it's located in an area (typically, a large city) for which this information is available. And in addition to including photos in the email messages it sends, MacTrak can upload the photos to your Flickr account (making them public or private, as you prefer). At your request, the company also works with the police to help them recover your computer by using the information provided in the email messages.

TweetMyMac

Unlike the other products listed here, the free TweetMyMac (http://themacbox.co.uk/tweetmymac) isn't primarily a security program but rather remote-control software that lets you send commands to your Mac from almost any computer or cell phone in the world using specially constructed Twitter messages. But among the things you can do with TweetMyMac are obtaining your Mac's current IP address, getting a screenshot or a photo from the built-in iSight camera, turning on the screensaver, logging out (or simply locking your Mac's user account), saying something using a text-to-speech system, and even executing arbitrary shell commands. Using a combination of these messages, you can perform most of the activities offered by stand-alone tracking software.

Undercover

Undercover, a $49 program developed by Belgian company Orbicule (www.orbicule.com/undercover), has a feature set roughly similar to that of BAK2u's Verey software — but without the repeated password prompts. Every six minutes, Undercover checks in with Orbicule's servers, but no identifying information is transmitted unless you report the computer as stolen by sending the company a unique code you should have received by email after installing the software. Once you do that, Undercover begins sending not only your Mac's location information and photos from its iSight camera but also screenshots (the assumption being that whatever the thief may have typed on the screen — in an email message or chat window, for example — could help to identify who's using the computer). Orbicule works with the ISP to which the Mac is connected to narrow down the computer's exact location and then contacts the police with the information to help them recover it.

In the event that the police are unable to recover your Mac, Undercover switches into another mode. It simulates a hardware failure in an attempt to induce the thief to sell the computer or take it to a repair shop. Once Orbicule determines that the computer has changed hands (which is particularly obvious if your Mac happens to report the IP address of a known reseller or Apple service provider), it signals Undercover to display a notice on the screen stating that it's been stolen — including the company's contact information (not yours) and the promise of a finder's fee if the device is returned, which Orbicule covers. In addition to displaying a message on the screen, Undercover sets your Mac's volume to its highest level and uses the built-in speech synthesizer to shout the message to anyone listening.

VigiMac

Like Adeona, VigiMac (www.vigimac.com) is a free tool for tracking your Mac. It's less sophisticated than the other options listed here — no iSight photos, screenshots, Wi-Fi location, or simulated screen problems. In fact, the program is the epitome of simplicity. It consists of two files: an 18-line shell script that sends your Mac's serial number — or, if that can't be determined, the MAC (Media Access Control) address of its AirPort card — to VigiMac's server (in the process informing them of your Mac's IP address) and a property list file that instructs the Mac OS X launchd process to run the tracking script every three minutes. After installing the software, you register your Mac's serial number on VigiMac's website. Then, whenever you want to track your Mac, you can send VigiMac an email message or type your ID and password on its site. You're responsible for providing any information you obtain on your own to the police.

Tip

When using any tracking software (commercial or otherwise), it's best to provide some way for the thief to actually use your computer rather than locking them out entirely. The more time they spend sitting in front of the screen and connected to the Internet, the better your chances of collecting the information you need to track the computer. Therefore, be sure to turn on a guest account or set up an extra standard account with no administrator privileges and no password (see Chapter 3). That way, your personal data still has some protection. ■

Using command-line software to track a Mac

In lieu of installing commercial tracking software, you can roll your own if you feel so inclined. The procedure boils down to two steps:

- First, write a shell script that performs whatever sort of tracking activities you want.
- Then, use cron or launchd to schedule the script to run at the interval of your choice.

If you're already comfortable working in the Mac OS X command line, know some shell scripting, and have experience scheduling tasks to run with a command-line tool, this is a piece of cake; simply refer to some of the suggestions here for a few specific commands you might want to use. If your Unix is a bit rusty but you don't mind tinkering, start with the prepackaged files I provide at the end of this section and then, if you feel adventurous, modify them to meet your needs. In any case, this isn't a good option for anyone averse to using the command line. Sticking with one of the prepackaged commercial or open-source solutions is a much better use of your time.

Your script can include any of numerous commands; what I provide here are some examples of components you might want to include in your script. When working in a Unix shell, there are typically numerous ways to do just about anything, so you may well be able to come up with a more clever or efficient way of performing any of these tasks.

Getting your Mac's public IP address

The most important piece of information you need for tracking your Mac is its public IP address. (If it's behind a NAT gateway, it has a private IP address too, such as 10.0.0.1, but the public address — the address of the router or gateway itself — is what's most useful in tracking your Mac down because it's unique and can usually be traced to a specific geographic location.)

The easiest way to find the public IP address of your Mac is to use the Unix curl command to consult one of the websites that reports this information. For example, either of these commands would work (type them into Terminal to test them):

```
curl -s http://www.whatismyip.com/automation/n09230945.asp
```

or

```
curl -s http://www.showmyip.com/simple/
```

To save information to a file, use the greater than (>) symbol followed by a file name:

```
curl -s http://www.showmyip.com/simple/ > filename.txt
```

You may not need to do this if you intend to pipe the information to another program, such as `mail`.

Getting your Mac's serial number

If you install a tracking script on more than one computer — or if you want evidence of your stolen Mac's serial number to provide to the police — you can get your Mac's serial number with this line (note that capitalization is important):

```
system_profiler SPHardwareDataType | grep Serial
```

Getting the MAC address of your Mac's AirPort card

Every network interface on your computer has a unique *MAC* (Media Access Control) address, which is a string of characters that can serve as another way of identifying your computer. (I should say the MAC addresses are theoretically unique because it's easy enough for someone to *spoof*, or forge, a MAC address. But it's relatively unlikely that a thief would go to the bother of doing that with your Mac.)

This command returns the MAC address of the network card located at interface en1, which is usually (but not always) the built-in AirPort card:

```
ifconfig en1 | grep ether | tail -c 19
```

If you're not sure your AirPort card is located at en1, type **ifconfig** (with no arguments) to list all your Ethernet interfaces.

Capturing images from your Mac's iSight camera

If you want to replicate the feature many tracking programs have of snapping a photo (presumably of the thief) from your Mac's built-in iSight camera, the easiest way to do so is to download the free isightcapture program from www.intergalactic.de/pages/iSight.html.

You can install this anywhere, but I suggest putting it in /usr/local/bin.

Then, to use it, you simply run it and give it the pathname of the resulting image file:

```
/usr/local/bin/isightcapture /usr/share/image.png
```

This takes a photo with your iSight camera, places it in /usr/share, and names it image.png. The green light next to the camera comes on briefly while the photo is being taken.

The author of `isightcapture` notes that the program doesn't work correctly when scheduled with `cron`; scheduling it with `launchd` does work, however.

Capturing screenshots

Do you like Undercover's trick of snapping images of what's on your screen? You can do it yourself by using the `screencapture` command, followed by the pathname of the resulting image:

```
screencapture /usr/share/screen.png
```

Mailing information to yourself

Once you've collected the information you want, what do you do with it? One option is to send yourself email messages with the information you've found. Sending email from the command line can be either trivially easy or frustratingly complex, depending on what software you've installed on your Mac, what restrictions your ISP places on email, how elaborate you want the messages to be, and so on. For the purposes of this brief overview, I provide just a few examples that use the Unix mail program built into Mac OS X. This isn't necessarily the best or most flexible method, but it's the easiest.

To send a message with the contents "contents" and the subject "subject" to user@domain.com, you could use the following:

```
echo "contents" | mail -s "subject" user@domain.com
```

For a more practical example, if you wanted to mail your Mac's IP address (without having to save it to an intermediate file first), you could do it this way:

```
curl -s http://www.showmyip.com/simple/ | mail -s "subject" user@
    domain.com
```

Or if you saved information (perhaps your Mac's IP address, MAC address, and serial number) to a file, you could send it as follows:

```
cat filename.txt | mail -s "subject" user@domain.com
```

If you want to mail yourself graphics (images from your iSight camera or screenshots), the simplest way to do so is to use the uuencode utility. Images sent this way may appear as garbage characters in some email clients — Gmail, for example, doesn't display the images in its web interface, whereas Apple Mail does.

To send a file named `img.png` (located in the same directory as the script), type the following:

```
uuencode img.png img.png | mail -s "subject" user@domain.com
```

And if you want your message to include text as well as a graphic, add text like so:

```
(echo "contents"; uuencode img.png img.png) | mail -s "subject" user@
    domain.com
```

Sending information to an FTP server

If you have access to an FTP server, you can also upload the information you capture to a pre-determined location on that server. FTP is an intrinsically unsecure protocol, so don't use this method to send any confidential information.

Cross-Ref

For more on the security risks of transferring files with FTP, see Chapter 7. ■

To upload a file to an FTP server with the username "username" and the password "password," type this:

```
curl -T filename.txt -u username:password ftp://ftp.domain.com/
```

If you're storing information in a local file that keeps being overwritten and you'd like to append the data to the file on your FTP server each time, type the following:

```
curl -T filename.txt -a -u username:password ftp://ftp.domain.com/
```

Sending information to a web server

If you run your own web server and have access to its error logs, you can have your tracking script attempt to get a specially named nonexistent file on your server and then search your logs for that special name.

For example, the following command would request a nonexistent document called `iwasstolen` at the domain `www.domain.com`. Without having to supply any additional information, you automatically log the public IP address of the computer making the request:

```
curl -s "http://www.domain.com/iwasstolen > /dev/null"
```

You can get much more elaborate than this with the `curl` command — filling in web forms, uploading photos, and more. To learn everything `curl` can do, see its documentation at `curl.netmirror.org/docs/manual.html`.

Wrapping it all up

Once you've finished writing your script, be sure you store it in a place where it's unlikely to be discovered accidentally (and where it can run even if no user is logged in). Also, give it an innocuous file name. For example, you might store it in `/usr/bin` or `/usr/local/bin` with the name `ztk.sh`. And make sure it's readable and executable:

```
sudo chmod 755 ztk.sh
```

Scheduling a script to run automatically

Mac OS X contains two main mechanisms for scheduling activities: `cron` and `launchd`. `cron` is the same on Mac OS X as on other varieties of Unix and can be configured in the same way, but `launchd` provides greater flexibility (and is compatible with the `isightcapture` utility).

You can learn all about `cron` from numerous websites, such as `www.macosxhints.com/article.php?story=2001020700163714`. You can also download a free GUI tool called Cronnix from `www.macupdate.com/info.php/id/7486` to help you configure `cron`.

To learn about using `launchd`, read an article I wrote for *Macworld*: "Launch Your Mac" (`www.macworld.com/2006/01/secrets/februarygeekfactor/`). Once again, there's a free program you can download to help you configure `launchd`: Lingon (`http://sourceforge.net/projects/lingon/`).

Example files

One way to put several of these commands together into a simple script is the following, which collects the computer's current public IP address, its serial number, and a photo from its iSight camera and then sends them to you via email. Type the following into a text file, store it in `/usr/bin` with the name `ztk.sh`, and change its permissions to 755 (as just described). In the last line, there should be no return, just a space, between `/usr/share/image.png` and `image.png`:

```
#!/bin/sh
# Send the public IP address, serial number, and iSight photo
# from this Mac to user@domain.com
ipadd=`curl -s http://www.showmyip.com/simple/`
serial=`system_profiler SPHardwareDataType | grep Serial`
/usr/local/bin/isightcapture /usr/share/image.png
(echo IP address: $ipadd "\n" $serial; uuencode /usr/share/image.png
    image.png) | mail -s "Reporting In" user@domain.com
```

To try this out, type the following in Terminal:

```
sudo /usr/bin/ztk.sh
```

and type your administrator password when prompted.

To run this script every 30 minutes by using `launchd`, create a text file with the following contents, name it `com.wiley.ztk`, put it in `/Library/LaunchDaemons`, and then restart your Mac:

```
<?xml version="1.0" encoding="UTF-8"?>
<!DOCTYPE plist PUBLIC "-//Apple//DTD PLIST 1.0//EN" "http://www.
    apple.com/DTDs/PropertyList-1.0.dtd">
<plist version="1.0">
<dict>
  <key>Label</key>
  <string>com.wiley.ztk</string>
  <key>ProgramArguments</key>
  <array>
        <string>/usr/bin/ztk.sh</string>
  </array>
  <key>RunAtLoad</key>
  <true/>
```

```
  <key>StartInterval</key>
  <integer>1800</integer>
</dict>
</plist>
```

Tracking a Mac with Back to My Mac

Even without any sort of tracking software installed, you may be able to learn the location of a stolen Mac, take pictures using your iSight camera, and perform other tasks that make life difficult for the thief. In a few well-publicized cases, users who had configured their Macs to use Mac OS X's Back to My Mac feature were able to log in to their stolen Macs remotely, retrieving information that led police to the person who had swiped it.

Back to My Mac ordinarily lets you log in to a remote Mac to share files or control the screen — for example, to fetch a document you left on your Mac at home or to run an application that's only on your work Mac. Behind the scenes, Back to My Mac enables one of your Macs to figure out how to contact another one, without knowing the remote IP address and even, in most cases, whether the remote Mac is behind a NAT gateway.

This technique comes with a few significant qualifications:

- You must be a member of Apple's $99-per-year MobileMe service (www.me.com).
- You must have turned on Back to My Mac before your Mac was stolen.
- Your stolen Mac must connect to the Internet directly or via hardware that supports Universal Plug and Play (UPnP) or NAT Port Mapping Protocol (NAT-PMP), two protocols a router or gateway can use to direct connections dynamically to particular computers.
- When you connect to your stolen Mac with Back to My Mac, you risk being discovered by the thief.

Although these are nontrivial issues, this is nevertheless a powerful technique that can in some cases enable you to recover a Mac when all else fails.

First, assuming you've already signed up for a MobileMe account, set up Back to My Mac:

1. **Choose ⇨ System Preferences to open System Preferences and then click MobileMe to open the MobileMe pane.**
2. **Click the Account tab and then verify that it says "Signed into MobileMe."** If not, type your MobileMe credentials in the fields provided and then click Sign In.
3. **Click the Back to My Mac tab.**
4. **If you see a button labeled Stop and a message that Back to My Mac is on, skip to step 5; otherwise, click Start.** The window should then look like Figure 2.2.

FIGURE 2.2

FIGURE 2.2

When Back to My Mac is running, you see this message on the MobileMe pane of System Preferences. If you see a Start button instead, click it to activate Back to My Mac.

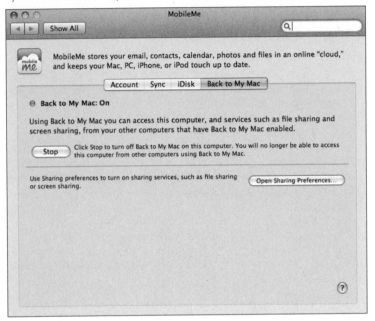

Note

If the Back to My Mac pane displays a warning that your router doesn't support NAT-PMP or UPnP, it means you can't test Back to My Mac now, but it could still be the case that if your Mac is stolen, the thief's network would support them and you'd be able to use this technique. ∎

5. Choose View ⇨ Sharing to switch to the Sharing preference pane.

6. **Click the check boxes for at least one or more of the following, as shown in Figure 2.3: Screen Sharing, File Sharing, and Remote Login.** If you turn on all three options, you increase your options for monitoring your Mac remotely, but you also open up more potential security holes (although you can reduce that risk considerably by allowing only yourself access to the shared resources by using your username and password).

7. Close System Preferences.

Cross-Ref

For more on sharing options, see Chapter 7. ∎

FIGURE 2.3

Turning on File Sharing, Screen Sharing, and Remote Login gives you the greatest range of options for tracking a stolen Mac using Back to My Mac.

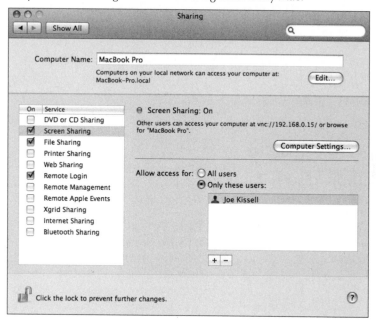

Suppose your Mac is stolen and you want to find out who's using it. You must use another Mac on which you've signed in to the MobileMe preference pane (as just described) with the same username and password. Keep an eye on the sidebar of your Finder windows. If you see the name of your stolen Mac show up there, you know that the thief has connected it to the Internet and that Back to My Mac is active. Then, you can try any of the following.

Share your Mac's screen

If you turned on Screen Sharing, you can get a live view of what's happening on your stolen Mac's screen — and even run applications (or perform other mischief). To do this, select your Mac from the sidebar of the Finder window and then click Share Screen. Supply your MobileMe credentials if prompted, and you should see the screen of your remote Mac.

This is a powerful capability, but beware: If the thief notices the pointer moving on the screen and strange things happening, your efforts to spy on your own Mac could be cut short. All it takes to stop you is disconnecting from the Internet or deselecting one check box in System Preferences. So, a word of advice if you ever attempt this: After connecting, watch your stolen Mac's screen for a while, keeping your pointer outside the Screen Sharing window. Take no action (except perhaps pressing ⌘+Shift+3 to take screenshots) until you've verified that nothing has happened for several minutes — likely signaling that the thief isn't looking at the screen.

Once you're connected, work quickly to discover your remote Mac's public IP address, which you should then share with the police. The easiest way to get it is to open a web browser and visit a site such as whatismyip.com.

Your next step, if you have the opportunity, is to take a picture using your stolen Mac's iSight camera. An easy way to do this is to open Photo Booth (which is located in /Applications), click the red camera icon at the bottom of the window, and then quickly quit the program. By default, Photo Booth stores pictures in ~/Pictures/Photo Booth, so you can navigate to that location by using File Sharing or open Mail and then email the photo to yourself if it shows anything useful.

Because screen sharing involves significant risk of being discovered, a safer (if geekier) approach is to connect to your Mac silently with SSH, which I describe in just a moment.

Retrieve (or delete) files

If you turned on File Sharing, you can copy important files (including, perhaps, any photos you took with Photo Booth) to the Mac you're currently using, and you can also delete any particularly sensitive files you don't want the thief to be able to see.

To do this, select your Mac from the sidebar of the Finder window. If you don't already see the message "Connected as:" followed by your username, click Connect As, type your username and password, and then click Connect. Then, navigate to the files you want and drag them to the Mac you're now using — or drag files to the Trash and then choose Finder ➪ Empty Trash.

Open an SSH session

If you turned on Remote Login, you can type a few commands into Terminal and get all sorts of information about your stolen Mac without alerting the person currently using it. Follow these steps:

1. Open Terminal, which is located in /Applications/Utilities.

2. Choose Shell ➪ New Remote Connection to open the Connect to server dialog box, as shown in Figure 2.4.

3. In the Service list on the left, select Secure Shell (ssh). If your stolen Mac is accessible via Back to My Mac, it appears in the Server list (possibly under a Discovered Servers heading).

4. In the User field, type a username (ideally, the username of an administrator account) that has access to the Mac to which you're connecting.

5. Select your remote Mac from the Server list and then click Connect. A new Terminal window opens with an SSH connection to your remote Mac.

6. Type your password when prompted.

At this point, you can use any of the commands listed earlier in this chapter to get information about your Mac, take iSight photos and screenshots, and even mail files to yourself.

FIGURE 2.4

To open an SSH session to a remote Mac via Back to My Mac, select it in the list on the right, type your username, and then click Connect.

Buying Computer Insurance

In this chapter, the main focus is protecting your Mac from theft or recovering it if it's stolen. If you're unable to recover a stolen computer, you may lose the data that's on it, but a good insurance policy at least reimburses you for most of the cost of the hardware itself.

Your existing homeowner's, renter's, or business insurance may provide coverage against loss of your computer equipment. But be sure to read the fine print carefully — you may be surprised at what limitations and exclusions it contains. For example, your policy may cover theft but only if the computer is stolen from your home and not if it's stolen when you're traveling with it. Some policies specifically exclude or limit reimbursements for high-value articles, which may include your Mac. And accidental damage is unlikely to be covered at all.

If you need insurance that covers your computer equipment in ways that your existing policies don't, think about getting a separate computer insurance policy.

The best-known purveyor of insurance specifically for computers is the Safeware Insurance Agency (www.safeware.com), based in Columbus, Ohio, and underwritten by the American Bankers Insurance Company of Florida and the American Reliable Insurance Company. Safeware offers policies to residents of the United States and Canada, with optional worldwide coverage, for protection of desktop and laptop computers, peripherals, and mobile devices.

continued

continued

Note

U.K. residents might want to investigate computer insurance policies available from JS Insurance (www. jsinsurance.co.uk/computer_insurance) **or Insure and Go** (www.insureandgo.com). ■

One of the interesting features of Safeware policies is that many of them cover not only theft and damage from disasters such as fire and flood when the equipment is located in your home or office but also theft from unattended vehicles (to a limited extent), damage from drops, falls, and liquid spills, and other common sources of loss. Policies are available for individuals, small businesses, educational institutions, and large corporations.

The exact cost of a Safeware policy depends on numerous variables, such as the value of the equipment you want to cover, where it's used, and where you live. However, roughly speaking, individuals can get a policy with good basic coverage of a single Mac system (even a fairly expensive one) for a few hundred dollars or less per year — typically less than the cost of an AppleCare Protection Plan policy (an extended warranty program that covers factory defects but not accidental damage or theft). That makes Safeware (or a comparable policy from another company) a smart investment, especially for people who travel extensively with a laptop.

Summary

In this chapter, I covered some of the ways to prevent your Mac from being stolen or to recover it if it is. I described a variety of locks and enclosures you can use to physically secure a Mac as well as alarms that can go off if your Mac is moved or separated from you by more than a small distance. I discussed ways of marking your Mac to identify it and aid police (or anyone else who might stumble upon your missing computer) in returning it to you, such as tracking stickers and marking it with your driver's license number. And I covered several techniques that you can use to track a Mac that's gone missing by using special software or Back to My Mac to discover its whereabouts and provide information the police can use to recover it.

Working with User Accounts

Mac OS X is an inherently multi-user operating system, even if only one person ever uses a particular computer. Each user has an account — and in addition, there are numerous built-in accounts that aren't normally visible to users. This chapter begins with an overview of what accounts have to do with security. I describe what accounts are, how to configure them, and how they relate to the pervasive notion of permissions.

How Accounts Affect Security

A great many Mac OS X security features revolve crucially around the concept of accounts. Although accounts in and of themselves are neutral with respect to security, they can be configured to put formidable barriers between malicious users (or software) and your computer's valuable data and resources.

So, what is an account, how does it work, and what exactly does it have to do with security?

The notion of accounts

The word *account* harks back to a time before personal computers, when the customary way of using a computer was for many people to share a single CPU — either by taking turns or by logging in simultaneously from simple terminals that consisted of little more than a keyboard, display (or printer), and network connection. In this sort of environment, having an account on a computer meant having permission to access it (with a username and password) and storage space for one's files and programs, which would be uniquely identified. Each user's activities could be logged, time limits and other restrictions could be put in place, and (if necessary) any user could even be billed according to the level of resource use. (Nowadays, most of us have accounts on numerous websites and other online services that amount to a similar kind of resource sharing.)

In the early days of the Mac, the concept of an account had no place. Unlike some of its predecessors, the Mac was more like an appliance. Only one person could use it at a time, and likely as not, a given Mac would have just one user in total. Over time, however, it became clear that multiple people frequently used a single Mac, and Apple reinstated the notion of accounts as a way these multi-user Macs could, at least in a limited fashion, keep certain files and resources segregated and private from other users.

With Mac OS X and its Unix core, the Mac has come full circle with the notion of accounts. Now, instead of accounts being awkwardly grafted onto an inherently single-user operating system, you have somewhat the reverse: an inherently multi-user operating system retrofitted to behave, at least superficially, more like a single-user computer. Accounts aren't optional, and their presence may intrude into your work from time to time, but the fact that the operating system was designed top to bottom to respect and exploit this division of resources provides considerable security.

What a Mac OS X account is

At its most basic level, an account in Mac OS X is a number — 501, for example. (Technically, this number is known as the *UID*, or user identifier; there's also a *GID*, or group identifier.) Every one of the million or more files on your Mac has an owner, which is the person or system process that created it or is responsible for it. If your account number is 501 and a file is owned by user 501, that makes you the file's owner. Likewise, every program that runs on your Mac, of which dozens or hundreds may be active at any one time, has an owner — the user (human or virtual) that started the program and has the authority to use its output or stop it.

Because numbers aren't terribly memorable or user-friendly, Mac OS X refers to accounts in two other ways. First is the short username (for example, joe), which is usually used to identify an item's owner in the user interface. Even though a file may in fact be owned by user 501, Mac OS X ordinarily tells me it's owned by joe if that's the short name associated with that particular number because it's easier to use and understand. But I still have the option, in some cases (such as when changing file ownership in Terminal), to issue commands using the numerical account identifier if I know it and care to use it.

Each account also has a long username, such as Joe Kissell, which lets users interact with their Macs using the terms most familiar to them from the real world rather than the shorter (if easier to type) numeric or alphabetic names Mac OS X uses internally.

Because one of the functions of accounts is to identify who's using the computer, each account may include a number of additional pieces of information — of which the most important is a password. A person or process with the username (long, short, or numeric) and password corresponding to an account gets permission to use any of the resources associated with the account. Typing your username and password when asked to do so is called *authenticating*, which means nothing more than identifying yourself to Mac OS X (or another computer system).

When you create an account for a new user on your Mac, Mac OS X helpfully sets aside a storage area exclusively for that user — the *home folder*, which is stored in /Users/*short-username*. Each user's home folder starts out the same, with subfolders for common files such as Documents, Music, and Pictures; users can add to these folders and modify them as needed. For the most part, every file or folder the user creates anywhere inside the home folder is automatically marked as being owned by that user. Mac OS X also assumes that each user wants to be able to store customized preferences for everything from the Desktop background to the ways individual features in his or her favorite programs behave. So, it puts user-specific preference files in a subfolder of the user's Library folder (/Users/*short-username*/Library/Preferences).

Note

Because it's often necessary to refer to one's own home folder, I use a standard shorthand to do so: the tilde (~) character. So, if your short username is joe, then while logged in, your home folder (/Users/joe) is ~, and your Documents folder is located at ~/Documents. ■

So, although user accounts can involve a great many files, permissions, and features, at their core, they boil down to these basics: an identifier (name or number), a password, and a home folder.

How accounts work

Accounts work in conjunction with permissions (described next) to specify who has the authority to perform various activities. It's not enough to say that Bob owns one file on a Mac whereas Cindy owns another if either user can freely open, run, or delete any file owned by the other. Instead, every file specifies not only its owner but several other key pieces of *metadata*, or extra information about the file beyond its actual content — including what activities the owner is allowed to do with that file and what activities other users are allowed to do with it. Mac OS X is designed to enforce these permissions rigidly: Only a user who has (by one means or another) permission to do something with a given file can do so.

As a result, if Cindy owns a file called bobisaloser.txt, and if that file's metadata says that only Cindy has read access, then Bob can't open it, however much he might want to — unless he knows Cindy's password or the password of an administrator who can access Cindy's files.

This concept of ownership and permissions doesn't just involve the files created by individual human users; it applies to every single file — including, notably, all those that make up Mac OS X itself. That means, as counterintuitive as it may sound, that you don't own all the files on your own Mac, even if you're the sole user and have an administrator account. For example, many files that make up Mac OS X itself are owned by a user called root and have permission settings that prevent any ordinary user from changing or deleting them. That's a very good thing because it means you can't accidentally delete files that would prevent Mac OS X from running properly.

The principle of least privilege

Limited access to root-owned files is just one example of an underlying concept called the *principle of least privilege*, which essentially means that every process and every user should have only as much authority as they need. For example, Bob obviously needs to be able to read documents he creates, but he doesn't necessarily need to be able to read Cindy's documents or modify parts of the operating system. If your Mac is running a web server, the server needs to be able to read certain files and send information over the network, but it doesn't need to be able to delete files belonging to other users or run other programs that have nothing to do with the server. The core files that make up the operating system need the authority to do just about anything, but everything else should be restricted as much as possible, with elevations in privilege granted or exceptions made only when clearly necessary.

A Mac's administrator could certainly subvert the principle of least privilege by changing the permissions of private files or granting other users liberal access to system resources. But under ordinary circumstances, Mac OS X comes reasonably close to the ideal, albeit with a few compromises that enhance usability or work around other problems. This arrangement has some important implications:

- Each user's files are isolated from those of other users, increasing privacy.
- Critical system processes are (partially) isolated from each other and from user accounts to minimize potential damage from hacking or malware.
- Users can't install software that could potentially endanger the security of the whole computer or of other users without administrative privileges.
- Sharing of files and other system resources across a network can be restricted to only those users with explicit permission.

Understanding POSIX Permissions

As I mentioned, Mac OS X, as a variety of Unix, labels each and every file and folder with a series of permissions. Leopard and Snow Leopard follow the POSIX standard, which specifies, among other things, a way to express permissions. Most other varieties of Unix also use POSIX permissions.

Read, write, and execute

To begin at the simplest level, POSIX permissions include three main capabilities for any item: read (abbreviated r), write (abbreviated w), and execute (abbreviated x). Read, of course, means open a file and see what's inside. Write permission implies permission to modify or delete a file or folder. Execute permission means, in the case of a program, permission to run it — or, in the case of a folder, permission to list its contents.

Read, write, and execute permissions for a file or folder appear as a simple cluster of three characters, always in the same order: rwx. If all three characters are present, then a user has read, write, and execute permission. If any character is replaced with a hyphen (-), it means the user doesn't have that permission. So, r-x means permission to read and execute but not write; rw- means permission to read and write but not execute; r-- means permission to read but not write or execute.

User, group, and other

In fact, you never see just one cluster of rwx characters; they always come in threes: rwxrwxrwx. Although r, w, and x always mean the same thing, they apply to different sets of users:

- The first set of three characters applies to the item's owner (or *user*, in POSIX parlance) — abbreviated u.

- The middle set of three characters applies to the item's group (abbreviated g), which is to say a group of users also considered to own the file.

- The final set of three characters applies to all other users (abbreviated o).

Note

When I say permissions always come in threes, that's an oversimplification. Technically, they come in fours, with the fourth set referring to three additional bits that can be on or off: the set UID, set GID, and sticky bits. I discuss these briefly later in this chapter, but you don't need to understand them to make sense of basic permissions. ■

Let's look at a few permission specifications with spaces added to divide them into user, group, and other categories.

```
rwx r-- r--
```

In this formulation, the user has permission to do anything — read (r), write (w), or execute (x), whereas the group and other users have permission only to read.

```
r-- -w- --x
```

I can't think of any reason someone would do this, but these permissions mean that only the user can read the file, only the group can write the file, and others can execute it but not read or write.

```
rw- rw- rw-
```

Here, user, group, and others — in other words, everyone — can read and write the item, but no one (not even the owner) can execute it.

```
rwx r-x r-x
```

In this common set of permissions, anyone can read or execute the item, but only the owner can write it.

Viewing file permissions

Although every file in Mac OS X has specifications for these permissions, they don't appear in this format in the graphical interface. To see all the details, open Terminal, located in /Applications/Utilities, and type **ls -l**. (The ls command means list, and the -l flag means long, which is to say showing important details such as permissions rather than just file names.) The screen shows something like this:

```
total 0
drwx------+   3 joe   staff   102 Jan 25 19:58 Desktop
drwx------+   4 joe   staff   136 Jan 25 19:58 Documents
drwx------+   4 joe   staff   136 Jan 25 19:58 Downloads
drwx------  23 joe   staff   782 Jan 25 19:58 Library
drwx------+   3 joe   staff   102 Jan 25 19:58 Movies
drwx------+   3 joe   staff   102 Jan 25 19:58 Music
drwx------+   4 joe   staff   136 Jan 25 19:58 Pictures
drwxr-xr-x+   5 joe   staff   170 Jan 25 19:58 Public
drwxr-xr-x    5 joe   staff   170 Jan 25 19:58 Sites
```

For now, let's look at just one line, the one for Desktop:

```
drwx------+   3 joe   staff   102 Jan 25 19:58 Desktop
```

The string at the beginning should look familiar, except that there's a d at the beginning and a + at the end. The d means this item is a directory (folder); if it were an ordinary file, it would instead look like -rwx------+. The + at the end means that that item has an access control list (ACL), which I describe at the end of this chapter — you can safely ignore it for now. So, the permissions for this item say that the owner can read, write, or execute (list the contents of) the Desktop folder but that the group and others have no access. And who is the owner? It's joe, the first name in the line; staff is the group. (You surely guessed that the date and time show when that item was last modified. As for the other numbers, the one to the left of the user is the number of items in the directory, whereas the one to the right of the group is the size, in bytes, of the item. But those numbers aren't pertinent to our current discussion, so you can pretend they're not there.)

Octal permissions

The usual way of displaying permissions, with single-letter abbreviations (r, w, x), makes them easy to read. But when it comes time to manipulate permissions, they're frequently referred to in a different format that's more computer-friendly: *octal*, or base-8, notation.

To put it in its simplest possible terms, expressing permissions in octal notation means substituting the number 4 for every r, 2 for every w, and 1 for every x — and then adding up those numbers separately for user, group, and other. Let me illustrate. Say the user's permissions are:

```
r-x
```

Because r is equivalent to 4 and x is equivalent to 1, that adds up to 5; the user's permissions, expressed in octal, are 5. Conversely, if I told you that the user's permissions were 3, you could deduce that they're really this:

```
-wx
```

That's because the only combination of 4, 2, and 1 that can give you 3 is 2 (w) plus 1 (x).

Now, look at a whole string for user, group, and other (with spaces added for readability):

```
rwx r-x r--
```

The user's permissions (rwx) add up as follows: r (4) + w (2) + x (1) = 7. The group's permissions (r-x) add up like this: r (4) + x (1) = 5. And permissions for other (r) are simply 4. Thus, the octal permissions for this entire item are 754.

Reversing the process, if I told you that a file had permissions 644, you could break it down as follows. Because 6 can only be the combination of r (4) and w (2), the user's permissions are rw-. The group and others both have permissions of 4, which is r — read only — so they're r--. Thus, the full permissions for this item are:

> rw- r-- r--

Note

I mentioned earlier that permissions have another set of three bits (set GID, set UID, and sticky bit); these can also be represented by an octal number. So, you may see permissions such as 0644 or 1755, in which the first number indicates the state of these other characteristics. ■

Modifying file permissions

To change a file's permissions (or *mode* in Unix parlance), you use the chmod (change mode) command in a Terminal window. To learn about the many ways in which you can use this command, type **man chmod** to view its manual page. I hit some of the highlights here.

You can use chmod in either of two basic ways. In the first way, you simply add or subtract permissions for user (u), group (g), or other (o) by using the + or - characters. This is known as chmod's *symbolic* mode. For example, say you come across a file named abc with these permissions:

> r--r--r--

To add write permission for the owner, type **chmod o+w abc**, which means change the permissions for file abc such that the owner (o) adds (+) write (w) permission. You can change permission for more than one entity at once; to give both the owner (o) and group (g) execute permission, type **chmod og+x**. You can also change more than one permission at a time; to give others both write and execute permission, type **chmod o+wx abc**. To remove a permission, switch to minus (-): typing **chown go-wx** removes write and execute permissions for the group and others.

A quicker way to change a file's permissions is to use octal notation, described previously, in what chmod refers to as *absolute* mode. Absolute mode also lets you instantly specify combinations that would take two or more passes with the first method — such as removing execute permission for user and group while adding write permission for group and other. To use octal notation, simply determine the final permission you want the item to have, expressed in octal, and type **chmod** followed by the octal number and the file name. For example, earlier I showed that octal 644 is equivalent to r--r--r--. Therefore, to change abc to have that set of permissions (regardless of what they are now), you could type **chmod 644 abc**.

Note

If you're not the owner of the file whose permissions you're trying to modify or a member of a group with write access to the file, you must precede chmod with the sudo command (described later in this chapter) to temporarily gain permission to make the change. ∎

Modifying file ownership

The chmod command can change permissions for a file or folder but not for its owner. To change a file's owner, use the chown command:

```
chown joe abc
```

This reads: "Assign the user named joe as the owner of file abc." You can change a file's group at the same time by putting a colon and the group's name after the owner. For example, to change the owner of the file abc to joe and the group to geeks, type this:

```
chown joe:geeks abc
```

You can also change the group without changing the owner by leaving out the owner but keeping the colon:

```
chown :geeks abc
```

As with changing permissions, you must already have suitable permissions to change an item's ownership. More often than not, this requires using sudo to temporarily assume root privileges.

Using the Get Info window

So far, I've discussed file permissions only as they appear in Mac OS X's command-line interface. The Finder also lets you see and modify permissions but only to a limited degree — for example, you can't change a file's execute permission in the Finder nor can you assign ownership to a hidden user account, such as root or www.

To see the Finder's representation of permissions for a file or folder, select it and then choose File ➪ Get Info (or press ⌘+I). In the bottom of the window that opens is the Sharing & Permissions section (shown in Figure 3.1), which shows you the current permissions and enables you to change them.

In this example, the file's owner (user), represented by the icon with one silhouette, has read and write privileges for the file. The file's group (admin, in this case), with the double silhouette, has read-only access, as does everyone else (others, with the triple silhouette).

To change permissions in this window, you must first click the lock icon and authenticate with your username and password. For any given entity, you can choose a different permission level by clicking the text in the Privilege column and choosing a different value from the pop-up menu. For the user and group, your only options are Read & Write or Read only; for the everyone (others) option, you can also choose No Access.

FIGURE 3.1

The Sharing & Permissions section at the bottom of the Finder's Get Info window displays and lets you modify basic information about an item's permissions.

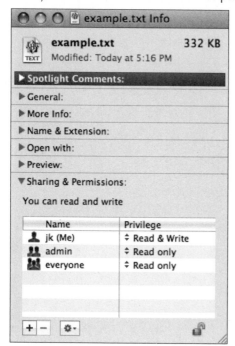

To add a user or group, click the Add (+) button at the bottom of the window and select one of the users or groups shown in the Accounts pane of System Preferences or define a new user. To remove a user or group, click the Remove (–) button. Because POSIX permissions permit a file to have only one user and one group, if you add more, they're defined by using ACLs (discussed at the end of this chapter).

If a file's owner or group isn't one that's visible in the Accounts preference pane, it appears in this list as unknown. Similarly, if a user or group has nonstandard privileges (such as an ACL), the Privilege column simply says custom.

If you find this interface too limiting but still want to manage permissions in a graphical environment, you can use any of several Mac OS X applications that give you much more detailed access to ownership and permissions. Examples include the following:

- FileXaminer by Gideon Softworks, shown in Figure 3.2 (www.gideonsoftworks.com/filexaminer.html, $10)

- PathFinder, Cocoatech's $40 Finder replacement (http://cocoatech.com)

Both of these utilities let you set read, write, and execute permissions for owner, group, and others simply by clicking a check box or button. They also let you select users and groups that don't appear in the Finder's Get Info window. In addition, FileXaminer has an Advanced view in which you can modify the set UID, set GID, and sticky bits (covered later in this chapter).

FIGURE 3.2

FileXaminer lets you modify permissions for a file or folder without using Terminal.

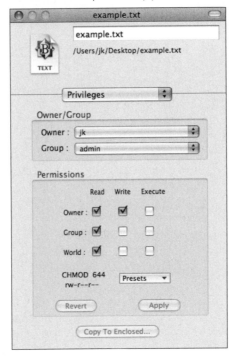

Using the umask

When you create a new file in Mac OS X, that file gets certain permissions by default: `rw-r--r--` (644) — everyone can read it, but only the owner can write it, and no one can execute it. Likewise, folders get default permissions of `rwxr-xr-x` (755). These defaults are changeable, either system-wide or per-user, by way of a strange mechanism called a *umask* (a template that specifies how permissions are to be set) — if you have some good reason to do so. For example, you may prefer that new folders you create not be readable by everyone by default, which can increase your privacy somewhat on a multi-user Mac.

You might imagine that the way to change the defaults would be to change an octal value in a preference file somewhere, such as replacing a 755 with a 750. In fact, the process is more obtuse by a couple of degrees, although it still has a certain elegant logic to it. To understand how the default mechanism works, you need to learn two new concepts: binary representations of permissions and bit masks.

Binary permissions

In addition to expressing permissions as letters (for example, `rwxr-xr--`) and as octal (754), there's yet another way to think of them: in binary. This is also simple because each r, w, and x is in a fixed position. So, to convert permissions to binary, simply replace each letter with a 1 and each hyphen with a 0. Thus, the following pair is equivalent:

```
rwx r-x r--
111 101 100
```

As with octal representations of permissions, it works the other way too. If an item has permissions of 110110110 you can see almost at a glance that it's the same as `rw-rw-rw-` or 666 (readable and writable by everyone but executable by none).

Bit masks

A *bit mask* is a sequence of binary numbers, such as `000010010`, that can filter or adjust the values of other sequences. You can think of a bit mask as being like a piece of paper with a row of squares. Some of those squares contain a number, and others are cut out. When you lay the piece of paper on top of another page that has a similar row of numbers, some of the numbers from the original show through (where there are cutouts), while others are blocked. To get the masked set of numbers, you just read what you see, which includes some values from the original (bottom) sheet and some values from the mask.

The analogy between a paper mask and a bit mask isn't quite perfect, but here's how a bit mask works:

- A 0 in the mask means: "Keep the existing value." In other words, it's like a cutout in a paper mask.

- A 1 in the mask means: "If the original is 1, make it 0; if it's already 0, it stays 0." In other words, it's like a 0 written on a square in a paper mask, which is sort of counterintuitive in that a mask value of 1 always leads to a final value of 0!

Let's look at some concrete examples. Suppose you have a file whose original permissions are `110110110` (`rw-rw-rw-`). You then apply a bit mask with the value `000010011`. It would look like this (again, spaces added for readability):

```
110 110 110 (original)
000 010 011 (mask)
110 100 100 (final)
```

Reading from top to bottom, you can see that wherever a 1 in the original encounters a 0 in the mask, it stays a 1 afterward. Whenever a 0 encounters a 0 in the mask, it also stays a 0. When a 1 encounters a 1 in the mask, however, as in the middle digit of each group, it turns into a 0.

And when a 0 encounters a 1 (as in the very last digit), it remains a 0. In short, a change in a bit's value occurs only if both the original and the mask have a value of 1 for that bit. A bit mask never turns on (1) a bit that's originally off (0).

Umasks

A umask is a bit mask for user permissions, and it's applied automatically when you create a new file or folder. The value to which it's applied — the original, or base permissions — is hard-coded into the operating system. Base permissions are as liberal as possible so that masks (which can only reduce permissions or keep them the same, not add them) have plenty to work with.

Files have base permissions of 110110110, or rw-rw-rw-, which is logical because it's the maximum range of options that would generally be possible for a file (executable files being the exception to the rule). Folders, on the other hand, have base permissions of 111111111, or rwxrwxrwx. Again, that's logical because the x when applied to a folder means permission to list its contents.

The default global umask in Mac OS X is 000010010. If you apply this mask to the base value for a file, you get 110100100, or rw-r--r--; recall from earlier in this chapter that this is, in fact, the default set of permissions for new files you create. Likewise, apply the default umask of 000010010 to the base folder permissions of 111111111, and you get 111101101, or rwxr-xr-x.

Note

The umask isn't the only thing that influences what permissions for a new file or folder may be. Individual applications can override the umask, for example. In some cases, the permissions of the parent folder in which the item is located also affect its value, as does the sticky bit (described just ahead). ■

I've described bit masks in binary to make them easier to comprehend, but let me throw in one final twist: Mac OS X always expresses bit masks in octal! So, although you need to grasp what's happening behind the scenes in binary, when you actually see or use a umask or other bit mask, it's in octal — a bit mask of 000010010 is expressed as 022.

Now, getting down to the bottom line: You can modify the umask for an individual user, with the result that the default permissions for files and folders created by that user in the command line changes. In addition, you can modify a different umask used by ordinary Mac OS X applications.

To change the Unix umask for the user account under which you're currently logged in, do the following:

1. **Open the file ~/.bash_profile (assuming you use the default bash shell) in your favorite command-line or GUI text editor.** If you use a different default shell, edit the corresponding profile file instead.

2. **Type umask followed by a space and an octal representation of the new umask you want.** For example, to apply a umask of 000110110, which would make default permissions for new files rw------- (110000000) and new folders rwx--x--x (110001001), you'd type **umask 066**.

3. **Save and close the file.** The change takes effect with the next shell session you open.

To change the Mac OS X application umask for the user account under which you're currently logged in, in Leopard only, not Snow Leopard, do the following:

1. Using `sudo` (described later in this chapter), open your favorite command-line or GUI text editor and then create the following file: `/etc/launchd-user.conf`.

2. As in the previous set of steps, type the word umask followed by a space and an octal representation of the new umask you want.

3. **Save and close the file.** The new umask applies immediately.

Caution

Changes to the umask shouldn't be made lightly, even if you feel confident they'll increase your security, because the software you use may assume default permissions and may misbehave in various ways if permissions aren't as expected. In particular, you should never attempt to change the global umask (by editing `/etc/launchd.conf`) because it could result in critical system files having permissions that are too restrictive to prevent functioning or so open that they present a security risk. ∎

The other permission bits

For the sake of completeness, I want to mention — but not go into detail about — three other components of POSIX permissions that I've largely ignored to this point. In addition to read, write, and execute permissions for user, group, and others, each item can have one, two, or all three of the following bits set:

- **Set UID bit.** This bit applies mainly to executable files. Its primary purpose is to affect the owner of the process when these files run. When this bit is set and the file is executed, the process is owned by whichever user owns the file rather than by the user who opened it. If a file's set UID bit is set (turned on), an `S` appears in the user's execute (`x`) slot; for example, `rwSr-xr-x`.

- **Set GID bit.** This bit has exactly the same effect on executable files as the set UID bit does, except that it sets the process's group owner (GID) to the group owner of the file. A file whose set GID bit is set displays an `S` in the group's execute (`x`) slot; for example, `rwxr-Sr-x`.

- **Sticky bit.** This bit, when applied to a folder, affects who can rename or delete files inside it: It can only be the file's owner, the owner of the folder itself, or root — and only if that user has write permission for that folder. When the sticky bit is set, the final character in a permission string becomes a `t`; for example, `drwxr-xr-t`.

As with other permissions, you can use `chmod` to change these bits. In symbolic mode, typing **chmod +s** *filename* turns on both the set UID and set GID bits for the file `filename`; typing **chmod -s** *filename* turns both bits off. To add or remove the sticky bit from a folder, type **chmod +t** *foldername* or **chmod -t** *foldername*, respectively.

Alternatively, if using `chmod` in absolute mode, you can substitute the value 4 for set UID, 2 for set GID, and 1 for sticky bit and then append the resulting number to the beginning of an octal permission string. For example, typing **chmod 1755** *foldername* would give the folder permissions `rwxr-xr-x` and set its sticky bit.

Tip

In this very brief look at POSIX permissions, I mention only the basics. For a friendly, readable discussion of permissions that goes into far more detail, read the ebook *Take Control of Permissions in Leopard* by Brian Tanaka (`www.takecontrolbooks.com`). ■

Types of Accounts

Earlier in this chapter, I described what an account is, and in the last section, I explained how the user and group names associated with accounts apply to files and folders. There's yet another piece of the puzzle though: the variety of account types as they appear in Mac OS X.

Depending on how you want to slice it, you could think of Mac OS X as having two, three, or as many as eight or more different account types. However you want to categorize them, account types are important because they indicate what sorts of actions are required, permitted, or prohibited for that sort of user (including but not limited to POSIX permissions).

In a moment, I describe all the different account types, but to help you get your bearings, here's the overall hierarchy, broken down into the smallest reasonable chunks. There are two basic account types for users: administrator and standard. Managed, guest, and sharing only accounts are technically sub-varieties of standard accounts — making a total of five types so far. Two other account types don't show up at all in Mac OS X's graphical interface: root (an all-powerful account that you can optionally turn on for command-line access only) and system accounts, which various parts of Mac OS X use behind the scenes to divvy up tasks and permissions. The final account type is a group, which isn't really an account itself but rather a list of related accounts. I list it here because it sometimes appears in lists of account types.

Administrator accounts

Traditionally, in the Unix world, an administrator is the person who keeps a computer (or a whole collection of computers) running — someone who installs and updates software, configures machines for network access, manages user accounts, and generally handles all those important background tasks that let ordinary users get their work done. This person has the authority to make any necessary changes to the computer and to determine who else can do what.

Because Mac OS X is a variety of Unix, every Mac must also have an administrator, which is someone whose account gives them the authority to manage all those essential configuration and maintenance tasks. If you're the only person who uses your Mac, that's you — even if you have no idea what Unix is!

Apple kept the concept of an administrator but designed Mac OS X in such a way that ordinary users don't normally need to be aware of this fact. The first account you set up (when you buy a new Mac or install Mac OS X) is automatically an administrator account. It lets you do anything you might need to do, without any restrictions other than occasional prompts to type your password. An administrator account has all the same folders, files, and capabilities as any other account, just with an extended range of authority — your administrator password lets you do things that a standard user's password won't. For example, an administrator can do all the following:

- Read or modify any file, including those belonging to other users
- Delete any file, including ones that would render it inoperable
- Install software of any kind
- Change all system preferences, including those that apply to all users
- Create, modify, and delete accounts for other users

Authentication Details

Mac OS X asks for your credentials frequently, especially when installing new software. In general, all you do is type your username and password and then click OK. Most people do this without paying careful attention to what's being requested, and if you've just double-clicked an installer, it's self-evident that this installer is what's asking for permission to run. But if you aren't sure why you're seeing an authentication dialog box or which particular program is seeking which kind of permission, click the disclosure triangle next to the word Details to reveal more information, as shown in this figure.

Click the Details disclosure triangle to find out exactly what permissions are being requested.

At the bottom of the window is the program requesting permission (click it to see exactly where on your computer it's located), and just above it is the type of permission it's requesting. Although the rights aren't spelled out in plain English, you can usually get an approximate sense of what a program wants to do; for example, in the figure shown here, the installer wants to install something in the /System folder with root user permissions.

Standard accounts

Standard accounts are plenty powerful: They let users freely read, modify, and delete files of their own; install software for their own use; modify preferences that apply only to their accounts; and access most of the computer's shared resources (such as its network connection and public folders).

Where they differ from administrator accounts is in a few added restrictions. Standard users can't do the following:

- Read, modify, or delete other users' files
- Install software for use by all users
- Modify certain system-wide preferences
- Add, modify, or delete user accounts

Mac OS X has no standard accounts by default; you must create them yourself. You can turn an administrator account into a standard account (or vice versa) merely by clicking a check box or two and typing a password, with the one qualification being that your Mac must always have at least one administrator account.

Even though Mac OS X creates an administrator account for you by default, most experts recommend using a standard account except when you specifically need to perform some administrative activity, such as installing software. Along with the power of an administrator account comes the capability to inadvertently do serious damage, and that power could also apply to, for example, malware running under the administrator's account.

Cross-Ref

For more on switching your Mac from a setup with a single administrative user to an administrator account plus a standard account, see Chapter 1. ■

Managed accounts with parental controls

The next account type is the managed account, which is in fact a standard account with additional (and variable) restrictions. For several years, Apple has used the term *parental controls* to describe the restrictions that can be placed on managed accounts, because the original intent of this account type was to give parents a way to restrict their children's computing activities. However, as Mac OS X has evolved, this term has become somewhat of a misnomer. Sure, parents can still create accounts that limit what their kids can do, but managed accounts have many other uses too. With them, you can create customized experiences of Mac OS X for schools, libraries, cybercafés, and other public places; you can set up a simplified, less-cluttered account for yourself; or you can do things like block websites that even the adult members of your household might not want to see.

I describe how to work with managed accounts later in this chapter. Some of the things an administrator can change about managed accounts include the following:

- Which applications can run
- Whether the Finder appears in a simplified form with fewer menus and icons
- Whether the user can burn CDs and DVDs, modify printers, change the items in the Dock, or change the account password
- Whether the Dictionary application shows "naughty" words
- Which websites the user can visit (or which should be blocked)
- Which addresses the user can contact via email or instant messaging
- Allowable times, dates, and durations for using the computer
- What information about the user's computer usage is logged

Guest account

The guest account is just like a managed account in most respects. It starts with all the capabilities of any standard account, but an administrator can set limits on how it can be used. There's one crucial difference though: When you log out of the guest account, Mac OS X deletes all its files and preferences. When you log in again, you start fresh with a clean environment. As such, it's perfect for a guest who needs to use a Mac temporarily but doesn't require long-term storage of files or personalized options.

Leopard and Snow Leopard have just one guest account, which is disabled by default. To enable it, follow these steps:

1. Choose ➪ System Preferences to open System Preferences and then click Accounts to open the Accounts pane.

2. Click the lock icon in the lower-left corner of the pane, type an administrator's username and password, and then click OK.

3. Select Guest Account in the list on the left (even if it's dimmed), as shown in Figure 3.3.

4. Click the Allow guests to log into this computer check box. Optionally, to give guest users access to the shared folders on this Mac, click the Allow guests to connect to shared folders check box.

5. To configure the guest account as a managed account, click the Enable Parental Controls check box, click Open Parental Controls, and then follow the instructions provided later in this chapter.

6. Close System Preferences.

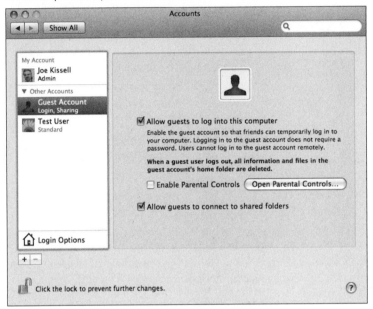

FIGURE 3.3

Enable the guest account and configure its settings by choosing Guest Account from the Accounts pane of System Preferences.

Sharing Only accounts

As the name suggests, a Sharing Only account allows someone to access shared resources — but nothing else — on this Mac. As a result, a Sharing Only user can't log in to your Mac directly — only over a network. The resources to which you can grant Sharing Only users access are:

- Screen Sharing
- File Sharing (via AFP, SMB, or FTP)
- Remote Login
- Remote Management
- Remote Apple Events

Merely creating a Sharing Only account doesn't grant a user any access to your Mac. You must then use the Sharing pane of System Preferences to turn on the types of sharing you want to use and assign users (and groups) access to individual shared items. You can also use the Finder's Get Info window to change users' access to individual items.

Cross-Ref

For more on working with shared resources, see Chapter 7. ∎

The root account

As in all varieties of Unix, Mac OS X has a special account type known as the root account, which gives its user nearly limitless power over the computer. A person logged in as root can read, modify, or delete any file, install any software, and make changes to any other account on the computer.

But wait — doesn't the administrator account have all those same capabilities? Yes and no. By default, certain kinds of activities can be performed only after typing an administrator password, which is to say you must type it repeatedly for each individual protected action you want to take. Other activities require even an administrator to jump through certain hoops — for example, an administrator can't ordinarily open files belonging to another user in the Finder but can get access to those files in Terminal by typing **sudo -s** (described later in this chapter) to temporarily assume root privileges. And individual administrative users can be barred from using sudo to accomplish certain tasks.

Not so with the root user. Once you log in to Mac OS X with your root password, you can do almost anything you want without being prompted for your password again and without having to work around any built-in security controls. Every file is directly accessible, either through the Finder or through Terminal, for you to do with as you please.

The root user isn't quite omnipotent, however. For example, the Mandatory Access Controls built into Leopard and Snow Leopard prevent even the root user from directly deleting the files in a Time Machine archive while using Terminal. (Because Mandatory Access Controls work behind the scenes and are accessible only to developers, I don't cover them in this book.) In addition, if another user has encrypted files — including keychains, FileVault archives, and other encrypted disk images — the root user is powerless to decrypt those files without knowing their passwords (although the root user can, of course, delete the files).

Because the root account has so much power, which could enable a person or program to cause untold damage to the system, Apple has disabled it by default in Leopard and Snow Leopard. Although I can imagine some extraordinary situations in which it might conceivably be necessary to log in as the root user — for example, in cases of hacking or extreme system corruption where ordinary administrator access is locked out — I have never personally encountered a problem that could be solved in no other way. So, unless you have some specific and urgent need for the root account and know exactly what you're doing, I strongly recommend leaving it disabled.

Tip

Even without enabling the root account, an administrator can still open a shell session in Terminal as the root user by typing sudo -s **or** sudo -i **(both explained later in this chapter).** ■

If you must enable the root user, you can do so by following these steps:

1. **Open Directory Utility, which is located in** `/Applications/Utilities` **in Leopard and in** `/System/Library/CoreServices` **in Snow Leopard.**

2. **Click the lock icon, type an administrator's username and password, and then click OK to authenticate.**

3. **Choose Edit ⇨ Enable Root User.** If you haven't previously enabled the root user, a dialog box opens in which you're prompted to type and verify a password and then click OK.

If you want to disable the root user account, follow the same steps except choose Disable Root User in step 3. Mac OS X remembers the password you previously assigned to root and uses it again if you re-enable the account.

System accounts

In addition to the various kinds of user accounts described previously and the root account, Mac OS X uses a variety of other accounts, which are normally hidden, to run certain processes. You can't modify these accounts nor can you, in ordinary circumstances, use them yourself. But I mention them because you may run across them from time to time, and you should understand that they exist to give Mac OS X greater control over security because they effectively constrain the range of things a given piece of software can do.

To see a list of all the accounts on your Mac (including these special, hidden system accounts), open Terminal, located in /Applications/Utilities, and type **dscl . -list /Users**. In Leopard and Snow Leopard, that list includes a few dozen entries. Most of these special accounts exist only to run the program with which they're associated — for example, _installer, _spotlight, and _www. The list also includes an account called daemon (which is used to run certain background services) and one called nobody (which is used for processes that require extremely limited permissions).

One place you're likely to notice these special accounts is in Activity Monitor, located in /Applications/Utilities, which can list all the processes currently running on your Mac along with the account (shown in the User column) that owns each process.

Groups

The last account type (of a sort) is the group, which is a collection of individual accounts that share certain attributes in common. By creating groups and assigning various combinations of users to them, you can quickly and easily grant or deny a number of people the authority to use various system resources.

One common way of using groups is in the context of file sharing. For example, suppose you have one folder that you want only the users Apple, Banana, and Cherry to be able to read and another folder you want to make available only to Circle, Square, and Triangle. Create a group called Fruits that contains the first three users and another group called Shapes that contains the other three. Then, assign the group Fruits read access to the first folder (while prohibiting access for those not in the group), and do the same with the second folder and the Shapes group. If you later realize that you want to give Date access to the same folder as Apple, Banana, and Cherry, all you have to do is add that user to the Fruit group. If you decide that Circle, Square, and Triangle should all be able to modify the folder their group is assigned to, you simply change the group's access for that folder to Read & Write.

Although you can have any number of groups with any number of members in each, and although any user can be a member of many different groups, a given file, folder, or volume in Mac OS X can be owned by only a single user and a single group (of which that user is usually a member).

In cases where you need more detailed control over access to resources, you can use ACLs, described at the end of this chapter.

Just as Mac OS X contains a number of hidden system accounts, so it includes numerous hidden groups. For example, there's a built-in group called admin that contains every user with an administrator account, another called staff that contains every user with a standard account, and another called wheel that should contain only the root user. (The root user, however, should be a member of every group.)

Configuring an Account

Adding, deleting, and editing accounts and groups in Mac OS X are straightforward processes, but you have a number of options to consider.

Creating a new user

To create a new user account of the administrator, standard, managed, or sharing only variety, follow these steps:

1. Choose ⤳ System Preferences to open System Preferences and then click Accounts to open the Accounts pane.

2. If the lock icon in the lower-left corner of the pane is in the locked state, click it, type an administrator's username and password, and then click OK.

3. Click the Add (+) button below the list of accounts to open a dialog box showing options for the new account.

4. From the New Account pop-up menu (refer to Figure 3.4), select the account type you want to create.

Note

You can convert most account types to most other types after the fact. For example, you can turn a standard user into an administrator by clicking the Allow user to administer this computer check box or into a managed user by clicking the Enable Parental Controls check box. However, you can't convert any sort of user account to a Sharing Only account or vice versa. ■

5. **Fill in the Name field.** This can be anything, but it's normally used for a person's first name and last name. Spaces are permitted. Optionally, you can also edit the Short Name field. By default, Mac OS X takes the contents of the Name field, turns it into lowercase, and removes any spaces — for example, John Smith in the Name field becomes johnsmith in the Short Name field. However, you may prefer something more compact, such as john or js because a shorter short username can enable you to log in, authenticate, and perform various commands in Terminal with fewer keystrokes.

Tip

In any login or authentication window, you can type either the short or long username. ■

6. **Type and verify a password in the appropriate fields.** Optionally, you can type a password hint. The dialog box says Recommended because this can help prevent the user from being locked out of the account due to a forgotten password. However, I recommend against using a hint because it reduces your security by giving an attacker help in guessing your password. If you do supply a hint, try to use something obscure that would help the user but not necessarily clue in an attacker.

Cross-Ref

For more on choosing a good password, see Chapter 6. ■

7. **If you want this user's account to be protected by FileVault, click the Turn on FileVault protection check box.** However, because you can always enable FileVault later and because it's often not a good idea, I suggest leaving this check box deselected for now. FileVault doesn't apply to Sharing Only accounts.

Cross-Ref

For more on FileVault, see Chapter 13. ■

FIGURE 3.4

In the New Account dialog box, you specify the type of account, short and long usernames, password, and an optional password hint.

New Account:	Standard
Name:	John Smith
Short Name:	john
Password:	••••••••• 🔑
Verify:	•••••••••
Password Hint: (Recommended)	
	☐ Turn on FileVault protection
(?)	(Cancel) (**Create Account**)

8. **Click Create Account.**

9. **Close System Preferences.** When you create a new user account, Mac OS X makes a new home folder (/Users/*short-username*) for that user, and inside that, a set of default folders such as Documents and Library are created. This doesn't apply to Sharing Only users, who can't log in locally, or to the guest account, whose folders are created dynamically on each use and deleted immediately thereafter.

Setting user options

After initially setting up a user account, you can modify its options and attributes as needed. To set the user options for an account, follow these steps:

1. **Choose System Preferences to open System Preferences and then click Accounts to open the Accounts pane.**

2. **If the lock icon in the lower-left corner of the pane is in the locked state, click it, type an administrator's username and password, and then click OK.**

3. **Select the account you want to modify in the list on the left, configure the options you want as described shortly, and then close System Preferences.**

The options you can modify fall into two categories: basic options (which you can see without doing anything special) and advanced options.

Basic options

The basic options available vary according to the type of account you've selected.

For all account types except guest:

- **User Name.** This is the user's long username (for example, Joe Kissell), not the short username (joe, jk, joekissell, or the like).

- **MobileMe User Name.** If the user is a MobileMe member, you can type his or her MobileMe username here. If you've previously done so, the window shows the username and a Change button you can use to modify it. Setting this up here is optional, but it saves the user a configuration step later on.

- **Change (or Reset) Password.** The current user's account has a Change Password button; for all other users, it's Reset Password. To change a password, click this button, type your old password (applies only to the current user), and then type and verify a new password (and an optional password hint). (For accounts with FileVault turned on, you must also type the master password.) Then, click Change Password.

For standard and guest accounts:

- **Enable Parental Controls.** To make this a managed account, click the Enable Parental Controls check box and then click Open Parental Controls to set up specific restrictions. You can't set up parental controls for the current user or for an administrator account. If you click the Enable Parental Controls check box for an administrator account, an alert asks if you want to disable administrator access and requires that you log out and log back in.

For standard, administrator, and managed accounts:

- **Administrator privileges.** Click the Allow user to administer this computer check box in order to make this user an administrator; click to deselect it to remove administrator privileges. If you click this check box for a managed account (one with Enable Parental Controls selected), an alert asks if you want to disable parental controls and requires that you log out and back in again.

For the current user's account only:

- **Address Book Card.** Click the Open button (in the Password pane) to open Address Book and jump directly to the card with your information on it.
- **Login Items.** Click the Login Items tab to see a list of files, folders, and applications that open automatically every time you log in. To add an item, you can either drag it into the window (from the Applications folder or elsewhere) or click the Add (+) button, navigate to the item, and then click Add. For applications (only), click the Hide check box next to the item in the list to make it open in the background.

Advanced options

Beyond the obvious and visible changes you can make to a user account, there are several others that are a bit harder to find. But if you select an account and Control+click it, you can choose Advanced Options from the context menu, which displays a dialog box like the one shown in Figure 3.5.

FIGURE 3.5

The Advanced Options dialog box lets you change attributes of an account that could be potentially harmful; use with care.

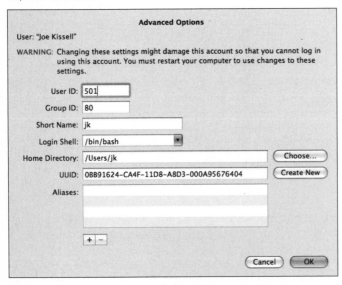

As the dialog box says, changing these settings could result in damage to the account, so you shouldn't change anything here unless you're sure you need to — and you should be sure you have a good backup first.

The following options can be modified in the Advanced Options dialog box:

- **User ID and Group ID.** These are the UID and GID associated with your account name, and ordinarily, they shouldn't be changed.

- **Short Name.** Although you can change the short username for your account here, it could have unexpected consequences. (For example, if a program's preference file references your account by short username rather than by UID, it may not work correctly after making the change.) In most cases, adding an alias is a much safer option.

Tip

If you must change the short username associated with an account, you have several options for doing so, all of which have their pros and cons. You can read a detailed article on the subject by Dan Frakes in *Macworld* at www.macworld.com/article/132693/2008/03/changeshortusername.html. ■

- **Login Shell.** If you prefer to use a shell other than bash (such as tcsh or zsh) when you access the Mac OS X command line via Terminal, choose it here. You can safely change this setting without causing any damage.

- **Home Directory.** This tells Mac OS X where your home folder is located; by default, it's at /Users/*your-short-username*. As with changing your short username, changing this location can cause significant problems, and I strongly suggest leaving it as is.

- **UUID.** Your regular user ID (UID) is a number, such as 501, that's unique across all users on your Mac. However, in some cases, a program or network device may need to refer to your user account using a number that's unique everywhere. Hence, the UUID, or Universally Unique User Identifier. This number is generated automatically based on the MAC address of your computer's Ethernet card and the time and date. In the extraordinarily unlikely event that you have some special reason to create a new UUID, click Create New.

- **Aliases.** An alias, in this context, is essentially an alternative short username. So, if your short username is johnsmith, and if no other user on your Mac has the short username john, you can add john as an alias here (or even j, for that matter) and then use that shorter name when you log in or whenever you're asked to type your credentials. To add an alias, click the Add (+) button and then type the new name. To remove an alias, select it and then click the Remove (–) button. You can safely add aliases or remove aliases you've previously added without causing any other damage, but don't remove any existing aliases (which may consist of long strings of letters and numbers).

Creating groups

Compared to the range of options available for users, groups are extremely straightforward. They basically have two attributes: a name (which, of course, corresponds to an underlying GID, or group identifier) and a list of members.

To create a group, follow these steps:

1. Choose ➭ System Preferences to open System Preferences and then click Accounts to open the Accounts pane.

2. If the lock icon in the lower-left corner of the pane is in the locked state, click it, type an administrator's username and password, and then click OK.

3. Click the Add (+) button below the list of accounts to open a dialog box showing options for the new account.

4. From the New Account pop-up menu, choose Group.

5. Type a name for the group and then click Create Group.

6. With the group selected in the Accounts preference pane (as shown in Figure 3.6), click the check box for each user you want to include in the group.

7. Close System Preferences.

FIGURE 3.6

After creating a group in the Accounts pane of System Preferences, add or remove group members by clicking or deselecting the corresponding check boxes.

You can repeat these steps to create additional groups, and you can change a group's members at any time by choosing the group and then clicking or deselecting the check boxes next to user-names. To delete a group, select it and then click the Remove (–) button.

Cross-Ref

For more on assigning groups to shared resources, see Chapter 7. ■

Adjusting Login Options

The Accounts pane of System Preferences, in addition to letting you add, delete, and modify users and groups, contains a number of settings involving the login window (where you type your username and password to log in to Mac OS X) and overall account behavior. Some of these have important security implications. To review and modify your login options, follow these steps:

1. Choose ⓧ⇨ System Preferences to open System Preferences and then click Accounts to open the Accounts pane.

2. If the lock icon in the lower-left corner of the pane is in the locked state, click it, type an administrator's username and password, and then click OK.

3. Click Login Options (at the bottom of the account list). Your window should then look something similar to Figure 3.7.

4. After changing any settings, close System Preferences.

FIGURE 3.7

Options relating to how the login window appears and other overall account behaviors can be adjusted in the Login Options view of the Accounts preference pane. The Snow Leopard version is shown here; in Leopard, it looks slightly different.

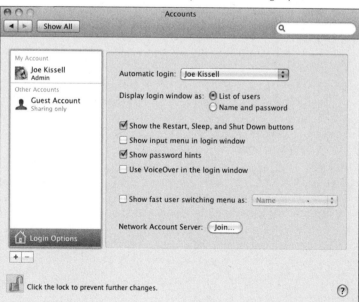

75

The options you can adjust are as follows:

- **Automatic login.** If you're the sole user of this Mac — and especially if you only use it at home or in a private office — you can opt to have Mac OS X log in to your account automatically when you turn on the computer or restart. To use this feature (which is enabled by default), choose a username from the pop-up menu, and type that user's credentials when prompted. But beware: This is a significant security risk because it means anyone with physical access to your computer can easily access any of your files. And if your keychain uses the same password as your user account, it's even less secure because your keychain unlocks automatically when you log in. So, think carefully before enabling this feature.

- **Display login window as.** If you click the List of users radio button (the default), then every time you turn on, restart, or log out of your Mac, the login window displays a list of all the user accounts, each with its own picture. To log in, you click a user and then type the corresponding password. This slightly reduces the amount of typing required, but it could also give useful information to a hacker — instead of having to guess both a username and a password, the hacker would only need to guess a password. Therefore, clicking the Name and password radio button, which provides empty fields for both pieces of information, is slightly more secure.

- **Show the Restart, Sleep, and Shut Down buttons.** This is a convenience feature that may or may not be useful, depending on how the Mac is used. If users normally log out immediately after use but without turning off the Mac, this option provides the capability to restart, shut down, or put the Mac to sleep without first having to log in (or manually turning off the power).

- **Show Input menu in login window.** The Input menu enables users to switch between keyboard layouts and input methods. If anyone using the Mac might need an alternative input method to type a username or password, click this check box.

- **Show password hints.** When you set up an account, you can optionally specify a hint that helps users remember their password if they forget it. Because these hints could also help an unauthorized person to access the computer, you can prevent the hints from being displayed in the login window for any user by clicking this check box to deselect it.

- **Use VoiceOver at login window.** VoiceOver is Apple's text-to-speech feature that speaks whatever text the mouse pointer is currently hovering over. If you or someone else using this Mac has difficulty reading the text in the login window, click this check box; otherwise, leave it deselected.

- **Fast user switching.** With fast user switching, a user can remain logged in while one or more other users also log in. A subsequent user can choose his or her account from a menu at the right of the menu bar and authenticate to begin a new session. Meanwhile, the first user's session remains running but hidden. Applications that were running continue to do so, windows remain open, and so on — but the second user can't see or access the first user's session. Fast user switching makes it quicker and easier to switch between user accounts, but because users need not log out when another logs in, this mode of using a Mac requires more RAM and can put more of a drain on the CPU. To enable fast user switching, click the Enable fast user switching check box (Leopard) or the Show fast user switching menu as check box (Snow Leopard); then, choose from the pop-up menu whether the menu bar should display the current user's Name, Short name, or Icon.

- **Network Account Server (Snow Leopard only).** To configure Mac OS X to retrieve user information from an Open Directory or Active Directory server, click Join, click the Add (+) button, choose a directory type from the pop-up menu, type the server's name or IP address, click OK, and then click Done.

Cross-Ref

For more on using directory services, see Chapter 26. ∎

Using Parental Controls

Mac OS X's parental controls enable an administrator to impose various limits on a managed account. Although the feature was originally designed for parents to restrict how their children can use a Mac, it's also useful in numerous other contexts — whenever common sense, company policy, or other considerations dictate that particular activities should be strictly controlled.

Parental controls can apply to any non-administrator account. To configure them, choose ➪ System Preferences, click Parental Controls, and then select an account. The settings you can adjust fall into several categories.

Enable or disable parental controls

If the account isn't already enabled for parental controls, click Enable Parental Controls. To remove parental controls, click the pop-up Action menu at the bottom of the account list and then choose Disable Parental Controls for *User Name*.

Remote management

You can adjust parental controls from another computer, which is useful for administrators of large Mac installations as well as for parents whose children have their own Macs. To enable this capability, you can either click the Manage parental controls from another computer check box (visible only if the account doesn't already have parental controls enabled) or click the pop-up Action menu at the bottom of the account list and then choose Allow Remote Setup.

Once you've enabled remote setup, if you go to the Parental Controls preference pane on another Mac on the same local network, the remote Mac should appear in the account list. Select the computer, type the name and password for an administrator on the remote computer, and then click OK to log in. The managed users on the remote computer then appear in the account list, and you can adjust their settings just as you would for a managed user on your local Mac.

System

Click the System tab (shown in Figure 3.8) to manage features relating to the Finder and other applications:

- **Use Simple Finder.** When this check box is selected, the user's version of the Finder displays a limited number of menus, menu commands, and Dock icons. Because the Simple Finder is very simple indeed, it's appropriate only for beginning users.

FIGURE 3.8

The System pane of the Parental Controls preference pane lets you configure access to the Finder, applications, and system-wide features.

Note
If the Use Simple Finder check box is selected, you can select which applications are available to the user, even if the Only allow selected applications check box is deselected. ∎

- **Only allow selected applications.** If you want the managed user to be able to run only certain applications, click this check box and then in list that follows, click the check box next to each application you want to allow.

Caution
Even if an application's check box is deselected in this list, it may be possible for the user to run it in some situations. For example, if Safari is deselected, the user won't be able to launch Safari directly, but clicking a URL in an email message may still launch it. ∎

- **Can administer printers.** When this check box is deselected, the user can switch printers and adjust printer settings.

- **Can burn CDs and DVDs.** Click this check box to enable the computer to record optical discs.

- **Can change password.** With this check box selected, the user can change the password for this account. When it's deselected, only an administrator can change it.

- **Can modify the Dock.** If you want to make sure the Dock displays only a fixed set of icons, click this check box to deselect it. When it's selected, the user can add or remove Dock icons.

Content

Click the Content tab (shown in Figure 3.9) to exercise limited control over website and dictionary content:

- **Hide profanity in Dictionary.** This option applies only to the built-in Dictionary application. When selected, it prevents Dictionary from displaying the definitions of words Apple deems profane. Of course, it doesn't prevent someone from knowing that the words exist or even searching for them.

FIGURE 3.9

The Content pane lets you restrict a user's access to profanity in the Dictionary application and to a limited range of websites.

- **Website Restrictions.** Click the radio button corresponding to one of the following three options for controlling access to websites:

  - **Allow unrestricted access to websites.** No restrictions.

  - **Try to limit access to adult websites automatically.** When this radio button is selected, Mac OS X attempts to identify likely pornographic websites and prevent any web browser from accessing them. However, it may misidentify some sites — either blocking or allowing them incorrectly. To explicitly allow or prohibit particular sites, click Customize and then add URLs in either the Always allow these sites or Never allow these sites list.

  - **Allow access to only these websites.** If you want to restrict the managed user to visiting only a specific, short list of permitted sites, click this radio button. To add a site, click the Add (+) button, choose Add bookmark from the pop-up menu, and type the site's URL and name. To remove a site, select it and then click the Remove (–) button.

Mail & iChat

Click the Mail & iChat tab (shown in Figure 3.10) to restrict how the user can send and receive email and instant messages:

- **Limit Mail.** Click this check box to control the addresses the user can communicate with by using the Mail application. This restriction isn't ironclad. For example, if the user is still permitted to visit a site in Safari that offers web-based email, which entirely bypasses this control.

- **Limit iChat.** Click this check box to limit the people with whom the user can carry on chats in iChat.

- **Address list.** If you've enabled limits on Mail, iChat, or both, click the Add (+) button to add someone with whom the user may communicate. In the dialog box that opens, type a first and/or last name and one or more email, AIM, or Jabber addresses; repeat for as many users as you want.

- **Send permission requests.** When this check box is selected, any attempt (incoming or outgoing) to communicate via email or iChat with an unauthorized user results in an email message going to the address you fill in here. You can then choose to allow or disallow communication with that person.

FIGURE 3.10

On the Mail & iChat pane, you can select which addresses the user can communicate with by email and instant messaging.

Time Limits

Click the Time Limits tab (shown in Figure 3.11) to restrict use of this account to certain times or durations:

- **Weekday time limits.** Click the Limit computer use to check box and move the slider to determine the total amount of time the user can be logged in to the account on weekdays.

- **Weekend time limits.** Click the Limit computer use to check box and move the slider to determine the total amount of time the user can be logged in to the account on weekends.

- **Bedtime.** Click the check boxes next to School nights, Weekend, or both and then set time ranges during which the user isn't permitted to be logged in.

FIGURE 3.11

On the Time Limits pane, choose when and for how long the user may be logged in.

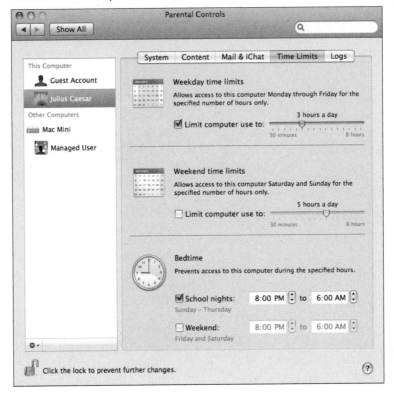

Logs

Finally, click the Logs tab (shown in Figure 3.12) to see what the managed user has been up to:

- **Show activity for.** Choose a time range from this pop-up menu to determine how far back activity logs go.

- **Group by.** Select a Log Collection from the left. Then, choose Website, Application, Contact, or Date from this menu to sort the logged information in that category.

- **Log Collections.** Mac OS X automatically tracks the four kinds of information listed here: Websites Visited, Websites Blocked, Applications (which applications are launched), and iChat (entire transcripts of instant messaging sessions). First, select a collection. Then, select a specific log from the Logs list and then click Open to view it. To restrict access to a website, application, or iChat contact that appears in the log, select it and then click Restrict.

FIGURE 3.12

The Logs pane lets you view some of the user's logged activities.

Using the Sudo Command

From time to time, any Mac user may need to perform certain tasks that would ordinarily require root access. Earlier, I advised against enabling the root account, but if you did enable it, actually logging in as root is dangerous — even for advanced users — and should be done only on those rare occasions when no alternative exists. Fortunately, there's another — and somewhat safer — way for non-root users to temporarily obtain root access for individual commands: the Unix command-line tool sudo.

First things first: sudo is short for "superuser do," and although it's supposed to be pronounced "sue dew," no one will laugh at you if you pronounce it "pseudo." To oversimplify somewhat, if you're currently logged in as an administrator and you type **sudo** (and a space) before a command that requires root access, you're prompted for your password and then the command executes.

Although sudo is usually employed to execute a command as root, you can also use it to execute a command as another user. For example, you might do this if you wanted to create or modify a series of files that need to be owned by another user; sudo could be a simpler approach than changing the files' ownership after the fact.

This simple and powerful capability is also more complex than it may at first appear and can be implicated in subtle security risks. So, it pays to understand how it works and how to tailor it to your needs.

How sudo works

When you type a sudo command in Terminal, you're prompted for a password. Before your password is even checked, though, sudo consults a special file (/etc/sudoers) that lists the users permitted to use sudo and what they're permitted to do. If you're not in that list, no password you type is accepted, and if you attempt to perform a task that the sudoers file says you can't do, it won't work.

Once you've successfully typed your password and used the sudo command, Mac OS X remembers your password for the next five minutes. So, you can use additional sudo commands without typing a password each time, and each time you use sudo during that five-minute period, the timer resets. Once you've gone five minutes without using a sudo command, however, you're prompted for a password on your next use.

By default, Mac OS X puts the admin group in this file, with full privileges. That means any user with an administrator account can use sudo and thereby obtain root access.

Sudo syntax

Basic use of sudo couldn't be simpler. Simply type it before the command you want to execute with root access. For example, if you were to try editing the file /etc/hostconfig with the nano editor by typing **nano /etc/hostconfig**, you could open it (because all users have read access) but wouldn't be permitted to save it. So, instead, type **sudo nano /etc/hostconfig** and press Return. On your very first use of sudo (only), you see a warning like this one:

```
WARNING: Improper use of the sudo command could lead to data loss or
    the deletion of important system files. Please double-check your
    typing when using sudo. Type "man sudo" for more information.
To proceed, enter your password, or type Ctrl-C to abort.
```

Type your password and press Return to run the command. In this example, nano functions as usual, except that you won't see an error message when you try to save the file because you're running it as the root user.

You can continue using sudo followed by other commands without having to retype your password unless more than five minutes elapse since your last use of sudo or you end your shell session.

To use sudo to execute a command as another user, type a command using the following syntax: **sudo -u** *user command*, with *user* and *command* filled in with some appropriate value. For example, to create a file owned by the user chris, you could type **sudo -u chris touch filename.txt**.

The safest way to use sudo is the way I've described it here: one command at a time. If you have to execute a long series of commands as root, that does, of course, entail typing **sudo** over and over again. If instead you want to assume the identity of the root user — that is, opening a new shell session as root — you can do so with sudo, even if you haven't enabled the root user account.

To start a shell session as root, type **sudo -s** or **sudo -i**. The difference between these commands is subtle but important. If you type **sudo -s**, the new shell session preserves the environment of your existing shell — for example, if you're using the default bash shell, anything specified in your .bash_profile file, such as aliases and PATH variables, also applies to the root session, and you maintain the home directory of your existing account. On the other hand, **sudo -i** starts a clean session with the root user's home directory, environment, and even login scripts. Which one you use depends on your preferences and needs. For most people, **sudo -s** seems to produce the most agreeable result.

To end a session as root and return to your original user account, type **exit** and then press Return.

Beyond the simple usage I've described here, sudo has a long list of options. To learn about other ways of using sudo, type **man sudo** in Terminal.

Tip

On occasion, you may want to run conventional GUI applications in Mac OS X as root. Although you can open a Terminal session and launch them by using sudo, **an easier way to achieve this effect is to use a program called Pseudo** (http://personalpages.tds.net/~brian_hill/pseudo.html, **$15 shareware). Drag an application onto the Pseudo icon, type an administrator's password, and the application runs as root. ■**

Sudo limitations and risks

In most situations, the default Mac OS X configuration of sudo works just fine. However, it does require some caveats:

- If you walk away from your computer within five minutes of using sudo but without logging out or ending your Terminal session, another user with physical access could use sudo — and get full access to your Mac — without a password.

- Because sudo can effectively grant someone root access, it can be exceptionally dangerous in the wrong hands. For example, a malicious or merely inexperienced user — or perhaps a Trojan horse running under an administrator's account — could do irreparable damage and access any user's private information. So, you may feel it wise to restrict who can use sudo and in what contexts.

- In some settings, you may want the list of users with `sudo` capabilities to be different from the list of users with administrator accounts. For example, you may prefer that all users except a sole administrator have standard user accounts for normal use but still want to grant certain trusted users `sudo` authorization for performing certain command-line activities.

If you want `sudo` to function on your Mac in any way other than the default, you must modify the `sudoers` file.

Modifying the sudoers file

The only safe way to modify `sudoers` is using a program called `visudo`, which is a special version of the `vi` editor made just for editing the `sudoers` file. Some people love `vi`, but those accustomed to non-modal editors such as `pico/nano` or `emacs` (to say nothing of GUI text editors, such as TextEdit or BBEdit) may find `vi` and, therefore, `visudo` to be inscrutable. You can find good references to `vi` online — for example, at `www.cs.colostate.edu/helpdocs/vi.html`. Use the same commands to edit files with `visudo`. (To learn more about `visudo` in particular, type **man visudo**.)

Naturally, `visudo` must be run as root, so to invoke it, type **sudo visudo**.

Once you're in `visudo`, look for this section, which represents the core specification of who's allowed to do what:

```
# User privilege specification
root    ALL=(ALL) ALL
%admin  ALL=(ALL) ALL
```

This says: The root user (second line) and anyone in the admin group (third line; groups are designated by a % sign) can run all commands (the third ALL) on all hosts (the first ALL) as all users (the middle (ALL)). If you want to restrict a particular user, add another line after the ones shown here. Because the commands in this file are parsed in order, later commands can override earlier ones.

For example, if you want the user joe to be able to use `sudo` only to run the commands `kill` and `reboot`, you could add a line as follows:

```
joe     ALL= /bin/kill, /sbin/reboot
```

Or if you wanted to prevent the user joe from using `sudo` to get full root shell access, as described next, try something like this (all on one line), which disallows launching any shell with `sudo`:

```
joe     ALL=!/usr/bin/su, !/bin/sh, !/bin/ksh, !/bin/bash, !/bin/
    zsh, !/bin/csh, !/bin/tcsh, !/usr/bin/login
```

If you're modifying the `sudoers` file for just one or two users, adding lines like these is the easiest way to go. However, if you need to assign a wide range of different capabilities to various groups of users, hosts, and programs, line-by-line specifications would be awfully tedious. Luckily, the `sudoers` file lets you specify aliases for all these entities and then simply reference the aliases in the user privilege specification. You can also do fancy things such as specifying how much time may elapse, for a particular user, between password prompts or even set sudo to insult users if they use an incorrect password! To get the full scoop on what you can do, type **man sudoers** in Terminal.

Using Access Control Lists

The POSIX division of permissions into those for owner, group, and others works well in many cases, but it doesn't provide the sort of fine-grained control you may need in certain situations.

For example, suppose you want to assign permissions to a certain file as follows:

- Bob, the owner, can read, write, and execute it. (So far, so good: -rwx------ bob.)
- The group bcd, consisting of Bob, Cindy, and Dale, can read it but not change it. (Still possible with regular permissions: -rwxr----- bob bcd.)
- Only Evelyn, Fran, or Gil can delete the file. (Whoops — no way to express that using POSIX permissions, at least while keeping the previous settings.)
- The group consisting of Henry, Ilya, and Joachim can read the file and append information to the end but not change any other parts of the file. (This enters territory that POSIX permissions can't even touch.)

Luckily, Leopard and Snow Leopard have an additional mechanism for specifying detailed permissions that cover all these cases and go far beyond. This mechanism is called an *access control list*, or ACL.

What's an access control list?

At the risk of stating the obvious, an ACL is a list — associated with a given file, folder, or volume — that specifies which users can access it and in what ways. The ACL is normally invisible, and in fact, Leopard and Snow Leopard don't provide any convenient way to see or modify the contents of an ACL without using Terminal. But once you know what to look for and where to find it, ACLs can give you tremendous control over file access.

An ACL doesn't replace regular permissions but rather supplements them. When considering whether a user has access to do something with a file, Mac OS X first looks at the ACL for that file, if any. If there is none or if the ACL doesn't apply to the particular combination of user and activity in question, Mac OS X then looks at the POSIX permissions for the file and follows those.

Configuring access control lists

In Leopard and Snow Leopard, ACLs are enabled by default on your startup volume. They may or may not be enabled on other volumes you have mounted. To enable ACLs on a volume named Media, type the following command in Terminal:

```
sudo /usr/sbin/fsaclctl -p /Volumes/Media -e
```

Viewing an ACL

To see whether any items in the current directory already have ACLs specified (and, if so, what they are), use a variant of the `ls` command: Type **ls -le**. You might see a listing like the following:

```
drwxr-xr-x+  2 jk  staff     68 Jan 26 01:30 foldername
    0: user:joe allow add_subdirectory,readattr,writesecurity
```

The plus (+) at the end of the permissions string indicates that the folder has an ACL attached, and the line below it spells out what the ACL contains. In this example, it says that the user joe is allowed to do three things: add a subdirectory to this folder (`add_subdirectory`), read its attributes (`readatttr`), and change its ownership and permissions (`writesecurity`).

Note

If you select a file, folder, or volume in the Finder that has an ACL and choose File➪ Get Info, the Sharing & Permissions portion of the window lists the user or group name with Custom in the Privilege column. So, you can tell that an item has an ACL in the Finder but not get any details on what its specific privileges are or modify them. ■

Modifying an ACL with chmod

Once ACLs are enabled, the default way to add, change, or remove an ACL for an item is to use the `chmod` command, just as you do for changing other permissions. You use the +a flag to add an ACL entry, +a followed by a number to add an entry in a specific order, or −a to remove an entry.

After `chmod +a`, `chmod +a#`, or `chmod -a`, you type the following: within quotation marks, a user or group name, either `allow` or `deny`, and the permission to modify; and after the closing quotation mark, the name of the file or folder. For example:

```
chmod +a "joe allow delete" filename
```

This command adds an ACL that reads: Allow the user joe to delete the file `filename`. You can also add or remove more than one attribute at a time by separating them with commas:

```
chmod +a "joe allow delete,chown" filename
```

Note

Entries in an ACL apply in order: The first matching entry is used, and anything following that is ignored. That's why you may need, in certain cases, to pay attention to the order in which permissions are listed. To indicate that a certain entry should be, for example, third in the list, specify it like this: `chmod +a3 "joe allow delete" filename`. ■

Access control list options

You can change quite a few different kinds of permissions with an ACL. In each case, you add or remove permission by using the `chmod` command as just described. The following lists are adapted from the manual page for `chown` (to read it, type **man chown** in Terminal).

Permissions that apply to files, folders, and volumes:

- `delete`. Delete the item.
- `readattr`. Read basic attributes (including ownership, permissions, and ACLs).
- `writeattr`. Write basic attributes.
- `readextattr`. Read extended attributes.
- `writeextattr`. Write extended attributes.
- `readsecurity`. Read extended security information (ACLs).
- `writesecurity`. Write security information (ownership, permissions, and ACLs).
- `chown`. Change user and group ownership.

Permissions that apply only to folders and volumes:

- `list`. List the contents of the folder or volume.
- `search`. Search the folder or volume for files by name.
- `add_file`. Add a file.
- `add_subdirectory`. Add a subfolder.
- `delete_child`. Delete an item in the folder or volume.

Permissions that apply only to files:

- `read`. Read the file.
- `write`. Write the file.
- `append`. Write the file, but do so in such a way that changes can be made to parts of the file that haven't already been written (typically, the beginning or end).
- `execute`. Run the file as a script or program.

In addition to these permissions, an ACL for a volume or folder can specify *inheritance* — that is, whether an entry should be carried over to any newly created files or folders inside it. Inheritance options are as follows:

- `file_inherit`. Files inherit this ACL.
- `directory_inherit`. Folders inherit this ACL.
- `limit_inherit`. A newly created subfolder inherits this ACL, but that copy of the ACL doesn't have the `directory_inherit` permission, so it won't pass on the inheritance to further subfolders.
- `only_inherit`. The entry is passed on to new files and folders but doesn't apply to the current folder or volume.

Using GUI tools to modify ACLs

However functional chmod may be for modifying ACLs, it's not the most convenient way to do it, especially if you don't spend lots of time in Terminal. Fortunately, you have more than one option for editing ACLs using a conventional Mac OS X application.

One option is a free program called Sandbox (www.mikey-san.net/sandbox), shown in Figure 3.13. Although Sandbox works perfectly well — and the price is right — you should be aware that it works only on folders and volumes, not on individual files.

Another option, which costs €7 (roughly US$9) but lets you modify ACLs for files as well as folders and volumes, is TinkerTool System (www.bresink.com/osx/TinkerToolSys.html). This program is a more-advanced version of the free TinkerTool, which lets you modify a variety of hidden system settings. TinkerTool System's ACL Permissions pane contains the controls you need. To edit an ACL, drag a file, folder, or volume to the top of the window and then click Details at the bottom to show all your options, as shown in Figure 3.14.

Sandbox provides a convenient graphical interface for viewing and modifying ACLs on folders and volumes.

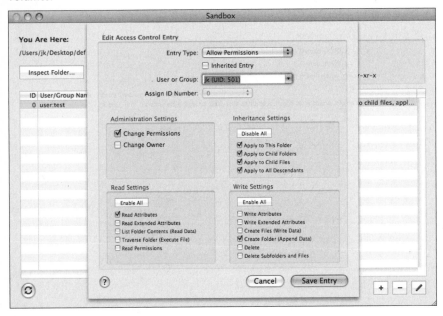

FIGURE 3.14

TinkerTool System lets you view and modify ACLs for files, folders, and volumes without opening Terminal.

Summary

In this chapter, I took you on an extensive tour of the Mac OS X accounts in their many facets. I explained how accounts work and what they have to do with security. Because permissions interact with accounts in such a crucial way, I described POSIX permissions at some length. I then explained the several varieties of user accounts you can create in Mac OS X and discussed how to configure each one, including managing an account with parental controls and setting overall login options. I explained how an administrator can temporarily gain root access by using the sudo command. And I rounded out the discussion on accounts with an overview of ACLs, which provide much more control than POSIX permissions.

Configuring Basic Security Settings

In one way or another, this entire book is about configuring and using your Mac in such a way that your privacy is maintained and your data is secure. Some ways of protecting your security require the use of third-party software or modifications in your behavior. But a number of security steps require nothing more than a few mouse clicks in one preference pane or another.

Accordingly, this chapter is about all those basic security settings. For the most part, everything you do in this chapter involves changing settings in Mac OS X's System Preferences.

General Settings

As you might expect, most of the security-related features built into Mac OS X are configured in the Security pane of System Preferences. That preference pane is, in turn, divided into three tabs: General, FileVault, and Firewall. In this section, I describe the settings you can adjust in the General pane.

Requiring a password to wake a computer

Even if you have Mac OS X configured to require your password when you log in (as described next), that single act of authenticating can last indefinitely — until you manually log out, restart, or shut down. If you leave your Mac on all the time, that means your account (possibly including your keychain) is nearly always unlocked, and anyone else who walks up to your computer could get access to your confidential information. By default, this behavior applies even when your computer goes to sleep or when your screen saver activates.

To illustrate why this might be a bad idea, suppose you have a laptop and, as you travel between home and office, you put it to sleep instead of shutting it down so you can get back to work as quickly as possible. Now, in transit, your Mac is lost or stolen. Merely opening the lid lets anyone see whatever's on your computer; the protections afforded by requiring you to log in with your password disappear.

You can reduce this risk with just a few clicks. Follow these steps:

1. Choose ⍙ System Preferences to open System Preferences and then click Security to open the Security pane.

2. If the lock icon in the lower-left corner of the pane is in the locked state, click it, type an administrator's username and password, and then click OK.

3. Click the General tab, which is shown in Figure 4.1, and then depending on your operating system, do one of the following:

   - **In Snow Leopard:** Click the Require password check box and then choose a time period from the pop-up menu (ranging from Immediately to 4 hours). This time period is the amount of time the computer must be asleep or the screen saver active before you're prompted to type your password.

   - **In Leopard:** Click the Require a password to wake this computer from sleep or screen saver check box. If automatic login (see just ahead) is enabled, an alert appears to recommend that you turn it off. Click Yes to turn off automatic login. (Clicking No means that someone who was blocked by this password prompt could simply restart your Mac to get full access.)

4. **Close System Preferences.**

With this setting enabled, Mac OS X presents an authentication window, prompting you for your username and password, whenever your Mac wakes up from sleep or when you begin using it again after the screen saver has kicked in.

Caution

One situation in which this setting has no effect is when your display is asleep (as opposed to the entire computer being asleep or the screen saver being active). Waking your display doesn't result in a password prompt. You can set your display to sleep in the Energy Saver pane of System Preferences or by clicking Hot Corners in the Screen Saver pane of the Desktop & Screen Saver pane. ∎

I suggest enabling this setting if you work in a busy office, if you use a laptop outside your home or office, or, if for any other reason, other people you may not trust completely could have physical access to your Mac. On the other hand, if you use your Mac only at home or in another location that's physically secure, turning on this feature requires you to expend more effort without actually improving your security.

FIGURE 4.1

The General pane of the Security pane of System Preferences includes a number of common preferences, including requiring a password to wake the computer. This pane differs somewhat between Leopard and Snow Leopard; the Snow Leopard version is shown here.

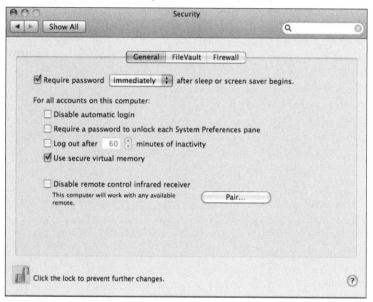

Disabling automatic login

When you set up Mac OS X for the first time, it configures the computer to log in automatically using your initial administrator account whenever you turn the computer on. This is the most convenient arrangement for an individual user, and it poses no significant security threat if you're the only person with access to your Mac. However, in all other cases — when you take your Mac on the road, for example, or if you ever leave it unattended in a spot where other people could walk up and turn it on — I recommend disabling automatic login so that no one can easily get to your personal files without knowing your username and password. And if you've chosen to make your keychain password the same as your login password (which means your keychain unlocks automatically when you log in), it's even more crucial for you to disable automatic login in order to protect all your passwords.

Cross-Ref

For more on automatic login and overall account settings, see Chapter 3. ■

To disable automatic login, follow these steps:

1. Choose ⌘ ⇨ System Preferences to open System Preferences and then click Security to open the Security pane.

2. **If the lock icon in the lower-left corner of the pane is in the locked state, click it, type an administrator's username and password, and then click OK.**

3. **Click the General tab.**

4. **Click the Disable automatic login check box.** If automatic login was previously enabled for a particular user in the Accounts pane of System Preferences, that setting is removed.

5. **Close System Preferences.**

If you later deselect the Disable automatic login check box to re-enable the feature, an alert appears, as shown in Figure 4.2. To set up a particular user to log in automatically, click Open Accounts, authenticate if required, and choose that user's name from the Automatic login pop-up menu. Type that user's password when prompted and then click OK.

FIGURE 4.2

If you re-enable automatic login after disabling it, this alert appears to remind you that this change alone doesn't set a particular user's account to log in automatically.

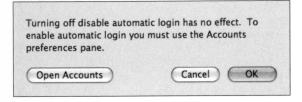

Note
You can also disable automatic login in the Accounts preference pane by clicking Login Options and choosing Disabled from the Automatic login pop-up menu. ∎

Locking System Preferences

Some of Mac OS X's preferences apply separately to each user, whereas others apply system-wide, although if you look through the panes of System Preferences, you may see no obvious clues as to which preferences are which. If you're the only person who uses your Mac, there's no problem treating all preferences equally. However, on a multi-user Mac, especially one in a public space, such as a school or library, you probably don't want just anyone to be able to change the computer's network settings, turn off the firewall, or manipulate other settings that could reduce security or usability. As a result, the preference panes that alter system-wide settings require an administrator's credentials to use and are called the secure preference panes in Apple's terminology. The following are the secure preference panes:

- Accounts
- Date & Time
- Energy Saver
- Network
- Parental Controls
- Print & Fax
- Security
- Sharing
- Startup Disk
- Time Machine

The Accounts preference pane requires authentication by an administrator for certain activities (adding or deleting accounts, for example), but individual non-administrator users can change their own settings (such as modifying the Login Items list) without authenticating. To unlock any locked preference pane, click the lock icon in the lower-left corner of the pane, type an administrator's username and password, and then click OK.

In Leopard, by default, when an administrator unlocks any one of the secure preference panes, all the panes remain unlocked until the current user logs out, shuts down, or restarts. (In Snow Leopard, authentication remains in effect for some panes but not others when you close and reopen System Preferences.) However, you can lock the secure preference panes in such a way that when an administrator unlocks one, they're all unlocked only until System Preferences is closed.

To lock system-wide preferences in Leopard so that an administrator's password is required in each session, follow these steps:

1. Choose System Preferences to open System Preferences and then click Security to open the Security pane.
2. If the lock icon in the lower-left corner of the pane is in the locked state, click it, type an administrator's username and password, and then click OK.
3. Click the General tab.
4. Click the Require a password to unlock each System Preferences pane check box.
5. Close System Preferences.

To reiterate, after adjusting this setting, the only difference in behavior is in how long the authentication sticks: With this feature turned on, authentication remains valid only until System Preferences is closed. Therefore, after adjusting any preferences, you (the administrator) should be sure to quit the application.

Setting automatic logout

If you're the sole user of your Mac, configuring it to require a password when you log in, wake up the computer, or disable the screen saver is generally enough to keep others with physical access to your computer from accessing your files when you're not looking. But you can add yet another barrier to unwanted use by ensuring that it automatically logs out any user after a pre-determined period of inactivity. In a multi-user environment or whenever security demands that you take no chances that anyone could use your Mac during your absence, turn on this feature.

To set up automatic logout, follow these steps:

1. Choose ⇨ System Preferences to open System Preferences and then click Security to open the Security pane.

2. If the lock icon in the lower-left corner of the pane is in the locked state, click it, type an administrator's username and password, and then click OK.

3. Click the General tab.

4. Click the Log out after X minutes of inactivity check box.

5. Set a number of minutes by clicking the up and down arrow buttons or by typing a number into the box. (The minimum value is 5 minutes; the maximum value is 960 minutes. In most cases, a value of between 10 and 30 minutes makes a reasonable compromise between security and convenience.)

6. Close System Preferences.

With this set, Mac OS X watches for keyboard or mouse activity and starts a timer as soon as it stops. Press another key or move the mouse, and the timer resets. If the timer reaches the value you set, Mac OS X displays an alert (shown in Figure 4.3) warning that the user will be logged out in 60 seconds. If the user doesn't respond to the alert, the system logs out that user (which entails quitting all open applications) and displays the login window.

FIGURE 4.3

When your Mac is set to log out users after a period of inactivity, this warning appears, giving you up to 60 seconds to say you want to stay logged in after all.

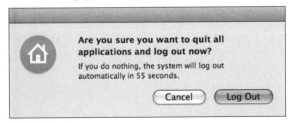

Note

For the purpose of this feature, passive activities (such as listening to music or watching a movie) don't count as activities. So, Mac OS X may log you out right in the middle of your favorite show if you don't respond to the alert. ■

However, this feature may not always work as you expect. In particular, you can't log out (manually or automatically) if an application has an open document with unsaved changes. When Mac OS X attempts to quit the application in order to log out, a dialog box opens asking if you want to save the changes, and if no one responds to that prompt, logout doesn't occur. The same is true if an application is busy or stuck or for any reason refuses to respond to the system's instruction to quit; if Mac OS X can't gracefully quit all applications, it doesn't log you out. Therefore, if you do use this feature, don't count on it being 100% reliable.

Remember, this setting affects all users on the Mac. Be sure to inform the other users of what this setting is and how it works.

Secure virtual memory

Mac OS X's virtual memory system regularly swaps portions of RAM onto and off of your hard disk. This happens more frequently if you have a small amount of RAM, if you run many applications at once, or both, but even if you have plenty of RAM and run few applications, Mac OS X always uses at least some virtual memory.

Because your RAM can contain, in theory, just about anything — including anything you've copied to the Clipboard, passwords you've typed, and other potentially sensitive information — so can your virtual memory. Therefore, regardless of other security measures you may have taken, an attacker who can examine the virtual memory swapfiles on your disk can potentially learn all sorts of confidential things. In fact, even after information in a swapfile has been erased, it can sometimes be recovered, meaning that private information that happened to be in RAM weeks or months ago could still be sitting on your hard disk for anyone with the necessary know-how to read.

One solution to this problem is to ask Mac OS X to encrypt your virtual memory swapfiles; Leopard and Snow Leopard refer to this as using secure virtual memory. The process of encrypting information as it's written to disk and decrypting it as it's read back into RAM is completely transparent and in most cases happens so quickly that it causes no noticeable performance degradation. Because there's no practical downside to turning this feature on, I recommend that everyone do so.

Note

If you use software that encrypts your entire boot volume (see Chapter 13), that includes your swapfiles, so turning on secure virtual memory offers little if any additional benefit. ■

To activate secure virtual memory, follow these steps:

1. Choose ⌘ ⇨ System Preferences to open System Preferences and then click Security to open the Security pane.

2. **If the lock icon in the lower-left corner of the pane is in the locked state, click it, type an administrator's username and password, and then click OK.**

3. **Click the General tab.**

4. **Click the Use secure virtual memory check box.** A notice appears stating that you must restart your Mac for this change to take effect.

5. **Choose ◆ ➪ Restart to restart your Mac.**

If you later decide to deactivate secure virtual memory, repeat these steps, clicking to deselect the Use secure virtual memory check box in step 4.

Location Services settings

In Snow Leopard, Apple introduced Location Services, a system-wide mechanism that enables your Mac to determine its geographical location (within limits) and lets various applications access this information for various reasons. For example, if this feature is enabled, your Mac can optionally set its time zone based on your current location and then update it automatically as you travel. However, you may not want applications to be able to discover your location, as that can reduce your privacy in some situations.

Location Services are enabled by default in Snow Leopard. To disable them, follow these steps:

1. **Choose ◆ ➪ System Preferences to open System Preferences and then click Security to open the Security pane.**

2. **If the lock icon in the lower-left corner of the pane is in the locked state, click it, type an administrator's username and password, and then click OK.**

3. **Click the General tab.**

4. **Click the Disable Location Services check box.**

5. **Close System Preferences.** The change becomes effective immediately.

Infrared receiver settings

Most recent Mac models have a built-in infrared receiver designed to work with an Apple Remote. You can use the remote to control iTunes, Front Row, DVD Player, or other media applications. By default, your Mac works with any Apple Remote, although if you have more than one, you can pair a particular unit with your Mac so that you need not worry about accidentally controlling the wrong device with a given remote.

If you haven't paired your Mac with a particular remote, it's possible that someone else could control your Mac's volume, play media, and cause other interruptions. And if you've installed the iAlertU software to set off an alarm when your Mac is moved, it can be enabled and disabled with your Apple Remote — meaning someone else could potentially disable your alarm software to make it easier for them to steal your Mac.

Cross-Ref

For more on iAlertU, see Chapter 2. ■

Note

The controls applicable to an infrared receiver appear in the Security preference pane only if your Mac has an infrared receiver! ■

To associate your Mac with just one remote, follow these steps:

1. Choose ➪ System Preferences to open System Preferences and then click Security to open the Security pane.

2. If the lock icon in the lower-left corner of the pane is in the locked state, click it, type an administrator's username and password, and then click OK.

3. Click the General tab.

4. **Click the Pair button.** If the button says Unpair, the computer is already configured to use just one Apple Remote.

5. Following the instructions that appear, hold your Apple Remote near your computer and then press and hold the remote's Menu and Next (forward) buttons at the same time until a graphic appears on your Mac's screen to confirm that the devices are paired.

6. Close System Preferences.

Even if you've restricted your Mac to recognize just one remote, someone could potentially emulate that remote with another device. Although the chances of this happening are, shall we say, remote — and although someone launching iTunes with a rogue remote doesn't pose any obvious threat to your Mac's data or your privacy — you may nevertheless want to eliminate the possibility altogether, just to ensure that you never lose control. To disable the infrared port altogether, follow these steps:

1. Choose ➪ System Preferences to open System Preferences and then click Security to open the Security pane.

2. If the lock icon in the lower-left corner of the pane is in the locked state, click it, type an administrator's username and password, and then click OK.

3. Click the General tab.

4. Click the Disable remote control infrared receiver check box.

5. Close System Preferences.

Common Criteria

An internationally recognized set of security standards called Common Criteria enables manufacturers and purchasers of computer equipment to verify that numerous basic security criteria are met. (You can learn more about Common Criteria by visiting the Common Criteria Portal at `www.commoncriteria portal.org`.) Numerous government agencies and other organizations require that the computers and software they buy be certified as compliant with Common Criteria and their settings be configured according to its guidelines.

Implementing Common Criteria standards on a Mac involves following certain procedures (such as choosing good passwords and logging out at the end of each session) in addition to setting a variety of preferences — mostly those described in this chapter — according to the requirements spelled out in Apple's Configuration & Administration Guide, available in PDF form from `www.apple.com/support/ security/commoncriteria/`. Some of those guidelines are stricter than what I recommend in this book.

From the same URL, you can also download Apple's Common Criteria Tools, which can enable an administrator to confirm that your Mac is configured properly and add logging and auditing of numerous events that affect your Mac's security.

FileVault

The FileVault feature in Leopard and Snow Leopard lets users encrypt their entire home folders. FileVault uses the AES-128 encryption standard, which is what the U.S. government specifies for protecting secret documents. As of 2009, AES has never been broken, and projections are that a brute-force attack would take all the computers on the planet, working together, longer than a human lifetime. Although FileVault itself has a variety of weaknesses, its encryption method is more than adequate for protecting any files you may have on your Mac, as long as you choose a good password and keep it safe.

Cross-Ref

Before turning FileVault on, see Chapter 13. ∎

How FileVault works

Before you can use FileVault, Mac OS X requires you to specify a master password, which can be used later on to access any account on your Mac protected with FileVault, even if the user's login password is forgotten. This password should be different from your administrator password and from any individual user's login password. It should also be kept extremely safe.

When you activate FileVault for a given user, Mac OS X creates an encrypted disk image, copies all the folders and files from the existing home folder (`/User/`*short-username*) onto the disk image, deletes the original home folder (optionally overwriting the data to prevent it from being recovered later), and then performs a bit of behind-the-scenes magic to make all references to the home folder point to the encrypted disk image.

Note

Because FileVault begins by creating a copy of the user's entire home folder, it needs quite a bit of free disk space — at least equivalent to the size of the existing home folder. ∎

The end result of all this is that when you log in to a FileVault-protected account, Mac OS X also mounts the disk image so that you (and any Mac OS X software) can read all the information in your home folder. Merely mounting the disk image doesn't decrypt the whole thing, however; Mac OS X decrypts the specific items it needs, on the fly, as they're read into RAM. When you log out (or shut down your computer), Mac OS X unmounts the encrypted disk image so that its contents can't be read at all.

FileVault gives you no control over which files are encrypted: It always and only encrypts the contents of your home folder. This means, on the one hand, that many files are encrypted that may not be at all sensitive, such as your iTunes library. But it also means some potentially private files aren't encrypted. For example, anything stored in the /Library folder — caches, log files, and system-wide preference files, to name a few — and anything in folders you've created at the root level of your hard disk remain unencrypted. Therefore, if you do use FileVault, you should be careful to store private documents only in your home folder or one of its subfolders, but you should also be aware that some applications may store private data elsewhere without asking your permission.

Setting up FileVault

To set up FileVault for the user who's currently logged in, follow these steps:

1. **Choose ➪ System Preferences to open System Preferences and then click Security to open the Security pane.**

2. **If the lock icon in the lower-left corner of the pane is in the locked state, click it, type an administrator's username and password, and then click OK.**

3. **Click the FileVault tab, which is shown in Figure 4.4.**

4. **If you see a message that says "A master password is not set for this computer," click Set Master Password, type and verify a password in the fields provided, type an optional hint, and then click OK.**

5. **Click Turn On FileVault.** Mac OS X first checks to see that you have enough free space to encrypt your home folder. If you don't, it informs you that you must delete some files before continuing.

6. **When prompted, type the user's password and then click OK.** A warning, as shown in Figure 4.5, appears.

FIGURE 4.4

Turn on FileVault for the current user in the FileVault pane. If you haven't already done so, you must first set a master password for the computer.

FIGURE 4.5

This warning lets you know that encrypting your home folder will take awhile and provides a couple of additional FileVault options.

7. **You can optionally click the Use secure erase check box.** This ensures that after the FileVault disk image is created, your previously unencrypted files are securely erased, but it can add several hours or more to the time required to activate FileVault.

8. **Leave the Use secure virtual memory check box selected and then click Turn On FileVault.** Mac OS X encrypts your home folder, which may take anywhere from seconds to hours, depending on its size. It then displays the login window, where you can log in as the existing user or a different user.

9. **Close System Preferences.**

You can then use your account normally, for the most part, although some features (such as Time Machine) won't be fully functional. From time to time, when you log out of a FileVault-protected account (including restarting and shutting down), you may see an alert informing you that FileVault would like to recover unused disk space; click Continue to agree or Cancel to postpone recovering the space.

Cross-Ref

For more on the interactions between Time Machine and FileVault, see Chapters 8 and 13. ■

Firewall

In computer terms, a *firewall* is hardware or software that selectively blocks network traffic. Presumably, you never want to block all your Mac's network traffic; that would mean no web browsing, no email, no file sharing — no communicating with other computers at all. However, there are excellent reasons for blocking some network traffic. Many kinds of network attacks involve an outside computer attempting to send instructions to vulnerable programs on your Mac so they can install unauthorized software, use your computer to send out spam, spy on you, or simply crash your system. In some cases, hackers use robotic armies of hundreds or thousands of computers to methodically probe computers on the Internet, looking for just the right kinds of openings needed to wreak havoc.

The situation isn't as scary as it may sound though. By default, Macs run very little software that actively listens for outside network connections, and most of this software has other kinds of safeguards against misuse. Even without taking any special action, the real-world chances of becoming the victim of a random network attack are, for a Mac user, quite slim. On the other hand, as you install more third-party software, your risk increases. And hackers are constantly looking for new vulnerabilities to exploit, so a Mac that's safe today could be quite unsafe tomorrow.

In order to protect yourself against these potential threats, your first line of defense is Mac OS X's built-in firewall. In fact, Leopard and Snow Leopard have two firewalls, but only one of them is visible in the user interface, and it provides adequate protection for most people. Unlike conventional firewalls, which block outside traffic based on the IP address from which it originates or the port to which it's directed, the default firewall in Leopard and Snow Leopard blocks traffic based on the application to which the outside traffic wants to connect. This sort of firewall is known as an *application firewall* or a *socket-filter firewall*. It provides less control over filtering but is much easier to set up than other firewall types.

Cross-Ref

For more on the built-in firewalls and third-party firewall software, see Chapter 17. ∎

Mac OS X's application firewall affects only incoming network traffic; it has no effect on outbound requests or their responses. For example, you can continue using a web browser and email client even with the firewall configured to use its most restrictive setting because in cases like these, the software on your Mac is initiating the network connection.

To configure Mac OS X's application firewall, follow these steps:

1. Choose ⇨ System Preferences to open System Preferences and then click Security to open the Security pane.
2. If the lock icon in the lower-left corner of the pane is in the locked state, click it, type an administrator's username and password, and then click OK.
3. Click the Firewall tab.
4. **In Snow Leopard only, if the firewall is off, click the Start button to start it, and then click the Advanced button to show configuration options.** The corresponding options appear on the main Firewall pane in Leopard, as shown in Figure 4.6.

FIGURE 4.6

Set options for Leopard's application firewall in this pane.

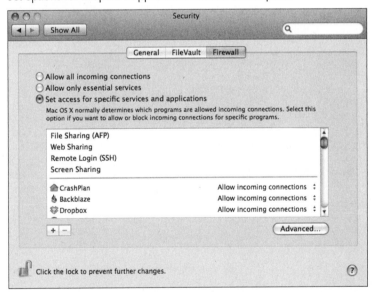

5. Do one of the following:

   - **In Leopard only, click the Allow all incoming connections check box.** This is another way of saying off; it blocks no connections and is therefore the least safe option. In Snow Leopard, the comparable option would be to leave the firewall off (or turn it off) in step 4.

   - **Click the Allow only essential services radio button (Leopard) or click the Block all incoming connections check box (Snow Leopard).** This is the most restrictive option; it permits incoming traffic only for DHCP (which enables your Mac to get an IP address, among other things), Bonjour (which makes your Mac visible to other computers on your local network), and IPsec (a secure Internet communications protocol). With this option selected, other computers can't access your Mac for file sharing, screen sharing, iTunes and iPhoto library sharing, or any other service.

   - **Click the Set access for specific services and applications radio button (Leopard) or click the Block all incoming connections check box, if it's already selected, to deselect it (Snow Leopard).** This is the most flexible option (see Figure 4.7). If you select this, the firewall automatically permits incoming connections for any services you've turned on in the Sharing pane of System Preferences (such as File Sharing or Screen Sharing). In addition, you can add other applications for which you want to explicitly allow or deny incoming access. For example, if you use Skype, iChat, or other software for text, audio, or video chats, you should add those applications here. To do so, click the Add (+) button, locate and select the application, and then click Add; repeat this process as necessary. By default, newly added applications are allowed incoming connections; click Allow incoming connections to the right of the application's name and choose Block incoming connections from the pop-up menu if you want to prevent a program from accepting connections.

6. **In Snow Leopard only, click OK to close the Advanced window.**

7. **Close System Preferences.** Mac OS X immediately begins allowing or blocking network traffic according to your settings.

Note

If you click the Set access for specific services and applications radio button and another application (one you haven't explicitly added to the list) tries to receive an inbound network connection, an alert like the one shown in Figure 4.8 appears. Click either Allow or Deny to add this application to the firewall's list, set to Allow incoming connections or Block incoming connections, respectively. ■

FIGURE 4.7

Set options for Snow Leopard's application firewall in this dialog box, which opens when you click the Advanced button in the Firewall pane.

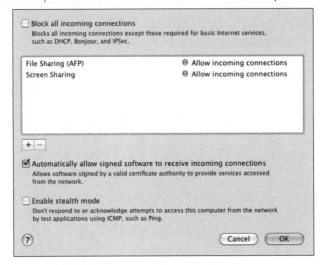

FIGURE 4.8

When the firewall is set to allow network access to only the applications you select, you may see alerts like this one asking whether applications not already on the list may receive inbound connections.

MobileMe Settings

MobileMe is Apple's suite of online services, including email, file sharing, web hosting, and synchronization of numerous kinds of data. Although you can use MobileMe with a Windows PC, an iPhone, or an iPod touch, it works especially well on a Mac in conjunction with features integrated into Leopard and Snow Leopard (and specific Mac OS X applications, including iLife and iWork).

Tip

I wrote an ebook all about MobileMe, which contains extensive information on all the service's features. You can find *Take Control of MobileMe* at www.takecontrolbooks.com/mobileme.html. ∎

You can configure each Mac OS X user account to tie into a single MobileMe account. (You can access more than one, but only one at a time can take advantage of certain account-wide capabilities, such as syncing.) Because MobileMe settings are user-specific, many of the security implications tied to a MobileMe account are determined by the security of your Mac OS X user account. However, you should be aware of several additional security considerations when using a MobileMe account in Mac OS X:

- Some of the data sent back and forth over the Internet between your computer and Apple's MobileMe servers isn't encrypted while in transit, making it vulnerable to *sniffing* (covertly observing network traffic). The good news is that MobileMe uses SSL to encrypt the connections between your Mac and Apple's servers when syncing data such as bookmarks, calendars, and contacts. If you use Mail for MobileMe email, it also uses SSL by default for IMAP and SMTP (although you can disable it). The bad news is that files copied to or from your iDisk aren't encrypted while in transit, although your user credentials are encrypted when you log in. In addition, if you use a web browser to access any MobileMe services, your session (again, apart from your initial login and your account information page) isn't protected by SSL, although Apple says it uses other mechanisms to ensure that sensitive data, such as email, can't be intercepted.

- Along the same lines, the files you put on your iDisk aren't encrypted while being stored on Apple's servers. So, in theory, an Apple employee or contractor could potentially examine any files you upload.

- If you keep a local copy of your iDisk on your Mac's hard disk, it becomes possible for an attacker with access to your disk to read the files stored there, even without knowing your MobileMe password.

- If you use the Back to My Mac features of MobileMe, you slightly increase the risk that an unauthorized person could access your files or take control of your Mac remotely.

The information that follows involves MobileMe settings that can influence your security or privacy in one way or another.

Account settings

The Account tab of the MobileMe pane of System Preferences, shown in Figure 4.9, lets you sign in to MobileMe or shows your member name if you're already signed in. If you want to be sure that all ties with MobileMe are severed — your iDisk isn't mounted in the Finder by default, syncing contacts and calendars with MobileMe is disabled, and so on — either leave this information blank (and skip the rest of this section) or click Sign Out and then confirm by clicking Sign Out again.

Most Mac users who are MobileMe members should remain signed in here because without the direct ties to Mac OS X that this setting provides, MobileMe offers much less utility. However, you should be aware of what information may be sent or stored in an unsecure way and then take appropriate steps to protect those pieces of data.

FIGURE 4.9

The Account pane of MobileMe preferences shows whether you're signed in; if you aren't, it lets you type your member name and password to sign in.

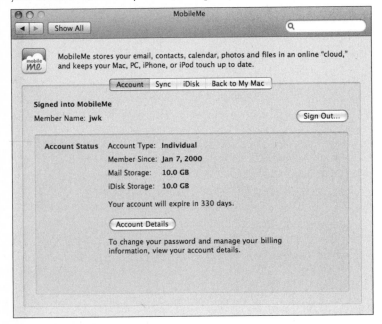

Sync settings

On the Sync tab of the MobileMe preference pane (shown in Figure 4.10), you choose which kinds of data are synchronized between this Mac and the MobileMe servers. By choosing the same settings on other Macs you own, you can then also sync the data between Macs.

According to Apple, all data that you can sync using these settings is encrypted during transit using SSL. In addition, your keychain files are always encrypted. However, the other data types, although they may be protected while on their way to and from Apple's servers, are stored there in an unencrypted form. That means someone at Apple or an attacker who could guess your password or otherwise break into Apple's servers remotely could conceivably access any of your private data — your contacts, appointments, and so on. Realistically, the chances of this happening are vanishingly small, but if you have extremely sensitive data in, for example, iCal or Address Book, you might want to think twice before turning on syncing for those data types.

FIGURE 4.10

You can sync numerous kinds of information between your Mac and the MobileMe servers; choose what you want to sync in this pane.

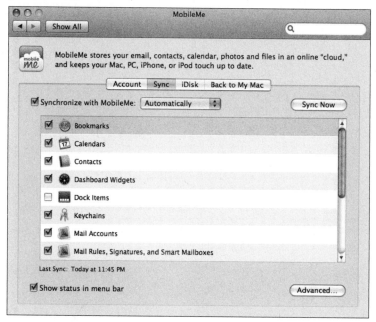

iDisk settings

As previously mentioned, data on your iDisk isn't encrypted — locally, on Apple's servers, or in transit. That's a limitation you must live with; if you want to store files on your iDisk that contain sensitive information, you should first put them on an encrypted disk image or encrypt them in some other way.

Cross-Ref

For more on encrypting files by using disk images and other methods, see Chapter 13. ■

In addition, if you store a local copy of your iDisk on your hard disk (so that you can get at your files even when you're offline), those files could potentially fall into the hands of anyone with physical access to your Mac, even if he or she doesn't have your MobileMe password. Once again, encrypting the files would address that concern, but your other option is to forgo syncing.

To turn off syncing, open the MobileMe preference pane, click the iDisk tab (as shown in Figure 4.11), and then click the Stop button at the bottom. Mac OS X puts the disk image it previously used for this purpose on your desktop in case you have any local files that weren't synchronized with the server. After verifying that all your files are on your iDisk, you can delete this disk image.

Besides offering you a private location to store files, your iDisk includes a Public folder in which you can place files you want to share with other people. By default, anyone who knows your MobileMe username can connect to this folder and download any files there. To restrict access to people who know a password, click the Password-protect your public folder check box, type and confirm a password, and then click OK. To prevent other users from uploading their own files to your iDisk, you can also click the Read Only radio button (in Leopard) or click the Allow others to write files in your public folder check box to deselect it if it's already selected (in Snow Leopard).

FIGURE 4.11

In the iDisk pane, choose whether to keep a local copy of your iDisk on your Mac for offline access. This figure shows the iDisk pane as it appears in Leopard; the Snow Leopard version is slightly different.

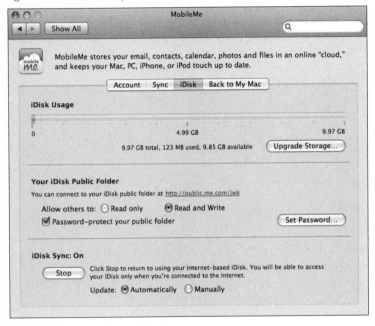

Back to My Mac settings

MobileMe includes several features, collectively known as Back to My Mac, that let you access a Mac you own that's in another location — even if there are intervening barriers such as NAT gateways and if either or both of the Macs are without a publicly routable IP address or domain name. The point of this fancy technology is to enable you to share a remote Mac's screen, copy files, or otherwise use its resources. For example, you might use it to fetch a file from your home computer while you're at work.

Back to My Mac uses MobileMe to provide a means of discovery and, in effect, a conduit for the two computers. For this magic to work, both computers must be turned on, awake, and logged in to MobileMe using the same set of credentials. In addition, Back to My Mac must be turned on, one or more sharing services must be enabled, firewalls (if any) on both ends must allow access to the necessary ports, and the router or gateway by way of which the remote Mac connects to the Internet must support one of the protocols (UPnP or NAT-PMP) that Back to My Mac uses. (Despite that seemingly long list of requirements, Back to My Mac usually works quite well — and transparently — in practice.)

Cross-Ref

For more on using Back to My Mac to track a stolen Mac, see Chapter 2. ■

As long as Back to My Mac is enabled (along with one or more shared resources), there's a small chance someone else who obtains or can guess your MobileMe credentials could log in to any of your Macs and take control of them or read your files. The best defense against this is to choose good passwords and keep them safe. Nevertheless, if you don't need the capabilities of Back to My Mac, it's safest simply to leave it turned off: Open the MobileMe preference pane, click the Back to My Mac tab (shown in Figure 4.12), and if the service is on, click Stop to stop it.

FIGURE 4.12

MobileMe's Back to My Mac feature, configured here, lets you reach your Mac even when it's connected to a remote network and you don't know its IP address. This figure shows the Back to My Mac pane as it appears in Leopard; the Snow Leopard version is slightly different.

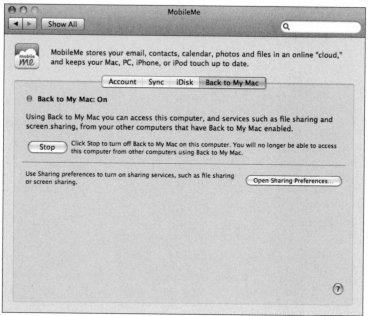

Energy Saver Settings

Mac OS X has a number of features that can reduce your Mac's use of electricity — extending battery life for laptops and reducing power costs for everyone. Some of these settings can also affect your Mac's security in subtle ways.

To adjust your Energy Saver settings, choose ⌘⇨ System Preferences and then click Energy Saver. What you see there depends on whether you're running Leopard or Snow Leopard and whether you're using a laptop or desktop Mac — and for laptops, which particular model you have. Desktop Macs, naturally, run only on AC power, whereas laptops have separate settings for running on battery or when their power adapter is plugged in. In addition, on some laptops, Leopard divides the settings for all computers into two groups — a Sleep tab and an Options tab — whereas Snow Leopard's Energy Saver preference pane has just one view (except for laptops, which require separate tabs for battery and AC power). Figures 4.13 and 4.14 show two of the possible variants. You may need to click a Show Details button show the Sleep and Options tabs.

FIGURE 4.13

The Energy Saver preference pane in Leopard is sometimes divided into Sleep and Options panes. This image shows the Sleep pane of the Energy Saver pane as it appears on some types of Mac laptops, with options at the top for choosing the power source.

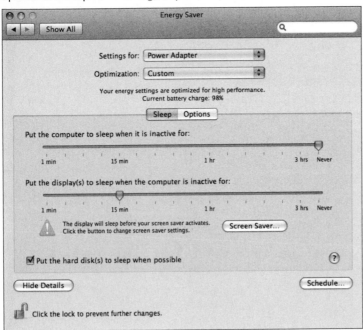

FIGURE 4.14

In Snow Leopard, the Energy Saver pane is organized differently. This is how it appears on a Mac laptop; on a desktop Mac, you would not see different settings for Battery and Power Adapter.

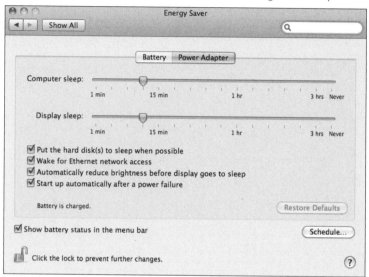

Setting computer, display, and disk sleep

You can use the sliders in the Energy Saver pane (on the Sleep tab, if present, in Leopard) to set the period of time after which your computer automatically sleeps (the top slider) and puts only the display to sleep (the bottom slider). You can also click the Put the hard disk(s) to sleep when possible check box to enable disks to stop spinning when not actively in use (with a slight decrease in performance, because you must wait for them to spin up when you need to read or write data).

Note

As I mentioned earlier in this chapter, even if you've configured your security settings to require a password when your Mac wakes from sleep, this doesn't apply when your display alone, not the entire computer, is asleep. Therefore, to avoid any ambiguity as to whether your Mac requires a password after the display goes dark, you can set Computer Sleep and Display Sleep to the same values. (If you don't require a password when waking from sleep, feel free to set Display Sleep to a shorter period of time.) ■

By clicking the Schedule button, you can optionally set a time when your Mac sleeps, restarts, or shuts down automatically. (It's disabled by default.) If you turn this feature on and choose Restart or Shut Down, be aware that an open, unsaved document in any application can prevent your Mac from restarting or shutting down. So, you should not count on this feature to prevent someone else from accessing your Mac when you're not present, unless you log out manually before leaving.

Waking for network access

When your Mac is asleep, normally you can wake it by pressing a key on the keyboard, pressing the Power button, or clicking the mouse. However, in certain situations, it may be helpful to wake up a sleeping Mac over a network. For example, if you use server-based backup software that runs on a schedule, it may need to wake up your Mac in order to back it up. Or an administrator may want to install software or perform other maintenance on a Mac that's too far away to conveniently wake up in person. For just such purposes, Macs include a feature called *Wake-on-LAN* (WoL), which keeps the Ethernet port minimally active when the computer is otherwise asleep and able to respond to a special signal that wakes up the computer.

Under Leopard, the uses to which Wake-on-LAN may be put are limited; someone wanting to wake a Mac remotely must use one of a handful of programs that can send out the proper kind of network packet, such as Retrospect version 8 or higher, Apple Remote Desktop, or the free WakeOnLan utility (`www.readpixel.com/wakeonlan/`).

Under Snow Leopard, Apple has expanded the capabilities of Wake-on-LAN so that one Mac can wake up another merely by attempting to access resources it's sharing (including file sharing, screen sharing, printer sharing, sharing media with iTunes or iPhoto, and so on). This enhanced capability, which Apple now refers to as Wake on Demand, even works over Wi-Fi connections in some situations. However, Wake on Demand is subject to a number of qualifications:

- Whether Wake on Demand is used over a wired (Ethernet) or wireless (Wi-Fi) network, your Mac must connect to the network via a recent-model AirPort Extreme (released in 2007 or later) or Time Capsule (released in 2008 or later), which must also have been updated to use firmware version 7.4.2 or later. This requirement is because Wake on Demand uses the base station as a proxy; it sends out messages on behalf of your sleeping Mac to convince other devices on your network that it's still awake; and when necessary it sends the Mac a special signal to wake it up.

- In order for Wake on Demand to work over Wi-Fi, if your base station uses WPA or WPA2 encryption (as it should), it must not be in Bridge Mode.

Cross-Ref
For more on the configuration of AirPort networks, including the connection mode and WPA/WPA2 encryption, see Chapter 16.

- Only newer Mac models support Wake on Demand over Wi-Fi. This apparently means all Macs released in 2009 or later, and some models released in 2008.

Tip
To learn more about Wake on Demand, including how to discover whether your Mac supports this feature over Wi-Fi, visit `http://support.apple.com/kb/HT3774`.

As useful as Wake-on-LAN (or Wake on Demand) may be, it can also pose a security risk in that it breaks the otherwise logical assumption that a sleeping computer is immune to having its files, screen, or other resources shared. If you've remained logged in to your Mac but put it to sleep, thinking that no one can access it over the network, someone could seize that opportunity to get at your computer behind your back.

The ways in which this feature is enabled or disabled depend on which operating system you're running.

If you're using Leopard, follow these steps:

1. Choose ⌘ ➪ System Preferences to open System Preferences and then click Energy Saver to open the Energy Saver pane.

2. If the lock icon in the lower-left corner of the pane is in the locked state, click it, type an administrator's username and password, and then click OK.

3. To enable Wake-on-LAN, click the Wake for Ethernet network administrator access check box (which is deselected by default). On some Macs running Leopard, this check box is located on the Options tab of the Energy Saver preference pane. The change takes effect immediately.

4. Close System Preferences.

If you're using Snow Leopard, follow these steps:

1. Choose ⌘ ➪ System Preferences to open System Preferences and then click Energy Saver to open the Energy Saver pane, as shown in Figure 4.15.

2. If the lock icon in the lower-left corner of the pane is in the locked state, click it, type an administrator's username and password, and then click OK.

3. To enable Wake-on-LAN, click the Wake for network access check box (if your Mac supports Wake on Demand over both Ethernet and Wi-Fi), the Wake for AirPort network access check box (if your Mac supports Wake on Demand only over Wi-Fi), or the Wake for Ethernet network access check box (if it supports Wake on Demand only over Ethernet). You may see a notice reminding you that you could hear your computer wake up occasionally; if so, click OK. The change takes effect immediately.

4. Close System Preferences.

In Snow Leopard's Energy Saver preference pane, you can choose whether your Mac wakes for (certain varieties of) network access. On some Macs running Leopard, this check box appears on a separate pane called Options.

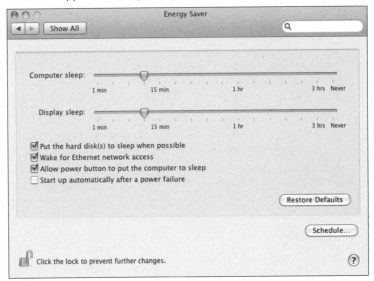

Spotlight Settings

Spotlight is Mac OS X's system-wide search feature, which relies on an index of all your files to deliver rapid search results. Because each folder is indexed individually, one user can't search for files inside another user's home folder. However, all users can search files located inside their own home folders as well as files located outside the /Users folder.

If you want to prevent Spotlight from indexing any files or folders, you can exclude them from searches. For example, you might do this for files that contain sensitive information you want to avoid indexing or for files that duplicate existing content (such as backups and caches).

To exclude data from Spotlight searches, follow these steps:

1. Choose System Preferences to open System Preferences and then click Spotlight to open the Spotlight pane.

2. Click the Privacy tab, which is shown in Figure 4.16.

3. Click the Add (+) button, choose a folder or volume, and then click Choose to add the item to the list. Repeat this step for every item you want to exclude. Spotlight excludes it from its index immediately.

4. Close System Preferences.

FIGURE 4.16

If you want the Spotlight index to exclude any folders or volumes, add them in the Privacy pane.

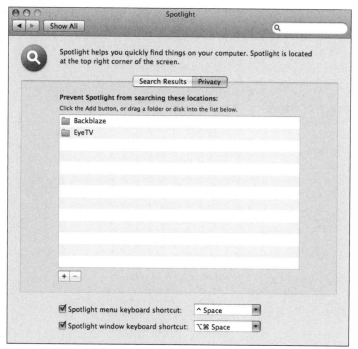

AirPort Preferences

Most Macs have a built-in AirPort card, which provides wireless network access via Wi-Fi (802.11) networks. Assuming the AirPort card is turned on (as it is by default) and all other settings are in their default states, whenever your Mac is disconnected from the Internet and encounters a Wi-Fi network, it asks whether you want to join that network (thereafter prompting you for a password if necessary). And you can freely switch between networks using the AirPort menu in the main menu bar (the one that looks like a striped wedge) or using the Network pane of System Preferences.

All this makes it convenient to stay connected to the Internet, and for single-user Macs (or portable Macs), it's most likely what you want. However, in some settings — for example, a school or office where Internet access must be tightly regulated — you may not want users to be able to freely switch between wireless networks. In these cases, you can lock down certain AirPort settings so that they can be changed only when an administrator's password is typed.

To configure your AirPort security settings, follow these steps:

1. Choose System Preferences to open System Preferences and then click Network to open the Network pane.

2. If the lock icon in the lower-left corner of the pane is in the locked state, click it, type an administrator's username and password, and then click OK.

3. In the list on the left, select AirPort.

4. Click the Advanced button to open a dialog box of AirPort settings.

5. Click the AirPort tab shown in Figure 4.17.

FIGURE 4.17

This Advanced dialog box in the Network preference pane lets you restrict access to AirPort networks. This figure shows the AirPort pane as it appears in Leopard; the Snow Leopard version is slightly different.

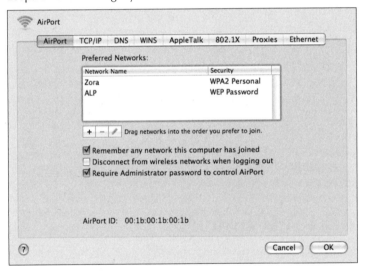

6. From the Preferred Networks list, select any existing networks to which you don't want this Mac to connect and then click the Remove (–) button.

7. **Under Leopard, click the Require Administrator password to control AirPort check box.** This ensures users can't connect to a new network without an administrator's password. Under Snow Leopard, click any or all of the following check boxes:

   - **Create computer-to-computer networks.** Prevents users on this computer from setting up ad-hoc Wi-Fi networks without an administrator's password

   - **Change networks.** Requires an administrator's password to connect to a new network

   - **Turn AirPort on or off**

8. **Optionally, click the Remember any network this computer has joined check box to deselect it.** With this deselected and the previous item selected, an administrator's password is required every time a network is joined, even if an administrator previously approved that network.

9. **Optionally, click the Disconnect from wireless networks when logging out check box (in Leopard) or the Disconnect when logging out check box (in Snow Leopard).** Choosing this ensures that even if one of a Mac's users is granted access to a wireless network, other users who log in later can't access it without explicit approval.

10. **Click OK and then click Apply.** The changes take place immediately.

11. **Close System Preferences.**

Assistive Device Access

Mac OS X was designed to be operated with a keyboard and mouse. However, some users are unable to use one or both devices, so as part of Apple's mandate to make their operating system as accessible as possible, they've built in hooks that enable controls to be manipulated by other means. For example, instead of manually clicking a button with your mouse, you might use software that simulates a click on the button in response to a verbal command or a customized input device of some kind. Almost every control in Mac OS X, including menus, radio buttons, check boxes, sliders, and other widgets, can be operated with software that mimics the effect of keyboard or mouse action, without having to refer to specific coordinates on-screen (which, of course, are highly variable).

The capability to use other software to operate on-screen controls isn't restricted to accessibility products. Speech recognition programs, mouse drivers, automation utilities, and even Apple's own AppleScript may need to be able to click a button or choose a menu command when no API (application programming interface) is available to trigger an action directly. In all these cases, software access to the user interface is possible only when the user has explicitly enabled it. Follow these steps to do so:

1. **Choose ▸ System Preferences to open System Preferences and then click Universal Access to open the Universal Access pane, as shown in Figure 4.18.**

2. **Click the Enable access for assistive devices check box near the bottom of the pane.**

3. **Close System Preferences.**

So, why would this be a security consideration? In theory, malware or a legitimate but malfunctioning program could wreak havoc on your Mac by clicking buttons and choosing menu commands. To make sure applications have this potential power only with your permission, Apple provides the Enable access for assistive devices check box.

I'm unaware of any programs that put this capability to malicious use, but I know of (and personally use) numerous programs that depend on this feature to provide important and useful capabilities. So, I recommend turning this feature on if any application you install asks you to do so, as long as you're confident that the software came from a reliable source.

FIGURE 4.18

For most people, enabling access for assistive devices in this preference pane is the appropriate setting.

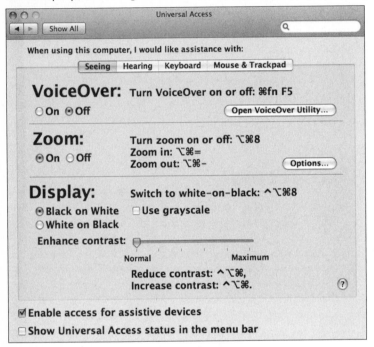

Software Update

Mac OS X's built-in Software Update mechanism provides an extremely easy way to obtain and install the latest versions of most Apple software (excluding paid upgrades). You can check for software updates manually at any time by choosing ➪ Software Update. To have Mac OS X automatically check for updates, follow these steps:

1. Choose ➪ System Preferences to open System Preferences and then click Software Update to open the Software Update pane.

2. On the Scheduled Check tab, shown in Figure 4.19, click the Check for updates check box and then choose a frequency (Daily, Weekly, or Monthly) from the pop-up menu.

3. Optionally, click the Download important updates automatically check box. This feature doesn't install any updates without your permission, but it downloads them to make installation faster and easier when the time comes.

4. Close System Preferences.

FIGURE 4.19

Schedule automatic software updates in this pane.

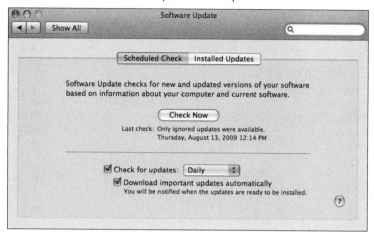

During a scheduled check for updates, if new versions are found, Mac OS X displays an alert like the one shown in Figure 4.20. This is a fabulously unhelpful message because it gives you no information about what is about to be updated or what potential consequences may arise. So, my advice is never to click Install first.

FIGURE 4.20

If you see an alert like this, be sure to click Show Details to find out what's about to be installed.

Instead, click Show Details. Mac OS X then displays a list of software to be updated, which may look something like Figure 4.21. Select an item in the list to read a description; note that some descriptions include links to web pages with further information. Then, to install all the updates shown, click Install *X* Items. (To omit any update, click the check box next to its name to deselect it. Or to tell Software Update to ignore any update entirely, select it and then press Delete.) Type your administrator password, click OK when requested, and then follow any remaining prompts (which may include restarting your Mac).

FIGURE 4.21

In this more-detailed view of available software updates, you can see which updates are available, get extra details on any of them, and deselect or delete ones you want to skip.

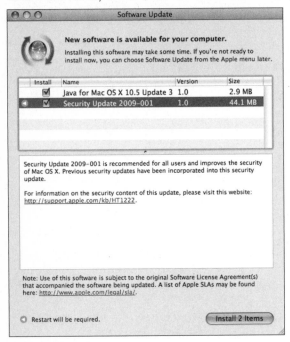

In terms of security, Software Update can be a mixed blessing. On the plus side, the feature lets you rapidly fix security holes and other serious bugs in Apple software. If you apply every update as soon as it's released, you greatly reduce your potential exposure to the newest hacks and exploits. On the minus side, software updates could themselves contain bugs or security holes. In a few rare cases, software updates have resulted in widespread data loss, crashes, and other problems. Although this might be aggravating for an individual user, it could be downright devastating to a large organization. So, do use Software Update, but use it judiciously.

To balance the pros and cons of Software Update, I suggest the following, especially for those who must make decisions about software updates for numerous Macs. First, set Software Update to check for new software as frequently as possible — once a day. When an alert appears on your screen to say that new software is available, carefully read its description, and if it includes links to a web page with additional details, be sure to follow the link.

But then quit Software Update without actually applying the updates. Wait a few days or a week, until you have enough free time to solve any problems you may encounter during the update process (or revert to a recent backup, if necessary). Do a quick check by using your favorite web search engine to see if users have reported any major problems with the update. If not, proceed with the installation, but if major problems do exist, consider holding off on that particular update until the following version is released.

Terminal

One final, small setting is worth knowing about. In Mac OS X's Terminal application, found in /Applications/Utilities and used to access a Mac's command-line interface or connect with other computers using SSH, there's a little-known option you might want to enable. If you choose Terminal ⇨ Secure Keyboard Entry, Mac OS X blocks any keystrokes you type in Terminal from being visible to other programs (the point being to protect you from keyloggers and similar malware). Once you choose this menu command, Terminal remembers your preference until you manually choose the command again to turn it off.

In certain situations, as when using macro utilities and other programs that rely on system-wide keyboard shortcuts, having this setting enabled prevents those keyboard shortcuts from working in not only Terminal but also in any other application that's running at the time. Quitting Terminal or turning off Secure Keyboard Entry solves the problem.

Summary

This chapter explored all of Mac OS X's basic security settings, including those made in the Security pane of System Preferences and several other kinds of preferences. I discussed general preferences, such as requiring a password to wake your Mac from sleep and disabling automatic login; how to use FileVault to encrypt the contents of your home folder; and how to adjust the settings of Mac OS X's application firewall. I covered security-related settings in the MobileMe, Energy Saver, and Spotlight preference panes, mentioned how to limit access to AirPort networks, and described the implications of enabling access for assistive devices. I also reiterated my advice to use Apple's Software Update mechanism to keep all the components of Mac OS X up to date.

The Mac OS X Keychain

To simplify the process of remembering and using passwords (along with other secure information), Mac OS X includes a system-wide mechanism known as the Keychain. The basic idea is that, as with a physical keychain, you can collect all your digital keys together in one place. All the information in your keychain is encrypted, and it can all be unlocked with a single password. As long as you can access your keychain, you can access all the individual keys (and the services they unlock).

Note

If you see the word Keychain capitalized, it generally refers to Mac OS X's keychain management system as a whole — the Keychain, as opposed to individual keychains. ■

The Keychain uses 168-bit Triple DES (TDES) encryption to protect all its contents. Although TDES is an older standard, it has never been cracked and is generally considered secure for the foreseeable future.

How Keychains Work

The keychain that you carry in your pocket or purse probably contains keys to your home, car, mailbox, and any other lock you need to open frequently. If you get a new key — to your office, filing cabinet, or whatever — most likely you'll put it on the same keychain. No matter what you need to unlock, you only have to worry about one object. As long as you have your keychain, you can open anything you need to access. The keychain itself isn't important, but it gains utility by keeping all your keys together.

IN THIS CHAPTER

Understanding what the Mac OS X Keychain mechanism does

Learning the types of data you can store in a keychain

Dealing with alerts asking for keychain access

Using a keychain with Safari

Managing your keychains with the Keychain Access utility

A keychain on your Mac serves a similar purpose; it lets you get at all your passwords in the same way. Unlike a physical keychain, though, your digital keychain can hold hundreds or thousands of items without becoming more cumbersome to use. Even if someone steals your keychain from your Mac, they can't use any of its keys without knowing your password, so it's safer too. And instead of fumbling for just the right key among many that look alike, you can depend on Mac OS X to automatically and instantly locate the right key at any given time.

By default, every user has a keychain called login, in which you can store passwords for any resources you need to access (and other confidential data). User keychains are stored in ~/Library/Keychains. In addition, each Mac has a keychain called System (stored in /Library/Keychains) that holds passwords needed by the operating system even when no user is logged in, such as the password to your wireless network. And finally, there are several keychains stored in /System/Library/Keychains that contain the special certificates Mac OS X needs to verify the validity of other certificates you may encounter. (I discuss certificates a few pages ahead.)

Note

Some older versions of Mac OS X gave the default keychain for each user the same name as that user's short username. So, if your short username was andrew, you'd have a keychain named andrew too. Although this practice changed years ago, if you've kept the same keychain through several system upgrades, it's possible that your default keychain has a name other than login. ■

You don't have to use your keychain at all, but chances are you've already done so without even realizing it. That's a testament to how seamless and invisible the process of using a keychain normally is. Whenever you access a secure resource, such as a file server or a password-protected wireless network, the authentication dialog box contains a check box like the one shown in Figure 5.1 that says Remember this password in my keychain (or similar wording). If you click that check box, the credentials you've typed are stored in your login keychain, and the next time you attempt to access that same server or network, Mac OS X supplies your password automatically, behind the scenes, with no user interaction required.

This automatic entry of passwords happens only when your keychain is unlocked, however. By default, your keychain is unlocked automatically when you log in (a rather insecure practice that I advise against). If your keychain happens to be locked at the time an application or service wants to access something inside it, an alert appears on-screen inviting you to type your keychain password to unlock it; if you do so, the password is delivered and your keychain remains unlocked until you log out, restart, shut down, or manually lock your keychain again — unless you've configured your preferences to lock your keychain automatically after a given period of time. (I discuss all these settings later in this chapter.)

The fact that you can unlock your keychain with a single password is somewhat misleading, though, because it suggests that whenever your keychain is unlocked, any application or website — or even a person who happened to sit down at your Mac — can freely see all your passwords. But that's far from the truth. In reality, your keychain provides several layers of security, and its locked or unlocked status is just the top layer.

FIGURE 5.1

When you connect to a network server for the first time, Mac OS X offers to save your username and password for the server in your keychain.

Each password or other item in your keychain has its own security settings. When you store something in your keychain and grant access to a particular application, only that application can use that password. For example, if you stored the password for your email server in your keychain when setting up an account in Mail, Entourage can't automatically get at that password; it must ask your permission. Although you can circumvent this process for any individual password if you choose to, it's cumbersome to do, and the default configuration helps to keep your passwords safe from unauthorized programs. And if you prefer even greater security, you can force a program to prompt you for your keychain password every time it tries to access something inside your keychain.

In addition, even if your keychain is unlocked, you (the keychain's owner) can't see any of the individual passwords stored there unless you type your keychain password each time. Again, you can alter this behavior for particular passwords, but the point is to keep your data safe from prying eyes.

In short, although a keychain lets you use a single password to unlock and enter all your other passwords, you may have to use that single password several times to peel back the various layers of security the keychain provides.

Note

Although Apple makes the Keychain available to any application that wants to take advantage of it, not all do. For example, Firefox and several other third-party web browsers use their own proprietary method for storing passwords. ■

What Keychains Can Store

Keychains are for keys, but what exactly does that mean? The digital data you can store securely in a keychain falls into several major categories.

Passwords

Without a doubt, the vast majority of items you store in your keychain are passwords of one kind or another. Each password in a keychain also includes the associated username (if any) and the location of the item — usually a URL or an IP address. A keychain may contain passwords such as the ones needed for the following:

- Local servers, including other Macs on your network using file sharing, screen sharing, and other shared services
- Remote file servers, including FTP servers and WebDAV servers, among many others
- Mail servers
- Websites (nearly any website that requires you to log in with a username and password)
- MobileMe
- Wireless networks
- AirPort base stations and Time Capsule devices
- Applications that use encryption or that must access password-protected network services on your behalf (including chat, blogging, synchronization, and telephony applications, among others)
- Encrypted disk images
- VPN services

Public keys, private keys, and certificates

Although passwords are fairly self-explanatory, some of the other objects stored in keychains may be less well-understood. The next set of items has to do with verifying someone's identity in a different manner than simply asking for a password.

Public key cryptography is a clever way of encrypting data without the sender and recipient ever having to exchange a password. Each user creates a pair of keys: one public (used to encrypt things) and one private (used to decrypt things). I give you my public key, post it on a website, or otherwise make it freely available, and if you want to encrypt something to send to me, you use my public key to do so. When I receive it, though, I can only decrypt it using my private key.

The same pair of keys can be used in a slightly different way to digitally sign files or email messages — confirming the identity of the originator and the integrity of the data without actually hiding its contents. If I sign a file using my private key, you can verify that it came from me, without being altered in transit, by using my public key.

Although in some forms of public-key cryptography the keys themselves are all anyone needs to encrypt, decrypt, sign, or verify data, it's often the case that another element comes into play: a special file called a certificate. If you send me your public key, how do I know that it's really yours? Maybe someone pretending to be you sent me his or her key, which just happens to have your name on it. To verify that keys do in fact belong to the entities (people or companies) using them, a trusted authority can certify them. A certificate contains (among other things) the digital signature of the trusted authority, and it's sometimes combined with a public key in a single file.

Who are these trusted authorities? Anyone — a business, educational institution, or even an individual — can become a certificate authority, meaning they can certify other people's keys. What prevents the system from becoming meaningless and chaotic is that every certificate authority must, in turn, be certified by a higher certificate authority. So, if I create Joe's Certificate Authority, my certificates must in turn be certified by another authority, perhaps my employer. My employer's certificate must in turn be certified by someone else, and so on up to a top-level or root certificate authority — a major security company such as VeriSign or Thawte.

Thus, if I use my certificate authority to sign Fran's public key and Cedric wants to verify that the key is legitimate, his computer must be able to follow the chain of signatures from Joe's Certificate Authority all the way up to VeriSign. His computer already contains a large selection of certificates from the major root certificate authorities (including VeriSign), so the entire process happens almost instantly.

Your keychain can hold public and private keys (your own and the public keys belonging to other people and companies) and certificates of various kinds. A System Roots keychain built into Mac OS X and another special keychain (usually hidden by default) called X509 Anchors contain the certificates of many well-known certificate authorities, including all the major root certificates.

Secure notes

A secure note is any text you want to keep encrypted in your keychain. Because secure notes can contain only unformatted text, they're best for brief, simple pieces of information, such as bank account numbers.

Understanding Keychain Alerts

Most keychain interaction is indirect: Either you're clicking a check box to indicate that you want a password to be stored in your keychain or you're responding to an alert asking for permission to use something in your keychain. These alerts come in several forms, and because they're so similar, it's easy to lose track of what they're truly asking and how you should best respond. Most keychain alerts fall into one of the following three categories.

Request to use your keychain

If your keychain is locked and an application wants to use something inside it, Mac OS X displays an alert similar to the one in Figure 5.2. Although the alert doesn't include the word *unlock*, it's actually asking you to unlock your keychain, which affects not only the application mentioned in the alert but everything else on your Mac that uses that keychain. Type your keychain password and then click OK to unlock your keychain or click Cancel to leave your keychain locked (which means you may have to manually type your password in whichever application is requesting it).

FIGURE 5.2

If an application wants access to something in your keychain while it's locked, you see an alert like this one; if you type your password and then click OK, you unlock your keychain.

Permission to use an existing item

When your keychain is unlocked and an application wants to use a password or other information in your keychain to which you haven't yet granted it access, you see an alert like the one in Figure 5.3. Click Allow to grant the application one-time use of the password, Always Allow to let it access this particular password indefinitely without prompting you again, or Deny to prevent access (in which case you must manually type the password).

In some cases, a similar alert appears but with an additional field in which you must type your keychain password, as shown in Figure 5.4. Later in this chapter, I describe how to configure a keychain item to request this additional level of authentication, which can protect you from unauthorized use of a password in cases when a keychain is already unlocked.

FIGURE 5.3

When an application asks for permission to use a password in your keychain, the alert that appears usually looks like this.

FIGURE 5.4

To add extra security, you can require that any application requesting permission to use a keychain item asks for your keychain password.

Alert that an application has changed

If an application is digitally signed (by its developer or in some cases by the Mac OS X application firewall), Mac OS X can detect when it's changed without authorization — for example, by a virus or other malware. Some changes, of course, are benign, as when an application that the developer didn't sign for one reason or another updates itself to a new version. However, if you've already granted a signed application access to a keychain item and the application changes without getting a new, matching signature, Mac OS X alerts you to this fact, just to be on the safe side.

As shown in Figure 5.5, the alert has text similar to the following: "The '*Application Name*' software on your computer has changed and wants to access your keychain. Do you want to allow this?" Click Allow to update the keychain item's entry to permit access to the application in its new form or Deny to prevent the modified application from accessing the keychain item. (The Always Allow button isn't available because that would essentially enable any future unauthorized changes in this application to go unnoticed.)

FIGURE 5.5

If a signed application changes unexpectedly, an alert like this one may appear.

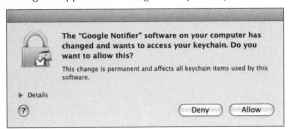

A variation on this alert may appear if the signature file itself (included within the application) has been altered since it was created. Because the signature is different, Mac OS X can't tell whether the rest of the application has changed, so you see a similar alert.

Safari and the Keychain

Many of the applications included with Mac OS X make use of the Keychain but none quite so extensively as Safari. If you configure Safari to do so, it can save usernames and passwords in your keychain for nearly any website you visit and restore them automatically when you return in the future. This capability can be a fantastic convenience feature, an aggravating annoyance, or a significant security risk, depending on how you use your Mac.

Safari's form-filling integration with your keychain is disabled by default. To enable it, follow these steps:

1. Open Safari, which is located in /Applications.
2. Choose Safari ➪ Preferences to open Safari's Preferences window, and then click AutoFill to open the AutoFill pane, which is shown in Figure 5.6.
3. Click the User names and passwords check box.
4. Close the Preferences window.

With this feature enabled, Safari offers to save usernames and passwords you type into forms on web pages as soon as you click the Log In (or equivalent) button. Click Yes to save the credentials to your keychain, Not Now to skip it (but let Safari ask again later), or Never for this Website to skip it and suppress future prompts for this site. The next time you visit a page for which your credentials are saved, Safari enters them automatically as soon as the page loads.

FIGURE 5.6

Safari's AutoFill preferences don't mention the keychain anywhere, but the middle option, when selected, lets Safari store usernames and passwords in your default keychain.

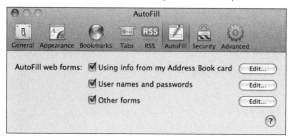

Cross-Ref

For more on AutoFill and its many capabilities — such as filling in personal information, including your name, address, and phone number — see Chapter 10. ■

Because Safari stores all these passwords in your keychain, you can view, edit, or remove them by using Keychain Access (described next). However, you also have limited access to these items from within Safari itself. To see your stored web form credentials in Safari, follow these steps:

1. Choose Safari ➪ Preferences to open the Preferences window and then click AutoFill to open the AutoFill pane.

2. Click the Edit button next to User names and passwords to open a dialog box similar to the one shown in Figure 5.7.

FIGURE 5.7

You can see a list of the sites for which you've saved passwords and remove any or all of the stored credentials — but not view the passwords themselves — from within Safari.

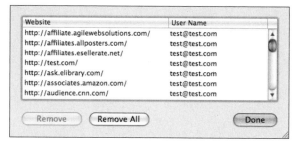

3. To delete an entry, select it and then click Remove, or to delete all entries, click Remove All.

Caution

When you click Remove All, Safari deletes all your web form passwords without asking for confirmation and without offering an undo capability. Click this button only if you're sure you want to remove all your web form passwords. ∎

4. Click Done and then close the Preferences window.

Note

Safari lets you see and remove credentials, but it doesn't show you what your passwords are. To see your passwords, you must use Keychain Access, which is described shortly. ∎

Safari's capability to store and restore passwords is impressive and easy to use, so what's not to like?

One consequence of saving every password without further interaction is that your keychain can accumulate passwords you'd prefer not to store, and you might not notice this fact until months later when randomly looking through your keychain items. If you want to store passwords for some sites but not others in your keychain, the only way to do so is to turn the feature on and off as needed — hardly convenient.

In addition, Safari never corrects or changes keychain entries; it simply adds new ones. So, suppose you visit Amazon.com and type what you think are your correct username and password, but the site rejects them. You try again, and on the second try, you get your credentials right. But if you look in your keychain, you can see that it stores both entries. In some cases, it can be difficult to tell which one is correct.

This problem also occurs if you use more than one set of credentials for a site. Type one set and Safari stores them; type another set on a different occasion and Safari stores those too. The next time you visit the site, Safari fills in the most recently stored credentials, which may or may not be the ones you want.

Finally, even if Safari's method for storing and saving passwords is exactly what you want, it may be unsafe. If you ever leave your keychain unlocked when you're away from your computer — or if you have your Mac set to log in automatically when it's turned on and unlock your keychain with your user account password — someone else could visit websites when you're not around, getting access to your accounts, making purchases in your name, and causing other trouble. Therefore, if you use a Mac in a shared environment — and especially if you don't take other measures to avoid unauthorized access to your keychain — it's best to leave the AutoFill feature for usernames and passwords disabled.

Note

If you want the capability to store multiple sets of credentials for any given website, you may want to use 1Password, described in Chapter 6. ∎

Using Keychain Access

Most of the time, you can store and use items in your keychain without ever actually seeing or directly interacting with your keychain itself. But you may need to change a password, delete an item, alter an application's permissions to use a keychain item, create a new keychain, or perform any of numerous other maintenance tasks on a keychain and its contents. You can do all this with a utility Apple includes with Mac OS X called Keychain Access.

To follow the instructions in this section, open Keychain Access, which is located in /Applications/Utilities.

Customizing the view

Keychain Access uses a familiar layout, with a sidebar on the left and a list view occupying the main part of the window, as shown in Figure 5.8.

You can adjust the view in several ways:

- To hide or show the list of keychains at the top of the sidebar, choose View ⇨ Hide Keychains or View ⇨ Show Keychains, respectively, or press ⌘+K to toggle the view. (I recommend leaving the list of keychains visible all the time.)

- To hide or show the details about the selected item just above the list, choose View ⇨ Hide Summary or View ⇨ Show Summary, respectively.

- To see the contents of a keychain, select it in the list of keychains.

- To show only the items of a particular type (such as certificates or passwords) in the selected keychain, select a category in the Category list in the lower portion of the sidebar.

- As in the Finder and other list-view windows, you can click a column heading to sort the list by that attribute (Name or Kind, for example); click it a second time to reverse the sort order. You can also rearrange or resize the columns using drag and drop.

- To search for an item, type part of its name or description into the search field on the toolbar. Search results (from all keychains and all categories) appear immediately.

The main Keychain Access window displays a list of passwords and other stored items in a standard list view.

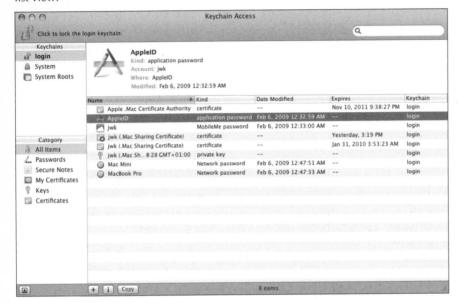

Keychain Access also offers an optional, system-wide menu that lets you perform common keychain-related actions without opening the Keychain Access application itself. To activate this menu, shown in Figure 5.9, choose Keychain Access ➪ Preferences, click the General tab, and then click the Show Status in Menu Bar check box.

If you explicitly activate it, the Keychain menu appears on your main menu bar, enabling you to lock or unlock keychains without opening a separate application.

The exact contents of this menu depend on how many keychains you have and their current states, but at a minimum, it contains the following commands:

- **Lock Screen.** Activates the screen saver, prompting you for your username and password to deactivate it.
- **Lock Keychain "login".** Locks your login keychain.
- **Open Security Preferences.** Opens the Security pane of System Preferences.
- **Open Keychain Access.** Opens Keychain Access.

If you have more than one personal keychain, the menu also shows commands to lock or unlock the additional keychains, in addition to showing a Lock All Keychains command.

Managing keychain items

The individual items in your keychain — the passwords, keys, certificates, and secure notes — can be viewed, edited, and deleted in several ways. After selecting a keychain (such as login) and the All Items category in the lists on the left, do any of the following:

- To view an item's contents, double-click it. The item opens in a new window, as shown in Figure 5.10. (Certificate windows are different, as I describe later in this section.)

FIGURE 5.10

Open an item in your keychain to view its details, including the username, URL, and password associated with it.

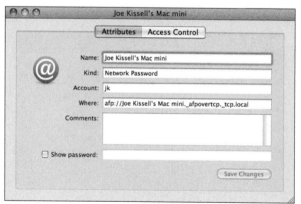

- In the Attributes pane, you can see and edit any of the information stored in the item, such as its name, the account name, and any URL associated with the item (shown in the Where field). To show the item's password, click the Show password check box. In the authentication window that opens, type your keychain password and then click either Allow (to show the password this time only but require authentication again the next time) or Always Allow (to show the password from now on whenever you click its check box, without requiring you to type the keychain password). To cancel display of the password, click Deny. After making any changes in the Attributes pane, click Save Changes. If prompted to do so, type your keychain password and then click Allow.

Note

It may seem confusing that you must type the keychain's password again to see something stored inside it, given that the keychain is already unlocked. This is an aspect of the Keychain's multi-level security (described earlier in this chapter). One advantage of this approach is that if someone were to walk up to your computer and look at your keychain while it's unlocked, he or she couldn't learn all your passwords (although he or she could, in some cases, use the passwords without learning them — for example, letting Safari enter them into web forms). ∎

Tip

If you want to get only an item's password, you can save a couple of steps by doing the following: Select the item in the list, Control+click it, choose Copy Password to Clipboard from the contextual menu, type your keychain password, and then click Allow or Always Allow. (In Snow Leopard, you can also select an item and choose Edit ⇨ Copy Password to Clipboard or press ⌘+Shift+C.) ∎

- In the Access Control pane, shown in Figure 5.11, you can determine which applications have access to the item:

  - Click the Allow all applications to access this item radio button to authorize any application on your Mac — currently or in the future — to get the contents of this item without asking your permission or even notifying you. This is an extremely insecure setting, and I recommend that you always avoid it.

  - Click the Confirm before allowing access radio button (the default setting) to show an alert every time a previously unauthorized application asks for access to this item. Ordinarily, this alert, shown earlier in Figure 5.3, has the familiar Allow, Always Allow, and Deny buttons. If the item is particularly sensitive, though, you can add another layer of security by clicking the Ask for Keychain password check box. With this check box selected, the alert asking for permission to use an item also contains a field for you to type your keychain password, as previously shown in Figure 5.4.

  - To grant a particular application access to this item without asking for permission each time, click the Add (+) button at the bottom of the window, navigate to the application, select it, and then click Open; to remove access for an application, select it and then click the Remove (–) button. When you answer Always Allow to a request for an application to use a particular item, that application (which may be Keychain Access itself) is added to this list automatically.

  After making any changes in the Access Control pane, click Save Changes. If prompted to do so, type your keychain password and then click Allow.

Note

Assigning access to keychain items is always on a per-item basis. For example, you can't give Mail or Safari access to all keychain items in one operation. ∎

- To delete an item, select it in the list and then press Delete. In the confirmation dialog box that opens, click Delete.

FIGURE 5.11

You can expand or restrict the ways various applications can access any given keychain item in this pane.

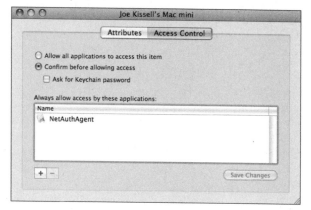

Managing keychains

In addition to managing the passwords and other individual items in a keychain, you can use Keychain Access to modify keychains themselves. The following actions are available:

- **Change a keychain's settings.** Select a keychain and then choose Edit ➪ Change Settings for Keychain "*Keychain Name*." The Change Keychain Settings window, as shown in Figure 5.12, opens, offering these options:

  - To lock your keychain automatically when you've been idle (no keyboard or mouse activity) for a period of time, click the Lock after *X* minutes of inactivity check box and then type (or use the up and down arrows to enter) a number of minutes.

  - To lock your keychain automatically when your Mac sleeps, click the Lock when sleeping check box.

  - If you use MobileMe to synchronize information between Macs and want to include the selected keychain among that synchronized data, click the Synchronize this keychain using MobileMe check box. If you have keychain synchronization turned on in the MobileMe pane of System Preferences, you can't turn off syncing for your login keychain, but you can turn syncing on or off separately for any other keychains you may have. (To jump directly to the MobileMe preference pane, click the MobileMe button.)

Note

In Leopard, Keychain Access may use the term .Mac in place of MobileMe. ■

Set options for automatic keychain locking and MobileMe sync in the Change Keychain Settings window.

After making any changes in the Change Keychain Settings window, click Save.

- **Change a keychain's password.** Select a keychain and then choose Edit ➪ Change Password for Keychain *"Keychain Name."* A password window opens, as shown in Figure 5.13. Type the keychain's current password, type and verify a new password in the appropriate fields, and then click OK. Performing this procedure with your login keychain makes your keychain password different from your account password, as a result of which logging in no longer unlocks your keychain automatically. This is a very good thing from a security standpoint, but it means the first time any application attempts to access an item in your keychain after you log in, you have to respond to an additional prompt (beyond the login window) to type the password that unlocks your keychain.

- **Create a new keychain.** Choose File ➪ New Keychain (⌘+Option+N). Type a name for the new keychain, and if you want to store it anywhere other than the default location (~/Library/Keychains), navigate to that location. Click Create, type and verify a password, and then click OK.

Note

Most people can get by quite well with a single keychain (the login keychain), and having more than one only provides additional complications. But if you have a set of passwords or other private information that you want to keep separate, protected with its own password, an additional keychain can do the trick. ■

FIGURE 5.13

When you change the password for a keychain, the window shows a visual indication of how strong your new password is.

- **Delete a keychain.** Select a keychain and then click Delete. In the dialog box that opens, shown in Figure 5.14, click Delete References to remove the keychain from the list in Keychain Access but leave the keychain file itself on disk. To also delete the file, click Delete References & Files.

FIGURE 5.14

When you delete a keychain from Keychain Access, you can choose whether to retain the keychain file itself on disk.

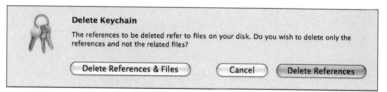

- **Set a default keychain.** If you want to use a keychain other than the login keychain as your default — the one in which all new passwords are stored automatically — select the keychain and choose File ⇨ Make Keychain "*Keychain Name*" Default.

- **Lock or unlock a keychain.** To lock a keychain, select it and then click the lock icon on the toolbar or choose File ⇨ Lock Keychain "*Keychain Name*." To unlock a keychain, select it and then click the lock icon or choose File ⇨ Unlock Keychain "*Keychain Name*." Type the keychain password and then click OK.

Note

You can't unlock the System keychain or any of the other keychains included with Mac OS X (such as X509 Anchors), not even with a root password. ■

Using secure notes

You can store any sort of text you want in your keychain, and because the entire file is always encrypted, the information is safe from anyone who doesn't know your keychain password. You might use this capability to store credit card numbers or other highly sensitive information.

To create a secure note, follow these steps:

1. **In Keychain Access, choose File ➪ New Secure Note Item (or press ⌘+Shift+N). The** dialog box shown in Figure 5.15 opens.

2. **Type a name for the note and its contents in the fields provided and then click Add.** Keychain Access adds the note to your list of keychain items, and you can access it later in exactly the same way as any other item.

FIGURE 5.15

Secure notes in your keychain can contain any text — but only unformatted text.

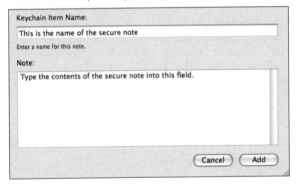

Note, however, that secure notes have several limitations:

- Everything must go in one field. If you want to store structured information (for example, with dates, account numbers, and URLs in different fields), you might prefer a third-party password manager, several of which offer this capability.

Cross-Ref

For more on third-party password managers, see Chapter 6. ■

- The note field accepts only unformatted text. If you paste text from another application, attributes such as font, size, and style are lost.
- You can't use an existing file as a secure note. To encrypt entire files, create an encrypted disk image or use a third-party tool that can hold encrypted files.

Cross-Ref
For more on creating encrypted disk images, see Chapter 13. ■

Working with certificates

The variety of certificate-related operations you can perform is long enough to fill its own book, but the vast majority of Mac users need to do just a few basic tasks. I describe those tasks here and also outline some of the less-frequent activities you may want to undertake on occasion.

Cross-Ref
For more on using certificates to sign and encrypt email, see Chapter 9. For more on using SSL certificates in Mac OS X Server, see Chapter 27. ■

Viewing a certificate

Certificates appear in your main list of keychain items along with your passwords, keys, and secure notes. If you want to filter the view so that it shows only certificates, select a keychain in the Keychains list and then select Certificates (or, for just your personal certificates, My Certificates) in the Category list. To see what's in a keychain, double-click it. A window like the one shown in Figure 5.16 opens.

Tip
Certificates always expire after a pre-determined length of time (which could in some cases be as long as decades in the future). When a certificate expires, it can no longer be used, but expired certificates aren't automatically removed from your keychain; they're merely hidden. To see expired certificates, choose View ➪ Show Expired Certificates. Or to hide them if they're already visible, choose View ➪ Hide Expired Certificates. An expired certificate is marked with a red X and its summary at the top of the window clearly says, "This certificate has expired" (also in red). ■

Most of the information in a certificate is highly technical and uninteresting to the general public, but you may find it useful to see, for example, what company issued the certificate and to whom and its dates of validity.

FIGURE 5.16

In a certificate window, you can view a long list of details about a certificate and who issued it.

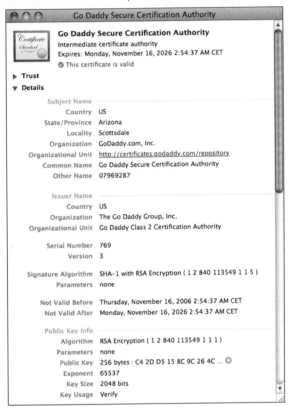

Adding a certificate

In most cases, certificates you encounter are added to your keychain automatically, as you use Mail, iChat, and other programs that access them. Occasionally, however, you may receive a certificate from another source that you want to add to your keychain. For example, if you work for a company that uses a self-signed certificate (one not certified by a higher-level certificate authority) to protect an internal website or other private resource, you may be asked to download and install a certificate manually.

To install a certificate, follow these steps:

1. **Double-click the certificate file to open it in Keychain Access — or if Keychain Access is already open, drag the certificate into the Keychain Access window.** The Add Certificates window, shown in Figure 5.17, opens.

2. **From the pop-up Keychain menu, choose the keychain in which you want to store the certificate.** If you're installing a root certificate, choose X509 Anchors.

3. **Click OK.**

When you install a new certificate, this window opens to let you choose which keychain to store it in.

Changing how a certificate may be used

Each certificate can be used for one or more purposes. A certificate intended to be used for signing email messages can't necessarily be used to secure an iChat session, and a certificate intended to encrypt web traffic by using SSL can't necessarily be used with a VPN server. In the vast majority of cases, a certificate's default settings are exactly what you want, but if you have a specific need to change one of a certificate's uses, you can do so by following these steps:

1. **Double-click the certificate in Keychain Access to show it in its own window.**

2. **At the top of the window, click the disclosure triangle next to the word Trust to show the trust settings, as shown in Figure 5.18.**

3. **To affect all the certificate's uses globally, choose Use System Defaults (recommended), Always Trust, or Never Trust from the When using this certificate pop-up menu.**

4. **To change a specific certificate use (such as Secure Sockets Layer or iChat Security), choose Always Trust, Never Trust, or no value specified from the corresponding pop-up menu.** The When using this certificate pop-up menu then reads Use Custom Settings.

5. **Close the certificate window.**

FIGURE 5.18

A certificate's Trust settings determine how it can be used on your computer.

Cross-Ref

For more on changing the settings for certificates used for SSL from within Safari, see Chapter 10. ■

Other certificate operations

Mac OS X includes command-line tools to perform a number of other certificate-related operations, and it also has a graphical program (hidden in /System/Library/CoreServices but easily accessible via Keychain Access) called Certificate Assistant that provides a friendlier, form-based interface for performing these tasks. Figure 5.19 shows the Certificate Assistant window in which you choose the task you want to perform.

To launch Certificate Assistant, open Keychain Assistant and then choose Keychain Access ⇨ Certificate Assistant ⇨ Open. (Or to jump to a specific task, choose one of the other commands in this submenu.)

Because the use of Certificate Assistant goes far beyond the basic functions of the Keychain, I don't cover its individual commands here. However, you can get more information about most of these tasks from the Mac OS X Help menu or from Apple's website:

- **Create a self-signed certificate:** http://docs.info.apple.com/article. html?path=Mac/10.5/en/8916.html

- **Create your own certificate authority:** http://docs.info.apple.com/article. html?path=Mac/10.5/en/9086.html

- **Use your certificate authority to issue new certificates:** `http://docs.info.apple.com/article.html?path=Mac/10.5/en/8917.html`

- **Request a certificate from a certificate authority:** `http://docs.info.apple.com/article.html?path=Mac/10.5/en/9087.html`

- **Set the default certificate authority:** If you've created more than one certificate authority, this command lets you choose which one is used by default when creating new certificates.

- **Evaluate certificates:** `http://docs.info.apple.com/article.html?path=Mac/10.5/en/9088.html`

FIGURE 5.19

The Certificate Assistant provides step-by-step instructions for creating certificates and certificate authorities, among other tasks.

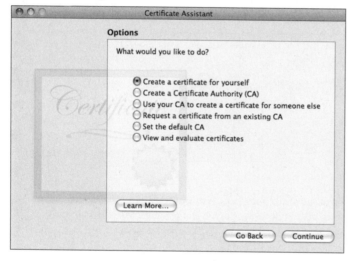

Cross-Ref

For more on specific uses of certificates, see Chapter 9 and Chapter 27. ■

Repairing damaged keychains

As you use your Mac, files — including your keychains — can become corrupted or damaged for any number of reasons. For example, if your Mac crashes at a particularly inopportune time, such as when data is being written to your keychain file, the information may not be stored correctly. Misbehaving applications, bugs in Mac OS X itself, and user error can also result in a damaged keychain file.

Keychain damage can manifest itself in several ways. For example, if you explicitly add a password to your keychain or grant an application access to a certain password and then continue to see repeated prompts to type the password or grant access to that application, it's likely that your keychain is damaged. If your keychain refuses to lock or unlock when you tell it to or if you begin seeing other unusual behavior regarding the way your Mac uses passwords, keychain corruption could be the cause.

Keychain Access has a built-in utility called Keychain First Aid that you can use to repair damaged keychains. Although it can't solve every problem, it's generally effective at eliminating the most common errors.

To use Keychain First Aid, follow these steps:

1. **Choose Keychain Access ⇨ Keychain First Aid (or press ⌘+Option+A).** The Keychain First Aid window, as shown in Figure 5.20, opens.

FIGURE 5.20

In the Keychain First Aid window, be sure to type your user account password, not your keychain password.

2. **Type your account username and your user account password — not your keychain password — in the fields provided.** If the password for your login keychain or any other keychain you've created is different from your account password and that keychain is locked, Keychain First Aid prompts you for that keychain's password as it runs.

3. **Click the Repair radio button and then click Start.**

Keychain First Aid analyzes all the keychains associated with your user account and repairs any damage it finds, reporting its progress in the log field at the bottom of the window.

Ordinarily, the default settings are appropriate for Keychain First Aid, but you can modify the way it functions by choosing Keychain Access ⇨ Preferences and then clicking the First Aid tab, shown in Figure 5.21.

FIGURE 5.21

The settings you select in this dialog box affect what happens when Keychain First Aid runs.

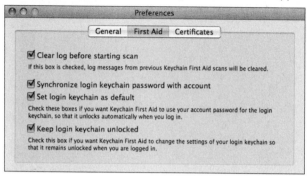

You can change the following behaviors, all of which take effect only when you run Keychain First Aid:

- **Clear log before starting scan.** When this check box is selected, Keychain Access erases the log of its previous run at the bottom of the window when you run it again.

- **Synchronize login keychain password with account.** Although any keychain can be the default, the login keychain has a special status in that it can unlock automatically when you log in if its password is the same as your user account password. When this check box is selected, if your login keychain has a different password from your account password, Keychain First Aid changes it to match your account password. I recommend against using this option because it defeats the security improvement you get by keeping those two passwords different.

Note

Password synchronization in Keychain First Aid happens only in one direction (changing your keychain password to match your user account password). Keychain First Aid can't change your user account password to match your keychain password. ∎

- **Set login keychain as default.** Click to select this check box to force Keychain First Aid to set your login keychain as the default if it isn't already.

- **Keep login keychain unlocked.** If you changed your keychain settings (as described earlier in this section) to lock when sleeping, after a period of inactivity, or both, clicking this check box turns off those settings. I recommend that you not use this option.

Resetting a keychain

If your keychain is damaged beyond repair or if you've forgotten its password and need to start over from scratch with a new keychain, follow these steps:

1. Choose Keychain Access ⇨ Preferences to open the Preferences window.

2. Click the General tab.

3. Click Reset My Keychain. A dialog box opens, prompting you for your password.

4. Type your user account password and then click OK.

5. Quit Keychain Access and then log out or restart. Mac OS X creates a new, empty keychain for you, sets it as your default, and uses it automatically when you next log in. Your previous keychain remains in `~/Library/Keychains`.

Summary

In this chapter, I described the Keychain, Mac OS X's system-wide mechanism for storing and delivering usernames, passwords, and other private data. I explained the design of the Keychain and what information it can hold, including the little-used secure notes. I showed what to do when an application requests access to your keychain, and I discussed the special connections between a keychain and Safari. Finally, I offered a tour of Keychain Access, Apple's utility for managing keychains and directly accessing their information.

Working with Passwords

A typical Mac user encounters requests for a password numerous times every day. Passwords pervade Mac OS X itself, appearing in a great many forms and serving a variety of purposes. In addition, the services to which you connect with your Mac — file servers, websites, wireless networks, and the like — usually require passwords. In fact, for most Mac users, the need to generate, remember, and fill in passwords occurs so frequently that the task becomes overwhelming. If you find yourself using the same password everywhere (perhaps even something as simple as your name or the word *password*), you're not alone. Unsafe as it may be, it's the only way some people have found to cope with password overload.

In this chapter, I get to the bottom of the password problem. How can you tell if a password is truly secure? Why does Mac OS X seem to need so many passwords? How can you choose safe passwords — and remember them all? If you've ever found the topic of passwords frustrating or perplexing, you should be able to find the answers you need here.

Understanding Passwords

Passwords existed long before computers. Do you want to cross the bridge, enter the castle, or get into the secret back room? Knowing the password proves to the guard, gatekeeper, or bouncer that you have the right to do so, even though he may have no idea who you are. The password is the secret piece of information, shared only with the most trustworthy people, that gives them access to otherwise private or hidden places.

Electronic passwords also give you access — although usually to information and digital resources rather than physical places. Nearly always, a computer system requires two pieces of information to be presented together. Your username or email address (which generally isn't secret) tells the machine who you claim to be, whereas the password (which is secret) verifies that you are in fact that person. These two pieces of information together are referred to as your *credentials*. Supplying your credentials — filling in the blanks with your username and password to identify yourself to the computer — is known as *authentication*.

Because a password is meant to remain secret, one of the most commonly asked questions is what makes a password secure. The answer is at once more complex and simple than you might imagine.

What makes a password secure?

You may have heard or read expert proclamations about what constitutes a secure password. For example, it must have a certain number of characters, or always include letters and numbers, or omit any words found in a dictionary. Although rules such as these aren't exactly wrong, they give an incomplete picture of the differences between a good password and a bad password.

The basic purpose of a password is to give you (the password's user) access to something while preventing all unauthorized people from getting access. Therefore, a good (or secure) password is one that fulfills those functions, and a bad (or insecure) password is one that doesn't. There's nothing magical about the password as such. Even if you had a 255-character password consisting entirely of random characters, that password wouldn't be secure at all if a hacker read it in an email message you sent. On the other hand, in certain contexts, a simple, memorable 6-character password is perfectly secure because the amount of time and effort needed to guess it would be far greater than the value someone could get by doing so.

Thus, a secure password is one that meets these criteria:

- **Accessibility.** It's memorable (or at least accessible) by you, the user — and anyone else who may need access to whatever's being protected.

- **Obscurity.** It's inaccessible and effectively unguessable by those who shouldn't have access to whatever's being protected.

- **Complexity.** It's sufficiently complex (given the design of the system and the way the password is implemented) to thwart automated attacks.

Some further explanation may help to clarify these criteria.

Accessibility

When it comes time to log in to your Mac, unlock your keychain, connect to your bank's website, or do whatever else you may need a password for, the password is useless if you can't remember it. As I describe later in this chapter, remember doesn't necessarily mean you store the password in your brain; you can use your keychain or a third-party password manager to remember it for you. You can also write down passwords or keep them in an unencrypted file, although, of course, you then face the need to keep other people from finding that paper or file. Writing down a password isn't necessarily a bad thing. Although you wouldn't want to put the password to your bank account on a sticky note attached to your monitor, you may very well want a co-worker or relative to be able to access your private accounts and information in the event that something happens to you, and for this reason, if your passwords aren't kept anywhere but in your head, that can in fact make you less secure.

Obscurity

As important as it is for you to be able to remember your password, it's equally important for unauthorized people not to know it. If you want to protect your Mac from being taken over remotely, using as your password your first name, or the name of your cat, or the string abc is mighty ineffective. So, not only should you choose a sequence of characters that no one else could guess, but you should also take precautions to prevent anyone else from accidentally finding or learning your password.

Complexity

I would never guess that your password is 111123 because, as a human being, that strikes me as an odd if not downright silly thing to choose as a password. However, put a computer to work trying to guess your password, and it can come up with that choice in seconds. When selecting passwords, you face the challenge of keeping not only people but machines from guessing them. It's trickier than it sounds, as I describe later in this chapter. Greater complexity is good for foiling computerized attackers, but it also makes more work for your brain and your fingers. So, in some situations, an appropriate level of complexity is much lower than what would be needed to fend off any possible attack.

Exploring password threats

To better understand how password complexity contributes to security, you should know a bit about the ways in which someone might try to defeat a password. An analogy might help to illustrate these techniques. Picture a padlock on the door to a building. Pretend that the building, the door, and the hasp are all impregnable — in other words, that the only thing keeping anyone out is that single lock. (Of course, in the physical world, as in the digital world, there's no such thing as completely impregnable, but use your imagination.) Bob holds the only key to the lock, and your job is to get in the building. How might you do it? The methods that apply to physical keys also apply to passwords, which function as digital keys:

- **Method 1: theft.** The easiest way to get past the lock, of course, is simply to use the key. If you break into Bob's house, pick his pocket or threaten him, and steal the key, you're in. Likewise, people can steal a password if they watch over your shoulder as you type it, read it on a piece of paper you've left out, or sniff it as it passes over an unencrypted wireless network.

- **Method 2: deception.** If you can trick Bob into opening the lock for you, you accomplish the same thing as if you had the key yourself. You might, for example, show Bob a fake ID to convince him that you have the authority to be in the building. A comparable technique in the world of computers is *phishing*, or creating websites that mimic those of a bank or other institution in an effort to trick you into typing your password so that an attacker can use it to access your account.

Cross-Ref

For more on protecting yourself from phishing attempts, see Chapter 10. ∎

- **Method 3: picking the lock.** Given the right tools and training, you may be able to pick the lock. The technique involves a combination of mechanics (knowing how the lock is designed) and finesse (experimenting using trial and error until the lock opens). This is all easier, of course, if the key follows a standard design. Likewise, someone can access a computer or account by guessing the password. Hackers know all the common passwords and patterns, and they invariably start with those. If your password is based on personal information such as your mother's maiden name, your anniversary, or your favorite band, a hacker can use what they know about you to make a list of likely password options — and then simply try them all.

- **Method 4: replicating the key.** Suppose the locking mechanism were so cleverly designed that all lock-picking techniques were rendered useless. With a well-equipped machine shop, you could try creating your own key from scratch. Of course, you wouldn't know the exact combination of peaks, valleys, ridges, and curves that might be needed to make your custom key work, so you'd have to try many combinations of shapes — perhaps thousands — to replicate a working key. In the physical world, such an undertaking would probably be a nonstarter, but a computer program can try millions of possible passwords in almost no time.

- **Method 5: breaking the lock.** If you can't obtain a key, get Bob to open the lock for you, pick the lock, or replicate the key, there's yet another method you might use to get into the building. You could try to break the lock itself. Maybe a bolt cutter or a sledgehammer would do the trick, or perhaps you discover that the lock has a flaw in its design such that if you put a little pressure here, twist a bit there, and jiggle it just so, it opens without any key at all. Similarly, on a computer, some of the encryption algorithms and other mechanisms that process passwords are themselves open to exploits of various sorts, in which someone can gain access to the protected computer or information without ever using the password itself.

Protecting yourself against the first two methods of attack (stealing and deception) requires common sense, attention, and perhaps a mildly suspicious attitude — and all of this is true regardless of how long or complex your password is. Protecting yourself from the fifth method (breaking the lock) means using only modern, proven encryption algorithms, although in many cases, the method your computer uses to lock information may be out of your control.

That leaves methods three and four (picking the lock and replicating the key), and this is where your choice of password becomes crucial. Assuming no one else can obtain your password or bypass the need for a password altogether, security comes down to picking a password that can't be guessed by a human being or a computer.

One logical policy would be to make sure every new password you create is sufficiently long, random, and complex that all the world's computers couldn't break it by brute force in your lifetime. If you plan to use password management software to remember and fill in all your passwords, that's an entirely reasonable approach because no harm could come from having passwords that are too long or too hard to remember. However, you certainly have to memorize (or write down) at least a few passwords, such as the master password used to unlock your keychain, and password managers can't be used in every situation.

Just how would a computer go about guessing your password? Two common approaches are dictionary attacks and brute-force attacks.

Dictionary attacks

One common means of hacking a password is a procedure known as a *dictionary attack*, so named because it involves (in theory at least) trying every word in a dictionary. Dictionary attacks exploit the reasonable assumption that the easiest passwords to remember are those found in a dictionary, so they simply try every word in order until they achieve a match. (Needless to say, hackers may employ dictionaries for languages other than English too.)

However, you should not assume that choosing a string of characters that isn't in any dictionary constitutes protection against a dictionary attack. For example, one common way of obfuscating passwords is to replace letters with similar-looking numbers — 4 stands in for A, 5 stands in for S, and so on. (This technique is part of an Internet dialect known as l33t, or leet; you can read more about it at `http://en.wikipedia.org/wiki/Leet`.) Although 4ppl3 (apple) isn't in the dictionary, hackers know that these sorts of substitutions are common, so dictionary attacks may include all those spelling variations of each word. In modern usage, a dictionary of this sort is simply a long list of words (and common strings of characters).

Similarly, merely appending a number to a common word (password1, joseph42) is such a common tactic that automated password-cracking programs try all such combinations early on; they're also sure to try keyboard patterns, such as xdrcft and iopjkl. However sneaky you may be in altering a common word or phrase or using an easy-to-remember pattern, chances are excellent that the people who write software to break passwords have seen it all before and have taken those alterations into account, including them on their dictionary list.

Brute-force attacks

If a dictionary attack fails, a hacker may resort to a much more comprehensive method of cracking a password called a *brute-force attack*. In a brute-force attack, a computer sequentially tries every possible combination of characters until the password is found.

In fact, brute-force attacks often involve not just one computer but dozens, hundreds, or even thousands working together. This sort of effort doesn't require a government agency with a building full of supercomputers; botnets consisting of hijacked PCs scattered around the world can accomplish the same thing.

However, before you begin panicking about armies of zombie computers trying to learn your PayPal password, bear in mind three important facts:

- The likelihood that someone would dedicate substantial computing resources to cracking a password is roughly proportional to the perceived value of doing so. In other words, if someone believes they can obtain the password to your bank account that holds millions of dollars, a brute-force attack is well worth the time and effort. But no one is going to mount such an attack to get your password for reading the *New York Times* online or vandalizing your MySpace page.

- A computer can, in theory, test thousands of passwords every second. But, in practice, this isn't always possible because of the way in which passwords must sometimes be entered. For example, if you send someone an encrypted file, an automated tool can try out different passwords with almost unlimited speed. But someone trying to log in to your Mac via SSH gets six opportunities to type a password per session (with delays before the last three tries). Mac OS X imposes a significant time penalty for guessing, massively reducing the rate at which an attacker could try passwords.

- Increasing a password's length and complexity makes it less vulnerable to a brute-force attack. In fact, even a ten-character password — if it's composed of randomly selected characters that include capital and lowercase letters, numbers, and punctuation — is unlikely to be discovered by any computerized method in your lifetime. I discuss the principles for creating attack-resistant passwords later in this chapter.

Identification versus security

When you set up online access to your bank account, you choose a username and a password. When you join a social bookmarking site such as Digg.com, you also choose a username and a password. In both cases, you have a set of credentials, but the uses to which they're put couldn't be more different. Your bank wants to keep your money safe, whereas Digg just wants to confirm your identity.

In reality, online bank access and a social bookmarking site represent points along a continuum of password uses. At one end of the continuum, the purpose is security — preventing anyone other than you from learning private information or controlling valuable resources. At the other end is identification — verifying that you are who you say you are but nothing else. In between are uses that mix the two elements to varying degrees. For example, you may have your address, phone number, and other personal information in your Facebook profile so that friends and family can access it. That information is somewhat valuable, but the consequences of an unauthorized person learning it would be less dire than if your bank account were compromised.

I mention this to point out that not all passwords are created equal. If you choose an easy-to-guess password for a discussion forum and someone else figures out what it is, the worst that could happen is that the intruder posts counterfeit messages in your name. And even if you use the same password for many different low-security applications, the likely risk of damage or loss in the event of your password being compromised is quite small. So, an argument can be made that in certain cases, a single, simple password is perfectly adequate.

However, the danger of using such an approach is that the line between identification and security is fuzzy at best. After all, what counts as private information? If your address and phone number are listed in the white pages, maybe you consider them public knowledge, not worth protecting with a strong password. But in some situations, seemingly innocuous information such as your ZIP code or date of birth could be enough to identify you to a marketer or help someone to steal your identity. At the time you choose a password, you may not be able to tell how much information it might be used to protect in the future or what the consequences may be of someone stealing or guessing it.

Some passwords are unambiguously high-security in nature. That list includes the following:

- Your Mac OS X user account password, especially on a multi-user Mac or if you use FileVault encryption

- Your keychain password and the password for any third-party software that stores or protects other passwords

- Passwords for your bank and any other institutions that deal with money

- Passwords that protect medical records or other sensitive personal data

- The passwords for your email accounts — because email is frequently used to confirm your identity when choosing or resetting other secure passwords

For some other password types, the picture is less clear, and you must consider on a case-by-case basis what your likely level of risk is. There's no harm in choosing a unique, secure password for every single service and site that asks for one; the only difficulty is that it takes effort to come up with all those passwords in the first place and remember them all. Later in this chapter, I explain several techniques that make both of these activities much easier. If the cost of using a secure password is no greater than the cost of using an insecure password, it makes sense to choose secure passwords every time.

Multifactor authentication

Because any password, no matter how complex, can potentially be stolen, intercepted, or guessed, an increasing trend in computer security is to add another type of information to the authentication process in order to decrease the overall risk. Security experts use the term *factor* to describe any of the following three categories of information that can be used for authentication:

- **What you know.** Information such as your username, password, and anything else that can be memorized.

- **What you have.** A physical object that identifies itself uniquely and is difficult or impossible to replicate, such as a USB token or smart card.

- **What you are.** Unique physical characteristics of a user, such as a fingerprint, retinal pattern, or hand geometry.

When more than one of these factors is required to confirm your identity, you're using *multi-factor authentication*. Two-factor authentication uses any two of these, such as a username and a fingerprint scan or a password and a smart card.

All the password mechanisms built into Mac OS X and most that you find on servers to which you connect are based solely on your username and password — single-factor authentication.

However, third-party software and services sometimes use multi-factor authentication. Later in this chapter, I describe several of the common hardware devices that can be used for multi-factor authentication on your Mac.

In some cases, your Mac itself can be used as an authentication factor of sorts (in the what-you-have category). For example, you can configure most wireless routers to allow access only to devices whose MAC addresses appear in a list. (Each Mac's MAC address is unique and hard-coded into its Ethernet hardware.) However, because MAC addresses are relatively easy to forge, this type of authentication turns into a what-you-know factor as soon as someone discovers your computer's MAC address.

Managing your passwords

In the discussion of what makes a password secure at the beginning of this section, I said that passwords must be accessible not only to you but to anyone else who may need to use them. I want to briefly elaborate on that point.

As much as none of us want to think about it, disasters do happen. You could get sick, or injured, or die suddenly. If that were to happen, how might someone else get access to critical information that you would normally provide? For example, your employer needs to know the passwords for the company's servers and other resources. A family member might need to get at insurance information, financial records, or your contact database. Your publisher might want to posthumously release that not-quite-finished novel still sitting on your hard disk.

Even though secrecy is generally important when it comes to passwords, you can have too much of a good thing. So, I don't recommend printing your passwords on a T-shirt, but I do suggest that you have a hard copy in some form. If you use a keychain or another password management tool (described later in this chapter), perhaps you only need to write down the master password that unlocks all the others. If you use some other system, you may need to write down all your passwords. Keep them in a safe place — which may be a safe-deposit box, or a locked drawer, or the margin of page 78 in your favorite novel, depending on how valuable the information is that you're protecting.

Whatever the case, make sure that anyone else who might need to use your passwords in an emergency knows not only where to find them but how to use them.

Security expert Bruce Schneier recommends keeping your most important passwords on a piece of paper in your wallet. Because your wallet is presumably always on your person or at least under your direct control, you greatly reduce the risk that someone could find your passwords without your knowledge (for example, while burglarizing your home or office). They're always handy when you need them, and a loved one would know where they are in an emergency.

The Varieties of Mac OS X Passwords

Mac OS X uses passwords in numerous different settings, each with its own purpose. In the next few pages, I list the most common places you find passwords on a Mac and explain each one's purpose.

Which characters can you include in these passwords? Unless otherwise noted, the following guidelines apply:

- For passwords that protect information or services on your Mac itself (your user account, keychain, disk images, and so on), you can use any character you can type on a U.S. English keyboard, including Option+key combinations. However, remember that you normally don't see your password when typing it (you usually see bullet characters or asterisks instead), so don't choose characters you're unable to type correctly without visual feedback.

- For passwords processed by other devices — a Wi-Fi access point, a web server, a network file server — you should generally stick with characters visible on a U.S. English keyboard: Capital and lowercase letters, numbers, and punctuation are usually acceptable, but any characters typed by using Option+key combinations should be avoided.

- As a general rule, it's wise to avoid the space character in a password, which can confuse a computer in certain situations (such as typing instructions on the command line in Terminal). Likewise, single and double quotation marks can sometimes be misconstrued, so it's safest not to use them.

User account passwords

Every user account in Mac OS X has its own password, sometimes referred to as a login password. Using the combination of a short or long username and password, users can log in using the Mac OS X graphical interface, a shell session in Terminal, or a remote SSH session. If you've configured your Mac to require a password when waking from sleep or turning off the screen saver, the user account password is the one required to do so. User account passwords can also be used when connecting to your Mac over a network for file sharing, screen sharing, and other types of remote access.

Cross-Ref

For more on how to configure user accounts — including administrator, standard, and managed accounts — see Chapter 3. ∎

Most software installers prompt you to type your account password, as in Figure 6.1; this permits them to store files inside your home folder. If an installer specifically requires an administrator's password, that means it wants to store files in a location for which a standard user account lacks write permission, such as the /Library folder.

FIGURE 6.1

Nearly every time you install software, an alert like this one prompts you to type your account password.

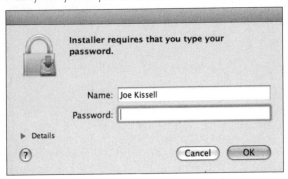

Note

In Mac OS X Server, you can set a password policy (either globally or per-user) that specifies requirements such as minimum password length and how often the password must be changed. See Chapter 26 for details. ■

Unless you manually change the password for your login keychain, it uses the same password as your Mac OS X user account, and it also unlocks automatically when you log in.

Passwords for administrators' accounts and most standard accounts should be as secure as possible to prevent anyone else from getting access to your files or taking control of your Mac. However, for less-secure account types — particularly managed accounts, which may be used by children, visitors, or others with limited access and privileges — you can safely pick a simple, insecure password because it's easier to remember and type, and little harm could come from someone using it without permission.

Note

Although it's possible for a user account password (even for an administrator) to be blank — meaning you can log in with your username alone — this is extremely insecure and not recommended. ■

FileVault master password

When you configure a user account to use FileVault, Mac OS X encrypts the entire contents of that user's home folder; typing the account's password enables the user to decrypt the information. When you set up FileVault for the first time, Mac OS X prompts you to supply a master password, which can enable an administrator to reset the account password for any user with FileVault enabled. If both the account password and the master password are forgotten, the files in the user's home folder can't be recovered.

Because the master password can provide access to any account, it should be chosen with particular care and should be different from all other passwords on the computer.

Cross-Ref

For more on FileVault, see Chapter 13. ■

The root password

A Mac's root account is a special hidden account that offers almost unlimited power to create, delete, or modify any file or setting on the computer. It's disabled by default and is needed only in highly unusual situations (such as advanced troubleshooting); even without the account being enabled, an administrator can get temporary root access from the command line by using the sudo command. If you do enable the root account, you should give it an extremely secure password.

Cross-Ref

For more on the root account and the use of sudo, see Chapter 3. ■

Keychain passwords

The Keychain is the Mac OS X system-wide storage mechanism for usernames, passwords, certificates, and other private information that must be kept encrypted at all times. Each user has at least one keychain and can create more as needed. As I mentioned earlier, the default password for each user's primary keychain is the same as the user's account password. If you leave this default in place, you should choose an especially strong account password (because logging in also unlocks your keychain, providing access to all the other passwords stored there), disable automatic login, and require a password when waking from sleep or a screen saver.

Cross-Ref

For more on the Keychain, see Chapter 5. For more on disabling automatic login and requiring the account password to be typed when waking from sleep or a screen saver, see Chapter 4. ■

Firmware passwords

As I describe later in this chapter, you can use a special utility to set a password in your Mac's firmware, which prevents users from booting the computer from another volume or otherwise bypassing the normal startup process. Firmware passwords are useful for Macs kept in public places, such as schools, museums, and libraries, because they can prevent vandalism and unauthorized access. However, someone who can open the computer physically can easily disable the firmware password, so it doesn't offer bulletproof protection.

Wi-Fi passwords

If you connect to the Internet wirelessly, using either an Apple AirPort base station or a third-party access point, the wireless network requires a password if it uses an encryption method such as WEP or WPA. When you type the password to join the network (in a dialog box that looks like the one shown in Figure 6.2), Mac OS X stores it in your keychain if the Remember this network check box is selected.

FIGURE 6.2

When you join a wireless network for the first time, you can have Mac OS X remember it (as it does by default). That means remembering not just the network's name but also its password, which is stored in your keychain.

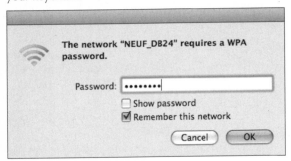

WEP encryption, which is no longer recommended because it's highly insecure, can use passwords represented either as plain text or as hexadecimal (base-16) characters. In general, if a password contains only the digits 0–9 and the letters A–F, it's hexadecimal. To use a plain text password, enclose it in quotation marks. To use a hexadecimal password, precede it with either $, 0x, or 0X; you may have to experiment to discover which of these works on any given system.

Cross-Ref

For more on wireless security, including the reasons you should never use WEP if you have a choice, see Chapter 16. ■

In addition to the password that a computer uses to gain Internet access, the AirPort base station (or other Wi-Fi access point) itself has a password, which is used for administrative access. (In the case of a Time Capsule, which also functions as an AirPort base station, the administrative password may also provide access to the shared disk.) If you're configuring your own base station, particularly one that's used in a dense urban area, be sure to choose a secure password to prevent someone else from hijacking the base station.

Disk image passwords

When you create a disk image in Disk Utility, you can optionally encrypt it with either 128-bit or 256-bit AES encryption. The password you select for an encrypted disk image can contain anywhere from 1 to 255 characters. When you open an encrypted disk image, you can optionally store its password in your keychain.

Cross-Ref

For more on using encrypted disk images, including those created by third-party security software, see Chapter 13. ■

Apple ID password

If you shop online at Apple.com or the iTunes Store, if you participate in the web-based discussion forums on the Apple site, or if you're a member of the Apple Developer Connection, you have an Apple Account, for which you need a username called an Apple ID and a password to go with it. Because your Apple account may contain personal information, including a credit card number, the password you use to protect it should be secure. Your password can be 6–32 characters in length.

To edit the information associated with your Apple ID or to sign up for one if you don't already have one, visit `https://myinfo.apple.com/cgi-bin/WebObjects/MyInfo.woa`.

Network passwords

The other computers to which you connect, including those on your local network and those found elsewhere on the Internet, often require a password of some sort. Examples include the following:

- Macs in your home or office that use file sharing, screen sharing, or other shared resources
- VPNs, which secure all network traffic between your Mac and a remote network

Cross-Ref
For more on VPNs, see Chapter 12. ∎

- The Apple MobileMe service, which provides email, file sharing, and other Internet services
- Websites, ranging from newspapers and discussion forums to financial and medical institutions
- Email servers
- FTP servers, file- and photo-sharing services, and other tools for transferring files between computers

Most of these network passwords can optionally be stored in your keychain.

Creating Good Passwords

I've read a great many procedures for creating secure passwords, and I've devised a few of my own. Lots of systems exist that purport to offer an easy-to-learn mechanism for creating passwords that would be difficult for a human (or even a computer) to guess, are long enough and complex enough to defeat most brute-force attacks, and yet are memorable. Although I provide a few examples ahead, the important thing to remember is that there's no single right way to create passwords. As long as you avoid making the mistakes that can compromise a password's security, the specifics of how you devise and remember passwords are entirely up to you.

Avoiding easily guessed passwords

So, what are the most common password mistakes? Whatever else you do, always avoid using the following, in any form, as a password — even in low-security applications:

- Names — your own or those of friends, family, pets, or places
- Dates of significant events (birthdays, anniversaries, and the like)
- Words and phrases someone might associate with you, such as your favorite color, food, or song
- Repeated characters, such as gggggg
- Easily typed patterns, such as mnbvcx
- Common passwords, such as password, password1, and 123456

Tip

You can find a list of the top ten passwords (at least according to one study) at www.modernlifeisrubbish. co.uk/article/top-10-most-common-passwords **and a list of the top 500 (according to another study) at** www.whatsmypass.com/?p=415. **Needless to say, you shouldn't use any of those passwords!** ■

If I wanted to discover your password, I might start by doing a few Google searches to find everything you've written online — all your blog posts, every tweet from Twitter, your profiles from every social networking site, and any other tidbit I can scrape together. In a matter of minutes, a computer could look through every word you've ever typed in a public place and come up with a list of likely password candidates. You might think that the name of your childhood sweetheart or your favorite movie quote is a secret, but you'd be surprised how much someone can discover with a bit of electronic detective work.

Going a step further, the only way to avoid a dictionary attack is to avoid all the words in a dictionary — any dictionary — along with common variations and simple combinations. (One of the most common passwords of all is letmein, which is extremely unsafe despite being a combination of three separate words.)

If that's the list of don'ts, what about the list of dos? I turn next to the subject of figuring out how to make an adequately secure password.

Password length and complexity

Suppose a program asks you to type a password consisting of just one digit from 0 through 9. Whichever number you choose, you know that someone else has a 1 in 10 chance of randomly guessing your password the first time, and a 100% chance of guessing it in 10 tries.

Now imagine that your password can still be only one character long, but it can contain any digit, any capital letter, or any lowercase letter, for a total of 62 choices. No matter what character you choose, you know that the chances of someone else guessing it randomly are much lower, and the total number of tries needed, on average, is much higher. The larger the pool of characters from which you choose your password, the harder it is to crack.

Next, double the length of your password to two characters. If each character can be any of 62 possibilities, the total number of combinations rises to 62 × 62, or 3,844. Every time you add one character to your password, you increase the number of possible combinations exponentially.

Cryptanalysts use the term *entropy* to describe the randomness of a password, which is to say how difficult it would be to guess by brute force. Entropy is based partly on the size of its character pool and partly on its length. (Identifiable patterns and repeated characters reduce a password's entropy, whereas randomly selected characters result in higher entropy.) A long password, made entirely of digits, may have the same entropy as a much shorter password consisting of letters and numbers. The key to choosing a password that's highly resistant to automated attacks is to make its entropy as high as possible.

To increase the entropy of a short password, include as many different types of characters as you can — capital and lowercase letters, digits, punctuation (such as #, ?, or *), and, if permitted, special characters, such as π (Option+p), Å (Option+Shift+a), and ƒ (Option+f). On the other hand, an easy-to-remember password such as "I ate 14 pies on Sunday!" (24 characters) has very high entropy by virtue of its length and character set (even though it includes words found in a dictionary).

In short, there's no single right answer to how long a password should be in order to be secure; it depends on what's in the password. A 10-character password, randomly created from all available character types, should be strong enough to resist any brute-force attack given current technology. If you use words or patterns to make your password easier to remember or if you use a smaller character set, the length should increase accordingly. For example, a password that uses all lowercase letters should be at least 14 characters long if the letters are randomly selected and perhaps twice that if they constitute an English phrase.

Password mnemonics

Your goal in creating a password is to have one with high entropy, which means that it appears (to an attacker) to be random. If you create a truly random password (or have a program create one for you), though, it can be very difficult to remember, and it's important for certain passwords (such as your Mac OS X user account password) to be memorable. So, the trick is to use a system that results in an apparently random password but one that has an underlying pattern that helps you to recall it.

No single technique is perfect or right for everyone, but I can show you two examples of ways to create complex yet memorable passwords.

Use a sentence

Although dictionary attacks are effective on individual words and short phrases, they're generally ineffective against longer sentences (or passphrases) because each word significantly multiplies the number of possible options to check. So, whereas the password "password" is terrible, the password "I can never seem to remember my password" is fairly good, mathematically speaking. All those extra characters take longer to type, but they don't require a lot of effort to memorize.

Note

There's no technical difference between a password and a passphrase; some people prefer the term passphrase because it implies a password that's long and complex enough to resist dictionary or brute-force attacks. ■

Even though a sentence is intrinsically more complex than a word, you can make it safer still by doing any or all of the following:

- **Avoid the obvious.** If you have a favorite slogan, catchphrase, or movie quote, that's something an attacker might guess, even if it's quite long. Don't use it as a password.

- **Add other character types.** Use capital and lowercase letters, numbers, and punctuation in your sentence — all of which can be entirely natural. So, "My cat, Cindy, has 9 lives!" or "What show is on channel 27, Ralph?" are good examples.

- **Make intentional mistakes.** If someone catches on to the fact that you use a sentence as a password — or if dictionary attacks advance technologically — you can improve the chances of keeping your password secure by introducing intentional misspellings or other errors. For example: "I always mispel, words On my 1st attempt!"

Obfuscate phrases

If you're looking for a more compact password, you can squeeze all the advantages of a memorable sentence or phrase into a mere eight or ten characters. Try something along the following lines:

1. **Begin with a complete sentence you can remember easily, such as a favorite quote.** For example, the sentence you start with could be, "The only thing we have to fear is fear itself." Sentences with at least eight words and preferably ten or more are best.

2. **Type just the first letter of each word.** For example: Totwhtfifi. (You could instead use the second letter or the last letter, although those are harder to remember and type quickly.) Passwords comprising the first letter of very common phrases, poems, quotes, or lyrics, such as NMWYGTYA (no matter where you go, there you are) are fair game to appear on the lists used by dictionary attacks and should be avoided.

3. **Change capitalization.** Use whatever system you can remember, such as capitalizing every third letter (TotWhtFifI) or only the consonants (ToTWHTFiFi).

4. **Throw in a number or two and some punctuation.** Although, as I said earlier, using l33t to substitute numbers for letters won't stop a dictionary attack, it's an entirely fine way to make a random-looking password even more so. For example, replace o with 0 (zero), h with #, and I with 1: T0tW#tFifl.

And that's it! You have a high-entropy password that's compact yet reasonably easy to remember.

Using patterns safely

As you read earlier in this chapter, not every password needs to be perfectly secure. For passwords that serve only to identify you and not to protect private information, you can afford to use a simpler approach that requires even less effort than the methods previously mentioned to create and remember passwords. Even for the least secure passwords, I never recommend simple words such as *toasters*, but what you can do is create a simple pattern that lets you almost instantly generate a new password for each new site or service.

One approach is to come up with a short string, such as 13cheeses, that includes an easily remembered word and a number. Then, to create a new low-security password, combine that string in some way with a portion of the name of the site or service you're accessing. For example, if you're making a password for your online subscription to the *New York Times*, you might make your password 13chenyteses; because nyt is buried in the middle of your existing word, it looks like a random string of letters. However you arrange the characters, if you do it the same way every time, you'll find the passwords extremely quick to create.

An even better approach is to take the name of the site to which you're creating and modify it according to a fixed formula. So, if you're creating a password for `www.cooksillustrated.com`, you might start with the name, minus the www, the com, and the two dots (cooksillustrated), reverse the letters (detartsulliskooc), take out the vowels (dtrtsllskc), and capitalize a couple of letters (DtrtsllskC). As before, if you use exactly the same system with every site, you'll find that the process of making passwords soon becomes almost automatic, and even though something like DtrtsllskC doesn't exactly trip off the fingers, it's memorable as long as it adheres to your pattern.

But remember, although strings such as 13chenyteses and DtrtsllskC may appear random, any moderately skilled hacker would be able to decode them (and, by extension, many of your other passwords) given two or three examples that follow your pattern. So, I must reiterate that you shouldn't use these techniques to create passwords for any application in which your money, private data, or other valuable resources are being protected.

Reusing passwords

I know some people who use the same password for everything — Mac OS X user account, bank website, Twitter account, you name it. Although I admire the Zen-like simplicity of this approach, it's an appallingly dangerous habit. Suppose someone watched over your shoulder as you typed an innocuous password into your laptop or iPhone and then wondered "What if?" and tried the same password on your PayPal or Amazon.com account. It can and does happen. If I were in the hacking business and wanted to guess any of your passwords, the very first thing I'd try is any existing password of yours I already knew.

So, the safest practice, without a doubt, is to never reuse the same password twice. However, no matter what sort of nifty pattern you've come up with for creating and remembering passwords, it's unquestionably more difficult to keep track of many passwords than just a few. As with everything, you must balance your need for security with your need for convenience.

If your memory is so bad or your time so short that you can't be persuaded to produce lots of unique passwords, you should at minimum have a few passwords that you reuse, selectively, for different applications. For example, you could have one password that you use only for the lowest-security situations, a second that you use whenever some personal data (such as your phone number or birthday) is involved, and a third password that you use only for high-security applications, such as banking and making online purchases. That way, at least if someone discovered your Facebook password, your life's savings wouldn't be in jeopardy.

Although I can't officially recommend reusing passwords, I should at least mention that if you plan to do this, you should make each one count. Even if you have only three passwords, if each one is long and complex, you decrease the chances that any of them can be guessed or otherwise compromised.

Using Password Assistant

If you're having trouble coming up with good passwords on your own, you can always let your computer generate them for you. Passwords created by software are likely to be less memorable than those you come up with yourself, but they're also likely to be more random (and therefore harder to break).

Mac OS X includes its own password generator, although you could easily miss it. In some of the windows where Mac OS X asks you to type a new password, a small square button with a key appears next to the password field. Click this button, and a floating window called Password Assistant opens. An example of the key icon next to a password field is shown in Figure 6.3; the Password Assistant window is shown in Figure 6.4.

In this dialog box (shown when you create an encrypted disk image in Disk Utility), as in several other locations in Mac OS X, a key-shaped icon appears next to the Password field. Click it to open Password Assistant.

FIGURE 6.4

The unassuming Password Assistant window is a full-featured password generator, complete with an indicator of any password's relative strength.

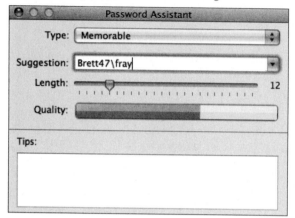

The icon for opening Password Assistant appears in the following places:

- Keychain Access, in the Change Password dialog box
- The Accounts pane of System Preferences, in the New Account and Change Password dialog boxs
- The Security pane of System Preferences, in the FileVault Master Password dialog box
- Disk Utility, in the password dialog box that opens when you create an encrypted disk image
- The login window, when you reset a user's password
- AirPort Utility (for selecting a Wi-Fi password and a base station password)

Unfortunately, it doesn't appear in other places, such as the Firmware Password Utility or in web browsers. However, a tiny, free utility from Code Poetry (www.codepoetry.net/products/passwordassistant) lets you open the Password Assistant window as a stand-alone application so that you can generate passwords — even if the icon isn't present. The utility is also called Password Assistant, although in reality, it's a Password Assistant Assistant!

As soon as you open the Password Assistant window, a suggested password appears, along with a colored bar that represents (one measure of) its strength. (Longer and greener bars are stronger; shorter bars — those colored red, orange, or yellow — are weaker.)

You can adjust the length of the suggested password by moving the slider left or right. The minimum number of characters is 8, and the maximum is 31.

You can also select any of several password styles from the Type pop-up menu:

- **Memorable.** Two English words, separated by one or more digits and one punctuation mark

- **Letters & Numbers.** Capital and lowercase letters plus digits 0–9

- **Numbers Only.** Digits 0–9

- **Random.** Random combinations of capital and lowercase letters, digits, and punctuation marks (but no Option+key special characters)

- **FIPS-181 Compliant.** Pronounceable strings (lowercase letters only) that are nevertheless not dictionary words

- **Manual.** When you choose Manual, Password Assistant doesn't generate its own passwords but does measure the strength of passwords you type yourself.

As you change the password type and length, the suggested password changes automatically, and the strength indicator updates dynamically. If you don't like the suggested password, you can click the pop-up menu control to its right to see more suggestions. As you choose, type, or modify passwords, tips may appear in the field at the bottom of the window offering ways you can improve the password's strength or noting weaknesses (words from the dictionary, patterns, and the like).

Using Third-Party Password Utilities

In addition to Password Assistant from Apple, numerous third-party utilities exist to help you generate, store, and use passwords. In this section, I describe just a representative sampling of such applications, with a longer description of one particularly powerful and useful tool called 1Password.

Password generators

One category of tools does nothing but create new passwords for you, much like Password Assistant does. They vary in complexity, ease of use, and number of features, but the following examples are all free, so you can download them and see if any of them are to your liking:

- Arcana: www.tekuris.com/products/arcana

- Make-a-Pass widget: http://andrew.hedges.name/widgets/

- PassForRandom: http://gnuserver.se/~netzach/netzach/software.php

- Password Generator: www.vonderborn.com/passwort_generator_software.php

- PwdGen: www.softhing.com/pwdgen.html

Password managers

The other major category of password utilities is password managers, sometimes referred to as password vaults or wallets. Although most of these utilities can generate new passwords, their main purpose is to provide a secure way to store, search, and use them, with a single master password protecting hundreds or thousands of other passwords.

Of course, the Keychain does all these things already, and it's included with Mac OS X, so why would you want a different application? For one thing, the Keychain Access user interface leaves something to be desired; third-party applications typically provide a cleaner and friendlier way to access your passwords. Also, although Keychain Access lets you store free-form notes, it isn't ideal for holding structured information such as credit card numbers and serial numbers, and some users prefer to keep all such secure data in one place. Some third-party password managers offer additional helpful features, such as iPhone synchronization, automatic entry of passwords into web forms (even if you're not using Safari), categorization and grouping of passwords, and various ways to import and export data.

Cross-Ref

For more on Keychain Access, see Chapter 5. ■

The following is a small selection of the password managers that run on Leopard and Snow Leopard:

- **AllSecure.** This utility stores passwords, bank account numbers, and other private information — and even entire documents — protecting them with strong encryption. For web form credentials, you can click a button to open the site in your web browser and fill in your username and password automatically. Includes a password generator: `www.edgerift.com/products/allsecure/`, $39.

- **Brieftasche.** Named after the German word for wallet, this tool stores passwords and other private data in user-defined categories. Doesn't include a password generator, however: `http://myownapp.com/site/moapp3.0/applications_leo/tools/brieftasche/brieftasche.html`, €9 or roughly US$11.

- **Password Repository.** This password manager focuses on color-coded categories, keywords, and searching to help organize and find passwords but doesn't include a password generator: `www.pomola.com/products_passwordrepository/passwordrepository.html`, $25.

- **Passwords Plus.** Another tool for storing private data of all kinds, Passwords Plus includes templates for dozens of data types, from credit cards to medical information. It also features a password generator: `www.dataviz.com/products/passwordsplus/`, $29.99.

- **PasswordWallet.** Available for numerous platforms, including Mac OS X, iPhone/iPod touch, and Windows, PasswordWallet lets you store private information, open URLs while automatically filling in credentials in your browser, and generate new passwords using the attributes of your choice: `www.selznick.com/products/passwordwallet/mac/`, $20.

- **Pastor.** The ultimate no-frills password manager, with an extremely simple interface, a built-in password generator, and a version available for the iPhone: `www.mehlau.net/pastor/`, free.

- **The Vault.** A simple, multi-platform password manager, with password generator included: `www.thevaultweb.com`, $29.95.

One password manager not included in that list deserves its own special mention: 1Password (`http://agilewebsolutions.com/products/1Password`, $39.95). Like the others, 1Password (which you can see in Figure 6.5) stores secure data of many types, has an easy-to-use interface, lets you categorize passwords the way you want, and has a powerful built-in password generator, which is shown in Figure 6.6. It's also available for the iPhone.

FIGURE 6.5

The main 1Password window lists all the passwords you've created. You can also store and view credit card and bank account information and free-form notes, and you can organize your passwords into folders.

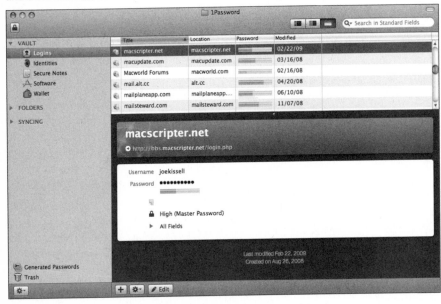

Several features, however, make 1Password unique among password managers. Of these, the most significant is that it includes plug-ins for every major Mac browser: Safari, Firefox, Camino, Flock, OmniWeb, DEVONagent, WebKit, Fluid, and iCab — plus NetNewsWire, an RSS reader.

With these plug-ins installed, you can fill in your credentials (or even credit card information) from within your web browser. As soon as you come to a page for which you've saved a password, you can fill it in almost instantly by using a menu command or a keyboard shortcut (even if 1Password isn't running). By contrast, most other password managers with browser integration force you to switch back to the utility, find the site for which you want to fill in credentials, and then click a button — a far more cumbersome process. 1Password's browser integration also lets you create new passwords, fill them in, and save them in a single step, without having to launch the application itself. And because all your browsers use a single database, passwords you save in one browser are available in all the others.

In addition, 1Password stores personal information (such as your address and phone number) and lets you define multiple identities (for example, home and work) so that you can fill in the same set of fields in different ways, depending on your needs at the moment. It also lets you store multiple sets of credentials for any given website so that you can log in under multiple usernames if needed.

1Password stands head and shoulders above other password managers on Mac OS X, and it also provides much greater flexibility and ease of use than Keychain. If you need to remember more than a handful of passwords, it's an extremely helpful tool.

FIGURE 6.6

1Password's password-generation tool, which you can open from within your web browser, is among the most versatile available on the Mac.

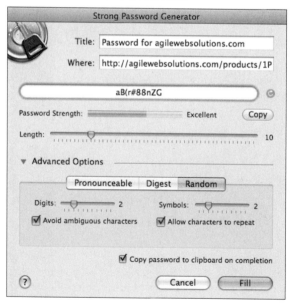

Resetting an Administrator's Password

The process for changing an administrator's password is ordinarily the same as changing any other password. But what happens if you forget your administrator password? Under normal circumstances, you can't change a password without knowing what it was before.

Mac OS X provides two ways to reset a forgotten administrator password. Use the first, which is quicker and easier, if you (or someone else who can assist you) can access the administrator account used when Mac OS X was first set up. Use the second if the computer has only one administrator account or if the password to the original administrator account has been forgotten.

Using the original administrator account

Although your Mac can have any number of administrators, one particular administrator account — the one that you created when you first installed Mac OS X or set up a new Mac — has a special status (even if you've since changed its password or other characteristics). The current password to that account — and only that account — can be used to reset the password for any other administrator account on your Mac.

If you have access to the original administrator account on the Mac or can enlist the aid of someone who does, follow these steps to reset the password of another administrator account:

1. Choose ➪ System Preferences to open System Preferences and then click Accounts to open the Accounts pane.
2. If the lock icon in the lower-left corner of the pane is in the locked state, click it, type (or have someone else type) an administrator's username and password, and then click OK.
3. Select the administrator account whose password you need to change and then click Reset Password. A dialog box opens.
4. In the fields provided, type and verify a new password and optionally type a password hint. If the other user has FileVault enabled, you must also type the master password.

Cross-Ref
For more on FileVault and master password, see Chapter 13. ■

5. Click Reset Password.
6. Close System Preferences.

Using a Mac OS X Install DVD

If you don't have access to the password for the Mac's original administrator account, your other option is to start the Mac from a Mac OS X Install DVD and use a special command in the installer to reset the password for an administrator account. Follow these steps:

1. If you've previously turned on a firmware password (as discussed elsewhere in this chapter), turn it off now.

2. Insert your Mac OS X Install DVD — either one that came with your Mac or a retail copy you purchased separately.

3. **Choose ⇨ Restart and then immediately hold down the C key until the Apple logo appears.** Wait a few minutes for the installer to open.

4. **After making a selection in the language selection window, choose Utilities ⇨ Reset Password.** The Reset Password window opens.

5. Select your startup volume.

6. **From the pop-up menu below the list of volumes, choose the administrator account whose password you want to reset.** Be careful not to choose the account System Administrator (root), which is the root account and not an administrator account.

7. Type and verify a new password for that account, optionally supply a password hint, and then click Save.

8. Click OK, choose Reset Password ⇨ Quit Reset Password followed by Mac OS X Installer ⇨ Quit Mac OS X Installer, and then click Restart.

Your Mac should now start from its hard disk. If you previously had a firmware password set, you should consider turning it back on.

Note

When you use either of these procedures to change an administrator password, you change only the login password — not the keychain password for the user in question. If that user's keychain password was set to the same as the administrator password, the keychain then no longer unlocks automatically when that user logs in. If the user can't remember the keychain password previously used, the keychain must be discarded and re-created from scratch (see Chapter 5). ■

Caution

The fact that an administrator password can be reset without already knowing another administrator password for a given Mac should give you pause. Although this is undeniably a useful feature in an emergency or when a sole user's password is genuinely forgotten, you can see that it's a huge security risk: Anything protected by the administrator password (potentially nearly everything on the computer) is open for access to anyone with sufficient physical access to perform these steps. Therefore, to minimize the chances that someone else could reset an administrator password for a machine you control, be sure to set the firmware password (discussed next), and on desktop Macs, use a security cable to prevent others from opening the case (see Chapter 2). ■

Using a Firmware Password

Firmware is software built into your Mac itself that contains (among other things) enough logic to enable the computer to boot and to perform certain basic tasks even when no disk is present with an installation of Mac OS X. Intel-based Macs use a firmware framework called EFI (extensible firmware interface), whereas PowerPC-based Macs use an older standard called Open Firmware.

One of the features built into both types of firmware is the capability to limit the ways in which a Mac can be started. Ordinarily, you can hold down one of several keys during startup to boot from another volume (such as an external hard disk or an optical disc) or perform any of several other administrative tasks that bypass your Mac's normal startup process. Because these procedures can bypass any security features you've enabled on your main startup disk, Apple provides a way to disable all these special startup shortcuts. To do so, you activate a firmware password.

When the firmware password is set, holding down any of the following keys at startup has no effect:

- **C.** Starts up from the internal optical drive.
- **D.** On Intel-based Macs only, starts up from the Diagnostic volume of a Mac OS X Install DVD.
- **N.** Starts up from a NetBoot server.
- **T.** Starts up in Target Disk Mode (for Macs that have FireWire).
- **Shift.** Starts up in Safe Boot mode.
- **⌘+S.** Starts up in Single-user mode.
- **⌘+Option+P+R.** Resets the Parameter RAM (PRAM).

In addition, you must type the firmware password when holding down the following keys at startup:

- **Option.** Shows the Startup Manager, which lists all valid boot volumes.
- **⌘+Option+O+F.** On PowerPC-based Macs only, starts up in Open Firmware.

To set, change, or remove a Mac's firmware password, you must use a program called Firmware Password Utility. For unknown reasons, this tool isn't installed as part of Mac OS X, and you can't download it separately. The only way to obtain it is to find it on a Mac OS X Install DVD. Moreover, even on the DVD, it's hidden by default, so you can normally run it only by booting from the DVD. Because this is a time-consuming extra step, I recommend using the following procedure to copy it onto your hard disk:

1. **Insert your Mac OS X Install DVD.**
2. **In the Finder, choose Go ⇨ Go to Folder and then type the following path:**

   `/Volumes/Mac OS X Install DVD/Applications/Utilities`

3. **Click Go.** The hidden Utilities folder from your DVD opens.
4. **Drag the Firmware Password Utility to your** `/Applications/Utilities` **folder (or another location of your choice).**

Once the utility is installed, follow these instructions to use it:

1. **Open Firmware Password Utility from whichever location you installed it in.**

2. **Click Change.** The window reveals new controls, as shown in Figure 6.7.

FIGURE 6.7

In the main Firmware Password Utility window, click the Require password to change firmware settings check box and then type a password (twice) to protect your Mac from being started in a way that bypasses the normal process.

3. **Click the Require password to change firmware settings check box.**

4. **In the fields provided, type and verify a firmware password and then click OK.** An authentication window opens.

Note

Your Mac recognizes only the first eight characters of a firmware password. Therefore, it's important to make those characters count — be sure to include at least one capital letter, lowercase letter, number, and punctuation mark. ∎

5. **Type an administrator's username and password and then click OK to authenticate.**

6. **Quit Firmware Password Utility.**

Although the change takes place immediately, it has an effect only during the startup process, so it begins protecting your Mac as of its next restart.

Firmware passwords are easy to get around if you can physically open a Mac. The trick is simply to change the amount of RAM in the Mac — such as adding or removing a module. When you next turn on the Mac, the firmware password is no longer in effect. You can't do this, however, with Macs whose RAM is soldered to the logic board or those Macs that lack expansion slots (such as the MacBook Air).

Using Smart Cards, Tokens, and Biometric Authentication Devices

Earlier in this chapter, I described multi-factor authentication, in which you identify yourself based on not only something you know (for example, a password) but also something you have (a physical object with unique characteristics), something you are (a physical feature, such as a fingerprint), or all three. You can implement some types of multi-factor authentication by adding third-party hardware to your Mac, thus adding an extra layer of security to your account password (or other passwords).

Before I describe some of these devices, however, I should mention that hardware-based authentication isn't necessarily multi-factor. For example, the front door of the apartment building in which I live has an electronic lock that can be opened either by typing a code (something I know) or by using an RFID key fob (something I have). Because the lock requires just one method, not both, it's only single-factor security. Similarly, you can install a fingerprint reader on your Mac that lets you authenticate by swiping your finger instead of typing your password, which is a convenience feature but is still single-factor authentication. However, if you configure the reader's software to work only if you type a password and also swipe your finger, it becomes multi-factor authentication.

Smart cards and tokens

A smart card is a small device (typically the size and shape of a credit card) that contains its own microprocessor and memory and stores a unique identifier. Smart cards are designed to be very difficult to copy or forge, and for this reason, some bank debit and credit cards use this technology to supplement or replace information stored on a magnetic strip (which is relatively easy to duplicate). Government agencies and other large, security-conscious organizations often mandate the use of smart cards, along with a password or PIN, for logging in to computers. In Leopard and Snow Leopard, smart cards can be used not only to log in but also to unlock a keychain or FileVault volume; in addition, you can configure Mac OS X to automatically lock the system when the smart card is removed.

In a corporate setting, smart card access is often managed over a network. When you insert your card and type your PIN, your Mac checks in with a server to verify that your card is valid. That way, if your card were lost or stolen, an administrator could immediately disable its use.

Some smart cards are packaged as stand-alone USB devices (called tokens or dongles), but many require a separate smart card reader, a piece of hardware that usually connects via USB, a PC card slot, or an ExpressCard slot. Although Mac OS X contains drivers for most common smart card readers, you must also configure the operating system to require smart card use for authentication. Apple provides a 16-page PDF document called Smart Card Setup Guide that contains complete instructions; you can download it from http://images.apple.com/server/macosx/docs/Smart_Card_Setup_Guide.pdf.

Tip
Although less secure than a conventional smart card, you can also use software to make an existing USB flash drive (or even an iPod or iPhone) function as a secure token. An example is the $29 Rohos Logon Key (`www.rohos.com/mac-os-x/`). ■

One-time password tokens

Another type of device for providing what-you-have authentication is the one-time password (OTP) token, which creates passwords you can use only once. For example, PayPal and numerous banks offer secure tokens that generate a new number every 30 or 60 seconds. To log in, you must type not only your username and password but the current number from the device (which is time-synchronized with the institution's servers). If you type the wrong number or the right number but too late, you can't access the site.

Biometric devices

Biometric information is anything about your body that can be measured; the term is usually applied to characteristics that uniquely identify you and are also easy for a machine to detect: fingerprints, iris and retina patterns, and hand geometry, to name a few examples. Biometric data can be used as the what-you-are authentication factor, and when used in combination with other factors, it can significantly increase a system's security.

As of the time this book was written, I was aware of only one company that offered biometric readers compatible with Mac OS X. The UPEK Eikon and Eikon To Go (`http://upek.com/solutions/eikon/default.asp`) are compact, USB-based fingerprint scanners that can be used for either single-factor authentication (substituting for your password) or two-factor authentication (both password and fingerprint scan required). Either way, you can use a fingerprint to log in, fill in your credentials in an authentication dialog box, or unlock your keychain. The company has stated that support for unlocking 1Password keychains is also planned.

Summary

This chapter covered the basic facts every Mac user should know about passwords. I explained the factors that make a password more or less secure and why different sorts of passwords are appropriate in different situations. I listed the various types of passwords Mac OS X uses, including their strengths and weaknesses. Because virtually every Mac user is asked repeatedly to choose and type passwords, I explained some of the ways in which you can select hard-to-crack passwords without expending too much time or mental effort. One way I showed how to do this is to use Password Assistant or a third-party password generator and use your keychain (or another tool) to store and fill in the passwords when needed. I mentioned how to reset a forgotten administrator's password, described the use of a firmware password on a Mac, and finished the chapter with a discussion of hardware devices that can increase your security by supplementing or replacing conventional password prompts.

Securely Sharing System Resources

Mac OS X makes it easy to share a long list of system resources — you can share files, optical discs, printers, scanners, control of your screen, your Internet connection, and even spare CPU cycles with just a few clicks. You can also turn your Mac into a web server, share data and connectivity using Bluetooth devices, and use any of several mechanisms to access your Mac remotely.

The benefit of all this sharing is that other people can easily get at the information and devices you want them to be able to use, and you can use your own Mac even if it's at home and you're at the office. However, as you might expect, all this wonderful openness comes with a price. The more resources you share, the more ways are open for an unscrupulous person (or computer program) to access them in ways you want to avoid.

This chapter describes the main built-in mechanisms by which Mac OS X can share data, all of which are controlled in the Sharing pane of System Preferences. In addition to listing the ways you can share resources, I hope to shed light on how to do so with as little risk as possible.

Using Shared System Resources Wisely

When you activate any of the shared resources in the Sharing pane of System Preferences, you run a server of sorts: You make a certain kind of information available to other computers running the right sort of client software, provided that they can reach your Mac over a network (and, in most cases, have the necessary credentials). In fact, there may be any number of barriers preventing another computer from taking advantage of your shared resources — including a too-strict firewall setting on your Mac or a router or gateway that uses NAT (network address translation) and thereby hides your Mac's public IP address. Nevertheless, the fact remains that the more services you run and make available to other computers, the more potential paths exist by which someone could exploit bugs, hack into your system, steal data, and otherwise put your Mac to illicit use.

Therefore, let me begin this chapter by offering two pieces of blanket advice that apply to all these shared resources (and I echo this advice several other times in this chapter, just to make sure it sinks in):

- **Share resources only when necessary.** All shared resources are disabled by default, but many Mac users like to turn some or all of them on just in case. I won't deny that there are rare situations in which having a shared resource turned on can save the day, but these situations occur far less frequently than hacking and exploit attempts. All things being equal, your odds of keeping your Mac and its data safe increase if you turn on only those services you actively use — and, better yet, only during the times you actively use them.

- **Limit access to shared resources.** In most cases, you can opt to share resources with all users or only with specific users, and in some cases (notably File Sharing), you have even more granular control over what is shared, how, and with whom. Whenever possible and feasible, restrict access only to trusted individuals — and even then, only to the particular resources they need.

Note
You may recognize these two pieces of advice as a reformulation of the principle of least privilege, discussed in Chapter 3. It's true: Always start by granting the minimum amount of access necessary and then add on as required. ■

DVD or CD Sharing

When Apple introduced the MacBook Air in 2008, it was the first Mac in many years not to include an internal optical drive, even as an option. You can buy an external SuperDrive to go with it, but what happens if you don't have one and you need to start your Mac from a CD or DVD? Apple's answer is clever: You put the disc in another computer (Mac or PC) and share it over the local (wired or wireless) network.

Although you can use conventional file sharing (described later in this chapter) to share an optical disc over a network, DVD or CD sharing is different in that it treats the shared disc exactly as though it were directly connected to your Mac. That means, among other things, that you can boot from it, which isn't true of optical discs shared as regular network volumes.

Mac OS X 10.5.2 and later versions include the software needed to share an optical disc; Windows users can download comparable software from Apple. But whereas any Mac with an optical drive can activate DVD or CD sharing to make that drive available to others, under Leopard, only a Mac without a built-in optical drive can see and use the shared drive.

To make your optical drive available to other Macs on the local network without an optical drive, follow these steps:

1. Choose ⌘ ⇨ System Preferences to open System Preferences and then click **Sharing** to open the Sharing pane.

2. If the lock icon in the lower-left corner of the pane is in the locked state, click it, type an administrator's username and password, and then click OK.

3. In the list on the left, click the On check box next to DVD or CD Sharing. Your Mac's optical drive becomes available immediately on the network (as long as it contains a disc).

4. Optionally, with DVD or CD Sharing selected in the list on the left, as shown in Figure 7.1, click to select or deselect the Ask me before allowing others to use my DVD drive check box. When this is selected, users wanting access to your optical drive must click a button to request access, and you must respond to an on-screen alert.

FIGURE 7.1

To let users of Macs without optical drives use the one in your Mac over the network, turn on DVD or CD Sharing.

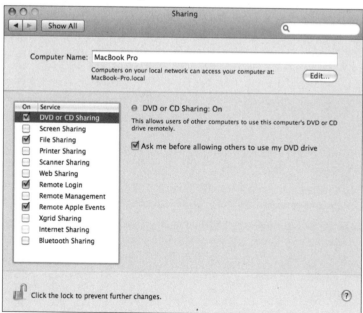

With your drive shared, if someone else on your local network using a Mac without a built-in optical drive wants to use the disk, that person must do the following:

1. **In any Finder window, select your optical drive, which is listed under Devices.**

2. **If the Ask to Use button is present, click it.** When the person with the shared optical drive grants permission, the disc becomes available.

Screen Sharing

Screen sharing is a generic term used for any system that lets you see and control another computer remotely — putting an image of its screen on your display and using your own keyboard and mouse to control it just as though you were sitting in front of it. This capability is essential for system administrators and anyone else called upon to do remote troubleshooting; it's also useful for people with more than one computer in different locations, such as one at home and another at work. If you want to run programs on a remote computer, see what's on its screen, or do more extensive operations than you can accomplish with file sharing or remote login via SSH, screen sharing is just what you need.

For many years, it's been possible to do this using third-party software, such as Timbuktu or the open-source VNC. Using such software, you can even control a Mac from a Windows PC or vice versa. Leopard and Snow Leopard include a version of VNC that offers comparable capabilities, and thanks to Apple's Bonjour networking and Back to My Mac, you can often share another Mac's screen without knowing its IP address or domain name.

Of all the ways in which you can share resources on your Mac, screen sharing is the most powerful — it gives the person on the other end potentially unlimited control. Of course, if you're sitting in front of a Mac that someone else is controlling, you can turn off screen sharing, disconnect the network cable, or turn off the computer. But if you're not physically present, all bets are off. So, you should exercise the utmost caution when activating screen sharing to avoid unwanted intrusions.

To enable Screen Sharing on your Mac, follow these steps:

1. **Choose ⇨ System Preferences to open System Preferences and then click Sharing to open the Sharing pane.**

2. **If the lock icon in the lower-left corner of the pane is in the locked state, click it, type an administrator's username and password, and then click OK.**

3. **In the list on the left, click the On check box next to Screen Sharing.** Screen Sharing becomes active immediately at the address listed on the right side of the pane, as shown in Figure 7.2.

4. **To determine who can control your screen, click one of the following two radio buttons:**

- **All users.** When this is selected (as it is by default), the credentials for any user with an account on your Mac can be used to log in. This setting doesn't mean that someone can control your screen without a password.

- **Only these users.** To restrict access to particular users, click this radio button. Then, click the Add (+) button, select one or more users or groups, and then click Select. The selected users are added to the access list. I strongly recommend selecting this option and adding as few people as possible (perhaps only yourself) to the list.

FIGURE 7.2

Activate screen sharing to give yourself (or someone else) the capability to see and control your screen from another computer.

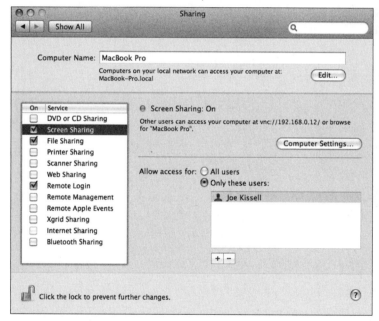

5. **To adjust other screen-sharing settings, click Computer Settings to open the dialog box shown in Figure 7.3.** You can adjust the following options:

- **Anyone may request permission to control screen.** To permit people who aren't on the access list to request permission to control your screen, click this check box.

- **VNC viewers may control screen with password.** When this check box is selected and a password is filled in (as your user account password is by default), a remote user, whether or not on the access list, can use VNC to view or control your screen by typing the password.

Note

This information explains only the server side of screen sharing — how to make your screen available to another computer. The other half of the operation — controlling the screen on another Mac with this feature enabled — is covered in Chapter 11. ■

FIGURE 7.3

Adjust other screen-sharing settings in this dialog box.

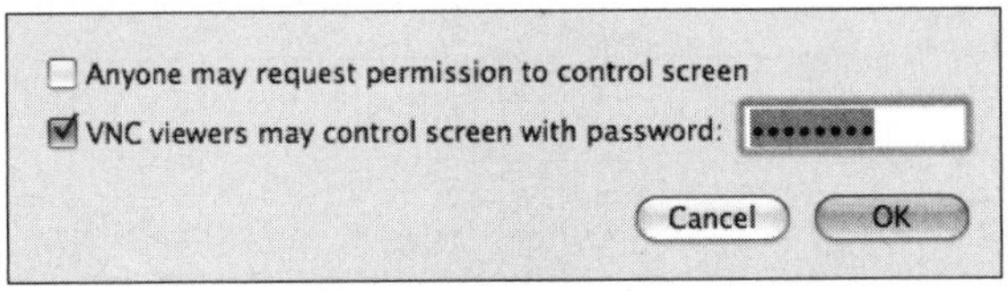

☐ Anyone may request permission to control screen
☑ VNC viewers may control screen with password: ●●●●●●●●

(Cancel) (OK)

File Sharing

Of all the sharing features built into Mac OS X, File Sharing is the most commonly used and has been around the longest. By turning on File Sharing, you can enable other users to access selected folders on your Mac according to the criteria you specify, and you can access any of your own files when using another computer. File Sharing can use AFP (Apple Filing Protocol), FTP (File Transfer Protocol), SMB (Server Message Block), or any combination of these.

As with all shared resources, File Sharing works as long as other computers can see your Mac over the network. Barring any restrictive firewall or router settings, that should always be true on your local network. If your Mac has a publicly routable IP address (or uses port forwarding), File Sharing can reach it over the Internet, and if you use Back to My Mac, you may be able to contact your Mac remotely even if it's behind a NAT gateway.

Cross-Ref

For more on port forwarding, see Chapter 15. For more on Back to My Mac, see Chapter 4. ■

Activating File Sharing

You can turn File Sharing on with just a few clicks, but after you do so, be sure to read the remainder of this section to learn what settings you may want to adjust.

To activate File Sharing, follow these steps:

1. Choose ⌘ ➪ System Preferences to open System Preferences and then click Sharing to open the Sharing pane.

2. If the lock icon in the lower-left corner of the pane is in the locked state, click it, type an administrator's username and password, and then click OK.

3. **In the list on the left, click the On check box next to File Sharing.** File Sharing becomes active immediately at the address listed on the right side of the pane, as shown in Figure 7.4.

FIGURE 7.4

To turn on File Sharing, click the On check box next to its name.

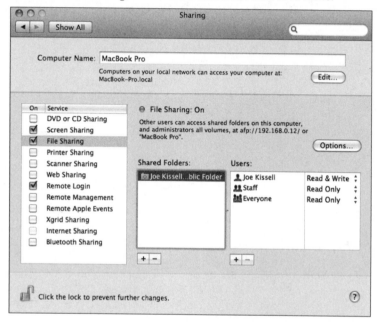

Initially, File Sharing makes files available only by using AFP (Apple Filing Protocol). As long as File Sharing is on, anyone with an administrator account on your Mac can access the entire startup disk via AFP — and any other mounted volumes, including external hard disks and even optical discs — subject to the usual permissions attached to each account. That is, an administrator can browse the same folders and access the same files over file sharing as when sitting in front of the computer. Other users' files are off-limits, but folders such as /Applications and /Library are visible. Regardless of what other folders you share, options you set, or permissions you specify, as long as AFP is enabled and File Sharing is on, all administrators continue to have these privileges.

In addition, File Sharing by default makes available the Public folder (~/Public) for the current user, with Read & Write access for the user and Read Only access for everyone else. You can modify the folders that are shared, with whom, and with which permissions, as I discuss shortly.

Note

Every Mac OS X user account automatically has a Public folder (`~/Public`), which is designed for items the user is comfortable sharing with anyone. Inside this folder is another folder called `Drop Box`. This is the default location for files and folders uploaded by users with write-only access to shared folders; users without Read & Write access can put items inside this folder but can't see its contents. These same folders can be used — even with File Sharing turned off — to share files among user accounts on a single Mac. ■

Choosing file-sharing protocols

File Sharing can use any or all of three common file-sharing protocols: AFP, FTP, and SMB. Which protocol(s) you use depends on your needs and your security requirements.

AFP

The default method of file sharing, AFP, provides the best security and performance of the three protocols. For sharing files with other Mac users — especially over a local network — AFP is without question the right choice because AFP properly copies all the metadata that may be associated with Mac OS X files, including ownership and permissions, ACLs, and resource forks.

FTP

FTP is a common protocol for transferring files over the Internet. If you have an account with a web-hosting provider, FTP is likely to be the method you use to upload files to your website, and the protocol you use to download software and other files found on websites is also often FTP. FTP is the most universal of the three supported protocols, but it's also the least secure. Transfers aren't encrypted, and neither is your login itself. When you connect to an FTP server that requires a username and password, your credentials are sent in cleartext. Anyone snooping on your Internet connection could learn your password with virtually no effort and could then use that password to log in to your Mac by using another method (such as SSH or screen sharing), potentially causing all sorts of harm. In addition, FTP isn't guaranteed to keep all the metadata from Mac files intact. For these reasons, you should use FTP only if absolutely necessary, and you should set up a special user account, with extremely limited access, just for FTP to avoid sending your regular account password over an insecure connection.

SMB

Just as AFP is the norm for Macs, SMB is the standard on Windows computers. SMB is a mature protocol and significantly more secure than FTP. If you want to make it as easy as possible for people running Windows to access files on your Mac, SMB is the right choice.

Besides sharing particular files and folders via SMB, you can enable user account sharing. What this means is that you can individually enable user accounts on your Mac for SMB access such that if someone running Windows logs in to your Mac over SMB using the username and password for his or her account on your Mac, he or she gets access to all the same files and folders he or she would if he or she logged in locally. However, the design of SMB is such that if you enable user account sharing, the way Mac OS X is required to store user account passwords for use with SMB makes them, in theory, slightly easier to crack if someone with access to your Mac were sufficiently skilled and motivated to do so.

Toggling file-sharing protocols

To change which file-sharing protocols are used, follow these steps:

1. With File Sharing selected in the Sharing pane of System Preferences, click Options to open the dialog box shown in Figure 7.5.

2. Click the check box(es) corresponding to the protocol(s) you want to enable to select them; to turn off a protocol, click to deselect it.

3. Click the On check box for one or more account names in the list at the bottom of the window to share that user account via SMB.

4. Click Done.

FIGURE 7.5

Use this dialog box to specify which file-sharing protocol(s) are used and, for SMB, whether to activate user account sharing for one or more users.

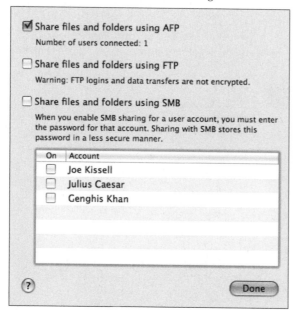

Changing which items are shared

If the only users who use File Sharing with your Mac are those with administrator accounts, you need not take any further action because administrators always have access to all folders (again, subject to the usual account permissions restrictions). If you want to share particular folders for access by other people, follow these steps:

1. **Click the Add (+) button under the Shared Folders list.** A file selection dialog box opens.

2. **Navigate to the folder (or volume) you want to share, select it, and then click Add.** The folder appears in the Shared Folders list, with default access permissions (which you can change, as described in the next section), and is immediately available on the network.

3. **Repeat steps 1 and 2 to share other folders.**

To stop sharing a folder, select it and then click the Remove (–) button. When the confirmation alert appears, click OK.

Granting access to users and groups

For each folder or volume you've shared explicitly (that is, for each one that appears in the Shared Folders list), you can specify which user(s) and group(s) can access it and with what permissions. To change access for a shared folder, follow these steps:

1. **Select an item in the Shared Folders list.** The Users list shows the users and groups with access.

2. **To add access for a user, click the Add (+) button below the Users list to open a dialog box with a list of the users and groups on your Mac, as shown in Figure 7.6.**

FIGURE 7.6

Select users and groups from this list to give them access to shared folders and volumes.

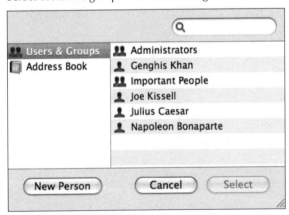

3. **Select one or more users or groups and then click Select.**

4. **If you want to grant access to someone not already on the list, click New Person, and in the dialog box that opens, type a username, type and verify a password, and then click Create Account.** Doing this creates a sharing only account for that user, and you can then select that user's name in the list.

Cross-Ref

For more on user accounts and groups, see Chapter 3. ■

5. **To change sharing permissions for a user or group, click the permission to the right of the user's name and choose Read Only, Read & Write, or Write Only (Drop Box) from the pop-up menu.** For the Everyone group (which refers to everyone other than the specified users and groups), you can also choose No Access to turn off all sharing access.

Note

In general, stick with the default setting of Read Only unless you're sure that a certain user or group needs write access, and if you do grant write access, do so for as small a group as feasible. ■

6. **To remove sharing access for a user or group, select the user or group in the Users list and then click the Remove (–) button.** You can't remove access for a folder's owner or for the Everyone group (although you can set Everyone to No Access).

All changes you make to user permissions take effect immediately.

Printer Sharing

Many printers have built-in Ethernet or Wi-Fi interfaces so that multiple computers can connect to them at once over a network. However, networking capabilities typically increase a printer's price, and some of the most popular (and least expensive) printers have only a USB connection, which normally means they can be used by the computer they're plugged into.

The Mac OS X printer-sharing feature lets any Mac with a connected printer function as a print server — accepting print jobs from any other Mac on the network and directing them to the printer, with the end result being the same as if the printer were directly connected to the other Mac.

Printer sharing presupposes that you've connected a printer to your Mac and configured it in the Print & Fax pane of System Preferences. As long as you can print from your own Mac to a printer directly connected to it, you're all set to enable printer sharing. (If you haven't yet configured a printer and need help doing so, open the Print & Fax pane of System Preferences and then choose Help ⇨ Print & Fax Help for complete instructions.)

With at least one printer configured, you can share it by following these steps:

1. **Choose ⇨ System Preferences to open System Preferences and then click Sharing to open the Sharing pane.**

2. **If the lock icon in the lower-left corner of the pane is in the locked state, click it, type an administrator's username and password, and then click OK.**

3. **In the list on the left, click the On check box next to Printer Sharing.** Your printer immediately becomes available on the network. With Printer Sharing selected from the

list on the left, as shown in Figure 7.7, the right side of the pane shows the printers connected to your Mac.

4. **To disable sharing for any particular printer without turning off printer sharing altogether, click the check box next to its name to deselect it.**

With a printer shared, other Macs on your local network can use it by following these steps:

1. **On another Mac, choose ⌘ ⇨ System Preferences to open System Preferences and then click Print & Fax to open the Print & Fax pane.**

2. **If the lock icon in the lower-left corner of the pane is in the locked state, click it, type an administrator's username and password, and then click OK.**

3. **If the shared printer doesn't already appear in the list of printers on the left, click the Add (+) button at the bottom of the list.** The Add Printer window, as shown in Figure 7.8, opens.

4. **With the Default button selected on the toolbar, select the name of the shared printer.** If the printer's driver doesn't appear in the Print Using pop-up menu, choose Select a driver to use from that menu and then select the driver you want.

5. **Click Add to add the printer to the list in the Print & Fax pane of System Preferences and then close the Add Printer window.**

FIGURE 7.7

Any printers that work with your Mac can also be shared with other users on your local network by turning on printer sharing.

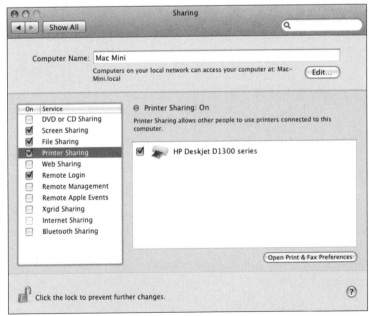

FIGURE 7.8

In this window, select a printer and its driver to add it to your Mac's list of available printers.

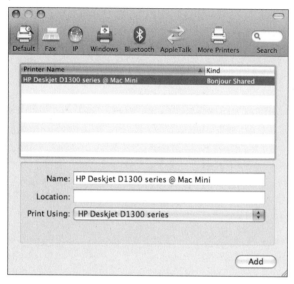

Thereafter, the newly added shared printer appears as a valid printer in all Print dialog boxes on the other Mac, as long as the Mac to which it's connected is turned on and awake.

Even though printer sharing doesn't require the use of a username or password, it poses no significant security risk for the person doing the sharing; the worst thing that could happen is that someone else uses up your paper and ink or toner! However, when you've configured your Mac to use a printer connected to another Mac as one of two or more options, you should be careful to choose the right printer when printing sensitive documents; you could inadvertently print something inappropriate on another person's printer.

Scanner Sharing

A small and little-discussed addition to the Sharing preference pane in Snow Leopard is a Scanner Sharing option, which lets your Mac share certain USB-attached scanners over the network in the same way as it can share a printer. (Leopard also supports scanner sharing, but using an entirely different procedure, as I explain later.) As with printer sharing, scanner sharing assumes you've already connected a scanner to your Mac and configured it in the Print & Fax pane of System Preferences.

Note

Many, but not all, USB scanners are supported. To see a list of the scanners for which Snow Leopard includes drivers, see `http://support.apple.com/kb/HT3669`.

With a scanner configured and turned on, you can share it by following these steps if you're running Snow Leopard (instructions for Leopard appear later):

1. Choose ⌘ ⇨ System Preferences to open System Preferences and then click Sharing to open the Sharing pane.

2. If the lock icon in the lower-left corner of the pane is in the locked state, click it, type an administrator's username and password, and then click OK.

3. **In the list on the left, click the On check box next to Scanner Sharing.** Your scanner immediately becomes available on the network. With Scanner Sharing selected in the list on the left, as shown in Figure 7.9, the right side of the pane shows the printers connected to your Mac.

4. **To disable sharing for any particular scanner without turning off scanner sharing altogether, click the check box next to its name to deselect it.**

With a scanner shared, other Macs on your local network that are running Snow Leopard can use it by following these steps:

1. On another Mac, choose ⌘ ⇨ System Preferences to open System Preferences and then click Print & Fax to open the Print & Fax pane.

2. If the lock icon in the lower-left corner of the pane is in the locked state, click it, type an administrator's username and password, and then click OK.

3. If the shared scanner doesn't already appear in the list of printers on the left, click the Add (+) button at the bottom of the list. The Add Printer dialog box (which also applies to scanners) opens.

4. With the Default button selected on the toolbar, select the name of the shared scanner. If the scanner driver doesn't appear in the Print Using pop-up menu, choose Select a driver to use from that menu and then select the driver you want.

5. Click Add to add the scanner to the list in the Print & Fax pane of System Preferences and then close the window.

If you're running Leopard, you can still share a scanner, but the procedure is different. On the Mac to which the scanner is connected — assuming it's already configured and turned on — follow these steps:

1. Open Image Capture, which is located in `/Applications`.

2. Choose Devices ⇨ Browse Devices to open the Device Browser window, and then click the Sharing button. A dialog box opens.

3. Click the Share my devices check box.

4. Optionally, type a new name for your devices, a password, or both.

5. Click OK to close the dialog box.

6. Back in the Device Browser window, click the Shared check box next to each scanner you want to share.

7. Quit Image Capture.

FIGURE 7.9

By turning on scanner sharing, you can share a USB-connected scanner with other Macs on your local network.

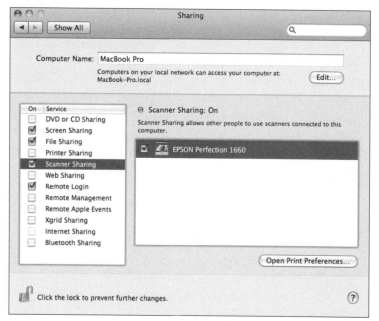

To use a scanner that has been shared on another Mac on your network if you're running Leopard, follow these steps:

1. Open Image Capture, which is located in /Applications.

2. Choose Devices ⇨ Browse Devices to open the Device Browser window.

3. Click the triangle next to Remote Image Capture Devices, if necessary, to show its contents and then click the Connected check box next to the scanner you want to use.

4. Quit Image Capture.

Web Sharing

Thanks to Mac OS X's built-in web-sharing feature, every Mac can function as a web server (at least in a limited sense). Web sharing is based on Apache, the most popular and widely used open-source web server on the planet. Thus, it offers outstanding performance, compatibility, and flexibility. That doesn't necessarily mean you can do without a conventional web-hosting service, but for simple applications, site testing, or an Intranet server for a small business, it can be a good fit. And each person who has a user account on the Mac automatically gets a personal website. As with all sharing features, though, running a web server on your Mac entails some potential security risks.

Activating Web Sharing

To activate Web Sharing, follow these steps:

1. **Choose ⇨ System Preferences to open System Preferences and then click Sharing to open the Sharing pane.**

2. **If the lock icon in the lower-left corner of the pane is in the locked state, click it, type an administrator's username and password, and then click OK.**

3. **In the list on the left, click the On check box next to Web Sharing.** With Web Sharing selected in the list on the left as shown in Figure 7.10, the right side of the pane shows the URLs for your Mac's main home page and your personal home page.

That's it! Your Mac is now a web server.

To view the website on the Mac that's running the server, click one of the URLs in the Web Sharing view of the Sharing preference pane or type the following in your browser's address bar: **http://127.0.0.1/**. Either way, you should see something like Figure 7.11.

To see an individual user's home page, use the same address followed by a tilde (~) and the user's short username. Users' home pages initially look like Figure 7.12.

Publishing web pages

Initially, your websites have simple placeholder pages. To publish pages using web sharing, create HTML documents using the tool of your choice and then put them inside `/Library/WebServer/Documents` (for your Mac's main site) or `~/Library/Sites` (for personal sites).

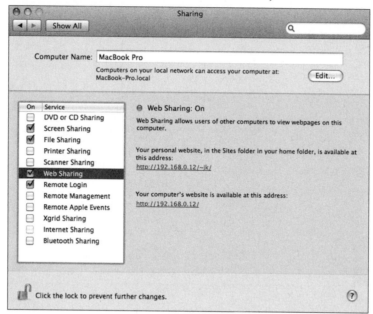

FIGURE 7.10

Your Mac can become a web server in one click — just activate web sharing.

Making your web server visible to the outside world

Your Mac's web server is visible to other Macs on your local network, but most computers connect to the Internet by using a router, gateway, or another device that assigns private IP addresses using NAT, which means that unless you jump through some additional hoops, no one from outside your local network can view your web pages.

Although a complete discussion of how to do this is beyond the scope of this book, one method is to configure your router or gateway to forward all requests for port 80 (used by the web server) to your Mac and then use your Mac's public IP address to access it from outside your network. (To learn your Mac's public IP address, type **http://whatismyip.com/** in your web browser.) If you also want to make your Mac accessible using a domain name, which is more memorable than an IP address (and which, unlike your IP address, isn't subject to change over time), you can use a dynamic DNS service, such as the one offered at no charge by DynDNS (www.dyndns.com).

FIGURE 7.11

The default home page for your Mac as a whole looks like this.

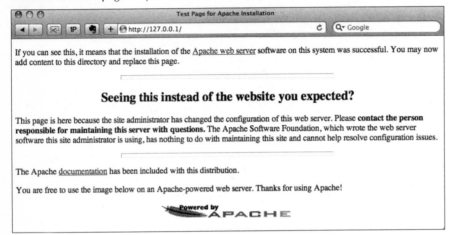

FIGURE 7.12

User-specific default home pages are slightly more interesting.

Web-sharing negatives

Although powerful and easy to use, using web sharing on a personal Mac isn't necessarily ideal for running public websites for the following reasons:

- In order to make websites available whenever a visitor might want to view them, the computer running them should be turned on and awake all the time; that may not be the way you prefer to use a personal Mac.

- Making a Mac that's behind a NAT gateway available to the public can be awkward. On the other hand, a web server not visible to the public is difficult to exploit — and therefore quite safe!

- If your website receives a lot of traffic, it can slow down the other activities you use your Mac for; conversely, if you keep your Mac busy with other tasks, it can reduce the performance of the web server.

- When you're running a web server that's visible to the public, you give would-be attackers another potential avenue to exploit. As long as your site contains nothing but simple HTML and media files, you face little risk, but if you add web forms, scripting (by using, for example, PHP or Perl), or a database engine, you must take into account all the associated dangers.

Cross-Ref
For more on web server security, see Chapter 18. ∎

If you want to use a Mac as a web server, you'll get the best results if the Mac is used only as a server and if it has its own publicly routable IP address and domain name.

Remote Login

You can log in to a Mac in a number of different ways, but in the context of the Sharing pane of System Preferences, Remote Login refers to one particular sort of remote access: using SSH (secure shell). When you activate Remote Login, you turn on Mac OS X's built-in OpenSSH server, which means that you or someone else can connect to your Mac remotely using the command-line `ssh` program or any of various methods that use SSH as a conduit for other services. You or the person connecting remotely must know your Mac's IP address or domain name and must have a valid username and password for a user account on your Mac. In addition, your Mac must either be directly connected to the Internet or, if connected via a NAT gateway, be available via port forwarding or a comparable router configuration.

Cross-Ref
For more on port forwarding and related techniques, see Chapter 15. ∎

If you feel comfortable using SSH and can easily imagine situations in which you might want to use it to connect to your Mac from another computer, then by all means turn on Remote Login. However, if you never use SSH, it has no value and should be left disabled because an attacker who knows or can guess your username and password could potentially use an SSH connection to view files on your Mac and even, in extreme cases, take over your computer.

To activate Remote Login, follow these steps:

1. **Choose ❖ ➪ System Preferences to open System Preferences and then click Sharing to open the Sharing pane.**

2. **If the lock icon in the lower-left corner of the pane is in the locked state, click it, type an administrator's username and password, and then click OK.**

3. **In the list on the left, click the On check box next to Remote Login.** OpenSSH immediately becomes active at the address listed on the right side of the pane, as shown in Figure 7.13.

FIGURE 7.13

To enable yourself (or other users) to connect to your Mac via SSH, activate Remote Login.

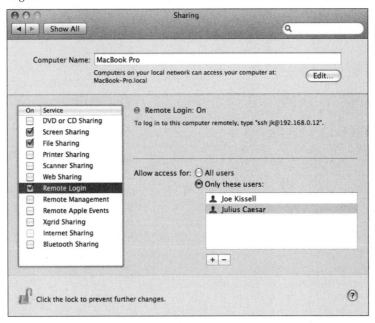

4. To determine who can access your Mac remotely over SSH, click one of the following two radio buttons:

- **All users.** When this is selected (as it is by default), the credentials for any user with an account on your Mac can be used to log in. This setting doesn't mean that someone can log in without a password.

- **Only these users.** To restrict access to particular users, click this radio button. Then, click the Add (+) button, select one or more users or groups, and then click Select. The selected users are added to the access list. I recommend selecting this option and adding as few people as possible to the list.

Cross-Ref

For more on connecting to a remote Mac by using SSH, see Chapter 11. ■

Remote Management

Apple Remote Desktop (www.apple.com/remotedesktop) is a commercial program that allows an administrator to perform a variety of administrative and maintenance tasks on another Mac — on the same network or elsewhere on the Internet. In addition to File Sharing and Screen Sharing, Apple Remote Desktop lets an administrator install software remotely, run Automator actions, get detailed reports of the remote computer's usage, and search remote computers using Spotlight, among other activities.

For Macs that are managed remotely, this feature must be enabled, and the administrator should decide what level of access is appropriate. If your Mac isn't administered remotely using Apple Remote Desktop, you should leave this feature turned off.

To enable an administrator to connect to and manage your Mac using Apple Remote Desktop, follow these steps:

1. Choose ⇨ System Preferences to open System Preferences and then click Sharing to open the Sharing pane.

2. If the lock icon in the lower-left corner of the pane is in the locked state, click it, type an administrator's username and password, and then click OK.

3. In the list on the left, click the On check box next to Remote Management. A dialog box with a number of options, as shown in Figure 7.14, opens.

4. Click to select the check boxes indicating the capabilities you want a remote administrator to have and then click OK. In most cases, the person connecting to your computer with Apple Remote Desktop will choose the necessary capabilities and select them or have you select them.

5. **To determine who can manage your Mac remotely using Apple Remote Desktop, click one of the following two radio buttons shown in Figure 7.15:**

   - **All users.** When this is selected (as it is by default), the credentials for any user with an account on your Mac can be used to manage your Mac.

   - **Only these users.** To restrict Apple Remote Desktop access to particular users, click this radio button. Then, click the Add (+) button, select one or more users or groups, and then click Select. The selected users are added to the access list.

6. **To adjust other remote management settings, click Computer Settings to open the dialog box shown in Figure 7.16.** You can adjust the following options:

   - **Show Remote Management status in menu bar.** When this check box is selected, a system-wide menu appears; the menu shows you when an administrator is connected and enables you to send the administrator a message.

   - **Anyone may request permission to control screen.** To permit people who aren't on the access list to request permission to control your screen, click this check box.

   - **VNC viewers may control screen with password.** When this check box is selected and a password is filled in (as your user account password is by default), a remote user, whether or not on the access list, can use VNC to view or control your screen by typing the password.

   - **Computer Information.** To include any particular information about your Mac in the System Overview Report shown in Apple Remote Desktop, type it into one or more of these fields.

   After making any changes in this dialog box, click OK.

7. **If you later want to adjust any of the settings you made in step 4, click Options to open the same dialog box.**

As soon as you activate Remote Management, an administrator can connect to your Mac by using Apple Remote Desktop.

FIGURE 7.14

Most administrators probably want all these capabilities, but you can restrict what an Apple Remote Desktop user can do in this dialog box.

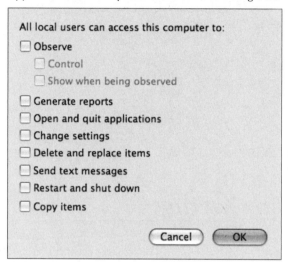

FIGURE 7.15

Select which administrators can manage your Mac using Apple Remote Desktop.

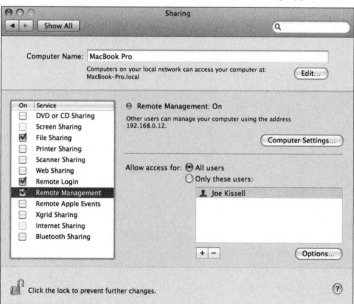

FIGURE 7.16

Configure additional options for remote management in this dialog box.

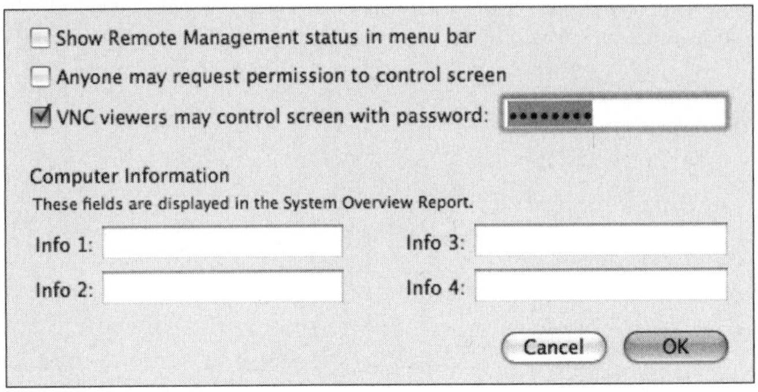

☐ Show Remote Management status in menu bar

☐ Anyone may request permission to control screen

☑ VNC viewers may control screen with password: ●●●●●●●●

Computer Information
These fields are displayed in the System Overview Report.

Info 1: [＿＿＿＿＿]   Info 3: [＿＿＿＿＿]

Info 2: [＿＿＿＿＿]   Info 4: [＿＿＿＿＿]

(Cancel)   (OK)

Remote Apple Events

AppleScript, the user-level scripting system that has been built into Macs since long before Mac OS X, enables users to automate repetitive actions, extend applications' abilities, and even create full-fledged, stand-alone applications using a relatively simple English-like language. Behind the scenes, AppleScript communicates with Mac OS X and individual applications using a lower-level messaging system called Apple Events.

In most cases, AppleScripts are designed to perform activities on the Mac on which they're running, just like any other application. However, AppleScript has the capability to tell other Macs to perform the same sorts of actions, with only slightly more code than is required to send the messages to one's own Mac. For example, AppleScript could instruct another Mac on your network to shut down, display an alert, or play a song in iTunes.

In order for AppleScript to work on a remote Mac, the computer running the script must be able to reach the remote Mac via TCP/IP, it must supply a valid username and password, and the Mac to which it's connecting must have Remote Apple Events enabled.

As with all sharing features discussed in this chapter, you should turn on Remote Apple Events only if you're certain you need it. A hacker who knew your Mac's IP address and a valid username and password could wreak all sorts of havoc, and it's best to leave all unnecessary avenues of attack closed off.

To enable Remote Apple Events, follow these steps:

1. Choose ★ ➪ System Preferences to open System Preferences and then click Sharing to open the Sharing pane.

2. If the lock icon in the lower-left corner of the pane is in the locked state, click it, type an administrator's username and password, and then click OK.

3. **In the list on the left, click the On check box next to Remote Apple Events.** The window should look like Figure 7.17.

4. **To determine who can send Apple Events to your Mac remotely, click one of the following two radio buttons:**

   - **All users.** When this is selected (as it is by default), the credentials for any user with an account on your Mac can be used to send Apple Events to your Mac.

   - **Only these users.** To allow only certain users to send Remote Apple Events to this Mac, click this radio button. Then, click the Add (+) button, select one or more users or groups, and then click Select. The selected users are added to the access list.

5. **Optionally, to permit Apple Events to be received from Macs running Mac OS 9, click Options, click the Allow events from Mac OS 9 check box, type and verify a password for Mac OS 9 computers to use when connecting, and then click OK.**

Remote Apple Events access immediately becomes available.

FIGURE 7.17

If you want to use AppleScript to perform actions on your Mac from another computer, turn on Remote Apple Events.

Xgrid Sharing

Xgrid is an Apple technology that lets multiple Macs combine their CPUs to reduce the amount of time it takes to perform computationally intensive tasks. Just as a single Mac may have multiple CPUs or cores that work together as one, an Xgrid setup may have dozens or even thousands of CPUs working in concert. One way of using Xgrid is to configure participating computers to devote their CPU time to a distributed task only when they're idle so that the shared processing doesn't interfere with any local computing tasks.

An Xgrid setup requires three different categories, or roles, of Macs. The *controller* is the Mac that manages the jobs, sending portions of the processing tasks to the other participating computers and compiling the results. The *client* is the computer that submits a task to the controller; the client need not actively participate in the processing or even be turned on while the task is being performed. And finally, there are *agents* — the individual Macs doing the actual work as requested by the client and divvied out by the controller.

Any Mac can be an agent; this requires just a couple of clicks in the Sharing pane of System Preferences (described next). To learn about the process of writing Xgrid-aware software, read Apple's Xgrid programming guide at `http://developer.apple.com/mac/library/documentation/MacOSXServer/Conceptual/Xgrid_Programming_Guide/Introduction/Introduction.html`. And to get complete details on setting up a controller, submitting jobs with a client, and managing Xgrid networks, read the PDF document "Xgrid Administration and High Performance Computing" at `http://images.apple.com/server/macosx/docs/Xgrid_Admin_and_HPC_v10.5.pdf`.

To enable your Mac to be an Xgrid agent, follow these steps:

1. **Choose ⟳ System Preferences to open System Preferences and then click Sharing to open the Sharing pane.**

2. **If the lock icon in the lower-left corner of the pane is in the locked state, click it, type an administrator's username and password, and then click OK.**

3. **In the list on the left, select Xgrid Sharing (but don't click its check box yet).**

4. **From the Authentication method pop-up menu, choose the type of authentication (Password, Single Sign On, or None) you want to use.** Your Xgrid administrator can tell you the right choice, but with a setting of None, your Mac could theoretically be used without your knowledge or permission in any Xgrid network. Although that would only result in a slowdown on your Mac — not a risk to your data or privacy — you should still avoid that choice if possible.

5. **If you choose Password, type a password in the field provided.**

6. **Click the On check box next to Xgrid Sharing in the list on the left.** Your Mac immediately becomes available as an Xgrid agent. The window should now resemble Figure 7.18.

7. **Optionally, to configure additional Xgrid settings, click Configure, which displays the dialog box shown in Figure 7.19.** The following options are available:

    - Click to select the Use first available controller radio button to make your Mac available as an agent to any Xgrid controller or click to select the Use a specific controller radio button and then choose a controller from the pop-up menu to make your Mac available only to a specific controller. You can also type a controller's IP address or domain name into this field.

    - Click the Only when this computer is idle radio button if you want to limit your Mac's Xgrid participation to when you're not using your computer, ensuring that performance doesn't decrease when you're present. Or click the Always button if this Mac is used only as an Xgrid agent.

8. **Click Done to close the configuration dialog box.**

FIGURE 7.18

Your Mac can become part of a supercomputer containing hundreds or thousands of nodes by turning on Xgrid.

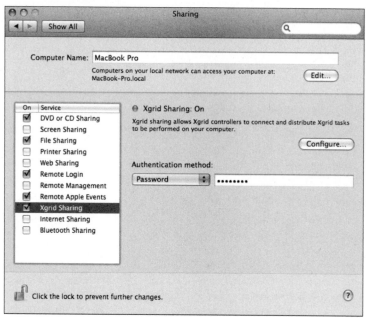

FIGURE 7.19

If you're using your Mac for things other than running Xgrid, you can make sure Xgrid is active only during idle times.

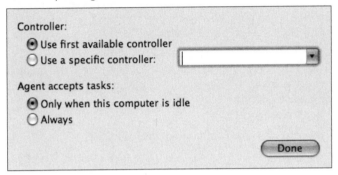

Internet Sharing

Given how ubiquitous Wi-Fi has become, many Mac users never even think about plugging an Ethernet cable into their computers in order to get Internet access. You can connect many computers to a single AirPort base station or another Wi-Fi access point without ever having to worry about running out of cables or connectors for them to plug into.

However, in some circumstances, one computer may have Internet access while other nearby devices don't. For example, consider these scenarios:

- Your Mac connects to the Internet via Ethernet. You want to connect another Mac to the Internet too, but you have only a single Ethernet port and no router, hub, gateway, or wireless access point. (This is a common situation when traveling, for example.)

- Your Mac connects to the Internet via Wi-Fi, but a friend's PC, which lacks a Wi-Fi card, can't connect.

- You use your cell phone as a modem (as described later in this chapter) in a location without other forms of Internet access, and you want to share that connection with a friend.

In these and other similar situations, you can enable a Mac to function as a basic router and even as a Wi-Fi access point, as long as it has some means of connecting to the Internet and an available interface with which another computer can connect. All it requires is selecting the interface with which your Mac currently connects to the Internet, the interface(s) through which you want to permit others to share your connection, and, in some cases, a couple of other options.

To share your Internet connection, follow these steps:

1. Choose System Preferences to open System Preferences and then click Sharing to open the Sharing pane.

2. If the lock icon in the lower-left corner of the pane is in the locked state, click it, type an administrator's username and password, and then click OK.

3. In the list on the left, Select Internet Sharing (but don't click its check box yet).

4. From the Share your connection from pop-up menu on the right, choose the interface through which your computer currently has Internet access.

5. **From the To computers using list, click the On check box next to one or more interfaces through which other users will be able to connect.** For example, if your Mac connects to the Internet via Ethernet, you might choose AirPort (to create a wireless network), FireWire (to enable someone else to get Internet access using a FireWire cable), or both.

Caution

You shouldn't share an Internet connection with computers using Ethernet unless you're sure no other source of Internet access exists on the same Ethernet network. For example, it's fine if your Internet access is via AirPort and you're sharing it with a single Mac only via a directly connected Ethernet cable, but not if you're sharing your connection over an Ethernet network that may have its own Internet connection. If you enable Ethernet as an outbound interface, a warning appears to remind you of potentially dire consequences, such as disrupting network service and having your service terminated. ■

6. Optionally, if you're sharing a connection via AirPort, click AirPort options to open a dialog box, as shown in Figure 7.20, in which you can specify several additional options:

    *   **Network Name.** If you want your ad hoc wireless network to have a name (SSID) other than your computer's name, type it here.

    *   **Channel.** Choose a channel from the pop-up menu or, for best results in most cases, leave it set to Automatic.

    *   **Enable encryption (using WEP).** To prevent others from connecting to your network without using a password, click this check box and then type and confirm a password in the fields provided (noting the instructions at the bottom of the window regarding password length). Choose the desired key length from the WEP Key Length pop-up menu.

7. Click OK to close this dialog box.

FIGURE 7.20

You can turn your Mac into a basic AirPort base station, but you're limited in the capabilities you can use — such as WEP encryption only, not WPA.

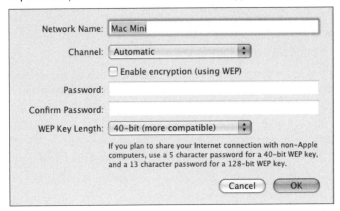

Caution

Using Internet sharing, your only option for encrypting a wireless network is WEP, which is easily cracked. Although it's better than nothing and worth turning on, you should be aware that information sent over this wireless connection can easily be intercepted by others nearby, unless the computer connecting to you also uses a VPN. ■

Cross-Ref

For more on WEP security, see Chapter 16. For more on using a VPN, read Chapter 12. ■

8. **Click the On check box next to Internet Sharing in the list on the left.** An alert appears, confirming that you want to share your Internet connection.

9. **Click Start.** The Sharing window should now resemble Figure 7.21.

With Internet sharing active, any Mac that connects to yours with the interface you specified should automatically get Internet access, assuming default settings in the Network pane of System Preferences.

To deactivate Internet sharing later, return to this window and then click the On check box next to Internet Sharing to deselect it.

FIGURE 7.21

When Internet sharing is active, the window shows which connection is being shared and over which interfaces.

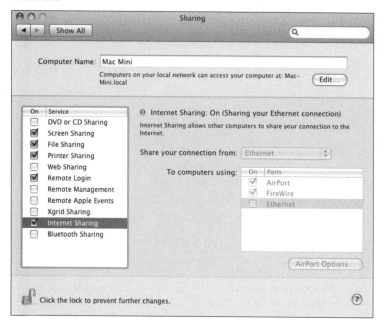

Bluetooth Sharing

The final category of sharing in the Sharing pane of System Preferences is Bluetooth. Bluetooth is a wireless communication standard designed for relatively low-speed data transfer over short distances. It's often used for peripherals such as keyboards, mice, and headsets. All current Macs have Bluetooth transceivers, as do the vast majority of cell phones and many other electronic gadgets. Although Bluetooth doesn't have the bandwidth or range of Wi-Fi, because it's so common and so easy to set up, it's an ideal way to share files and data when other routes are unavailable.

Bluetooth security depends primarily on the concept of pairing. When you pair two devices, they confirm their identity to each other and thereafter can freely exchange information. Unpaired devices may be able to see each other but usually can't connect. For example, if you want to use a Bluetooth headset with your cell phone, you must perform a procedure that stores information about your phone in your headset and vice versa. If this procedure weren't required, someone else could use his or her headset to listen in on your conversations!

Pairing, in turn, requires that one device be able to detect the other and learn its name and unique identifier. When a Bluetooth device broadcasts its ID so that other devices can detect it, it's said to be *discoverable*. Typically, you make a device discoverable only for a short period of time (perhaps two or three minutes) — just long enough to pair it. Although the procedures for pairing vary according to the type of device being used, the usual procedure is for the device initiating the connection to ask the other device to type a passkey. For example, if you ask your Mac to pair with a Bluetooth cell phone, you must press a particular sequence of numbers on the cell phone in order to verify that it's under your physical control.

Once two devices are paired, the ways in which they can exchange information depend on the capabilities of the two devices and their settings. In some cases, for example, you can transfer files such as pictures and movies between a Mac and a cell phone; in others, you can share a cell phone's Internet connection with your Mac or vice versa. (The iPhone, although it includes Bluetooth, offers very little in the way of sharing capabilities.)

The full list of ways in which your Mac can use Bluetooth is quite long, but for the purposes of this chapter, I focus on just two areas. First, I describe sharing files via Bluetooth — either with another Mac or with some other device, such as a phone. And second, I explain how your Mac can use a Bluetooth-enabled cell phone to connect to the Internet.

Sharing files via Bluetooth

If your Mac and another Bluetooth device are paired, assuming the other device offers file-sharing capabilities, you can copy files in either direction between the two devices. Although there are other ways of achieving the same end result, the best way to accomplish this is to make sure the devices are already paired before attempting to share files. In order to receive files from another device, you must then turn on and configure Bluetooth sharing on your Mac.

Pairing a Bluetooth device with your Mac

Because the exact procedure for pairing depends on the type of device, I provide only general instructions for doing so here. Follow these steps to pair your Mac with another Bluetooth device:

1. **Choose ⇨ System Preferences to open System Preferences and then click Bluetooth to open the Bluetooth pane.**

2. **Click the Show Bluetooth status in the menu bar check box at the bottom of the window to show the menu.**

3. **Follow the manufacturer's instructions to make the other device discoverable.** If the other device is a Mac, you can make it discoverable by choosing Discoverable from the Bluetooth menu (if it isn't already selected).

4. **From the Bluetooth menu, choose Set Up Bluetooth Device.** The Bluetooth Setup Assistant, as shown (after the Introduction screen) in Figure 7.22, opens.

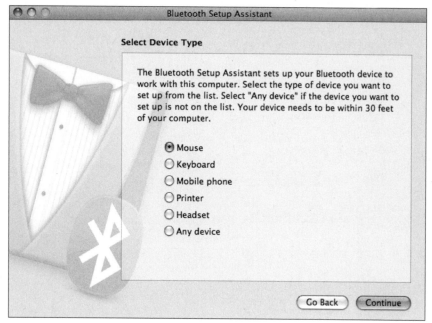

FIGURE 7.22

In the Bluetooth Setup Assistant (the second screen is shown here), you can configure a mouse, keyboard, phone, or another device to connect to your Mac via Bluetooth.

5. **Follow the prompts to pair your device.** Once the device is paired with your Mac, it appears on the Bluetooth menu.

Setting up Bluetooth Sharing

If you want to send a file to a paired Bluetooth device, such as a cell phone or PDA, you can skip this section. However, if you want your Mac to be able to receive files sent by the other device, follow these steps:

Note

For the best balance of security and convenience, I recommend leaving all these settings at their defaults. ■

1. Choose ⇨ System Preferences to open System Preferences and then click Sharing to open the Sharing pane.

2. If the lock icon in the lower-left corner of the pane is in the locked state, click it, type an administrator's username and password, and then click OK.

3. In the list on the left, click the On check box next to Bluetooth Sharing. The window should now look something like Figure 7.23. Your Mac immediately becomes available as a destination for shared files over Bluetooth.

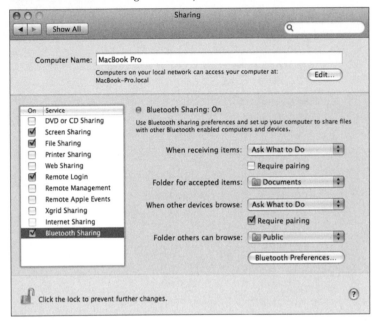

FIGURE 7.23

Turn on Bluetooth Sharing to enable your Mac to receive files shared via Bluetooth.

4. **Optionally, you can adjust any of the settings on the right side of the window:**

- **When receiving items.** This pop-up menu determines what happens when a Bluetooth device attempts to send you a file. Choose Ask What to Do (the default) to see an alert when someone tries to send you a file; you can then accept or decline each file individually. Choose Accept and Save to automatically save incoming files to the folder you designate (in the next option) without having to approve each one. Choose Accept and Open to do the same but also open a saved file in its default application after it's been copied. Or choose Never Allow to block all reception of files. To require devices to be paired before they can send you files, click the Require pairing check box.

- **Folder for accepted items.** By default, the folder in which received files are stored is set to ~/Documents; to change it, choose Other from this pop-up menu, select the folder you want to use, and then click Open.

- **When other devices browse.** If the other device supports browsing, it can look through all the files in any single folder you designate and download any of those files. To let other devices browse and download items from this folder freely, choose Always Allow. To block browsing, choose Never Allow. To show an alert when someone wants to browse (so that you can grant or deny requests as they occur), choose Ask What to

Do (the default setting). To require devices to be paired before they can browse, click the Require pairing check box if it isn't already selected.

- **Folder others can browse.** By default, your browsable folder is set to ~/Public; to change it, choose Other from this pop-up menu, select the folder you want to use, and then click Open. Your Mac is now ready to receive files via Bluetooth.

Sending or receiving files over Bluetooth

Once your devices are paired, you can send files from your Mac to the other device or send files from the other device to your Mac.

To send a file from your Mac to the other device, follow these steps:

1. **Choose Send File from the Bluetooth menu.** A file selection dialog box opens.
2. **Navigate to find the file you want to send and then select it.**
3. **Click Send.** The Select Bluetooth Device window opens.
4. **Select the device to which you want to send the file and then click Send.**

The file is copied to your other device. To send a file from the other device to your Mac, follow the instructions provided by the other device's manufacturer. If the other device is also a Mac, follow the steps in the previous set of steps and choose your Mac as the destination in step 3. If you've configured your preferences to require confirmation before receiving a file, an alert appears on your screen, as shown in Figure 7.24. Click either Accept or Decline; if you click Accept, the file transfers to your designated folder for receiving files. When the file has finished copying, an alert appears (or if you've set your preferences to open incoming files automatically, the file opens).

FIGURE 7.24

An alert like this one lets you decide whether to receive files someone tries to share with you via Bluetooth.

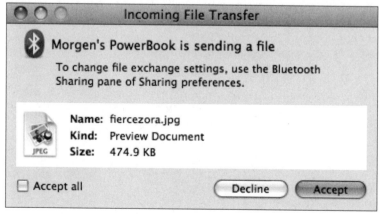

Sharing an Internet connection via Bluetooth

Earlier in this chapter, in the discussion of Internet sharing, I described how you can share your Mac's Internet connection over other network interfaces, which could include Bluetooth. One application of this capability would be to give a Bluetooth-enabled device, such as a PDA, access to the Internet by way of your Mac's wired or wireless Internet connection. Likewise, you can use Internet sharing to make an Internet connection provided to your Mac by your cell phone available to other computers. However, there's one missing piece in that story, which is what I describe here: how to enable your Mac to connect to the Internet by using your cell phone as a modem.

I should say at the outset that this configuration works only with certain combinations of cell phones, carriers, and data plans. If you have a cell phone that supports Bluetooth tethering (as the feature is sometimes called), if your cell phone carrier permits this use, and if your data plan includes this option (which sometimes requires paying an additional fee), you can use your Mac to dial into your cell carrier's network and connect to the Internet, with Bluetooth serving as the conduit between your phone and your Mac.

Note

iPhones running iPhone Software 3.0 or higher can be tethered as long as your carrier supports it and you have a suitable data plan. As of late 2009, AT&T had not yet enabled a tethering option for iPhone users in the United States, although that may have changed by the time you read this book. ■

To get this working, you must first configure your cell phone properly. Unfortunately, I can't help you there — the variety of phones and plans makes it impossible to give you any guidance. Contact your carrier or visit its website for instructions. While you're at it, be sure to get the list of parameters you must enter on your computer.

Given a properly configured phone, however, which has already been paired with your Mac, you can follow these steps to set up your Mac to use the phone as a modem:

1. Choose ⇨ System Preferences to open System Preferences and then click Network to open the Network pane.

2. If the lock icon in the lower-left corner of the pane is in the locked state, click it, type an administrator's username and password, and then click OK.

3. In the list of services on the left, select Bluetooth, as shown in Figure 7.25.

4. In the fields on the right, type the connection information provided to you by your cell carrier.

5. Click Advanced, and in the dialog box that opens, click the Modem tab and then select your phone's vendor and model from the pop-up menus.

6. Click each of the remaining tabs (DNS, WINS, Proxies, and PPP), filling in any additional settings provided by your cell carrier, and then click OK.

7. Click Apply to save the settings.

8. To connect to the Internet using your cell phone, click Connect.

FIGURE 7.25

Select Bluetooth in the Network pane of System Preferences and then type the parameters provided by your cell carrier to use your cell phone as a modem.

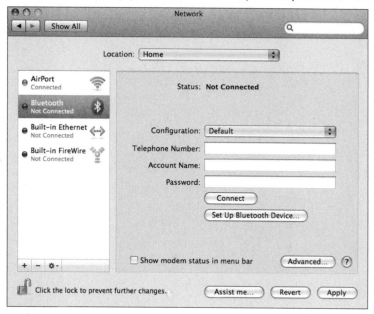

When your Mac is connected to the Internet via your cell phone, the data you send and receive is subject to interception, although not quite as easily as if you were using unencrypted Wi-Fi. To encrypt your data, you can use a VPN, but keep in mind that cellular data connections may be slow to begin with, and a VPN only makes them slower.

Cross-Ref

For more on VPNs, see Chapter 12. ∎

Summary

This chapter described many of the ways in which your Mac can share data and resources with other computers and how to do so as safely as possible. I described sharing your Mac's optical drive with others and explained how one Mac can control another's screen. I discussed file sharing at some length, including how to set up users and groups and how the various file-sharing protocols differ in the security they provide.

I showed how one Mac can share its printers and scanners with other users and how to use your Mac as a simple web server. I also discussed how one Mac can log in to another remotely using SSH, how remote management tools work, and how and why one Mac might want to send an Apple event to another. I mentioned Xgrid, which enables multiple Macs to combine their resources to solve processor-intensive problems. I showed how to share your Mac's Internet connection with other computers and explored some of the ways in which Bluetooth facilitates sharing data and resources.

Backing Up Your Mac

O f all the security measures you can take to protect the data on your Mac, backups are among the most important. Think about all the valuable information on your hard disk: photos of your kids, years worth of email correspondence, your unfinished novel, business and tax records, and countless other files. If your Mac were to be stolen; if its data were to be damaged by a hacker, malware, or simple user error; if a disaster such as a fire or an earthquake were to strike; or if some electronic or mechanical error were to make your machine nonfunctional, you could lose any or all of it. Good backups provide peace of mind and enable you to recover from almost any type of data loss.

Even if you don't need to be convinced to back up your Mac, the specifics of how you go about doing so may be unclear. There are lots of products claiming to be the ultimate backup solution and lots of ways you can approach the problem of how to keep your data safe. In this chapter, I provide an overview of the backup landscape, help you decide what to back up and how, and address some of the common myths and misunderstandings about backups.

Backup Basics

In the simplest possible sense, a backup is another copy of some piece of data. In the physical world, you might photocopy a piece of paper; on your computer, you do the equivalent by making a copy of a file. The great thing about digital copies is that, unlike photocopies, they're absolutely identical to the originals. A lost or damaged original would therefore be of no consequence as long as you have a backup.

Continuing with the photocopy analogy, suppose you've made a copy of a will, a contract, or some other important legal document. You probably wouldn't keep the photocopy with the original because if your office were burglarized or the building burned down, the original and the copy would both be gone. Common sense dictates that the copy — the backup — be stored somewhere else.

The same is true when backing up digital files. If I duplicate a document and store the duplicate on the same hard disk, I have a tiny bit of protection; if the original file were somehow damaged or deleted, I could use the copy. However, anything that affected the entire disk would also affect my backup. Storing the backup on another drive inside the same computer is a notch safer; storing it on an external drive is safer still; and storing a copy in an entirely different location is best of all. Better yet, I could maintain more than one backup copy — for example, one that I keep near my computer (for convenience) and another I store in a separate location (for safety).

In a way, that's all there is to backups. Make a copy of your data on some other media. Ideally, do it again, keeping the second set of media in a different location. Repeat as needed.

However simple that may sound, the devil is in the details. You may well wonder which data you should back up, to what sort of media, and how often. You must also think about how many copies of your data to keep and whether (or when) to erase old copies when making new ones. In the next few pages, I explore some of these essential basic topics.

Note

This chapter provides basic guidance about backing up your Mac, but because of the wide variety of possible backup scenarios and the breadth of backup hardware, software, and services available, I can cover only a small portion of the overall picture here. To learn much more about backups, read my ebook *Take Control of Mac OS X Backups* (www.takecontrolbooks.com/backup-macosx.html). ∎

What to back up

The hard disk of a typical Mac may contain upward of a million files, including those that make up Mac OS X itself, user-created documents, and assorted other files. Copying files takes time, and the copies themselves take up space on your backup media. So, it's fair to ask which of these files one must actually back up.

The best answer is all of them. If you back up every file on your disk, you eliminate the possibility of inadvertently leaving out the one obscure item that, weeks or months from now, may turn out to be critically important. For this reason, by default, Time Machine backs up every single file on your disk (as do many other backup programs). The main downside to this approach is that your backup media (a hard disk, in the case of Time Machine) must be at least as large as — and ideally much larger than — the volume you're backing up, and that can involve some expense and clutter.

Another entirely reasonable answer, at least for those who haven't added a great deal of third-party software and who have another Mac available, is the contents of your home folder. By default, Mac OS X and third-party applications store all your documents, photos, music, preferences, and other user-created data in one or another subfolder of your home folder (/Users/*your-short-username*). So, backing up that folder (for each of the users on a Mac if there's more than one user) should, in most cases, catch all the most crucial data. Of course, because this doesn't include Mac OS X itself or any applications, you must go to the effort of reinstalling a good bit of software (or switching to another Mac) if your entire hard disk dies or becomes otherwise unavailable. And it doesn't account for any data you may have chosen to store outside your home folder.

If storage space is at a premium for some reason, you could consider backing up only the particular folders (such as ~/Documents) or files you use or modify most actively. However, I recommend against this approach because it leaves too many potential avenues for data loss.

Which media to use

Most modern backup programs — at least those geared toward individual users — assume that you'll be backing up your files to a hard drive (which may be directly connected or mounted over a network). Hard drives offer the highest potential capacity and fastest speed of any backup media, are relatively inexpensive, and make it possible to create a backup from which you can start up your Mac if necessary. For all these reasons, hard drives are the ideal backup media for most people.

If you have to back up more than a handful of Macs, the total storage capacity you need may quickly outstrip what any individual hard drive can hold. You can combine two or more drives to form a *RAID*, or Redundant Array of Independent Disks (described later in this chapter), but at a certain point, it may become impractical to maintain the necessary total amount of storage even on a RAID, particularly if you want more than one copy of your backups. In this situation, a tape library may be the best choice. You can purchase a mechanism that contains one or more drives that write to digital tape (with storage capacities in the hundreds of gigabytes per cartridge) and that can automatically swap tape cartridges when they become full. Tape backups lack the convenient random access of hard drives, and although tape cartridges themselves don't cost much, the drive and library mechanisms can be quite expensive. But for businesses that must back up truly massive amounts of data — and maintain multiple copies of it — they make a good solution.

At the other end of the spectrum, if your budget — or the amount of data you want to back up — is extremely limited, you may consider optical discs (any of the numerous varieties of recordable CDs and DVDs). Optical discs are more durable than hard drives (they won't break or endanger your data if you drop them or get them wet, for example), although the data on them degrades over time, making them potentially unreliable for long-term storage. They're also less expensive than hard drives, on a cost-per-gigabyte basis. But because they're much slower than hard drives, have a much smaller capacity, require considerable manual effort to manage, and are unable to create a bootable duplicate of your entire Mac disk, they make a less-capable choice overall.

How often to back up

There's no single right answer to the question of how often you should back up. But in general, you should ask yourself how much time you could afford to spend redoing work, reinstalling software, and the like in the event of data loss. If you're on such a tight schedule that it would be a hardship for you to lose even an hour's worth of work, then you should back up every hour (or more frequently). If, on the other hand, you use your Mac recreationally and seldom make significant changes to files that would be difficult to reconstruct, perhaps a weekly backup would be adequate.

Virtually all backup software can perform *incremental* backups. This means that the software initially copies all the files you want to back up, but the next time it runs, it backs up only the files that have been modified or added since the last time. So, although the first run may take hours or even days, subsequent runs tend to be quite fast — sometimes minutes, sometimes mere seconds. Incremental backups mean there's little downside to more-frequent backups, particularly if the software is designed to run in the background and not noticeably slow down your Mac while it's backing up.

Note

You may also hear about differential backups, which are similar to incremental backups except that on each run after the initial run, the software copies everything that has changed since the very first backup. Differential backups take longer to run, but they make restoration faster (at least when restoring from tapes) because the backup software doesn't have to step through each incremental backup to restore all your files to their most recent state. ∎

Versioned backups

Picture this: Your backup software creates a copy of your entire hard disk. Time passes, during which you change just one file. Now the backup software runs again, and because it's backing up incrementally, it copies just that one changed file. The question is: What does it do with the copy of that file that was already on your backup media? One way of doing backups is to overwrite that file so that your backup contains only the most recent version of every file on your disk. Another way is for the backup software to keep the old file (perhaps moving it, renaming it, or storing it in a special format) and then add the new file. That way, you can restore not only the most recent version but also any previously backed up version of a file. In this book, I use the term *versioned backups* to refer to a backup scheme in which multiple versions of your files are maintained. You may also hear this sort of backup referred to as, among other things, an *archive* — borrowing the term from a special type of storage file sometimes used to hold all your backed-up files. Note, however, that some backup programs use the term *versioned* to mean something different from what I describe here, whereas others use *archive* to mean a backup in which files are copied to your backup media and then deleted from the source.

Versioned backups protect you from user error (accidentally changing or deleting a file) as well as from computer error (program crashes, file corruption, and the like). Even if you think you never need to go back to an earlier version of a file, I strongly recommend some form of versioned backups for everyone. (Time Machine, along with most other modern backup software, automatically creates versioned backups.)

Bootable duplicates

Another style of backup is the *bootable duplicate*, which also goes by a variety of other names, including *clone* and *mirror*. In a bootable duplicate, your backup software creates a complete copy of all the files on your hard disk, storing them on another hard disk in such a way that you can start up and run your Mac from the other disk. Because many of the files that make up Mac OS X are hidden, have special ownership and permissions, or have other unusual attributes, merely copying the contents of one disk to another (in the Finder or by using another program) won't make the two identical. Backup software has to jump through a number of special hoops for the resulting copy to be bootable. Many Mac backup programs, although not all, can create bootable duplicates, and a few do only this. A bootable duplicate must be stored on its own volume, and in general, it's not possible for a bootable duplicate to also be a versioned backup; the two types of backup must be maintained separately.

Offsite backups

Although a single backup copy of your data is good, it's better to have more than one copy. For example, your backup media could develop errors or could be lost or stolen, so having a secondary backup (or even more than one) is prudent. Better yet, as I mentioned earlier, you should keep an extra copy somewhere else — somewhere sufficiently distant from the original that it will be safe from any catastrophe that might endanger your computer and any media nearby. An *offsite backup* could mean physically moving an extra hard drive or a stack of tapes or optical discs to another location from time to time, or it could mean backing up your files over the Internet to another building or even another country. One way or another, keeping an extra copy of your data in a secondary, safe location is extremely important; I return to this matter later in this chapter.

Choosing Backup Software

You know that you should back up your Mac, and you know generally what end result you want to achieve, so which backup software do you choose? Years ago, when few backup programs existed for Mac OS X and even fewer had a full range of features, the choice was simple. For most people, in fact, Retrospect (once published by Dantz but now owned by EMC) was the only option worth considering.

Retrospect is still worth considering, but now it's just one of a vast and rapidly growing range of alternatives. Even poring over the specifications of every backup program — much less trying all of them out — requires far more time than most of us have.

Tip

I've compiled a list of more than 100 Mac backup programs, complete with extensive feature comparisons, that you can use to help evaluate your many options and decide what best meets your needs: www.takecontrolbooks.com/resources/0014/. ■

Therefore, what I present here is a short list of questions to consider when looking for backup software, along with some examples of applications that may provide the capabilities you need. You may have additional requirements that go beyond what I mention here, and new or updated backup software may be available by the time you read this, but these features should provide a starting point for making a decision. In any case, bear in mind that you may get the best results from using a combination of two or more programs, each suited to a particular task.

How many computers are you backing up?

Broadly speaking, Mac OS X backup software can be divided into two major categories: consumer programs designed mainly to back up a single computer and enterprise programs designed to back up lots of computers. (There's some overlap, which is to say that some programs optimized for a single Mac can scale up to handle several, and some programs intended to be used for a large network also work just fine on single Macs.) If you're backing up just one Mac, the three Macs in your home, or the ten Macs in your small office, choosing something from the former category makes sense. On the other hand, if you need to back up dozens, hundreds, or thousands of Macs, you need to use a product built from the ground up to handle that sort of configuration.

In the consumer category, there are dozens upon dozens of options, including (to pick just a few prominent examples) the following:

- Time Machine (built into Leopard and Snow Leopard)
- CrashPlan and CrashPlan+ (www.crashplan.com)
- Personal Backup (www.intego.com/personalbackup)
- Data Backup (www.prosofteng.com/products/data_backup_info.php)
- Tri-Backup (www.tri-edre.com/english/tribackup.html)

All of these can handle backing up a single Mac or, with varying degrees of difficulty and success, a small network.

In the enterprise category — software designed for large businesses and priced accordingly — there are fewer options overall. Here are some examples:

- BRU Server (www.tolisgroup.com/products/bruserver)
- CrashPlan PRO (www11.crashplan.com/business)
- NetVault: Backup (www.bakbone.com/products/netvault_mac)
- PresSTORE (www.archiware.de)
- Retrospect Workgroup and Retrospect Server (emcinsignia.com/products/smb/retroformac/comparison)

Some of these enterprise programs come in more consumer-friendly versions too: BRU LE is designed to handle one Mac, whereas Retrospect Desktop can back up the Mac it's installed on plus up to two others (or more, with the purchase of additional licenses).

The thing to keep in mind is that using consumer-oriented backup software for a large network leads to nothing but pain and frustration, whereas using enterprise software on a small network requires you to spend more money and effort than necessary.

Note

Many of the backup programs that run on Mac OS X are also available in versions for other platforms. If you want to use just one program to back up Macs along with Windows or Linux computers, look for multi-platform backup software. ∎

What type(s) of backup do you need?

The majority of Mac backup programs can create versioned backups (although this feature may go by various names). Fewer can create bootable duplicates, but a handful of programs offer only bootable duplicates (and no other type of backup). As of late 2009, only three programs (to my knowledge) offered the capability of creating bootable duplicates over a network: Carbon Copy Cloner, ChronoSync, and Retrospect. If you prefer to keep all your backup media in one central location (or to use a single physical drive, divided into multiple partitions, to store all your bootable duplicates), this rare capability may come in handy.

Crucially, keep in mind that many programs that refer to themselves as backup software offer neither versioned backups nor bootable duplicates. Although they may copy your data onto other media, this is a primitive sort of backup better described as file synchronization. Because so many programs offer more-advanced features, I'd steer clear of these programs as backup tools.

What media will you use?

All the backup software mentioned in this chapter can store your backups on a hard drive. Most of them can also use network volumes as destinations. However, support for optical media and tape drives varies from excellent to nonexistent. When it comes to optical media, Retrospect has the best support, followed at some distance by Data Backup and Personal Backup, with other options further down the scale. Retrospect also has generally good support for tape libraries, as do the various versions of BRU.

How should data be restored?

You've just discovered that a file is missing, you need an old version of a file, or your entire hard disk is unreadable. You have backups, but how exactly do you go about recovering that data? Time Machine (described just ahead) makes the restoration process not only easy but fun, as you zoom back in time in a 3-D star field, select the file you want, and then click a Restore button. Other programs give you something similar but with less theatrics — navigate through a list, select what you want, and then click a button. However, some applications make you jump through lots of hoops to get back your files, and a few offer no restoration capabilities at all, forcing you to manually dig through folders on a backup drive looking for the files you want to restore and then drag them back to your main disk. In short, there's a huge range of variation when it comes to restoring your data, and it's well worth trying out a program's restoration interface before deciding to entrust your backups to the software.

If you use client-server backup programs (including some versions of Retrospect and most enterprise backup applications), restoration of files is typically handled on the server side by an administrator. This means individual users can't simply select a missing file and then click a button to get it back. This may be unavoidable in cases where tape libraries are used and the data can't all be kept online at once, and some administrators may prefer keeping this sort of control away from end users. But because it increases the total amount of time and effort needed to restore data, it's another factor worth considering when choosing a backup approach.

What other special features do you need?

Among the many other features frequently found in backup programs, the following may be especially worth considering:

- **Compression.** Some backup programs compress the data stored on your backup media to save space and, when backing up over a network, reduce the time required to transmit all your files.

- **Encryption.** If you plan to store your backup media in a location outside your physical control, consider a backup program that offers encryption so that no one who might obtain access to your backups can read their contents without your password. Most programs that support backing up files over a network also have an encryption feature. One notable exception is Time Machine, which neither compresses nor encrypts its backups.

- **Deduplication.** Programs designed to back up multiple Macs over a network to a single archive (including CrashPlan and Retrospect) often offer a feature called *deduplication*, which simply means storing only one copy of any given piece of data. For example, if you have two identical copies of a file on your Mac, the software stores just one copy; likewise, if two or more Macs have identical files (such as those that make up Mac OS X itself), the software can still store just one copy. This greatly reduces storage space requirements and makes backups go faster because less data must be copied.

- **Block-level or byte-level incremental updates.** Historically, most backup software has operated on a file level: If a file changes, the whole file gets backed up the next time the backup runs. This can introduce problems when backing up very large (multi-gigabyte) files that change frequently, especially over a network: Backups take a long time to complete and fill up their storage media quickly. Some backup programs — including CrashPlan, QRecall (www.qrecall.com), and almost all Internet backup services (described later in this chapter) — address this problem by offering *block-level* or *byte-level incremental updates*, which means that after the initial backup, they copy only the portions of files that have changed. (A block is a small unit of disk storage, typically 4K on a Mac; a byte is equivalent to a single character.)

- **Rolling (or rotating) backups.** When your backup disk becomes full, Time Machine automatically purges older files to make space for new ones. Numerous programs offer their own versions of this capability, typically with more control than what Time Machine offers. For example, you may be able to set a backup program to keep just the most recent five copies of any particular file or to automatically delete all backups older than 90 days. A few backup programs don't perform incremental backups — they copy every file, every time — but they do so without deleting older files, letting you specify how many full backups to keep.

- **Appropriate scheduling.** Backup software is most effective when it runs automatically, without your manual intervention. In years past, conventional wisdom held that backups should be scheduled to run in the middle of the night, under the assumption that an active backup would take a long time, during which it would slow down one's computer to the point that it's nearly unusable. Although that's still true of some backup software, most modern Mac backup programs can run almost invisibly in the background without dragging down your computer's performance significantly, and in many cases, incremental backups take just a few minutes anyway. Numerous backup programs have abandoned the notion of an explicit schedule altogether and instead simply look for file changes constantly, backing up any new or changed data immediately.

Bottom-line recommendations

Taking all the previous information into consideration, what backup software do I recommend?

For individual users, Time Machine (described next) is an excellent choice for versioned backups, and either SuperDuper! or Carbon Copy Cloner is perfect for bootable duplicates. Other good all-around choices — all of which handle versioned backups as well as bootable duplicates — include Data Backup, Personal Backup, and Tri-Backup.

For backing up a handful of Macs, my current favorite is CrashPlan+, which lacks the slick interface of Time Machine but offers compression, encryption, and a long list of other powerful features, including the capability to back up to your friends' computers over the Internet. Alternatively, Retrospect 8 can handle just about any backup task you throw at it and scales up to dozens or thousands of computers — but it costs more and has a steeper learning curve.

In any case, before making a final decision, I suggest that you review the information at `www.takecontrolbooks.com/resources/0014/`, download demo versions of the products that seem to fit your needs best, and try them out to see how well they perform and how easy they are to use.

In terms of enterprise backup for Mac, BRU and Retrospect are the best-known names, although some of their competitors are also quite robust. Because enterprise requirements and specifics vary so much, I can make no blanket recommendations — except to say that you should carefully compare each product's specifications with your company's backup policy.

Using Time Machine

For individual users, Time Machine offers the easiest possible way to create a versioned backup of an entire hard disk. In some cases, it can be configured with a grand total of one click. It's fast and efficient (particularly under Snow Leopard), works with local drives or over a network, makes file restoration a piece of cake, and even provides a way of restoring an entire disk if your hard drive should fail entirely.

To be sure, Time Machine isn't for everyone. Because it lacks compression, deduplication, and block-level incremental updates, its backups occupy a considerable amount of disk space; this makes it less than ideal for backing up more than a few Macs over a network to a central location. In addition, it can't create bootable duplicates, encrypt your backups, or back up to certain kinds of network volumes. However, the majority of Mac users don't need any of those capabilities, and because the software comes with Leopard and Snow Leopard, it makes an obvious first choice for a great many people.

How Time Machine works

Fundamentally, Time Machine asks for just one piece of information: What volume do you want to use to back up your Mac? As a result, every time you connect a new hard drive to your Mac, an alert pops up on the screen (as shown in Figure 8.1) asking if you want to use this volume as a destination for Time Machine. If you click Use as Backup Disk — that's the single click I mentioned a moment ago — you do three things at once: designate that volume as your destination, turn on Time Machine, and stop all future alerts when you connect new hard drives. You can also opt to back up to a network volume, although mounting a shared network volume doesn't produce an automatic alert.

After you turn on Time Machine, the software automatically runs in the background, making a complete copy of your startup disk (and any other locally mounted volumes) on your selected destination volume. Thereafter, it runs once an hour, updating your backup with whatever files were added or changed since the last run. Unless you hear your disk clicking or happen to notice a spinning clock icon in your menu bar, you may not even notice that Time Machine is doing anything.

If the backup drive is unavailable when Time Machine would otherwise run, it simply waits until the drive is online again, and then performs its next backup. This is especially important for laptops that may not have continuous access to the external or network volumes where backups are stored.

FIGURE 8.1

Setting up a backup doesn't get easier than this. To turn on Time Machine and tell it to use this newly connected disk, click Use as Backup Disk.

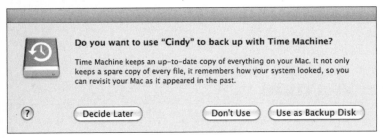

Time Machine automatically purges your backups from time to time. It always keeps the last 24 hourly backups, the last backup of each day for a month, and the last backup of each week for as long as possible. When your destination disk gets full, Time Machine begins deleting your oldest weekly and daily backups as necessary to make space for new backups.

If you need to restore a file that's been backed up, all you do is click the Time Machine icon in your Dock, use the controls on-screen to skip back to an earlier state of one of your folders, select what you need, and then click a button. I describe restoring data in more detail later in this chapter.

Time Machine offers only a few options you can configure, making it simple to use but less flexible than other programs. You can change the destination disk, exclude particular files or folders from your backups, prevent Time Machine from running automatically every hour, choose whether to back up while your laptop is running on battery, and turn on or off the status menu and the alert that appears when backups are deleted to save disk space. But that's about it.

Choosing hardware for Time Machine

Time Machine always stores its backups on a hard drive of some sort, but that still gives you a number of options:

- **Local hard drive.** Any locally attached hard drive can be a destination for Time Machine. That includes a secondary internal drive (on Macs that can accommodate one) and external USB, FireWire, or eSATA drives. For that matter, anything that identifies itself to your Mac as an external drive can work, including a RAID and even the popular Drobo device (www.drobo.com). Drives must be formatted as Mac OS Extended (Journaled) — either the case-sensitive or case-insensitive version — and drives over 512 GB in size must be partitioned using the GUID Partition Table or Apple Partition Map (and not Master Boot Record, the default for PC hard drives). You get the best results if you choose a larger hard drive rather than a smaller one and a faster interface rather than a slower one (for example, FireWire 800 is faster than either FireWire 400 or USB 2.0). Apple recommends that a Time Machine volume not be used for anything else.

- **Hard drive attached to another Mac.** Time Machine can also back up your Mac over a wired or wireless network. For this to work, you must have a Mac running Leopard, Leopard Server, Snow Leopard, or Snow Leopard Server, and it also must have a drive shared using the Apple Filing Protocol. (Time Machine doesn't work with FTP or SMB shares.) The requirements for disk format and partitioning are the same as for locally attached drives.

- **Time Capsule.** Apple's Time Capsule is a device that combines an 802.11a/b/g/n Wi-Fi access point, an Ethernet switch, and a network-accessible hard drive in a single unit. It also includes a USB port, which you can use to add one or more external drives (or to share a printer). Macs on your network can back up to a Time Capsule either wirelessly or over Ethernet.

Note
If you attach an external hard drive to an AirPort Extreme base station (a configuration called an AirPort Disk), that disk shows up as a possible destination in Time Machine. However, Apple doesn't officially endorse or support using an AirPort Disk as a Time Machine destination, and anecdotal evidence suggests that this is an unreliable setup. ■

- **Other options.** Officially, Time Machine doesn't support other destinations, such as third-party *NAS* (network-attached storage) devices, which are basically one or more hard drives with a network interface. However, at least one manufacturer (LaCie) offers several such products that it claims work correctly with Time Machine. Others may follow.

Locally attached hard drives provide the best performance, with far better throughput than what you'd get with a wired Ethernet connection or an 802.11n wireless connection. However, a network-based option may be more convenient, especially for users of laptops who don't want to be tethered to an external drive all the time. Storing backups on a network device also lets you back up multiple computers to a single drive, reducing the number of devices you need (although that single drive may need to be quite large).

The main advantage of a Time Capsule over a drive attached to a computer is that you need not keep another Mac on, awake, and available for backups all the time. Because a Time Capsule duplicates the features of an AirPort Extreme base station, it can also reduce the total number of devices you need in your home or office. On the other hand, if you already have a Mac running all the time (a server, for example), you can save money by simply adding a hard drive to that Mac and then letting that hold your Time Machine backups.

Configuring Time Machine

If you didn't use the one-click setup when connecting your drive, you can set it up by following these steps:

1. Choose ⌘ ➪ System Preferences to open System Preferences and then click Time Machine to open the Time Machine pane, as shown in Figure 8.2.

FIGURE 8.2

Time Machine has only a few user-configurable options, which you can set in this preference pane.

2. **Click Choose Backup Disk (in Leopard) or Select Backup Disk (in Snow Leopard).** A dialog box opens in which all eligible disks currently mounted on your Mac are listed.

3. **Select the volume you want to use and then click Use for Backup.** Time Machine becomes active immediately, and your first backup begins in two minutes.

4. **Close System Preferences.**

If you later want to use a different disk to hold your backups, repeat these steps, except that the Choose Backup Disk (or Select Backup Disk) button in step 2 becomes the Change Disk button.

Ordinarily, Time Machine backs up everything — every single file on your startup disk as well as every single file on any other locally attached (internal or external) hard disks. Time Machine doesn't back up mounted network volumes or optical discs. Backing up everything is the safest practice because it means you can return your entire disk to a functional state if anything goes wrong and get back every file. However, in a couple of circumstances, you may want to exclude certain items from your backups:

- **You have very large files that change often.** If your disk contains multi-gigabyte files that change constantly, that means Time Machine must back them up almost every time it runs. The result is that you rapidly fill up your backup disk, and in some cases, each hourly backup may take so long to complete that you're nearly always in the process of backing up. Examples of files that fall into this category are Entourage's database and the virtual disks used by programs such as Parallels Desktop and VMware Fusion.

- **You're short on backup disk space.** Your backup disk needs enough capacity to back up all the files on your Mac plus extra space to hold multiple versions of your files and new files that you add. If you don't have or can't afford a sufficiently large backup disk, you may have to omit certain items so that your backups can fit in the space you have.

Along with excluding items from your backups, Time Machine lets you choose whether backups should occur when your laptop is running on battery power and whether you want to see an alert when your backup disk is full and Time Machine begins purging older files. You configure all these things in Time Machine's Options dialog box.

To set your preferred Time Machine options, follow these steps:

1. **Choose ⌘ ⇨ System Preferences to open System Preferences and then click Time Machine to open the Time Machine pane.**

2. **Click Options to open the Options dialog box.**

3. **In the Options dialog box (as shown in Figure 8.3), click the Add (+) button, navigate to the file or folder you want to exclude, select it, and then click Exclude.** Repeat this step to exclude more items.

4. **Optionally, to enable Time Machine to back up your laptop when it's not plugged in to AC power, click the Back up while on battery power check box.**

5. Optionally, to see an alert when your backup disk is full and Time Machine begins removing older files, click the Warn when old backups are deleted check box (in Leopard) or the Notify after old backups are deleted check box (in Snow Leopard).

6. Click Done and then close System Preferences.

FIGURE 8.3

To exclude files or folders from your Time Machine backups, add them to the list in this dialog box. This figure shows the dialog box in Leopard; the Snow Leopard version differs slightly.

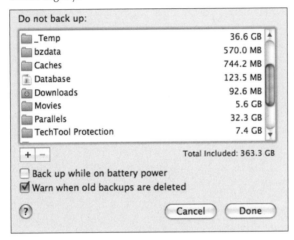

Tip

Besides excluding files from Time Machine, you can also manually delete items that have already been backed up. To delete all instances of a single file or folder, navigate to that item in the Finder and then click the Time Machine icon in your Dock. When the time travel display opens, select the item you want to remove and then choose Delete All Backups of "File Name" from the Action pop-up menu on the toolbar, type your password when prompted, and then click OK. To delete an entire snapshot (all the files backed up in a particular hourly run), follow the same procedure but choose Delete Backup from the Action pop-up menu. ∎

Managing Time Machine behavior

For most people, Time Machine requires no manual interaction. It automatically runs every hour, removes old backups as necessary, and remains mostly invisible until you want to restore files. If you have a reasonably fast computer and, for network backups, a reasonably fast network, Time Machine's operation should be nearly undetectable.

With slower Macs, slower hard disks, slower network connections, or some combination of these, you may find that Time Machine bogs down your computer while it runs or reduces network performance. And if you're sensitive to noise, you may be put off by the clattering of your hard drive as it stores your backups. In cases such as these, you can back up manually with Time Machine instead of relying on its once-an-hour schedule.

Note

Apple provides no official way to adjust the Time Machine schedule to anything other than once per hour. If you'd prefer that it ran once every six hours or only overnight, you're out of luck. You can adjust the interval, however — at your own risk — by modifying Time Machine's preference file. An easy way to do this is to use a free utility called TimeMachineScheduler (www.klieme.com/TimeMachineScheduler.html), **which lets you set the backup interval to anywhere from 1 to 12 hours, specify the times of day during which Time Machine can run, and adjust other options that affect Time Machine's user interface.** ■

To use Time Machine manually, choose ❖ ➪ System Preferences, click Time Machine, and then click Off. Then, whenever you want to initiate a backup, you can either Control+click the Time Machine icon in the Dock and then choose Back Up Now or click the Time Machine icon in your menu bar (as shown in Figure 8.4) and then choose Back Up Now from the menu.

If the Time Machine menu doesn't appear in your menu bar, choose ❖ ➪ System Preferences, click Time Machine, and then click the Show Time Machine status in the menu bar check box.

FIGURE 8.4

The Time Machine menu lets you run backups manually, even when Time Machine is turned off.

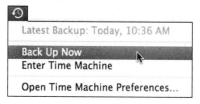

Restoring data from Time Machine

Backups are of no value if you can't restore your data when a problem arises, and when it comes to restoring individual files and folders, Time Machine has one of the most convenient and easy-to-use interfaces of any backup software. You can also restore data from within Mail, Address Book, or iPhoto to recover individual pieces of data without having to know where the underlying files are stored on your disk. And you can use Time Machine to restore an entire disk, if necessary.

Restoring individual items in the Finder

The usual way to restore something in Time Machine — an individual file or folder — is by following these steps:

1. **In the Finder, navigate to the folder where the item you want is stored (if you're looking for an old version) or where it used to be stored (if it's been deleted).**

If you're unsure where the item is (or was), type a portion of its name into the Spotlight search field on the toolbar of any Finder window.

2. **Click the Time Machine icon in the Dock.** As Time Machine activates, your Finder switches into a time travel display in which the current folder appears against a starry background, with earlier versions behind it, receding into the distance. Figure 8.5 shows an example.

FIGURE 8.5

Travel back in time in this 3-D star field to recover files and folders that Time Machine has backed up.

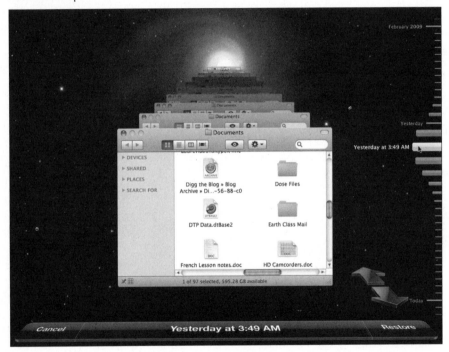

3. **Navigate back to an earlier state of the folder in one of the following ways:**

   - Click the arrows in the lower-right corner of the screen to move backward or forward through time. With each click, you go to the next backup in which the folder's contents were different from the one you're currently looking at.

   - Move your mouse along the right edge of the screen to see the dates (or times) of each backup Time Machine currently stores and then click to select a backup.

4. **When you find the item you're looking for, select it and then click Restore.** The Time Machine view disappears, and Time Machine copies the file or folder back to its original location. However, note the following:

   - If the folder to which you're restoring the item already contains a file or folder of the same name, Time Machine displays an alert asking what you want to do. Click Keep Original to cancel restoring the item, retaining the version currently in the folder. Click Replace to overwrite the current file with the restored backup. Or click Keep Both to rename the current file and also restore the backup.

   - If you want to restore an item to a location other than the one it came from, select it and, instead of clicking Restore, choose Restore "*filename*" to from the Action pop-up menu on the toolbar, navigate to the spot you want to store the recovered item, and then click Choose.

Restoring data in Mail, Address Book, and iPhoto

At present, three Apple applications — Mail, Address Book, and iPhoto — enable you to restore Time Machine backups from within the application. (Other supported applications may appear in the future.) The basic procedure is the same as restoring files in the Finder, except that you can restore individual Mail messages, Address Book contacts, or photographs without knowing where the corresponding files are on disk.

To restore data from within any of these programs, follow these steps:

1. **Navigate to the location where the data used to be or where the current, incorrect information is.**

2. **Click the Time Machine icon in the Dock.** The time travel display opens, with copies of your application's window rather than the Finder window receding into the background.

3. **Navigate to an earlier backup, just as in step 3 in the previous set of instructions.**

4. **When you find the item you're looking for, select it and then click Restore.** In Address Book and iPhoto (but not in Mail), you can also restore all the data from that particular backup by clicking Restore All. The Time Machine view disappears, and Time Machine copies the item back to its original location.

Restoring an entire disk

Although Time Machine can't create a bootable duplicate, it does copy every file on your disk, so it can restore a disk to an earlier (and bootable) state. However, the process to do so is somewhat involved and time-consuming. To restore an entire disk, follow these steps:

1. **Insert your Mac OS X Install DVD.**

2. **Restart your Mac and immediately hold down the C key until the Apple logo appears.**

3. **When the installer runs, select your language on the initial screen.**

4. **If your backup is stored on a Time Capsule to which you connect wirelessly, select your Time Capsule's name from the AirPort menu and then type your password if prompted to do so.**

5. **Choose Utilities ⇨ Restore System from Backup to open a screen in which you can initiate the restoration process, and then click Continue.**

6. **Select your Time Machine disk and then click Continue to advance to the next screen.**

7. **If the disk you selected has backups for more than one Mac, choose the one whose backups you want to restore from the Restore From pop-up menu.**

8. **In the list of backups, select the one you want to restore and then click Continue to advance to the next screen.**

9. **Select your Mac's internal disk as the destination and then click Restore.** You may see an additional prompt asking to confirm that you want to restore your data. Time Machine then restores all your data. The process may take several hours. When the process is complete, follow the on-screen instructions to restart your Mac.

Creating Bootable Duplicates

In addition to the versioned backups you can get with Time Machine or other comparable programs, a complete backup plan should include bootable duplicates, which can enable you to get back to work almost instantly in the event of a serious disk problem.

What's a bootable duplicate?

As I said at the beginning of this chapter, a bootable duplicate is a copy of your entire startup disk, created in such a way that you can boot your Mac from it. Back in the days of Mac OS 9 and earlier, you could create a bootable disk simply by dragging your System Folder from your startup disk to another disk and then opening and closing the copied folder to *bless* it, or get the system to recognize it as valid. However, those days are long gone. If you were to drag all the visible files from your Mac OS X startup disk to another disk, you'd miss all the crucial invisible files that make up the Unix core of the operating system. And even if you did manage to copy those invisible files, they'd almost certainly have their ownership and permissions altered during the copy process in such a way that the end result would no longer be a bootable system. Add to that a few special maintenance tasks (comparable to blessing a System Folder in Mac OS 9), and you have an operation that's too complex and error-prone to attempt by hand.

Fortunately, numerous backup programs know just what to do and can put all the right things in the right places and in the right way. I discuss some of these programs just ahead.

Note
Even the best backup programs don't copy every single file from your startup disk when creating a bootable duplicate — they intentionally leave out certain items, such as cache files and other data, that Mac OS X prefers to re-create from scratch on a new volume. ■

But a bootable duplicate requires more than the right software. You also need the right hardware. In order for a backup to be bootable, it must be stored on its own volume — that is, a disk or a partition on a disk. You can't boot from a disk image or a network volume; therefore, even if you stored a perfect copy of Mac OS X in such a location, it wouldn't serve as a bootable duplicate. Similarly, although you could instruct your backup software to copy everything from your startup disk into a folder on another volume, the result wouldn't be bootable. The duplicate must have the volume all to itself, and that volume must be attached locally.

When I say "attached locally," I'm referring to a hard drive connected to your Mac via FireWire or USB — or installed inside your Mac and connected via SATA or IDE, depending on the interface your Mac uses internally. (No Macs currently ship with built-in eSATA connectors. Some third-party eSATA cards support booting from an eSATA drive, but not all do.)

Note

Intel-based Macs can boot from either USB or FireWire external drives. FireWire (of either the 400 Mbps or 800 Mbps variety) provides better performance than USB 2.0, but not all new Macs have FireWire ports. PowerPC-based Macs, on the other hand, can boot from FireWire drives but not from USB drives. ∎

The two most popular programs for creating bootable duplicates are SuperDuper! and Carbon Copy Cloner. I describe these next.

Tip

To reduce the number of drives you have to buy and manage, consider using a single large drive for both versioned backups and bootable duplicates. Use Disk Utility to divide the disk into two partitions, direct Time Machine (or your other backup software) to use one of them, and then store your bootable duplicate on the other. ∎

Using SuperDuper!

SuperDuper!, from Shirt Pocket Software (http://shirtpocket.com/), is renowned for its simplicity, its clarity, and the reassuring, plain-English explanations it provides of what is about to happen. Although it can do a few tricks besides creating bootable duplicates, that's its main feature and its forte. The program costs $27.95, although its basic functionality is free; after paying for and registering the program, you unlock additional (extremely important) features, such as scheduled backups and the capability to update a duplicate incrementally instead of having to recopy every file every time. The instructions that follow are based on the full paid version.

To duplicate your startup disk with SuperDuper!, follow these steps:

1. **After installing SuperDuper! (in the location of your choice), double-click its icon to launch it.** The main SuperDuper! window, as shown in Figure 8.6, opens.

2. **If the lock icon in the lower-left corner of the pane is in the locked state, click it, type your username and password, and then click OK.**

3. **From the Copy pop-up menu on the left, choose the name of your startup disk (the one you're copying from).**

4. From the To pop-up menu on the right, choose the name of your destination disk (the one you're copying to).

5. Choose Backup - all files from the Using pop-up menu.

6. Click Options to switch the window to its Options view, as shown in Figure 8.7.

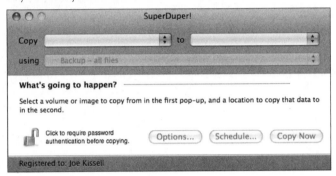

FIGURE 8.6

The SuperDuper! window initially shows just a few options; more information appears as you make your selections.

7. **In the General pane, choose Smart Update** *Destination* **from** *Source* **from the During copy pop-up menu.** This isn't strictly necessary for your initial backup, but it saves tremendous time on subsequent backups, and because you may be scheduling future backups in the next step, it's best to choose this now.

8. **Choose Quit SuperDuper! from the On successful completion pop-up menu and then click OK.**

9. **Optionally, to schedule this duplication procedure to recur on a schedule, click Schedule to open the Scheduled Copies dialog box, as shown in Figure 8.8.**

10. **Click to select the days on which you want the backup to occur, select a time by using the Start copying at controls, and then click OK to close the Scheduled Copies dialog box.**

11. **Back in the main SuperDuper! window, which should now resemble Figure 8.9, click Copy Now.** SuperDuper! duplicates your disk — a process that may take anywhere from several minutes to several hours — and then quits automatically.

At the end of the duplication process, your destination disk contains a complete bootable copy of your startup disk. I explain how to use the copy later in this chapter.

FIGURE 8.7

In this dialog box, specify the options with which you want SuperDuper! to create a duplicate.

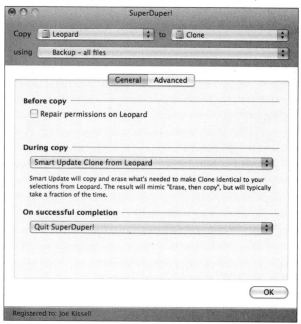

FIGURE 8.8

To schedule SuperDuper! to update your bootable duplicate automatically, select one or more days and a time in this dialog box.

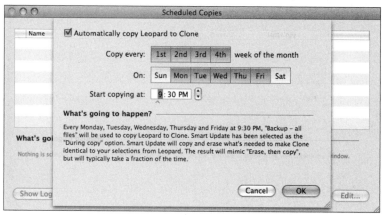

Note

Whether or not you opted to schedule recurring backups in step 9, you can use SuperDuper! manually at any time to clone one disk to another. ■

FIGURE 8.9

Once you've specified all the options that you want SuperDuper! to use, you can create a duplicate by clicking Copy Now.

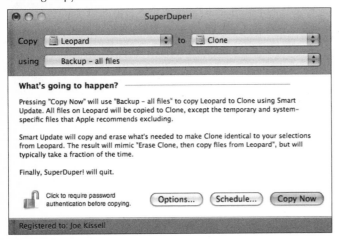

Using Carbon Copy Cloner

Shortly after the initial release of Mac OS X, developer Mike Bombich released Carbon Copy Cloner, the first genuinely easy-to-use tool for creating a bootable duplicate. Over the years, this utility has undergone significant transformations. It now rivals SuperDuper! in ease of use and remains rock solid in reliability. And it's even free (donations requested).

Although Carbon Copy Cloner lacks some of the advanced features of SuperDuper!, it does offer one significant benefit: the capability to create a bootable duplicate over a network. You can't boot from the duplicate over the network — you must directly connect the drive to your Mac in order to boot from it — but this capability makes it convenient to create duplicates of all the Macs in your home or business to a central location. Creating duplicates over a network requires a number of steps I don't cover here; consult the Carbon Copy Cloner documentation for complete details.

To duplicate your startup disk with Carbon Copy Cloner, follow these steps:

1. **After installing Carbon Copy Cloner (in the location of your choice), double-click its icon to launch it.** The main Carbon Copy Cloner window, as shown in Figure 8.10, opens.

2. **If the lock icon in the lower-left corner of the pane is in the locked state, click it, type your username and password, and then click OK.**

3. **From the Source Disk pop-up menu, choose the name of your startup disk (the one you're copying from).**

4. **From the Target Disk pop-up menu, choose the name of your target disk (the one you're copying to).**

5. **From the Cloning options pop-up menu, choose Incremental backup of selected items.** This isn't strictly necessary for your initial backup, but it saves tremendous time on subsequent backups, and because you may be scheduling future backups in the next step, it's best to choose this now.

6. **Click the Delete items that don't exist on the source check box.**

7. **Optionally, to schedule this duplication procedure to recur on a schedule, click Save Task to open the Backup Task Scheduler window, as shown in Figure 8.11.**

8. **Using the controls in the Schedule pane, select how often you want the schedule to run.** To change the schedule's name, double-click the word Untitled and type a new name.

9. **Click Save and then close the window.**

10. **Back in the main Carbon Copy Cloner window, which should now resemble Figure 8.12, click Clone.** Carbon Copy Cloner duplicates your disk — a process that may take anywhere from several minutes to several hours. When the process completes, quit Carbon Copy Cloner.

At the end of the cloning process, your target disk contains a complete bootable copy of your startup disk. I explain how to use the copy just ahead.

FIGURE 8.10

Like SuperDuper!, Carbon Copy Cloner has a simple, straightforward interface.

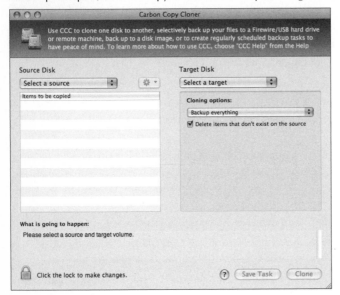

FIGURE 8.11

In the Backup Task Scheduler window, you can tell Carbon Copy Cloner when to automatically update your duplicate.

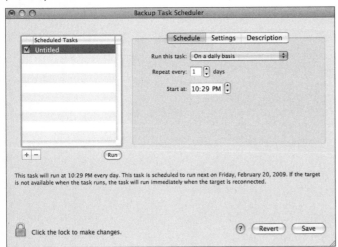

FIGURE 8.12

Once you've set up the options you want in Carbon Copy Cloner, just click Clone to duplicate your disk.

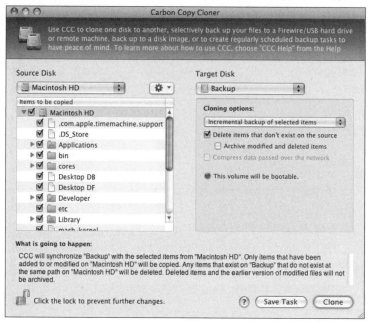

Other options

Of the utilities that do nothing but create (and update) bootable duplicates, SuperDuper! and Carbon Copy Cloner have especially well-earned reputations for reliability and ease of use. However, dozens of other backup applications also offer this capability, including full-featured backup programs such as Data Backup from Prosoft, Retrospect from EMC, Personal Backup from Intego, and Tri-Backup from Tri-Edre.

Two other notable utilities that can make bootable duplicates are ChronoSync ($40; from Econ Technologies; www.econtechnologies.com/pages/cs/chrono_overview.html) and Disk Utility from Apple. ChronoSync, which was designed mainly as a file synchronization tool, gained the capability to create bootable duplicates — even over a network — in version 4.0, released early in 2009. Although it's not quite as easy to use as SuperDuper! or Carbon Copy Cloner, it has a long list of powerful features that the others lack.

Disk Utility can also create bootable duplicates, but because it can't update them incrementally or run on a schedule, it's not ideal for frequent use. However, if you want to duplicate your startup volume with Disk Utility, follow these steps:

1. Open Disk Utility, which is located in /Applications/Utilities.

2. In the list on the left, select any hard disk.

3. Click the Restore tab.

4. From the list on the left, drag your startup volume into the Source field.

5. From the list on the left, drag your destination volume into the Destination field.

6. **Click the Erase destination check box.** The window should now resemble Figure 8.13.

7. **Click Restore.** Disk Utility copies the source volume onto the destination volume, a time-consuming process.

8. When the copying process has completed, quit Disk Utility.

FIGURE 8.13

Disk Utility doesn't have the clearest interface for creating a bootable duplicate, but the window should look something like this.

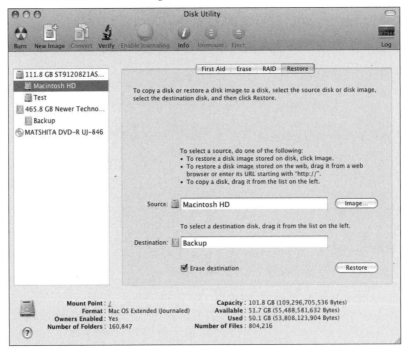

Starting up from a bootable duplicate

If your main startup disk dies or for any other reason you want to start up from your bootable duplicate, first connect it to your Mac. Then, follow these steps:

1. **Power on your Mac (if it's turned off) or restart it (if it's already on) and immediately hold down Option until the Apple logo appears.** The window displays icons for each disk attached to the computer on which your Mac sees a valid startup volume.

2. **Using the mouse or the arrow keys, select the external hard drive containing your duplicate.**

3. **Press Return.** Your Mac boots from the selected disk.

At this point, your Mac should behave exactly as it did when you created (or updated) your bootable duplicate. You can now use your Mac normally or, if need be, run disk repair utilities on your startup disk.

If your internal disk is badly damaged and you want to replace its data with what's on your duplicate, use SuperDuper! or Carbon Copy Cloner, following all the same steps as you did originally — but choosing your external volume as the source and your normal internal startup disk as the destination.

Note

If you updated your versioned backups more recently than your bootable duplicate, you may also need to restore any recently modified files using Time Machine or whichever backup software you use to bring your newly restored startup disk completely up to date. ∎

Using Internet Backup Services

An increasingly popular way to back up your Mac is to use one of the growing number of Internet backup services. To oversimplify somewhat, backing up over the Internet is much like backing up to another server on your local network, except that your files are stored in a data center somewhere far from your home or office. Internet backup services offer numerous benefits but also suffer from some noteworthy drawbacks, so for most people, they're best seen as a supplement to local backups rather than as a replacement.

Internet backup basics

Conceptually, Internet backup services do nothing more than move the hard disk on which backups are stored from your home or office to a big, noisy, climate-controlled room full of servers far away. The software most online backup providers use is similar to desktop backup software in that it stores multiple versions of your files, lets you choose what to back up (or exclude) and how often, and also offers a convenient way to restore your data — often along with a few additional features.

To keep your data safe and minimize the amount of information that must be sent over the Internet, online backup services tend to use software that offers encryption, compression, block-level or byte-level incremental updates, and deduplication (all described earlier in this chapter). In addition, many of them offer *bandwidth throttling* (enabling you to reduce the amount of upstream bandwidth used to back up files) and continuous operation (backing up files as they change, or shortly thereafter, rather than waiting for a scheduled backup).

The major benefit of Internet backups is that they're automatically stored offsite. No matter what tragedy were to befall your computers, their data would still be safe — in another city or possibly even another country. Such services are a benefit to laptop users who spend a lot of time on the road, in that backup and restoration are possible wherever you can find a broadband Internet connection. And most backup software in this category is of the set-and-forget variety, requiring little or no manual involvement.

The biggest downside is speed. Most broadband Internet connections in the United States have much less bandwidth available for uploads than for downloads. Upstream bandwidth of 1 Mbps or less is common, with real-world throughput typically much lower — and that bandwidth must be shared by any other applications you use that send data over the Internet. Even under ideal conditions, it could take almost five days to upload 50 GB of data over a 1 Mbps connection, and if you have more data, a slower connection, or both, your first full backup can easily take several weeks. And although restoring files may be much quicker than backing them up, it could still take several days to restore all your data.

Note

If you have an enormous amount of data to back up online and a relatively slow Internet connection, ask your Internet backup provider if they offer a seeding service, whereby you make an initial full backup onto a hard drive and ship it to them so that only incremental updates must travel over the network. ■

Besides the time it takes to back up your computer, relying on online backups means you're relying on your Internet connection. If your connection goes down for any reason, you can't back up or restore your files. And because online backups are typically used for only a portion of one's files (to save cost and time), you increase the chances that some file you need wasn't included in your backup.

For all these reasons, online backups make the most sense as a secondary backup — an insurance policy in case something goes wrong with your main, locally stored backups. As long as you have a local backup, it's not a serious problem if your first full backup over the Internet takes a long time or if your connection isn't always available. But relying solely on an Internet backup service is unwise.

Choosing a provider

Before entrusting your data to an online backup provider, you should review their terms of service, read reviews, and try them out with a small amount of data. (Most services offer a free trial period or ongoing free backups of 1 or 2 GB of data.) When evaluating a service, ask yourself these questions:

- **Does the pricing make sense?** Some services offer flat-fee pricing for unlimited data from a single Mac; some charge by the gigabyte; still others offer hybrid plans. Consider the amount of data you need to back up and the number of computers, bearing in mind that the total data stored will increase over time.

- **How easy is the software to use?** Try restoring several different kinds of files, from different dates, to get a feel for the restoration process.

- **Are business-grade features available?** If you're backing up many Macs in a business setting, you probably want capabilities such as centralized administration and restoration as well as the option to use your own servers (instead of or in addition to the ones offered by the backup provider). Several online backup services have separate offerings for individuals and businesses.

- **What are the company's future prospects?** Because online backups probably won't be your only backups, it wouldn't be the end of the world if the company hosting them went out of business — but it would be an inconvenience. Consider how long the company has been in business and its reputation, and read independent reviews and opinions if possible.

The range of companies offering online backup services is constantly growing, and their offerings and prices change frequently. So, although the specifics of this list may have changed by the time you read this, it should give you a representative sampling of what's likely to be available. Among the better-known online backup services are:

- **Backblaze.** A relative newcomer to the online backup world, Backblaze (`www.backblaze.com`) offers unlimited storage of backups from a single computer for $5 per month. You can restore files over the Internet or request that the company deliver your data overnight on a DVD or external hard drive.

- **BackJack.** BackJack (`www.backjack.com`), based in Canada, is the oldest Internet backup provider for the Mac. The company offers plans for individual, small business, and enterprise users. Pricing for individual plans is considerably higher than most competing services, however.

- **CrashPlan.** Using the free CrashPlan software (from Code 42 Software) or the more-powerful $59.99 CrashPlan+ software (`www.crashplan.com`), you can back up your computer to a hard disk, another computer you own, a friend's computer anywhere on the Internet, or the company's datacenter (CrashPlan Central). Online backups start at $54 per year ($4.50 per month) for unlimited data from a single computer or $100 per year ($8.33 per month) for unlimited data from multiple computers; discounts are available for multi-year subscriptions. In addition, the company offers CrashPlan PRO for business, a backup system that can use a business's own servers, the Code 42 servers, or both for backups.

- **Dropbox.** Primarily designed for file sharing and syncing, Dropbox (`www.getdropbox.com`) can also be used for backups and for storing multiple versions of each uploaded file. The service offers 2 GB of free storage, 50 GB of storage for $9.95 per month, or 100 GB of storage for $19.99 per month.

- **Mozy.** Mozy (`www.mozy.com`), owned by a subsidiary of EMC (the company that develops Retrospect), offers online backups for individuals (MozyHome, $4.95 per month for unlimited data from a single computer) and businesses (MozyPro, $3.95 per desktop license or $6.95 per server license plus $0.50 per gigabyte per month).

- **steekUP.** steekUP (`http://steekup.com/`), based in France, provides full-featured online backups with storage amounts ranging from 1 GB (free) to 100 GB ($99.90 per year or $169.90 for two years).

- **S3 and JungleDisk.** S3 (Simple Storage Service; `http://aws.amazon.com/s3/`) from Amazon provides inexpensive file storage on the Amazon servers, with pricing based on the amount of data you store and transfer. But the storage isn't directly accessible with most backup programs, so the best way to get to it is by using JungleDisk (`www.jungledisk.com`), a program that costs $2 per month and provides user-friendly access to S3 storage space as well as complete backup capabilities.

Note

You can see feature comparisons of these and other online backup services in the tables I offer at `www.takecontrolbooks.com/resources/0014/`. ■

Managing Backup Media

In this chapter, I focus on backup methods that use hard disks as the storage medium. But whether you use disks, tapes, or optical discs, the same basic rules apply to handling and storing your backup media. Even the most thorough, diligent backups are worthless if the media on which they're stored is lost or damaged.

Offsite backups

The first rule of managing your backup media is to have at least two copies of all your data and to keep those copies in different places. One reason for keeping multiple backups is that any particular disk or tape can fail randomly, but it's much less likely that two or more backups would fail at the same time. But keeping all your backups in one location is like keeping all your eggs in one basket. If your home burns down or your office is burglarized and all your backups are right there near your computer, they'll all be gone, and you'll be out of luck. Therefore, common sense dictates that one of your copies should be kept somewhere else — preferably someplace reasonably far from the source.

One way to achieve this end — multiple copies, with at least one offsite — is to make two or more physical copies of everything and move one of them to another spot on a regular schedule (such as once a week). In the case of a Time Machine backup or a bootable duplicate, this could mean using one backup hard drive for a week and then unplugging it, plugging in a different one that you'll use for the following week, taking the first drive to another location, and repeating this procedure each week.

Another option is to use an Internet backup service as your offsite backup. Because the servers are already located in another building — and almost certainly one that's highly resistant to fire, theft, and other threats — you can get your data offsite without having to move anything physical. If you have to back up massive amounts of data, this approach may be infeasible due to the cost of online backups and the time required to move that much information over the Internet. But for modest amounts of data, Internet backups can save considerable trouble.

Keeping media comfortable

Both local copies and offsite copies of your data should be kept in an environment that discourages deterioration. Specifically, cool (but not freezing), dry, dark places are good; heat, moisture, and light are bad. Magnetic media (tapes and disks) should also be kept well clear of magnets and strong electrical fields, and hard disks should be protected from excessive vibration. So, a safe-deposit box, a fireproof safe, or even a sturdy desk drawer could be a good storage spot; a cold garage, a car's glove compartment, or a sunny windowsill would not.

Testing and recopying media

Regardless of what media, software, or backup techniques you use, another cardinal rule of managing your media is to perform test restores regularly. Over time, backup media can develop errors, and backup software can malfunction (failing to write data correctly in the first place). So, at least once a month, spot-check each piece of backup media by attempting to restore a few random files. If restoration fails, replace that media immediately.

In addition to testing your backups, keep in mind that all storage media have finite life spans. Magnetic particles on a hard disk won't hold their charge forever, and optical media degrades over time. Some brands of optical media are rated as *archival* storage, meaning they should in theory retain their data for several decades or longer, but these kinds of media haven't been around long enough for these claims to be verified empirically. So, for any data you expect to keep around for an extended period of time, consider recopying it onto fresh media every two to three years.

RAID and Data Redundancy

The acronym RAID stands for Redundant Array of Independent (or Inexpensive) Disks. In a RAID, two or more physical disks are combined in any of numerous ways to behave as a single disk. RAIDs come in many flavors, each designed to meet certain needs.

For example, in a striped, or RAID 0, array, data is divided evenly among all the disks; because portions of each file can be written to and read from multiple disks in parallel, overall performance increases. However, if any disk in a RAID 0 array were to fail, all the data would be lost because no single disk contains a complete copy of any file.

Note
Because RAID 0 arrays don't provide any data redundancy, I don't discuss them further in this book. ■

In a mirrored, or RAID 1, array, identical data is written to two or more disks at once. That means that if any disk in the array were to fail, all the data would still be intact; if the faulty disk were replaced, it could rebuild its mirror from the other disk(s) still in the array.

In a concatenated RAID, also known as JBOD (Just a Bunch of Disks), two or more disks appear as a single large volume whose capacity is the total of all member disks. (For example, two 1 TB disks function as a single 2 TB disk.) If one of the disks fails, its files become unavailable, but the files on the other disk(s) could still be accessed.

Many other sorts of RAIDs exist, including several varieties that combine the virtues of striping, mirroring, and/or concatenation, often by setting aside some space on each disk for redundant data storage. RAID 5, for example, is a striped array in which some space on each drive is set aside for *parity* (blocks of data that enable the array to rebuild missing blocks from any member disk).

The logic needed to tie multiple disks together to behave as one can come from hardware or software. For example, you can buy stand-alone enclosures that hold several disks and which handle all the formatting, management, and read/write channeling necessary for a RAID to function; you can also get a PCI Express card with similar capabilities for a Mac Pro or Xserve. Mac OS X itself includes the software necessary to create several types of RAID from individual disks attached to a Mac, with the operating system performing the necessary management. A program called SoftRAID (http://softraid.com/) offers a number of additional features, including better monitoring and management of RAIDs.

Mirrored RAIDs and backup

RAIDs serve many useful purposes and are worth serious consideration for their role in protecting your data. However, don't confuse a mirrored RAID with a backup. Although a mirrored RAID can give you two identical copies of your data (much the same as a bootable duplicate provides for your startup disk), the fact that both copies are updated at the same time means that if a file is accidentally deleted on one, it's deleted on the other. If a file is corrupted on one, it's corrupted on the other. If your directory develops faults, that also affects both disks. A two-disk mirrored RAID does just one thing: It protects you from disk failure. Even if one disk dies entirely, you can continue your work without any interruption whatsoever. But unlike a bootable duplicate, it doesn't provide you with the capability of returning to an earlier state of your disk.

You can, however, get the benefits of a bootable duplicate by using a mirrored RAID that includes at least three identical disks. With such a RAID, you can disconnect any one disk, and the remaining two (or more) continue to function normally. The disk you disconnect can serve as your bootable duplicate; if you rotate that disk into your array while rotating another one out (for example, once a week), the newly added drive automatically rebuilds itself to become identical to the others still in the array. In this way, you can get the best of both worlds without having to run separate software.

Do you need a RAID?

If you already have a bootable duplicate, do you need a RAID too? The answer depends on several factors:

- **How important is single-volume capacity?** With some types of RAID, you can create a single volume with a much higher capacity than any single disk available on the market.

If your Mac has 2 TB of storage and you want to back it all up using Time Machine, for example, you need to store it on a disk larger than 2 TB (the largest single-disk capacity as I write this). A RAID can give you a single 4 TB or 6 TB volume, perhaps with redundant storage to protect you against the failure of one of the drives.

- **How much downtime can you afford?** For servers and other mission-critical applications, in which you can't afford to have a computer offline for even a few minutes, a RAID enables a system to keep going even after a catastrophic disk failure, whereas locating, attaching, and booting from a duplicate can take some time — not to mention the additional time that may be required to update the duplicate to include the latest data from your most recent versioned backups.

- **What is your budget?** Hard disks cost money, and the software or hardware necessary to combine multiple disks into one may cost considerably more. For the cost of a two-disk RAID, you may be able to afford three or four stand-alone disks, which may ultimately provide more flexibility.

- **How long do you plan to keep your disks in service?** I've owned hard disks that functioned flawlessly for seven years or longer and others that died in their first year of use. Despite manufacturers' claims of average mean time between failures (MTBF), there's no guarantee that any given disk will last for any given period of time, but older disks are more likely to fail than newer ones. If you expect to keep disks in continuous service for more than three years or so, a RAID becomes an increasingly wise choice.

Choosing a RAID system

If you've determined that a RAID is right for you, the number of options from which you can choose is staggering. Here are some of the most prominent examples:

- **Disk Utility.** Mac OS X's Disk Utility can create a level 0, level 1, or concatenated RAID as well as RAIDs that combine these features (for example, a RAID of four or more disks in which multiple mirrored RAIDs are striped together, known as RAID 10). Because it's included with the operating system, the price is right. Because your Mac's processor must manage the RAID, it can have a small adverse effect on the performance of other applications on your Mac. I provide basic instructions for creating a RAID with Disk Utility just ahead.

- **SoftRAID.** The primary competitor to Apple's built-in RAID feature is SoftRAID, which costs $129. SoftRAID doesn't offer RAID 10 or other combination RAID setups, but it's far easier to use than Disk Utility, especially in that you can add a disk to a RAID without reformatting it. It also offers better read performance in some configurations and faster rebuilding of mirrored RAIDs as well as more helpful monitoring than Disk Utility.

- **RAID Cards.** If you have a Mac Pro or an Xserve, you can buy a PCI Express Card with the capability of creating a RAID with up to four internal drives and, in some cases, external drives too. The Apple RAID Card supports not only RAID 0, RAID 1, and JBOD but also RAID 5 and RAID 0+1, two ways of combining some of the benefits of mirroring and striping. This card avoids putting strain on your Mac's processor, and it includes options that software alone doesn't, but it works only with internal drives and is expensive for what it offers. Third-party RAID cards, such as the CalDigit RAID Card (www.caldigit.com/ RAIDCard), support both internal and external drives and offer many additional features.

- **Drobo.** A device called the Drobo (www.drobo.com) lets you install up to four hard drives of any capacity (eight in the DroboPro) and upgrade them at any time; the device dynamically configures a RAID to use whatever disks happen to be available. (Most RAIDs require all disks to be the same size and force you to manually configure them if you make any changes to your hardware setup.) The Drobo is essentially a fancy RAID 5 device that's especially friendly to use and easily expandable. Because the Drobo is a hardware RAID, its performance is higher than software-based RAID. Its price is higher too, but not as high as the Apple RAID Card.

- **Other RAID Assemblies.** Although the Drobo is popular for its convenient setup and use, it's not the only game in town. Other manufacturers, such as Buffalo Technology (www.buffalotech.com) and G-Technology (www.g-technology.com), offer RAID drive assemblies that hold two or more disks and use various types of RAID schemes.

Configuring a RAID with Disk Utility

If you have two or more hard disks (internal or external) attached to your Mac, Disk Utility lets you combine them into a RAID. Before you do this, keep in mind that creating a RAID with Disk Utility reformats the member disks; don't attempt this on a disk that already contains any data unless you're sure it's safely backed up. Also, be aware that if you want your startup disk to be a member of the RAID, you must perform this procedure while booted from another volume (such as your bootable duplicate or a Mac OS X Install DVD).

To create a RAID with Disk Utility, follow these steps:

1. **Open Disk Utility, which is located in** /Applications/Utilities.

2. **In the list on the left, select one of the disks you want to include in the RAID.**

3. **Click the RAID tab.**

4. **Drag all the disks you want to use in the RAID from the list on the left (shown in Figure 8.14) into the RAID set on the right.**

5. **Type a name for the RAID in the RAID Set Name field and then choose a format (normally Mac OS Extended (Journaled) is best) from the Volume Format pop-up menu.**

6. **From the RAID Type pop-up menu, choose whether you want a Mirrored, Striped, or Concatenated RAID Set.**

7. **Select the first disk in the set.** The RAID Type menu changes to Disk Type.

8. **Select either RAID Slice (an ordinary RAID member) or Spare (for a disk that remains unused until one of the other disks fails, at which time it's automatically rebuilt to take over).** Repeat this step for each disk.

9. **Click Options to open the dialog box shown in Figure 8.15.**

FIGURE 8.14

Use the RAID pane in Disk Utility to combine two or more disks into a single logical volume.

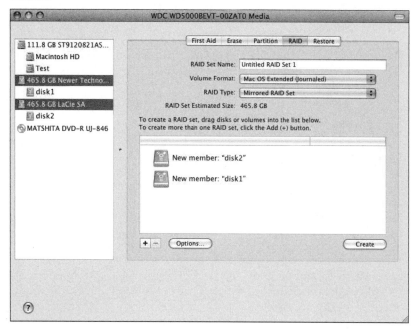

FIGURE 8.15

Select the block size for your RAID — and optionally turn on automatic mirroring — in this dialog box.

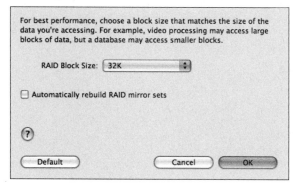

10. Following the instructions in the dialog box, choose a block size from the RAID Block Size pop-up menu, and if you're configuring a mirrored RAID, click the Automatically rebuild RAID mirror sets check box, and then click OK.

11. **Click Create.** Disk Utility creates the RAID.

12. **Quit Disk Utility.**

To learn about other ways of creating a RAID in Disk Utility, including combining striped and mirrored arrays, choose Disk Utility Help from Disk Utility's Help menu.

Summary

In this chapter, I explained why and how to back up your Mac. I began by covering the basic questions of what you should back up, how often, to what media, and in what form — and emphasized the importance of being able to easily restore backed-up files. I listed some of the most important criteria to consider when choosing backup software. For those who choose to use Time Machine, I provided a thorough description of how to back up and restore data with this utility built into Leopard and Snow Leopard.

I also explained how to make bootable duplicates of your Mac's startup disk, described the virtues and pitfalls of backing up your data over the Internet, and talked about managing your backup media (including offsite copies). Finally, I discussed the use of RAIDs to provide protection against drive failure and how this is different from a backup.

Part II

Protecting Your Privacy

Securing Email, Chat, and Voice over IP

Your Mac enables you to communicate over the Internet in many different ways. When it comes to one-on-one conversations with other people (or companies), the most common modes of communication are email, instant messaging (along with its audio and video chat variants), and voice over IP (VoIP), which can extend audio chats to people using conventional telephones. In all these cases, your Mac is the conduit through which you may send or receive highly personal or confidential information. This chapter covers ways of preventing that information from being intercepted in transit (and, in the case of email, being read while stored on a server somewhere).

The important thing to keep in mind about all these forms of communication is that even though you may think you're talking (or typing) directly to another person, the data doesn't go from one computer straight to another; it travels through numerous routers, gateways, and servers — each one potentially vulnerable to snooping, sniffing, or other unwanted attention. Because you can't control every portion of the network between your computer and the other person's, you may have to take special steps to ensure that your private data remains private.

Understanding Email Security

To understand how to send and receive email securely, you should know a bit about the ordinary, insecure methods of exchanging email. As I outline the typical path a message takes on its way from sender to recipient, notice the many points at which your data is effectively out in the open.

IN THIS CHAPTER

Learning the ins and outs of email security

Encrypting email logins and message transfers

Securely checking email over the web

Encrypting messages end to end and using digital signatures

Reducing the influx of junk mail

Discovering where email came from

Encrypting instant messaging sessions

Preventing others from hearing audio transmitted over the Internet

---

Suppose Pat composes a message to send to Sandy. For starters, there's a copy of the message somewhere on Pat's computer, and although it may be stored in any of several different formats, it's essentially cleartext that anyone who looks in the right place could read.

When Pat clicks Send, his email program contacts an SMTP (Simple Mail Transfer Protocol) server where he has an account (such as one run by his ISP, his employer, or another email provider). In most cases, the SMTP server asks Pat's email program for his username and password to make sure he has permission to send messages, and those credentials may be sent over the network in cleartext. Once Pat has been authenticated, his email program transmits the message, again in cleartext, to his SMTP server.

Now the message is sitting on Pat's SMTP server, and it may stay there for as little as a fraction of a second or as long as several days. During the time it's there, anyone with access to the SMTP server could read Pat's message, and if the server is automatically backed up (as it likely is), one or more copies of Pat's message could be kept indefinitely.

Pat's SMTP server next tries to contact Sandy's SMTP server in order to deliver the message. If that server isn't immediately available, the message may have to pass through one or more intermediate servers on its way. If all goes well, Sandy's SMTP server eventually accepts the message. Once again, the transfer involves the cleartext traveling across the Internet and being stored (and possibly backed up) on a server — or on several servers.

Next, Sandy's email program checks in with her ISP or email provider to retrieve Pat's message. Although the server used SMTP to receive the message, Sandy's email program uses a different protocol — usually POP (Post Office Protocol) or IMAP (Internet Message Access Protocol) — to download the message to her computer. This exchange requires Sandy's email program to send her username and password, which may be sent as cleartext.

Note
Not all email communication passes through multiple servers. If Pat and Sandy both have email accounts on the same mail server (for example, they both work for the same employer), that eliminates many of the potential hops a message might make in transit. However, that all changes if Pat or Sandy uses the mail server to exchange messages with someone outside the company. ■

Finally, the message arrives on Sandy's computer, where she may read it immediately and then delete it or save it. Needless to say, Sandy could also make one or more backups of the message.

In this overview of the process, I've left out lots of details, such as the fact that a message may travel over a wireless network from Pat's computer to his AirPort base station, then over a DSL line to his ISP, then over an Internet backbone to his email provider, and so on, all the way to Sandy's computer. The point is: Email messages can go through a lot of steps on their way from sender to receiver. At any point along the way, they can be stored, indefinitely, in a way that anyone with access to the computers can freely read their contents. And because the credentials of either or both user can be sent across the Internet in cleartext, anyone who intercepted them could access all of someone's incoming or outgoing mail from then on.

The way email works has often been compared to sending a postcard in the mail. The mail carrier who picks up the card from the mailbox and any of the dozens of other people who may handle it on its way to the addressee can read whatever's on it. They may not do so, of course, but nothing's stopping them; and even if they don't read the text on the card, they certainly read the recipient's name and address so they know where to deliver it. If someone with access to the mail in transit were so inclined, he or she could alter the text on the postcard, destroy it, send the recipient an entirely different postcard, or engage in other mischief. Naturally, any such tampering is illegal — but illegal behavior happens all the time.

If all that sounds a bit scary, it should. The vast majority of the world's email communication is sent, received, and stored (in many different places) in cleartext, and untold numbers of people — from system administrators to government agencies — can read all that text with ease.

That's not to say someone actually does read all your email. The sheer volume of email sent and received every day makes it highly unlikely that any particular message passes before the eyes of someone who shouldn't see it. Unless someone is specifically targeting you (because, for example, they believe you send or receive especially valuable or dangerous information), the probability of your mail falling into the wrong hands is small. Nevertheless, people do win the lottery, get struck by lightning, and experience other rare events. To avoid becoming one of those statistical anomalies, you can and should take steps to minimize the number of opportunities the bad guys have to get to your email.

Because email must normally travel over numerous networks and through multiple servers on its way from sender to recipient, you should think about every link in that chain. Some are inherently more vulnerable than others. For example, it's far more likely that someone would intercept a message when it's traveling from your computer to your ISP (especially if you're connected to an open Wi-Fi hotspot) than when it's traveling between your ISP's mail server and the recipient's. Depending on the nature of the email you send and receive, you may decide that only the riskiest links are worth protecting.

The following are your primary options for keeping email private during (and after) its journey; I describe each in considerably more detail later in this chapter.

Using secure authentication

The first step is making sure that when you log in to your SMTP, POP, or IMAP server, your username and password aren't sent over the network in cleartext. Most email servers support (but don't necessarily require) methods of logging in that send your credentials over the network in an encrypted form. Doing so prevents anyone who may be observing network traffic between your computer and your mail server from discovering your password, which means that although they may be able to see future messages while in transit, at least they won't be able to log in as you and see messages that are stored on the server — or send out messages using your account.

Using SSL for sending and receiving email

Most email providers support the use of SSL to encrypt messages as they travel between your computer and your mail server (in either direction). If you use SSL, anyone sniffing network traffic is unable to see the contents of your messages as they travel to and from your computer. The same goes for the recipient. Because SSL provides much better protection than merely using secure authentication, it's a very good idea. However, beware of these limitations:

- Although you can control whether SSL is used between your Mac and your mail server, you can't control what happens on the other end (the recipient of mail you send or the sender of mail you receive).

- SSL keeps network traffic encrypted, but it doesn't alter the message contents. So, once a message has traveled from your Mac to a mail server, it's stored on the server in cleartext.

- Even if both sender and recipient use SSL, messages are sent from one mail server to another in cleartext.

In other words, if both sender and recipient use SSL, the message is protected during transit over the final, and most vulnerable, link in each direction. But there may still be multiple, unencrypted copies of the message sitting on various mail servers, and in theory, someone who had access to any portion of the network between the mail servers could also see the cleartext version of the message while moving from one to the other.

Note
Instead of or in addition to SSL for email, you can encrypt your entire Internet connection by using a VPN, as described in Chapter 12. But, like SSL, that protects a message only on a portion of its journey. ∎

If sending email in the ordinary way is analogous to sending postcards in the mail, using SSL is a bit like sealing a letter in an envelope. You can be reasonably sure that the postal carrier who picks up the letter and the one who delivers it won't read its contents, and the volume of letters passing through the postal system makes it improbable that anyone else will either — although someone at an intermediate post office could in theory steam open the envelope and take a look inside.

Signing email messages

When you write a letter that you send by postal mail, you typically sign it. The signature serves as proof that you wrote it and are aware of its contents. Even though it's possible to forge signatures and change the contents of letters, it's somewhat difficult to do so quickly and convincingly, and for most ordinary purposes, a signature is adequate to confirm the identity of the sender.

In email too, you may want to be sure the recipient can verify that you — and not a forger — sent an email message and that it wasn't tampered with after you sent it. Digital signatures offer both these capabilities and are much harder to forge than handwritten signatures.

Encrypting email messages

Because using SSL (or any other method of encrypting network traffic) still leaves messages vulnerable to interception in transit or to inspection on a server somewhere, the best way to keep a message private all the way from sender to recipient is to encrypt it. If Pat encrypts a message before sending it to Sandy, the only two places the message should ever exist in cleartext form are Pat's computer and Sandy's computer. It's a bit more complicated than that in that Sandy's email program may or may not store the message on disk in cleartext, and if it does, her backup software may or may not encrypt it before storing it elsewhere, but these are comparatively minor details.

To return to the postal analogy, encrypting email messages is like writing a letter in a very complex code. Whether or not the letter were in an envelope, anyone who saw its contents wouldn't be able to tell what it meant without having the key to decode the message.

Encryption offers the highest security, but it also involves the most bother. Think back over your lifetime and try to recall how many coded letters you've sent or received in the mail. Unless you're a professional cryptographer or an amateur code enthusiast, that number is probably not far above zero. Most of us assume that merely putting a letter in an envelope and entrusting it to the postal service provides adequate security most of the time, whereas encoding or decoding a letter first would be time-consuming and inconvenient. The same goes for email. Even though a computer can encrypt or decrypt a message much more easily than you could do by hand, the process still involves extra steps, extra time, and extra bother for both parties.

Encrypting data on your disk

I'd be remiss if I didn't mention one last weak link in the chain. Encrypting email protects it while in transit, but depending on your software and settings and those of the other party, it may not protect your messages while stored on the sending and receiving computers. In other words, if I send you an encrypted message, my email client most likely stores an unencrypted copy on my hard drive, as does yours. This fact is a good reason to supplement encrypted email with encrypted file storage of one sort or another.

Cross-Ref

For more on encrypting files on your hard drive, see Chapter 13. ■

Logging In Securely

The first potential security hole in your email setup involves the credentials you use to log in to check and send email. Needless to say, whoever can guess or steal your password can log in to your account — checking your email and sending email in your name. Because your username is usually either your email address or the portion of the address before the @ sign, only your password is truly confidential, and it pays to keep it that way. And yet, by default, many email clients send this information in cleartext over the Internet when logging in to mail servers, and it's easily intercepted by anyone with access to any of the network segments between your computer and the server.

Several methods are available to encrypt your credentials in the process of logging in to your mail server, so that even if someone is eavesdropping on your network traffic, at least that crucial information remains hidden. As long as your ISP or email provider supports secure logins (as most do), you should make use of this capability. Be sure to check with your provider to see which method(s) of secure login they support, such as MD5 Challenge-Response, NTLM (NT LAN Manager), or Kerberos.

Note

If you use SSL to send and receive mail, as described later in this chapter, your logins are already encrypted, even if your client appears to be configured to use an insecure login method. ■

Secure logins don't mean your email itself is encrypted, but they do mean that the only data eavesdroppers could read is what's transferred in the particular session(s) they're watching rather than all your email (as would be the case if your password were known).

Secure logins in Mail

You must configure secure logins separately for incoming (POP or IMAP) servers and for outgoing (SMTP) servers. Exchange servers don't offer secure login separately from SSL, but as with other account types, if you enable SSL for an Exchange account, you get secure login too. In addition, if you have more than one email account, you must configure secure logins separately for each of them. Each email client has its own method for doing this.

To configure Mail to log in to a POP or IMAP account securely, follow these steps:

1. With Mail running, choose Mail ⇨ Preferences to open the Preferences window, click Accounts to show the Accounts pane, and then select an account in the list on the left.

2. Click the Advanced tab.

3. From the Authentication pop-up menu, choose either MD5 Challenge-Response, NTLM, Kerberos Version 5 (GSSAPI), or (for POP accounts only) Authenticated POP (APOP), as specified by your email provider.

4. Repeat the previous steps for each of your accounts that supports secure logins.

5. Close the Preferences window and then click Save when prompted to save your changes.

To configure Mail to log in to an SMTP server securely, follow these steps:

1. With Mail running, choose Mail ⇨ Preferences to open the Preferences window, click Accounts to show the accounts pane, and then select an account in the list on the left.

2. Click the Account Information tab.

3. From the Outgoing Mail Server (SMTP) pop-up menu, choose Edit Server List to open the SMTP Server List dialog box.

4. Select an SMTP server in the list at the top of the dialog box.

5. Click the Use Secure Sockets Layer (SSL) check box.

6. If your username, password, and authentication method aren't already filled in, enter them according to your email provider's instructions.

7. If (and only if) your email provider has told you to use a special port for SSL, click the Use custom port radio button and then type the port number into the adjacent field. Ordinarily, SMTP uses port 465 for SSL and 25 or 587 for unencrypted connections.

8. Click OK, close the Preferences window, and then click Save when prompted to save your changes.

Secure logins in Entourage

To configure Entourage to log in to an IMAP or POP server securely, follow these steps:

1. With Entourage running, choose Tools ⇨ Accounts to open the Accounts window, double-click an account name to open the Edit Account dialog box, and then click the Account Settings tab.

2. Click the Click here for advanced receiving options button to open a pop-up window with additional options.

3. Click the Always use secure password check box.

4. Click the close box in the corner of the pop-up window and then click OK to close the Edit Account dialog box.

5. Repeat the previous steps for each of your accounts that supports SSL.

To configure Entourage to log in to an SMTP server securely, follow these steps:

1. With Entourage running, choose Tools ⇨ Accounts to open the Accounts window, double-click an account name to open the Edit Account dialog box, and then click the Account Settings tab.

2. Click the Click here for advanced sending options button to open a pop-up window with additional options.

3. Click the SMTP server requires authentication check box.

4. If you use the same credentials for SMTP as for IMAP or POP (the usual case), click the Use same settings as receiving mail server radio button. Otherwise, click the Log on using radio button, type your username and password into the fields provided, and then click the Save password in my Mac OS keychain check box.

5. Click the close box in the corner of the pop-up window and then click OK to close the Edit Account dialog box.

6. Repeat the previous steps for each of your accounts that supports SSL.

Secure logins in Thunderbird

Thunderbird 3.x offers your choice of secure authentication, secure connection (using SSL), or both. In Thunderbird 2.x, there's no explicit way to enable secure authentication independently of a secure connection, so if you're using a pre-3.0 version of Thunderbird, skip ahead to the next section to learn about using SSL. To configure Thunderbird 3.x to log in to an IMAP or POP server securely, follow these steps:

1. **With Thunderbird running, choose Tools ⇨ Account Settings to open a dialog box for configuring settings.**

2. **In the list on the left, select Server Settings under one of your accounts.**

3. **Under the heading Security Settings, click the Use secure authentication check box.**

4. **Repeat step 3 for each of your accounts that supports SSL.**

5. **Click OK to close the window.**

To configure Thunderbird 3.x to log in to an SMTP server securely, follow these steps:

1. **With Thunderbird running, choose Tools ⇨ Account Settings to open a dialog box for configuring settings.**

2. **In the list on the left, select Outgoing Server (SMTP).**

3. **In the list on the right, select an SMTP server (of which you may have only one) and then click Edit to open a configuration dialog box.**

4. **Click the Use secure authentication check box.**

5. **Click the Use name and password check box and then type your username into the User Name field.**

6. **Click OK to close the window.**

7. **Repeat steps 3 to 6 for each SMTP account you have and then click OK to close the Settings dialog box.**

Using SSL for Incoming and Outgoing Mail

A secure login is essential, but by itself, it's not enough. Even without having your password (and thus being able to snoop on all your mail at any time), an interloper could read the text of any email message that passes between your computer and your mail server in either direction. However, if that part of the message's path is encrypted, it blocks one of the most obvious avenues of attack.

The usual means of encrypting email between client and server is SSL — the same technology that banks and other institutions use to secure web pages. SSL is a form of public-key cryptography, which means that each side has a pair of keys: the other party's public key (used to encrypt outgoing data) and his or her own private key (used to decrypt incoming data). To oversimplify somewhat, this scheme means that unless someone knows (or can guess) your password, which protects your private key, the odds against that person being able to decrypt your messages are astronomically high.

Cross-Ref

For more on public-key cryptography, see Chapters 5 and 13. ■

Note

Although SSL was succeeded by a more modern version of the protocol called TLS (Transport Layer Security), and although your email client may support either version, most email software still uses the SSL terminology. ■

How SSL works for email

For you to use SSL, your ISP or email provider must support it. Most do nowadays, and some in fact no longer support unencrypted sessions. But the only way to know for sure is to check with your provider — the information is usually easy to find on an FAQ or support web page. You may also see additional information about how to configure your client to use SSL, including which port to use, whether you must specify a different server address, and other details; be sure to take note of all this.

When you configure your client to use SSL, you're setting it up to encrypt all the email that passes between the client and a particular server. It's important to understand that your client generally makes two independent connections: one to a POP or IMAP server for incoming mail and the other to an SMTP server for outgoing mail. Exchange accounts are different in that the same server can be used for incoming and outgoing mail, so a single SSL setting applies to both. Even if both servers have the same address and even if they're running on the same physical computer, your email client sees them as separate. So, you could, for example, use SSL for IMAP but not for SMTP. I can't think of any good reason to do so; rather, I mention this to caution you that you should always set up SSL in two places — incoming and outgoing mail — for each of your accounts.

As I mentioned earlier, if your email session is encrypted using SSL, that includes your login, even if the login method is otherwise insecure (such as the "password" method). However, you should remain aware of the limitations of SSL. Because it affects only the traffic between your email client and your email server, your message could still be stored on the server and transmitted to the recipient in cleartext. So, you shouldn't assume that a message is safe from one end to the other just because you use SSL; its purpose is only to keep the communication between your client and your server private.

Configuring SSL for incoming mail

As elsewhere in this chapter, I provide basic instructions for configuring the three most popular Mac OS X email clients: Mail, Entourage, and Thunderbird. If you use another client, consult its documentation for instructions on using SSL. What follows are directions for setting up incoming (POP and IMAP) accounts for SSL; later, I describe the analogous process for outgoing (SMTP) accounts.

Incoming SSL in Mail

To configure Mail to use SSL for incoming mail, follow these steps:

1. With Mail running, choose Mail ⇨ Preferences to open the Preferences window, click Accounts to open the Accounts pane, and then select an account in the list on the left.

2. Click the Advanced tab, shown in Figure 9.1.

3. Click the Use SSL check box.

4. If (and only if) your email provider has told you to use a special port for SSL, type its number into the Port field. Ordinarily, IMAP uses port 993 for SSL, POP uses port 995, and Exchange 2007 uses port 443.

5. Repeat the previous steps for each of your accounts that supports SSL.

6. Close the Preferences window and then click Save when prompted to save your changes.

FIGURE 9.1

Turning on SSL for incoming mail is usually as easy as clicking a single check box. This figure shows the window as it appears for a POP account; IMAP and Exchange accounts differ slightly.

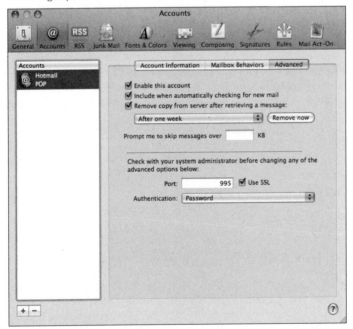

Incoming SSL for POP or IMAP in Entourage

To configure Entourage to use SSL for incoming POP or IMAP mail, follow these steps:

1. With Entourage running, choose Tools ➪ Accounts to open the Accounts window, double-click an account name to open the Edit Account dialog box, and then click the Account Settings tab.

2. Click the Click here for advanced receiving options button to open the pop-up window shown in Figure 9.2.

FIGURE 9.2

In this pop-up window, click the This IMAP service requires a secure connection (SSL) check box to enable SSL for this IMAP incoming mail account.

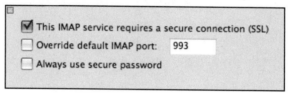

---

3. Click the relevant check box for your account:

   • **For IMAP accounts.** This IMAP service requires a secure connection (SSL)

   • **For POP accounts.** This POP service requires a secure connection (SSL)

4. If (and only if) your email provider has told you to use a special port for SSL, click the Override default IMAP port, Override default POP port, or Override default DAV port check box and then type the port number into the adjacent field. Ordinarily, IMAP uses port 993 for SSL and POP uses port 995.

5. Click the close box in the corner of the pop-up window and then click OK to close the Edit Account dialog box.

6. Repeat the previous steps for each of your accounts that supports SSL.

Incoming SSL for Exchange in Entourage

To configure Entourage to use SSL for incoming Exchange mail, follow these steps:

1. With Entourage running, choose Tools ➪ Accounts to open the Accounts window, double-click an Exchange account name to open the Edit Account dialog box, and then click the Advanced tab.

2. In the Exchange server section, click the This server requires a secure connection (SSL) check box.

3. If (and only if) your email provider has told you to use a special port for SSL, click the Override default port check box and then type the port number in the adjacent field. Ordinarily, Exchange 2007 uses 443.

4. Click OK to close the Edit Account dialog box.

5. Repeat the previous steps for each of your Exchange accounts that supports SSL.

Incoming SSL in Thunderbird

To configure Thunderbird to use SSL for incoming mail, follow these steps:

1. With Thunderbird running, choose Tools ⇨ Account Settings to open the settings dialog box.

2. In the list on the left, select Server Settings under one of your accounts, as shown in Figure 9.3.

3. From the Connection security pop-up menu, choose SSL/TLS.

4. If (and only if) your email provider has told you to use a special port for SSL, type that number in the Port field. Ordinarily, IMAP uses port 993 for SSL, and POP uses port 995.

5. Repeat steps 2 to 4 for each of your accounts that supports SSL.

6. Click OK to close the Account Settings window.

FIGURE 9.3

Turn on SSL for an incoming mail account (an IMAP account is shown here) in Thunderbird's Account Settings window.

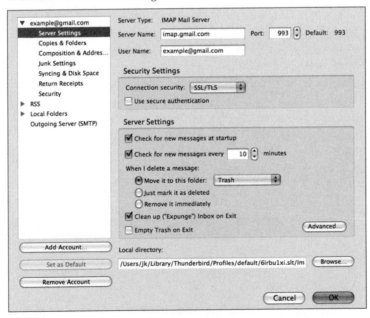

Configuring SSL for outgoing mail

As I did with incoming mail, I provide instructions here for configuring Mail, Entourage, and Thunderbird. Other email clients follow similar procedures.

Outgoing SSL in Mail

To configure Mail to use SSL for outgoing mail, follow these steps:

1. With Mail running, choose Mail ⇨ Preferences to open the Preferences window, click Accounts to open the Accounts pane, and then select an account in the list on the left.

2. Click the Account Information tab.

3. From the Outgoing Mail Server (SMTP) pop-up menu, choose Edit Server List to open the SMTP Server List dialog box.

4. Select an SMTP server in the list at the top of the dialog box and then click the Advanced tab, shown in Figure 9.4.

5. Click the Use Secure Sockets Layer (SSL) check box.

6. If your username, password, and authentication method aren't already filled in, enter them according to your email provider's instructions.

7. If (and only if) your email provider has told you to use a special port for SSL, click the Use custom port radio button and then type the port number in the adjacent field. Ordinarily, SMTP uses port 465 for SSL and 25 or 587 for unencrypted connections.

8. Click OK, close the Preferences window, and then click Save when prompted to save your changes.

Outgoing SSL in Entourage

If you're using an Exchange account in Entourage and have configured it to use SSL for incoming mail, that setting also applies to outgoing mail; no further steps are necessary. To configure Entourage to use SSL for outgoing mail with an SMTP server, follow these steps:

1. With Entourage running, choose Tools ⇨ Accounts to open the Accounts window, double-click an account name to open the Edit Account dialog box, and then click the Account Settings tab.

2. Click the Click here for advanced sending options button to open the pop-up window shown in Figure 9.5.

3. Click the SMTP service requires secure connection (SSL) check box.

4. If (and only if) your email provider has told you to use a special port for SSL, click the Override default SMTP port check box and then type the port number in the adjacent field. Ordinarily, SMTP uses port 465 for SSL.

5. **If you use the same credentials for SMTP as for IMAP or POP (the usual case), click the Use same settings as receiving mail server radio button.** Otherwise, click the Log on using radio button, type your username and password in the fields provided, and then click the Save password in my Mac OS keychain check box.

6. **Click the close box in the corner of the pop-up window and then click OK to close the Edit Account dialog box.**

7. **Repeat the previous steps for each of your accounts that supports SSL.**

FIGURE 9.4

For each SMTP server Mail is configured to used, check the Use Secure Sockets Layer (SSL) check box if your email provider supports SSL. Exchange 2007 servers don't appear in this list.

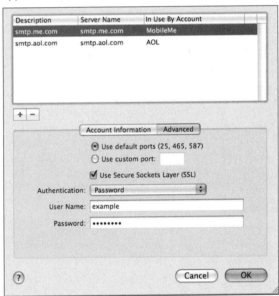

FIGURE 9.5

For each account you have configured in Entourage, use this pop-up window to configure security for outgoing messages.

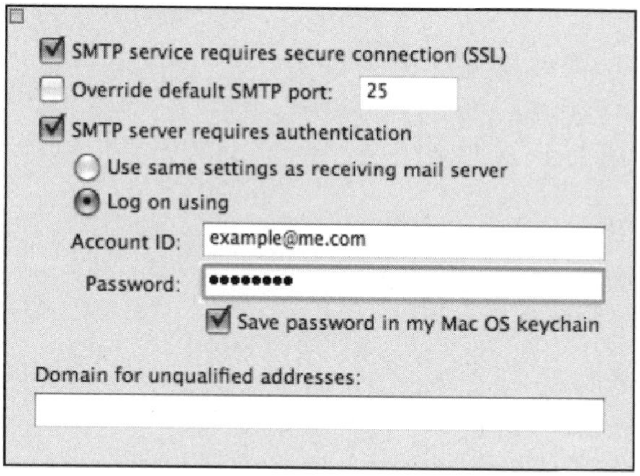

☑ SMTP service requires secure connection (SSL)
☐ Override default SMTP port: 25
☑ SMTP server requires authentication
  ○ Use same settings as receiving mail server
  ● Log on using
  Account ID: example@me.com
  Password: ••••••••
  ☑ Save password in my Mac OS keychain

Domain for unqualified addresses:

Outgoing SSL in Thunderbird

To configure Thunderbird to use SSL for outgoing mail, follow these steps:

1. With Thunderbird running, choose Tools ⇨ Account Settings to open the settings dialog box.

2. In the list on the left, select Outgoing Server (SMTP).

3. In the list on the right, select an SMTP server (of which you may have only one) and then click Edit to open the dialog box shown in Figure 9.6.

4. In Thunderbird 2.x, click the radio button corresponding to the type of secure connection your email provider supports (SSL is the preferred choice, followed by TLS); in Thunderbird 3.x, choose the desired type of connection from the Connection security pop-up menu (with SSL/TLS being a better option than STARTTLS, assuming your provider supports it).

5. Verify that the Port field says 465. If it doesn't, type 465 in the field, unless your email provider has given you a different port number for secure SMTP, in which case type that number instead.

6. Click the Use name and password check box and then type your username in the User Name field.

7. Click OK to close the window.

8. Repeat steps 3 to 7 for each SMTP account you have and then click OK to close the Settings dialog box.

FIGURE 9.6

To configure an outgoing account in Thunderbird for SSL, make sure the bottom portion of this dialog box is filled in as shown (with your own username, of course). This image shows the appearance in Thunderbird 3.x; earlier versions are somewhat different.

Using SSL for webmail

Most email providers offer a webmail option so that you can check your email using a web browser when you're away from your regular computer, and in a few cases, that's the only way of accessing your mail. A number of services, including Hotmail and Gmail, initially offered only web-based email access but later added access via POP, IMAP, or both.

In the previous section, I described using SSL to encrypt email sent and received with an email client such as Mail or Entourage. But it's equally important to encrypt your email when using a web-based email interface — whether on your own computer or on a public computer. Otherwise, everything you send and receive could be intercepted and read; the fact that it's delivered via HTTP rather than POP, IMAP, or SMTP doesn't afford it any particular protection.

Because every webmail system is different, I can't provide instructions that work with all of them. However, I offer some tips for several popular email providers just ahead. But in general, if you're about to log in to your webmail page and notice that the URL begins with http:// instead of https:// and there's no lock icon in your browser window, your credentials won't be encrypted when you log in — and that's a definite danger sign.

Gmail

Gmail offers a secure sign-in page so that your credentials are encrypted in transit, but for years the default setting was to use standard, insecure web pages. Google has announced that they're considering switching to completely secure Gmail connections, but if they haven't yet made that change by the time you read this, you can change a setting that forces all future sessions to be encrypted in their entirety. To do so, follow these steps:

1. **In a web browser, type** www.gmail.com **and then log in as usual.**

2. **Click the Settings link at the top of the page.**

3. **In the Browser connection section at the bottom of the General pane (displayed by default), click the Always use https radio button and then click Save Changes.**

4. **Click the Sign out link to disconnect.**

When you next log in, the entire session occurs on a secure (`https://`) web page.

Hotmail

Hotmail from Microsoft offers a secure login page at `https://login.live.com/`; alternatively, if you visit the standard login page, you can click a link labeled Sign in using enhanced security to go to the secure login page. However, either way, your login is encrypted. Hotmail currently doesn't offer a way to encrypt your entire webmail session.

MobileMe

When you go to `www.me.com` to log in to MobileMe, the site redirects you to a secure page for typing your credentials. Thereafter, although the URLs of the pages don't begin with `https://` and no lock icon appears, Apple says that all the data transfer is nevertheless encrypted behind the scenes using the site's AJAX (asynchronous JavaScript and XML) interface. Although this is tricky to verify without using special tools that watch network traffic, if you view the source of a MobileMe Mail page in your browser, you can see that none of the text of your email messages appears.

Yahoo! Mail

Like Hotmail, Yahoo! Mail offers optional secure logins. If you go to `http://login.yahoo.com/`, Yahoo! redirects you to a secure page for typing your credentials. However, also like Hotmail, Yahoo! doesn't offer fully encrypted sessions.

But there's a trick you can use if you don't mind a very minimalist interface. Instead of visiting the regular Yahoo! site, go to `https://us.m.yahoo.com/p/mail`. This secure version of the site, which is entirely encrypted, is designed for mobile users (accessing the site via a cell phone or other device with a small screen), but it can also be used in a conventional desktop web browser.

Digitally Signing and Encrypting Email

Even if both the sender and the recipient of an email message use SSL to connect to their respective mail servers when sending and receiving mail, someone could read the messages while they're stored on either of the servers (or their backups), and could intercept them as they travel from one server to another. The only way to be sure that your message can't be read by anyone except you and the person on the other end is to encrypt it, which keeps it safe from end to end, regardless of whether you log in securely, use a VPN, or take any other security measures.

Separate from encryption is the question of integrity. How do you know that a message actually came from the party who claimed to send it? And how do you know that someone else didn't tamper with it on its way? Both of these questions are addressed by digital signatures. When you digitally sign a message, your email client appends your certificate (which includes your public key — but not your private key) along with a *digest* of the message, which is basically an encrypted *checksum* of the message text (a number calculated from the contents in such a way that any change would yield a different result). Because the receiving client can verify whether the message text and its digest match, it can tell whether the message has been altered. And by checking the authenticity of the certificate, the receiving client can confirm that the claimed sender was the real sender. For any given outgoing message, you can sign it, encrypt it, or both.

Note

Don't confuse digital signatures (as described here) with the signatures you can include at the bottom of an outgoing message with your contact information, favorite quote, or other text. Digital signatures are usually not visible to the recipient, whereas ordinary email signatures are considered part of the message text itself. ∎

Ideally, every email message you send and receive would be signed and encrypted, but doing so would introduce some practical difficulties. Chief among these is how to ensure that the recipient and only the recipient can decrypt messages sent to him or her. If anyone could decrypt the messages, they might as well not be encrypted! For example, suppose I use a password to encrypt a message that I send you. You need to know the password to decrypt the message, but how do I send you the password securely? I could tell you in person if you're nearby or I could deliver it by phone or mail, but all those methods are awkward, and they're all subject to eavesdropping.

To overcome this difficulty, most email encryption schemes involve some form of public-key encryption. SSL, described earlier in this chapter, also uses public-key encryption, but the underlying mechanism is different because the client and the server can exchange information in real time, which isn't true of an email message's sender and recipient. Each party has a pair of keys: a public one, freely shared, that the other party can use to encrypt (but not decrypt) a message, and a private one, which can only be used to decrypt an incoming message. If I send you my public key, you can then send me an encrypted message, and because public keys are only used for encrypting, I can circulate the key freely without worrying that someone might learn it and be able to decrypt a message intended for me.

There's still a problem, though, in that if I want to send you an encrypted message, I need your public key, and there's no single, central repository for all the world's public keys — nor any guarantee that a given individual even has a public key. In addition, because numerous, mutually incompatible systems exist for securing email with public-key encryption, both users may not have software installed that can handle the type of encryption used on the other end.

One way of addressing the compatibility issue is to use an encryption standard called *S/MIME* (Secure/Multipurpose Internet Mail Extensions), which most modern email clients support, including Apple Mail, Entourage, and Thunderbird, among many others. That leaves the problem of getting the other user's public key, and the usual way of accomplishing this is to have the other person send you a signed (but not encrypted) message. Because the message includes the sender's public key, you then have what you need to encrypt any outgoing message to that person. Unfortunately, you must generally repeat this procedure, manually, for each recipient to whom you want to send encrypted messages.

Users of Pretty Good Privacy (PGP) software (or its relative GPG — GNU Privacy Guard, also referred to as GnuPG) can have their email clients automatically connect to keyservers that store public keys for vast numbers of people, thus eliminating the need to exchange keys manually in advance. However, because these keyservers work only with PGP/GPG (and therefore require the installation of additional third-party software beyond one's email client), the odds that the person with whom you want to communicate has the necessary software are much lower than with S/MIME. Various proposals have been advanced to extend S/MIME to use a mechanism comparable to PGP's keyservers, but none have been implemented on a wide scale yet.

When and why to encrypt your email

The unfortunate reality is that most of the people and companies with whom you exchange email won't be able to deal with encrypted messages. Using encrypted email isn't difficult, but it does require some setup steps (plus, in some cases, installation of extra software), and most people either can't or won't go to this extra effort. So, in order to exchange encrypted email, the first thing you need is an understanding with the person on the other end. You need to agree on which type of encryption to use and, if it's S/MIME, you need to obtain personal certificates (as described ahead) and exchange your public keys. Once you've done this, exchanging encrypted email with that person is a piece of cake, but it's a process you must go through with each of your correspondents.

Why and with whom might you go through all this bother?

If you must exchange highly confidential information by email and especially if you and the other person don't have the luxury of connecting to the same mail server (which affords some security because it presents fewer open avenues of attack), encrypting email is a good idea. This applies to situations such as government contractors discussing sensitive projects, doctors and attorneys sharing privileged information, and communication with a banker or accountant where large sums of money are involved. In short, whenever your personal safety, your career, your reputation, or your bank account (or someone else's) could be jeopardized were an email message to fall into the wrong hands, encryption is well worth the effort.

However, bear in mind that the use of encrypted email messages may signal to some people that you have something valuable to hide. If I were a hacker intercepting your email transmissions, for example, and I noticed that all (and only) messages to a certain address were encrypted, I may become curious about what this special information is, and I may therefore start looking for ways of obtaining your private key, guessing your password, or doing anything else that might lead me to your secrets. So, one could argue that the more broadly you use encryption (even for trivial information sent to friends and family members), the less suspicious any particular use of encryption becomes. You must decide for yourself how practical it is to follow that advice.

Using S/MIME in Apple Mail

Apple Mail isn't the only email client to support S/MIME — most do — but because of the ways it's integrated with the Mac OS X Keychain, it provides the simplest way to get S/MIME signing and encryption capabilities on a Mac. Once you've obtained a personal certificate, you can sign an outgoing message with one click, and assuming you've already obtained someone else's public key, you can encrypt messages just as easily.

Note

To learn about using S/MIME in Entourage, see www.entourage.mvps.org/smime/. For Thunderbird, read http://kb.mozillazine.org/Getting_an_SMIME_certificate, followed by http://kb.mozillazine.org/Thunderbird_:_FAQs_:_Install_an_SMIME_Certificate.

Obtaining a personal certificate

The first step in using Mail's encryption and signing features is to obtain a personal certificate, which includes a private/public key pair tied to your email address. You can encrypt a message as long as you have the recipient's public key — even if you don't have your own — but as the process would be one-way only, it makes the most sense for both parties to have certificates.

Certificates are supplied by *certificate authorities*, which are organizations that vouch for (certify) the identities of other people and organizations. Any company or individual can become a certificate authority, but unless a certificate authority is itself certified by a higher-level certificate authority (in a chain going all the way up to so-called root certificate authorities), one's certainty of the identity of a certificate holder is limited to one's trust in the certificate authority that granted the certificate.

Note

In lieu of becoming your own certificate authority, you can also create what's called a self-signed certificate (by using a tool such as Keychain Access), in which you simply vouch for yourself with no opportunity for outside verification. Although self-signed certificates work in Mail, they provide less security than personal certificates supplied by a certificate authority because nothing prevents someone from faking the information they contain. ∎

Because of this chain-of-certification mechanism, the standard process for obtaining a certificate is rather involved and expensive. The certificate authority must receive and validate extensive evidence proving that the applicant (a person or organization) is who he or she claims to be and that his or her email address hasn't been forged, spoofed, or intercepted. Only then can it truly vouch for the applicant because in so doing, it's effectively putting not only its own reputation but also that of any higher-level certificate authority at risk.

However, outside corporate and government environments, all the time, cost, and paperwork associated with getting a certificate is too much to expect for individuals who want to exchange email securely. So, there's a less-involved option, which is speedy and often free: the personal certificate. Anyone can get a personal certificate with a few minutes' effort of filling out forms and responding to email messages. The catch? In granting a personal certificate, a certificate authority certifies only that the email address associated with the certificate is the one used to request it. Depending on the provider, personal certificates may not include your name or any other identifying information, only your email address. And even if they do, they typically contain a qualification to the effect that the holder's persona has not been validated, meaning that you haven't proven to the certificate authority that you are who you claim to be.

Caution

S/MIME encryption isn't foolproof. Someone else with access to your email account could request and receive a personal certificate tied to your email address and use that certificate to sign messages supposedly from you — and also give out the public key associated with that certificate to let other people send encrypted messages that you, the actual account owner, wouldn't be able to decrypt. It's essential to take additional measures to protect your email passwords and the connections over which you send and receive email (using SSL, for example). ■

For years, the best-known supplier of free personal certificates was Thawte, the second-largest certificate authority (after VeriSign, its parent company). However, Thawte discontinued offering personal email certificates in November 2009. At the time this book was published, the best remaining option for free certificates was InstantSSL (`www.instantssl.com/ssl-certificate-products/free-email-certificate.html`), which resells certificates offered by Comodo (`www.comodo.com`), the next-largest certificate authority after VeriSign/Thawte. VeriSign itself also offers personal certificates (`www.verisign.com/authentication/individual-authentication/digital-id`), but they're not free; the company charges $19.95 per year.

In the steps that follow, I describe how to obtain and install a personal certificate from Comodo via InstantSSL. If you use a different certificate authority, the exact procedure differs somewhat, but the end result should be the same: a personal certificate in your keychain. This procedure is extremely straightforward — you're mainly responding to a series of simple questions. To obtain your personal certificate, follow these steps:

1. **Type** www.instantssl.com/ssl-certificate-products/free-email-certificate.html **in a web browser.**

2. **Near the top of the page, click the Get It Free Now! button.** A new window opens.

3. **In the form shown in Figure 9.7, type your name, email address, country of residence, and password.** Leave the Key Size (bits) set to 2048 (High Grade).

4. **After reviewing the Subscriber Agreement, click Agree & Continue.** Assuming all your information was typed correctly, the site displays a window saying "Application is successful!" Comodo then processes your request and sends you an email message when your certificate is ready.

5. **When you receive the email message from Comodo, an example of which is shown in Figure 9.8, click the Click & Install Comodo Email Certificate button.** Doing so

opens a new browser window or tab, and your browser downloads the certificate. If Safari is your default browser and you have its preferences configured to open safe files after downloading, Keychain Access opens automatically and imports your new certificate. You can then close Keychain Access as well as the open browser window.

Your keychain now has a personal certificate for the email address you selected.

Type the requested personal information on this page of Comodo's Secure Email Certificate application.

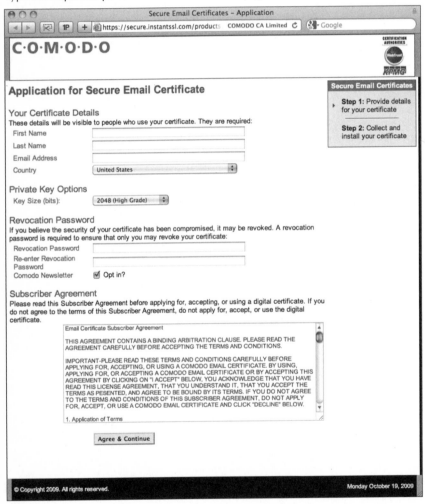

FIGURE 9.8

To retrieve your personal certificate, click the button in this email message.

Signing a message

To digitally sign an outgoing message — which appends your certificate (including your public key) to the message and enables the recipient to verify that you sent it and that it wasn't altered on the way — follow these steps:

1. In Mail, choose File ⇨ New Message to open a new message window.

2. **Verify that the buttons for encryption and digital signatures are visible.** By default, they appear in the lower-right corner of the header portion of the message window, as shown in Figure 9.9. The one on the left (which encrypts the message) looks like a padlock, and the one on the right (which signs the message) looks like a starburst-shaped seal. If the buttons aren't there, click the unlabeled pop-up menu icon in the lower-left corner of the header and then choose Customize. Click the check box next to the encryption and digital signature buttons and then click OK.

3. **Address and compose your message as usual.**

4. **If the digital signature button has an X in it, click it, which replaces the X with a check mark.**

5. **Click Send.** The first time you sign or encrypt a message with your certificate, a keychain request appears, as shown in Figure 9.10. Click Allow (to let Mail access the certificate in your keychain just this once) or Always Allow (to let Mail access the certificate in your keychain whenever it needs it). Mail then sends your signed message.

FIGURE 9.9

The two tiny buttons just above the message area on the right side of the window enable you to encrypt (left) and sign (right) this outgoing message.

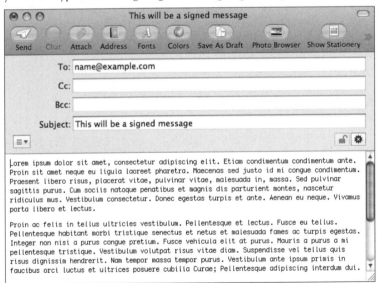

Although email clients vary in how they handle the receipt of signed messages, what usually happens is that a banner or other indicator appears in the recipient's message window to indicate that the message was signed, and your certificate is stored (automatically, in the case of Mail) on the recipient's computer, making it possible for him or her to send you encrypted messages.

FIGURE 9.10

Mail requests your permission to use a certificate in your keychain for signing or encrypting a message.

Caution

Once you've signed a message, the digital signature button remains selected by default in all future messages. This can be a problem because some email clients can't process or display signed messages properly, and digital signatures tend to wreak havoc with mailing list software. Therefore, to avoid accidentally sending a signed message to the next person (whenever that may be), I recommend opening a new message window, clicking the digital signature button to deselect it, and then immediately closing the window. This turns off the digital signature until you manually reselect it. ■

Encrypting a message

To encrypt an outgoing message, you must have the recipient's certificate in your keychain. If the other party has previously sent you a signed message, that should already be the case. If not, ask the other person to send you a signed message. When you open it, Mail adds his or her certificate to your keychain and then you can proceed with these steps:

1. **In Mail, choose File ⇨ New Message to open a new message window.**

2. **Verify that the buttons for encryption and digital signatures are visible.** If not, follow step 2 in the previous set of instructions to add them.

3. **Address and compose your message as usual.**

4. **If the encryption button shows the icon of an unlocked padlock, click it, which changes the icon to a locked state, as shown in Figure 9.11.**

5. **Click Send.** If a keychain alert appears, click Allow (to let Mail access the certificate in your keychain just this once) or Always Allow (to let Mail access the certificate in your keychain whenever it needs it). Mail then sends your encrypted message.

Note

The encryption button is disabled unless the message's To field contains a recipient whose certificate is in your keychain. ■

As with signed messages, email clients vary in how they handle the receipt of encrypted messages. In general, the recipient's email client decrypts the message automatically, displaying in the message window some indication that the message was encrypted.

Note
You can also sign an encrypted message, and doing so adds an extra measure of security because it provides a way for the recipient to verify the source and integrity of the message. ▪

FIGURE 9.11

It's subtle, but the lock icon changes to a closed shape and darkens slightly when it's selected to signify that you want to encrypt this outgoing message.

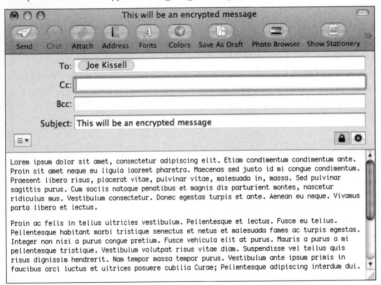

Working with incoming signed or encrypted messages

Mail handles incoming signed or encrypted messages transparently, unless they contain an error of some sort or were modified during transit. If you receive a signed message, Mail adds a Security header (just below the To header) that says Signed and has the starburst seal icon. If you click this icon, Mail displays information on the sender's certificate, as shown in Figure 9.12.

Similarly, incoming encrypted messages have a Security header that says Encrypted (with a padlock icon). Messages that are both signed and encrypted have both messages in the Security header.

Other than those subtle indicators that a message was signed or encrypted, Mail treats such messages specially only in two situations:

- **Searching.** You can choose whether the contents of encrypted emails are included in your Spotlight index, which makes them searchable both from within Mail and by using the system-wide Spotlight menu. The message headers are always available for searching, even when messages are encrypted. To let Spotlight search encrypted messages, choose Mail ⇨ Preferences, click General to open the General pane, and then click the Encrypted Messages check box, as shown in Figure 9.13. To disable indexing of encrypted messages, click the check box to deselect it.

- **Rules.** If you create rules in Mail to filter your messages, you can have a rule look for a signed or encrypted message and then take a special action based on that attribute. To create a rule, choose Mail ⇨ Preferences, click Rules on the toolbar to open the Rules pane, and then click Add Rule. From any pop-up menu in the top section (which contains rule criteria), you can choose either Message is Encrypted or Message is Signed.

FIGURE 9.12

When you click the icon next to the word Signed in a message header, Mail displays a dialog box like this one in which you can verify the identity of the sender.

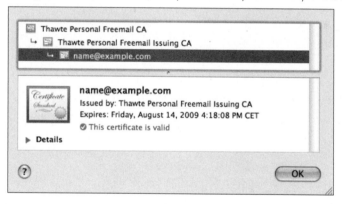

FIGURE 9.13

To enable Spotlight to search encrypted messages, make sure the Encrypted Messages check box is selected.

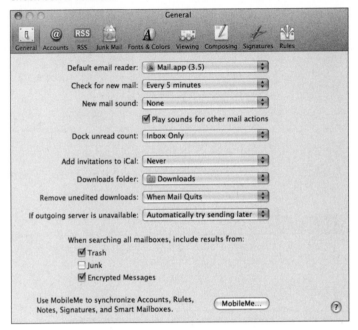

Using PGP or GPG for encrypted email

PGP is a popular and secure public-key encryption tool, which adheres to an open, public standard called OpenPGP. Although PGP has undergone many changes and evolutions over the years, currently PGP-branded software is sold by PGP Corporation (www.pgp.com), and numerous other companies and individuals make compatible products that also use the OpenPGP standard. Of these, the best known is the open-source GPG project.

Mac versions of GPG software products are distributed under the moniker Mac GPG (http://macgpg.sourceforge.net). Unfortunately, the email component of GPG, GPGMail, currently works only under Leopard and earlier, not Snow Leopard, and the developer has no plans to offer a Mac OS X 10.6–compatible version in the future, although that could change — or another developer could take up the project. So, Leopard users wanting PGP encryption capabilities can either pay for a nicely designed, fully supported, integrated package or download a set of free tools with somewhat fewer features and a less-polished interface.

Either mechanism provides the same end result: the capability to easily exchange strongly encrypted email messages with other users of OpenPGP-compatible software. As of late 2009, the commercial PGP software is the only good option for Snow Leopard users, but if you're using Snow Leopard and are interested in GPG, it's worth checking to see if an update or alternative is available.

As described earlier in this chapter, PGP uses keyservers to automate the exchange of public keys so you can encrypt a message to someone without previously having received a signed message from that person or having manually obtained his or her certificate in some other way. No one is required to use such keyservers, though, and it's possible to exchange public keys manually if you prefer to do so.

PGP and GPG require some initial setup steps, but on the whole, they're less complicated than obtaining and installing a personal certificate. After you install and configure the software and create a key, you can sign and encrypt messages in Mail as easily as with its built-in S/MIME method.

Because both programs include extensive documentation, what follows is simply a high-level overview of the steps involved in using them.

PGP

To use the PGP Corporation's commercial product for signing and encrypting your email with Apple Mail, follow these steps:

Note

PGP also supports signing and encrypting messages with Microsoft Entourage. ∎

1. **Purchase and install PGP Desktop Email, PGP Desktop Home, or PGP Desktop Professional for Mac from PGP** (`http://na.store.pgp.com/macstore.html`). All products include email encryption. The Home and Professional versions add support for encrypting entire volumes, among other capabilities. At the end of the installation process, the installer prompts you to restart your Mac.

Cross-Ref

For more on using PGP to encrypt folders, disk images, and entire volumes, see Chapter 13. ∎

2. **Open Mail, choose Mail ⇨ Preferences to open the Preferences window, click Accounts to open the Accounts pane, select each of your accounts in turn in the list on the left, and then turn off SSL for incoming and outgoing mail because PGP adds its own SSL security and the two can't be used at the same time.**

3. **Quit Mail.**

4. **Open the PGP Desktop application.** The Setup Assistant runs, walking you through all the basic configuration steps — including creating and optionally publishing a public/ private key pair.

5. **Open Mail.** One or more alerts like the one shown in Figure 9.14 appear. In each one, leave the Yes, secure this email account radio button selected and then click Continue. Confirm that your account name and PGP key are correct and then click Finish.

FIGURE 9.14

After you install PGP Desktop and open Mail, you see an alert like this for each of your email accounts.

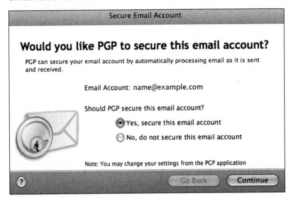

By default, PGP Desktop uses *opportunistic encryption*. This means that when you attempt to send a message, PGP checks to see if the recipient has a public key in your PGP keyring or on the PGP keyserver (called the PGP Global Directory). If so, it automatically signs and encrypts the message; if not, it sends the message unencrypted. To ensure that PGP doesn't let a message go out unencrypted (in case no valid public key can be found), include [PGP] in the subject line. If you want more control, you can set up a series of security policies in the PGP Desktop application that function much like rules in Mail: They look for certain criteria in outgoing messages and then take the action you specify (signing, encrypting, and using the keys of your choice) when a match is found; policies also specify what to do if no recipient key can be found (for example, blocking the message or sending it unencrypted).

If you open a message that has been encrypted with PGP, Mail initially displays the encrypted contents, as shown in Figure 9.15. Click the Decrypt button, type your passphrase, and then click OK to show the decrypted version of the message.

FIGURE 9.15

Incoming messages that were encrypted with PGP look something like this initially (which is also what a hacker would see); click the Decrypt button to decode the message by using your private key.

GPG

To use the open-source GPG software for signing and encrypting your email with Apple Mail under Leopard (remember, these instructions may not work with Snow Leopard), follow these steps:

1. Type http://macgpg.sourceforge.net **in a browser, download the latest versions of the following items, and then install them according to the instructions provided:**

   - GNU Privacy Guard (you can use either the version hosted on this site or the newer version, 2.x, hosted at `https://sourceforge.net/project/showfiles.php?group_id=248469`)

- GPG Keychain Access
- GPG Preferences

2. Type www.sente.ch/software/GPGMail **in a browser, download the latest version of GPGMail, and then install it according to the instructions provided.**

3. **Open the GPG Keychain Access application, choose Key ⇨ Generate, and then follow the steps in the Make a New Key Assistant to create a key.**

4. **Open Mail, choose Mail ⇨ New Message, and then do one or both of the following:**

   - To sign the message, click the Signed check box in the header portion of the message window or choose Message ⇨ PGP ⇨ Sign New Message.

   - To encrypt the message, click the Encrypted check box in the header portion of the message window or choose Message ⇨ PGP ⇨ Encrypt New Message.

5. **Click Send.** GPG prompts you for the passphrase associated with your key. Type it and then click OK.

If you open a message that has been encrypted with PGP, GPG prompts you for your passphrase. Type it and then click OK to decrypt the message.

Stopping Spam

Spam, or junk email, has reached such epidemic proportions that it has put some people off of email altogether. For many people, spam constitutes upward of 90% of incoming mail, making it difficult to find legitimate messages and wasting enormous time.

There's no question that spam is annoying, but it's also a security issue. That's because among all the ads for medications and get-rich-quick schemes, spam may also include viruses, Trojan horses, and malware of other kinds; it may also contain phishing attempts, in which someone tries to induce you to type your passwords or other private information on bogus websites.

For these reasons and more, it behooves anyone concerned about privacy and security to take steps to reduce or eliminate spam.

If your Mac is on a corporate network and all your incoming email is filtered by your employer's mail server, you may have little spam to contend with — at least in your business account. However, most people encounter at least some spam, and even if your company keeps your professional email mostly spam-free, you may not have the same good fortune with your personal email accounts.

Understanding spammers

As you're trying to determine your strategy for fighting spam, you should have in mind who — or what — you're up against. It's natural to assume that every spam message is sent out by an individual or a company with something to sell, so your opponent is a (presumably rational) human.

But that's a faulty image. In reality, the majority of spam is sent out by huge automated systems that don't function according to what we commonly think of as logic.

For example, suppose I wanted to sell you pirated software, and my goal were to get as many people as possible to visit a website to make a purchase. If I completely lacked scruples, how might I go about this?

First, I'd construct a website that would be difficult to trace back to me. I might even create a temporary, disposable site that's intended to work for just a few days and then disappear.

Next, I'd craft an email message with sender and subject lines that look innocent and make it likely that you want to see what's in the message. The subject may be completely misleading, of course, because the point is to get you to read the message.

Now comes the interesting part. I could buy, very cheaply, lists of millions of email addresses and plug them into my own email program. But sending all those messages would take a long time, and my ISP would probably notice that suspicious behavior and shut me down. So, instead, I'd pay someone else to send out the messages for me, and there are numerous shady organizations that run server farms to do exactly that. Recipients would never know I was the message's originator because they were sent by a third party on my behalf. In fact, almost all spam messages have fake senders — if you tried to reply, your message may bounce or it may go to a completely innocent person. Many spam messages, in an effort to evade spam filters, put your own email address in the From field so they appear to have been sent by you!

It's true that your email address may be on one or more of the many lists circulating around the Internet that spammers use frequently. However, spammers may also simply try every single potential address at a given domain, and you can get spam without being on any list. Doing this requires lots of computing power, but that's easy to come by.

One extremely common technique is to use so-called zombie machines to send out spam. First, spammers craft viruses or Trojan horses designed to turn unsuspecting users' computers into email-sending robots. They spread that malware far and wide, and as soon as a computer becomes infected, the spammers send it a message to distribute and a list of addresses (or instructions for generating random addresses). It does its thing silently, in the background, until the user — or the user's employer or ISP — figures it out and shuts it down, perhaps by installing antivirus software. As you read this, millions of zombie machines are sending out spam messages by the billions.

It may be that only one message in a million results in a sale, but because messages are so inexpensive to send — and there are so many potential targets — the economy of scale means that spamming is still a profitable enterprise.

In short, you're not up against a human being or a company. You're up against a massive army of mindless robots that happily keep sending out messages regardless of how many of them ultimately get through. Bouncing a message or asking to be removed from a mailing list does no good because the robots on the other end don't care, and even if you did manage to get removed from one list, thousands of other spammers may still have (or may be able to figure out) your address.

Learning basic spam-filtering concepts

The job of a spam filter is conceptually simple: separate junk mail from good mail. Mail that's clearly good goes right into your inbox, whereas messages suspected to be junk might be saved for you to inspect later, mixed in with the rest of your mail but tagged in some way to mark them as suspicious, or even (in extreme cases) deleted immediately.

However, in practice, the task of figuring out which email is spam is extremely complex. One reason for this is that spammers have become extremely clever, making many junk messages look convincingly real and working around the common clues spam filters know to look for. As filters get better, spammers change their tactics, resulting in still more cycles of development on both sides.

Although the specifics may change over time, the basic principles of filtering out spam have remained pretty consistent over the years. The following are some of the key concepts you should know about spam filtering.

Where filtering occurs

A spam filter can be used at any of several places along the path between a message's sender and your inbox, and you may have filters at more than one of these stages:

- **Server-based filters.** Your mail server may have a spam filter that integrates with the server program itself. This lets the mail server intercept and possibly set aside the spam before it's delivered to your email client. MobileMe, Gmail, and most major ISPs and email providers offer some variety of server-based spam filtering. Such filters may or may not give you any control over which messages are considered spam or what actions are taken with those that are.

- **Client-based filters.** Your email client may have built-in spam filtering (on the Mac, Entourage and Mail do, as do several others), and you can install add-ons that integrate with your email program to enhance or replace its spam-filtering capabilities. Client-based filters tend to provide the maximum level of configurability and control, although they don't prevent spam from being downloaded to your computer.

- **Proxy filters.** A proxy filter is a program that checks your email, filters out spam, and then sends whatever's left to your client. In other words, it stands between your client and the server instead of integrating directly with either. You can obtain proxy filters that run on your Mac or on the same computer as your mail server software. You can also subscribe to proxy services online; to use such a service, you give it the necessary information to check your mail server and then configure your email client to fetch mail from the proxy server rather than directly from your mail server. Another form proxy filters can take is stand-alone appliances that you install on your local network between your outside connection and any client computers. Devices like this, such as the Barracuda Spam Firewall (www.barracudanetworks.com/ns/products/spam_overview.php), can often filter spam for an entire network without requiring any explicit reconfiguration of email client settings.

False negatives and false positives

Spam filters are never perfect; they can only judge the probability that a message is spam. If a message scores above a certain arbitrary point, after taking into account whatever criteria the filter checks for, it's considered spam; below that, it's considered legitimate. But some good messages might have attributes that make them look spam-like, pushing their scores over the limit, whereas some spam messages might look so innocuous that they fall below the limit.

A *false negative* is a spam message that your spam filter misses, mistaking it for a good message. A *false positive* is the opposite: a legitimate message that your spam filter mistakenly thinks is junk. Every spam filter produces a certain number of false positives and false negatives. The more messages that are identified incorrectly (in either way), the lower the filter's overall accuracy.

When your spam filter produces a false negative, it means a spam message shows up in your inbox. As long as it doesn't happen too often, the only consequence is that you must select the message and delete it — a minor irritation. However, false positives are more problematic. Imagine that someone sends you a legitimate message, but it doesn't appear in your Inbox because your spam filter thinks it's junk. That message is most likely in a junk mailbox or sequestered in some other location with all the rest of your suspected spam. Unless you check that mailbox carefully from time to time (or you find out by some other means that the person was trying to contact you), you might never get the message. Manually sorting through hundreds or even thousands of spam messages looking for the odd false positive is no fun, but it's often a necessity.

Filtering strategies

How does a spam filter go about determining whether a message is spam? It's a surprisingly tricky process, and a great many techniques and algorithms have been tried, with varying degrees of success. Some of the most common strategies are these:

- **Pattern matching.** A spam filter can look for words, phrases, domain names, and other patterns in the headers or body of a message that are strong predictors of spam. For example, names of certain prescription drugs, along with common intentional misspellings of them, are likely signs of spam, and filters may contain long lists of sophisticated wildcard sequences that help to identify such patterns. Although pattern matching can be quite powerful, it can be labor-intensive to update, and in some cases, only the spam filter's developer can update the patterns.

- **Statistical analysis.** Instead of (or in addition to) using fixed patterns, spam filters may use statistics to determine what's spam. Several methods of statistical analysis exist, including one technique called Bayesian analysis (used by numerous third-party spam filters) and another called Adaptive Latent Semantic Analysis (LSA), used by Mail. Statistical filters look at large numbers of existing spam messages and large numbers of legitimate messages, noticing things like how often certain words and phrases are used in each sort of message. Crucially, statistical filters learn as you use them. Whenever they encounter a new message, its attributes are added to the filter's statistical database of good and bad message characteristics. If the filter makes a mistake, you can correct it, and that new information updates the database accordingly, making it less likely to misidentify similar messages in the future.

- **Blacklists.** A blacklist (also known as a blocklist) is just what it sounds like: a list of senders from whom email is never accepted. The list may include individual senders or even entire domains. Some spam filters update their blacklists to block all future messages by any sender who sends you a message you confirm as spam, but this is of questionable value because most spammers use a given From address only once (or forge the address so the message appears to come from you or from someone else in your domain you wouldn't want to block from sending you mail). Sometimes better results are obtained by using dynamically updated public blacklists, sometimes known as Realtime Blackhole Lists, or RBLs. The idea is that your filter can check in with the RBL and, if it sees a message from a sender or domain many other people have identified as sending spam, it can reject the message. The problem with this approach is that sometimes numerous people incorrectly identify legitimate mail as spam, blacklisting the sender — and getting removed from a public blacklist can be a complicated process.

- **White lists.** A white list is the opposite of a blacklist: a list of senders' email addresses or domains from whom you always accept email. Anyone on the white list (which may be or include the contents of your address book) is automatically exempted from the spam filter. White lists can avoid false positives from people you know and trust, but they can sometimes be circumvented by spammers forging addresses so they appear to come from people on your white list.

- **Challenge/Response.** A more drastic approach to spam filtering, called challenge/response, is being offered by an increasing number of ISPs, proxy services, and client-side filters. It works like this: I send you a message, and your mail server (or a proxy filter) checks to see if I'm on its white list. If not, it holds on to the message instead of delivering it to you. It then sends me a message (the challenge) asking me to reply, click a link taking me to a web page, or perform some other action to prove that my From address is valid and that I'm a human being and not a robot (the response). If I succeed, the mail server passes the message on to you and adds me to the white list so I won't have to respond to challenges for future messages. If not, it assumes the message is spam and eventually deletes it. Purveyors of challenge/response systems claim that they offer virtually 100% protection from spam, because spammers almost never respond to challenges. Although they're indeed highly effective in keeping an inbox spam-free, they pose a significant risk of false positives. Most people receive a significant number of legitimate email messages from automated systems (banks, utilities, companies from whom purchases are made, and the like) that are unable to respond to challenges and whose email addresses you may not necessarily know in advance in order to put them on your white list. So, lots of important email might not get through to you. Meanwhile, legitimate senders tend to find challenge email messages highly annoying, and some may be so irritated that they don't bother responding. Challenge/response filtering presents a negative image to friends, family members, and clients, and the loss of goodwill may counteract much of the benefit they provide.

What happens to suspected spam

Spam filters take a variety of approaches when they encounter suspected spam. Among the common results are these:

- **Add a header.** Server-based spam filters often add one or more headers to an email message. These are normally invisible, but they can tell your email client to take special action or display the message in a special style.

- **Change the subject.** A spam filter may add [SPAM] or some similar tag to the beginning of the message's subject to alert you to its potential junk status.

- **Move the message.** One of the most common actions, which may occur in combination with adding a header, is moving the message to a junk or spam mailbox — either on the server or in your email client.

- **Sequester the message.** Proxy filters typically have their own, separate storage area for suspected spam, and you must consult this list (either on a website or in a separate program running on your Mac) to look for false positives.

- **Bounce the message.** When a mail server bounces a message, it returns it to the sender, marking it as undeliverable. Bouncing is useful when the sender has misaddressed the message or when the recipient's address has changed. But bouncing spam is almost entirely useless because the messages are usually sent from invalid addresses that can't receive mail, and even if the bounce does get through, the spammer is unlikely to see any value in going to the effort of removing your address from a mailing list. Bouncing a message from your email client is even less effective because the message's headers show that it was in fact delivered to you, thus confirming to the sender that your address is valid.

- **Delete the message.** Of course, a filter could also simply delete the message so that you never see it under any circumstances. In most cases, this makes sense only for messages that have such a high score that they're indisputably spam; deleting messages with any uncertainty as to their status could lead to grief for both the sender and the recipient.

Configuring your email client's spam filter

Even if you use server- or proxy-based spam filters, some spam messages are bound to slip through, so it never hurts to activate the spam filter built into your email client. If you have no other source of spam filtering, client-based filters may or may not be adequate on their own, but at a minimum, they provide some improvement. I provide instructions here for configuring the three most popular Mac email clients: Mail, Entourage, and Thunderbird; if you use another client, consult its documentation for instructions on activating and configuring its spam filter.

Apple Mail

Mail's built-in LSA junk filter requires setup and ongoing training to work effectively. Although you can use it in a variety of ways, I recommend configuring and using it as follows:

1. **With Mail running, choose Mail ⇨ Preferences to open the Preferences window and then click Junk Mail to open the Junk Mail pane, shown in Figure 9.16.**

2. **Click the Enable junk mail filtering check box if it's not already selected.**

3. **Click the Move it to the Junk mailbox radio button.**

4. Make sure the Sender of message is in my Address Book and the Sender of message is in my Previous Recipients check boxes are selected but that the Message is addressed using my full name check box isn't (it is by default).

5. Click the Trust junk mail headers set by my Internet Service Provider check box if it's not already selected.

6. Close the Preferences window. As new messages arrive in your inbox, Mail automatically moves those it considers spam to your junk mailbox.

7. As new mail arrives, if any spam messages appear in your inbox (false negatives), select them and then click the Junk icon on the toolbar to update Mail's junk filter and move the messages to your junk mailbox. Likewise, check your junk mailbox from time to time, and if you find any legitimate messages there, select them, click the Not Junk icon on the toolbar to update the junk filter, and then move them to your inbox or another location. As you train the junk mail filter in this way, it becomes more accurate over time.

FIGURE 9.16

For most people, the settings shown here are the optimal way to configure Mail's built-in Junk Mail filter.

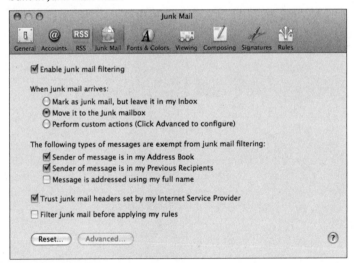

Microsoft Entourage

Entourage has a built-in spam filter, and although Microsoft doesn't disclose what methods it uses, it appears not to be based on statistical analysis. Instead, Entourage provides several ways to adjust the behavior of the spam filter, including changing its sensitivity and adding senders to a blacklist or white list. You can use a button or menu command to move messages into or out of your junk mailbox if they've been misidentified, but this doesn't necessarily improve the accuracy of the filter in the future. Microsoft does, however, release periodic updates to Entourage that include revised spam-filtering capabilities.

To set up Entourage's spam filter, follow these steps:

1. **With Entourage running, choose Tools ⇨ Junk E-mail Protection to open the Junk E-Mail Protection dialog box shown in Figure 9.17.**

2. **Click the High radio button.** This setting results in the best compromise between avoiding false positives and avoiding false negatives.

3. **Optionally, to add domains to Entourage's white list, click the Safe Domains tab and then type one or more domain names, separated by commas.** The Safe Domains list is designed for entire domains, not specific email addresses.

4. **Optionally, to add a particular sender or domain to Entourage's blacklist (categorizing it all as spam automatically), click the Blocked Senders tab and then type one or more email addresses or domain names, separated by commas.**

5. **Click OK to close the dialog box.**

As new mail arrives, if a spam message appears in your inbox (a false negative), select it and then click the Junk icon on the toolbar to move it to the junk mailbox. Or to move the message to the junk mailbox and also add its sender's email address to your blacklist, choose Message ⇨ Block Sender.

FIGURE 9.17

Entourage offers relatively little in the way of customizing its junk email filter, but for most users, the High setting strikes the best balance.

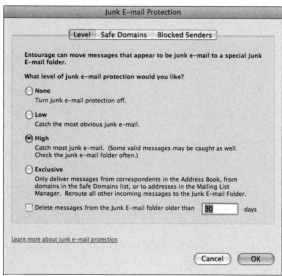

You should check your junk mailbox from time to time to see if it contains any false positives. If you find a legitimate message, select it and then click the Not Junk button on the toolbar. In the dialog box that opens, shown in Figure 9.18, you have three options to choose from:

- **Add sender to the Address Book.** Click this radio button and then click OK to add the sender to Entourage's Address Book (which constitutes part of its white list).

- **Classify all messages sent from the sender's domain as "not junk".** Click this radio button and then click OK to add the domain name to Entourage's Safe Domains list (the other part of its white list).

- **Just classify this message as "not junk".** Click this radio button and then click OK to move the message to your inbox without changing any white list settings.

FIGURE 9.18

When you tell Entourage that a suspected spam message is legitimate after all, it offers you these choices to determine how similar messages are handled in the future.

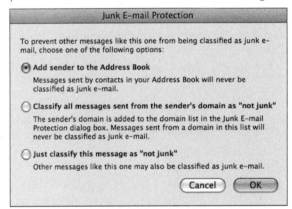

Mozilla Thunderbird

Thunderbird is a popular, free, open-source, multi-platform email client, featuring a built-in Bayesian spam filter. Using the spam filter requires three sequences of steps. First, you must enable the junk filter and set its basic parameters for each account. Next, you must configure overall preferences for the way junk mail is handled. And finally, you must train the filter.

To enable and set up the junk filter, follow these steps:

1. **With Thunderbird running, choose Tools ⇨ Account Settings to open the settings dialog box.**

2. **In the list on the left, select Junk Settings under the address of your email account, as shown in Figure 9.19.**

3. Click the Enable adaptive junk mail controls for this account check box.

4. In the Do not mark mail as junk if the sender is in list, click the check boxes next to Personal Address Book and Mac OS X Address Book to select them.

5. Click the Move new junk messages to check box.

6. If you already have a top-level mailbox in your IMAP account called Junk or if you have a local mailbox called Junk, click the "Junk" folder on radio button and then select the location of your junk mailbox from the pop-up menu. Otherwise, click the Other radio button, use the pop-up menu to select the mailbox you use to store spam, and then click OK.

If you have more than one email account in Thunderbird, repeat these steps for each account.

FIGURE 9.19

For each email account, the Thunderbird junk filter must be enabled here and then trained in order to separate good messages from spam.

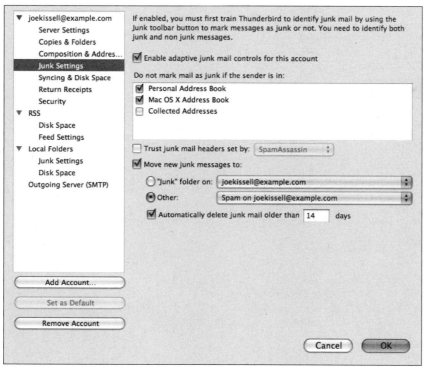

Next, configure Thunderbird's global preferences for handling junk mail by following these steps:

1. Choose Thunderbird ➪ Preferences to open the Preferences window, click Privacy (in Thunderbird 2.x) or Security (in Thunderbird 3.x) to open the Privacy (or Security) pane, and then click the Junk tab, shown in Figure 9.20.

2. Click the **When I mark messages as junk check box.**

3. If you think you might have some future need for messages you manually mark as junk, click the **Move them to the account's "Junk" folder radio button.** Otherwise, click the Delete them radio button.

4. Click the E-mail Scams tab and then click the **Tell me if the message I'm reading is a suspected email scam check box** if it's not already selected.

5. Click the Anti-Virus tab and then click the **Allow anti-virus clients to quarantine individual incoming messages check box** if it's not already selected. This feature comes into play only if you have third-party antivirus software installed.

Cross-Ref

For more on antivirus software, see Chapter 14. ■

6. Close the Preferences window.

FIGURE 9.20

Set global preferences for the way Thunderbird handles junk mail in this preference pane.

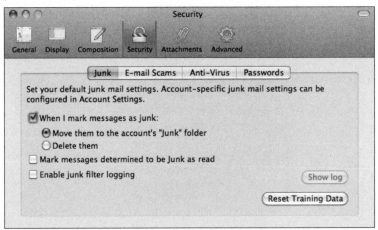

Finally, you must train the filter by following these additional steps:

1. **Select some good email messages and then choose Message ⇨ Mark ⇨ As Not Junk.** How many you select is up to you, but the more you select, the more accurate your results are.

2. **Select some spam messages and then choose Message ⇨ Mark ⇨ As Junk.** Again, the number of messages you select isn't fixed, but selecting more makes your filter more accurate.

3. **As new messages are delivered, use the procedures in steps 1 and 2 to correct Thunderbird if its filter generates any false positives or false negatives.** This ongoing training helps keep the filter as effective as possible.

Using third-party spam filters

The spam filters built into Mail and Entourage aren't bad, but for some people, they may not be adequate. In practice, even after training the Mail junk mail filter diligently on thousands of messages, it still makes mistakes a significant percentage of the time, and because the Entourage filter relies on updates from Microsoft to improve its algorithm, it can also be less accurate than you may prefer.

Of course, the degree to which this matters depends on your spam volume. If you receive only ten spam messages per day, having just one slip through the filter — an accuracy rate of 90% — isn't bad. But if you receive 1,000 spam messages each day, a 90% hit rate means you still end up with 100 annoying spam messages in your inbox that you have to cull manually.

Several third-party tools that run on Mac OS X provide spam filtering that's considerably more accurate than what's built into any email client. They fall into two broad categories: plug-ins and proxy filters. The two that function as plug-ins are by far the best choices, assuming you're using a compatible email client.

Plug-in spam filters

The following anti-spam programs integrate directly into your email program:

- **SpamSieve.** This $30 program by Michael Tsai works with Mail, Entourage, and almost every other Mac OS X email client (`www.c-command.com/spamsieve/`). Its accuracy is consistently well over 99%, and it's both extremely easy to use and highly configurable for those who like to tinker. SpamSieve incorporates a Bayesian filter, blacklist, white list, and a variety of other spam-catching technologies. When used with Mail, it adds commands (and associated keyboard shortcuts) to the Message menu to train the filter by identifying good and bad messages, including those that have been misidentified. The manner of integrating with other applications varies.

- **Personal Antispam.** Intego's $49.95 Personal Antispam (`www.intego.com/personal Antispam/`) works only with Mail and Entourage but provides excellent results with those two programs. Like SpamSieve, it features Bayesian filtering along with a blacklist, white list, and numerous other features. And it likewise adds menu commands and keyboard shortcuts to the email clients with which it integrates, enabling easy training. However, in addition to being more expensive than SpamSieve, it installs several background components (including a system-wide process to check for updates, a System Preferences pane, and a startup item that forces you to restart your Mac after installing the software) that I've found to be unnecessarily intrusive.

Proxy spam filters

The remaining three programs all run independently of your email client. They check your email and sort out the spam and then you configure your client to retrieve your email from the proxy. As such, they work with any email client, but they also require you to run a separate program all the time, and the lack of direct integration makes them all much more cumbersome to use. The proxy filters available for Mac OS X are the following:

- **Purify.** Purify is the most sophisticated of the three proxy spam filters for Mac OS X. It includes what the developer calls a Bayesian-type filter and a long list of other spam-checking techniques. It's also the only one of these three that appears to be in active development (`www.hendricom.com`, $29.95).

- **Spamfire.** This program from Matterform Media (`www.spamfire.com`) also includes a Bayesian filter, a blacklist, and a white list. It costs $39.95, not including subscriptions to filter updates, which vary in price. It works reasonably well with POP accounts but less effectively with IMAP accounts.

- **SpamSweep.** SpamSweep ($24.95 from Bains Software, `www.bainsware.com/spamsweep/`) includes a Bayesian filter and other anti-spam measures but offers very little in the way of configurability. It's also awkward to train and offers no support for IMAP accounts.

Other spam-filtering strategies

If you've taken advantage of any server-based filtering that your ISP or email provider offers and have added a properly configured third-party spam filter to your Mac, but you still see more than an occasional spam message in your Inbox, you have a serious spam problem indeed. I can suggest a couple options you might pursue to restore email sanity.

Find a better email provider

Not all ISPs and email providers offer spam filtering, and of those that do, not all are of high quality. If your current mail server lets too much spam through, consider switching to another one. Google's Gmail service has excellent spam filtering, for example, and can be used with your own domain if you so choose (see `www.google.com/a/cpanel/domain/new`). The Apple MobileMe service (`www.me.com`) also offers respectable server-based spam filtering.

Use an alias

As you use the web, you're inevitably asked to provide your email address over and over again — for making purchases, when signing up for discussion forums and online services, and when asking for product support, for example. Most companies to whom you provide your address are responsible and use it only for the stated purpose. But sometimes, a website sells its list of addresses to another organization, and once an address starts circulating on spammers' lists, the volume of spam you get can only increase.

One approach you can take to reduce spam from such sources is to give your actual email address only to co-workers, friends, family members, and clients — real people, in other words. Whenever you're asked to provide an address for an online purchase or otherwise make it available to an impersonal entity, use an alias — a temporary or disposable address that points to your main address. You can then watch your incoming mail, and if you see spam coming from that special address, you know that it's been compromised, and you can cancel the address or add a rule (filter) to your email client to reject any future mail sent to that address.

MobileMe members can create up to five aliases to their email accounts. To do so, log in at `www.me.com`, click the Mail icon on the toolbar, and then choose Preferences from the pop-up Action menu (the one with the gear icon). Click Aliases on the toolbar and then follow the instructions to add, change, or remove an alias.

You can also create your own alias on the fly — regardless of your email software or provider — with this handy trick. Take your email address and insert a plus (+) sign and some text between your username and the @ sign. For example, if your address is `name@domain.com`, an alias could be `name+shopping@domain.com` or `name+lists@domain.com`. If someone sends mail to one of these addresses, it's delivered to you because most mail servers ignore the plus sign and anything after it in a username. But your email client can still see it, so you can set up a rule to take special action when a message arrives with a plus sign in the To address. Before giving out such an address, send a test message to yourself to verify that this method works with your mail server.

Alternatively, you can use a service such as spamgourmet (`www.spamgourmet.com`), Spamex (`www.spamex.com`), Sneakemail (`http://sneakemail.com`), or Spam Motel (`www.spammotel.com`) to generate new disposable email addresses whenever you need them. Generally, services like these enable you to completely cancel an email address when the need arises so that it no longer forwards mail to your account.

Tip
I cover anti-spam options for users of Apple Mail in vastly more detail in my ebook *Take Control of Spam with Apple Mail* (`www.takecontrolbooks.com/spam-apple-mail`). ∎

Examining Message Headers and Source

What you see when you read an email message in your inbox may be only a small portion of what the message actually contains. In order to make messages more readable and friendly looking, your email client usually hides some parts of the message and interprets others. For example, if the message contains HTML tags to display text in a special font or to include a graphic with a clickable link to a web page, your email client most likely shows you the styled content the sender intended rather than the cluttered, difficult-to-read underlying code.

Normally, what your email client shows you is exactly what you want. However, occasionally, you may be unable to tell if a message is legitimate or you may receive something so troubling that you feel obligated to report the sender to the authorities. In cases such as these, you need to be able to look behind the scenes to what's really inside your messages. You can do this by examining the message's headers, source, or both.

Message headers

Every email message includes two key parts: the content and the *headers*, lines of text that provide information such as who sent the message, to whom, on what date, and with what subject. Most email clients display just a few of these headers (typically From, To, Date, and Subject) while hiding the rest, which includes all sorts of technical details about the path the message took between sender and recipient and notifications that any of the intermediate mail servers or spam filters may have added. These extra headers, which would normally be distracting to see, can often provide enough information to determine whether a message is spam or not and who its real sender was. So, it pays to know how to view them and at least a few of the basics of how to interpret them.

Viewing message headers

Virtually every email client has a simple command for viewing all the headers of the currently open email message:

- **In Mail:** Choose View ➪ Message ➪ Long Headers. The previously hidden headers appear in the header portion of the window.

- **In Entourage:** Choose Message ➪ Internet Headers. The headers appear in a separate window.

- **In Thunderbird:** Choose View ➪ Headers ➪ All. The previously hidden headers appear in the header portion of the window.

Understanding message headers

Although nearly all messages share a few headers in common, email clients, servers, spam filters, and plug-ins can add more of their own in a variety of formats and orders. Therefore, I can't predict exactly what you may see when you look at a message's headers, but a typical set of headers may look something like the following:

```
Return-path: <noreply@domain.com>
MIME-version: 1.0
Content-transfer-encoding: 8BIT
Content-type: text/html; charset=utf-8
Return-path: <noreply@domain.com>
Received: from smtp-abc000 ([10.10.10.10]) by imap.example.com with
    ESMTP id <EDCBA@imap.example.com> for name@example.com;
    Sun, 11 Jan 2009 18:03:29 -0800 (PST)
Original-recipient: rfc822; name@example.com
```

```
Received: from smtp.provider.com ([22.22.22.22]) by smtp.example.com
    with SMTP id <ABCDE@smtp.example.com> for name@example.com
    (ORCPT name@example.com); Sun, 11 Jan 2009 18:03:28 -0800 (PST)
Received: from 12345.localisp.com [66.66.66.66] by
    smtp.provider.com; Sun, 11 Jan 2009 18:03:25 -0800 (PST)
To: "Your Name" <name@example.com>
Subject: Mystery Message
Date: Sun, 11 Jan 2009 13:42:08 +0100
From: "Read This Now" <noreply@domain.com>
Message-ID: <12345678.090123@domain.com>
X-Mailer: MailXSender
```

As you can see, each header goes on its own line; those that are longer than the window is wide may wrap onto one or more additional lines, which are typically shown indented. Headers begin with the header name (such as Return-path or Received), followed by a colon and the contents of the header.

The Received header

In terms of understanding a message's provenance, the most important headers are those that begin with Received. These detail the path the message took from the sender's computer, through one or more SMTP servers, to your email provider's POP, IMAP, or Exchange server. In the best cases, they provide an IP address that you can trace back to a single individual; at the very least, they should give you a good idea of the area and perhaps the organization where the message originated.

Received headers may appear in chronological or reverse-chronological order; you can usually tell which by examining the time stamps at the ends of each one — although, keep in mind that the message may have traveled through multiple time zones, so some translation may be necessary, and that any given server's clock could be out of sync with the others.

By looking at the sequence of Received headers in the previous example, you can see that the earliest time stamp is in the third Received header:

```
Received: from 12345.localisp.com [66.66.66.66] by
    smtp.provider.com; Sun, 11 Jan 2009 18:03:25 -0800 (PST)
```

This line says that the message originated at a computer with a domain name of 12345. localisp.com and an IP address of 66.66.66.66. That could be the sender's home computer or router, a webmail server, or a computer on a corporate network (among other options), but if this line shows up, it's usually a good indication of where the message started its journey. You can use an IP address lookup tool such as the one at http://cqcounter.com/whois to determine the geographical location of this or any other IP address and also the name of the entity to which it's assigned. This line also says that the domain name of the SMTP server that accepted the message from the sender was smtp.provider.com; once again, you can look up this name to determine what and where it is.

After that, the message took its next hop:

```
Received: from smtp.provider.com ([22.22.22.22]) by smtp.example.com
    with SMTP id <ABCDE@smtp.example.com> for name@example.com
    (ORCPT name@example.com); Sun, 11 Jan 2009 18:03:28 -0800 (PST)
```

In this move, it traveled from the `smtp.provider.com` server (which you now know has the IP address `22.22.22.22`) to `smtp.example.com`. This second hop is most likely the SMTP server your email provider uses to receive incoming mail, although some messages go through several other intermediate servers. In this example, because the domain name of the mail server and that of your email address are the same (`example.com`), you know for sure that it's your email provider's server.

Finally, the message makes one last, small move:

```
Received: from smtp-abc000 ([10.10.10.10]) by imap.example.com with
    ESMTP id <EDCBA@imap.example.com> for name@example.com;
    Sun, 11 Jan 2009 18:03:29 -0800 (PST)
```

Because the name of the server in this header is `imap.example.com`, and in the previous example, it was `smtp.example.com`, you can tell that your email provider uses one server to accept incoming mail and a different one to store and deliver those messages to you (in this case, by IMAP). This final hop simply transferred the message from one server at your email provider to another.

The X-Mailer header

Although any header may contain something of interest, one you should look for particularly is the X-Mailer header. In the example, it reads as follows:

```
X-Mailer: MailXSender
```

The X-Mailer header — which isn't guaranteed to be in any message, I should point out — tells you what software sent the message. In this case, the software was called MailXSender, which a quick web search tells me is a program designed mainly for sending messages to large mailing lists. So, that strongly suggests the sender might be a spammer. For a list of X-Mailer headers commonly associated with spam, see `http://postfixmail.com/blog/?p=303`.

You can also learn other interesting things from the X-Mailer header — sometimes by doing web searches on the name of the software. For example, all these are programs that run only on Macs:

```
X-Mailer: Apple Mail (2.930.3)
X-Mailer: CTM PowerMail version 6.0 build 4587 English (intel)
    <http://www.ctmdev.com>
X-Mailer: Mailsmith 2.2
```

These run only on Windows computers:

```
X-Mailer: Microsoft Outlook, Build 10.0.6838
```

```
X-Mailer: Microsoft Outlook Express 6.00.2900.2180
X-Mailer: UnityMail
```

And this one is available only in Chinese, which again gives you a clue as to the sender's origin:

```
X-Mailer: FoxMail 4.0 beta 2 [cn]
```

The absence of an X-Mailer header doesn't mean the message is spam, but an X-Mailer that doesn't make sense given the message content or what you know about the alleged sender could help you determine that the message isn't genuine.

Message source

Headers alone don't tell the whole story of an email message, especially when it's sent in HTML or rich text, in which case, information can be hidden from most email clients. The most prominent example is a phishing attempt, in which a message claiming to be from your bank, PayPal, eBay, or another large organization asks you to click on a link to verify or confirm your account. If you were to do so, you'd be taken to a fake website whose only purpose is to collect usernames, passwords, and other personal information from unsuspecting victims — enabling someone to steal your money, your identity, or both. The link may simply say Click here (or words to that effect) or it may contain a URL. But how do you know the text of the link truly represents the domain to which the link points? For that, you must examine the message source.

Cross-Ref
For more on phishing, see Chapter 10. ■

As with displaying message headers, almost all email clients make it easy for you to see the source of the currently open message:

- **In Mail:** Choose View ➪ Message ➪ Raw Source. The source appears in the message window.
- **In Entourage:** Choose Message ➪ Source. The source appears in a separate window.
- **In Thunderbird:** Choose View ➪ Message Source. The source appears in a separate window.

In the source view, you can usually see all the underlying codes used to generate the text that appears in the message's normal view. Some messages contain two or more segments, each with the content in a different version (for example, a plain text version and an HTML version), so you may have to scroll to see the portion that interests you. Be aware, however, that some messages are encoded in such a way that when viewing the source, you see nothing but a string of random-looking characters, so viewing the source doesn't always show you what you want to see.

If you suspect that a message is a phishing attempt, scan the source for the link text that appeared in the normal view of the message. If the domain name doesn't match, if it points to a numeric IP address, or if it seems suspicious in any other way, don't click the link!

iChat Security

Mac OS X's iChat software offers an easy way to exchange real-time text messages (instant messaging), chat using audio or video, transfer files, and share photo albums, movies, presentations, and other multimedia data across the Internet. It works with MobileMe accounts as well as with AIM (AOL Instant Messenger), Google Talk, and Jabber accounts — and with other Macs on your local network via Bonjour.

iChat includes two categories of security settings. First, you can specify, for some account types, which users can or can't contact you and whether anyone can see that you're idle. And second, MobileMe users can encrypt iChat sessions in their entirety to avoid the possibility of chats being intercepted in transit.

Adjusting iChat privacy settings

To change iChat's privacy settings, follow these steps:

1. With iChat running, log in to each of your accounts if you haven't already done so.

2. Choose iChat ⇨ Preferences to open the Preferences window and then click Accounts to open the Accounts pane.

3. In the Accounts list on the left, select any MobileMe, Mac.com/.Mac, or AIM account. Privacy settings don't apply to other account types.

Note
Even though MobileMe replaced .Mac, as far as iChat is concerned, Mac.com (.Mac) and MobileMe are still two separate things. When you use an @mac.com address, that's considered .Mac (in Leopard) or Mac.com (in Snow Leopard), not MobileMe. When you use an @me.com address, that's MobileMe.

4. Click the Security tab, shown in Figure 9.21.

5. To prevent iChat from changing your status from Available to Idle if you haven't used your Mac in the last 10 minutes (which can alert people who have you on their Buddy Lists that you're not at your desk), click the Block others from seeing that I am idle check box.

6. Click one of the radio buttons under Privacy Level, according to your preferences:

   - **Allow anyone.** Lets anyone who knows your ID see your status and initiate a chat with you

   - **Allow people in my Buddy List.** Lets only those in your Buddy List see your status and initiate chats

   - **Allow specific people.** Blocks everyone except those you specify from seeing your status and initiating chats. To add someone to the list, click Edit List, click the Add (+) button, and then type an AIM ID or an email address ending in @mac.com or @me.com, as shown in Figure 9.22. Repeat as necessary and then click Done.

- **Block everyone.** Blocks everyone from seeing your status and initiating chats

- **Block specific people.** Allows everyone except those you specify to see your status and initiate chats. To add someone to the list, click Edit List, click the Add (+) button, and type an AIM ID or an email address ending in @mac.com or @me.com, as shown in Figure 9.22. Repeat as necessary and then click Done.

7. **Repeat steps 3 to 6 for each MobileMe, Mac.com/.Mac, and AIM account you have.**

8. **Close the Accounts window.** Changes you've made take effect immediately.

FIGURE 9.21

In iChat's Security pane, you can determine (among other things) whether someone can see when you're idle.

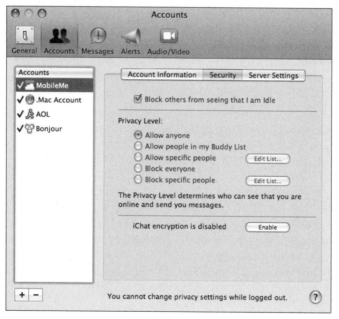

FIGURE 9.22

If you want to allow only a select few people to initiate iChat sessions with you, add their email addresses to this list.

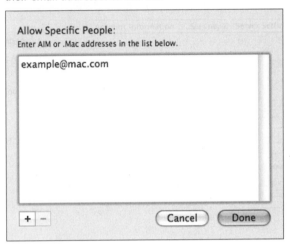

Allow Specific People:
Enter AIM or .Mac addresses in the list below.

example@mac.com

Using encryption for iChat

MobileMe offers encryption for iChat, which means that all the data sent and received with iChat is encrypted — not just text but audio, video, and other data too. It's an excellent way to ensure that your iChat communication remains private, but it works only when both parties (or all parties, in the case of multi-user chats) are logged in with MobileMe (or Mac.com/.Mac) accounts and when all parties have encryption enabled.

To enable iChat encryption, each user should follow these steps:

1. With iChat running, choose iChat ➪ Preferences to open the Preferences window and then click Accounts to open the Accounts pane.

2. In the Accounts list on the left, select any MobileMe or Mac.com/.Mac account.

3. Click the Security tab.

4. At the bottom of the window, if you see a message that says iChat encryption is enabled, you don't need to do anything further — just close the window.

5. Click Enable. A new window, shown in Figure 9.23, opens.

6. Leave the Enable iChat encryption check box selected and then click Continue.

7. On the next screen, click Done.

8. Wait for a few moments until the iChat Preferences window says iChat encryption is enabled and then close the window.

Assuming both (or all) parties of a chat are logged in using MobileMe/Mac.com/.Mac and have encryption enabled, chat windows show a lock icon in the title bar (and say Encrypted Chat initially) to confirm that the sessions are encrypted.

Note

In addition to offering encryption for email, PGP (described earlier in this chapter) can encrypt text-based instant messaging sessions and file transfers in iChat. This avoids the need for both parties to use MobileMe/Mac.com/.Mac accounts but imposes other restrictions — the other user must also have PGP installed and be using either iChat or, on Windows, AIM. PGP doesn't encrypt audio or video chats. ■

FIGURE 9.23

Enabling iChat encryption requires just a few clicks for MobileMe members — leave this check box selected, click Continue, and then click Done.

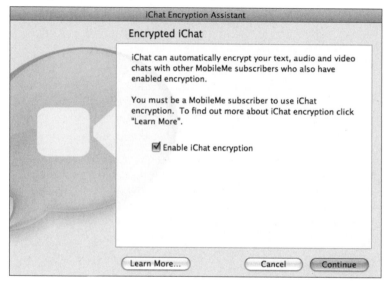

Securing Instant Messaging and Voice over IP with Third-Party Software

iChat started out as a text-based instant messaging system and later added audio and video capabilities. Dozens of third-party Mac applications also offer some combination of text, audio, and video chat features. Closely related to audio chat is *voice over IP* (VoIP). In its broadest sense, VoIP refers to any method of conducting real-time audio conversations over an IP network (such as the Internet), but the term is more often applied to systems that use the Internet to carry audio conversations to or from conventional telephone networks. Most VoIP software lets you use your Mac as a telephone, placing calls to (and/or receiving calls from) regular telephone numbers.

As previously described, iChat lets you encrypt your conversations (of whichever variety) as long as all participants are using MobileMe or .Mac accounts and have encryption enabled. However, most instant messaging and VoIP programs offer no encryption capabilities. Someone with access to Internet traffic between you and another participant could conceivably watch your text messages in real time, listen to the audio of the conversation, and watch the video. The real-world risk of your communication channel being compromised is small, but even so, if you have anything especially sensitive to discuss, an unencrypted digital stream isn't the wisest way to do so.

Unfortunately, most instant messaging and VoIP software doesn't include encryption, even as an option. If encrypted iChat isn't an option for one or more of the participants or if you need to communicate securely with someone on a conventional telephone network, you have several choices. Because this category of software is advancing rapidly, you may have many more choices than what I list here, but these should give you a start.

Skype

Skype (www.skype.com) is a free application that resembles iChat in that it can be used for text, audio, and video chats. But unlike iChat, Skype can be used to reach ordinary telephone numbers (SkypeOut) and can also receive incoming calls placed by conventional telephones (SkypeIn). SkypeOut and SkypeIn are optional services, requiring additional fees, but they give your Mac the capability to make and receive phone calls almost anywhere in the world.

All Skype communication is automatically and transparently encrypted. So, if you're using Skype to communicate with another Skype user, you can rest assured that the data is encrypted end to end. And unlike iChat, Skype doesn't use a central server to mediate conversations, so connections occur directly between the two clients — eliminating another possible point where data could be intercepted. However, Skype encryption ends (or starts, as the case may be) with the connection to the telephone network. Audio sent over an analog telephone line isn't encrypted, so if you use Skype to talk to someone on a regular telephone, someone could tap into the phone line on the other end and listen to both sides of the conversation.

Zfone

Zfone (http://zfoneproject.com) is a new application invented by Phil Zimmerman, who created Pretty Good Privacy (PGP). It's essentially an encryption add-on to existing VoIP software. So, if you want to use a computer-to-computer instant messaging or VoIP program that lacks encryption, such as Yahoo! Messenger (http://messenger.yahoo.com/) or Gizmo5 (http://gizmo5.com/), Zfone offers a way to do so — as long as the person on the other end also has Zfone installed. Zfone is available for Windows and Linux as well as Mac OS X.

The biggest limitation to Zfone is that it doesn't directly work with conventional telephones — you must have a device running the Zfone software on both ends. Various manufacturers are developing hardware that lets you use Zfone in conjunction with standard telephones connected to VoIP services, such as Vonage (with no computer required), but such devices may not be widely available for some time — and even when they are, you can carry on encrypted telephone conversations only if the other party is using a Zfone-enabled device.

Adium

Adium (`http://trac.adiumx.com/wiki/AboutAdium`) is a free, open-source instant messaging program that works with a variety of services (including AIM/iChat, MSN Messenger, and Jabber). It includes OTR (Off-the-Record) encryption capabilities, but you can encrypt a conversation only if the other person also uses OTR software. Adium is currently a text-only instant messaging application, although the developers have plans to add audio and video capabilities in the future.

Psi

Psi (`http://psi-im.org/`) is another free, open-source text chat program, available for Mac OS X, Windows, and Linux. It currently supports only the Jabber protocol. Psi offers two types of encryption. It has the built-in capability to encrypt the data flowing between any participant and the Jabber server. And if both parties have the free GPG software installed (`www.gnupg.org`), you can encrypt conversations from end to end.

Summary

This chapter covered various ways to keep person-to-person communication on your Mac private. I began with an overview of email security and then moved on to explain how to prevent your passwords — as well as the contents of your incoming and outgoing messages — from being intercepted in transit. I explained how to digitally sign messages so the recipient can confirm the sender (and that the message hasn't been tampered with) and how to encrypt messages to prevent them from being read while stored on a mail server.

Because junk mail isn't merely annoying but can also contain viruses, phishing attempts, and other security threats, I described several ways of reducing spam as well as ways to discover more about a message's origins. I then showed how to encrypt instant messaging sessions as well as audio communication using voice over IP.

Browsing the Web Securely

T he word *browse* sounds so innocent, evoking images of strolling up and down the aisles of a library or bookstore or flipping through the pages of a catalog. What could be safer? But when it's the web you're talking about, browsing suddenly takes on a whole new range of meanings. Now the visions you see may be those of pop-up windows, stolen personal information, rude anonymous commenters, and unreliable rumors — all surrounded by so many ads, you can barely find any useful information.

The web can be a safe and useful place or it can be a jungle with perils at every turn. The quality and security of your web-browsing experience depend on many factors, including the sites you visit, the software you use, and the ways you choose to interact with the information you encounter. As with most matters of security, a little common sense goes a long way. The more you understand about the risks you face and the tools and techniques with which you can conquer them, the safer you'll be.

Note

Although there are more than a dozen web browsers that run under Mac OS X, in this chapter, I provide specific instructions only for the two most popular ones: Safari from Apple and Firefox from Mozilla. If you prefer another browser, consult its documentation for instructions on performing similar activities. ■

The Challenges of Secure Browsing

As the Internet's most visible feature, the web attracts hundreds of millions of visitors every day. Wherever you get a large crowd of people together, there are bound to be some shady characters looking to make a quick buck or just cause trouble, and the web is no exception. Unfortunately, the interconnected nature of the web makes it tricky to avoid danger altogether.

In order to browse the web safely and securely, one must consider and take measures to address (through software, behavior, or both) a number of issues.

Privacy

Picture the simplest possible web activity: visiting a single web page. Merely by typing a URL in your browser, you set in motion a series of actions that can reveal private information to other people. For example, any or all of the following could (and often do) happen:

- The web server you visit records the time and date of your visit, which page you viewed, details about which browser and operating system you used, the resolution of your display and how many colors it supports, your browser's default language, the last page you visited, and your IP address — which can in turn reveal your ISP and your geographical location, sometimes right down to your street address. The server may also calculate your connection speed and, if you visit more than one page, track how much time you spend on each one. Some servers collect even more information.

- The web server may write information to a file on your disk called a cookie so the next time you visit the site (or, in some cases, an entirely different site), the server can tell that you're the same person who visited previously. Cookies can be used for a wide variety of reasons — most quite legitimate and some entirely nefarious — as described later in this chapter.

- If you happen to type any information into a form on the page you visit, that information may be stored on the server and shared with other people or companies.

- Your browser keeps a record of the page you visited in its history list, and your computer may keep other sorts of logs detailing your Internet activities. Browsers typically cache graphics (to enable pages to load faster the next time) and sometimes other data too. Often, your computer also indexes every word on the web page so you can search later for text on a page you visited and retrieve its URL. In some cases (generally with the addition of third-party software), your computer can preserve on your disk a complete copy of every page you visit, without further interaction. And if the site you visited used a plug-in (such as Flash or QuickTime), the plug-in itself may log or cache information even if your browser doesn't.

- Your local ISP, at the other end of your broadband or dial-up connection, may also keep a log of every website you visit, along with times and dates.

- Potentially, a government agency, a hacker, or some other party could covertly monitor some portion of the Internet between your computer and the server, thus obtaining all the information about your visit. Similarly, if anyone obtained access to your computer — physically or over the Internet — they could read your browsing history, logs, and similar information.

The frightening thing is that even though your name, email address, home address, and phone number don't show up anywhere in this list, they can often be inferred. Perhaps you mentioned in a blog post that you live across from a certain park, and you brag on your Facebook profile that you've got a 30-inch display on your Mac. Those facts alone, combined with the information you reveal to every website you visit, could be enough to identify you uniquely to anyone who cared to look closely enough at server logs and do a bit of research. Once someone knows who you are and what websites you visit, he or she could use that information to try to sell you things, to steal your identity, or even, in extreme cases, to blackmail you.

Keep in mind that this private information is spread out. You can wipe details about your browsing history off your computer, but that doesn't prevent them from being stored on a web server. You can block a web server from detecting or storing certain kinds of data, but that doesn't necessarily prevent your ISP or an intermediate party from seeing the information. In short, the very act of visiting any web page exposes potentially private information to people who may not treat it with care.

I want to emphasize that in this description, I don't assume that you're doing anything improper or unseemly. Whether you visit a site promoting a radical political cause or disney.com, you record and potentially expose the same information. Of course, if you do frequent questionable or controversial sites, you can assume that your level of risk increases accordingly. Although a site may be scrupulous about protecting visitors' privacy, some information can leak out — and in most cases, even strict privacy policies don't prevent sites from logging the sort of standard visitor data just described. And if you use the web to access your email, edit files and photos, and do other tasks traditionally associated with desktop applications, you expose yourself even further to privacy breaches.

Fraud

Because the web is so often used to buy and sell things, to conduct banking, and to engage in other financial transactions, opportunities for fraud are rampant. At one end of the spectrum are phishing sites, which exist for the sole purpose of capturing information that can enable someone to steal your money, make purchases in your name, or otherwise defraud you. At the other end are perfectly legitimate sites that collect your credit card information for purchases or subscriptions — but then inadvertently expose your data when their own servers are hacked into, a disgruntled employee goes digging through a database, or someone loses a laptop with customer information. When you send your financial information over the web, no matter how trustworthy the recipient may be or what security measures they put into place, there's always a small chance that your data could fall into the wrong hands.

Your web browser itself (or third-party add-on software) can add yet another complication. Many tools exist to enable you to store contact information, credit card numbers, and other personal details — and use that information to fill in the forms you encounter so often on the web with just a keystroke or two. That's a tremendous convenience, but it also creates an additional security risk because if anyone else obtains access to your computer and can discover the password with which you protect that personal information (or, worse, if you leave it unlocked), your financial assets are just as much at risk as if someone obtained the information from a web server.

Malware

Viruses, worms, spyware, and other malware may be transmitted by email or placed directly on your computer by someone who has found a way to hack in remotely. But the web is another way to spread malware — particularly Trojan horses, which are programs that perform malicious activities but are disguised as (or bundled inside) useful applications, such as games or video players. If a site can persuade you to download and run such a program that you think is helpful in some way, they've used you as an accomplice in spreading their malware.

Cross-Ref

For more on malware, see Chapter 14. ■

Inappropriate content

The web has given all new meaning to free speech. Any imaginable word, image, or information — no matter how disturbing, offensive, or otherwise objectionable one might consider it — can easily be found (and, in fact, can hardly be avoided). Although the typical reaction people may have is simply to ignore or navigate away from anything they dislike, inappropriate content becomes a more serious issue in certain situations.

First, if children use or have access to the web on your Mac, you may (as a parent or guardian) prefer that they not be exposed to certain kinds of content. Even if it's impossible — and perhaps undesirable — to shield a child completely from all potentially corrupting influences, most adults would agree that some limits should be placed on what young children can see and read.

Cross-Ref

For more on parental controls, see Chapter 3. ■

But even adults may want to avoid some kinds of information on the web, especially at work. The frequency of the acronym NSFW (not safe for work) as a warning label on websites and blogs should be sufficient evidence that employers typically frown on the use of business computers, during work hours, to view sites that are clearly non-work-related and which could offend one's co-workers. If viewing a website could lead to the loss of your job, that certainly counts as a security issue — job security!

The problem for children and adults alike is that one can't always know before visiting a site what its contents are. You might find an interesting-looking link on a blog or search engine and follow it quite innocently, only to find something inappropriate on the other end. If you accidentally stumble onto a site that's extremely inappropriate, information about that visit is stored in your browsing history, server logs, and other places just as if you'd gone there intentionally. You may have difficulty convincing an employer, spouse, or parent that the visit was inadvertent.

Of course, what's inappropriate depends on the person and the context. Apart from information that's indisputably illegal, dangerous, or defamatory, there are countless sites displaying content that one person may bristle at, whereas another may find it entirely benign (or that may be legal in one jurisdiction but not in another). But there's a class of sites that I'll go out on a limb and label "unsavory" — those that traffic in porn, online gambling, pirated software and media, and the like — that tend to be problematic regardless of their actual legality. Although there's no direct cause-and-effect relationship, anecdotal evidence suggests a strong correlation between such sites and the incidence of other concerns described here (privacy breaches, fraud, malware, and pop-up windows, for example). It's very much like the real world: Although a crime can happen anywhere, if you walk down certain streets at certain times of the day, your odds of becoming a victim increase.

Annoyances

Beyond obvious concerns of privacy and security are issues that appear at first glance merely to be annoying. Nearly every web user encounters irritations such as the following:

- **Advertising.** Many websites wouldn't exist if it weren't for the income they receive from advertising, and there's nothing wrong with that in and of itself. But when ads are too numerous, too pushy, or too distracting, they begin to cross the line from a necessary evil to an evil necessity.

- **Pop-up (and pop-under) windows.** A special (and specially hated) variety of advertising is the pop-up window, which tries to grab your attention by coming between you and the page you're trying to view. Because many browsers have included effective blockers that prevent conventional pop-up windows from appearing, an increasingly common tactic is to use Flash or other mechanisms to put pop-up-like ads in front of a page's content that don't actually create a new window. Another variant is the pop-under window, in which a new window appears behind your browser window so that you see it only after you've closed the page you're viewing.

- **Flash.** Adobe's Flash technology can enrich web browsing with movies, animations, and complex user interfaces. Flash is terrific for certain applications, but an unfortunate number of sites misuse it, increasing the time it takes for pages to load, distracting viewers with unnecessary bells and whistles, and making users jump through extra hoops to get to the information they want.

- **Sounds.** Some web pages begin playing music, movies, recorded speech, or other sounds as soon as they load — and, often, they provide no obvious way to turn off the sound. Besides being annoying, such pages can be embarrassing in business environments.

All these things and many more detract from the experience of using the web, but they also carry security implications. Every ad you see could produce another line of data in a server log (even if you don't click on it), and many of them write to or read from cookies on your disk to track your behavior. In some instances, Flash can store or transmit private information about you without your knowledge, and some versions have had significant security flaws. And simply visiting a page with sound can tell those around you something about your browsing habits that you may not want them to know.

Using SSL Encryption

By default, all information that moves between your web browser and a web server (in either direction) is sent over the Internet in its raw, unencrypted form using HTTP (Hypertext Transfer Protocol). Ordinarily, this is no problem because most of the information on the web is, by definition, public, and most of the information sent by your web browser simply contains requests for that information. However, because it's relatively easy for someone to observe Internet traffic as it travels between browser and server, unencrypted HTTP isn't a safe way to transmit sensitive information, such as passwords, bank account numbers, and medical records.

Most sites that let you send or receive any sort of private information use SSL to encrypt the entire session between your browser and the server so that if anyone were to intercept the data, all he or she would see is a seemingly random stream of scrambled characters. SSL-protected sites use the HTTPS protocol (S for secure), and thus their URLs begin with the scheme `https://` rather than `http://`. In addition, when you're connected to a secure website, your browser usually displays the icon of a locked padlock — often in the corner of the window, in the title bar, or (in the case of Safari 4, for example) in the tab corresponding to that page.

Note

SSL isn't the only way of securing data sent and received by web pages, but it's the most commonly used. Apple's MobileMe service, for example, uses SSL only for the login page but thereafter uses a proprietary, behind-the-scenes method of encrypting data. ■

SSL was invented by Netscape, and after going through three major revisions (versions 1, 2, and 3), it was superseded by a similar but open standard called TLS (transport layer security). Most modern web servers and browsers support both SSL and TLS. Although the two aren't interoperable, if a browser tries to initiate a TLS session and the server supports only SSL, both automatically drop back to using SSL. From the user's point of view, there's no difference in behavior between SSL and TLS, and even though TLS is technically the modern standard, the term *SSL* is often used to refer to either system.

Cross-Ref

For more on SSL, see Chapter 9. ■

The decision whether to use SSL isn't usually in the hands of the person browsing the web — it's determined by the server's configuration. In most cases, if a site supports SSL, visitors are automatically redirected to an `https://` link, at least when you get to the portion of the site where you must log in and thereafter send or receive private information. However, some sites offer secure logins only as an option, so if you see a link or button that says Log in securely or words to that effect, it's always a good idea to click it. Occasionally, sites offer, but don't advertise, SSL capabilities. If you're about to type a password or other private information and notice that you're not on a secure page, try manually adding an s after the `http` in the URL and reloading to see if a secure version of the page is available.

Caution

Get in the habit of looking for the padlock icon before typing information on any web form, especially passwords. If a site doesn't offer SSL encryption, be aware that any data you send using the form could be compromised. Contact the site owner to inquire about an SSL version of the site. ■

As useful as SSL is, you should also be aware of some relatively uncommon but potentially serious risks when using seemingly secure sites. Suppose you're on a site that uses SSL, and you can verify this by the presence of the padlock icon and `https://` at the beginning of the URL. That means the page you're currently viewing was sent to you encrypted. However, it's possible that the encrypted page includes some elements that were delivered by other, SSL-less servers; these items could be as insignificant as graphics or style sheets or, in theory, sensitive text data that's in fact being sent to you unencrypted. Firefox can display an explicit warning when it encounters such pages; to enable it, choose Firefox ➪ Preferences, click Security, click Settings, click the I'm about to view an encrypted page that contains some unencrypted information check box, and then click OK.

Another potential concern is that the padlock icon and URL don't tell you anything about the next page you visit on the site. A careless web designer could design a form in such a way that even though the form is delivered to your browser in an encrypted form, the destination to which the form data is sent when you submit it is a plain HTTP URL — which would mean the information you typed into the form is sent unencrypted despite the fact that the form itself is encrypted! To guard against this, Safari includes a preference, enabled by default, that warns you if you try to submit data using such a form. To find the preference, choose Safari ➪ Preferences and then click Security. The Ask before sending a nonsecure form from a secure website check box at the bottom of the window should be selected. Firefox doesn't check for this situation specifically, but it does offer a broader warning when you submit any unencrypted form information (even if the site doesn't use SSL at all). To enable this warning, choose Firefox ➪ Preferences, click Security, click Settings, click the I submit information that's not encrypted check box, and then click OK.

Despite these rare issues, SSL is an extremely important and effective means of protecting your data, and if it were used on every single site, the risks of having information intercepted or stolen would decrease dramatically. So, why don't more sites use SSL? For one thing, it's not trivial to set up. The website owner must go through a sometimes expensive process to obtain (and periodically renew) an SSL certificate and must also perform a series of steps to install it and configure the web server properly — all of which may be easy enough for an experienced systems administrator but beyond the means or ability of nontechnical people. But SSL is expensive in another sense: It puts an additional processing burden on the server to encrypt or decrypt all the data it exchanges. This means a given server can't handle as many requests at once or (to look at it from another point of view) that more processing power is needed to handle a given number of requests. Either way, that translates into increased cost for the site owner, especially if the site receives a large volume of traffic.

Cross-Ref

For more on using SSL to protect pages served by your Mac running Mac OS X Server, see Chapter 27. ■

Checking a certificate

When you connect to a page that's protected with SSL, your main concern is normally just to see that the padlock icon is there and that no warning messages have appeared. However, any site can obtain an SSL certificate, and the fact that your communication is encrypted doesn't guarantee that the site itself is legitimate or that its owners are trustworthy. If you have any doubts about the authenticity of an SSL-protected site or the identity of the person or organization running it, you can get more information by examining the site's SSL certificate.

The certificate lists, among many other things, the name and location of the entity that requested it and the certificate authority that issued it. If you see that the certificate is self-signed and you don't know or trust the organization or individual who issued it, you should think twice before typing any personal information on the site.

When you're connected to an SSL-protected site in Safari, you can view its certificate by clicking on the padlock icon (which appears in the top-right corner of the window). A dialog box opens, as shown in Figure 10.1. Click the disclosure triangle next to the word Details (and other triangles beneath it) to reveal further information about the certificate.

FIGURE 10.1

When you click the padlock icon at the top of an SSL-protected page, you can see details about the site's certificate.

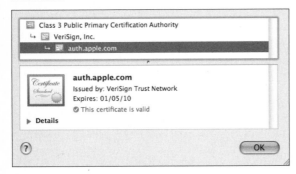

When you're connected to an SSL-protected site in Firefox, you can view its certificate by choosing Tools ⇨ Page Info (⌘+I), clicking the Security tab, and then clicking View Certificate.

Responding to certificate warnings

On occasion, you may connect to a web page and see a certificate warning in your browser. For example, Safari displays a dialog box like the one shown in Figure 10.2, whereas Firefox puts a message in the main window, as shown in Figure 10.3. Warnings like these mean your browser has determined that something isn't quite right about the certificate and that you should proceed with caution.

Most certificate warnings turn out to have harmless causes. That's not to say the site owner shouldn't remedy them but rather that they don't constitute a security risk. One common cause is when an organization uses a certificate that was created for one server on another one. Most SSL certificates are tied to specific server names (for example, `www.domain.com`), and if a site owner uses the same certificate with another domain (say, `secure.domain.com`), that mismatch produces a warning. Other common causes for warnings are expired certificates and self-signed certificates (often issued by smaller organizations, especially for internal use, in order to save money and bother).

FIGURE 10.2

When a site's certificate doesn't match what Safari expects to see, the browser displays a warning like this one so that you can determine if the site is legitimate before proceeding.

FIGURE 10.3

Firefox makes it impossible to miss warnings about certificates that might be problematic.

If you see a certificate warning in Safari, you have the following options:

- Click Continue to accept the certificate for this one visit only.

- Click Cancel to not connect to the site.

- Click Show Certificate to see what's in the certificate and to show additional information, as shown in Figure 10.4. Click the disclosure triangle next to Details to learn who requested and granted the certificate, among other information. If you're satisfied that the page is safe to visit and you want to trust this certificate not just now but also in the future, click the disclosure triangle next to Trust, choose Always Trust from the When using this certificate pop-up menu, and then click Continue. Safari adds the certificate, along with the access privileges you selected, to your keychain.

If you see a certificate warning in Firefox, click the Or you can add an exception link, which displays additional information and two more buttons. Click Add Exception to open a dialog box in which you can take additional action. Click Get Certificate to show what Firefox considers problematic with the certificate, as shown in Figure 10.5, and then click View to see the contents of the certificate itself. If you want to trust this certificate from now on, click Confirm Security Exception.

FIGURE 10.4

You can display more details about a certificate that caused a warning in Safari. To learn still more, click the disclosure triangle next to Details.

FIGURE 10.5

When you click Get Certificate, Firefox fills in this window with information about what caused the certificate warning.

Keeping Form Information Safe

Earlier, I explained the importance of checking to see that a web page is protected with SSL before typing any personal information in a form. Crucial as that is, it's not the only factor determining whether your form information is safe. You must also consider how the information is stored and accessed on your Mac.

Most web browsers — and numerous third-party utilities — include facilities for storing usernames, passwords, addresses, account numbers, and other such data commonly used on web forms and then inserting the information for you automatically or on demand. Automatic form-filling features save you typing, reduce the need to remember passwords, and ensure accuracy when typing data. But the flip side of this convenience is that anyone else with physical access can also fill in web forms automatically using your data — thus compromising your security and privacy and possibly your money — unless you take explicit steps to protect this information.

If you're the only person who uses your Mac and if you keep it in a safe place where no one else can access it, you may find that implementing additional security measures is more bother than it's worth. But in shared or public environments or when there's a significant risk of your Mac being stolen, protecting form data is extremely important.

Using your browser's form-filling feature

Every browser handles form filling in its own way, but what typically happens when you turn on an AutoFill feature is that when you submit a form, the browser takes note of what information you've filled into each field and saves it for you — either automatically or after a confirmation prompt — so that when you visit the same form or a similar form in the future, you can fill in all that data quickly. When you return to a page for which you've saved form data, you may be able to fill in the fields with a keystroke or two or by choosing a menu command or clicking a button.

Some browsers store usernames and passwords in your keychain, whereas others have a built-in database of some kind. Because your keychain isn't designed for holding other types of structured information, though, such as contact details and credit card numbers, those sorts of data usually go somewhere else.

Safari

Safari's AutoFill feature comprises three categories of data, each of which can be enabled or disabled separately:

- **Contact information.** First, there's your personal contact data, such as your name, address, and phone number, which Safari retrieves automatically from your personal card in Address Book. AutoFill of contact data is enabled by default.

- **Usernames and passwords.** Credentials for the websites you visit are stored in your keychain. This option is disabled by default.

- **Other forms.** Anything that isn't personal contact information, a username, or a password goes into a third category, which is also enabled by default. Safari stores this data separately, in the file ~/Library/Safari/Form Values. The file is encrypted, and Safari stores the decryption key in your keychain.

Note

Other form data may include search terms, account identifiers, URLs, site preferences, and any other miscellaneous data that wouldn't appear in your Address Book card. However, Safari respects the HTML autocomplete="off" HTML form attribute often used on sites that collect credit card numbers and other sensitive data; any form element marked with this tag won't be stored, regardless of your Safari settings. ■

To configure AutoFill, follow these steps:

1. With Safari running, choose Safari ⇨ Preferences to open the Preferences window and then click AutoFill to open the AutoFill pane, as shown in Figure 10.6.

2. To enable Safari to use your Address Book data (from your personal card only), click the Using info from my Address Book card check box. To disable this feature, click the check box to deselect it. To open your personal card in Address Book to add, remove, or change any of its information, click Edit.

FIGURE 10.6

In this preference pane, you can turn on or off any of the three types of AutoFill that Safari offers.

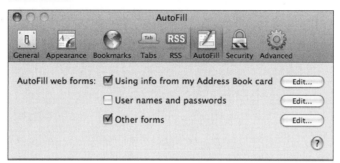

3. **To enable Safari to save and fill in usernames and passwords, click the User names and passwords check box.** To disable this feature, click the check box to deselect it. To see the websites for which you've stored credentials and their associated usernames, click the Edit button. You can then select any item and then click Remove to delete it from your keychain or click Remove All to delete all of them. However, to see the password associated with any item, you must open `/Applications/Utilities/Keychain Access`.

4. **Click Done to close the list of credentials.**

5. **To enable Safari to save and fill in other form data, click the Other forms check box.** To disable this feature, click the check box to deselect it. To see the sites for which you've stored this data, click the Edit button. You can then select any item and then click Remove to delete it or click Remove All to delete all of them. However, note that Safari offers no way whatsoever to view or edit this other form data. Click Done to close the list of websites and then close the Preferences window.

Once AutoFill is turned on, its operation consists of two phases: collecting form data (except for your Address Book card, which it doesn't modify) and filling it in. The behavior depends on the kind of data you fill in.

For usernames and passwords, as soon as you type your credentials on a site and then click the Submit button, Safari displays an alert like the one shown in Figure 10.7. To save this set of credentials in your keychain, click Yes. To continue with the form submission without letting Safari store your credentials, click Not Now. To prevent Safari from saving your credentials now and from prompting you to save them for this particular website in the future, click Never for this Website.

FIGURE 10.7

Even though you've turned on the Safari AutoFill feature for usernames and passwords, you must explicitly agree to each set of credentials before Safari stores them in your keychain.

For other form data, Safari silently stores the information in the background as you fill in forms and then click the Submit button.

When you're viewing a web form for which Safari has previously stored data — or which asks for personal information stored in your Address Book card — you can fill in that data in any of three ways:

- Choose Edit ⇨ AutoFill Form or press ⌘+Shift+A. Safari fills in all the form values for which it can find matching fields. This may not be all of them, and sometimes, Safari fills in fields you'd rather leave blank, so you should always double-check what's filled in and make any necessary edits before submitting the form.

- Click in any of the form fields and type the first character of the data that goes in that field. For example, because my first name is Joe, I could click in a First Name field and type J. Safari immediately fills in that field with the rest of the name or other data. If it's correct and you want to accept it, press Tab; Safari then also fills in all the other form fields on the page. Again, be sure to check these before submitting the form. If any of the data is incorrect or if you don't want to accept Safari's guess, simply keep typing the rest of the field's contents.

- If a page has username and password fields, Safari fills in your credentials automatically as soon as the page loads; you need take no action at all (unless the credentials are incorrect, in which case you must manually replace them with the right information).

Safari's default settings — AutoFill turned off for usernames and passwords but turned on for contact and other data — are reasonably safe, especially because it normally doesn't store credit card information. If someone were to walk up to your machine when you weren't around and visit a few websites, it's unlikely they could find out much about you that isn't already available in some other easily accessible way (such as looking in your Address Book). So, to the extent that those two AutoFill features make web browsing more convenient, they're generally worth leaving on. However, do note that unless you activate Private Browsing mode (as described later in this chapter), Safari may store form information you type on any site you visit — along with the site's URL — and this information could conceivably reveal details about your browsing history to others with access to your Mac.

Using AutoFill for usernames and passwords is a bigger risk because it means that anyone with physical access to your Mac could log in (as you) to any website for which you've saved your credentials — including, perhaps, your bank, PayPal, eBay, or other sites that deal with money. You can minimize the risk by setting your keychain to lock automatically after a period of inactivity or when your Mac goes to sleep. But in a shared or public environment, the safest course of action is to leave this feature turned off. Alternatively, a third-party form-filling tool (discussed ahead) may give you finer-grained control over when and how form data is collected and used as well as how it's secured.

Cross-Ref

For more on changing the settings for keychain locking, see Chapter 5. ■

Firefox

The Firefox browser uses a proprietary database, rather than the Keychain, to store usernames and passwords that can be automatically filled in later. This information can be viewed and edited within the browser. Firefox also has a second storage area for other form data, which may include your contact information; this second database also stores everything you type into the Firefox search bar.

The Firefox database of passwords is encrypted, but oddly, it's not password-protected by default. That means someone who obtained the database file alone couldn't read your passwords directly from the file, but merely opening Firefox on your computer grants anyone unrestricted access to the database's contents from within the browser. Therefore, it's best to set a password to encrypt your passwords, as described just ahead.

To configure Firefox's form data settings, follow these steps:

1. **With Firefox running, choose Firefox ⇨ Preferences to open the Preferences window and then click Security to show the settings shown in Figure 10.8.**

2. **To let Firefox collect usernames and passwords you type into form fields, click the Remember passwords for sites check box (it's selected by default).** To disable collection of passwords, click the check box to deselect it. If you've previously instructed Firefox never to remember the password for a particular domain (as described shortly), click Exceptions to view which sites are blocked from this feature. To remove a site from the list, select it, click Remove, and then close the window.

3. **To password-protect the password database Firefox uses — an extremely good idea — click the Use a master password check box; and in the dialog box that opens, type and confirm a password, click OK, and then click OK again to acknowledge that the password has been saved.** After each launch, Firefox then prompts you for this password the first time you attempt to save or fill in form data.

4. **Click the Privacy button on the toolbar and then do one of the following:**
   - To enable Firefox to save information you type in form fields and in the search bar, click the Remember what I enter in forms and the search bar check box (it's selected by default) and then close the Preferences window.

- To disable the feature, click the Remember what I enter in forms and the search bar check box to deselect it and then close the Preferences window.

FIGURE 10.8

On the Security pane of the Firefox preferences window, you can configure how it deals with form data.

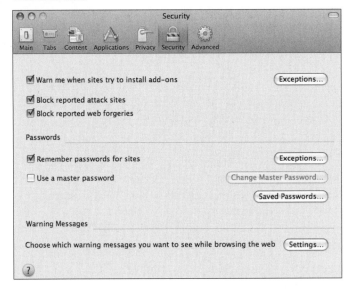

As in Safari, filling in form data automatically requires two steps — collecting the information and then entering it into forms.

If you selected Remember passwords for sites in step 2 in the previous set of steps, Firefox notices when you submit your username and password at a new site and displays a bar just above the top of the page content with the label Do you want Firefox to remember the password for "*username*" on *sitename*? To save the password in the Firefox database, click Remember. To continue browsing without letting Firefox store your credentials, click Not Now. To prevent Firefox from saving your credentials now and from prompting you to save them for this particular website in the future, click Never for this Site.

To see what credentials you've previously stored in this way and to change or delete them, choose Firefox ⇨ Preferences, click Security, and then click Saved Passwords. The window that opens initially lists only the URLs and associated usernames; to also display your passwords, click Show Passwords, type your master password (if any), and then click OK. To delete any item, select it and then click Remove; to delete all items, click Remove All.

If you selected Remember what I enter in forms and the search bar in step 4 in the previous instructions, Firefox does so automatically and silently as you fill in forms and search by using the search bar. Firefox doesn't offer an interface where you can see and edit all this form data in one place.

When collecting form data, Firefox requires an extra step to store usernames and passwords while remembering other form data automatically. But when filling in previously stored data, the reverse is true. When you load a page for which Firefox has previously stored a username and password, it fills in your credentials automatically. To fill in other form data, click in one of the fields and then type the first letter of something you previously typed in that field or press the down arrow key. Firefox displays a pop-up list of potential matches. Using the arrow keys, highlight the one you want and then press Return. Repeat this procedure for each field you want to fill in.

Firefox's method of storing and filling in miscellaneous form data is about as safe as Safari's; under ordinary circumstances, you run little risk from using this feature. However, the way Firefox handles usernames and passwords is a bit riskier. Because Firefox's default configuration is to prompt you to store passwords when you type them, because they're ordinarily stored without being protected by a further password, and because they're filled in automatically when you load a site, there's a significant chance that someone else could access your data online if he or she got physical access to your computer. If you choose to use Firefox to store your credentials, be sure to set a master password and to quit Firefox when you're not using it or when you step away from your computer. Or use a third-party password utility (discussed next) that offers greater security.

Third-party web form password tools

In lieu of using your browser's built-in form-filling capabilities, you can opt for a third-party tool. There are several advantages to such tools:

- **They're browser-independent.** Safari and Firefox don't share form data with each other (nor do most other browsers), so if you happen to save a password or other form information in one browser and then visit the site in a different browser, you have to type the data from scratch again. Most third-party utilities instead give you a centralized database that works across various browsers.

- **They offer greater security.** Third-party tools typically give you a greater degree of control over what information is stored and when and how it's filled in. They may also let you keep your form data encrypted even when your keychain or Firefox password manager is unlocked.

- **They're more flexible.** For entirely understandable security reasons, Safari and Firefox don't normally store credit card information and other highly sensitive information. But you may want to be able to fill in such information when shopping online, as long as you can store and access your financial data in a secure way. Third-party tools let you do this — not just with credit cards but also with serial numbers and other kinds of confidential data.

Some examples of third-party form-filling tools follow.

Note

The utilities I discuss here are also general-purpose password managers, and as such, I mention some of them in the context of generating and storing passwords in Chapter 6.■

1Password

1Password, from Agile Web Solutions (`http://agilewebsolutions.com/products/1Password`, $39.95), is a general-purpose utility for creating, storing, and accessing passwords, bank account information, and other private data. But it's particularly useful for storing credentials and any other information destined for web forms because it integrates thoroughly with every major Mac web browser. This integration lets you browse as you normally would, and when you happen to load a page that requires you to type credentials, you can insert them quickly with a keystroke or menu command, as shown in Figure 10.9.

If you haven't encountered the site before, you can create, save, and type a new password in a single step, as shown in Figure 10.10, or save other form data you type in your browser without any extra effort. Among 1Password's other tricks is the capability to store and fill in information for as many credit cards and addresses as you need — all of which, again, requires nothing more than a simple menu selection.

FIGURE 10.9

When you arrive at a web page with a form, click the handy 1P menu in your browser's toolbar (or menu bar) to show options for filling in the form.

FIGURE 10.10

1Password's built-in password generator makes it easy to come up with secure passwords — and save them automatically for future use.

Other password utilities

As much as I like and recommend 1Password, it's not the only game in town. Several other password managers also let you store your passwords outside your browser and then fill them in with a few clicks. I list a few examples just ahead. These utilities vary tremendously in the specifics of their interfaces, but they all share a couple of traits. First, recording form data is an entirely manual process — unlike 1Password and the form-filling features built into Safari and Firefox, they can't grab data you've already filled in on a web page.

Second, you must access web pages and their associated credentials from within the application, not from your browser. For example, you might click a button or choose a menu command in the utility that opens a certain site in your default browser and then (possibly after an additional click or keystroke) fills in your credentials. If you've already loaded a page in your browser, you can't simply ask one of these utilities to fill in your username and password on the fly. You must first launch the utility (if it's not already running) and then use its command to reload the page in question. This lack of integration makes all these tools less convenient for those who spend most of their time in a web browser, but if you only occasionally visit sites that require form information and if you tend to visit a relatively small set of sites all the time, it may be a reasonable approach.

- **AllSecure.** As of late 2009, this password utility works only with Safari, but the developer has promised support for other browsers in the future. AllSecure stores not only passwords and web form data but also entire documents. To use a password in a web form, you double-click the password item in AllSecure and then click a button to open the web page and insert your credentials (www.edgerift.com/products/allsecure/, $39).

- **PasswordWallet.** PasswordWallet is a capable but no-frills password utility that's also available for iPhone/iPod touch and Windows. To open a URL and type a password, just click an icon next to the item in PasswordWallet (www.selznick.com/products/passwordwallet/mac/, $20).

- **Web Confidential.** Web Confidential has been around for many years and is also available for Mac OS 9 and Windows (www.web-confidential.com, $20). It manages all sorts of private information, including credit cards, bank accounts, and serial numbers, and offers strong encryption. You can also jump directly to any web page for which you've stored a password using the program's Dock menu.

Protecting Yourself from Harmful Downloads

I have some good news and some bad news. First the good: Regardless of which browser you use or how sketchy a site you visit may be, you can't accidentally catch a virus or install any harmful software simply by clicking a link on a web page. You can download software with a click, and if it's compressed, it may decompress automatically — sometimes converting, in the process, from a disk image into an application or installer. And some kinds of downloaded files, such as PDFs and graphics, may open automatically in Preview or another suitable program. Even so, the mere act of downloading a file can't, all by itself, cause any malware to infect Mac OS X because you can't run a downloaded application in Mac OS X simply by clicking a web link.

Note
By default, Safari opens certain kinds of files it considers safe after downloading them — PDF files, sounds, word-processing documents, disk images, and so on. To disable this behavior, choose Safari ➪ Preferences to open the Preferences window, click General to open the General pane, and then click the Open "safe" files after downloading check box to deselect it. Then close the Preferences window.

Another piece of good news: Both Safari and Firefox (among other browsers) can alert you if you attempt to visit a site that's known to contain malware, assuming you have the right preferences turned on (as they are by default). In Safari, choose Safari ➪ Preferences, click Security, and then verify that the Warn when visiting a fraudulent website check box is selected. If not, click it. In Firefox, choose Firefox ➪ Preferences, click Security, and then confirm that the Block reported attack sites check box is selected; if not, click it. With these settings in place, if you navigate to a site that's been reported as distributing malware, an alert appears — the one for Safari is shown in Figure 10.11, while the one for Firefox is shown in Figure 10.12. However, I should warn you that neither browser knows of all possible malware sites, so although you should heed these warnings if you see them, they're no guarantee that you'll never encounter malware on the web.

That brings me to the bad news. Notice that I said you can't install malware just by clicking a web link. That doesn't mean you can't download it, as you well may if you encounter a site with malware that your browser hasn't warned you about. And once you do, you can install the malware by manually double-clicking a downloaded application. The problem is that once you've downloaded a program, you may not be able to tell whether it's entirely legitimate or a catastrophe waiting to happen. Because it's just as easy to run an installer that puts bad software on your Mac as it is to run a perfectly good installer, Mac OS X's built-in safeguards against running software directly from a web page can take you only so far.

FIGURE 10.11

Safari warns you of sites that may contain malware with a page that looks like this.

Anti-malware software can certainly scan downloaded files and warn you against anything that might be problematic, but there are other steps you can take — and that Mac OS X takes for you — to reduce your risk.

Cross-Ref

For more on anti-malware software, see Chapter 14. ∎

First and foremost, it's always wise to download software only from trusted sources. Developers with familiar names (whether larger or small) are usually safe bets, as are sites like VersionTracker (`www.versiontracker.com`) and MacUpdate (`www.macupdate.com`). If you're tempted to download software from an unknown site, do a bit of clicking to make sure you can discover the identity of the person or company that developed the software, their contact information, and, if possible, reviews or discussions of the software on sites other than the one where the software is found. Commercial software available via newsgroups, BitTorrent, and other peer-to-peer file-sharing networks is usually pirated, and if you're serious about keeping your Mac free from malware (to say nothing of following the law), you should steer clear of such sources. These steps alone can help you avoid most dangerous software downloads.

FIGURE 10.12

Navigate to a site in Firefox that's been reported as containing malware, and you see a warning like this.

Safari, Mail, and iChat all add a special, invisible tag to downloaded applications as well as to disk images that contain them. The first time you double-click an application stored on a tagged disk image, Mac OS X displays a warning like the one shown in Figure 10.13. The intent of this warning is to remind you that the file was downloaded and to urge you to check its source before continuing to run or install it. The message displays the domain name of the site from which the software was downloaded; if it's unfamiliar to you, that's a danger sign. To double-check the site, click Show Web Page. If you're satisfied that the software is legitimate, click Open to continue opening it. If you want to trust every file on this particular disk image from now on, click the Don't warn me when opening applications on this disk image check box before clicking Open. To cancel opening the application, click Cancel.

If, instead of opening a downloaded program directly from a disk image, you copy it to your disk first — or if it wasn't stored on a disk image in the first place — Mac OS X displays a simpler warning, as shown in Figure 10.14, the first time you try to open it. Click Open to continue opening the application, which also causes Mac OS X to consider it safe to open in the future, or click Cancel to stop opening it.

FIGURE 10.13

When you first open a program on a disk image you downloaded with Safari, Mail, or iChat, Mac OS X displays this alert to confirm that you know the item's origin.

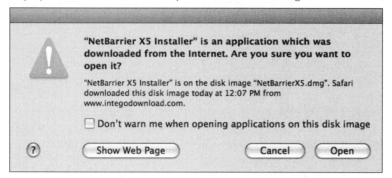

FIGURE 10.14

If you copy an application from a downloaded disk image to another folder before opening it the first time, Mac OS X displays an alert like this one.

In Snow Leopard, Apple does all this and also goes a step further. When you open a disk image downloaded with any of the most popular browsers or email programs (or with iChat), the operating system checks for certain malware programs, such as common Trojan horses. If any are found, you're alerted to move the disk image to the Trash rather than continuing to open it. Although this falls short of a full-fledged anti-malware feature, it's at least a start, and Apple can deliver definitions for new malware programs to check for via Software Update. But remember, this feature applies only to certain kinds of downloads (not to files that arrive on your Mac in any other way), can't scan your Mac for existing malware or remove it for you, and is quite limited in the range of malware it checks for.

Protecting Yourself from Phishing Schemes

The term *phishing* has already appeared several times in this book. It describes a type of scam in which someone sends out bait — usually in the form of an email message — in an attempt to lure unsuspecting people to a phony website, where they're asked to type a password or other private information. The fake website may look just like a real one to which they're accustomed (a bank website or PayPal, for example), and the message may warn of dire consequences if the person doesn't confirm or verify his or her account details or do something of that sort. If you go along with the request and type your personal information, the phisher then uses it to log in to your account, pretending to be you — collecting private information, transferring money to themselves, or stealing your identity. Phishing is big business, and the people who perpetrate such scams have become increasingly clever and convincing. But you can protect yourself from phishing attempts with a combination of good sense and the right software.

The best way to avoid phishing attempts is to never click links in email messages from unknown sources — and to be skeptical even about known sources (such as your bank) because From addresses can be forged. If you have any doubt at all about a message, the safest thing to do is to manually type the URL of the site in question into your browser, log in the usual way, and check your account status to see if there are any problems or alerts. If there aren't and if you still think the message might be legitimate, call or email the customer service department of the institution in question to ask about the message.

Checking source URLs

One way technology can help to thwart phishing is to verify that the URL you're visiting is the one you think you're visiting. Phishing sites often use domain names that visually appear to be legitimate but which in fact use one or more foreign characters that look the same as English letters but are interpreted differently by a computer. So, unless you manually typed www.paypal.com, for example (or selected a bookmark you created earlier in your browser), you could be viewing a completely different site whose URL simply looks like that. Fortunately, most modern browsers (including current versions of Safari and Firefox) can automatically check for such misleading domain names and warn you if you try to visit them. Browsers can also consult online databases of previously discovered phishing sites (whatever their domain names) and block them entirely or display warnings if you stumble across them.

In Safari, these anti-phishing measures are activated by default. To confirm that protection is on, choose Safari ⇨ Preferences, click Security, and then verify that the Warn when visiting a fraudulent website check box is selected. If not, click it. In Firefox, choose Firefox ⇨ Preferences, click Security, and then confirm that the check box Block reported web forgeries is selected; if not, click it.

Note
The Warn when visiting a fraudulent website check box in Safari also guards against sites known to contain malware, as discussed earlier in this chapter.

Using Extended Validation certificates

Another technique phishers sometimes use to give visitors a false sense of security is to install an SSL certificate on their site — meaning you see both an `https://` URL and a locked padlock icon in your browser. But anyone can get an SSL certificate, and although that can ensure that the information you send and receive is encrypted, it doesn't guarantee that the site on the other end is legitimate or even what it claims to be.

A recent standard that's designed to address this issue is the Extended Validation (EV) SSL certificate. In terms of identifying the company running the site and encrypting data, this type of certificate works just like any other SSL certificate. But in order to obtain an EV certificate, a company must go through elaborate security and verification procedures (and no small expense) to verify who it is and that its business is legitimate. It's extremely unlikely that a scammer would be able to pass these stringent requirements — or would even bother to try. Therefore, if a site is protected with an EV certificate, you can be quite confident that it's a legitimate site and not part of a phishing scheme.

How do you tell if a site uses an EV certificate? Just look at the address bar in your browser. Browsers that support EV certificates (including all recent versions of Safari and Firefox) display the name of the company that owns the certificate in green next to the URL. For example, if you visit an EV-protected site in Safari, its address bar looks like Figure 10.15, and if you visit such a site in Firefox, it looks like Figure 10.16. In either case, click the green company name to show information about the certificate.

FIGURE 10.15

When you visit a web page protected with an Extended Validation SSL certificate, Safari puts additional information in the address bar.

FIGURE 10.16

Firefox uses a more prominent method than Safari to show a site's Extended Validation status.

Using a password manager to fill in data

Yet another way to avoid phishing sites is to use your browser's form-filling feature or a third-party password manager such as 1Password or AllSecure to store and fill in your passwords instead of typing them by hand or using copy and paste. When you store credentials with any of these tools, they're tied to the URL of the site where they're used. The software fills in your credentials only if the URL you're currently visiting matches the URL in your keychain, password manager, or other utility. So, if you use the appropriate command to fill in your credentials and nothing happens (or you get an error message), that's a warning signal that the site you're looking at isn't truly the one with which your credentials are associated.

Using third-party anti-phishing software

If you use a browser that lacks anti-phishing features, or if you're unsatisfied with the way the existing features work, you can use third-party software to watch for fraudulent sites. Here are two examples of programs that can do this:

- Norton Confidential for Mac, part of Norton Internet Security for Mac (`www.symantec.com/norton/macintosh`, $79.99), includes Phishing Protection. This feature adds a toolbar to most Mac browsers (including Safari) showing an indication of the page's trust-worthiness or suspiciousness, based on sites that have been verified by Symantec as fraudulent and those that match patterns that indicate likely fraud.

- Trend Micro Smart Surfing for Mac (`http://us.trendmicro.com/us/products/personal/smartsurfing-mac/`, $49.95) can detect websites known to perpetrate phishing attacks or spread malware. You can also add individual sites manually to lists of blocked or allowed sites.

Covering Your Browsing Tracks

Your Mac keeps detailed records of your activities on the web, and anyone else who looked at the right files could determine a great deal about how and where you've been spending your time. To state the obvious, this means (among other things) that your spouse could tell that you've been viewing porn or looking for a fling, your employer could tell that you've been goofing off on the job, and law enforcement agencies could tell that you've been downloading pirated software. Not that you'd ever do such things, of course!

But it's not just people who engage in questionable activities on the web who might want to cover their browsing tracks. Suppose someone stole your computer. Would you want the thief to know all the websites you visited in the past month — however innocent they may be? Or imagine you're a journalist researching terrorist organizations. Would you worry that a government investigator could draw the wrong conclusions about you by looking at your browsing history? Or maybe you simply want to keep details about gift shopping, trip planning, or other surprise activities secret from an inquisitive family member.

You may have any number of reasons to keep other people from learning about your browsing activities, however legal and ethical they may be. Whatever the case, you should know what information your Mac typically stores as you browse the web and how to protect the privacy of that data if you feel it's important to do so.

Note

Protecting the records stored on your Mac is just part of the equation — there's also the matter of preventing information about your browsing activity from being stored elsewhere on the web. I turn to that issue later in this chapter. ■

The browsing records your Mac stores

Earlier in this chapter, I mentioned the variety of information you store on your Mac every time you visit a website. That list of items is worth repeating — and expanding on. Depending on your software and settings, any or all of the following pieces of information could be saved on your Mac for each site you visit:

- **URL.** Browsers record the URL of every single page you visit on the web to make it easy to go back to them immediately afterward (using your browser's Back button) or even days later (using the history menu or list). You can usually configure the maximum size or age of your history file in your browser's preferences, but it's not uncommon for a browsing history to stretch back a week or more.

- **Bookmarks.** Needless to say, if you manually bookmark a page, your Mac stores that information on disk too — and doesn't delete it unless you do so manually.

- **File download information.** When you download a file from a website, your Mac stores not only the file itself but a record of the file name and where it came from — in your browser's download history. Depending on your settings, this history may be purged immediately or when you quit — or never.

- **Cookies.** Many websites use cookies to help them operate more effectively or, in more dubious cases, to track your activities on the web. Cookies are stored in text files on your Mac unless you take steps to block them or erase them.

- **Form AutoFill information.** As discussed earlier in this chapter, your browser may record anything you type into a form field on a web page.

- **Search history.** If you use the search field built into your browser, a list of the search terms you typed is, by default, stored on your Mac.

- **DNS information.** In order to connect to a website, your Mac must consult a DNS server, which converts the site's domain name (such as www.apple.com) to an IP address (such as 17.112.152.32). This all happens behind the scenes — almost instantaneously in most cases. In order to speed up future connections to the same domain name, a component of Mac OS X called the DirectoryService daemon keeps a cache of the recent domain lookups. This cache — which includes not only the domains you accessed via a web browser but those your Mac contacted via any means — stretches back over a relatively short period of time, but it could still give someone who sat down at your computer when you weren't looking the URLs of websites you visited within the last hour or so.

- **Cached images and page data.** Web browsers keep local copies of images on the pages you visit in order to speed up loading the next time, and in some cases, they keep copies of the entire page. As with your browsing history, you can often configure the maximum size of a cache so that older cache items are deleted automatically, but even small caches can reveal interesting things about where you've been on the web and what you've seen there. Safari also stores thumbnail images of each web page you visit to use in its Top Sites view.

- **Favicons.** The tiny icons that appear next to the URL in your browser's address bar are called *favicons* (as in favorite icons). Your browser also keeps a cache of these.

- **Indexes of page content.** Every time you visit a page in Safari, Spotlight stores an index of all the text on that page. So, you can perform a Spotlight search for text that was on a page you visited days ago, and the URLs of matching pages show up in the list. Although Spotlight doesn't store the original text of the page, it does have a record of what words were on it.

- **Plug-in data.** If you visit sites that use browser plug-ins, such as Flash and QuickTime, the plug-ins themselves may store logs or even cached media, regardless of your browser settings. Similarly, if you use 1Password to manage passwords for web forms, it keeps a log of each time a password is created, saved, or used — including the page's URL.

In some cases — particularly if you've installed additional caching, filtering, or monitoring software — even more data can be stored.

Prevention versus cleanup

All the data about your web browsing that's stored on your Mac is there for a reason. It's there to speed up your browsing, help you find information, enable you to repeat searches more quickly, and keep records of any problems that occur. So, it all has a benign purpose, but because most of this information is stored transparently in the background as you browse, you can easily build up a massive catalog of your activities that could, without your explicit permission or awareness, endanger your privacy. Anyone with access to your computer has a long list of ways in which he or she could find out where you've been on the web.

In light of all this data, if you visit any websites that you'd rather not have records of, you have two basic choices: either prevent your browser or other software from storing it in the first place or delete it as soon as possible after it's been stored. Each approach has its pros and cons, and in most cases, the best approach is a combination of the two.

If you turn off as many of your browser's data-collection features as possible, you avoid ever having certain information written to your disk at all, and that's a good thing because once data is written to your disk, it's hard to be sure it's erased entirely. For example, if your backup software runs between the time the data is written and when it's deleted, you've got an extra copy that you may not have thought of. So, prevention is, to some extent, the best policy.

Unfortunately, prevention isn't always complete or perfect. Although you can turn off some data-collection features, you can't turn off everything — at least without disabling crucial capabilities of your browser. And certain sites won't work if you disable features they depend on, such as cookies or plug-ins.

You could, of course, leave some or all of the data-collection features turned on and then erase the data later. Although after-the-fact cleanup is crucial for, at minimum, the bits you can't prevent your computer from saving, it's a tedious and error-prone process if done manually. You can make the task much easier by using any of several cleanup utilities (discussed later in this chapter), but these don't always catch every piece of potentially incriminating information, and conversely, they often throw out the baby with the bathwater, deleting useful, important things along with the data you want to get rid of. In addition, they don't always erase the data securely, meaning it could potentially be read by a file recovery utility.

Cross-Ref

For more on securely deleting files — and overwriting free space on your disk — see Chapter 13. ∎

Therefore, my general advice is to selectively prevent your Mac from storing certain information and to supplement this prevention with regular (automated or manual) cleanup.

Managing cookies

Of all the data your Mac stores when you browse the web, none is so controversial as the cookie, and because of its specially interesting status, it's worth a separate discussion.

First, just what is a cookie? Unlike the delicious snack food of the same name, an HTTP cookie is nothing more than a piece of text. A web server sends the text to your browser, and your browser stores it in a file on your disk. Later, the web server may ask to see that cookie again, and if it does, your browser sends it back. Fundamentally, that's all there is to it.

The next question is why a web server might want to store text on your computer. The reason stems from the fact that every request for a web page is independent from every other request. Although the experience of browsing through a site may seem like a continuous whole to you, the server doesn't see it that way. Web servers often receive thousands of requests for pages every second, and they can't generally tell with any certainty whether two requests came from the same person. Because many computers may share an IP address, a web server can't determine just by looking at a plain request for a page whether it came from the same user who requested another page on the site a few seconds ago. Cookies are one way to solve this problem because they give the web server a hook to identify a user from one request to the next.

In case it's not obvious why a server would need to keep track of who's accessing it, let me give you an example. Suppose you log in to a site such as MobileMe or Gmail to check your mail. You type your credentials so the site knows who you are and can deliver the correct content to you. A few moments later, you want to go to another page on the same site — perhaps to upload a photo or change your preferences. When you click the link to that other page, how does the server know that it's still you making that request so that it can deliver the page with your personal content?

It checks a cookie that it set on the first page you visited. Because the data in that cookie is the same from page to page, the server doesn't have to ask you to log in separately for each page, and it can always be sure that it's delivering the right content to the right person. Without cookies, shopping sites couldn't keep track of which user added which item to a shopping cart, web-based applications such as word processors and photo editors would be useless, and much of what we know and love about the web would simply be impossible.

In short, cookies are extremely useful for solving an otherwise difficult problem and enabling all sorts of convenient capabilities on the web.

So, why all the fuss? Well, in addition to the virtuous use for which cookies were originally intended, they can be called upon to serve a sneakier role. Ordinarily, a cookie is written and read only by a single website. But some sites share cookies in order to track where a user has been. For example, suppose you visit a site that sells hammers, and that site sets a cookie on your Mac that says, "This person looked at hammers on Tuesday." The next day, you go to another site that sells screwdrivers, and because the two sites are partners, it checks the cookie the first site set. So, the screwdriver site knows you're also interested in hammers, and it adds a bit of text to the cookie, which now records your visits to two different sites. On Thursday, you visit a third site that uses the same cookie — maybe a hardware store. Before you've clicked on anything, that store knows you've looked elsewhere recently for hammers and screwdrivers, so the first thing it does is present ads for those and similar hand tools. This, to oversimplify somewhat, is what makes a cookie a *tracking cookie* — it records data about visits to multiple sites, revealing to each one where you've been previously.

Web-based advertising services that place their ads on thousands of different sites often use tracking cookies so that they can tell which other partner sites a visitor has been to, which ads he or she has seen, and what kinds of products or services he or she might be interested in. That in itself isn't terrible because, in fact, you may appreciate seeing ads for items you want to buy. But the problem is that you don't know if or when this tracking is happening. You never explicitly agreed to give Bob's Hardware Store the information that you visited Hammers 'R' Us two days ago, and you most likely assumed that whatever you did there was between you and that site. So, tracking cookies could be considered a breach of privacy, and depending on what sites you visit and how the tracking cookies are used, you can end up giving away a significant amount of information about your browsing history.

As a result, you may want to delete or even disallow tracking cookies (if you can figure out which ones those are). But even ordinary cookies could contain your username, password, or other personally identifying information. Although that's fine when you're the only person using a computer, it can reveal to other people details you may want to keep secret, particularly if you're using a public or shared computer. Likewise, if you've been to (or plan to visit) any sites that could be considered incriminating for one reason or another, you should delete any cookies associated with them.

Each browser offers its own set of tools (some more extensive than others) for dealing with cookies, and if you find those tools inadequate, third-party software can often help.

Safari

Safari offers some basic control over cookies. To use Safari's cookie-related features, follow these steps:

1. **With Safari running, choose Safari ⇨ Preferences to open the Preferences window and then click Security to open the Security pane.**

2. **In the Accept Cookies portion of the preferences window, click a radio button to select one of these three options:**

   - **Always.** Safari accepts all cookies. This provides the greatest convenience but the least privacy.

   - **Never.** Safari blocks all cookies. Some sites won't work at all (and those that don't generally display an error message saying that they require cookies), whereas others offer only partial functionality. On the other hand, you're guaranteed not to store any tracking cookies that could compromise your privacy.

   - **Only from sites I visit.** Safari accepts cookies from the sites you visit but not from other domain names. For example, if you visit `fredshardware.com` and it displays an ad that was delivered by `peteshammers.com`, you might get a cookie from `fredshardware.com` but not from `peteshammers.com`, which is presumably an advertising site. Although this setting doesn't offer complete protection against tracking cookies, it offers the best compromise from among the three choices you have.

3. **To see and manage the cookies Safari has previously stored, click Show Cookies to open a dialog box similar to the one shown in Figure 10.17.** In this dialog box, you can see basic information about each cookie. To delete one, select it and then click Remove; to delete them all, click Remove All. To search for a cookie (by domain name or cookie name), type the text you want to find in the search field at the top of the dialog box; Safari dynamically filters the display to show only matching cookies.

FIGURE 10.17

Safari offers a few basic tools for viewing and removing cookies it's stored.

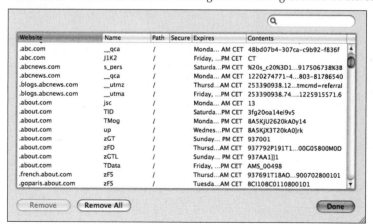

Although you can drag the resize control in the lower-right corner of the dialog box to make it larger, sort the list by clicking on a column header, and search by using the search field, this display is still limited in that you can't always see the entire contents of a cookie, which can be extensive. You can't search by cookie contents either. In addition, a given domain may store its cookies using one or more of several formats, such as `domain.com`, `.domain.com`, and `www.domain.com`. This can make it difficult to know whether you've found all the cookies associated with a given domain. For greater control, use a third-party cookie tool, as described ahead.

Firefox

Firefox's built-in cookie management capabilities appear at first glance to be similar to those of Safari, but they offer considerably more flexibility and control. To configure Firefox's cookie behavior, follow these steps:

1. **With Firefox running, choose Firefox ⇨ Preferences to open the Preferences window and then click Privacy to open the Privacy pane.**

2. **In the Cookies portion of the preferences window, you can set the following options:**

   - **Accept cookies from sites.** If this check box is selected (as it is by default), Firefox accepts cookies, subject to any restrictions imposed by the further settings in this window. To prevent Firefox from storing cookies except as expressly permitted, click this check box to deselect it. The Keep until pop-up menu, described ahead, provides a way to accept only specific cookies even if this check box is selected.

   - **Exceptions.** If the Accept cookies from sites check box is selected, you can still block cookies from certain domains. Likewise, if the check box is deselected, you can still selectively permit certain domains to store cookies. To permit a site to store cookies, click the Exceptions button, type the URL of a website, and then click Allow. To allow a site to store cookies only until you quit Firefox, click Allow for Session instead. To block a site from storing cookies if Accept cookies from sites is selected, type its URL and then click Block. You can also configure Firefox to add exceptions to this list automatically by choosing Ask me every time from the Keep until pop-up menu.

   - **Accept third-party cookies.** If the Accept cookies from sites check box is selected, you can prevent Firefox from storing cookies from domains other than those of the sites you visit (typically advertising services) by clicking the Accept third-party cookies check box to deselect it.

   - **Keep until.** Every cookie includes an expiration date, beyond which it no longer functions and should be deleted by your browser. However, these dates are sometimes decades in the future. To control how long a cookie sticks around, choose an option from this pop-up menu. Choose They expire (the default) to keep them until their built-in expiration date. Or choose I close Firefox to delete all cookies when you quit Firefox. The third option is to choose Ask me every time, which means each time a site tries to set a cookie, Firefox displays an alert like the one in Figure 10.18. Click Allow to store the cookie (adding it to the Exceptions list with an Allow status); click Allow for Session to store it only until you quit Firefox; click Deny to block the cookie (adding it to the Exceptions list with a Deny status); or click Show Details to see the cookie's contents and expiration date. Because some sites set several cookies, you can avoid seeing multiple copies of this alert by clicking the Use my choice for all cookies from this site check box before clicking one of the buttons.

FIGURE 10.18

Alerts like this may seem intrusive at first, but they help you to stay in control of what cookies Firefox accepts.

3. **To see and manage the cookies Firefox has previously stored, click Show Cookies to open a window like the one shown in Figure 10.19.** In this dialog box, you can see basic information about each cookie. Cookies are grouped by domain name; click the disclosure triangle next to a domain name to see all its cookies. Select a cookie to show its details at the bottom of the window. To delete a cookie, select it and then click Remove Cookie; to delete them all, click Remove All Cookies. To search for a cookie (by domain name or cookie name), type the text you want to find into the Search field at the top of the dialog box; Firefox dynamically filters the display to show only matching cookies. When you're finished, close the Cookies window and the Preferences window.

Given Firefox's wide range of options, what's the best combination of settings? Blocking all cookies makes the web nearly unusable, so that's an unwise choice. Allowing cookies from third-party sites is virtually never necessary and often an insecure practice. Although somewhat intrusive, the safest procedure is to manually allow or deny cookies from each site you visit. Therefore, I suggest leaving the Accept cookies from sites check box selected, deselecting the Accept third-party cookies check box, and choosing Ask me every time from the Keep until pop-up menu. When you visit a site for which you're willing to store cookies, click the Use my choice for all cookies from this site check box and then click Allow to add the domain to your permanent list of exceptions. If you're asked to store cookies for an advertising domain, do the same except click Deny to block that domain permanently.

FIGURE 10.19

Firefox's cookie list organizes cookies by domain name and lets you view or remove them.

Third-party cookie management software

Safari and Firefox can block websites from storing cookies in the first place, but once cookies are on your computer, several third-party programs offer ways of managing them that go beyond the capabilities built into Safari or Firefox. A few examples include:

- **CocoaCookies.** This free utility (`http://ditchnet.org/cocoacookies/`) provides a list of the cookies saved by Safari and other applications that use Mac OS X's system-wide cookie storage (including Shiira and NetNewsWire). In CocoaCookies, as in Safari, you can sort cookies and delete them individually or en masse. But unlike Safari's simple list, CocoaCookies groups cookies by domain, as shown in Figure 10.20, and lets you search cookies' contents as well as their domains and names — optionally using regular expressions for sophisticated pattern matching. You can even edit a cookie directly if you know what you're doing.

- **Internet Cleanup.** Cookies are among the many kinds of private data this suite of tools can erase. You can view and delete cookies from all your browsers (individually or collectively), edit cookies, and mark certain cookies to be deleted automatically or to be protected from automatic deletion when they appear on your computer (`http://my.smithmicro.com/mac/cleanup/index.html`, $29.99).

The Opt-Out Dilemma

Many of the major advertisers on the Internet, in an effort to be kind, reasonable, and accommodating to those with privacy concerns, offer website visitors a way to opt out of the use of tracking cookies. These advertisers don't go out of their way to publicize this fact or make it easy to find though — and as a visitor to any given web page, you may not even be able to tell which advertising networks are responsible for the ads you see.

To address this problem, a group called The Network Advertising Initiative offers a helpful web page at www.networkadvertising.org/managing/opt_out.asp, where you can opt out of dozens of tracking cookies with a couple of clicks. The site also provides more information about each of the participating advertisers. If you choose to opt out in this way, you must do so separately in each browser you use.

And what mechanism do these advertisers use to identify the fact that you've opted out of tracking cookies? Cookies, of course! What you're actually doing when you opt out is accepting a cookie that tells the advertisers' servers not to store tracking information in cookies sent to you in the future. A few of the advertisers may still put information in the opt-out cookies that can be used to identify you, but that's a less serious, if still irritating, concern.

The fact that a cookie is used to block a certain usage of cookies leads to a dilemma. If you delete all your cookies, you also, in so doing, delete the cookies you deliberately set in order to avoid being tracked! And even setting the opt-out cookies in the first place requires that your browser be set to accept third-party cookies.

Some of the third-party cookie software discussed in this chapter, including Internet Cleanup and NetBarrier, lets you mark certain cookies as protected so that they won't be erased along with the rest when you use those programs' cookie-deletion features. If you use Firefox, a free extension called Targeted Advertising Cookie Opt-Out, or TACO (https://addons.mozilla.org/en-US/firefox/addon/11073), can do essentially the same thing.

Apart from one of those solutions, though, if you have to choose between deleting cookies altogether (with the risk of deleting opt-out cookies) and keeping all your opt-out cookies (at the risk of also keeping tracking cookies), the safer of the two courses is simply to delete all your cookies. Although that deletes the opt-out cookies, it also deletes any tracking information they would otherwise have blocked.

- **MacCleanse.** This program can delete cookies (and many other kinds of private data) from most Mac browsers, optionally overwriting the data securely to prevent it from being recovered (www.koingosw.com/products/maccleanse.php, $19.95).

- **MacScan.** Designed to scan for and delete all sorts of spyware, MacScan (http://macscan.securemac.com/, $29.99) has two features that relate to cookies (in that tracking cookies could be construed as spying on you). First, it provides the option to delete all cookies, as do several other utilities discussed later in this chapter. But it also lets you scan your computer specifically for tracking cookies, as shown in Figure 10.21, and delete those without touching the other cookies on your disk.

FIGURE 10.20

CocoaCookies provides a more flexible view than Safari of the cookies used by most Cocoa-based web browsers.

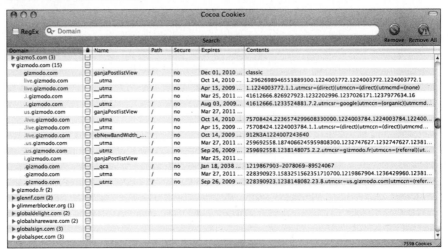

- **NetBarrier.** This multi-purpose security application (www.intego.com/netbarrier/, $49.95), which is discussed in numerous other contexts in this book, has an unusual feature for dealing with cookies: Although it doesn't block your browser from receiving or storing them, it can block your browser from sending stored cookies back to the sites that request them, unless you've added their URLs to a list of trusted sites. Because the process of adding sites is manual and somewhat awkward, this feature is best used only on occasions when you have a particularly strong need to protect your privacy as you browse. A second application called Washing Machine, included with NetBarrier, lets you view, edit, and delete the stored cookies from all your browsers in a single location.

FIGURE 10.21

MacScan can search for and list any cookies that contain tracking information. You can then delete any or all of them.

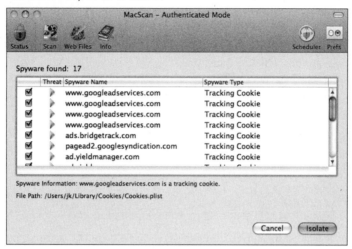

Using Safari's Private Browsing feature

Sometimes merely blocking cookies isn't enough; you want to be sure your browser records no information at all about your web-browsing activities that someone could later discover. When that's what you want, you can use Safari's Private Browsing feature, or, as it's often called (only half-jokingly), "porn mode." To activate this mode, choose Safari ⇨ Private Browsing. In the dialog box that opens, shown in Figure 10.22, click OK.

FIGURE 10.22

The alert that appears when you activate Safari's Private Browsing mode reminds you of exactly what information will be kept private.

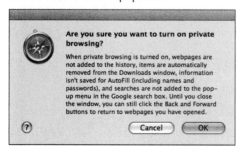

While in Private Browsing mode, Safari makes the following changes to its normal data-collection procedures:

- **History.** The URLs of sites you visit aren't added to Safari's history list. However, Safari does keep a temporary cache of recent sites so that you can still use the Back and Forward buttons to navigate to other sites you visited in this session. That cache disappears when you close the window.

- **Cache.** Images and other data from web pages you visit (such as favicons) aren't written to disk in Safari's cache, and page content isn't indexed by Spotlight.

- **Cookies.** Any cookies set by sites you visit while in Private Browsing mode are deleted automatically when you turn off Private Browsing or quit Safari.

- **Downloads.** If you download files while in Private Browsing mode, the items you download are removed from the Downloads list immediately. The downloaded files themselves aren't deleted though.

- **AutoFill.** Information you type into form fields isn't stored for Safari's AutoFill feature while in Private Browsing mode. However, you can still use AutoFill to fill forms with data you've previously saved.

- **Searches.** Terms you type into Safari's search field aren't recorded in Safari's Recent Searches list.

You can manually deactivate Private Browsing by choosing Safari ➪ Private Browsing again. Regardless, Private Browsing always turns itself off when Safari quits. So, if Safari should crash while you're in Private Browsing mode and you relaunch it, you must manually turn the feature back on. Safari provides no visual indication that you're in Private Browsing mode (except a check mark next to that menu command), so it would be easy to assume the feature is still active when it's not.

Tip

To launch Safari with Private Browsing mode already activated, you can use a free AppleScript utility called Safari PB, available from `http://tomx.890m.com/.` ■

Although Private Browsing certainly does decrease the amount of private information Safari stores, you should be aware that it doesn't completely prevent information about your browsing session from being recorded. In particular, plug-ins will continue to cache and log data. For example, if you visit sites that use Flash, Safari's Flash plug-in may cache information about the sites you visit. Or if you use the free Glims plug-in (`www.machangout.com`) to enhance Safari's capabilities, terms you type into the search field are preserved. In addition, the Directory Service cache still includes the domain names of sites you visit. Later in this chapter, I discuss how to delete some of this extra data.

Using Safari's data removal features

When you don't use Private Browsing, Safari accumulates quite a bit of data about your browsing activities. You can remove this data after the fact by using either of two commands (one of which affects only Safari's cache and the other of which can zap just about anything).

Empty Cache

To empty Safari's cache, choose Safari ⇨ Empty Cache and then click Empty Cache. When you do this, Safari deletes all the page content it has cached, including images found on web pages you've visited. However, this command doesn't delete Safari's thumbnail images of pages (used for the Top Sites view), favicons, browsing history, or other information Safari downloaded during the course of your browsing. To delete this additional data, you must use the Reset Safari command.

Reset Safari

When you want to delete more than just Safari's cache, you can use a much more powerful command: Safari ⇨ Reset Safari. When you choose this command, the window shown in Figure 10.23 opens. By default, all the check boxes are selected; click the check box next to any item you don't want to delete to deselect it. Then, click Reset to delete the still-selected items.

The Reset Safari command is powerful, but you shouldn't use it indiscriminately. If you leave every check box selected, the command wipes out not only tracking cookies and recent browsing history, which may compromise your privacy, but extremely helpful things, such as ordinary cookies, usernames and passwords from your keychain, and form AutoFill data. If you delete these items, understand that they're completely gone and unrecoverable; you'll have to type your credentials and other form data manually the next time you visit any site for which you previously stored such information.

FIGURE 10.23

The Reset Safari command displays this dialog box, which lets you choose which types of information to delete.

Handling private data with Firefox

Firefox also has features that enable you to prevent certain private data from being stored in the first place or to clean it up afterward.

Preventing Firefox from storing private data

Firefox, beginning with version 3.1, has a Private Browsing mode that's nearly identical to what Safari offers. To use this feature, choose Tools ➪ Start Private Browsing (⌘+Shift+P) and then click Start Private Browsing in the dialog box that opens. Firefox saves your current tabs and windows (so you can return to them later) and then closes them, opening a new window in which you can begin your private browsing session. It also puts the words "(Private Browsing)" in the window's title bar to remind you that this mode is active.

Tip

If you're using a version of Firefox earlier than 3.1, you can get comparable functionality by installing either of two free plug-ins: Stealther (`https://addons.mozilla.org/en-US/firefox/addon/1306`) or Distrust (`https://addons.mozilla.org/en-US/firefox/addon/1559`) — but an even better option is simply to upgrade to a newer version of Firefox. ∎

Like Safari, Firefox prevents all data (browsing history, caches, search terms, and so on) from being written to disk while in Private Browsing mode and stores some information (such as newly set cookies and the list of pages you've visited recently) temporarily in RAM, deleting them when you choose Tools ➪ Stop Private Browsing or when you quit Firefox. Also like Safari, Firefox can't prevent plug-ins or the DirectoryService process from storing some information about your web visits, so that data must be purged manually (as I describe later in this chapter).

Cleaning up Firefox's private data

Just as Safari has a command to clear its cache and another to delete a wide variety of private data, so does Firefox, although they function a bit differently.

To clear Firefox's cache, choose Firefox ➪ Preferences, click Advanced, and then click the Network tab, as shown in Figure 10.24. Click the Clear Now button and then close the Preferences window.

To remove other private data (analogous to the Reset Safari command), choose Tools ➪ Clear Recent History. In the window that opens, shown in Figure 10.25, begin by clicking the check boxes next to the types of data you want to erase to select them. From the Remove pop-up menu, choose how far back you want to delete data (for everything, choose My entire history). Then, click Clear Private Data. The window closes automatically.

Note

In versions of Firefox before 3.1, the procedure to clear private data is a bit different. Choose Tools ➪ Clear Private Data, select what you want to delete, and then click Clear Private Data Now. ∎

Tip

You can also configure Firefox to delete private data automatically each time it quits. To do this, choose Firefox ➪ Preferences, click the Privacy button on the toolbar, and then click the **Always clear my private data when I close Firefox** check box. To adjust which data is cleared when you quit, click Settings, which displays a dialog box similar to the one shown when you choose the Clear Recent History command. ■

FIGURE 10.24

Among the controls in the Advanced pane of Firefox's preferences window is one to clear its cache.

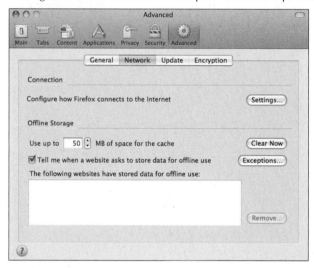

FIGURE 10.25

You can erase a variety of private data on command with Firefox's Clear Recent History command.

Using third-party web privacy software

Because the privacy features included in most browsers offer limited control — and because you can easily forget to use them — a number of third-party programs let you go much further. These tools provide automated ways to restrict the information browsers store on your disk, clean it up afterward, or both, and in some cases can watch for and block certain kinds of content being sent from or received by your browser in real time.

Most of these programs also have features that fall into other categories of safe browsing (deleting cookies, browsing anonymously, blocking content, stopping malware, and so on) and therefore also appear elsewhere in this book. In this section, I discuss only the features relating to blocking your browser from storing private data or removing it once it's been stored.

NetBarrier

Intego's NetBarrier (www.intego.com/netbarrier/, $49.95) includes many tools to protect your privacy. Of particular interest here is the included Washing Machine application. In addition to deleting cookies (as mentioned earlier), Washing Machine, shown in Figure 10.26, can clear the browsing histories, download histories, caches, and even bookmark lists maintained by almost any browser. It even offers the option of secure deletion, overwriting the information so that it can't later be recovered with special software. It can also schedule automatic deletion of private data to occur on a schedule. Except for cookies, though, it's an all-or-nothing affair for any given combination of data type and browser; you can't, for example, delete only certain bookmarks or a limited period of browsing history.

Internet Cleanup

As its name implies, Internet Cleanup (http://my.smithmicro.com/mac/cleanup/index.html, $29.99) is designed to remove most traces of your Internet activities from your Mac's disk. This suite of tools includes two that are pertinent here. Internet File Finder, shown in Figure 10.27, searches for cookies, history files, cache files, and form data stored by most browsers as well as data stored system-wide by the Flash Player plug-in. You can then view, edit, and delete individual found items or simply have Internet File Finder delete everything it finds. A second tool, Web History Finder, offers the same capabilities but only for the files that store your browsing history.

MacCleanse

An all-purpose privacy tool, MacCleanse (www.koingosw.com/products/maccleanse.php, $19.95) can delete dozens of kinds of data, including cookies, browsing and download histories, caches, and favicons from a variety of Mac web browsers, instant messaging programs, and other software. It also deletes system-wide caches, logs, and other files that may contain private data, and you have the option to securely erase deleted content.

FIGURE 10.26

NetBarrier's Washing Machine application lets you search for and delete a variety of private data from nearly any browser.

MacPrivacy

When you run MacPrivacy (www.itechprofessionals.com/software/mac-privacy.html, $15), a tiny padlock icon appears on your main menu bar. Click this icon to open a menu of MacPrivacy commands, shown in Figure 10.28. Of particular interest here, the Clear Browsers command erases browsing history, download lists, and caches from Safari and Firefox, and the Clear Video Players command removes QuickTime and VLC caches (although not the Flash cache). In addition, the Clear All command erases the Directory Services (DNS) cache and the contents of the Clipboard.

FIGURE 10.27

In Internet Cleanup's Internet File Finder window, you can search for several types of private data from all popular web browsers.

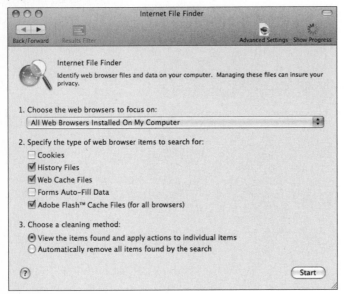

FIGURE 10.28

The unobtrusive MacPrivacy menu gives you one-click access to several powerful deletion features.

MacScan

Using the Web Files pane of MacScan (`http://macscan.securemac.com`, $29.99), shown in Figure 10.29, you can remove cookies, browsing history, download lists, and caches from any or all of the listed browsers. However, MacScan doesn't offer secure deletion of these files.

FIGURE 10.29

Among its other tricks, MacScan can search for and delete most private data stored by web browsers.

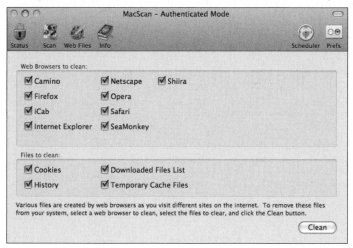

NetShred X

NetShred X (`www.mireth.com/pub/nxme.html`, $24.95), shown in Figure 10.30, can securely erase cookies, passwords, browsing history, download lists, and caches from all popular browsers — and, for several browsers (including Safari and Firefox), favicon files. You can configure which sorts of data you want to delete and from which browsers; which of several types of secure deletion you prefer; and whether you want deletion of the data to occur automatically on a schedule.

FIGURE 10.30

In NetShred X's Preferences window, you can select which kinds of data will be securely deleted.

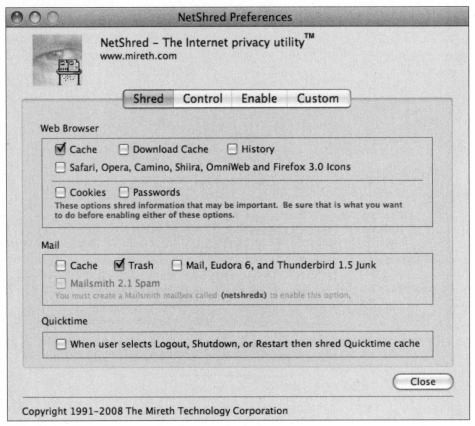

Cleaning up other browsing traces

Elsewhere in this chapter, I mention that some browser plug-ins have their own methods and locations of storing data. They don't respect your browser's Private Browsing mode, and most Internet cleanup applications skip right over any caches, logs, or other information they save on your disk. As a result, if you want to get rid of such data, you must know where to find it and how to delete it yourself. You may have any number of plug-ins, and each one may store this data in a different location, but I focus here only on the plug-ins most likely to cache data you'd rather keep private — those used to display Flash, Silverlight, and QuickTime content in your browser.

Caution

The overwhelming majority of content on the web can be viewed using the plug-ins that are included as part of Mac OS X. If a website prompts you to install another plug-in, take a moment to learn about its source. If it's from a major company such as Microsoft (as in the case of Silverlight), you're probably safe, but be circumspect about installing plug-ins from unknown providers — such software has been known to contain Trojan horses. ■

Another potential privacy hole mentioned earlier is the Directory Service cache, which stores a limited number of domain names your computer recently looked up and is also usually ignored by cleanup software. That is also easy to delete if you know how.

Tip

A general tip about all these plug-ins: Keep them up to date. As developers discover bugs and security holes, they release updated versions of their software, which can reduce your risk of privacy breaches. ■

Flash data

Adobe's Flash Player, a plug-in included with Mac OS X, lets you view videos, animations, and interactive content, such as fancy navigation systems. In order to function effectively, Flash often caches data on your disk using a feature called Local Shared Objects (LSOs). But some sites use this storage mechanism to record the equivalent of cookies, which enable them to keep track of you as you use the site without relying on your browser's regular cookie mechanism. Although Flash includes safeguards that prevent sites from reading each other's content (thus eliminating worries that these cookie-like items can track your behavior across sites), they may nevertheless store data you'd rather keep to yourself. Even more worryingly, although you can set Flash Player not to cache data for the sites you visit, it still keeps a record of the URLs for Flash-enabled sites you load.

To prevent Flash Player from storing data locally, follow these steps:

1. **Type** www.macromedia.com/support/documentation/en/flashplayer/help/settings_manager03.html **in a web browser.** The web page that opens contains embedded controls that affect Flash Player's settings on your computer.

2. **Move the slider all the way to the left (None), click the Never Ask Again check box, and then click the Allow third-party Flash content to store data on your computer check box to deselect it.**

3. **In the Table of Contents on the left side of the web page, click the Website Storage Settings Panel link.** This displays a page showing the sites for which your computer is already storing data.

4. **Click Delete all sites to remove all this data from your disk.**

5. **Click the Global Security Settings link in the Table of Contents and then click the Always deny radio button.** This prevents sites that use an older form of security from potentially obtaining private information about you.

6. **Close your browser window.** All changes take effect immediately.

Note

While you're on this page, it's worth exploring the other links in the Table of Contents, which let you change other Flash Player settings, such as which sites may activate your computer's camera and microphone. ∎

Even with these changes made, however, Flash Player records a small amount of data about the sites you visit, including their URLs. To delete all this data, drag the following two folders to the Trash and then empty the Trash: `~/Library/Preferences/Macromedia/Flash Player/#SharedObjects` and `~/Library/Preferences/Macromedia/Flash Player/macromedia.com/support/flashplayer/sys`. Unless you automate this procedure using a shell script, AppleScript, or other automation utility, you must do this manually each time you want to erase stored Flash Player data.

Tip

If you use Firefox as your browser, you can install a free extension called BetterPrivacy (`https://addons.mozilla.org/en-US/firefox/addon/6623`) that can automatically delete Flash LSOs when you quit Firefox. A free Safari add-on called ClickToFlash (`http://rentzsch.github.com/clicktoflash/`) lets you prevent Flash content from loading at all unless you specifically allow it for a given page or domain. ∎

Silverlight data

Another way of displaying rich, interactive media in a browser is to use Microsoft's Silverlight plug-in. Silverlight offers capabilities comparable to those of Flash and uses a similar mechanism (called isolated storage) to save data on your disk. As with Flash LSOs, sites can't access each other's Silverlight isolated storage data, so it can't be used to track your behavior beyond the site that wrote the data. Another factor in Silverlight's favor is that it doesn't store the URLs for sites you visit in an obvious, human-readable fashion. Nevertheless, you may not want this invisible data lying around because it could contain information about your web activities.

To delete Silverlight's isolated storage, drag the following folder to the Trash and then empty the Trash: `~/Library/Application Support/Microsoft/Silverlight/is`.

The QuickTime cache

When you view online QuickTime content (such as a movie trailer or video podcast) in your browser, QuickTime can optionally store a copy of the media on disk (in `~/Library/Caches/QuickTime/downloads`) so that you can watch it again without having to wait for it to download a second time. In Leopard — but not in Snow Leopard — you can turn this preference off, restrict the volume of data QuickTime stores, or delete the existing cache with a few clicks.

To manage your QuickTime cache in Leopard, follow these steps:

1. Choose ⟹ System Preferences to open System Preferences, click QuickTime to open the QuickTime pane, and then click the Browser tab.

2. **To prevent QuickTime from storing downloaded content on disk, click the Save movies in disk cache check box to deselect it.** If it's selected and you want to keep it

that way, you can adjust the maximum amount of space this cache can occupy (with a minimum of 100MB) by moving the Movie Download Cache Size slider.

3. **To remove files QuickTime previously downloaded, click the Empty Download Cache button.**

4. **Close System Preferences.**

Tip

NetShred X, mentioned earlier in this chapter, can be set to securely delete your QuickTime cache every time you log out, shut down, or restart. ■

The Directory Services cache

Among the many caches Mac OS X maintains as it goes about its ordinary business is the Directory Services cache, created by a background process known as the DirectoryService daemon. One type of information this cache stores is a list of all the domain names your computer has recently looked up — which can include not only websites you've visited but mail servers, online backup services, and other remote computers to which your Mac has connected. The cache doesn't stretch back very far, but it may still contain private information.

To see what's currently in your Directory Services cache, open Terminal, located in /Applications/Utilities, type **dscacheutil -cachedump -entries host**, and then press Return.

The Terminal window displays the cache contents. To delete everything in the cache now, type **dscacheutil -flushcache** and then press Return.

Note, however, that you can't turn off this cache; as soon as you delete its contents, it immediately starts filling up again with new DNS requests.

Browsing Anonymously

The previous section discussed how to make sure your Mac doesn't keep detailed records of what you've been doing on the web. But even if you turn off every sort of logging on your Mac, delete every cookie, and use cleanup software to erase every last trace of your activities, none of this hides what you're doing from the servers on the other end — or anyone who can observe Internet traffic between your computer and a server. To make it as unlikely as possible that anyone could figure out who you are or to connect web visits to you personally, you can take a number of additional steps to mask your identity as you browse.

I should point out, though, that all the anonymous browsing options I cover here involve compromises. In many cases, browsing speed is reduced considerably, some site features that depend on being able to identify you uniquely may not work, and the mere fact of using these techniques may raise the suspicions of anyone who may be monitoring your web activities. Whether or to what extent you use these techniques depends largely on how you weigh anonymity against convenience.

What information you normally reveal

To reiterate and expand on what I said earlier in this chapter, you can reveal a great deal of information about yourself when you visit a website, including any or all of the following information:

- Your IP address (which can be used to determine your geographical location, your ISP, and other interesting facts about you)
- The date and time of your visit
- The last page you viewed
- Your operating system's name and version number
- Your browser's name and version number
- Your browser's default language
- The dimensions of your browser's window
- Whether your browser has Java, JavaScript, or cookies enabled
- Which plug-ins your browser has installed
- Your display resolution
- The number of colors available on your display

This happens because your browser automatically sends certain data to every web server it contacts (which enables the server to fulfill its request), and servers typically keep a log of every access request. In addition, the page you're viewing may contain special code to deliver extra information about the site's visitors.

Here's a somewhat simplified example of what might get stored in a web server access log when someone requests the page index.html. You don't need to worry about the specifics of how to parse all this data; just notice what's here:

```
12.34.56.78 - - [29/Mar/2009:18:46:38 +0200] "GET /index.html
    HTTP/1.1" 200 1286 "http://someplace.com/file.html" "Mozilla/5.0
    (Macintosh; U; Intel Mac OS X 10.6; en-US; rv:1.9.0.8) Gecko/20$
12.34.56.78 - - [29/Mar/2009:18:46:38 +0200] "GET /je=true&sw=1920&sh
    =1200&sd=24&la=en-US&co=true&ww=1110&wh=952&p=Gears%20
    0.5.15.0&p=Adobe%20Acrobat%20and%20Reader%20Plug-in &p=Java%20
    Plug-in%20for%20Cocoa &p=Silverlight%20Plug-In&p=QuickTime%20
    Plug-in%207.6 &p=RealPlayer%20Plugin.plugin &p=Shockwave%20Flash$
```

The first line contains a typical set of data that a browser may send to a server, including the IP address of the requester, the date and time of the request, the file being requested, the page from which you were referred to this URL (http://someplace.com/file.html), and the browser version (which includes the name and version of the operating system it's running on).

The second line appears because this particular HTML page contains some embedded JavaScript code that collects more information than your browser normally gives out and embeds that information into a special, additional request that's sent to the server (as though it were downloading another page — except it's a nonexistent page). Thanks to this extra (and very common) reporting mechanism, the server log now knows that the user who requested `index.html` a fraction of a second earlier has JavaScript enabled (otherwise the script wouldn't run, and this entry wouldn't be there); Java enabled (`je=true`); screen dimensions of 1920 × 1200 (`sw=1920&sh=1200`); a 24-bit-color display (`sd=24`); a default language of American English (`la=en-US`); cookies enabled (`co=true`); browser window dimensions of 1110 × 952 (`ww=1110&wh=952`); and a bunch of plug-ins installed, including Google Gears, Adobe Acrobat Reader, Microsoft Silverlight, and Apple QuickTime.

Again, it's not necessary to concern yourself with the details of the log entry, and the format may vary considerably depending on what web server is used and how the JavaScript reporting code is written. The main point is simply that the operator of a web server can learn quite a bit about you every time you visit a web page. Most website operators use this information to help them understand their visitors and tailor the content they provide to the visitors' needs. But the more outside parties are able to learn about you, the greater the risks to your privacy, and certainly, some unscrupulous website operators collect this data for less than wholesome reasons.

Note

You can reduce the amount of information your browser sends to servers by turning off JavaScript in your browser. However, because so many sites rely on JavaScript for navigation and other crucial features, the downsides probably outweigh the benefits. You can mask this information by using a proxy server or filtering software, as I discuss later in this chapter. ■

Hiding your IP address by using anonymous proxy servers

Of all the facts you reveal about yourself when browsing the web, the one you should be most concerned about is your IP address. All the other details your browser sends could be the same for a great many people, but very few people (and in many cases, only one) use a given IP address at any given time. It could potentially be used to track you down personally, so if you want to be certain that the websites you visit can't keep records enabling them — or a third party — to tell what you were doing, you should take steps to hide your IP address. Because the process of hiding your IP address can be awkward and can sometimes slow down browsing, you may want to do so only when visiting sites where you're particularly concerned about privacy.

You can hide your IP address in a number of ways, each of which involves the use of one or more computers besides your own and the server. The first of these approaches is using something called a *proxy server*. Simply put, a proxy server is a computer that receives requests from a client, passes them on to a server, and then reverses the process with the information that's returned. It's a go-between for sending and receiving information. Because the proxy server and not your own computer contacts the website you're trying to reach, it looks to the web server as though your requests are coming from the proxy server's address, and that's what gets stored in its logs. As a bonus, using proxy servers often hides other details about your computer (such as the referrer, operating system, and browser) and can sometimes block cookies, Flash content, JavaScript, and other kinds of data. On the other hand, if a proxy server does permit content such as Flash and JavaScript, you should be aware that those features can potentially reveal your IP address or other private details.

Note

Proxy servers can perform other functions besides hiding IP addresses, such as caching content to reduce bandwidth usage and filtering out objectionable material. But the only usage that concerns us here is anonymizing web browsing — hence, the term anonymous proxy servers. ■

The simplest way to try this out is to visit one of the many websites that offer anonymizing services. Type the URL of the page you want to visit in a form on the site, and it forwards your request and returns the result — usually in another frame of the same window. A few examples of services that work like this are Ninja Cloak (`www.ninjacloak.com`), Proxify (`http://proxify.com`), The Cloak (`www.the-cloak.com`), US UK.info (`http://usauk.info`), and Catchitforu.info Proxy (`http://catchitforu.info`). Be aware that services of this sort are typically ad-supported (which means tolerating extra ads and possibly weird page layout in exchange for privacy), although some of them offer paid, ad-free subscriptions.

Note

An anonymous proxy server may put limits on the quantity of data or the types of files you can transfer. Some types of web-based activities, such as watching streaming videos, are usually impossible with proxy servers. ■

If you want the flexibility to use your browser's bookmark list, switch between browsers, and view web pages without additional frames in your browser window, you can configure your Mac (or a particular browser) to send all web traffic directly through a proxy server. The first thing you need is the address of an anonymous proxy server. You can find a detailed and regularly updated list of public proxy servers at `www.publicproxyservers.com`. Before configuring Mac OS X to use a server on this list, be sure to visit the server's website to check out its terms of service, privacy policy, and features — and to see if it requires a fee or registration.

Safari and most other browsers use system-wide proxy server settings. To configure these, follow these steps:

1. Choose ⇨ System Preferences to open System Preferences and then click Network to open the Network pane.

2. Select your current network interface in the list on the left, click the Advanced button on the right side of the window to open a dialog box with additional settings, and then click the Proxies tab, as shown in Figure 10.31.

3. Choose Manually from the Configure Proxies pop-up menu.

4. Click the Web Proxy (HTTP) check box.

5. Type the proxy server's domain name or IP address in the Web Proxy Server field and the port it uses (provided by the server operator) in the field to its right. If the server requires a username and password, click the Proxy server requires password check box and then type your username and password in the fields provided.

6. Click the Secure Web Proxy (HTTPS) check box and then repeat step 5.

7. Click OK to close the configuration dialog box and then close System Preferences. All web traffic to and from Safari now flows through the selected proxy server until you

go back to the Network preference pane and deselect the Web Proxy and Secure Web Proxy check boxes.

Firefox requires that you configure its own preferences to use a proxy server. To do this, follow these steps:

1. **With Firefox running, choose Firefox ➪ Preferences to open the Preferences window, click Advanced to open the Advanced pane, and then click the Network tab.**

2. **Click the Settings button to open a configuration dialog box for proxy servers.**

3. **Click the Manual proxy configuration radio button and then type the IP address for your proxy server in the HTTP Proxy field and its port in the Port field.**

4. **Click OK to close the configuration dialog box and then close the Preferences window.**

FIGURE 10.31

In this somewhat hidden and mysterious-looking dialog box within the Network preference pane, you can configure proxy servers used by Safari and other applications.

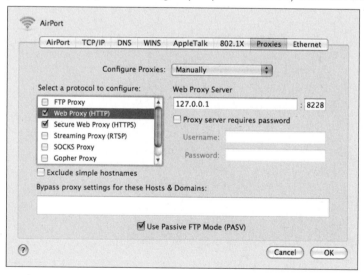

If all that sounds like more trouble than you care to go through regularly, one way to simplify this procedure is to download and install a program called NetShade (`www.raynersoftware.com/netshade`, $29), shown in Figure 10.32. With one click, NetShade selects a public proxy server from a long (and dynamically updated) list, modifies the settings in your Network preference pane, and connects you. You can disconnect (reverting your Network preferences) just as easily. When you purchase NetShade, you also get a one-year subscription to the developer's private proxy server, which provides better performance and privacy than public proxy servers.

Another option is a program called Proxifier (www.proxifier.com, $39.95), which lets you configure multiple proxy servers and switch between them easily without having to use System Preferences. Proxifier supports several different types of proxy servers and can be used for all your Internet traffic, not just web browsing.

Although proxy servers provide a simple solution to a tricky privacy problem, they can't guarantee complete anonymity. One reason is that although the web server doesn't know your real IP address, the proxy server does, at least while it's handling your page request. So, the server operator could potentially tell which sites you're visiting, and if the server keeps an access log, someone else could learn your browsing history after the fact. Proxy servers differ greatly in their policies about whether or how long they keep logs and under what circumstances they may make them available to outside parties. For that matter, unless you research the provider of your proxy services carefully, you could be inadvertently giving away your personal data to an advertising firm, government agency, or hacker, making your browsing less private instead of more private!

NetShade makes it easy to connect to any of a long list of anonymous proxy servers.

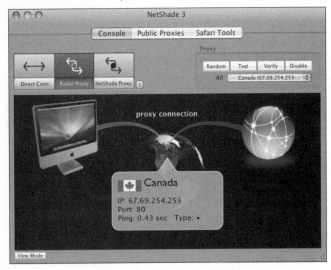

Yet another potential problem is that although proxy servers modify the IP address your browser sends to a server when it requests a page, they can't control what your web browser plug-ins may do. A clever Flash site, for example, could theoretically coerce Flash Player on your Mac into discovering and reporting your real IP address. So, you'll be safer when using proxy servers if you avoid sites that rely on plug-ins.

By the way, if you use a VPN to connect to the Internet, the VPN also acts as a proxy server, masking your IP address. This doesn't necessarily do any more to ensure your anonymity than a conventional proxy server, but it's sometimes a useful option in that it does more than redirect your Internet traffic — it encrypts all the traffic, and because it affects your entire connection, it can be used for applications (such as streaming video) that might not work with a proxy server.

Cross-Ref

For more on VPNs, see Chapter 12. ∎

Hiding your IP address by using onion routing

A proxy server puts one computer between you and a web server, but as I just said, that doesn't guarantee your anonymity. Beyond the risk of someone reading the proxy server's logs and connecting your real IP address with the sites you visited, there are various other methods someone could use to infer that a certain request came from you, regardless of what the server thinks your IP address was. To address some of these shortcomings, there's a more complex variation on the idea of a proxy server: a process called *onion routing*, a system originally designed by the U.S. Navy.

In an onion routing network, every request for a web page is encrypted and then sent through one or several intermediate nodes before going to the server. Each time a request travels between nodes, it's wrapped in an additional layer of encryption (hence the onion image), and the request is decrypted only by the last node in the network, which sends it on to the web server. Because of this configuration, none of the nodes except the first (the one closest to the requester) can know who originally made a request, and none except the last (the one closest to the web server) can know what page was being requested. When the web server responds with the requested data, it's sent back along the same path (once again, with multiple layers of encryption).

The best-known onion routing network is Tor (www.torproject.org), a name that also refers to the software needed to participate in the network. Versions of Tor are available for Mac OS X, Windows, and Linux; all are free and open source. You can download Tor from www.torproject. org/easy-download.html.en; what you get is a package that includes not only Tor itself but also Vidalia (an easy-to-use graphical application for configuring and controlling Tor), Privoxy (a proxy application, discussed elsewhere in this chapter), and Torbutton (which lets Firefox users turn Tor on or off with a single click).

After downloading and installing the Tor package according to the instructions provided at www. torproject.org/docs/tor-doc-osx.html.en, you can connect to the Tor network simply by opening the Vidalia application, shown in Figure 10.33 (although much more extensive customization is possible if you so choose). However, you must also tell your browser to use Privoxy as your proxy server because it serves as a conduit to connect your Mac to the Tor network. In Firefox, with Torbutton installed, this requires merely clicking the text Tor Disabled in the lower right corner of the window; when it changes to Tor Enabled, you're all set. If you use Safari, you must configure the Network pane of System Preferences to connect to the proxy server 127.0.0.1 on port 8118, following the instructions earlier in this chapter. Either way, from then on, all your web requests are routed through Tor until you disable it.

As useful as onion routing is, it does have some downsides. For one thing, it's even slower than using proxy servers, and the speed may vary a great deal from one request to the next. In addition, your IP address could still potentially be discovered through the use of plug-in exploits, as it can with proxy servers. Last but not least, onion routing hides your IP address but encrypts only the data you exchange with web servers during part of its journey. The link between the outermost node of the onion-routing network and the web server must always be unencrypted, and if that node is compromised (or run by an untrustworthy person), all the data you send and receive can be seen.

One final note on this subject: Although not exactly the same as onion routing, a comparable service called JonDonym (`www.jondos.de/en/`) routes users' requests for web pages randomly through a series of encrypted servers to hide the IP address of the computer that originated the request. The Mac software needed for the service, JonDo (as in John Doe) is free, but membership in the JonDonym network requires prepayment, which ranges from 2 euros, or roughly US$3 (for up to 200 MB of data transferred over a maximum of 3 months), to 40 euros, roughly US$53 (for up to 6500 MB of data transferred over a maximum of 2 years).

FIGURE 10.33

Vidalia lets you turn Tor network access on or off with a single click.

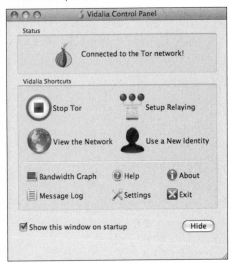

Masking other browser details

Some of the methods of anonymizing your IP address also, at least optionally, hide other browser data, such as your browser type, operating system, and the site you most recently visited. The Tor bundle for Mac OS X, for example, offers all these capabilities via a prebuilt configuration file for Privoxy, and most anonymous proxy servers offer some of them.

You can also mask some of this extra information without hiding your IP address. For example, in NetBarrier, choose View⇨Surf and then select Information Hiding to show a series of check boxes that enable you to conceal some information normally sent while browsing. To prevent information about your operating system and browser from being sent to web servers, click the Hide information about my computer and Web Browser check box. To prevent web servers from learning which website you came from to get to their site, click the Hide information on the last Web site visited check box. Changes take place immediately; you can then quit NetBarrier.

Internet Cleanup also offers one concealment feature. In Internet Cleanup's main window, click NetBlockade to open the NetBlockade configuration window, shown in Figure 10.34. If the Blocking Is button says Off, click it so that it says On. Then, to block web servers from knowing the URL of the page you last visited, choose Block All from the Referrers pop-up menu. The change takes place immediately; you can then close the window and quit Internet Cleanup.

FIGURE 10.34

The NetBlockade module of Internet Cleanup offers, among other things, a way to block referring web pages from appearing in the logs of web servers you visit.

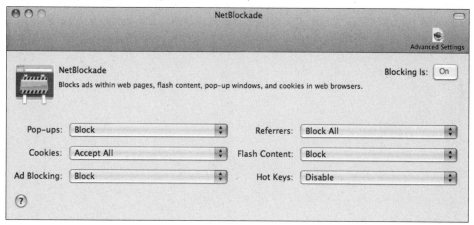

Blocking Ads, Pop-up Windows, and Flash

Speaking as someone who runs several ad-supported websites, I understand how crucial advertising is to keep interesting and useful websites available and free. On the other hand, as someone who visits dozens of websites every day, I also recognize that ads can be intrusive and irritating — and, if used to collect information about my browsing habits, a threat to my privacy. Although I think that, on the whole, ads do more good than harm, others may not share that opinion. And even the most ardent supporters of advertising must concede that there's a limit to what's reasonable. Small, tasteful ads are one thing; pages covered with obnoxious blinking banners, pop-up windows, and animated overlays are something else.

As a result, a number of options exist for blocking ads that would otherwise appear as you browse the web — either by setting blanket policies or by selectively disallowing content from particular domains. Your browser itself may offer some ad-blocking capabilities, and third-party software can provide additional filtering. In a similar vein, there are a number of methods for blocking Flash content (animations, movies, and other dynamic content), whether it's used for advertising or some other purpose.

Using browser settings

Safari and Firefox have limited ad-blocking capabilities built in. If you find these insufficient, you can use third-party utilities to go much further; I discuss these later in this chapter.

Safari

Safari has a built-in pop-up window blocker. To activate it, choose Safari ➪ Block Pop-Up Windows (⌘+Shift+K); to turn it off, choose the same command again. When this command is active, Safari prevents sites from loading pop-up (or pop-under) windows automatically, although they can still load in direct response to something you do, such as clicking a link or button.

It's extremely rare to find a site that can bypass Safari's blocker and equally rare (although not unheard of) to find sites that won't function properly with this feature enabled. However, as I mentioned earlier in this chapter, some sites superimpose ads on web pages without actually causing the browser to open a new window (even though the ad may resemble a window and may even be movable within the page limits and have its own close button). Safari may be unable to block such ads, but fortunately, they're much less common than conventional pop-up/pop-under windows.

Firefox

Firefox can block most pop-up windows, as Safari can, but it also lets you configure exceptions for certain sites and lets you block images by default if you prefer. In addition, it gives you explicit control over certain JavaScript behaviors often associated with ads and other pop-ups.

To configure Firefox's ad-blocking features, follow these steps:

1. **With Firefox running, choose Firefox ➪ Preferences to open the Preferences window and then click Content to open the Content pane, as shown in Figure 10.35.**

2. **To prevent pop-up windows from opening on their own, click the Block pop-up windows check box (if it's not already selected).** When this check box is selected, you can exempt certain sites from pop-up blocking by clicking Exceptions, typing the URL of the site, and then clicking Allow.

3. **To prevent images from loading when you visit new pages, click the Load images automatically check box to deselect it (if it's currently selected).** Again, you can let certain sites display their images by clicking Exceptions and then adding their URLs. Because images are used for much more than ads, I recommend leaving this check box selected unless you're using an extremely slow Internet connection and pages load too slowly otherwise.

FIGURE 10.35

Firefox has a few basic ad-blocking capabilities built in, which you configure on this pane of its Preferences window.

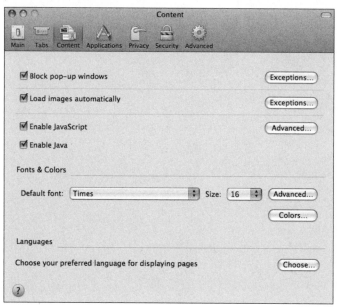

4. **To enable Firefox to use JavaScript, click the Enable JavaScript check box (if it's not already selected).** With JavaScript enabled, you can customize certain settings by clicking the Advanced button, which displays the dialog box shown in Figure 10.36.

FIGURE 10.36

Some JavaScript behaviors are used most often by annoying ads; you can enable or disable them in this dialog box.

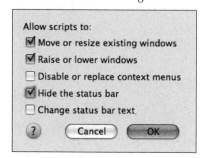

5. **In the Advanced pane, click any of the check boxes to select or deselect them, as you prefer.** To eliminate the most annoying behavior often found in windows that use JavaScript, make sure at least the following items are deselected: Move or resize existing windows, Raise or lower windows, and Hide the status bar.

6. **Close the Preferences window when you're done.**

Using Hostal

Another way of blocking ads relies on something called a *hosts* file, and it's an elegant, old-school approach that's often surprisingly effective.

Ordinarily, when you connect to a server of any kind on the Internet, your Mac sends the domain name you want to contact to a *DNS* (domain name system) server, which returns the numeric IP address of the server in question. Your web browser, email program, or other Internet application then uses the numeric address to connect to the server. However, before the DNS system existed, each computer maintained a simple text file listing all the servers it might need to connect to, with each computer's IP address and domain name on its own line. This list is known as the hosts file.

What's interesting about this file is that if you happen to have one on your Mac in the appropriate location (`/private/etc/hosts`), your Mac consults it first — before sending an address to a DNS server for resolution. So, suppose a web page contains the URL of an ad hosted by a third party on a server such as `www.myadvertisingservice.com`. If you put that domain name in your hosts file and associate it with a nonexistent IP address such as `0.0.0.0`, your browser never even bothers to look up its address using DNS. It simply assumes the server is down and displays nothing where the ad would otherwise be.

You could do a bunch of searching and try to come up with a list of every ad server you might want to block and manually create a hosts file in Terminal. But a much easier way to do this is to pick up a copy of Hostal (`www.northernsoftworks.com/hostal.html`, $9.99), which can do all that work for you. It comes with two long lists of domain names — one that contains ad servers and the other that contains adult sites you might want to block. With a few clicks, you can add any or all of these domain names to your hosts file, preventing any browser (or other program) on your computer from displaying any content from them.

After you've downloaded and installed Hostal, follow these steps to use it:

1. **Open Hostal from wherever you installed it.**

2. **To turn on Hostal, choose File ➪ Enable Hostal.**

3. **Click the Ad Filters tab, shown in Figure 10.37, and then click Enable All to select all the preconfigured ad servers.** To deselect a server, click the check box next to its URL in the On column.

4. **Choose File ➪ Save to save your updated hosts file.** The selected sites are immediately blocked.

Hostal lets you add to your hosts file a long list of domain names that deliver advertising to your browser, blocking their content from appearing.

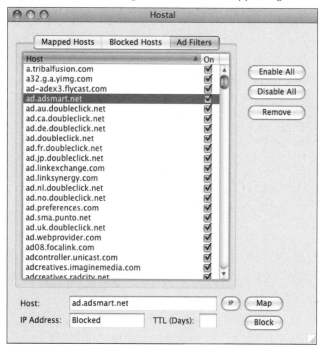

5. **Optionally, to also use Hostal to block adult sites, click the Blocked Hosts tab, click Enable All, choose File ➪ Save again, and then quit Hostal.** As long as your hosts file is in place, Hostal itself need not be running.

Hostal has a number of additional interesting features too, which you can read about on its website.

Using other ad-blocking software

If the capabilities of your browser and Hostal alone still let through more advertising than you're happy with, you can use any of numerous other programs, which take different (and sometimes more aggressive) approaches to blocking advertising. Because the process of blocking ads is closely related to other privacy-protection steps, several of these programs appear elsewhere in this chapter and in other parts of this book too.

Some of the programs that include ad-blocking capabilities among their features are the following:

*   **PithHelmet.** PithHelmet is a plug-in that works only with Safari. It lets you configure the way Safari treats cookies, JavaScript, plug-ins, and other web features on a site-by-site basis

(or following pattern-matching rules) instead of globally as Safari normally does. It also lets you block ads, images, pop-up windows, animations, music played from MIDI files, and similar annoyances — again, for only the sites or types of sites that you choose — and, if you have sufficient geek savvy, perform other fancy substitutions and transformations. (`http://culater.net/software/PithHelmet/PithHelmet.php`, $10)

- **Privoxy.** I mentioned Privoxy earlier in the context of proxy servers, because indeed that's what it is, but in fact, its main raison d'être is to function as an ad blocker. At your request, it looks for URLs matching certain patterns and references to graphics that are in the sizes commonly used by ads and then blocks them. It can also block cookies from being set, prevent pop-ups, and perform numerous other web-filtering tricks. Unfortunately, setup and configuration is far from simple. If you like to tinker and don't mind spending hours learning about Privoxy's features and rule syntax, you can do some powerful things with it, but it's not for the technologically timid. (`www.privoxy.org`, free)

- **AdBlock.** If Firefox is your browser of choice, you can install this extension to gain extensive control over ads and other annoyances. You can block ads on individual sites or subscribe to any of several free services that supply AdBlock with the URLs of common ads and ad servers so that most ads are blocked automatically. AdBlock can also prevent Flash and Java content from appearing. (`https://addons.mozilla.org/en-US/firefox/addon/1865`, free)

- **GlimmerBlocker.** If you like the idea of using an ad-filtering proxy server but find Privoxy too much to wrap your head around, try GlimmerBlocker, shown in Figure 10.38, instead. It installs as a preference pane and is extremely easy to use — you can activate it with a single click, and adding or modifying rules is extremely straightforward. Turning on GlimmerBlocker even configures your Network preference pane to use it as a proxy automatically, and turning it off removes the proxy setting. GlimmerBlocker can keep most static, animated, and Flash ads from appearing on pages in Safari; unfortunately, it doesn't support other browsers. (`http://glimmerblocker.org/`, free)

- **NetBarrier.** The big daddy of Internet filtering software for Mac, NetBarrier from Intego contains a Banners Filter, which can block images based on rules you define — such as patterns of characters in the URL or hostname — by replacing them with empty blocks the same size. It works with all browsers, although it may take some experimentation and tweaking to get it to block all and only the content you want to hide. (`www.intego.com/netbarrier/`, $49.95)

- **Internet Cleanup.** This utility package focuses mainly on cleaning up private data after the fact, but its included NetBlockade program can block pop-ups, cookies, ads, referrers (preventing a site from knowing which page you came from), and Flash content. You can use pre-defined patterns or add your own to specify which sorts of ads on which sites should be blocked or shown and which sites may show Flash content when it's otherwise blocked. (`http://my.smithmicro.com/mac/cleanup/index.html`, $29.99)

- **SafariBlock.** This Safari-only plug-in is an attempt to replicate the functionality AdBlock provides for Firefox. (`http://code.google.com/p/safariblock/`, free)

FIGURE 10.38

GlimmerBlocker has extensive filtering capabilities, but even its default settings are quite helpful.

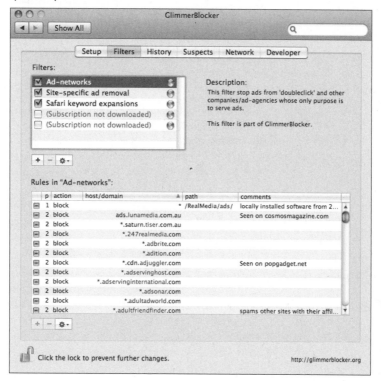

Blocking Other Undesirable Content

Blocking advertising is one thing; blocking entire categories of websites from loading at all is a different matter. The desire to do this comes up most often for parents who want to prevent their children from seeing certain kinds of sites, for public institutions such as libraries that want to do the same for all their patrons (but especially children), and for companies that want to restrict what sorts of sites their employees can view at work.

Mac OS X's built-in parental controls offer some filtering of web content, but this capability isn't as thorough, flexible, or bulletproof as some users prefer. Hostal, covered earlier, also lets you block sites with adult or other undesirable content, but it works only with the specific sites on its list (or those you add manually) — it can't dynamically determine which sites may contain offensive material.

Cross-Ref

For more on using Mac OS X parental controls, see Chapter 3. ∎

If you want to go further in blocking sites with questionable content from appearing in browsers on your Mac, you can try one of the following software packages:

- **ContentBarrier.** This program blocks all Internet software on your Mac from accessing sites or using protocols (such as file-sharing protocols) that you deem unsafe or unfit. You can configure different settings for each user and can even manage your Mac's settings remotely. (`www.intego.com/contentbarrier/`, $49.95)

- **KidsGoGoGo X.** In addition to blocking adult content in programs such as web browsers, RSS readers, and iTunes, this software forces searches performed using search engines such as Google to return safe search results, offers parental monitoring features, and keeps a record of all information sent or received online. (`www.makienterprise.com/kggg/kidsgogogo.html`, $30)

- **Safe Eyes.** With this software installed, you can block access to web content in any or all of 35 categories, including nudity, pornography, drugs, and games. It can block users from searching for certain keywords, selectively restrict access to certain YouTube videos, and filter email, instant messaging, and other Internet content. (`www.internetsafety.com/safe-eyes-parental-control-software.php`, $49.95)

- **Trend Micro Smart Surfing for Mac.** In much the same way as the other products in this list, Smart Surfing lets you block any or all of 28 categories of websites. In addition to specifying which categories to block, you can add individual sites to an Approved or Blocked list. (`http://us.trendmicro.com/us/products/personal/smartsurfing-mac/`, $49.95)

Summary

This chapter explored the problem of keeping your personal information from falling into the wrong hands when browsing the web. After detailing some of the reasons web browsing is often insecure, I described the use of SSL to encrypt communication with specific sites. I explained how best to store the personal information (including usernames and passwords) that you type into web forms and discussed ways of avoiding malware and phishing schemes. Because your Mac itself stores considerable information about your web activities, I showed how to keep that data private and also investigated ways of keeping your identity secret from the sites you visit (and anyone watching your web traffic). I rounded out the chapter with a look at ways to block ads (which sometimes enable advertisers to track you) from appearing in your browser.

Securely Accessing Other Computers

A part from email and web browsing, discussed earlier in this book, you may have any number of different reasons to access another computer. You may need to exchange files with a client, customer, or employer or upload files to a web server. You may also need to control another computer remotely — either by sharing its screen or via a command-line interface using Terminal.

Each of these ways of connecting to another computer carries certain security risks. There's the usual, all-purpose worry that someone could eavesdrop on your connection and see what you're doing online or steal your password and thereby get access to the same remote computer. But some ways of connecting to remote computers are inherently less secure or otherwise more problematic than others, and it pays to know what your options are and what specific risks or benefits each one involves.

Transferring Files

If you're copying files between computers on your local network, you can be reasonably confident that you're safe from eavesdropping — at least if you use a wired Ethernet network or a Wi-Fi network protected with WPA or 802.1x encryption, along with a NAT gateway of some kind — and that's true regardless of which protocol you use. However, if you want to transfer files to or from computers outside your local network, you should think more carefully about security because merely having a username and password isn't necessarily enough to keep your data (and your credentials) safe.

In this section, I discuss several of the protocols used for transferring files to and from remote computers. Then, I show how to use these protocols in the Finder (to the extent the Finder supports remote transfers) and other popular applications.

FTP, SCP, SFTP, and FTPS

The first thing many people think when they hear FTP is something along the lines of, "Oh, yeah, that's how you download software from websites." Even though it's less often the case than it once was, it's true that many websites that distribute software still store those files on a server separate from the web server where the HTML files reside; if you click a link that starts with `ftp://`, you're downloading a file from an FTP server. FTP, or *File Transfer Protocol*, was in existence long before the web, and because it was an established, reliable way of transferring files, a lot of people stuck with it. Because it's so widely known, used, and supported, you're likely to run into it in other situations too. If you run your own website, you may use FTP to upload HTML files to it, for example. And FTP is still commonly used by publishers, graphic design studios, and other organizations that need to get lots of large files to or from their customers or clients.

FTP is perfectly effective at getting a file from one place to another. The problem with FTP is that it's inherently insecure. When you connect to an FTP server, your username and password (if any) and the files themselves are all sent in the clear, without any encryption or other security. Anyone who can watch (or sniff) the traffic between your computer and the FTP server can see everything you upload or download as well as get your credentials for unhindered access to the server in the future. Even using a VPN, as helpful as that may be, doesn't guarantee security all the way to the server if the server isn't on the same local network as the VPN. For these reasons, most security experts recommend avoiding FTP if at all possible and instead using any of a variety of comparable but secure protocols, such as SCP, SFTP, or FTPS. Some FTP servers also support one or more of these other protocols, so you can simply change the settings in the application you use to transfer files. In other cases, switching to a different protocol involves convincing a network administrator to install or turn on software with secure transfer capabilities.

Because initials such as FTP, SCP, SFTP, and FTPS often get mixed up with each other, here are some basic descriptions to clarify what the terms mean and how they differ:

- **File Transfer Protocol (FTP).** This is a long-established mechanism for sending and receiving files over a TCP connection.

- **Secure Copy (SPC).** This is a simple protocol for securely transferring files over an SSH connection. Although SCP is a more recent protocol than FTP, it's more advanced only in the sense of being more secure. Other than that, it has much less functionality. For example, to get or send a remote file or folder, you must know its exact path on the server; you can't get a directory listing over SCP. SCP transfers are typically done in a command-line environment, such as Terminal, rather than in a graphical application.

- **SSH File Transfer Protocol (SFTP).** Despite the fact that the name includes FTP, SFTP isn't based on FTP at all but is an entirely separate protocol, which combines the security of SSH with a similar range of flexibility to that offered by FTP. Like SCP, SFTP depends on an existing SSH (secure shell) implementation for its security, but unlike SCP, it allows users to get directory listings, delete remote files, and interact with the server in other ways.

- **FTPS.** The initials FTPS are generally interpreted to mean FTP over SSL, although some people refer to this protocol (somewhat confusingly) as FTP Secure. FTPS is an extended version of FTP that sends commands and data over an SSL connection.

- **FTP over SSH.** Not to be confused with FTP over SSL, FTP over SSH tunnels ordinary FTP through an existing SSH connection. This usage is somewhat awkward and is therefore fairly uncommon, given the more convenient alternatives.

Although all these protocols except plain FTP can be used to transfer files securely, if you have a choice, I suggest going with SFTP, which is the most common and convenient of the methods that offer directory listings and other important features. But read on to learn about still other file transfer options.

WebDAV

WebDAV, short for Web-based Distributed Authoring and Versioning, is a mechanism by which one can manage files on another computer using HTTP (the same transport mechanism used for delivering web pages). It was originally intended to allow groups of web developers to work together more easily on large projects in that it could not only let them list, upload, download, and edit files but would also prevent one user from changing a file that's in use by another, keep track of multiple versions of files, and perform other management functions.

But even though more effective web development was the impetus for WebDAV, this technology has also been put to other, less flashy uses. It offers all the features needed to function as a remote file system, so you can mount a WebDAV server in the Finder just as you would any other remote server (as I explain just ahead) and interact with the files as though they were on a local disk. In fact, if you're a MobileMe member, this is exactly how Mac OS X connects to your iDisk. It looks and acts like any other disk, but in the background, it uses WebDAV to communicate with the server.

In case you're wondering why this should be interesting or why yet another file-transfer mechanism was needed, one of the key features of WebDAV is that because it uses HTTP, it normally transfers data over port 80. So, in situations where an ISP, company, or local firewall blocks access to certain ports for security reasons or to restrict what its users can do, WebDAV almost always remains a viable option because blocking port 80 would also mean blocking access to the web.

Also, like HTTP, WebDAV traffic can be secured using HTTPS (which normally uses port 443). In general, you should always opt for the secure version of WebDAV if it's available. Nothing changes about the way you access it except for the slightly different address, but all the traffic between your computer and the WebDAV server is encrypted. Unfortunately, Apple doesn't offer HTTPS access to the MobileMe iDisk.

Other protocols

Servers on your local network (which may include other Macs and PCs with File Sharing turned on, network-attached storage devices, and other such gadgets) most often use other protocols for transferring files. Although all of these also work over the Internet, you're less likely to encounter them when accessing remote computers. Some of the most common protocols are these:

- **AFP.** Apple Filing Protocol is Apple's primary mechanism for sharing files between Macs, although some other operating systems and third-party devices also support it. Of all the network protocols supported by Mac OS X, AFP is the one most likely to transfer all the special Mac-specific metadata (ownership, permissions, resource forks, extended attributes, and so on) intact, because it was the only one designed expressly for the Mac.

Cross-Ref
For more on AFP, see Chapter 12. ■

- **SMB.** Whereas AFP is the primary network protocol for file sharing on Macs, Server Message Block is the primary local networking protocol under Windows. It also goes by the more user-friendly name Microsoft Windows Network. Most network-attached storage (NAS) devices and other stand-alone home or small-business file servers use SMB as their networking protocol.

Cross-Ref
For more on SMB, see Chapter 7. ■

- **NFS.** The Network File System is yet another networking protocol — this one most common on Unix systems of various sorts, although support for NFS is also built into Mac OS X and Windows.

AFP and SMB traffic is sent unencrypted, and NFS offers encryption only as an option. Mac OS X versions 10.2 through 10.4 offered the option of secure AFP connections using SSH, although this was awkward to configure and not entirely reliable. Starting with Leopard, secure AFP is no longer an option. Someone sniffing the network traffic between your Mac and the server could see all the data that's transferred. Therefore, except for the secure version of NFS, these protocols aren't safe ways to transfer files to or from computers outside your local network unless you use some other method of encrypting the connection, such as manually setting up an SSH tunnel (which I describe later in this chapter) or, better yet, using a VPN to connect to the network where the server is located.

Remote file transfers in the Finder

Perhaps the easiest way of transferring files to or from remote computers is to use the familiar interface of the Finder, which can connect to servers using the following protocols, mounting their shared volumes so that they're accessible just like any other Mac disk:

- AFP
- FTP

- NFS
- SMB
- WebDAV

First, of these protocols, only WebDAV and NFS natively offer encrypted versions; for all the others, the connections you make in the Finder are unencrypted unless you use Back to My Mac (as I describe in a moment), a VPN, an SSH tunnel, or some comparable method of network security. Second, although the Finder can mount FTP servers, it provides read-only access to the files. If you want to upload files to an FTP server, you must use a third-party file-transfer program (discussed later in this chapter).

To connect to a remote network server in the Finder, follow these steps:

1. **Choose Go ⇨ Connect to Server or press ⌘+K.** The Connect to Server window, as shown in Figure 11.1, opens.

FIGURE 11.1

This simple window lets you connect to a wide variety of local and remote file servers, including AFP, SMB, and WebDAV servers.

2. **In the Server Address field, type the URL of the server to which you want to connect.** In other words, type the scheme representing the networking protocol (such as `ftp://`, `https://`, or `smb://`) followed by the domain name or IP address of the server — for example, `afp://server-name.com`.

3. **Click Connect.** If the server to which you're connecting requires authentication, a dialog box similar to the one in Figure 11.2 opens.

4. **Type your username and password in the appropriate fields (optionally clicking the Remember this password in my keychain check box to store your credentials in your keychain) and then click OK.** The remote volume mounts on your desktop, and a new window opens to show the volume's contents.

To disconnect from the remote volume, drag its icon to the Trash. You can also select the volume and then press ⌘+E.

If you're a member of Apple's MobileMe service and have enabled both Back to My Mac and File Sharing on another Mac, you can connect to the other Mac and transfer files in the Finder exactly as you would if it were on your local network. When you do, although the connection uses AFP for file transfer, it's securely encrypted.

Cross-Ref

For more on Back to My Mac and File Sharing, see Chapter 7. ■

FIGURE 11.2

When you type your credentials to connect to a file server in the Finder, you can save the information in your keychain so that you need not type your password again.

WebDAV File System Authentication

Enter your user name and password to access the
server at the URL "https://some-webdav-server.com."

Your name and password will be sent securely.

Name

Password

☐ Remember this password in my keychain

Cancel   OK

Using file-transfer software

In cases where the Finder lacks support for a protocol you want to use (or, in the case of FTP, prevents you from uploading files) — or when you need advanced features, such as automatic synchronization of local and remote folders or queued transfers — you can turn to a third-party file-transfer program. There are many to choose from; the ones I list here are among the most popular. All these programs support FTP, SFTP, and FTPS, along with other protocols as listed:

- **Captain FTP.** A full-featured file-transfer tool, Captain FTP (shown in Figure 11.3) supports WebDAV as well as Amazon.com's S3 (Simple Storage Service), which uses a proprietary system for transferring files. It offers a two-pane view of local and remote files (or files on two different servers) and can automatically synchronize or mirror pairs of folders. (`http://captainftp.xdsnet.de/`, $29)

- **Cyberduck.** This free, open-source program supports FTP, FTPS, SFTP, SCP, WebDAV, and Amazon S3, among other protocols (`http://cyberduck.ch/`).

- **Fetch.** Fetch, shown in Figure 11.4, is one of the oldest and best-known FTP clients for the Mac, easily recognizable due to its trademark animated running dog pointer, which appears during file transfers. The program works with FTP servers that use GSSAPI (an interface to the Kerberos security system, which lets you authenticate securely and encrypt data transfers without using a password) and can warn you before sending your password insecurely, regardless of which protocol you use (`http://fetchsoftworks.com/`, $25).

- **Interarchy.** This file-transfer application, shown in Figure 11.5, supports WebDAV (with or without SSL) as well as SCP (highly unusual for a graphical application), regular and secure versions of Amazon S3, and even (using some clever Perl magic) direct file transfers over SSH, even when the server doesn't explicitly support any other file transfer protocol. Interarchy can automatically mirror files between local and remote folders and has a long list of other advanced features. (`http://nolobe.com/interarchy/`, $59)

FIGURE 11.3

Captain FTP offers a two-pane interface for transferring files to and from remote servers.

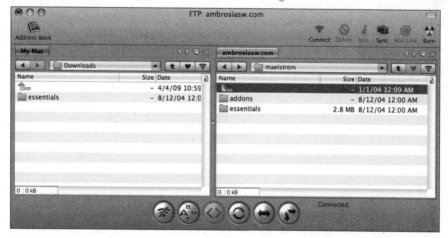

FIGURE 11.4

The beloved, iconic running dog pointer appears in Fetch during file transfers.

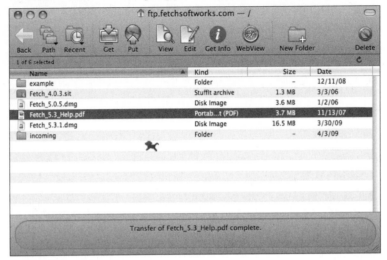

FIGURE 11.5

Interarchy displays remote files in a single window similar to the Finder's List view.

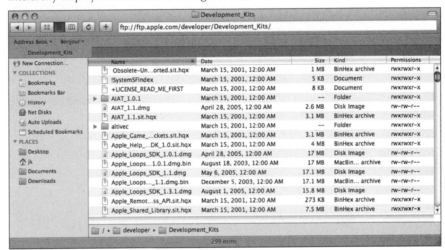

- **Transmit.** Transmit, shown in Figure 11.6, is my personal favorite of these applications — it doesn't have the longest feature list, but it's easy to use and extremely reliable. The program supports WebDAV (with or without SSL) as well as Amazon S3 and lets you configure its interface in a variety of ways, including a two-pane view in which you can easily compare files between local and remote folders. Transmit includes support for syncing your Favorites (bookmarks for sites you visit often) with your other Macs using MobileMe, automated file synchronization between local and remote folders, a built-in editor for text files, and numerous other capabilities. (www.panic.com/transmit/, $29.95)

FIGURE 11.6

Transmit provides a simple, straightforward interface for connecting to a variety of remote file servers.

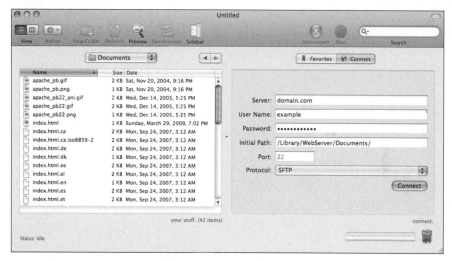

Controlling Another Computer Remotely

From the comfort of your Mac (even if it's a laptop on a park bench), you can view the screen of another computer and control it using your own keyboard and mouse as though you were sitting right in front of it. The reverse is also true, given the appropriate sharing and firewall settings — someone can view your Mac's screen and control it from another computer. Screen sharing, as this process is called, is extremely powerful, and for that reason, you should take particular care to ensure that no one can intercept your credentials or the actual screen data while it's in transit. Although there are several different ways to go about sharing a screen, the specific precautions you must take are somewhat different for each.

Using Mac OS X Screen Sharing

Screen sharing requires two software components: a server running on the remote computer, which makes its screen available to others, and a client running on the local computer, which lets you connect to and control the screen of the server. The most widely used protocol for sharing screens is VNC (Virtual Network Computing), and in general, any client or server based on the VNC standard can communicate with any other VNC system, regardless of platform or brand.

Every Mac running Mac OS X 10.3 Panther or later has built-in client software for Apple Remote Desktop, a remote administration tool described just ahead, which uses VNC for screen sharing. Because (in a confusing twist of terminology) the Apple Remote Desktop client functions as a VNC server, this means you can observe and control the screen of any such Mac without having to install extra software on it — assuming the service is turned on and you have the necessary credentials to connect to that Mac.

Meanwhile, VNC client software, which you use to connect to the remote computer sharing its screen, has been built into Mac OS X since version 10.5 Leopard. That software is called Screen Sharing, following Apple's rather uninventive pattern of naming applications after their functions. Because Screen Sharing uses VNC, you can use it to view and control the screen of any computer, running any operating system, as long as it has VNC-compatible server software installed and activated.

Cross-Ref

For more on Screen Sharing, see Chapter 7. ∎

Screen sharing in Leopard and Snow Leopard takes on a few different forms:

- You can use it to control the screen of another computer on your local network.
- If you're a MobileMe member, you can use Back to My Mac to control the screen of another Mac that's also logged in to the same MobileMe account, even if it's located around the world.
- You can manually run Screen Sharing to connect to any computer with an active VNC server.

Of these usages, the first two are fairly common, whereas Apple has made the third quite obscure, but all three are easy to use once you know how.

Using Screen Sharing locally

To view and control the screen of another Mac on your local (wired or wireless) network that has Screen Sharing enabled, follow these steps:

1. **In the Shared section of the sidebar in any Finder window, select the Mac whose screen you want to view, as shown in Figure 11.7.**

FIGURE 11.7

Macs on your local network with File Sharing or Screen Sharing enabled appear in the Shared section of the sidebar in any Finder window.

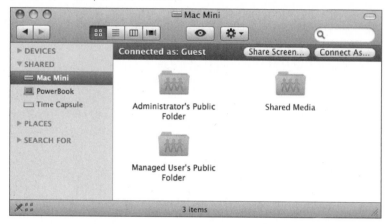

2. **Click the Share Screen button.** The location of the button in the window may vary depending on which view — Icon, List, Column, or Cover Flow — you're using. If you haven't already stored your credentials for the other computer in your keychain, an authentication dialog box opens. Type your username and password (as configured on the other Mac), optionally click the Remember this password in my keychain check box , and then click Connect. The other Mac's screen appears in a new window, similar to the one shown in Figure 11.8.

3. **Operate the other Mac just as you would your own Mac — your keyboard and mouse now act as the other Mac's keyboard and mouse, as long as the Screen Sharing window is in the foreground.**

Here are a few tips for interacting with another Mac using Screen Sharing:

- To send the information on your Mac's Clipboard to the other Mac (so that you can paste there something you copied locally), choose Edit ➪ Send Clipboard or click the rightmost of the two clipboard icons on the toolbar. To copy the contents of the other Mac's clipboard onto your current Mac's Clipboard, choose Edit ➪ Get Clipboard or click the leftmost of the two clipboard icons on the toolbar.

- Because screen sharing uses a considerable amount of network bandwidth, performance can sometimes be sluggish over a slow network, so Screen Sharing lets you choose whether responsiveness or display quality is more important to you. For a faster display (at the loss of some visual quality), choose View ➪ Adaptive Quality. For a crisper display (which may be less responsive), choose View ➪ Full Quality.

- If the computer to which you're connecting has a larger display than the one you're sitting in front of, Screen Sharing can either scale down the other computer's display (with a loss of quality) or show you only a portion of the other computer's display (meaning you'd have to scroll to see parts of it). To scale down the display to fit on your screen, choose View⇨Turn Scaling On. To keep the remote display at full size, with scroll bars to move around as necessary, choose View⇨Turn Scaling Off. You can also toggle scaling on and off by clicking the leftmost button on the toolbar.

- Although you can control the other Mac with your keyboard and mouse, you won't hear any sounds it plays (unless it happens to be nearby) — they still come through the other Mac's speaker, not yours. Likewise, the other Mac's microphone and iSight camera, if any, pick up audio and video from that Mac, not from the one you're using to control it.

- When the client Mac is running Leopard, most system-wide keyboard shortcuts — such as ⌘+Shift+3 (to take a screenshot), ⌘+spacebar (to display the Spotlight search field), and ⌘+Option+Esc (to force-quit an application) — apply only to your local Mac, not to the remote Mac. Under Snow Leopard, these keyboard shortcuts work correctly on the remote Mac.

FIGURE 11.8

When you control another Mac's screen with Screen Sharing, it appears on your Mac's screen in a simple window like this one.

Using Screen Sharing with Back to My Mac

If you're a MobileMe member and have more than one Mac (such as a home Mac and a work Mac or a desktop Mac and a laptop you travel with), you can use MobileMe's Back to My Mac feature to view and control one of your Mac's screens from another Mac — even if one or both of the computers use dynamic IP addressing or are behind a NAT gateway or firewall. Back to My Mac enables the two Macs to communicate with each other, and once they do, you can use Screen Sharing exactly as you would if they were on the same local network.

This feature works only if both Macs are logged in to MobileMe using the same username. In addition, before you can use this capability, you must activate Back to My Mac on both Macs and enable Screen Sharing at least on the Mac that you'll access remotely. To do so, follow these steps:

1. **On each Mac, choose ⇨ System Preferences to open System Preferences, click MobileMe to open the MobileMe pane, and then click the Back to My Mac tab, as shown in Figure 11.9.**

FIGURE 11.9

Back to My Mac must be turned on in this preference pane before it can be used for remote file sharing or screen sharing.

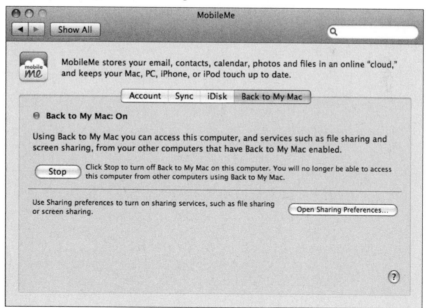

2. **If the window doesn't already say Back to My Mac: On, click the Start button to enable Back to My Mac.**

3. **On the Mac you'll access remotely, also click the Open Sharing Preferences button and then confirm that the Screen Sharing check box is selected.** If it isn't, click it.

4. **Close System Preferences.**

Thereafter, as long as both Macs are connected to the Internet (assuming the use of routers and other hardware compatible with the protocols Back to My Mac uses), the remote Mac appears in the Shared section of Finder window sidebars, just as it does when it's on the same local network. The icon may be slightly different, however. To share its screen, use the same procedure described earlier for sharing a local Mac's screen.

Using Screen Sharing with any VNC server

As long as you're connecting to another Mac that appears in Finder sidebars, Screen Sharing is just one click away. However, if you want to use Screen Sharing as a client to connect to other VNC servers, you must launch the application separately. For whatever reason, Apple chose not to put Screen Sharing in the `/Applications` folder with the rest of your applications but instead hid it in an unusual place: `/System/Library/CoreServices`. If you browse to that folder, you see Screen Sharing (among other tools). If you think you'll use it often and don't want to dig that deep for it each time, you can drag it to your Dock or create an alias in `/Applications` or another convenient spot.

In any case, using Screen Sharing as a stand-alone application is extremely simple. Follow these steps:

1. **Open Screen Sharing, which is located in** `/System/Library/CoreServices`.

2. **In the window that opens, shown in Figure 11.10, type the domain name or IP address of the VNC server to which you want to connect.**

FIGURE 11.10

The interface for starting a new connection in Screen Sharing is about as simple as they come: nothing but a field to type the other computer's address.

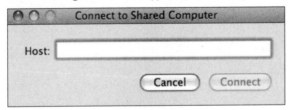

3. **Click Connect.** If the VNC server requires a username, password, or both, a prompt opens; type your credentials as requested and then click Connect. A new window opens, showing the remote computer's desktop.

Screen Sharing security considerations

VNC isn't inherently very secure, as I discuss later in this chapter. But Screen Sharing adds some extra security features to the VNC protocol that can make it much safer:

- When one Mac is controlling the screen of another Mac with Screen Sharing (whether locally or remotely and whether or not using Back to My Mac), as long as both computers are running Leopard or later, credentials are sent in a securely encrypted manner, regardless of the password's length, as are keystrokes sent from the client to the server.

- You can optionally encrypt all screen-sharing data traveling between two Macs running Leopard or higher, although doing so could significantly decrease performance, especially over a low-bandwidth connection. To enable encryption for all data, open the Screen Sharing application, choose Screen Sharing ⇨ Preferences to open the Preferences window, as shown in Figure 11.11, and then click the Encrypt all network data (more secure) radio button. Then, close the preferences window.

FIGURE 11.11

The oft-overlooked preferences in Screen Sharing let you determine, among other things, whether to trade security for speed.

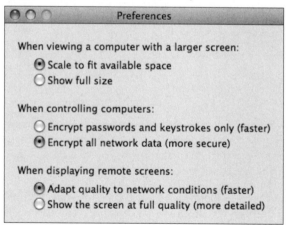

However, because both the client and the server must participate in encryption, if you're controlling the screen of a computer running an earlier version of Mac OS X or another operating system, the data may not be encrypted. Read the discussion on using VNC, presented later in this chapter, to learn about the risks and how to mitigate them.

Using Apple Remote Desktop

Apple Remote Desktop (ARD) is a commercial application that enables an administrator to centrally manage large numbers of Macs over a local or remote network. ARD lets you install and update software remotely, transfer files to or from the managed computers, provide remote technical support, get detailed reports of application usage, and perform numerous other administrative tasks. Just one of the many ways in which an administrator can interact with one of the managed Macs is to control its screen using essentially the same mechanisms — and the same built-in VNC server software — as Screen Sharing. In other words, you can think of Screen Sharing as a minimalist subset of ARD.

Note

To learn more about Apple Remote Desktop, visit Apple's ARD website at `www.apple.com/ remotedesktop.` ∎

One of the handy features ARD includes that isn't part of ordinary Screen Sharing is drag-and-drop file transfer. In other words, you can drag a file or folder from the desktop of your Mac directly onto the desktop of a Mac whose screen you're controlling instead of having to connect separately using File Sharing. Likewise, you can copy and paste data seamlessly between the administrator's Mac and the remote Mac. ARD also offers Curtain Mode, which lets the administrator see the remote Mac's screen but keeps the display hidden from anyone looking at it in person.

Apple Remote Desktop includes an extensive PDF Administrator's Guide (nearly 200 pages long), which details how to observe and control clients' screens and perform all the other management tasks the software offers.

Using VNC

You should already know that VNC is a widely used standard for screen sharing, available not only on Mac OS X but also on most other platforms, including Windows and Linux. Although Mac OS X has built-in VNC-compatible server and client software, you can also use third-party VNC software if you prefer a different interface or range of features.

Unlike Screen Sharing and Apple Remote Desktop, which use additional mechanisms in Mac OS X to provide encryption and security for screen-sharing activities, VNC itself offers no encryption for the screen video data, mouse movement, and keystrokes sent over the Internet. As a result, an eavesdropper could conceivably intercept that data and watch what you do (including capturing keystrokes you send, even if they're not visible) with the remote computer. In addition, although the mechanism for logging in to a remote VNC server protects one's password with basic encryption, it's a form that's easily defeated, meaning that someone could learn your credentials and thus be able to control the remote computer in the future. You can decrease that risk by using a password longer than eight characters, but some VNC software doesn't allow longer passwords.

Fortunately, however, the two major third-party VNC programs for Mac OS X offer their own encryption mechanisms, and if you need to control the screen of a remote computer that's not protected in some other way, either of these programs provides a safe way to do so:

- **JollyFastVNC.** JollyFastVNC (`www.jinx.de/JollysFastVNC.html`, free), shown in Figure 11.12, is a VNC client that lets you connect to any computer running a VNC server. It can secure connections using SSL (if the server supports it) or by creating an SSH tunnel — without the need for additional software or a trip to Terminal.

- **Vine.** Vine includes both server (Vine Server, free) and client (Vine Viewer, $35) components (`www.testplant.com/products/vine_viewer`). Both run only on Mac OS X, but Vine Viewer is also compatible with VNC servers that run on other platforms, such as Real VNC (Windows and Linux) and Tight VNC (some other varieties of Unix). Vine Viewer, shown in Figure 11.13, offers SSH tunneling for secure connections as well as the capability to capture screenshots or movies of the remote screen. When Vine Viewer is used to connect to Vine Server, you can copy and paste not only formatted text but even entire files between the two computers.

FIGURE 11.12

In the foreground, the JollyFastVNC configuration window; in the background, the window of a Mac being controlled (which is even more minimalist than the window in Screen Sharing)

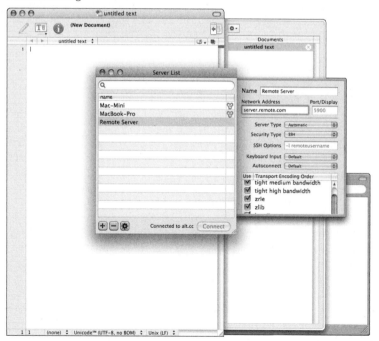

FIGURE 11.13

The controls in Vine Viewer's toolbar let you capture movies or screenshots of the remote computer.

Using Timbuktu Pro

Long before VNC was a gleam in a programmer's eye, Timbuktu (now developed by Netopia, a division of Motorola) enabled Mac and Windows users to control screens of remote computers, with all the bells and whistles (www.netopia.com/software/products/tb2). The current incarnation, Timbuktu Pro (shown in Figure 11.14), is available for both platforms, and each computer must have a license, whether functioning as a client or as a server. Pricing varies by platform and according to how many units you buy, but a single-user license can be as much as $94.95.

That may sound like a pretty unattractive price compared to products like Screen Sharing (free with Mac OS X) or Vine, but to some extent, you get what you pay for. The Timbuktu Pro proprietary protocol generally provides better performance than VNC; it also offers a wealth of features and a wide range of options for configuring its behavior. Like ARD, Timbuktu Pro lets you drag and drop files between client and server windows. Like Vine, Timbuktu Pro can capture movies or screenshots of the remote computer. And like Screen Sharing with Back to My Mac, it lets two computers communicate through firewalls, NAT gateways, and other barriers — as long as both are running Skype and you know the Skype username under which the remote computer is logged in.

In addition, Timbuktu Pro lets you configure multiple user accounts, with varying levels of access for each one. It has modes in which you can observe another computer's screen without controlling it and in which you can transfer files between computers without seeing the other screen at all. Timbuktu Pro gives you extremely fine-grained control over network bandwidth usage too; for example, letting you choose how many colors or shades of gray are transmitted over the network, regardless of the computer's display settings. Best of all, Timbuktu Pro has built-in support for SSH, so you can guarantee secure connections between the computers.

Apart from the cost, the most significant negatives of Timbuktu are that it doesn't interoperate with VNC and it's not available for Linux. It also lacks some of ARD's remote management and software installation features and has a somewhat cumbersome and outdated interface. But if your need for remote computer control extends beyond what you can get with Screen Sharing or Vine and you don't need the extensive management capabilities of ARD, Timbuktu Pro may be just right.

FIGURE 11.14

Timbuktu Pro puts some controls on the border around the window showing the computer being controlled, but most of its power is hidden away in a series of menu commands and other windows.

Using SSH for Remote Login

Years ago, the standard way to log in to a remote computer in order to run programs on it was to use a protocol called Telnet. You opened a window in a Terminal emulator program, typed **telnet** followed by another computer's domain name or IP address, typed your credentials, and you were in (via a command-line interface). Telnet still exists, but it's fallen into disuse because it doesn't offer encryption and has numerous other security vulnerabilities that put your data (and, in fact, the entire remote computer) at too great a risk. The most common replacement is SSH, which also provides a command-line interface to a remote computer but encrypts the connection.

Cross-Ref

For more on enabling Remote Login on your Mac so that another computer can use SSH to log in to it, see Chapter 7. ■

Using SSH with password authentication

In order to connect to a remote computer using SSH, you must have an account on that computer, and it must be running some variety of SSH software. If the other computer is a Mac, you can connect to it with SSH as long as it has Remote Login activated in the Sharing pane of System Preferences. Virtually all Unix computers have SSH capabilities built in, although it's less common on Windows PCs.

The simplest way to use SSH is to use password authentication, which (as the name suggests) means you type your username and password each time you log in, and the server checks them against its records to make sure you have permission to connect. Another means of authentication, which is more awkward to set up but more convenient in the long run, is key-based authentication, discussed in the following section.

To connect to a remote computer with SSH, follow these steps:

1. **Open Terminal, which is located in** `/Applications/Utilities`.

2. **Type** ssh, **a space, your username on the remote computer, an @ sign, and the domain name or IP address of the remote computer, and then press Return.** For example:

   ```
   ssh cindy@123.45.67.89
   ssh jk123@myworkmac.com
   ```

   If you haven't previously connected to this computer, you should see something like the following:

   ```
   The authenticity of host 'myworkmac.com
   (eb62::20c:26ae:edb2:48df%en0)' can't be established.

   RSA key fingerprint is c9:24:82:66:95:8b:b2:1e:4c:a2:e9:b1:6e:74:4
      3:da.
   Are you sure you want to continue connecting (yes/no)?
   ```

   If possible, confirm through some independent means (such as checking a secure web page or asking the server's system administrator) whether the fingerprint shown on your screen is the correct one — that is, that you're in fact connecting to the computer you think you're connecting to and your SSH session hasn't been compromised.

3. **If the fingerprint checks out or if you have another reason to trust that it's valid (which is almost always true on a local network), type** yes **and then press Return.** The remote computer responds with a message similar to the following:

    ```
    Warning: Permanently added 'myworkmac.com.,
    eb62::20c:26ae:edb2:48df%en0' (RSA) to the list of known hosts.
    ```

4. **When prompted to do so, type your password for the remote computer and then press Return.** Assuming the computer accepts your credentials, you can now run shell programs on it and interact with it just as you would in your own Mac's command-line environment — as shown in Figure 11.15 — subject to any restrictions on your permissions on the remote computer.

Tip

To learn much more about using the Mac's command-line interface for interacting with your own computer as well as remote computers via SSH, read my ebook *Take Control of the Mac Command Line with Terminal* (www.takecontrolbooks.com/command-line). ■

When you're finished with your remote SSH session, type **exit** and then press Return. You can then quit Terminal.

FIGURE 11.15

Interacting with another computer via SSH isn't flashy, but if you're familiar with command-line syntax, you can accomplish just about anything.

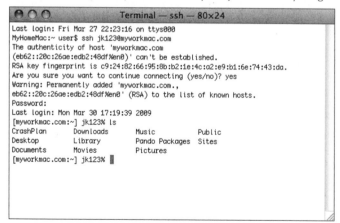

Man-in-the-Middle Attacks

The process of confirming the RSA key fingerprint for a remote SSH server and storing it on your Mac, as described previously, is somewhat awkward, and as a result, many people never bother confirming it at all. That's unwise because the point of the confirmation step is to prevent something called a *man-in-the-middle attack*, in which an attacker inserts his or her computer between yours and the server to which you're connecting, retransmitting all the data from your computer to the server and vice versa. By acting as a conduit, the attacker's computer can not only observe all the traffic that flows between your computer and the server but also intercept your credentials (enabling him or her to log in to the real server as you at any time) and even alter the information you send or receive in real time.

What makes such an attack possible is letting your computer accept the attacker's fingerprint as real, and it's a particular worry if the attack occurs the very first time you connect to a server. Once you store the (real) remote server's fingerprint, if you ever try to connect to a computer with the same IP address or domain name and the fingerprint no longer matches, SSH displays a prominent warning that your connection may have been compromised.

Using key-based authentication

In lieu of password authentication, you can use a method known as key-based authentication to connect to an SSH server. SSH can optionally use public-key encryption, in which you create a pair of keys: one public (which you put on the server) and one private (which you keep on your own computer). When your public key is on the server and your private key is in the appropriate spot on your Mac, SSH can use the two keys to confirm that you have access to the remote computer — as well as using those keys to encrypt and decrypt the data you send.

The usual reason given for choosing key-based authentication is to avoid the tedious step of having to type your password every time you connect. But whether or not you're prompted for a password depends on whether you use a password when creating your public/private key pair. If you choose not to create a password (to avoid the prompts), your keys are less secure, and one practical consequence of this is that anyone with physical access to your Mac could start an SSH session with a server that stores your public key without ever being prompted for a password.

However, in Mac OS X, there's a clever way to have your cake and eat it too. You can create a public/private key pair that uses a nice, strong password and then use that for authenticating your SSH sessions. But then, you can store that password securely in your keychain. As long as your keychain is unlocked (as it likely is when you're actively using your Mac), you won't be prompted for your password when connecting to an SSH server, but as soon as you lock your keychain — or it locks on its own, according to your settings in Keychain Access — your password is safe from anyone else who might use your Mac.

Cross-Ref

For more on keychain settings, see Chapter 5. ∎

To set up key-based authentication with an SSH server, follow these steps:

Note

These instructions are a variation of the ones Apple provides at `http://developer.apple.com/` `documentation/MacOSXServer/Conceptual/XServer_ProgrammingGuide/Articles/SSH.html`. **That page also provides an example of running a Perl script with multiple servers that use key-based SSH.** ■

1. Open Terminal, which is located in `/Applications/Utilities`.

2. To ensure that you have the necessary directory for storing SSH keys, type mkdir ~/.ssh and then press Return. If you see a message that says "File exists," you can safely ignore it and move on to the next step.

3. To create your public/private key pair, type ssh-keygen -t rsa -f id_rsa and then press Return.

4. When prompted, type a password and then press Return; confirm the password by typing it and pressing Return a second time.

5. To create the file in which the server stores your public key, type touch authorized_keys2 and then press Return.

6. Copy your key into the new file by typing cat id_rsa.pub >> authorized_keys2 and then pressing Return.

7. Adjust the permissions of the key file as SSH needs them to be by typing chmod 400 id_rsa and then pressing Return.

8. Use the scp (secure copy) command to upload your private-key file to the SSH server by typing scp authorized_keys2 *username@serveraddress*:~/.ssh/ (substituting your username and the server's domain name or IP address) and then pressing Return. Type your password when prompted.

This procedure must be followed only once for any given server. To add your public key to another server, repeat step 8 as needed.

Tip

A free program called SSH Helper (available from `www.gideonsoftworks.com/sshhelper.html`**) provides a more user-friendly way of creating public/private key pairs for use with SSH and installing public keys from other computers on your Mac. One thing the program doesn't do, however, is provide a means of transferring your public key to an SSH server and installing it there.** ■

Now, connect to the SSH server in the usual way (by typing **ssh** *username@serveraddress*). An alert appears, as shown in Figure 11.16, asking for your password. Type the password you created in step 4 — not your usual password for the SSH server. To save the password in your keychain (which I recommend), click the Remember password in my keychain check box. Click OK. Your SSH session begins as usual.

FIGURE 11.16

When using key-based SSH authentication, the password you want to type here is the one you used to create your key, not the one you'd normally use to log in to the SSH server.

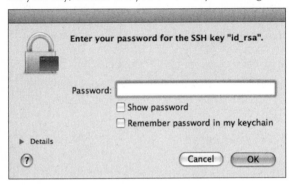

If you saved the password in your keychain, the next time you connect to that same SSH server, you won't be prompted for any password, assuming your keychain is unlocked.

Tunneling other services through SSH

The conventional way of using SSH, as previously described, is to connect to another computer using Terminal in order to run command-line programs. However, SSH can be used to secure any sort of network traffic between your Mac and another computer. When you create an SSH connection and then use it to encrypt another kind of network traffic, you're said to be *tunneling* the traffic through SSH.

For example, if you want to transfer a file to another computer using FTP, which is normally quite insecure, you may be able to open an SSH tunnel to the computer and route the FTP data through that tunnel. Because the SSH tunnel itself is encrypted, the same goes for all the data that passes through it. For this reason, an SSH tunnel is useful for any situation in which you must communicate with a server that doesn't natively offer a secure protocol for some type of service.

A secondary (or, for some users, primary) function of SSH tunnels is to change or mask the port used for a given type of Internet traffic. For example, if you're connected to the Internet through an ISP that blocks port 21 (used by FTP), you can bypass that restriction by sending the traffic through an SSH tunnel, which uses port 22 and is rarely blocked. The computer to which you've established the tunnel then routes the traffic out through port 21.

SSH Tunnels, Proxy Servers, and VPNs

If the description of an SSH tunnel sounds familiar to you, it may be because it's closely related to two other concepts described elsewhere in this book: proxy servers and VPNs. The three technologies overlap in a number of ways, although each has some distinct characteristics:

Cross-Ref

For more on proxy servers, see Chapter 10. For more on VPNs, see Chapter 12. ■

- **Type of traffic.** Generally speaking, an SSH tunnel applies to a single port, which is to say a single type of Internet traffic (although you can have as many tunnels as you need going at once). So, you can have an SSH tunnel for AFP traffic (port 548) or an SSH tunnel for web traffic (port 80), for example. The same is usually true of proxy servers: one proxy per port. VPNs, on the other hand, apply to your entire Internet connection.

- **Encryption.** Connections to proxy servers are usually unencrypted, whereas both SSH tunnels and VPNs are, by their nature, always encrypted.

- **Destinations.** The purpose of a proxy server is to intercept, reroute, and/or filter traffic between your Mac and other servers. It always functions as a go-between. With a VPN connection, your final destination may be within the network to which you're connecting (as when you're connecting to your corporate network from home to check your email) or it may be elsewhere on the Internet (as when you're using the VPN to protect your wireless network transfers when using an open Wi-Fi hotspot). SSH tunnels are most often used when your destination is the particular computer to which you've made the tunnel. As described ahead, you can use SSH to create a SOCKS proxy on your Mac, which produces approximately the same end result as using a VPN, because it routes all the Internet traffic to and from your Mac through the computer to which you've created the tunnel. The subtle distinction is that you're routing traffic through a single specific computer rather than through a network.

Setting up a basic SSH tunnel

Tunneling an application's traffic through SSH may sound very mysterious and complex, but it's straightforward once you understand the underlying mechanism. Essentially, there are just two parts to the procedure. First, you use a special version of the SSH command in Terminal to create the tunnel; the command specifies which port the service ordinarily uses and a new port, which you route it through temporarily. Then, set up the application to direct its traffic to that new port on your own Mac (rather than the usual port on the server) and connect as you normally would.

Because every application handles SSH tunnels slightly differently, I provide a few different examples here to give you an idea of how it's done. All these assume that you have an account on a remote computer running SSH.

Tunneling AFP through SSH

Suppose a remote server for which you have an SSH account also shares files via AFP (Apple Filing Protocol) and you want to connect to it securely. To do so, follow these steps:

1. **Open Terminal, which is located in** `/Applications/Utilities`.

2. **Type** ssh -L 5480:localhost:548 -f -N *username@serveraddress* **(substituting your user-name for the SSH server and its domain name or IP address) and then press Return.** If you haven't already set up key-based authentication with this server and saved your password in your keychain, type your password when prompted and then press Return. To oversimplify slightly, this command says to redirect all traffic sent to port 5480 (a random, unlikely-to-be-used port) on your Mac to port 548 (the usual AFP port) on the server specified (if you were going to redirect it to a different server, that server's IP address or domain name would take the place of `localhost`, which in this context refers to the SSH server) and to keep running in the background (the -f flag).

3. **In the Finder, choose Go⇨Server or press ⌘+K.**

4. **In the Connect to Server window that opens, type** afp://localhost:5480 **in the Server address field and then click Connect.** Mac OS X mounts the remote volume. Depending on the configuration of the server, you may also be prompted to type your credentials for file sharing and/or to select a volume to mount.

Let me point out some important concepts here. First, the port to which you're redirecting traffic in step 2 can be anything at all — as long as it's not already in use by some other process. Always pick a number higher than 1023 but below 49152. If you see an error message stating that the port you selected is in use, pick a different one.

Second, because the SSH tunnel itself makes the connection to the AFP server, you don't type the server's address when you want to use that service; you type **localhost** (referring to the computer you're currently using) followed by whichever port you specified in step 2.

Note
By default, SSH tunnels set up in this way remain open until you shut down or restart — or the remote server does. To close all SSH tunnels, type killall ssh in a Terminal window and then press Return. ∎

Tunneling screen sharing through SSH
Here's a second example. You want to share the screen of a remote computer running VNC on Windows or Linux. You have SSH access to the computer, and you want to secure your screen-sharing session. Follow these steps:

1. **Open Terminal, which is located in** `/Applications/Utilities`.

2. **Type** ssh -L 6000:localhost:5900 -f -N *username@serveraddress* **(substituting your user-name for the SSH server and its domain name or IP address) and then press Return.** If you haven't already set up key-based authentication with this server and saved your password in your keychain, type your password when prompted and then press Return. This command is identical to the one from the previous set of instructions, except that the port numbers are different. In this case, you're redirecting traffic sent to port 5900 (the default for VNC) to port 6000.

3. **Open Screen Sharing, which is located in** `/System/Library/CoreServices`.

4. **In the Host field, type** localhost:6000 **and then click Connect.** Screen Sharing displays the remote computer's screen. Depending on the configuration of the server, you may also be prompted to type your username, a password, or both before you can connect.

Tunneling SMTP through SSH

Finally, here's a more complex example just to give you a small taste of what else is possible. Suppose you're at a library with free Wi-Fi access and you want to send email using your ISP's SMTP server. Unfortunately, the library's ISP blocks port 25, usually used for SMTP — and in addition, the Wi-Fi connection is unencrypted. You can kill two birds with one stone by setting up an SSH tunnel to your Mac back home or at the office, which has Remote Login turned on (that encrypts the SMTP traffic) and then using that computer, for which port 25 presumably isn't blocked, to send mail to your ISP.

To route SMTP traffic through an SSH tunnel on an intermediate server, follow these steps:

1. **Open Terminal, which is located in** /Applications/Utilities.
2. **Type** ssh -L 1025:smtp.myisp.com:25 -f -N *username@serveraddress* (**substituting your mail server's address, your username for your remote Mac, which is functioning as an SSH server, and its domain name or IP address**) **and then press Return.** If you haven't already set up key-based authentication with this server and saved your password in your keychain, type your password when prompted and then press Return.
3. **Open your email program and change the account settings for the SMTP server such that the server's address is** localhost **and its port is** 1025.
4. **Try sending a message (even to yourself).** If everything is working correctly, it should go through without an error.

Cross-Ref

For more on setting up SMTP servers in popular email clients, see Chapter 9. ■

Using SSH Tunnel Manager

If you use SSH tunnels frequently and dislike mucking around in Terminal, you can download a free application called SSH Tunnel Manager (http://projects.tynsoe.org/en/stm) to simplify the process. With this program, shown in Figure 11.17, you simply fill out a form specifying all the parameters you want to use. In the example shown, it's configured to tunnel SMTP through SSH, as described in the previous set of steps. You can also choose among several encryption methods, have tunnels open automatically when you launch the application, and close individual tunnels by clicking an icon.

FIGURE 11.17

SSH Tunnel Manager lets you fill out a simple form to specify how you want an SSH tunnel to behave.

Tip

Another powerful and easy-to-use (although not free) SSH tunnel manager for Mac OS X is Meerkat (`http://codesorcery.net/meerkat`, $19.95). If you don't mind using the command line but would like a bit more automation than the procedures I outlined in this chapter, try the free tunnelopen Perl script (`http://hea-www.harvard.edu/~fine/OSX/tunnelopen.html`), which lets you open specific URLs through SSH tunnels.

Using SSH to create a local SOCKS proxy

Earlier in this book, I discussed the use of proxy servers for anonymous web browsing. But proxy servers can be used for a variety of purposes. One particular proxy protocol, called SOCKS (short for SOCKetS, believe it or not), is often used by organizations with strict firewall settings to manage and redirect all traffic bound for the outside world. SOCKS affects all Internet data — not just data sent on a single port — but unlike VPNs, SOCKS doesn't encrypt anything.

Note

For a convenient way to set up your Mac to route Internet traffic through a SOCKS proxy (without encrypting it), try MacProxy (`http://www.tidalpool.ca/macproxy/`, $19.99).

However, using another variant of the SSH command, you can combine the encryption of SSH with the multi-port awareness of SOCKS, giving you the best of both worlds (and, in a sense, a simple VPN). You create a local SOCKS proxy — running on your own Mac — and direct all your Internet communication through that proxy. This proxy, in turn, communicates with a remote computer via SSH, relaying all Internet traffic to and from remote servers securely.

To set up a local SOCKS proxy with SSH, follow these steps:

1. **Open Terminal, which is located in** `/Applications/Utilities`.

2. **Type** ssh -D 8080 -f -q -N *username@serveraddress* **(substituting your username for the SSH server and its domain name or IP address) and then press Return.** If you haven't already set up key-based authentication with this server and saved your password in your keychain, type your password when prompted and then press Return.

3. **Choose ⇨ System Preferences to open System Preferences and then click Network to open the Network pane.**

4. **Select your current network interface in the list on the left, click the Advanced button on the right side of the window to open a dialog box with additional settings, and then click the Proxies tab.**

5. **In Leopard, make sure Manually is selected in the Configure Proxies pop-up menu.**

6. **Click the check box next to SOCKS Proxy.**

7. **Type** localhost **in the Web Proxy Server field and then type** 8080 **in the field to its right.**

8. **Click OK to close the configuration dialog box, click Apply, and then close System Preferences.** All Internet traffic now flows through the selected proxy server until you go back to the Network preference pane and deselect the SOCKS proxy check box.

Summary

In this chapter, I covered the three main ways in which you might interact with another computer over the Internet and how to do so without any information being intercepted along the way. I first looked at ways to upload and download files securely using any of a variety of protocols. Then I provided an overview of secure screen sharing — using either the tools built into Mac OS X or third-party software. And, finally, I discussed the use of SSH for secure communications between computers, including how to use SSH to protect otherwise insecure types of data transfer.

Using Virtual Private Networks

O f all the ways in which you can protect your data as it flows over the Internet, one of the most effective is a virtual private network (VPN). Although the use of VPNs is common in the corporate world — especially for telecommuters and frequent business travelers — it's much less common among home and small-business users.

That's a pity because this single tool offers eavesdropping protection for a broad range of activities (including email, web browsing, and file transfers), even if no other security measures are taken. And for anyone who must use a wireless network with no security or with only WEP encryption, it's the only reliable way to ensure that all your network traffic is secure.

This chapter explains what a VPN is, describes the various flavors in which it may appear, and explains how to use such a network with your Mac.

What Is a Virtual Private Network?

Picture a group of computers networked together but not connected to the Internet (or any other outside network). The computers can share information with each other with complete safety because the only people who can access the information that moves across the network are those with physical access to one of those computers. That's a completely private network.

Most private networks do, in fact, connect to the outside world, but they generally do so by way of a firewall (and/or other mediating devices) that keeps most of the data on the network private, with exceptions only for certain crucial and closely controlled types of interaction. For example, a typical corporate firewall lets users on the local network connect to file and mail servers but blocks access to those same servers for people outside the network.

So, what happens if an employee needs to work from home or from a remote location? The remote user requires access to resources on the company's closed, private network but is kept out by the same mechanisms that block outsiders who shouldn't have access. The way around this problem is to set up a special, secure tunnel between the remote user and the private network, making it appear to the network that the remote computer is in fact connected locally. The user must supply credentials to join the network, and the entire connection is encrypted so that regardless of what sort of data passes back and forth through this tunnel between the private network and the remote user, it can't be read or used by anyone who might be tapping in to the connection. So, from the remote user's perspective, it's just like being connected to the private network without actually being there physically: a virtual private network.

I want to emphasize that a VPN connection applies to all Internet traffic sent or received by the remote computer. By contrast, when you use SSL to connect to a particular email or web server, when you use SFTP for file transfers, or when you use SSH to log in to a remote computer using a command-line interface, only those specific connections are encrypted while the rest of your Internet data is sent and received in the clear.

The fact that you've connected to a particular private network securely doesn't necessarily mean you can reach only computers on that network. Although that's certainly a possible configuration, VPNs are usually configured to also give remote users access to the Internet — just as they would have if they were on a computer attached to the network locally. In other words, by using a VPN, you can securely access not only a particular private network but also — within limits I mention just ahead — the Internet beyond.

Because a VPN encrypts all the Internet traffic between a remote computer and another network, it has uses beyond protecting corporate users on the go. For example, as I've mentioned several times in this book, open Wi-Fi networks and those that use only WEP encryption make extremely easy and attractive targets for hackers. But wrap all that traffic in a VPN, and it's invulnerable during the wireless portion of its journey. Even if you're sending email without an SSL connection to your mail server, for example, the use of a VPN would prevent anyone who can sniff your wireless traffic from knowing the contents of your messages. Anyone who worries about the security of his or her local Internet connection can benefit from using a VPN.

Cross-Ref

For more on protecting wireless Internet connections, see Chapter 16. ■

Another increasingly common use of VPNs is to bypass national firewalls in countries such as China and the United Arab Emirates, which prevent access to certain kinds of Internet traffic. For example, if you're a foreign journalist working in China and you want to be able to access websites that the Chinese government blocks nationwide because they're considered too subversive, a VPN lets you access those sites by way of a network in your home country.

VPNs also have an interesting secondary function: When used to provide a conduit to the Internet, they act as proxy servers, replacing the remote user's actual IP address with an IP address on the private network. In this way, they can partially disguise the origin of requests for resources such as web pages and, in some cases, make it appear to Internet servers that the person connecting to them is in a different geographical location.

For all the benefits of VPNs, they do have one significant limitation, which users shouldn't overlook: The encryption they offer goes only as far as the boundaries of the private network. In other words, suppose I'm in New York and I connect to a VPN in California — and then, using that connection, visit a web server in Colorado. All the data going to or from my computer is encrypted only between New York and California. The connection between the private network in California and the web server in Colorado is unencrypted (unless the web server offers SSL or another end-to-end encryption mechanism). The moral of the story is that although VPNs are great for protecting remote connections to private networks, they don't provide complete protection if you extend that connection to the Internet beyond the VPN.

VPN Varieties

Just as there are multiple protocols for transferring files over the Internet but with the same end result, there are numerous varieties of VPN, all of which aim to accomplish essentially the same thing. The protocols do differ in certain important details, however, and require somewhat different methods of configuration and use. This section covers only the most popular protocols — there are also a variety of others that you may occasionally encounter.

PPTP

Point-to-Point Tunneling Protocol, or PPTP, is a VPN protocol developed by Microsoft in association with several other vendors. It's by far the most commonly used type of VPN, and support for it is built into every major operating system, including Mac OS X and Windows. PPTP itself doesn't include encryption, but it's normally used along with an encryption protocol called Microsoft Point-to-Point Encryption (MPPE).

PPTP has a reputation for being insecure, although experts differ as to how legitimate that concern is. Early implementations of PPTP did in fact have a number of significant security holes, although most of those have been fixed and modern versions are far more secure than what was available a decade ago. As long as you choose a long, random password and keep it secure — and use the strongest possible encryption available with the particular version of PPTP to which you have access — it's difficult to show any significant specific security weakness. However, one caveat is that you may have no way of knowing which version of PPTP is being used on the other end of your VPN, and if it happens to be an old or buggy version, your connection could be at risk, even though the underlying security problems were solved.

L2TP over IPsec

Internet Protocol Security, or IPsec, is a set of protocols for authenticating and encrypting Internet traffic. Although it can be used on its own to create a VPN, it's typically paired with Layer 2 Tunneling Protocol (L2TP), a method of tunneling traffic (based in part on PPTP) that doesn't have any encryption features of its own. So, IPsec encrypts the connection packet by packet, and L2TP creates the tunnel through which the Internet traffic flows — hence, L2TP over IPsec (or L2TP/IPsec). As with PPTP, Mac OS X, Windows, and most other operating systems now include support for L2TP-over-IPsec VPNs without any additional software.

L2TP over IPsec is widely regarded as being more secure than PPTP — although also more complex and, therefore, more difficult as well as more expensive to install and manage on the network end. Because L2TP is slightly more processor-intensive on each end, network performance can in some cases be slightly less zippy than with PPTP.

Cisco IPsec

Networking giant Cisco sells a variety of routers and other devices that let companies provide VPN services to their users. Most of these products use the IPsec protocol, and prior to Snow Leopard, Mac users had to download and install Cisco's client software — widely regarded as difficult to use — to connect to a Cisco IPsec VPN. Although the Cisco client still works under Snow Leopard, support for Cisco IPsec VPNs is also built into the operating system. (Note, however, that the built-in client has fewer features than the Cisco client, so it may not be suitable for all situations.)

SSL/TLS and OpenVPN

Secure Sockets Layer (SSL) — or its closely related successor, Transport Layer Security (TLS) — is commonly used to encrypt email and web pages. Because this standard (or pair of standards, if you prefer — in common usage, the term *SSL* is used to refer to either) is mature, secure, supported on virtually every platform, and reasonably easy to implement, it was natural to find a way to use it for protecting more than just a single stream of data. As a result, some varieties of VPN can use SSL to encrypt the entire Internet connection between a computer and a remote network.

Cross-Ref
For more on protecting your email with SSL, see Chapter 9. For more on protecting web browsing with SSL, see Chapter 10. ■

Unfortunately, the term *SSL VPN* has (at least) two different meanings, and the two major senses are extremely different from one another in principle and in practice. Both have in common that they function at a higher level than PPTP or IPsec — instead of using low-level drivers built into the operating system, they use higher-level software that operates in what's known as user space (just like all ordinary applications you run on your Mac).

One type of VPN that uses SSL is the popular, open-source OpenVPN (http://openvpn.net/), of which free implementations are available for Mac OS X and almost every other major platform. When you connect to a remote network using an OpenVPN client, the effect is just what you'd expect from any VPN. Every Internet application, from email to online backup programs, automatically routes all its traffic through the VPN. All the data is encrypted, and if you use the VPN connection to contact servers beyond the VPN (that is, elsewhere on the Internet), they see your connection as having come from an IP address in the VPN, not from your actual IP address. OpenVPN is known as one of the fastest and most efficient types of VPN.

The other major sense of SSL VPN is a system in which you connect securely, using SSL, to a special proxy server using your web browser. Then, as needed (or as supported by the server on the other end), your browser automatically downloads special modules, often written in Java, that enable other services — email, FTP clients, instant messaging programs, and the like — to send and receive data over the secure connection. That way, without having to explicitly install or configure any other software, you can use a web browser, on any computer, for secure access to a wide range of services. Although this variety of SSL VPN is becoming increasingly popular for corporate use, and although it does permit remote users to access the network from any computer with an Internet connection, it's not a full-fledged VPN in the sense that it doesn't encrypt and tunnel all your Internet traffic; it works only with those specific services for which the VPN server offers support.

Zero-configuration VPNs

A new class of VPNs has recently emerged, for which (as far as I know) there's not yet a generally agreed-upon generic term — although they emphasize their self-configuring nature, so I'm calling them zero-configuration VPNs. Unlike most VPNs, which let you connect securely to an existing network (such as your corporate headquarters) or, indirectly, to the Internet, these VPNs are designed solely to enable a group of people to communicate securely with each other over the Internet.

For example, suppose Andy, Brenda, and Cam are in different cities and they want to chat with each other, play online games, or exchange files — but they don't want to risk anyone else being able to see what they're doing or run afoul of usage restrictions imposed by their ISPs. Andy could start a zero-configuration VPN, which requires little more than launching a program and picking a name and password for the network. Then, Brenda and Cam open their VPN software and join the same network by typing its name and password. The three people can then interact with each other privately — any data that travels between their computers is encrypted. Because he started the network, Andy can monitor it to make sure no one else tries to join; he can also change the password, bump participants off the network, or invite other users.

Although zero-configuration VPNs certainly have business applications, the most common usage at the moment seems to be sharing files without using any intermediate servers, manually encrypting files, or worrying that a third party might be able to see what data is being transferred.

Examples of zero-configuration VPNs for which Mac OS X software is available include Remobo (www.remobo.com) and Hamachi (https://secure.logmein.com/products/hamachi/vpn.asp?lang=en).

Choosing a VPN Provider

If you work for a company that uses a VPN, chances are that the corporate IT staff has provided ready-made instructions for connecting to it with your Mac. If so, you can skip this section and refer to the following section (about configuring your Mac for VPN access) only if you run into trouble with your setup. However, if you're in need of VPN capabilities and don't already have a company providing them for you, this section is for you.

As a Mac user, you may be looking into a VPN solution from any of several points of view:

- You work for a large company that wants to provide its employees with secure remote access to its local network.

- You want a way to access your home or small-office network securely from elsewhere in the world.

- As an individual user, regardless of your location, you want a way to encrypt all your Internet traffic — protecting it from eavesdroppers and, perhaps, adding anonymity by obscuring the actual IP address of its origin.

If you're in the first category, one option is to configure a Mac on your network to function as a PPTP or L2TP-over-IPsec VPN server using the VPN Services feature built into Mac OS X Server. You may also be able to find third-party VPN servers available for Mac OS X. Another option is to forgo the use of a Mac altogether and instead install a dedicated VPN appliance. Companies such as Barracuda Networks, Cisco, and Juniper Networks offer a tremendous variety of equipment that may serve your needs. The use of third-party VPN server software or appliances is beyond the scope of this book.

Cross-Ref
For more on configuring the Mac OS X Server VPN services, see Chapter 31. ■

People in the second category, whose main need for a VPN is to reach their home or small-office network, are best served by installing an inexpensive router with VPN support. Most of the following (just a few of many examples) can be had for a few hundred dollars or less:

- D-Link's DIR-130 wired (www.dlink.com/products/?pid=563) or DIR-330 wireless (www.dlink.com/products/?pid=564) routers

- Linksys's EtherFast BEFVP41 (www.linksysbycisco.com/US/en/products/BEFVP41) or BEFSX41 (www.linksysbycisco.com/US/en/products/BEFSX41) routers

- Netgear's VPN Firewalls, which come in wired (www.netgear.com/Products/VPNandSSL/WiredVPNFirewallRouters/) and wireless (www.netgear.com/Products/VPNandSSL/WirelessVPNFirewallRouters.aspx) varieties

- Netopia's 4600 Series (www.netopia.com//equipment/products/4000/4600_business_routers.html) or R-Series (www.netopia.com/equipment/products/r_series/) routers

All these routers and many others like them can secure your connection to your home network when using an open Wi-Fi hotspot or in any other situation where network security is in doubt, but keep in mind that as with all VPNs, they don't secure traffic that goes beyond your home or office network to the public Internet.

The final category of people is the one in which I suspect most readers find themselves. You want to protect the entire Internet connection of an individual Mac, although perhaps only in certain situations (such as when you're away from home, when living or working in a country that places restrictions on Internet access, or transferring unusually sensitive information), and you don't already have VPN service available from your employer. In these cases, you can choose from a wide variety of commercial VPN providers.

In a moment, I list a few prominent examples of companies selling VPN services, but first, I want to offer a word or two of caution. Not all VPN providers are created equal. They vary not only in cost, performance, and reliability but also in their security and trustworthiness. Some exist mainly to cater to people who want to download pirated media or software without being caught by their ISPs, view porn, gamble, or play games at the office without being caught by their employers, or engage in other such questionable activities. Anecdotally, my observation has been that when a VPN provider (or, for that matter, an anonymous proxy provider) has less of a business focus and more of a stick-it-to-the-man focus, the overall quality and longevity of the service tend to be low. There's also the possibility, however slim, that a seemingly innocent VPN service could in fact be run by (for example) the RIAA, MPAA, NSA, or some other organization whose gaze one might prefer to avoid — enabling them to easily collect the very information you're trying to keep private.

In short, don't choose a VPN provider without doing your homework. Carefully read its terms of service to make sure they square with the activities for which you want to use the VPN. Make sure the company offers technical support, educate yourself to the extent possible about its history, and try to find independent testimonials from people for whom the service has worked well.

With those warnings duly made, here are a few of the VPN providers you may want to investigate:

- **Hotspot Shield.** This free (yes, free) VPN service from AnchorFree (`http://hotspotshield.com/`) is based on OpenVPN but includes its own customized client software. The company also offers a version of its service for iPhones that uses L2TP over IPsec. When you're connected to the Internet with Hotspot Shield, your web browser displays ads at the top of the window; these ads are one of the ways the provider pays for the cost of the service. In my experience, Hotspot Shield has been reasonably solid, although less speedy and reliable than WiTopia's OpenVPN offering.

- **HotSpotVPN.** This provider (`www.hotspotvpn.com`) offers a variety of VPN packages, at prices ranging from $8.88 per month to $13.88. HotSpotVPN offers both PPTP and OpenVPN-based VPNs; the OpenVPN packages are a bit more expensive, although you can choose three different levels of encryption, which is unusual among VPN providers.

- **PublicVPN.** One of the oldest and most reputable commercial providers of VPN services, PublicVPN (`www.publicvpn.com`) offers PPTP and L2TP over IPsec VPNs — and has plans to offer an OpenVPN option in the future. The service costs $6.95 per month or $69.95 per year.

- **SecureNetics.** SecureNetics (www.securenetics.com) provides PPTP and OpenVPN services as well as SSH proxies for individual Internet applications. Prices range from $9.49 per month to $39.45 per month (with discounts for longer-duration commitments), depending on the level of service you want.

- **WiTopia.** Of the VPN providers I've tried personally, WiTopia (www.witopia.net) is my current favorite. WiTopia offers both OpenVPN and PPTP VPNs, with prices starting at $39.99 per year. Throughput (once you've found the optimal settings for your situation) is generally excellent, and the company takes its business very seriously (although without losing a human touch). A unique WiTopia offering — and one of the most interesting reasons to choose them — is an optional product they offer called CloakBox. This is a modified Linksys wireless/Ethernet router that uses OpenVPN to connect to WiTopia. Thus, every computer or other device you connect to the Internet through the CloakBox automatically gets full VPN access all the time. This means you don't have to run any VPN software on your Mac, and in addition, devices that can't run their own VPN software (such as certain VoIP telephones, game consoles, and Apple TV) can nevertheless benefit from a full-time VPN connection. CloakBox sells for $199, including one year of service; beyond the first year, service costs $99 per year.

Note

CloakBox is in a sense the opposite of the VPN routers mentioned earlier in this chapter — instead of letting you connect to your entire home network securely from the outside, it lets your entire home network connect securely to the Internet via WiTopia. ∎

- **World Secure Channel.** This VPN provider, based in Belize (http://world-secure-channel.com/), offers L2TP over IPsec connections. Although the cost of a simple (unencrypted) proxy connection is only $0.99 per day, the company charges $1,200 per year for ultra-high-bandwidth VPN connections with no usage limits.

Configuring Your Mac for VPN Access

As I've explained, VPNs come in a wide variety of shapes and sizes. Leopard contains built-in client software for two popular VPN types (PPTP and L2TP over IPsec) and Snow Leopard adds support for Cisco IPsec VPNs. In all cases, these settings are accessed through the Network pane of System Preferences, and it's not difficult to configure (although not necessarily obvious either). Third-party VPN utilities offer some capabilities missing in Mac OS X and also provide support for additional VPN varieties. This section provides an overview of the major ways to configure Mac OS X as a client for VPN access.

Using the Network preference pane

Mac OS X includes support for both PPTP and L2TP over IPsec (and, in Snow Leopard, for Cisco IPsec VPNs). You configure these using the Network pane of System Preferences. Although both protocols have a number of options, I describe only basic setup here.

To configure Mac OS X to use a PPTP, L2TP over IPsec, or Cisco IPsec VPN, follow these steps:

1. Choose ➪ System Preferences to open System Preferences and then click Network to open the Network pane.

2. If the lock icon in the lower-left corner of the pane is in the locked state, click it, type an administrator's username and password, and then click OK.

3. Click the Add (+) button at the bottom of the list on the left.

4. In the dialog box that opens, shown in Figure 12.1, choose VPN from the Interface pop-up menu, choose PPTP, L2TP over IPsec, or Cisco IPsec from the VPN Type pop-up menu, type a name for the service (or simply accept the default), and then click Create.

FIGURE 12.1

To create a new VPN configuration in the Network preference pane, begin by choosing the interface type (VPN) and the type of VPN in this dialog box.

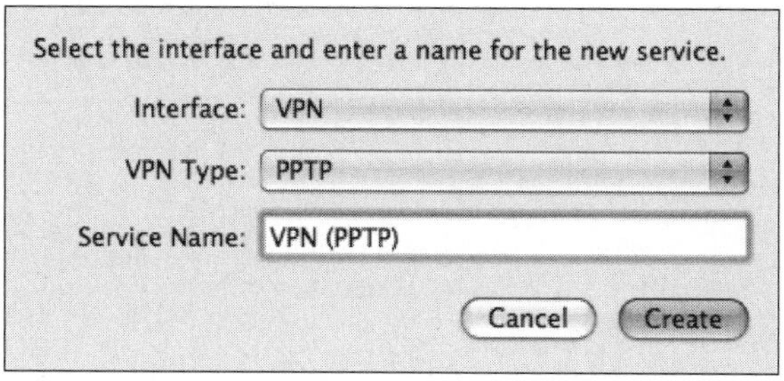

```
Select the interface and enter a name for the new service.

      Interface:  VPN                              ▲▼

      VPN Type:  PPTP                              ▲▼

  Service Name:  VPN (PPTP)

                              ( Cancel )  ( Create )
```

5. Type the rest of the information in the preference pane, as shown in Figure 12.2, as follows:

   1. From the Configuration pop-up menu, choose Add Configuration, and in the dialog box that opens, type a name for the configuration and then click Create.

   2. Type the address of the VPN server (as supplied by your VPN provider) in the Server Address field.

   3. Type your username (again, as supplied by the VPN provider) in the Account Name field.

   4. For PPTP VPNs only: From the Encryption pop-up menu, choose the level of encryption offered by the VPN provider or leave it set to Automatic (128 bit or 40 bit), which usually works regardless of the encryption level.

   5. Click Authentication Settings to open the authentication window.

6. If you use a password to authenticate (which is the typical method), type your password; otherwise, click the radio button corresponding to the type of authentication method you want to use and, for a certificate, click Select to locate the certificate. For L2TP over IPsec VPNs only: If you use a secondary authentication method, click its radio button and fill in any required information.

7. Click OK.

8. Click the Show VPN status in menu bar check box.

9. Click Apply and then close System Preferences.

FIGURE 12.2

To configure the settings for your VPN, fill in the fields on the right side of the window. This figure shows an example configuration for PPTP. The L2TP over IPsec VPN configuration is similar but lacks an Encryption pop-up menu; the Cisco IPsec configuration lacks Encryption and Configuration pop-up menus and adds a password field.

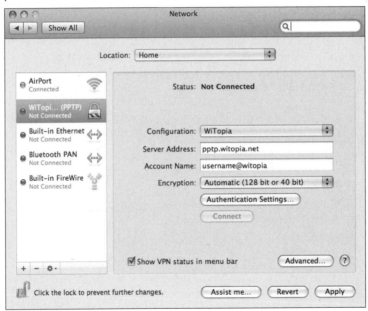

Your VPN is ready to go. To connect, click the VPN status icon in your menu bar and then choose Connect *name-of-service* from the menu. The menu indicates the current connection status. To disconnect, choose Connect *name-of-service* from the menu.

Using other VPN tools

If you need to connect to a different type of VPN, the provider generally includes complete instructions — and, often, preconfigured client software — to enable you to do so. For example, if you use WiTopia's OpenVPN service, the company sends you a personalized installer for an OpenVPN client called Tunnelblick (`http://code.google.com/p/tunnelblick`). Ordinarily, Tunnelblick is somewhat confusing to set up, but with WiTopia's customized software, you simply run the installer and then use a new icon on your menu bar to connect and disconnect. Similarly, if you use Hotspot Shield, you simply double-click the icon for the Hotspot Shield application and then click Connect; no other configuration is required.

In some cases, however, a provider may not include its own software or you may want extra features or options not included with the bundled software. Accordingly, I provide here just a few examples of third-party VPN tools and how to use them:

- **HamachiX.** Hamachi, mentioned earlier as an alternative variety of VPN, has software available for Mac OS X, but it's command-line-only and not terribly friendly to configure or use. If you're interested in Hamachi but want an easier way to access it, you can download HamachiX (`http://hamachix.com/`, free). When you run it the first time, it checks to see whether the official Hamachi command-line software is installed, and if not, it offers to download and install the latest version for you. You can then create and join your own networks using HamachiX's graphical interface, as shown in Figure 12.3.

FIGURE 12.3

In the HamachiX window, you can create private networks that others can join or you can join existing networks someone else has already created.

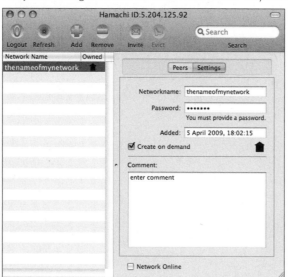

- **IPSecuritas.** Although Mac OS X includes support for L2TP over IPsec VPNs, its range of configurable options is limited. If you want full control over every conceivable parameter of an IPsec VPN, try IPSecuritas (www.lobotomo.com/products/IPSecuritas, free). As shown in Figure 12.4, it includes a wizard that automates IPsec configuration for a long list of popular VPN firewalls from more than a dozen manufacturers — although you can configure everything manually if you prefer.

FIGURE 12.4

This wizard, built into IPSecuritas, lets you quickly configure VPN settings for any of numerous common IPsec firewalls.

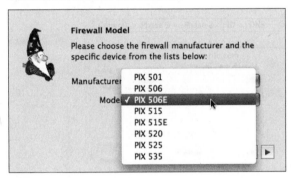

- **Shimo.** If you want an all-singing, all-dancing VPN client with all the bells and whistles, look no further than Shimo (www.shimoapp.com, $20.95). It supports every major VPN type, including PPTP, L2TP over IPsec, OpenVPN, and Hamachi. If you've previously set up any VPNs in the Network pane of System Preferences, Shimo uses those settings automatically, and Shimo can also import settings from most other client software. But the features Shimo adds beyond merely connecting and disconnecting are what make it interesting. For example, Shimo can be set to detect when you've selected a new location (using the ⌘⇨ Locations menu) or joined a different Wi-Fi network and to automatically connect to a particular VPN, as shown in Figure 12.5.

FIGURE 12.5

Shimo lets you associate VPN settings with network locations and Wi-Fi networks so that changing your location or joining a different network automatically causes the selected VPN to connect.

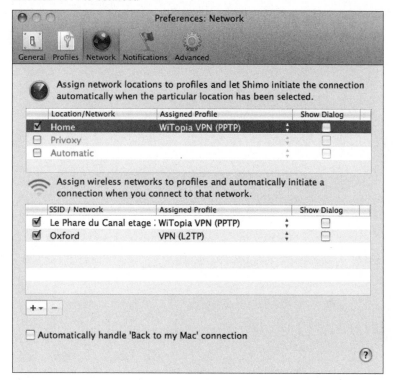

- **Viscosity.** Viscosity (www.viscosityvpn.com, $9), shown in Figure 12.6, is an OpenVPN client. Unlike Tunnelblick (whose configurations it can import), Viscosity provides a complete graphical interface for configuring all VPN settings. It also offers an optional semitransparent display showing a live graph of VPN usage, local and public IP addresses, and other information.

FIGURE 12.6

Viscosity provides a user-friendly graphical interface for configuring OpenVPN connections.

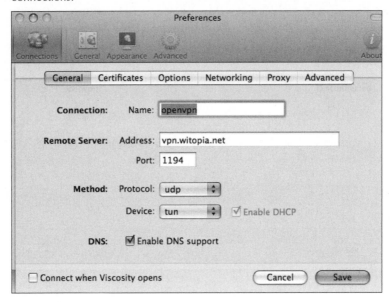

Summary

This chapter covered one of the most effective means available for securing your network access: using a virtual private network, or VPN. After explaining how VPNs work, I described some of the most common classes of VPNs and listed numerous providers of such services for people who don't already have access to one through their businesses. I described how to set up Mac OS X to use certain kinds of VPNs as well as basic configuration for several popular third-party VPN clients.

Encrypting and Securely Deleting Files

As long as your Mac is under your sole control, it's perfectly fine for all your files to be stored on your hard disk in their normal state — freely viewable without any special procedures. Unfortunately, it's difficult for anyone to guarantee that no one else will ever have physical access to his or her computer. There are the obvious cases — such as theft, a nosy roommate or co-worker, or a network intruder who has gained access to your disk — in which your data could slip from your control. But there are other situations that can affect even the most scrupulous and security-conscious person. What if your Mac breaks down, for example, and you need to take it in for servicing? An unscrupulous repairperson could read anything on your disk.

It's fair to ask whether that would even matter. Some people keep very little confidential information on their Macs, so it wouldn't be a particular problem if someone else gained access to it. At the other end of the spectrum, if your hard disk contains your company's business secrets, classified government information, or your patients' medical records, then it's clear that keeping it private matters a great deal.

What about the rest of us — those somewhere in between? Think about it this way: Would it bother you or any of your friends or family if the entire contents of your Address Book were made public? Would you be disturbed to know that a stranger could see years' worth of your family photos, read all your email, and discover every website you've visited in the past month? Even the least secretive of us would probably agree that all this sounds pretty creepy, and they provide good reasons to make sure these never happens.

The way to keep your data safe while it's sitting on your hard disk is to encrypt it — to scramble it in such a way that it looks like garbage to anyone without your password or key. Encryption comes in many forms, some of which are almost trivially easy to use, and others that require extra thought and effort. This chapter explores a variety of different approaches to encrypting some or all of your files. It also covers an oft-neglected step: securely erasing sensitive data you no longer need so it can't be recovered even by someone who has the skills and equipment to resurrect files you committed to the Trash months ago.

File-Encryption Basics

This book won't turn you into an expert in cryptology, but because encryption can be so useful — in so many different ways — in keeping the data on your Mac safe, it's definitely worth knowing a few of the fundamentals of the process.

Encryption algorithms

An encryption *algorithm*, also known as a *cipher*, is a particular method for encrypting data — a sort of mathematical formula that takes the input (sometimes called *cleartext*), processes it using a secret piece of information (a *key*), and produces encrypted output (sometimes called *ciphertext*). Over the centuries, thousands of encryption algorithms have been developed, ranging from the trivially simple to the breathtakingly elaborate. In the modern computing world, you're likely to run into at least a half-dozen common ciphers considered especially well-suited for encrypting and decrypting data on your Mac!

Two factors influence how secure (resistant to being broken) an encryption algorithm is. First is the design of the algorithm itself. Some have weaknesses or design flaws that could enable an attacker to decrypt data even without knowing the key. The other factor is the complexity of the key. If you use the world's most complex and powerful cipher but give it a simple key, such as the word "cat," it becomes almost trivially easy for someone to figure out how to decrypt your data. The best results come from combining solid, reliable algorithms with long, random keys.

I could spend many pages simply listing encryption algorithms and their variants, but I want to briefly acquaint you with just a few especially common ones:

- **AES.** The Advanced Encryption Standard is one of the world's most commonly used ciphers and one accepted by the U.S. government for protecting secret data. AES can use 128-, 192-, or 256-bit keys (see just ahead for a discussion of key length); these variants are commonly known as AES-128, AES-192, and AES-256, respectively.

- **Blowfish.** This fast, open-source encryption algorithm, designed by security expert Bruce Schneier, can use key lengths from 32 to 448 bits.

- **CAST.** The term *CAST* is used for a family of algorithms; the name comes from the initials of its developers, Carlisle Adams and Stafford Tavar. The original version, with a 128-bit key, was called CAST-128 or CAST5; a modern successor is CAST-256.

- **DES.** The Data Encryption Standard, which dates back to 1975, was formerly approved for use by the U.S. government and can therefore be regarded a forerunner to AES. But it supports only 56-bit keys, and because it's been shown to be breakable with relative ease and speed, it's no longer considered secure.

- **IDEA.** The International Data Encryption Algorithm, which uses 128-bit keys, is considered a highly secure cipher, and was designed as a potential replacement for DES.

- **Triple DES.** Also known as 3DES or TDES, this cipher is based on DES but applies the DES algorithm three times to each block of data, thus increasing the possible key size to 168 bits (that is, three separate 56-bit keys).

- **Twofish.** Designed by a team of cryptologists, including Bruce Schneier, Twofish is in the same family as Blowfish but considered more modern and advanced. Twofish can use key lengths up to 256 bits.

Passwords and keys

As previously mentioned, a key is a piece of information that a cipher uses to encrypt (and decrypt) data. If you encrypt two copies of the same data with identical ciphers but different keys, the resulting ciphertext is different; likewise, if you use the same key to encrypt two copies of some data with different ciphers, the results are different.

One form a key can take is a password (or passphrase). In other words, feed your password into an encryption algorithm to encrypt some data; then use the same password later to decrypt it. This example assumes a system in which the same key is used both for encryption and for decryption — a *symmetric* cipher. *Asymmetric*, or public-key, ciphers use one key to encrypt data and another one to decrypt it. A key can also be, among other things, a string of data stored on a token, a smart card, an electronic key, or another device.

An algorithm's key length is the longest key it can use. So, AES-128 can use a key that's 128 bits long. For those of you unaccustomed to thinking in binary, that translates to 16 characters. Likewise, a 256-bit key can be up to 32 characters in length.

When you choose a password for encrypting data, most encryption algorithms don't use the password itself as the key. Behind the scenes, the algorithms run your password through some mathematical functions that turn it into a number with the maximum key length the algorithm supports. This is done partly to protect your password from discovery (even if the key is cracked) and partly to make sure the key has exactly the right number of bits. If a cipher uses a 128-bit key but I type an 8-character (64-bit) password, the software performs its magic to give itself a longer and more secure key to work with. That means if someone attempts to break the encryption by trying every key, that person has a much wider range of possibilities to test. But if, instead, that person tries to break the encryption by testing passwords directly (running each one through the necessary process to derive a key), he or she might break the encryption sooner.

On the other hand, if I type a password that's longer than the supported key length (say, a 20-character password for a 128-bit cipher), the software typically discards the extra characters before deriving its key. The result would be that an attacker trying to decrypt my files by trying all possible password combinations would have just as much trouble as someone trying all possible key combinations.

The upshot of all this is that it's to your benefit to choose a password that's as long as possible — but no longer than the maximum key length supported by the algorithm you use. If you use 56-bit DES, a 20-character password is no safer than a 7-character password. However, with AES-256, a 32-character password is exponentially safer than a 31-character password!

For any given encryption algorithm, longer keys (and therefore, to a point, longer passwords) are more secure. However, as I stated earlier, not all algorithms are created equal. That means key length alone doesn't tell the whole story; one algorithm's 128-bit keys might be, in practice, just as secure as another's 256-bit keys if the 256-bit algorithm has flaws that reduce its effective strength. In other words, given the choice of a longer key length with a given algorithm, you should take it; but don't assume that cipher A is stronger than cipher B just because the former uses longer keys. For all practical purposes, any modern cipher with 128-bit or larger keys is secure against all but the most determined attacks — assuming you've chosen a good password.

Cross-Ref

For more on choosing good passwords, the trade-offs between password complexity and convenience, and the use of third-party password managers, see Chapter 6. ■

Choosing what to encrypt

How much you encrypt or whether you encrypt anything at all depends on several factors, including where you use your Mac, how sensitive the information on it is, what other security measures you've taken (protecting against theft, for example), and what your tolerance for inconvenience is.

Needless to say, the greater the confidentiality of your data and the less physically secure your Mac is, the more important it is to encrypt data. But you shouldn't overlook the convenience factor. In general, the larger the unit of data you encrypt, the more convenient it is in the long run. That is, it's less bother (in some senses, at least) to encrypt your entire disk than to encrypt just your home folder; it's less bother to encrypt your home folder than to encrypt a conventional folder; and it's less bother to encrypt a folder than to encrypt a single file. That may all sound counterintuitive, but it has to do with things such as the amount of manual effort required to encrypt and decrypt files and how often you have to type a password.

However, also keep in mind that how and when you use encryption depends on context. For example, in some situations, it may not make sense to encrypt even a very sensitive file when it's sitting on your hard disk, but if you transfer it to a flash drive to take it with you somewhere or if you send it to someone via email, FTP, or some other method, encryption suddenly becomes quite important because you lose the security otherwise provided by your normal computing environment.

With those thoughts in mind, consider the following units of data you could potentially encrypt, all of which are elaborated on later in this chapter:

- Individual files
- Individual folders
- A disk image

- Your home folder
- An entire volume
- Your startup disk
- A complete hard drive

As I describe ahead, there are good arguments for choosing any point along this continuum. The way you go about encrypting data depends on how much you want to encrypt and what combination of features and trade-offs works best for you.

Encryption pitfalls and misunderstandings

Encryption can sound like a magical process that makes your data impervious to discovery. But merely encrypting something doesn't necessarily make it safe. Encryption involves a number of potential holes and hidden dangers, and if misused (or trusted indiscriminately), it can cause more problems than it solves. Before you embark on an encryption crusade, however worthwhile your ultimate objective may be, keep in mind the following possible gotchas.

Forgetting the originals

In most cases, when you encrypt a file, you actually create an encrypted copy of the file, leaving the original intact. Even encryption programs that automatically delete the original after encrypting it often do so in such a way that the unencrypted file could later be recovered. Later in this chapter, I discuss secure deletion as a way to solve this problem.

Leaving files unlocked

Encryption protects data on your disk only when it's not actively in use. For example, your keychain is encrypted, but when you unlock it, you (or someone else) can freely access its contents until you lock it again or it locks on its own (based on your preferences). Similarly, if you encrypt a disk image, it's safe as long as it's closed, but when you mount it, its files become available to anyone with access to your computer. Therefore, you should always close, unmount, or lock encrypted files when they're not actively in use.

Choosing an insecure password

Poorly chosen passwords are the Achilles' heel of any encryption system. Longer, random (or seemingly random) passwords do a vastly better job at protecting your data than short or easily guessable passwords.

Forgetting your password

The flip side of choosing an insecure password (which might let someone else get at your data) is choosing a great password but then forgetting it (which prevents you from seeing your own data). If you're not sure you can remember your passwords, store them in your keychain or in a third-party password management program.

Cold Boot Attacks

No matter how carefully or thoroughly you've encrypted your data, it could still be vulnerable to certain kinds of clever attacks, one prominent example being a procedure known as a *cold boot attack*. This way of recovering encrypted data is based on two key facts. First, most encryption programs — and this includes the Mac OS X Keychain, FileVault, and most full-disk encryption tools — store the encryption key in RAM while you're using the data (while your keychain is unlocked, for example, or while you're logged in to your account). Second, although RAM loses its contents when you turn off the computer, this doesn't happen instantly; it can take up to a few minutes for the data to disappear.

In a cold boot attack, someone restarts your Mac (or shuts it down and immediately powers it back on), booting from an external device, such as a flash drive, and immediately uses special software to copy all the as-yet unerased contents of your RAM to a file. The attacker then scans that file for passwords that were temporarily stored in RAM, and using those, he or she can then log in to your account or access your encrypted files. A variation on the attack is to shut down your Mac, quickly remove the RAM modules, and then insert them into another computer, where their contents can be read. Either way, if the attacker chills the RAM (which is easily done by blasting it with ordinary canned air), it retains its data for much longer — sometimes upward of an hour — making the attack that much easier and adding another layer of literal meaning to the expression "cold boot."

Cold boot attacks are possible only when someone else has physical access to your Mac and when it hasn't been shut down for more than a few minutes. To guard against these attacks, take care to lock your keychain and eject encrypted disk images when they're not in use, shut down your Mac (instead of putting it to sleep) when it's outside your physical control, and consider using multiple layers of encryption, such as full-disk encryption plus encrypted disk images.

Not encrypting everything that needs protection

If you're working on a secret business plan or composing an illicit love letter, it's easy to see why that one particular file should be encrypted. But one of the most common mistakes in data security is overlooking data that may not appear, at first glance, to be confidential but which can contain extremely sensitive information. Here are some examples:

- **Virtual memory.** As you use your Mac, Mac OS X constantly swaps information between physical RAM and virtual memory on disk to improve performance. The result, though, is that something you thought was only fleetingly stored in memory (such as text you copied to the Clipboard) can be stored on disk — sometimes for hours, days, or longer.

Cross-Ref

For more on encrypting the contents of your virtual memory, see Chapter 4. ∎

- **Your Clipboard(s).** Speaking of your Clipboard, information that you copy or paste could be recovered, even if not stored in a virtual memory file, by using a cold boot attack (described above). And if you use any of the numerous utilities that offer multiple Clipboards, they almost certainly store their information on disk long after you copy it.

- **Cache files.** Many applications, from your web browser to your word processor, maintain cache files of recently (or frequently) accessed information to help them run faster. These cache files can contain a surprising amount of personal information.

- **The contents of your iDisk.** If you're a MobileMe member, you should be aware that anything you put on your iDisk is unencrypted (unless you manually encrypt it), and therefore anyone who knows your MobileMe user ID and your password can access anything on it.

- **Backups.** Some programs can store extra backup copies of your files as you work, possibly in locations you wouldn't expect. Also, some backup programs, particularly those that back up to Internet servers, keep caches of files on your disk, which may be unencrypted.

- **Spotlight.** Apple's system-wide Spotlight indexes could contain cleartext traces of data from files you've encrypted. Some encryption programs expressly delete such data.

Encrypting Individual Files and Folders

The most basic approach to encryption is to apply it only to the particular items that are especially sensitive. Although it would be extremely awkward to individually encrypt each file you use on a daily basis, encrypting specific files or folders makes sense when sending the info over the Internet (by email, FTP, or otherwise) or if you're using any other unencrypted transmission or storage method, such as employing a flash drive, external hard drive, or optical disc to move files from one location to another.

As mentioned earlier in this chapter, it's important to remember that when you encrypt a file or folder, you actually create an encrypted copy, leaving the original intact and unencrypted. The same is true if you decrypt a file or folder, modify it, and then re-encrypt it. Therefore, the safest practice to follow after encrypting something is to securely delete the original; for example, by dragging it to the Trash and choosing Finder➪Secure Empty Trash.

If this is the sort of encryption you want, you have many tools to choose from. Mac OS X includes command-line utilities that can encrypt files (as described in just a moment), although they're not terribly convenient to use. Numerous third-party vendors offer easy-to-use alternatives, with a wide variety of encryption algorithms, interfaces, and extra features. Regardless of which type of program you use to encrypt your files, consider the following factors when choosing an encryption tool:

- **Compatibility.** Will someone else have to decrypt this file — or will you have to decrypt it on another computer — and is suitable decryption software available on the target computer? If you choose a Mac-only encryption program, for example, you'll be out of luck if the recipient of a file has only Windows available.

- **Convenience.** How well does the program's interface fit in with your workflow? Be sure to download the program and try it out a few times with test data before committing to it for live use.

- **Sending a password.** The most securely encrypted file isn't secure at all if an attacker or thief learns its password. So, if you're sending an encrypted file to someone else, you must also find a secure way to let him or her know how to decrypt it. Sending a password in a cleartext email or writing it on a slip of paper is an insecure method. Better methods include sending it in an encrypted message, using Skype or another encrypted instant messaging service, or delivering the password orally in person.

Encrypting files on the command line

You can encrypt individual files using the `openssl` program included with Mac OS X, as long as you don't mind getting your hands dirty on the command line. Basic instructions follow; for more detail, type **man openssl** in Terminal.

To encrypt a file with `openssl`, follow these steps:

1. **Open Terminal, which is located in** `/Applications/Utilities`.

2. **Choose an encryption algorithm.** `Openssl` supports dozens of ciphers, and your choice is significant in that you must know which cipher was used to encrypt a file when you want to decrypt it later. To get a list of available ciphers, type **openssl list-cipher-commands** and then press Return. In this example, I use `des3` — that is, Triple DES.

3. **Type** openssl enc -des3 -salt -in *filename* -out *filename.enc*. Substitute des3 with your preferred cipher. The first *filename* is the name of the file you're encrypting, and the second *filename* is the name of the resulting, encrypted file.

4. **When prompted, type a password, press Return, retype the password, and then press Return again.** `Openssl` immediately encrypts the file.

5. **To decrypt the file later, type** openssl enc -d -des3 -in *filename.enc* -out *filename*. Again, substitute des3 with your preferred cipher, and replace the file name references with the file names.

6. **When prompted, type the password used to encrypt the file and then press Return.**

Encrypting files and folders with third-party software

Of the many Mac OS X applications that can encrypt individual files and folders, I've selected a small sampling to give you an example of your options:

- **BitClamp.** BitClamp compresses individual files using your choice of AES-256, 256-bit Serpent, or 448-bit Blowfish algorithms. Drag one or more files into the window, click Encrypt, type and confirm a password, and you're done. To decrypt files, double-click them and type your password (www.fastforwardsw.com/bitclamp/, $19.95).

- **Compress Files.** This utility compresses files and folders, storing them in any of numerous archive formats, including ZIP files and disk images. It can also create encrypted ZIP or 7-Zip archives and disk images and can optionally attach the encrypted and/or compressed files to outgoing email messages. It doesn't, however, handle decompression or decryption — for that, you need a compatible utility, unless you use a format for which Mac OS X includes built-in support, such as disk images (`www.apimac.com/compress_files/`, $14.95).

- **Drop Secure Pro.** Drop Secure Pro is available for Mac OS X, Windows, and Linux. As the name suggests, it lets you encrypt files, folders, and raw text by drag and drop. It offers no fewer than 15 encryption algorithms, including all the usual suspects (such as AES, Blowfish, IDEA, and Triple DES). You can optionally compress the items you encrypt using gzip or bzip2 compression (`www.dropsecurepro.com/08/`, $57).

- **FileWard.** This easy-to-use utility, which relies on the `openssl` tool built into Mac OS X, lets you encrypt files and folders as well as the contents of the Clipboard by drag and drop using any of the following algorithms: Blowfish, Cast5, Triple DES, DES-X, AES-128, or AES-256. After encrypting files, it securely deletes the unencrypted temporary files created by `openssl` (`www.northernsoftworks.com/fileward.html`, $9.99).

- **PGP Desktop Home and PGP Desktop Professional.** These security packages, which I discuss in more detail later in this chapter, offer a variety of ways to encrypt data. Among them is the option to encrypt individual files or folders, either with a password or using public-key encryption, which can eliminate the security concerns associated with sending someone else a password to decrypt a file (http://na.store.pgp.com/macstore.html, Home version, $99; Professional version, $239).

- **R10Cipher.** R10Cipher can encrypt files, folders, raw text (for example, to include in an email message), or the contents of your Clipboard using 128-bit Blowfish. It comes in versions for Mac OS X, Windows, and Linux, making it viable for exchanging files with people using other platforms (`www.artenscience.co.uk/r10cipher/`, £14 or roughly US$20).

- **StuffIt Deluxe.** This suite of file compression tools has existed, in one form or another, since the early days of the Mac and is also available on Windows. In its current version, you can compress and/or encrypt files and folders using either StuffIt Archive Manager or DropStuff (the latter of which, shown in Figure 13.1, is designed for quick drag-and-drop operations and also lets you create droplets — stand-alone applications with specific combinations of compression and encryption settings for particular tasks). With these products, you can encrypt files in the StuffItX format using any of four algorithms: 512-bit RC4 (the default), 64-bit DES, 448-bit Blowfish, or AES-256. You can also use StuffIt Deluxe to encrypt ZIP files (using only the AES-256 algorithm), but because of the way the ZIP format handles encryption, someone could see the names of the files and folders in an encrypted ZIP archive even without decrypting it (http://store.smithmicro.com/ProductDetails.aspx?pid=10825, $79.99).

- **Swizzler.** Swizzler uses AES-256 to encrypt individual files and folders. It's unobtrusive: To encrypt or decrypt a file, you Control+click on a file or folder and then choose Swizzle from the More submenu of the pop-up menu. A free version of the program works only with files less than 100 KB in size. Note, however, that despite being nearly invisible in actual use, Swizzler requires that you log out and log back in when installing it (http://wiredupandfiredup.co.uk/swizzler/, $9.99).

There's another category of software that can encrypt individual files and folders, but instead of storing them separately on disk, it stores them in a proprietary container, sometimes known as a vault. Often, such programs are used to secure not only files but notes, passwords, credit card numbers, and other random snippets of information. Obviously, such programs are more appropriate for securing data for your own use than for sending it to others. Two examples of software in this category are:

- **AllSecure.** This snippet keeper can store files, folders, notes, and other confidential information. When you add files to AllSecure, they're ZIP-compressed with AES-256 encryption. (www.edgerift.com/products/allsecure/, $25)

- **Yojimbo.** Yojimbo is a popular repository for random information of all kinds. When you store files or text notes, you can optionally encrypt them individually using AES-256 by clicking an Encrypt button and then typing your password. To view an encrypted item, as shown in Figure 13.2, click the View button and then type your password; to decrypt it permanently, choose Item⇨Decrypt and then type your password (http://barebones.com/products/yojimbo/, $39).

FIGURE 13.1

StuffIt Deluxe offers numerous compression and encryption options, including four encryption algorithm choices.

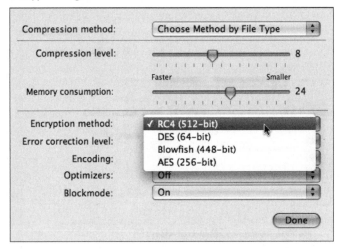

Note
Password managers, such as 1Password and even the Mac OS X Keychain, also create encrypted containers for storing data on disk, although they generally can't be used to store entire files. See Chapter 5 to learn about the Keychain, and see Chapter 6 for information on other password managers. ■

FIGURE 13.2

Any individual file in Yojimbo can be encrypted. To view an encrypted file, click View and then type your password.

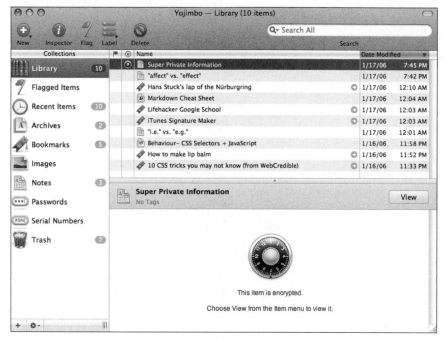

Working with Encrypted Disk Images

Mac OS X makes frequent use of *disk images*, special containers that look and act like single files when they're closed but when opened mount on your desktop like hard drives, revealing any number of other folders and files inside. Disk Utility, included with Mac OS X, lets you create and modify disk images of several types, each of which can optionally be protected with AES-128 or AES-256 encryption. By definition, any file you store on an encrypted disk image is encrypted, so you can use a single encrypted container to protect many files without having to worry about passwords or other settings for each one individually. Using the encrypted disk image requires merely double-clicking it and then typing your password; locking it again is as simple as ejecting the disk.

Because Mac OS X can create highly secure encrypted disk images without any extra software, it's a popular way to get this capability. Another popular option is PGP Desktop, which employs a different (and, arguably, easier-to-use) mechanism to create disk images with comparable capabilities. In addition, several third-party tools provide other ways of creating and using encrypted disk images (using Apple's disk format in some cases and a proprietary format in other cases).

Encrypting disk images with Disk Utility

Disk Utility can make robustly encrypted disk images that enable you to conveniently store any number of files securely and lock or unlock them almost instantly. Unlike folders, disk images remain encrypted on disk even while they're open. Although someone with access to your computer could still get at the files on a mounted (open) disk image, the advantage over encrypting a folder is that even as files change, they remain encrypted, so you need not go through repeated cycles of decrypting, modifying, re-encrypting, and securely deleting files.

The disk images Disk Utility creates can take various shapes:

- **Standard (read/write) disk image.** This is an ordinary disk image with a fixed size. In other words, if you make a 50 MB disk image, it offers 50 MB of capacity and takes up (a little more than) 50 MB on disk — even if it's completely empty.

- **Sparse disk image.** Unlike standard disk images, sparse images can grow as you add data to them. Instead of specifying a fixed total size, you specify a maximum size. The initial image is quite small, and as you add data to it, it grows as needed until it reaches the threshold you set.

- **Sparse bundle disk images.** Sparse bundles are similar to sparse images in that they can grow as needed. The difference is that instead of storing data in a single large file, sparse bundles store data in a series of 8MB files called bands, and all of these are wrapped in a special folder called a bundle that looks and behaves like an ordinary file. Because they consist of very small files (only a few of which typically change at any given time), sparse bundles work much better with most backup systems because only a few bands must generally be copied during each incremental backup run.

Creating and using encrypted disk images

To create an encrypted disk image in Disk Utility, follow these steps:

1. **Open Disk Utility, which is located in** `/Applications/Utilities`.

2. **Choose New ⇨ Blank Disk Image.** The New Blank Image dialog box, shown in Figure 13.3, opens.

3. **In the Save As field at the top, type the name you want your disk image file to have.**

4. **From the Where pop-up menu, select a location for the disk image file.** You can later move it wherever you want.

5. **In the Volume Name field, type the name you want the disk image volume to have when it's mounted.** This can be different from the file name.

6. **From the Encryption pop-up menu, choose either 128-bit AES encryption (recommended) or 256-bit AES encryption (more secure but slower).**

7. **From the Image Format pop-up menu, choose read/write disk image, sparse disk image, or sparse bundle disk image, as described earlier.**

8. **From the Volume Size pop-up menu, choose the capacity of the disk image.** For read/write disk images, the file size is approximately the same as the volume size; for sparse and sparse bundle disk images, this figure represents the maximum size to which the volume can grow. If you don't want one of the preset sizes, choose Custom, type a number, choose a measurement (such as MB or GB) from the pop-up menu, and then click OK.

9. **Leave the Volume Format and Partitions pop-up menus at their default settings and then click Create.**

10. **Type and confirm a password for the disk image and then click OK.** Disk Utility immediately creates the disk image, stores it in the location you chose, and then mounts it in the Finder. Depending on your preferences, you may see the icon for the mounted volume on your desktop, in the sidebar of Finder windows, or both. You can then quit Disk Utility.

FIGURE 13.3

Disk Utility offers an extensive range of choices when creating new disk images, but you need concern yourself with only a few.

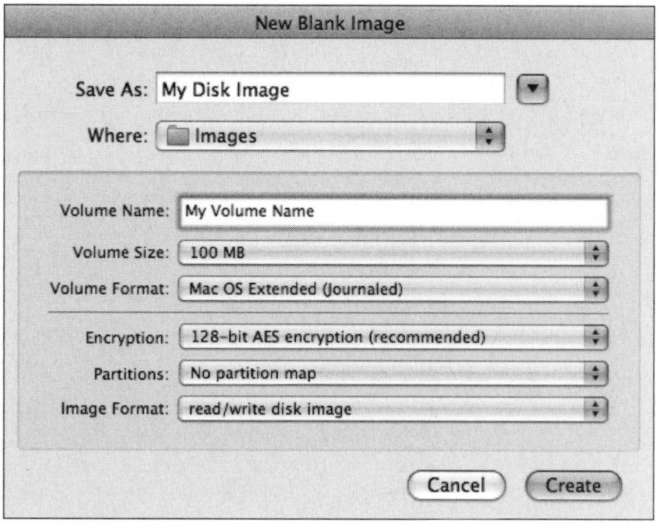

With your disk image mounted in the Finder, you can copy files to it or open files directly from it, exactly as you would if they were stored on an external hard disk or network volume. The volume's contents remain encrypted on disk at all times, although as long as the volume is mounted, anyone else with physical or network access to your computer could potentially see what's on it without needing a password. To unmount the volume so that future access requires a password, select it (the mounted volume, not the disk image file) and then choose File ➪ Eject *Volume Name* or drag the volume to the Trash.

Note

If you copy or move files from the disk image to another location (on your hard disk or elsewhere), they're automatically decrypted in the process. ■

To mount an encrypted disk image, simply double-click it. A password dialog box, as shown in Figure 13.4, opens. Type the password for the disk image and then click OK to mount it. To save the password in your keychain, which prevents this password prompt from appearing in the future as long as your keychain is unlocked, click the Remember password in my keychain check box before clicking OK.

FIGURE 13.4

A standard password dialog box opens when you double-click an encrypted disk image for which the password isn't already stored in your keychain.

Changing the password of an encrypted disk image

After creating a disk image, you can change its password if the need arises. To do so, follow these steps:

1. **Open Disk Utility, which is located in** `/Applications/Utilities.`

2. **Choose Images ⇨ Change Password to open the Select Image to Change Password dialog box, navigate to the disk image, select it, and then click Change.**

3. **If Disk Utility prompts you for the image's password, type it and then click OK.** A second password dialog box opens.

4. **Type and confirm a new password and then click OK.** Disk Utility changes the image's password but doesn't mount it. You can then quit Disk Utility.

Changing other attributes of an encrypted disk image

Finally, you can change other characteristics of the disk image, such as converting it to use a stronger or weaker version of AES encryption or a different disk image format. To modify an encrypted disk image in any of these ways, follow these steps:

1. **Open Disk Utility, which is located in** `/Applications/Utilities`.

2. **Choose Images ➪ Convert to open the Select Image to Convert dialog box, navigate to the disk image, select it, and then click Convert.** The dialog box shown in Figure 13.5 opens.

3. **Type a name for the modified disk image and then select a location from the Where pop-up menu.** You can keep the same name and location if you want to convert the image in place instead of creating a new file.

4. **From the Image Format pop-up menu, choose the format you want the image to have.**

5. **From the Encryption pop-up menu, choose either of the encryption methods or none for no encryption.**

6. **Click Save.** If you chose an encrypted format, type and confirm a password and then click OK. Disk Utility saves the disk image with your newly selected characteristics. You can then quit Disk Utility.

FIGURE 13.5

You can convert an existing disk image to any of numerous other formats, and increase or decrease the strength of encryption at the same time.

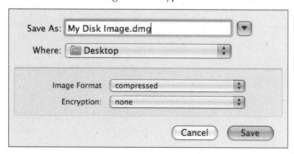

Encrypting disk images with PGP

PGP Desktop (`http://na.store.pgp.com/macstore.html`) is a multi-purpose security suite, available in several different configurations, that can encrypt email, instant messaging, files and folders, and even entire disks. Of relevance in this section is PGP Desktop's capability to create encrypted disk images (called virtual disks) using your choice of AES-256 or 128-bit CAST5 ciphers and secured either with a password or with your PGP public key (just like PGP's encrypted ZIP files). Like the sparse images Disk Utility can create, PGP's virtual disks start out small and grow, as needed, up to a preset maximum size.

Cross-Ref

For more on PGP and its use for securing email and instant messaging, see Chapter 9. ■

In everyday usage, a PGP virtual disk behaves almost identically to an encrypted image made with Disk Utility. However, apart from the cipher choices available, there are three key differences between the two systems:

- Whereas a Disk Utility disk image can be mounted on any Mac without the need for additional software, a PGP virtual disk can only be mounted on a computer with PGP's software installed, licensed, and running.

- The flip side of that requirement is that a given PGP disk can be used not only on another Mac with PGP installed but also on a Windows computer running PGP. Mac OS X's disk images can be opened only on Macs.

- A PGP virtual disk can have not just a single password but separate passwords for multiple users.

To create an encrypted disk image in PGP Desktop, follow these steps:

1. **Open the PGP application, which is located in** /Applications, **and then select PGP Disk in the sidebar, as shown in Figure 13.6.**

FIGURE 13.6

PGP Desktop offers an easy-to-use interface for creating encrypted disk images.

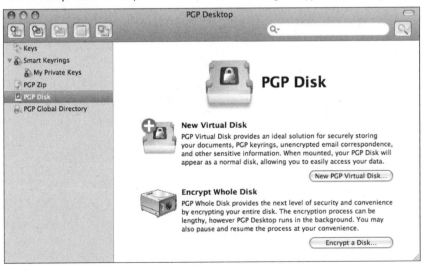

2. **Click New PGP Virtual Disk.** A new window, as shown in Figure 13.7, opens.

FIGURE 13.7

When configuring settings for a virtual disk, be sure to show the Advanced Options at the bottom of the window to be able to choose an encryption algorithm and disk format.

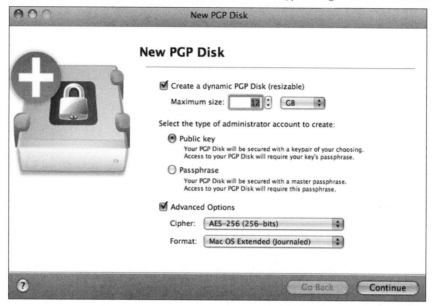

3. **For an automatically expanding virtual disk (the default, which I recommend), leave the Create a dynamic PGP Disk (resizable) check box selected.** For a fixed-size disk, click the check box to deselect it.

4. **In the Size (for fixed-size disks) or Maximum size (for resizable disks) field, type a number representing the capacity of the virtual disk (the maximum capacity to which it can grow in the case of resizable disks) and then choose a unit of measurement (KB, MB, or GB) from the pop-up menu.**

5. **Click either the Public key or Passphrase radio button to select the authentication method you want to use.** Passphrase is the more flexible option and the one I use for the remainder of these steps.

6. **Click the Advanced Options check box, revealing two more pop-up menus.**

7. **Choose the encryption algorithm you want to use (AES-256 or CAST5) from the Cipher pop-up menu, choose the disk format from the Format pop-up menu, and then click Continue.** In general, the disk format you choose should be the same as the format of your Mac disk, which is usually Mac OS Extended (Journaled).

8. **To configure a master passphrase for the disk, type your name in the Name field if it isn't already there, type and confirm a password in the fields provided, as shown in Figure 13.8, and then click Continue.**

FIGURE 13.8

Type and confirm a passphrase (a long password) for your encrypted disk image here.

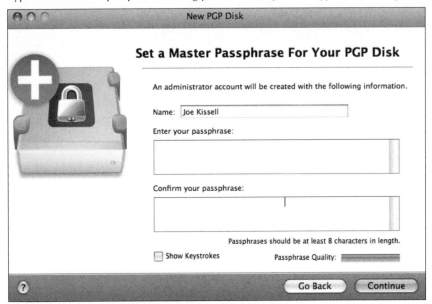

9. **Type a name for your virtual disk, navigate to the location where you want to store it, and then click Save.**

10. **In the summary window that appears, click Create.** PGP Desktop creates and formats the new virtual disk for you.

11. **Click Finish.** PGP Desktop mounts your new virtual disk in the Finder, and you can interact with it just as you would any other disk.

To unmount the volume so that future access requires a password, select it (the mounted volume, not the disk image file) and then choose File ➪ Eject *Volume Name* or drag it to the Trash. To remount it later, double-click it, type your password, and then click OK.

If you later want to change the characteristics of a PGP virtual disk — for example, using a different encryption algorithm or giving access to additional users — you can do so by selecting the disk in the sidebar of the PGP window and using the controls on the right side, as shown in Figure 13.9. Consult PGP's Help menu for detailed instructions on working with virtual disks.

FIGURE 13.9

You can adjust the features of an existing virtual disk, including changing its encryption algorithm.

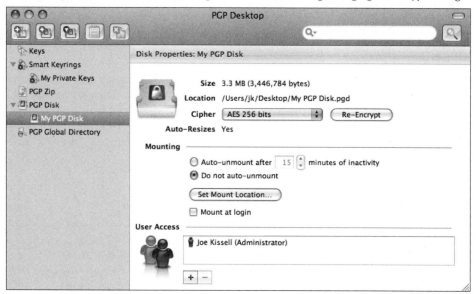

Using other encrypted disk image products

In addition to Disk Utility and PGP Desktop, a number of other programs can create and manage encrypted disk images. Most of these use the same formats as Disk Utility and simply add features, but TrueCrypt uses its own format. Examples of other tools you can use to create these images include:

- **Espionage.** Espionage takes existing folders and turns them into AES-128 or AES-256 sparse or sparse bundle disk images. It puts the original folder in the Trash but relies on the user to remember to empty it securely. Espionage hides the disk image itself in an obscure folder but puts an alias to it — which looks like a regular folder — back in the original location. The effect of all this is to make the process of interacting with encrypted disk images as similar as possible as interacting with regular folders, except for having to type your password when you open them. (`www.taoeffect.com/espionage/`, $24.95)

- **Ghost Sphere Pro.** This utility is designed primarily to hide files and folders in the Finder, protecting them by obscurity. However, unlike the less-expensive Standard edition of the program, the Pro edition also supports creating AES-128-encrypted standard or sparse bundle disk images and then hiding them so that they can't normally be seen or opened in the Finder. (`http://web.mac.com/spherecorner/shareware/Ghost_Sphere.html`, €30 or roughly $40 US)

- **Knox.** Knox creates AES-128 or AES-256 sparse disk images, and you can optionally exclude items on these images from being indexed by Spotlight. You can quickly access any of Knox's disk images using a system-wide menu, and you can configure Knox to back up the images automatically. In addition, Knox can reformat an external drive (such as a hard drive or a USB flash drive) to function as an encrypted disk using a special, hidden disk image. (www.knoxformac.com, $29.95)

- **TrueCrypt.** This free, open-source encryption package (www.truecrypt.org) creates disk images encrypted with your choice of AES-256, Serpent, or Twofish ciphers (or combinations thereof). In addition to making disk images that function similarly to those created by Disk Utility or PGP, TrueCrypt can encrypt an entire volume (although not, on Mac OS X, a boot volume) and can optionally hide an encrypted volume in such a way that it would be very difficult for an attacker to even discover its presence, much less gain access to its contents.

Using FileVault

In addition to offering encrypted disk images that you can create manually to protect any number of files, Mac OS X includes a mechanism called FileVault that puts an encrypted disk image — specifically, an encrypted sparse bundle disk image — to a special use. FileVault encrypts the entire contents of a user's home folder (/Users/*username*), which typically includes all the user's documents, email, photos, music, preferences, and other personal files. Because FileVault operates almost invisibly behind the scenes, it makes a convenient way to keep nearly all your personal files secure. However, it also has some noteworthy downsides, so it's not the best choice for everyone.

Cross-Ref
For more on FileVault, see Chapter 4. ■

FileVault virtues and vices

I wish I could offer either a blanket recommendation to use FileVault or a blanket warning not to, but it's not that simple. FileVault does some things brilliantly, which makes me quite enthusiastic about it at times, but it also has some significant failings and limitations that give me pause (enough so that I don't use FileVault on my own Macs). But your mileage may vary, so I present here some of the pros and cons of FileVault.

Great things about FileVault
The first great thing about FileVault is that it encrypts almost all your personal files without demanding any more interaction from you than would be necessary for encrypting a single file (and, typically, much less). Assuming you keep all your user-created data somewhere inside your home folder — which is the default location for just about everything and therefore the place it's most likely to be unless you take special steps to put it elsewhere — it's all protected automatically without your needing to worry about which sensitive files are stored where.

FileVault is also extremely easy to set up and use, compared to most other encryption software. You can turn it on with a few clicks (and a bit of waiting), and after that, you can go about using your Mac just as you ordinarily would without having to open special software, remember extra passwords, or go through any other obtuse procedures.

Because of the relatively low level at which FileVault operates and the way it's integrated into Leopard and Snow Leopard, it exerts a minimal toll on system performance. You need not constantly wait for files to be decrypted as they're opened or encrypted as they're saved; in most cases, all this happens so quickly behind the scenes that you won't perceive any slowdown at all.

Last but not least, FileVault uses reasonably secure encryption. It's not the best (as I detail in a moment), but it's good enough for most people in most situations — assuming you've chosen a long, random password, you keep it secure, and you exercise the usual precautions, such as locking your keychain after a period of inactivity. Unless the data on your computer is of sufficient value that a dedicated hacker or a government agency is willing to invest considerable time and money in breaking in, you're unlikely to suffer a data breach.

Less-than-great things about FileVault

As enticing as all those pros are, the list of things that might make you circumspect is longer.

First and most obviously, FileVault protects only the files and folders in your home folder. Even though that's generally most of your data, FileVault fails to encrypt a few significant things, any of which could potentially contain sensitive personal data — for example:

- Log files for system-wide processes, such as those stored in `/Library/Logs` and `/var/log`

- Certain cache and temporary files, such as those stored in `/Library/Caches` and `/tmp`, and the cache files stored by certain backup programs

- System-wide preferences, such as those stored in `/Library/Preferences`

- The contents of the `/Developer` folder, which is present if you installed Apple's Xcode Tools and which may contain code you've written

- Any other file or folder that you or a program you installed decided to store outside your home folder for any reason

Second, FileVault is only partially compatible with Apple's Time Machine backup software. For one thing, Time Machine backs up the contents of your home folder (again, that means your most important files) only when you're logged out of your account (so that the FileVault disk image is closed) — but your Mac is still running. That's an unusual usage scenario for many people. For another thing, Time Machine's 3-D "time travel" interface isn't compatible with FileVault, so if you want to restore files that were backed up, you must either restart from your Mac OS X Install DVD and then use it to restore your entire volume with Time Machine or else manually dig through oodles of archived folders and disk images to find the files you want. The upshot is that you can choose extremely easy, built-in, automatic encryption or extremely easy, built-in, automatic backups — but not both.

Next, there are certain incidental annoyances. For example, from time to time, when you log out, shut down, or restart your Mac, a dialog box opens stating that FileVault is using more space than necessary and would like to clean up the unused space. You can choose to ignore this request, but if you agree to it, you're committed; you can't do anything else with your Mac (such as toss it in your carrying case and walk out the door) until the cleanup has finished, and that process can take anywhere from minutes to hours.

Another concern about FileVault involves the master password you set as a safety net in case any individual user on the machine forgets his or her password. The user's security is only as good as the master password, over which the user may have no control — and in fact, even a good master password is less secure than it may appear because of weaknesses in the encryption method used to store it.

Even without compromising the master password, though, FileVault has been shown to be vulnerable to a variety of different attacks, particularly in cases where someone can gain temporary access to a Mac with FileVault enabled or where a poor password was chosen. FileVault has also fallen victim to the notorious cold boot attack, described earlier in this chapter.

Last but not least, even if FileVault had no security holes, technical limitations, or design flaws, it would, like any encryption system, be only as secure as you, the user, allow it to be. If, for example, you use FileVault but configure your Mac to log in automatically when it's turned on, the encryption is worthless because there are no barriers to someone simply pressing the Power button. If you put too much stock in FileVault security, you could be tempted to adopt unsafe computing habits that will leave you less safe overall than with FileVault disabled.

Deciding whether FileVault is for you

So, the list of negatives was a lot longer than the list of positives. Even so, FileVault might be an entirely reasonable choice (or, at least, superior to the alternatives) for some types of users. To discover whether you might be one of those users, answer these questions:

- **Do you need encryption at all?** This isn't the no-brainer question it may sound like. As discussed earlier, encryption may be more trouble than it's worth if your computer is kept in a secure environment and you've taken other precautions to ensure that unauthorized people can't access it in person or over a network. It's also irrelevant if you don't store any personal, financial, or other confidential information on your Mac — although most of us have at least some private information on our computers.

- **Can another encryption method serve your needs (almost) as well?** If you do need encryption, consider what kinds of data you need to keep safe. If that list includes items outside your home folder, you may need full-disk encryption (instead of or in addition to FileVault). If it includes only a limited subset of items in your home folder, a simple encrypted disk image (covered earlier in this chapter) may be a better solution.

- **Do you use a laptop?** Most laptop users move their computers around a good bit, including traveling with them. Laptop users are at a higher risk for physical theft, and if they use open Wi-Fi networks, they're also at a higher risk for network intrusions. Therefore, all else being equal, laptop users are more suitable candidates for FileVault than desktop users.

- **Do you have a great backup strategy?** Because of the limitations of Time Machine with FileVault, you should probably use a different application to back up your Mac. If you're willing to research and test other methods of backing up your Mac, FileVault makes a bit more sense; if you're committed to using Time Machine (or if you choose to live dangerously and not back up at all), using FileVault is most unwise.

- **Do you have another, non-encrypted account on your Mac — just in case?** That's a question that should answer itself. If you use FileVault for your main account, it's in your best interest to set up a second account on your Mac that has FileVault turned off. If your FileVault disk image develops errors and can't be mounted for some reason (which does happen occasionally), you could be locked out of your Mac entirely if you don't have another account to use while restoring your data from a backup.

If you've considered all those questions and decided that FileVault is a good solution for your needs, read on to learn about configuring and using it.

Configuring FileVault

Earlier in this book, I described the basic steps for setting up FileVault. I now want to expand on those instructions, including additional steps you should perform to reduce your risks of data loss, hacking, and other random problems.

Cross-Ref

For the abbreviated steps for setting up FileVault for the current version, see Chapter 4. ■

If you haven't recently done so, make sure you have a complete backup of your hard disk — a bootable duplicate — so that you can return your Mac to its pre-FileVault state if anything should go wrong. If your account (login) password is shorter than nine characters and not randomly selected, choose a stronger password. Then, to set up FileVault for the current user, follow these steps:

Cross-Ref

For more on backups, see Chapter 8. For more on changing your password, see Chapter 3. For more on choosing a secure password, see Chapter 6. ■

1. Choose **É ⇨** System Preferences to open System Preferences and then click Security to open the Security pane.

2. If the lock icon in the lower-left corner of the pane is in the locked state, click it, type an administrator's username and password, and then click OK.

3. To keep your future FileVault configuration as secure as possible against the most likely threats, begin by locking down a few system-wide settings (if you haven't done so already) by clicking the General tab, shown in Figure 13.10, and then doing the following:

FIGURE 13.10

Before turning on FileVault, make sure your other security settings are configured to make up for some of FileVault's inherent limitations.

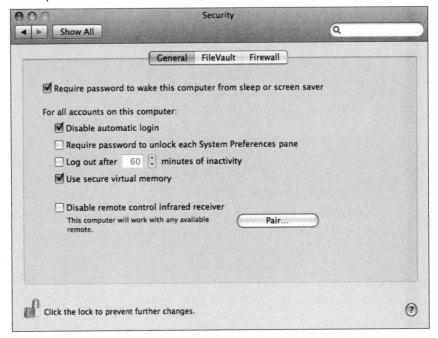

- Click the Require password to wake this computer from sleep or screen saver check box if it's not already selected.

- Click the Disable automatic login check box if it's not already selected.

- Optional but recommended: Click the Log out after X minutes of inactivity check box and then type a reasonable number (such as 30) in the field to make your Mac log you out of your account (securing your FileVault in the process) after that number of minutes with no activity.

- Click the Use secure virtual memory check box if it's not already selected.

4. **Click the FileVault tab.**

5. **If you see a message that says "A master password is not set for this computer," click Set Master Password, type and verify a password in the fields provided, type an optional hint, and then click OK.** Make sure you choose an exceptionally strong password — and one that's different from your user account password!

6. **Click Turn On FileVault.** Mac OS X first checks to see that you have enough free space to encrypt your home folder. If you don't, it informs you that you must delete some files before continuing.

7. **When prompted, type the user's password and then click OK.** A warning appears.

8. **Click the Use secure erase check box.** This can add several hours or more to the time required to activate FileVault but is advisable for the extra security it provides.

9. **Leave the Use secure virtual memory check box selected and then click Turn On FileVault.** Mac OS X encrypts your home folder, which may take anywhere from seconds to hours, depending on its size. It then displays the login window, where you can log in as the existing user or a different user.

10. **Close System Preferences.**

You can now use your account normally.

Encrypting an Entire Disk

So far, this chapter has covered encrypting individual files, folders, and disk images, up to and including one's entire home folder. In general, encrypting a large set of files rather than numerous smaller sets makes sense because it requires fewer passwords and less bother. But even encrypting your entire home folder can leave some sensitive files unprotected. So, why not simply encrypt everything on your disk — meaning you can lock or unlock every file at once? Indeed, you can do exactly that using any of several software packages.

Until relatively recently, however, this option was available only for non-boot volumes. You couldn't encrypt an entire Mac OS X startup disk because the infrastructure needed to load the software that could decrypt the data during the startup process didn't exist. However, thanks to Apple's move to Intel processors and the ingenuity of a few software companies, that formerly elusive capability is now also a reality.

Most means of encrypting an entire Mac OS X volume — startup disk or not — are geared toward large-scale enterprise use, and may be difficult for ordinary users to find and equally difficult for them to configure. PGP Whole Disk Encryption is a notable exception in that it's extremely consumer-friendly, as encryption software goes. These products also carry with them certain intrinsic limitations. For example, once you've started your computer and typed your password, all your files are freely accessible (in person or over a network) just as they would be if they hadn't been encrypted. Even putting your Mac to sleep doesn't lock them; you must actually turn off your Mac to do so. Thus, in some scenarios, whole-disk encryption actually provides less security than encrypting only part of your data. In addition, having your entire disk encrypted can make disk repair and other maintenance tasks more complicated.

Still, depending on your needs, whole-disk encryption may offer just the right combination of benefits, and it may also serve as a useful adjunct to other, more conventional means of encryption, filling in gaps that the other processes miss.

PGP Whole Disk Encryption

I've mentioned PGP's encryption products several times already in this chapter and elsewhere in this book. One of PGP's most recent — and most impressive — features is called Whole Disk Encryption (WDE), and it lets you encrypt any hard disk, flash drive, or similar storage device connected to your Mac, including the startup volume, which I focus on here.

The process of encrypting your startup disk with PGP is very similar to that of creating an encrypted disk image, as I explained earlier in this chapter. After going through the initial configuration process, which includes choosing a password, PGP encrypts your disk in the background as you work. The process can take quite a few hours (depending on the speed of your processor and disk, the size of your disk, and what other activities you're doing while the encryption is taking place), but it doesn't decrease your Mac's responsiveness much, and if you find it to be a problem, you can pause the encryption and resume it at your leisure.

Once your disk is fully encrypted, you never notice anything different in the way your Mac behaves — except at startup, when you're faced with a new password prompt, which appears before the Apple logo even graces your screen. After you type your password, Mac OS X loads, the login process proceeds as usual, and you can use your Mac in the way you always do. Apart from the controls for initially turning on encryption and logging in, PGP's WDE has no visible user interface. It simply does its thing, silently, in the background (its thing being keeping every last file on your Mac securely encrypted at all times). Although WDE works just fine for individual users, it's also designed to fit into the enterprise, where centralized configuration, deployment, and management are crucial. When deployed by a systems administrator, WDE offers a (very limited) back door of sorts, whereby if a user forgets his or her password, the administrator can issue a special token that works only once — and only on that computer — to enable the user to recover the data from the encrypted disk.

For all its benefits, WDE does have some noteworthy limitations. For one thing, it's incompatible with Boot Camp. If you want to run Windows on your Mac, you can use a virtualization program, such as Parallels Desktop or VMware Fusion, but because of the way your disk must be partitioned to work with Boot Camp, it's not supported. The company has said it hopes to be able to support Boot Camp in the future. Disk repair could also be a hassle. Because a PGP-encrypted volume can mount only on a computer that loaded the WDE driver on startup, you can't access the contents of your encrypted disk when starting up from a Mac OS X Install DVD or CDs or DVDs distributed with other disk-repair software such as DiskWarrior or TechTool Pro. So, if your disk develops problems and you want to repair it, the best course of action is to start your Mac from a bootable duplicate of your PGP-encrypted drive (which, of course, has the PGP software installed) and then run repair software from that disk.

Finally, WDE, like the other products in this section, authenticates and unlocks only at startup. That means once you type your password, all your data is freely available to anyone with physical or network access to your computer (unless it's also encrypted in some other way). Even putting your Mac to sleep doesn't lock it; unless you've configured Mac OS X to request your login password when your Mac wakes up, your disk continues to be accessible without any barriers.

So, WDE by itself provides limited protection to people who put their laptops to sleep, instead of turning them off, when moving them from place to place.

PGP Whole Disk Encryption is available as a stand-alone product, which costs $119 (`https://row.store.pgp.com/whole_disk_encryption_mac.html`); it's also included as part of PGP Desktop Professional (`https://row.store.pgp.com/desktop_pro_mac.html`, $199), although not with PGP Desktop Home or PGP Desktop Email. Volume discounts and annual subscriptions are also available. Having tried all three of the full-disk encryption products covered in this section, I can say with some conviction that PGP's is the most user-friendly by far as well as the one whose user interface is most Mac-like. It's the only one any individual can freely buy simply by clicking a few buttons on a website. It's also easy to use and includes thorough, clear documentation. Except for users or environments in need of a specific feature that only one of its competitors offers, PGP gets my personal recommendation.

Caution

PGP Whole Disk Encryption version 10, which was not yet shipping at press time, supports Snow Leopard; earlier versions do not.

Check Point Full Disk Encryption

Check Point was the first company (by a few months) to introduce a product that could encrypt a Mac's startup disk: Full Disk Encryption (FDE). The design and interface are based on the company's similar product for Windows, which had already been in the marketplace for some time, and the two are freely interoperable. Although individuals can supposedly, after a fashion, purchase single copies of FDE, it's not designed as a stand-alone product. The interface for setting it up and managing it is one only an IT geek could love, an example of which is shown in Figure 13.11. It's undoubtedly just what you'd want if installing the software on hundreds or thousands of computers at once, but the process of getting it up and running on a single Mac is far more cumbersome than either of the other two full-disk encryption products discussed here.

Because of its enterprise focus, support for centralized deployment and management is extensive. From a corporate viewpoint, FDE offers thorough yet fine-grained control over encryption practices. For example, an administrator can configure a global policy specifying how long a password must be, whether it must contain numbers or a mixture of cases, whether special characters and spaces are allowed, and other characteristics. Administrators can create profiles specifying various user and group configurations as well as install, update, or remove the software remotely. FDE users can authenticate with passwords, dynamic tokens, or both.

FDE offers support for Boot Camp — to a point: You can run Boot Camp Assistant to install a Windows partition after encrypting your disk but not before. If you already have Boot Camp installed, you must uninstall it, repartition your disk as a single volume, install FDE, encrypt your disk, and then reinstall Boot Camp (and Windows) from scratch. On the other hand, unlike PGP WDE, Check Point's product works only with internal drives — not with external FireWire or USB devices. Of interest to laptop users, FDE doesn't support Safe Sleep, a mode (turned on by default) in which the contents of your RAM is saved automatically to disk when you put your computer to sleep so that it's preserved — and you can return to exactly where you left off — even if your battery drains completely before the computer wakes up.

Just as PGP's WDE presents challenges for disk repair, so does FDE. A company representative told me that a way to address the problem is to connect the ailing Mac with a FireWire cable to another (healthy) Mac whose drive isn't encrypted and then restart the Mac with disk problems while holding down the T key to put it into FireWire Target Disk Mode. Then, its disk appears as an external disk on the other Mac, and after typing your password, you should be able to access it and repair it using the normal range of utilities. Of course, this trick doesn't work for Macs without FireWire ports.

Check Point claims that individuals can purchase FDE, which has a list price of $120, by contacting one of their partner vendors (http://partners.us.checkpoint.com/partnerlocator/), although I found it extremely difficult to do so in practice because the vendors are typically resellers accustomed to working only with large corporate accounts. Of course, if you're a large corporate account, you should have no problem!

FIGURE 13.11

This is just a tiny sample of the seemingly endless hierarchy in Check Point FDE's configuration interface, which looks more like the Windows registry than a typical Mac program.

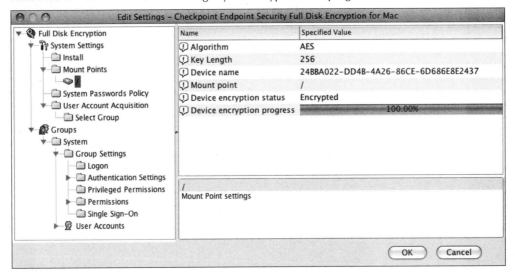

WinMagic SecureDoc

WinMagic's SecureDoc Disk Encryption for Mac, like Check Point FDE, is designed mainly for use in corporate settings. But its interface is much simpler than FDE's. In fact, in my opinion, it could do with a few more controls and more text to explain what to do. Like the other products listed here, it currently doesn't work with Boot Camp. If you've encrypted your home folder with

FileVault, you can install SecureDoc, and FileVault continues to work, but you can't activate — or deactivate — FileVault after SecureDoc is installed. On the other hand, SecureDoc not only works with internal drives and external USB or FireWire devices but also supports encryption of CDs, DVDs, and pretty much any other storage medium you can connect to your Mac. It also claims to support disk repair utilities, defragmentation utilities, and imaging tools (for creating files with a complete installation of Mac OS X for widespread installation).

The stand-alone version, for which the initial configuration window appears in Figure 13.12, is extremely easy to install and configure on an individual Mac, whereas the enterprise version has, as do PGP WDE and Check Point FDE, a full range of controls for centralized management. The product supports multi-factor authentication using devices such as smart cards and USB tokens, and support for biometric authentication (such as fingerprint scanners) is also planned. In addition, SecureDoc can tie into LDAP servers and other enterprise-wide services, using them to establish which users have access to which data. For example, if a user has encrypted a flash drive, that drive can be inserted and used transparently — without any additional password prompt — on any computer in the company with which that user has authenticated (using whichever methods the organization specifies). SecureDoc is also designed to enable an organization to easily and transparently encrypt data stored on personal devices employees have brought with them to the office.

FIGURE 13.12

When you first install SecureDoc, you can fill in some basic details here and then click a button to set your password.

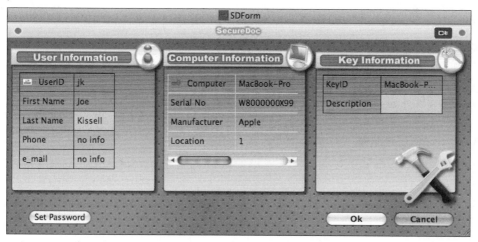

SecureDoc was the first product to offer support for self-encrypting drive mechanisms, which I discuss just ahead. Check Point and PGP are also reportedly working on adding support for self-encrypting drives. This means that if you put a self-encrypting drive in your Mac, you can use the SecureDoc driver to handle authentication and access (with its usual range of options) while the circuitry of the drive itself takes care of the actual encryption and decryption.

Like the other full-disk encryption products, SecureDoc is designed to prevent unauthorized access to your data when you log in or connect a device, but it doesn't prevent someone else from accessing your files while you're logged in nor does it lock your data when your Mac goes to sleep. In addition, its very transparency can be a problem in some situations; its minimalist interface makes it difficult to tell what's encrypted and what isn't and doesn't include documentation to explain what you should expect in day-to-day use or how to troubleshoot problems. It also took the longest of the three full-disk encryption programs, by a considerable margin, to complete the initial encryption of an entire disk.

Although WinMagic doesn't go out of its way to advertise this fact, the stand-alone version of SecureDoc for Mac is available for sale to individuals at a suggested retail price of $155. To purchase a copy, send an email message to sales@winmagic.com and identify yourself as an end user. Corporate customers can find all the information they need at `www.winmagic.com/products/securedoc_disk_encryption_for_mac`.

Using Hardware-Encrypted Drives

All the encryption options mentioned so far in this chapter are software-based. As a result, they all have certain inherent limitations. If the software becomes corrupted because of a disk error, for example, you may be unable to access your encrypted files. A malicious program could conceivably insinuate itself into your system between your encryption software and the operating system, capturing your password as you type it, decrypting data behind your back, or causing other mischief. Because the necessary software must run on the computer accessing the data, moving drives between systems (particularly on different platforms) can be challenging. And in the case of full-disk encryption programs, the time required to encrypt an entire volume (and the restrictions they sometimes place on partitioning) can be hard to swallow.

Wouldn't it be great if your storage device itself were somehow inherently encrypted so you don't have to mess with software at all? In fact, numerous hard drives and flash drives do have one sort or another of built-in encryption, which can solve many of the previously mentioned problems — albeit at a higher cost and with some additional usage complications.

Most devices of this sort fall into one of several major categories, as I discuss next.

Tip

Although these devices protect your data from unauthorized access, one peril they can't protect it from is fire! Although you can buy fireproof safes designed for keeping computer media cool, one model in particular, the FireKing MediaVault Data Container (`www.fireking.com/adesco_safes_data_mediavault.html`) is unique. It can hold one or two USB hard drives, which attach to cables that pass through the case. That way, you can use the drives for backups or other file storage while they're securely locked inside a fireproof safe (instead of having to disconnect and put away the drives when you're not using them). If your home or office happens to burn down when you're away, chances are your data will still be safe on the drives. ∎

Key-based enclosures

The first variety of fully encrypted external hard drives to appear on the market, key-based enclosures hold an ordinary, off-the-shelf drive mechanism but use special logic in the controller to encrypt all data written to the drive and decrypt all data read from it — if and only if an electronic key with a unique signature is inserted into the device. The physical keys contain the digital encryption keys and are designed to be virtually impossible to copy or forge. With the key inserted, the drive starts up normally; if you remove the key, it can no longer mount. You can generally remove the key after the disk has mounted without losing access to the data — as long as the drive isn't powered down. Even if the bare drive mechanism were removed from the enclosure, its data couldn't be read.

Key-based enclosures are, in theory at least, faster, more reliable, and less prone to errors and attack than software-based encryption methods. They may also be less susceptible to hacking than fingerprint scanners, some of which can be compromised with a variety of techniques much simpler (and less messy) than removing the fingertip of the user. On the other hand, because access requires only a key, you must take special steps to protect this physical object; it can't be stored in your memory like a password, and it can be lost — leaving you unable to read your own data.

Examples of key-based encrypted USB and FireWire drives (or enclosures) include the following:

- RadTech's Impact enclosures, available for 2.5-inch and 3.5-inch drives, with 64-bit or 128-bit encryption (`www.radtech.us/Products/Impact.aspx`)

- Rocstor's Rocbit drives, which also come in 2.5-inch (`www.rocstor.com/products/products-search.cfm?category=Mobile-Encrypted`) and 3.5-inch (`www.rocstor.com/products/products-search.cfm?category=Desktop-Encrypted`) configurations

- Rocstor's Rocsafe MX drives (`www.rocstor.com/products/rocsafe-mx.html`) use a smart card in place of a key and also include a numeric keypad for two-factor authentication — you can configure the drives to require both the physical key and the numeric password, greatly reducing the chances of someone gaining access to your data. This makes the drive a hybrid between key-based enclosures and keypad-based enclosures, which are covered next.

- SecureDisk enclosures (`www.cooldrives.com/usdriv.html`) for 2.5-inch and 3.5-inch drives, offered with either 40-bit or 128-bit encryption

Keypad-based enclosures

Instead of using a physical key to unlock the data on your drive, you can simply type your password directly, as long as the drive has a keypad to enable you to do so. An example of a keypad-equipped encrypted external drive is the Data Locker (`www.datalockerdrive.com/Products/`), which provides up to 256-bit encryption. Unfortunately, because the keypad offers only ten numeric keys, you must type a fairly long password to achieve the same level of security you could obtain with a much shorter, alphanumeric password. The keypad includes telephone-style letters on each key to help you remember complex passwords. Some models can be configured to *self-destruct* (automatically erase their data) after a certain number of incorrect password attempts.

Biometric enclosures

If you don't want to worry about losing a key or forgetting a password, there's yet another option: external drives with an integrated fingerprint scanner. Just swipe your finger across the scanner to unlock the information on the disk. Most such drives can be configured to accept fingerprints from multiple fingers (or people). Examples of biometric enclosures include these:

- The Ceelox HD3500 Fingerprint Hard Drive, a portable USB 2.0 drive with capacities ranging from 40 GB to 100 GB (`www.zvetcobiometrics.com/Business/Products/HD3500/overview.jsp`)

- LaCie SAFE hard drives, which come in a range of capacities in both portable (2.5-inch) and desktop (3.5-inch) sizes (`www.lacie.com/us/products/range.htm?id=10062`)

- MXI Security's Outbacker MXI Bio hard drives (`www.mxisecurity.com/mxi/categories/display/65`) and Stealth MXP Bio flash drives (`www.mxisecurity.com/categories/display/62`)

Externally authenticating enclosures

Still another broad category of devices includes hardware-based encryption of some kind but relies on desktop software for authentication. In other words, the drives typically have a special, protected partition that holds simple Windows and Mac OS X software that can be used to fill in your password so you can use the devices on nearly any computer without having to worry about installing software or giving up the benefits of hardware encryption. Examples of devices like this are:

- Buffalo Technology's MiniStation DataVault Portable Hard Drive (`www.buffalotech.com/products/external-storage/ministation/ministation-datavault-portable-hard-drive-with-full-disk-encryption-hds-phu2/`)

- MXI Security's Stealth M-Series (`www.mxisecurity.com/categories/display/87`), Stealth Mini (`www.mxisecurity.com/categories/display/66`), and Stealth MXP Passport (`www.mxisecurity.com/categories/display/64`) flash drives

Self-encrypting drive mechanisms

Finally, we come to drive mechanisms that have internal encryption circuitry, so that whether they're installed directly inside your computer (desktop or laptop) or in an external enclosure, you can take full advantage of hardware-based encryption. Like the externally authenticating enclosures just mentioned, these mechanisms, often called self-encrypting drives, need some way for a user to authenticate, but they don't include their own software. Instead, they rely on software supplied by computer vendors or other third parties to handle authentication (which may be anything from a simple password entry to multi-factor authentication, including tokens, biometrics, and the like) and centralized key management while performing low-level encryption themselves.

Seagate was the first manufacturer to deliver self-encrypting drives, available in its Momentus FDE line (for both desktops and portables). Somewhat later, a group of other manufacturers, including Fujitsu, Hitachi, and Samsung, developed a competing standard for self-encrypting drives called Opal. Although the underlying mechanisms are different, the end result for users is the same.

Self-encrypting drive mechanisms offer the fastest possible encryption and decryption. However, although such drives have been available in PC laptops for some time, they haven't made large inroads into the Mac world yet because of limited software support. As I write this, only WinMagic's SecureDoc offers a Mac-compatible front end for accessing such drives (without compatible authentication software, the drives can be used as ordinary, unencrypted drives), although Check Point and PGP have stated that they're also looking into developing support.

Securely Deleting Files

Normally, when you delete a file — either by dragging it to the Trash and emptying the Trash or by using the rm command in a Terminal window — Mac OS X doesn't erase it as such. It simply removes the file listing from its directory, making the space it occupies on disk available for other files. The effect, as far as you the user are concerned, is that the file is no longer there, and the free space on your disk increases by the size of the file. But in fact, the file's data is still right on your disk where it was before you deleted it, and with the right tools, you (or someone else) could recover its data (sometimes called undeleting a file).

Once a file has been overwritten with other data, however, all bets are off. Barring interventions by professionals with extremely expensive equipment and lots of time on their hands, data that's been overwritten is gone forever. Therefore, if you've deleted a file and want to make sure it's unrecoverable — or if you've encrypted a file and want to make sure the cleartext version is permanently eradicated — you must overwrite it. Unfortunately, because of the complexities of Mac OS X's file system, simply copying another file to the same folder doesn't work.

One way of securely deleting a file is to use a different deletion procedure than simply emptying the Trash normally. Using a special Finder command or a third-party program, you can overwrite a file as it's being deleted. If you've already deleted a file but didn't overwrite it, you can use a different procedure to overwrite all the free space on your drive, making any files that are still there unrecoverable.

Overwriting a file a single time — for example, with a long string of zeros — is adequately secure in the vast majority of situations. Overwriting files multiple times (especially if the pattern of bits recorded each time is different) can defeat specialized techniques that can sometimes detect residual traces of data on disks that have been overwritten just once. Experts disagree on just how many times a file should be overwritten to guarantee absolute security from any conceivable means of recovery, but most secure-deletion routines offer a choice of one pass, seven (good enough for the U.S. Department of Defense), or thirty-five (the so-called Gutman method, developed by researcher Peter Gutman, which supposedly results in the physical impossibility of data being recovered from modern magnetic media but which most people — including Gutman himself — consider overkill).

Using the Secure Empty Trash command

The easiest way to overwrite a file while deleting it is to drag it to the Trash and then choose Finder ➪ Secure Empty Trash. The Finder overwrites the data seven times, which takes about seven times as long as a normal deletion and is more than secure enough for almost anyone.

Note
Another way to securely delete files is to use the `srm` command in Terminal. For details, type `man srm` in a Terminal window. ▪

Erasing empty space with Disk Utility

If you've already deleted files such that the Secure Empty Trash command is no longer an option, you can use Disk Utility to overwrite all the free space on a disk — one time or many. This makes your data safely unrecoverable but can be extremely time-consuming, especially on large drives and more so if you choose multiple passes.

To erase your free space using Disk Utility, follow these steps:

1. **Open Disk Utility, which is located in** `/Applications/Utilities`.

2. **In the list on the left, select the volume whose free space you want to erase and then click the Erase tab.**

3. **Click the Erase Free Space button to show a dialog box with secure-deletion options, as shown in Figure 13.13.**

4. **Click the radio button corresponding to the number of times you want to overwrite your data.** The Zero Out Deleted Files option is almost always the best choice. If you're paranoid, choose 7-Pass Erase of Deleted Files and be prepared to wait a long time. If you're outrageously paranoid, choose 35-Pass Erase of Deleted Files and plan a nice long vacation while the process finishes!

5. **Click Erase Free Space.** Disk Utility overwrites your free space, showing a progress indicator and estimated time to completion. When it's finished, you can quit Disk Utility.

FIGURE 13.13

You can overwrite your free space up to 35 times, but I'd love to see someone actually recover data that had been overwritten only 34 times (or even a few).

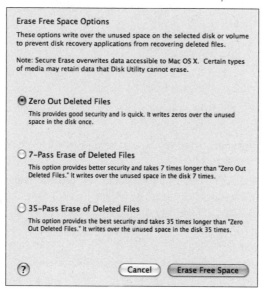

Erase Free Space Options

These options write over the unused space on the selected disk or volume to prevent disk recovery applications from recovering deleted files.

Note: Secure Erase overwrites data accessible to Mac OS X. Certain types of media may retain data that Disk Utility cannot erase.

- **Zero Out Deleted Files**
  This provides good security and is quick. It writes zeros over the unused space in the disk once.

- **7-Pass Erase of Deleted Files**
  This option provides better security and takes 7 times longer than "Zero Out Deleted Files." It writes over the unused space in the disk 7 times.

- **35-Pass Erase of Deleted Files**
  This option provides the best security and takes 35 times longer than "Zero Out Deleted Files." It writes over the unused space in the disk 35 times.

Cancel   Erase Free Space

Using third-party utilities

If you want more security or convenience than Secure Empty Trash offers, you can use any of several utilities, most of which offer drag-and-drop operation, some examples of which include:

- **AlienDestroyer.** AlienDestroyer (`www.aliencrypt.com/AlienDestroyer.html`, $10) securely deletes not only files and folders but also caches and browsing history stored by most web browsers.

- **Permanent Eraser.** This free utility (`www.edenwaith.com/products/permanent%20 eraser`) overwrites files 35 times and can also be used with rewritable CDs and DVDs.

- **PGP Shredder.** This tool is built into PGP Desktop Home and PGP Desktop Professional, covered earlier in this chapter.

Securely Erasing Disks

Just as Disk Utility can securely erase the free space on a disk, it can securely erase an entire disk — visible files and all. Of course, you wouldn't do this with disks you're actively using, but you might do it for disks you're about to sell, give away, transfer to another employee, or otherwise get rid of if they contain any personal data.

Tip

Before selling or disposing of a computer, you should securely erase its internal disk and then (if someone else will be using it) reinstall Mac OS X. To erase a Mac's internal disk, you must start up from another volume, such as an external hard drive containing a bootable duplicate or a Mac OS X Install DVD, and then run Disk Utility from that volume. ■

If you read the procedure earlier for erasing the free space on a disk, most of these steps should look quite familiar:

1. **Open Disk Utility, which is located in** `/Applications/Utilities`.

2. **In the list on the left, select the volume you want to erase (which can't, obviously, be your startup volume) and then click the Erase tab.**

3. **Click the Security Options button to show a dialog box with secure-deletion options, as shown in Figure 13.14.**

4. **Click the radio button corresponding to the way you want to erase the disk and then click OK.** The default option, Don't Erase Data, isn't what you want because it enables files to be recovered. As with erasing free space, the Zero Out Data option is usually ideal. Select 7-Pass Erase for extra security or 35-Pass Erase for the ultimate in data erasure if you have lots of time to kill.

5. **Click the Erase button and then click Erase again to confirm.** Disk Utility securely erases the entire volume, showing a progress indicator and estimated time to completion. When it's finished, you can quit Disk Utility.

Tip

This procedure is for hard disks only. If you want to destroy the data on an optical disc (CD or DVD), the safest and most reliable way is to shred it, using either a specially designed disc shredder or a heavy-duty paper shredder. Although you can also effectively destroy optical discs by putting them in a microwave oven for a few minutes, the smell is terrible and the fumes may be toxic. ■

Note

If you want extraordinarily secure deletions but can't wait for hours or days, another approach is to use a device called a degausser, which is basically a very powerful electromagnet designed for erasing disks. Degaussers tend to be expensive but securely erase entire disks quickly (often in a matter of seconds). One downside: Sometimes they go too far and render disks completely unusable. ■

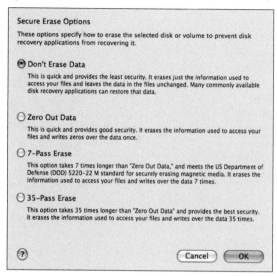

FIGURE 13.14

To securely erase an entire disk, select any option except the first one (which is selected by default).

Recovering Deleted Files

If you've deleted a file in the ordinary way (not overwritten), you may be able to recover some or all of it. This isn't guaranteed, and the process is sometimes complex and time-consuming, but this is what someone else could do who wanted to access your data.

The following are examples of programs that can recover, or undelete, files that have been deleted but not yet overwritten:

- **Boomerang Data Recovery.** Boomerang can restore not only individual files but even entire partitions. It can also reconstruct some RAIDs and recover data from iPods. The product is licensed based on the volume of data you want to be able to recover — for example, with the least-expensive ($39.95) license, you can recover 100MB of data. (www.boomdrs.com/macosx, Home edition, $39.95 and up; Professional edition, $349.95 for a one-year license)

- **Data Rescue 3.** This application can recover files from your computer's hard drive as well as from many digital cameras, iPods, and other storage devices. (http://prosofteng.com/products/data_rescue.php, $99)

- **File Recovery for Mac.** Like Data Rescue 3, this program can recover files from your Mac's disk and numerous other storage devices in cases where data has been accidentally deleted, disk errors have occurred, or a disk has been inadvertently reformatted. (www.applexsoft.com/mac-file-recovery.html, $99.95)

- **FileSalvage.** For recovering accidentally deleted files or those that have been made unreadable due to disk errors, FileSalvage offers a wide range of recovery options. (`www.subrosasoft.com/OSXSoftware/index.php?main_page=product_info&cPath=200&products_id=1`, $89.95)

- **OfficeSalvage.** This tool, essentially a limited subset of FileSalvage, is designed mainly for office-type files such as word-processing documents and spreadsheets. (`www.subrosasoft.com/OSXSoftware/index.php?main_page=product_info&cPath=200&products_id=5`, $49.95)

Note

SubRosaSoft.com, the developers of FileSalvage and OfficeSalvage, also make a heavy-duty data recovery tool for forensic experts (such as law enforcement personnel and academic researchers) called MacForensicsLab (`www.macforensicslab.com`). Prices start at $1,195, so it's not for basic personal file recovery, but its tools are among the most advanced available. ∎

- **R-Studio for Mac.** R-Studio has almost every imaginable file-recovery feature and supports volumes in nearly every format. An advanced version, R-Studio for Mac Network ($179.99), can even recover deleted files over a network. (`www.data-recovery-macintosh.com`, $79.99)

- **Stellar Phoenix Macintosh Data Recovery.** This utility supports a long list of file formats and works with memory cards, flash drives, and iPods in addition to hard drives. (`www.stellarinfo.com/mac-data-recovery.htm`, $129 and up)

- **TechTool Pro.** Unlike the other tools in this list, TechTool Pro is focused mainly on repair, not recovery. Nevertheless, it does have a limited capability to restore deleted files. (`www.micromat.com`, $98)

Summary

This chapter covered ways of keeping others from reading private data stored on your hard disk. I outlined the basic concepts of encryption, along with common pitfalls and misunderstandings. I then reviewed several third-party applications that can encrypt individual files and folders. To make it easier to encrypt and decrypt numerous items at once, an encrypted disk image is often a better choice; I explained how to create and use these with both Disk Utility and PGP.

I next covered FileVault, which uses a special encrypted disk image to store the contents of a user's home folder. When even that is insufficient, you can encrypt an entire volume — even your startup volume — using any of several third-party utilities. After you encrypt files (or when you delete unencrypted files), their original, easily readable data can remain on your disk unless you take special steps to overwrite them so they can't be recovered. I described how to do this and mentioned steps you should take when getting rid of an old Mac or media.

I wrapped up this chapter by demonstrating how to recover deleted files that haven't been over-written to illustrate the importance of secure deletion.

Part III

Network Security Fundamentals

Guarding against Malware

Every Mac comes with a fine collection of useful software for browsing the web, exchanging email, viewing and editing documents, managing media, and other essential tasks. Tens of thousands of other vendors — from huge corporations, such as Microsoft and Adobe, to individual shareware authors — offer a wealth of other tools for accomplishing nearly any conceivable computing task. But among this vast range of software choices are a few bad apples — programs whose purpose isn't to accomplish something useful for you but rather to steal your private information, take over your computer's resources, or simply cause trouble for its own sake. Much of it circulates covertly, so you may have it running on your Mac without even knowing it. This *malware*, or malicious software, can appear in many forms and come from many sources, but it's all bad news, and smart Mac users take steps to avoid it.

Fortunately, the number of malware programs that can run on your Mac is quite small, and in the majority of cases, they're easily avoided by a combination of common sense and some judicious preference settings. Even so, those unlucky enough to find their Macs infected with malware are in for pain and frustration, and odds are that the number of malware programs will only increase as time goes on.

This chapter describes the range of programs that can be considered malware as well as the range of defenses Mac users can employ to stop them.

The Varieties of Malware

In everyday speech, the word *virus* is often used as a catchall term for any kind of malware. But, in fact, a virus is something very specific and, on a Mac, very rare. It's not even necessarily the most destructive type of malware, despite the ominous associations of its name. Because the risks and the methods of protecting yourself vary tremendously from one kind of malware to another, it pays to understand a bit about the kinds of malware you could encounter.

As you review this list, keep in mind that it's not exhaustive — new kinds of malware and variants of old ones crop up all the time — and that a given piece of malware may fall into more than one category.

Viruses

In the simplest terms, a computer *virus* is a tiny, self-replicating program. Viruses aren't stand-alone programs like ordinary applications. Instead, they secretly attach themselves to files and applications on your computer. When you open an infected application (or certain types of infected files that include the capability of executing code, such as PDFs), the virus has the opportunity to run, and as it runs, it tries to copy itself into other files and applications — on your computer or on any available media (which may include network volumes). Those copies, in turn, also make copies of themselves.

Apart from copying themselves into files on network servers to which you're connected, viruses can't, of their own accord, move from computer to computer. They're ordinarily transferred when you email an attachment that's been infected or put an infected file on a server somewhere. The greater the number of infected files on your computer, the greater the chances that the virus can spread to other computers.

A program could meet the definition of a virus without actually doing any damage. In theory, a virus could do all the above and nothing else. It could be essentially invisible, and in fact, it could even be virtuous — performing some useful task. But, in actuality, almost every virus is designed not merely to replicate but to do some sort of damage — deleting or corrupting files, blocking network access, or harming your computer in some other way.

Because such a high percentage of the world's computers run Windows, and because earlier versions of Windows had security holes that made it particularly easy for viruses to spread, there are thousands of Windows viruses in circulation, some of them quite serious. Although viruses for Mac OS X have been demonstrated, as of the time this book was written, not one had been found in the wild (outside a controlled research setting).

Macro viruses

A number of popular programs include a built-in macro language — that is, a way to write programs that use that application's features without relying on any outside framework, such as AppleScript. These programs, usually called *macros*, are typically attached to or embedded in particular documents. For example, you may have a macro that performs certain text cleanup operations, and you may include this in the word-processing files that need it or in a template from which you create new files. Some macro languages can be used to write viruses that spread to other files used by the same application, and they can damage your documents, disrupt the operation of the software you're using, or even, in some cases, send out email messages in your name (containing an infected file as an attachment, naturally). Any virus written in an application's macro programming language and attached to a file like other macros is called a *macro virus*.

The two applications most commonly associated with macro viruses, by far, are Microsoft Word and Microsoft Excel, which have historically included support for a macro language called Visual Basic. Because these Microsoft Office applications are available on both Windows and Mac OS X, their macro viruses had the unusual and dangerous characteristic of running on either platform. However, in Office 2008, Microsoft had removed support for Visual Basic. If you're running Office 2008, Word and Excel macro viruses can't run on your Mac and therefore can't duplicate or do any damage. You can, however, still spread them by sending already-infected files to users of Windows PCs, on which the viruses can cause damage.

Microsoft Office 2004 and earlier versions did support Visual Basic macros, and Microsoft has also stated that a future release of the application suite will bring back Visual Basic support. So, if you have a version of

Office that supports macros, you're potentially vulnerable — many macro viruses exist, and some of them are quite nasty. Anti-malware software can usually eliminate macro viruses; alternatively, Word and Excel enable you to disable macros entirely or for particular documents.

Worms

Like viruses, *worms* are self-replicating programs. But they're far more insidious than viruses because they have the capability of spreading from one computer to another entirely on their own without attaching themselves to an application or waiting for a user to transfer an infected file to someone else. Worms sometimes look for open network ports on other computers and try to exploit holes and weaknesses in the programs that listen to those ports in order to copy themselves to the other computers and activate themselves once there so they can spread even farther.

Also, like viruses, worms can have any of a variety of functions, which can range from nothing at all, to installing zombie software (described in just a moment), to deleting files and causing other sorts of system damage.

Trojan horses

Like the eponymous wooden horse in which Greek soldiers hid in order to infiltrate the city of Troy, a *Trojan horse* (or simply *trojan*) in computer terms is a program that appears to be innocent or helpful but which conceals a dangerous payload. Trojan horses don't self-replicate like viruses or worms; they spread when people download them manually, believing them to be entirely legitimate software. A trojan can take almost any form (games, utilities, screen savers, video players, and so on) — whatever may entice someone to install and run the software.

In terms of potential damage, a trojan can do nearly anything; it's commonly used to install zombie software or remote-access software (which enables someone else to take control of your computer) or to cause network disruptions.

Zombie software

One of the many purposes to which a virus, worm, or trojan can be put is installing *zombie software* on your computer, which turns it into a remote-controlled server without your knowledge. When your computer is functioning as a zombie, someone else (perhaps in another country) can use it, along with thousands or even millions of other similarly infected computers, as part of a massive robotic network (or *botnet*) for sending out spam, sharing files illegally, running chat servers, or bombarding certain servers or networks with access requests to make them crash or prevent legitimate users from reaching them (a distributed denial-of-service attack, or DDoS).

Zombie software doesn't spread on its own; it's always delivered as the payload of some other sort of malware. However, it could persist on your computer even after the delivery mechanism has been found and deleted.

Spyware

The term *spyware* is a broad and somewhat vague one, referring to any sort of computer program that collects information about you or your computer and sends it to someone else without your knowledge and consent. Spyware could be a program that tracks websites you visit or tries to collect your passwords (perhaps using a keystroke logger, which is described ahead). It could also attempt to gather information about your habits and interests in order to display advertising; much adware (next in the list) is also spyware. Some people also categorize tracking cookies as spyware because they can report your browsing behavior on one site to another site without your knowledge.

Cross-Ref

For more on tracking cookies and how to deal with them, see Chapter 10. ∎

Like zombie software, spyware is usually delivered as the payload of a virus, worm, trojan, or other malware.

Adware

In its most general sense, *adware* is any software that displays advertising. Programs that run on their own and produce pop-up windows (even when you aren't in a web browser) with ads are the quintessential adware variety. However, not all adware is malware. For example, if you use Carbon Copy Cloner to duplicate your disks or Evernote to synchronize text and web page clippings, you see ads within the programs for third-party products. Because these programs are distributed for free, the developers use advertising as a way of defraying their costs. It's still adware in the sense that you see advertisements, but it's neither covert nor malicious in its intent. If you don't want to see the ads, you can simply stop using the program. Some ad-supported programs also offer an ad-free, paid mode.

Most covert adware is also spyware, and like other spyware, it typically arrives on your computer by way of another form of malware.

Keystroke loggers

A *keystroke logger*, or *keylogger*, is a program that — you're going to be shocked, I know — logs your keystrokes. So, everything you type, no matter where you type it, gets put into a big text file. Because this file doesn't show the text in context (a paragraph in a word-processing document, a username in a form field, an address in your email client, and so on), it might not look very readable or useful. But someone examining this log could read every password, credit card number, serial number, or other private piece of information you've typed, not to mention the contents of anything you typed into an email message or a web form. Keyloggers that send this information over the Internet without your knowledge are a very dangerous sort of malware that can lead to identity theft.

I should point out, however, that keyloggers aren't inherently evil. For example, parents may install keyloggers to monitor their children's activities, and writers who have suffered one too many crashes of Microsoft Word, resulting in lost hours of typing, may use this software to provide an alternative way of getting their work back. Keyloggers can also enable people who use their Macs in shared environments to see what, if anything, other people have been doing with their Macs. In other words, the underlying activity itself is neutral, but it can be used for either good or bad purposes.

Numerous keyloggers for Mac OS X are commercially available — all intended to be put to entirely legitimate uses. Some examples include:

- Aobo Mac OS X Keylogger (www.parental-controls-software.net/mac-keylogger-perfect-keylogger-for-mac-os-x.htm, $79.95)
- Perfect Keylogger for Mac (www.blazingtools.com/mac_keylogger.html, $34.95)
- Spector Pro (www.spectorsoft.com/products/Spector_Macintosh, $99.95)
- TypeAgent (www.typeagent.com, $29.95)

All these except TypeAgent can also take screenshots at regular intervals.

By the way, although this chapter is only about software, I'd be remiss if I didn't mention the existence of hardware keyloggers — devices that can be installed in one's computer or keyboard or placed inline between the two that record everything typed without any software involvement at all. Anti-malware programs offer no defense against such devices.

Rootkits

A *rootkit* isn't necessarily a specific program as such but rather a general term for any mechanism whereby malware can disguise itself to prevent detection — often, even by anti-malware programs. Early rootkits were designed to let unauthorized users obtain root access (that is, unfettered permission to change anything on the computer) without the knowledge of the computer's administrators, but today, the term is used more generally to describe any method of hiding the existence of malware or of system modifications that constitute a back door for an attacker. A rootkit can't grant itself root access in the first place, but if an administrative user can be tricked into installing malware that uses a rootkit, it can enable an attacker to assume root privileges later on. Any type of malware, including viruses, trojans, and worms, can spread — and then potentially be protected by — rootkits.

Macs as Malware Carriers

We've all heard of cases where someone is infected with a virus or bacteria and, although they don't get sick themselves (perhaps because of an especially strong immune system or a genetic anomaly), they instead act as carriers, passing on the illness to other people. In the digital world, the same thing can happen. A Windows virus or other malware can appear on your Mac but be unable to run or cause any damage because it wasn't designed to run on Mac OS X. However, if the malware finds its way from your Mac to someone running Windows, it can cause damage on their machine — and spread farther from there.

You may have noticed that I used vague, wishy-washy expressions such as "appear on your Mac" and "find its way" to another computer. But, in fact, any malware that's unable to run on your Mac is also unable to appear or spread by itself. So, what I'm really saying is that you could (presumably without realizing what you're doing) download malware, and you could then take some action that moves or copies it to someone else's computer. It can't "just happen," but you can, through ignorance, make it happen.

How might you do this? The most common way, by far, is to receive an email message containing a malware program as an attachment and then forward it to someone else. It probably goes without saying that email chain letters, get-rich-quick schemes, petitions, jokes, and other such messages that beg to be forwarded are likely sources of such malware. Another frequent source of malware is peer-to-peer file-sharing services, such as BitTorrent — especially when used for pirated media and software. You may think you're getting a movie, album, or application, but lots of widely shared media contains malware too. By sharing (or *seeding*) such files, you help to spread the malware to computers that may be more vulnerable than yours.

It's fair to ask whether you should even care about this. I've heard it argued more than once that malware protection is, by its nature, each individual's responsibility. So, if you pass on a virus to a Windows user who's foolish enough not to run software that can filter it out, that's not your problem. Others say that the malware ecosystem depends on a steady supply of oblivious or uncaring people and that if more of us decided to be good citizens, we could put significant barriers in the overall ability of malware to spread.

I can't speak to the ethics of the question, but my personal opinion falls somewhere in the middle. I wouldn't, for example, run anti-spam or antivirus software on my Mac for the sole purpose of preventing it from becoming a carrier. However, I use anti-spam software because it serves my own needs, and if it also happens to help other people, then I'm happy to provide that service passively. Similarly, I practice common-sense malware avoidance strategies, as explained later in this chapter, and those undoubtedly have the effect of preventing the spread of a certain amount of malware as a side effect.

Assessing Your Mac's Vulnerability

As I've stated several times, Mac OS X's vulnerability to malware is limited by the very small number of malware programs that can run on a Mac. Although more could certainly appear, the small number of malicious programs, combined with Mac OS X's inherent security features, make it reasonably safe from most malware even if you don't change your habits (as I discuss in the next section) or install anti-malware programs (covered later in this chapter).

Nevertheless, the situation of each Mac and each Mac user is a bit different from the next. Although it's true on the one hand that Macs are resistant to malware and on the other hand that exceptionally virulent malware could find its way onto nearly any Mac, certain factors increase or decrease your risk. You can roughly assess your individual vulnerability by taking stock of how many risky activities you undertake and how often.

Some of the things that can put your Mac at greater risk from malware are the following:

- **Gullibility.** I mean no disrespect to innocent and trusting individuals, but if you're trying to protect your security and privacy, credulity does one a disservice. If you're prone to believe most of what you read, even if you don't know (and have a good reason to trust) the source, you're more likely than most people to unwittingly participate in the spread of malware.

- **Visiting unsavory sites.** You know the sorts of sites I'm talking about: those that traffic in porn, online gambling, unsanctioned medications, pirated media and software, and other products and services of dubious legal or ethical status. Websites of these types tend to hold a special attraction for malware distributors.

- **File sharing.** As I explained in the previous section, downloading commercial items you haven't paid for using BitTorrent or other similar file-sharing mechanisms is a good way to pick up malware.

- **Using outdated software.** If you tend to ignore software updates, especially for Mac OS X itself, you're turning down security patches that can significantly decrease your vulnerability to malware.

- **Downloading software from unknown sources.** Most software you can download from the web is perfectly safe. But trojans in particular depend, for their distribution, on gullible people (see the first point) downloading and installing software, often from unsavory sites (see the second point). If you stick with the official sites of well-known software developers and vendors or sites that check all downloads for malware (such as www.macupdate.com and www.version-tracker.com), you're in good shape; but if you randomly download any software that looks interesting from any and every website, not so much. The same goes for software received from unknown sources via email, instant messaging, and other means.

- **Turning off security features and warnings.** Mac OS X includes a number of features (discussed throughout this book) designed to warn you against potential security problems or block undesirable content or network access. You can disable most of these features and warnings or leave those off that aren't turned on by default, but you do so at your own peril.

- **Reusing passwords.** If you have just one password (or a few) that you use for everything — logging in to your Mac, checking your bank accounts online, booking plane tickets, and so on — you have a higher-than-normal risk of suffering because of malware. Why? The more often you use a given password, the more likely it is to be captured by a keylogger or other spyware. Once the bad guys have your password, they can easily try it with a long list of popular sites and services. In other words, if the same password works in multiple places, the end result can be greater and broader damage.

Cross-Ref

For more on choosing good passwords and how to remember them, see Chapter 6. ■

- **Running a web server.** When you run a web server on your Mac, you invite (implicitly or explicitly) millions of people around the world to connect to your Mac over the Internet, making it more visible than it otherwise would be. Although serving plain HTML pages poses virtually no risk, web-based forms and dynamic sites that use PHP or other scripting languages provide additional avenues by which someone could attack your Mac. The same is true of other Internet services you can run on your Mac, such as FTP servers or remote login support.

Cross-Ref

For more on web server security, see Chapters 18 (for web servers running on the standard version of Mac OS X) and 30 (for web servers running on Mac OS X Server). ■

- **Working for the wrong employer or in the wrong profession.** I'm not saying there's anything wrong (ethically or morally) with working for a major bank, the government, a defense contractor, or (to pick a computer firm completely at random) Apple. What I am saying is that employees of certain companies or people who work in certain fields probably have information on their computers that would be especially valuable to an attacker — a thief, a foreign government, or an industrial spy. So, if you're such a person or work in such an industry, your Mac (especially if it's a laptop not currently connected to your company's internal network) makes an appealing target for malware and can result in especially serious data losses.

If few (or none) of these items describe you and if you also take most or all of the measures described in the next section, you're in extremely good shape and as unlikely as anyone to fall victim to malware. If, however, you do find that some of these items aptly describe you, your vulnerability is higher, and you should take appropriately stronger measures — which generally means installing and turning up the security settings on heavy-duty anti-malware software.

Common-Sense Malware Protection

The question of whether the average Mac user needs to install anti-malware software has been, for years, the subject of intense debate among industry authorities and pundits. Most Mac experts I know say it's unnecessary — and indeed a waste of time, money, and CPU cycles — unless your employer or some legal constraint requires you to install such software or you participate in high-risk computing (as described in the previous section).

Nevertheless, it's a tricky question to answer because there's so little Mac malware in the wild right now but no logical reason there couldn't be more (and worse) malware out there in the future. If the day comes when a nasty virus starts spreading rapidly among the world's Macs, it could very well be the paranoid and overcautious among us who escape unscathed, while the experts curse themselves for their carelessness. On the other hand, that day may never come, and in the meantime, you'll be spending money on annual software upgrades, waiting for disk scans to complete, and cluttering up your Mac with something that may have no real-world effect on your security.

My professional opinion, after working in the Mac world for more than 15 years and after considerable study and contemplation, is that almost everyone can protect themselves from almost every potential malware threat by adopting the following common-sense habits:

- **Use a NAT gateway.** If you connect directly to the Internet, by which I mean your Mac has its own publicly routable IP address (whether static or not), then, in theory, any other computer on the Internet can directly contact yours. And one of the reasons they may do so is to try to install malware or to communicate with malware that's already present. On the other hand, if you connect through a NAT gateway or router, such that the outside world sees the gateway's IP address, while within the network your Mac has a different, private address, then outside computers can, by default, contact only the gateway — not your computer specifically. Now, there are ways around this, and I don't mean to misrepresent a NAT as a magical or impenetrable barrier, but it's a reasonably effective first step. Luckily, the majority of DSL and cable modems are preconfigured to function as NAT routers and indeed many can't be used in any other way.

Cross-Ref

For more on NAT, see Chapter 15. For more on wireless security, see Chapter 16. ■

- **Turn on your firewall.** Mac OS X includes not one but two serviceable built-in firewalls, and if you find those to be inadequate for any reason, you can find a number of third-party choices. In any case, a firewall is another, much more powerful and flexible tool for keeping undesirable network traffic away from your Mac. It can close most of the holes a NAT gateway leaves and is especially important to use if you don't connect to the Internet using NAT.

Cross-Ref

For more on firewalls, see Chapter 17. ■

- **Stay up to date.** Malware works its dirty deeds by exploiting bugs and security holes in one's operating system or other software. Keeping all your software — especially Mac OS X itself — up to date with the latest fixes and security patches can plug the holes that enable malware to cause damage.
- **Use spam filtering.** One of the most common methods by which malware travels from one computer to another is in the form of email attachments. Most modern spam-filtering software also identifies malware and automatically prevents it from reaching your inbox.

Cross-Ref

For more on various options for stopping spam, see Chapter 9. ■

- **Be suspicious.** Before you click a link, advertisement, or download button — in an email message or on a web page — take a moment to consider the source. Do you know and trust whoever sent the message or created the website? Although you can rarely have 100% certainty about the provenance of a program, link, or web page, some neighborhoods online are seedier and less confidence-inspiring than others. If you have doubts about something, stay away until you can independently verify its legitimacy. If you refuse to cooperate with the bad guys who are trying to get you to download their malware-in-disguise, you've made a major step in protecting yourself.
- **Pay attention to warnings.** Safari and Firefox are configured by default to warn you when you visit a site that's known to contain malware. In addition, Snow Leopard checks for a limited range of malware when you open disk images that were downloaded via popular browsers, email programs, or iChat, and warns you if a download is known to be dangerous. Although these warnings don't cover every type of malware or every way it might get onto your Mac, it certainly pays to heed these warnings if they appear!

Cross-Ref

For more on the ways browsers and Snow Leopard warn you about potential malware, see Chapter 10. ∎

- **Use a password manager.** Whenever you type a password, you expose it to any keystroke-logging software that may be installed on your computer. Although there are other fine ways of avoiding such software, an extra precaution to avoid typing any keystrokes that a logger can intercept is to use your browser's form-filling feature or a third-party password manager, such as 1Password, to fill in passwords for you.

In the overwhelming majority of cases, if you faithfully do all these, your need to run anti-malware software is practically nonexistent.

Choosing Anti-Malware Software

Having taken all the preceding into account, if you feel that an automated approach to blocking, uninstalling, or scanning for possible signs of malware is the best approach — or if your employer or some legal requirement demands it but gives you a choice of which software to use — you have several good options. Although anti-malware programs on the Mac aren't as numerous as on Windows (which is only appropriate given how much lower the threat is), there are a number of products in this category with various combinations of features that may serve your needs.

Factors to consider

I wish I could say that one anti-malware program is as good as the next, allowing you to simply pick the one with the lowest price or the prettiest icon or some other easily discernable feature. But despite the fact that most of these programs share several traits in common, there's a great deal of variation among them, and your experience may be much more pleasant with some than with others.

Before you commit to or pay for an anti-malware program, I recommend that you download a trial copy, install it, figure out how to use all its features, and see how it works for a couple of weeks. More likely than not, the program won't actually discover any malware during that time, but you'll be able to tell how stable, speedy, and convenient the software is.

Among the factors you should keep in mind as you're selecting and trying out anti-malware software are the following:

- **Thoroughness.** Most anti-malware programs detect and eliminate the full range of malicious software (even if their names mention only virus), but a few focus only on Trojan horses, keystroke loggers, and other spyware. If spyware is your only concern, it's perfectly fine to use one of these, but keep in mind that it won't protect you against a virus or worm.

- **Prevention versus cleanup.** Most anti-malware programs can delete malicious programs and repair or undo the damage they caused. However, it's far better to prevent damage from occurring in the first place because not all damaged files can be recovered — and between infection and eradication, the malware has a chance to spread to other computers, send out spam, deliver your personal information to hackers, and cause other trouble. Ideally, you want both capabilities: *on-demand scanning*, in which the program looks at your entire disk or the folders you specify, searching for malware; and *on-access scanning*, in which the software looks for tell-tale signs of malware as you download or open files or when you mount a new volume on your Mac.

- **Performance.** All this scanning can take a long time, and if you have millions of files on your Mac, that's to be expected. But some programs are better than others at efficiently scanning files and watching for suspicious behavior — doing so quickly and without slowing down the other things you're doing on your Mac any more than absolutely necessary. Anti-malware software that bogs down your Mac so much that it interferes with your ordinary work and play is just asking to be turned off, at which point you lose the protection it provides.

- **Intrusiveness.** In addition to raw performance is how quietly or overtly software goes about its scanning. Some anti-malware programs focus on alerting you about every action they perform, making sure you're always aware of how safe they're keeping you — but doing so by producing an endless succession of pop-up windows, sounds, or other distracting notifications. Others stay out of your way, working silently in the background most of the time and alerting you only when something particularly important occurs. I, for one, prefer to avoid interruptions and alerts whenever possible, so I'm turned off by programs whose default settings make them highly intrusive.

- **Definitions and heuristics.** Because harmful software usually goes out of its way to avoid detection, anti-malware software usually relies on technical descriptions of particular pieces of known malware called *signatures* or *definitions* that enable the software to identify malicious programs — even though they may have misleading names, be stored in unusual locations, or disguise their nature in some other way. As new malware is discovered, new definitions are created, and as long as your anti-malware program has up-to-date definitions, it should be able to clear all the latest threats. Most programs let you download these updated definitions automatically on a schedule, which is a very good thing. However, it's always possible that you'll encounter some novel malware for which no definition yet exists. To guard against that possibility, some anti-malware programs include *heuristics* that look for the sorts of suspicious behavior that often indicate malicious activity — letting them block certain kinds of malware even if you're unlucky enough to be the first victim ever!

- **Reputation.** Beyond a program's effectiveness at stopping any particular piece of malware, you should consider the reputation of the company that sells it. I've heard about both good and less-than-admirable business practices from most of the developers of Mac anti-malware products. But what I care most about in this context is how efficient the companies are at identifying new threats and providing updates rapidly that can wipe them out. Whatever else you can say about the five leading developers listed here (Intego, Kapersky, McAfee, Sophos, and Symantec), it's clear that they have dedicated teams of smart, skilled researchers working hard to keep their customers' computers safe. If push came to shove, I'd feel more confident about one of those companies' products protecting my Mac from a major new virus than a product from a lesser-known developer.

ClamXav

ClamXav (www.clamxav.com) is a free anti-malware program based on the open-source ClamAV scanning engine. It's designed primarily to find and eliminate Unix malware (much of which, of course, could affect Macs too, based as they are on Unix). However, because the ClamAV database contains few if any definitions for Mac-specific malware, the program may miss viruses, trojans, worms, and other such programs that were designed expressly for Mac OS X. Although the underlying malware-scanning software is open source and maintained by a group of contributors, ClamXav itself is created and maintained by a single person named Mark Allan. For that reason, users of ClamXav may not receive the level of technical support or responsiveness to newly released threats that would be possible with commercial anti-malware programs.

Those qualifications aside, ClamXav, whose rather minimalist interface is shown in Figure 14.1, has most of the features found in the other products I describe here. It can scan your files as well as download updated malware definitions on demand (manually or on a schedule); in addition, it can optionally scan newly inserted media and watch designated folders (such as your Downloads folder) for the appearance of malware. When malware is found, ClamXav can quarantine or delete the infected files.

FIGURE 14.1

There's not much to see here, but this simple interface makes it much easier to use the ClamAV malware-scanning engine than the command line would.

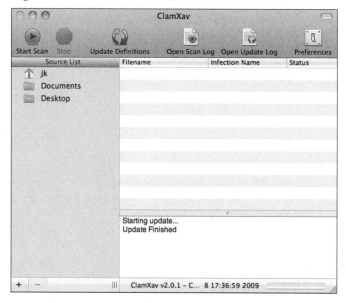

Intego VirusBarrier, Internet Security Barrier, and NetBarrier

Intego, a major developer of security software for the Mac (and, to a lesser extent, Windows), is based in Paris but also maintains offices in the United States and Japan. I've mentioned Intego's products for backing up your Mac, stopping spam, and protecting web browsing elsewhere in this book. So, it should come as no surprise that an anti-malware program is among their offerings. The product is called VirusBarrier (www.intego.com/VirusBarrier), and it's available by itself for $69.95 or in either of two Internet Security Barrier bundles (www.intego.com/isb/). The Backup Edition of this bundle ($99.95) includes VirusBarrier, NetBarrier, and Personal Backup; the Antispam Edition ($89.95) includes VirusBarrier, NetBarrier, and Personal Antispam.

VirusBarrier, shown in Figure 14.2, is a thorough, capable anti-malware program. It offers on-demand (manual or scheduled) and on-access scanning, which occurs as files are opened or saved. The program can also scan volumes when they're mounted and provides the option to exclude certain items from scanning.

You can update malware definitions manually or, using the included NetUpdate program, on a schedule. However, after the first year, you must pay an additional annual fee — or upgrade your software — to download the latest definition files. In normal operation, VirusBarrier is largely invisible, alerting you only when it's found a problem or when an update is available.

Another Intego program, NetBarrier (`www.intego.com/netbarrier`, $49.95), discussed in several other contexts in this book, also includes one particular anti-malware feature. The Trojans module, shown in Figure 14.3, watches for network activity matching a list of known Trojan horses, alerting you (and blocking the program's network access) when suspicious access occurs. You can individually enable or disable monitoring for any of the trojan behaviors in the list, but additions or updates to the list come only from Intego's software updates.

Cross-Ref

For more on NetBarrier's features for protecting web browsing, see Chapter 10. ∎

FIGURE 14.2

The interface for configuring and manually running VirusBarrier is rather flashy. But when the software is running in the background, you rarely see anything at all.

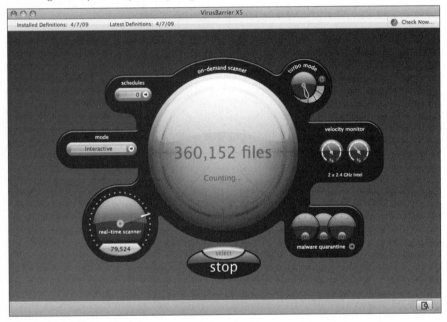

FIGURE 14.3

NetBarrier's Trojans module includes definitions for a number of common Trojan horses and can identify them by their network behavior.

iAntiVirus

PC Tools, a company that makes — you guessed it — PC utility software, offers a single Mac program called iAntiVirus (www.pctools.com/iantivirus). Surprisingly, though, it's not a part of their Windows antivirus software. In fact, it doesn't even scan for Windows malware. It was designed from scratch to look and act like a proper Mac application and to find and eliminate Mac-specific malware exclusively. It has a simple and clean user interface, as shown in Figure 14.4, and is among the least intrusive and resource-hungry Mac anti-malware programs. Best of all, it's free for personal use. For business use or if you want the option of getting technical support by telephone, you pay $29.95.

Like most other anti-malware programs, iAntiVirus can perform manual or scheduled on-demand scans; it also monitors new files for malware. You can choose where you want the program to scan and whether you want the scans to include running processes. Malware definitions can be updated automatically on a user-definable schedule.

FIGURE 14.4

For a PC company, PC Tools did themselves proud with this elegant preference pane for controlling iAntiVirus.

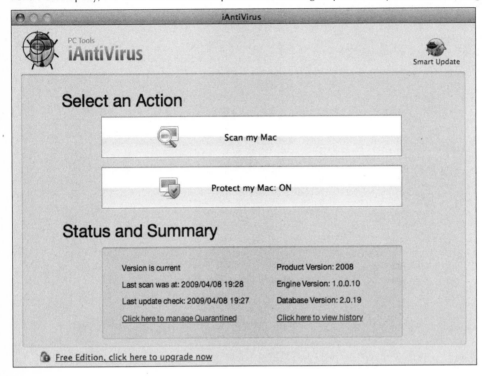

Internet Cleanup

Smith Micro's Internet Cleanup suite (www.smithmicro.com/default.tpl?group=product_full&sku=MIC5CD, $29.95) includes a tool called SpyAlert, shown in Figure 14.5, that's designed to find spyware, such as keystroke loggers. It doesn't locate viruses, worms, or other malware. When SpyAlert finds spyware, you can delete it or isolate it to prevent it from sending out personal information. Like other Internet Cleanup modules, SpyAlert can be run on demand or scheduled to run at intervals of your choice, but it doesn't watch your system in real time for newly downloaded spyware.

Cross-Ref

For more on Internet Cleanup, see Chapter 10. ■

FIGURE 14.5

The SpyAlert component of Internet Cleanup lets you scan your Mac for spyware.

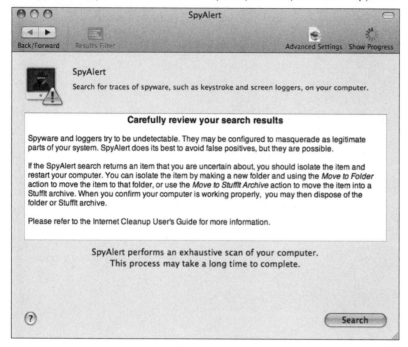

Kaspersky Anti-Virus for Mac

The latest company to offer anti-malware software for the Mac is Kaspersky, whose products have long been available on Windows. Kaspersky Anti-Virus for Mac (`www.kaspersky.com/kaspersky-anti-virus-for-mac`, $59.95) has features comparable to other software in this section, but because there is so little Mac malware, the company claims one of its biggest advantages is preventing your Mac from transferring malware to Windows users.

MacScan

Like Internet Cleanup (and unlike most of the products in this section), SecureMac's MacScan (`http://macscan.securemac.com/`, $29.99) doesn't look for viruses, worms, and every other kind of malware under the sun. Instead, this program focuses exclusively on eradicating spyware. According to the definition MacScan uses, malicious programs, such as Trojan horses, keystroke loggers, and remote administration programs, count as spyware, as do tracking cookies. Although programs such as worms and viruses could be used to spy on you too, the company doesn't claim that it rids your computer of all malware.

Note

MacScan can find and clear not only tracking cookies but browsing history, caches, and other temporary files you encounter while using the web, as I discuss in Chapter 10. ■

MacScan's simple, straightforward interface, shown in Figure 14.6, lets you perform manual or scheduled checks — of your entire disk (a full scan), your home folder (a quick scan), or the folder of your choice (a custom scan). The program can be set to automatically download updated spyware and tracking cookie definitions.

FIGURE 14.6

MacScan, focused as it is on spyware alone, has a clean, uncluttered interface with only a few options to configure.

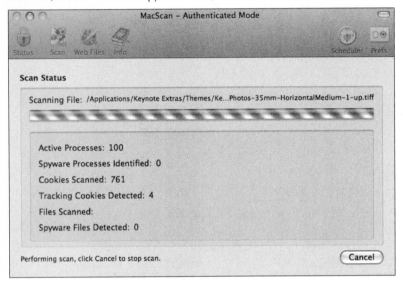

McAfee VirusScan

Several years ago, Apple offered a free antivirus program called Virex to all members of .Mac (as MobileMe was formerly known). That program, developed by security giant McAfee, later morphed into McAfee VirusScan (www.mcafee.com/us/enterprise/products/anti_virus/file_servers_desktops/virex.html) and in the process changed its character from a consumer program to an enterprise program. Although you can still buy VirusScan easily online, the minimum quantity is now three licenses (which cost $36.55 each for up to 25 units; the price goes down at larger volumes).

On the plus side, VirusScan, shown in Figure 14.7, is a capable program with a wide range of features and is well-supported by a company with tremendous antivirus expertise. You can scan files on demand (manually or on a schedule), and on-access scanning can be triggered when reading files, writing files, or both. Users can exclude specific files, folders, or volumes they don't want to have scanned. User-configurable preferences for virus-scanning behavior are quite thorough.

In addition to removing viruses and cleaning or deleting infected files, VirusScan offers a range of options for notifying you when it's found something troubling. Malware definition files can be delivered automatically according to a schedule you set, but the program can also scan for virus-like characteristics, enabling it to catch certain kinds of new malware for which definitions haven't yet been created.

On the minus side, VirusScan tends to be resource-intensive when scanning, especially when performing on-demand scans, so those are best scheduled for times when you're not actively using your Mac. Anecdotal evidence suggests that VirusScan may not be the most effective or reliable antivirus product and that technical support may be inadequate.

FIGURE 14.7

VirusScan's small control window, which you use only for manual scans and configuring preferences, is easy to understand. The large, friendly Start button is usually all you need to click.

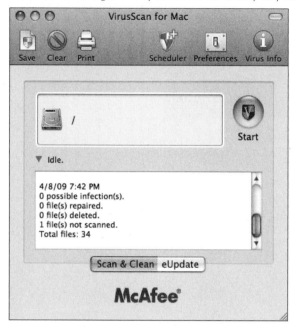

Norton AntiVirus for Mac

Symantec is one of the biggest names in computer security, and their Norton brand is well-known on both Windows and Mac platforms. Norton AntiVirus for Mac (`www.symantec.com/norton/macintosh/antivirus`) is available as a $49.95 stand-alone product or as part of the Norton Internet Security bundle ($79.95), which also includes a firewall and web-browsing protection software.

Norton AntiVirus, whose main window is shown in Figure 14.8, has pretty much every anti-malware feature you could ask for. It can perform manual or scheduled scans of any or all of the volumes mounted on your computer; you can manually exclude items you don't want it to scan or have it scan only in specific places. It can optionally scan most types of compressed files and offers automatic updating of malware definition files. When it finds an infection, Norton AntiVirus removes the malware, attempts to repair infected files, and quarantines any that can't be repaired.

By default, Norton AntiVirus scans every new or modified file — anything you download (from the web, in an email message, or via instant messaging), create, or modify — although you can modify this behavior to suit your needs. It can also automatically scan new volumes as they're mounted, including optical disks, disk images, iPods, external drives, and so on (again, you can specify what should or should not be automatically scanned). This scanning isn't invisible though; a window like the one shown in Figure 14.9 pops up whenever a scan is taking place. A vulnerability scanner also monitors your Mac for tell-tale signs of network access by spyware and other malware designed to exploit bugs and security holes in Mac OS X and popular third-party software.

Although I can't fault Norton AntiVirus for its flexibility or robustness, I found it to be among the most intrusive of the anti-malware programs I tried; it seemed as though something was always popping up on-screen to tell me that the program was scanning something. In addition, scans were often time-consuming and resulted in a perceptible slowdown of the computer while they were taking place.

FIGURE 14.8

Norton AntiVirus displays statistics and settings in this window, which also lets you scan your Mac's disk manually.

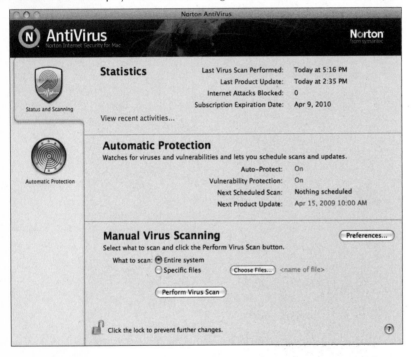

FIGURE 14.9

Assuming you use Norton AntiVirus's default settings, you see a window like this every time you mount a new volume, and it can take some time to disappear.

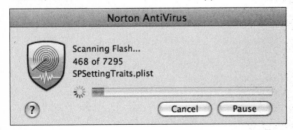

Sophos Anti-Virus

Of all the anti-malware programs discussed in this book, Sophos Anti-Virus (www.sophos.com/products/ enterprise/endpoint/security-and-control/8.0/mac) is by far the one most oriented toward enterprise use. If you're managing hundreds of Macs, that's a good thing because the software is designed for centralized installation, configuration, and updates on a corporate network. However, Sophos's licensing and distribution policies make this product a nonstarter for individuals and families. Not only is the minimum purchase three licenses, but you can't even buy those directly; you must locate and contact one of the company's distribution partners, request a quote, and go through a much more complicated procedure to obtain the software than simply clicking a few buttons in your web browser and typing a credit card number. Pricing depends on volume, license duration, and which specific edition of the software (or a bundle including other programs) you choose, and the company doesn't publicize its suggested pricing.

Those caveats aside, Sophos is a well-known and reputable supplier of security software, and Sophos Anti-Virus includes all the basics. It supports both on-demand and on-access scans, and users can exclude items that shouldn't be scanned. When the program finds malware, it removes it and tries to disinfect any files that have been modified. You can decide whether the program moves, copies, or deletes any infected files that could not be disinfected.

The Sophos Anti-Virus interface consists of two main parts: a stand-alone application, shown in Figure 14.10, whose old-school look and feel provides a functional, if not especially pretty, way to run manual scans. The program also adds a modern-looking pane to System Preferences for configuring background behavior; you can access either component using a system-wide menu.

FIGURE 14.10

It's not the most modern or elegant design, but it's serviceable: Click the play or stop button to start or stop a manual scan in Sophos Anti-Virus.

Trend Micro Smart Surfing for Mac

A more recent entrant into the Mac anti-malware game, Trend Micro's Smart Surfing for Mac (http:// us.trendmicro.com/us/products/personal/smartsurfing-mac/, $49.95) has a basic but serviceable malware scanner that can run in any of the usual modes (scheduled, on-demand, on-access, or manual). Because the program doesn't have a long track record, I can't make meaningful comments about its effectiveness or reliability.

Using Outbound Firewalls

Scanning the files on your disk (and new ones you download) is an effective way to locate known malware, eradicate it, and, in many cases, undo the damage it may have caused. However, one particular category of malware — spyware — has a sufficiently broad and vague definition that you could easily have programs installed that covertly send out information you'd prefer to keep private, even though the programs themselves wouldn't typically be considered illegitimate. If you're especially cautious (or paranoid), you might want to consider using special software that can watch for outgoing connections and either block you or alert you. Programs that can do this are known as *outbound firewalls* because they monitor connections your Mac initiates with other computers on the Internet, as opposed to conventional firewalls, which monitor inbound traffic from other computers trying to contact your Mac.

Although I understand the spirit of wanting to be fully in control of all information your Mac sends out to destinations unknown, I must admit to having a strong negative bias against outbound firewalls. It's true that such a program could identify a covert trojan or keystroke logger sending out your passwords or an ordinary application "phoning home," sending its developer details about your computer, your location, and other potentially personal details. However, in practice, much more than 99.9% of outbound Internet traffic is completely aboveboard and useful — it's there for a good reason. Having to respond to an alert whenever a program tries to access the Internet (even if it's just the first occasion, after which you approve future connections) is incredibly intrusive, especially because the number of programs that do this is extremely high, as is the frequency with which they do it. Outbound firewalls, in my experience, are more effective at creating fear and suspicion and distracting you from using your Mac normally than providing a useful service.

Consider just how common it is for software to contact another computer over the Internet. Among the many programs that make outbound Internet connections frequently in the course of normal operation are components of Mac OS X that handle MobileMe syncing and iDisk access; Skype, iChat, and other instant messaging and VoIP programs; Time Machine, when used over a network; online backup and file synchronization programs such as Dropbox, CrashPlan, and SugarSync; Apple's Software Update and the built-in software update mechanisms of countless other programs; Microsoft Office; anti-malware programs downloading new malware definitions; and, of course, your web browsers, email programs, and other conventional Internet software. In fact, virtually every utility designed to protect your privacy and security must itself access the Internet in order to do its job. The mere process of agreeing to exceptions for so many programs may actually make it more difficult to notice the extremely rare program that's trying to send out information it shouldn't.

With that enormous disclaimer out of the way, allow me to present four samples of the outbound firewall genre for your consideration.

Little Snitch

Probably the best-known outgoing firewall, Little Snitch (`www.obdev.at/products/littlesnitch`, $29.95) — unlike the others in this list — serves only this one purpose, instead of being a module in a suite of other Internet utilities. After you install it and restart your Mac, Little Snitch alerts you, by default, every time your Mac attempts to make an outbound Internet connection by displaying an alert like the one in Figure 14.11 (but showing the icon of the application making the request). You can then, with a click or two, choose to allow or deny the application access — just this once, until the application quits, or forever. At the same time, you can also decide how broadly to apply the rule you're creating that governs the application's behavior (restricting the application to communicating only with a particular server, only on a given port, both, or neither).

Note

The very first time you restart your Mac after installing Little Snitch, you may encounter a dozen or more alerts like this in a row, which is also true of other outbound firewalls. After you approve access for your most commonly used applications, the rate of alerts should slow down dramatically. ■

Little Snitch includes a number of preconfigured rules to allow outgoing access from some applications (such as Safari) and for any application communicating with other computers on your local network. As you approve or deny requests, that list of rules, shown in Figure 14.12, grows; you can also add or modify rules manually at any time.

FIGURE 14.11

Alert windows like this one, each showing the icon of the application requesting Internet access, appear frequently when running Little Snitch.

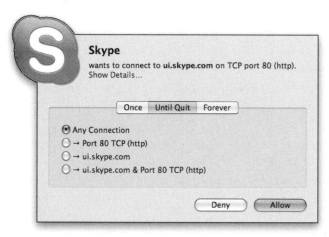

FIGURE 14.12

Little Snitch's main window displays a list of rules for allowing or blocking outbound Internet connections. You can add rules manually or by responding to automatic alerts.

NetBarrier

Yet another module of Intego's NetBarrier (www.intego.com/netbarrier, $49.95), which keeps popping up in this book, is Anti-Spyware. It doesn't scan your disk for spyware, as the company's VirusBarrier software does. Instead, it's an outbound firewall.

Anti-Spyware's default settings are quite liberal; you must explicitly tell it if, how, and to what extent you want it to intrude on your Mac's Internet communication. Intego recommends that you begin by manually adding applications to its list, as shown in Figure 14.13. For each application, you can allow or deny all outgoing access, allow or block access on a particular port, or ask to be prompted when the application tries to access the Internet (and you can decide whether the default behavior should be to block or allow access if you don't respond to the request within a reasonable time).

After configuring settings for your most commonly used applications, you can choose what action Anti-Spyware should take with other applications (or other types of requests by applications on your list) — again, you have the same options: allow, deny, ask but allow on timeout, and ask but deny on timeout. If you choose one of the ask options, an alert appears on-screen (by default, accompanied by a slightly scary buzzing sound), giving you buttons to allow or deny that request. Whichever choice you make, Anti-Spyware adds the application to its list, with your preferred setting.

FIGURE 14.13

For each application you've listed in NetBarrier's Anti-Spyware module, you can specify in what ways it's permitted to access the Internet.

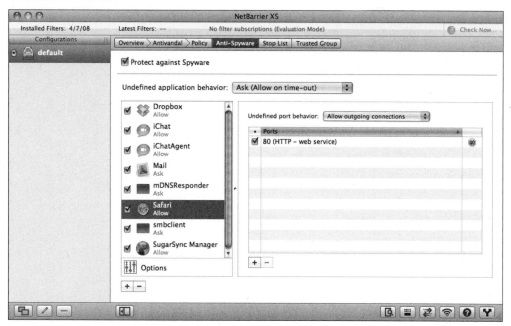

Norton Firewall for Mac

Norton Firewall, part of Norton Internet Security for Mac (www.symantec.com/norton/macintosh/internet-security, $79.99), can monitor both incoming and outgoing connections. The former feature is called Connection Blocking, whereas the outbound firewall is referred to as Application Blocking. Much like the other utilities in this list, Application Blocking lets you specify certain applications for which outbound access is allowed or denied, as shown in Figure 14.14. If an application not already on the list tries to access the Internet, an alert like the one in Figure 14.15 appears. Click Block or Allow to determine how this particular connection should be handled; to add your selection to the program's permanent list so you won't be prompted about future connections, click the Don't ask again for this application check box before clicking Block or Allow.

Cross-Ref

For more on Norton Firewall's inbound firewall features, see Chapter 17. ∎

FIGURE 14.14

Norton Firewall's Application Blocking module is an outbound firewall. This dialog box shows applications for which you've configured (allowed or blocked) outgoing Internet access.

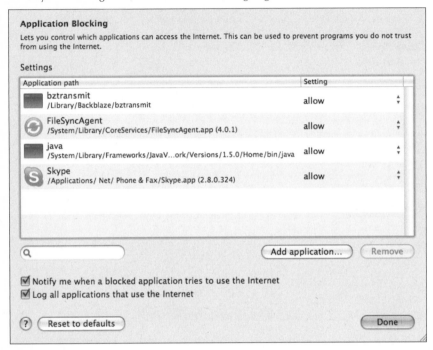

FIGURE 14.15

When an application not already on the Application Blocking list attempts outbound Internet access, a window like this one prompts you to decide how to handle the request.

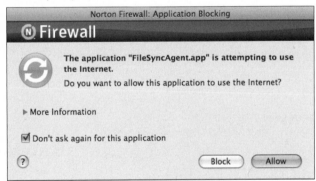

Internet Cleanup

Last but not least is Network SpyAlert, a component of Smith Micro's Internet Cleanup suite (www. smithmicro.com/default.tpl?group=product_full&sku=MIC5CD, $29.95). The outbound firewall feature of Network SpyAlert, called Program Control, is shown in Figure 14.16. As usual, you provide a list of applications, along with specifications for how they may or may not access the Internet, and when outbound access not matching one of your rules is attempted, you're prompted to approve or decline the request — adding that application to either list, with the settings you selected. Network SpyAlert provides extensive control over application behavior by name, port, protocol, and destination address.

FIGURE 14.16

Internet Cleanup's Network Spy Alert, like the other programs mentioned in this section, lets you specify outgoing Internet access privileges for each application.

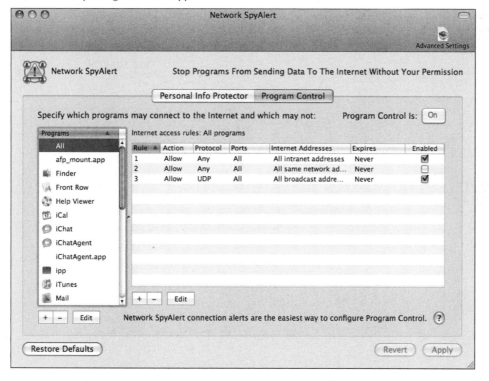

What Anti-Malware Software Can't Do

As you know from reading the rest of this chapter, I generally consider common sense a better way of protecting oneself from malicious software than anti-malware software. Without question, though, there's a place for anti-malware programs because they make up for a certain amount of human error and may protect your Mac against as-yet unimagined threats. But don't let the fact that a program is frequently scanning your disk for malware lull you into a false sense of security. Even the most sophisticated anti-malware program can't protect you against every conceivable danger.

Here are some examples of things anti-malware can't do:

- **Catch everything.** Even with the most up-to-date malware definitions and the most clever heuristics, it's conceivable that your anti-malware program will miss a particularly clever or insidious virus designed explicitly to avoid common forms of protection. Unlikely? Very much so. But not impossible. Likewise, even among the top anti-malware programs, differences in design could lead one program to overlook a virus that another one catches.

- **Protect you from yourself.** If you tell your anti-malware program not to scan a certain folder because it takes too much time, then, ipso facto, that folder becomes a potential safe haven for malware — especially if it happens to be, or contain, your `~/Downloads` folder, your `/System` folder, or your `/Library` folder. Similarly, if you turn off on-access scanning or other features that are intrusive or slow down your Mac, then however justified you may be in wanting to put the software in its place, you're also opening security holes. A determined (or simply inattentive) user can prevent even the best security program from doing its job!

- **Read your mind.** People differ tremendously as to what they consider spam, advertising, and spying, and anti-malware programs also differ in how they define such things. There's no guarantee that your idea of malware matches up perfectly with your software's, so it may report false positives, false negatives, or both. In addition, if you've installed parental monitoring or keystroke-logging software to serve legitimate needs, your anti-malware software may assume that it was put there without your knowledge and try to block it.

In short, if your situation demands the use of anti-malware software, by all means use it, but bear in mind the limits of its capabilities, and make sure you have good backups in place that you can fall back on if unrecoverable damage from malware does occur.

Securing Windows on a Mac

Now that Macs use Intel processors, it's easier than ever before to run Windows on your Mac — either using Apple's dual-boot Boot Camp solution or side by side with Mac OS X using a virtualization program, such as Parallels Desktop, VMware Fusion, or Sun's VirtualBox. Whether it's playing games or running business software, all these Windows-on-Mac scenarios let you do things that a few years ago would have required having a PC on your desk or using painfully slow emulation software, such as Virtual PC.

Along with all the benefits that come from being able to run the vast number of Windows-only programs out there comes a risk: Most of the world's malware is also designed exclusively for Windows! At minimum, therefore, you should take steps to protect your Windows installation against these outside threats, just as you would if you were running Windows on a PC. In addition, depending on which software you install and how you have it configured, you may expose your Mac's files and resources to threats from Windows-based malware, so you should be aware of the dangers and the techniques you can use to mitigate them.

Security risks with Boot Camp and virtualization software

With Boot Camp, you create a new volume on your Mac just for your Windows installation, and when you boot into Windows, your Mac OS X volume is read-only (in Snow Leopard; in Leopard, it's not visible at all). The downside of this arrangement is that you have to go through extra, sometimes awkward, steps to share files between the two platforms. But the benefit is that even if your Windows installation were to become infected with some atrocious malware, the worst it could do is damage the files on your Windows volume; Mac OS X itself and all the rest of the files on your Mac volume would be untouched. Although you should take reasonable precautions to protect your Windows installation itself (as I discuss ahead), you need not worry that Windows malware will take out your Mac.

I'm aware of two programs that aim to make file sharing easier by enabling Windows to see and interact with any Mac-formatted volumes connected to your system. One is called MacDrive (`www.mediafour.com/products/macdrive/`, $49.95), and the other — which also lets Mac OS X access NTFS-formatted Windows volumes for both reading and writing — is Paragon Software's NTFS for Mac OS X (`www.paragon-software.com/home/ntfs-mac/`, $39.95). If you have one of these programs installed, then regardless of its benefits for file sharing, you also incur a greater risk: Malware can potentially read, delete, or damage any file on any volume mounted on your computer. You should therefore take extra precautions, such as installing Windows anti-malware software.

The situation with virtualization software is a bit different. Ordinarily, your Windows installation lives on a special disk image. When you run Windows in a virtualization program, it treats that image as a hard disk, but as far as your Mac is concerned, it's just another file. So, once again, by default, Windows software has access to only your Windows volume, and any malware you encountered couldn't hurt the rest of the files on your Mac. However, in order to simplify sharing files between Mac OS X and Windows, all three major virtualization programs let you share folders or entire volumes from your Mac so that they appear in Windows (as local or network volumes, depending on the situation), and Windows software has, in most cases, unrestricted access to their files. When you do this, Windows malware can potentially cause damage to the items in the shared folders or volumes (although not elsewhere on your Mac).

Tip

I discuss sharing files between virtual machines and Mac OS X as well as go into much more detail about choosing and using Windows anti-malware software in my ebook *Take Control of Running Windows on a Mac* (`www.takecontrolbooks.com/windows-on-Mac`). ∎

Both Parallels Desktop and VMware Fusion can, if you choose, run an existing Boot Camp installation of Windows as a virtual machine instead of using a virtual disk. This arrangement is convenient for those who must sometimes run Windows in Boot Camp but at other times want access to their Windows software without having to reboot. In this configuration, you can choose to share any of your Mac's folders and volumes with Windows, just as when running a conventional virtual machine, so the same risks apply.

Protecting your Windows installation

Conventional wisdom says that anyone running any version of Windows on a computer connected to the Internet should use a firewall, at the very minimum, and preferably antivirus software too. In reality, the dangers of forgoing either or both of these precautions aren't as severe as they once were — partly because Windows itself has become much more secure in the last decade or so and partly because the majority of computers these days attached to home broadband routers use NAT, which provides a certain degree of protection against network intrusion.

Nevertheless, given the prevalence of viruses under Windows, a little extra caution never hurts. What follows is my suggested strategy, first for Boot Camp users and then for those using virtualization software.

Boot Camp strategy

Because Boot Camp requires at least Windows XP SP2, you're guaranteed to have a system that includes reasonable firewall settings and other basic security features that make it less prone to attack than any previous version. However, in general, newer versions of Windows are more secure still, so if you're committed to running XP, make sure you install Service Pack 3 (SP3). And if you can install Windows Vista or Windows 7, all the better; be sure to apply any available security updates.

Boot Camp doesn't natively provide a way to write to your Mac volumes unless you install third-party software, such as MacDrive or NTFS for Mac OS X. If you do, I suggest that it's worth the extra expense and bother to install Windows anti-malware software (see ahead).

In any case, I strongly suggest that you back up your Windows installation regularly. In general, Mac backup software won't back up your Windows volume, so your best bet is to use Windows backup software while running Boot Camp.

Virtualization strategy

When running Windows using virtualization software, your range of threats is slightly different, but you can take several measures to decrease your risk of being infected with malware and of passing the danger on to your Mac files if you do the following:

- **Use a modern version of Windows.** Because virtualization programs, unlike Boot Camp, can run old (and very insecure) versions of Windows, they provide the opportunity to expose yourself to unnecessary risk. If possible, use the newest version of Windows that will serve your needs and keep up to date with security patches.

- **Turn on your Windows firewall.** Newer versions of Windows have the system's built-in firewall turned on by default, which is as it should be. Because the firewall settings vary quite a bit from one version of Windows to another, check your online help for how to activate and configure the firewall in the version of Windows you're running.

- **Use NAT networking.** A virtual machine can use any of several methods to connect to the Internet. One way is to communicate directly to your router or gateway, getting its own IP address; this is typically called *bridged* networking. This setting provides the fastest network performance but increases your virtual machine's exposure, potentially making it more vulnerable to attack. A second way is called *host-only* networking; this means the guest operating system can communicate with the host (Mac OS X in this case) but can't see the network beyond. That's highly secure but impractical for most people. The third way — the default in all virtualization programs and my recommendation — is NAT networking, also called *shared networking*, in which your Mac functions as a NAT server, giving the guest operating system a private IP address.

- **Limit folder sharing.** Sharing folders or volumes from your Mac to your virtual machine makes it easy to work on your Mac files using Windows programs. However, the more folders you share, the more folders and files you expose to damage by any Windows malware you might encounter. Therefore, as a general rule, avoid sharing any folders you don't actively use within Windows, and in particular, don't share your whole Mac disk if you can avoid it.

  In Parallels Desktop, for example, if you choose Virtual Machine ➪ Configure, click the Options tab, and then select Shared Folders, as shown in Figure 14.17, you can see the options for sharing your Mac folders. From the Share these Mac folders pop-up menu, choose one of the three available options to determine what portion of your data is automatically shared. All disks is the riskiest option; Home folder only is much safer. (To turn off sharing, choose None.) Instead of sharing folders with this menu (or in addition), you can add one or more specific folders to share in the User-defined Mac OS X folders section; for each shared folder, you can also choose whether to give Windows read/write access or read-only access. Sharing only specific folders like this is the safest option.

- In VMware Fusion, if you choose Virtual Machine ➪ Settings and then click the Sharing icon to open the Sharing pane, as shown in Figure 14.18, you can configure how Fusion handles shared folders. Fusion makes it harder to share entire disks — which, from a security viewpoint, is a good thing! To share a particular folder, click the Share folders on your Mac check box and then add one or more folders to the list. As in Parallels, you can select whether each shared folder has read/write or read-only access in Windows.

Note

Independently of shared folders and volumes, Parallels and Fusion also offer an option to mirror several key folders (such as Desktop, Documents, and Music) between Mac OS X and their Windows counterparts. Although doing so may increase your risk of data loss by a tiny amount, the feature is extraordinarily useful — enough so that I'd say its utility far outweighs its risk. ■

- **Turn it off when you're not using it.** Finally, remember that malware can't harm your computer when it's not running! So, turn off Windows (or at least suspend the virtual machine) when it's not actively in use.

FIGURE 14.17

For each virtual machine you've configured in Parallels Desktop, the Shared Folders configuration pane lets you choose which folders or volumes from your Mac are available within Windows.

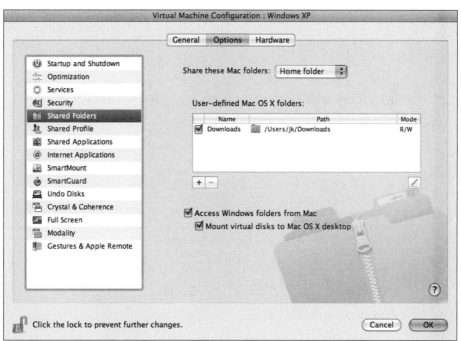

FIGURE 14.18

VMware Fusion lets you manually configure any folder or volume on your Mac to appear as a shared disk in Windows.

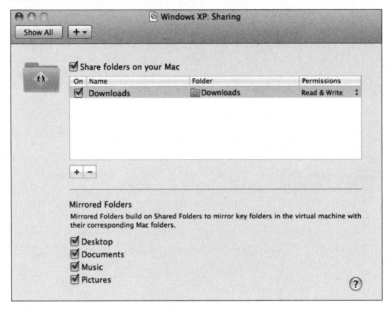

Choosing anti-malware software for Windows

If you're running Windows on your Mac (using whichever method) and you've decided that you need Windows anti-malware software, you have a vast number of choices — far more than on Mac OS X. Rather than list every choice in detail, I want to call your attention to a few options that stand out for one reason or another.

First, if you're using a virtualization program, you probably already have Windows anti-malware software. Parallels Desktop version 4 or later includes a free copy of Parallels Internet Security, a custom-branded version of the well-respected Kaspersky Internet Security suite, which contains a complete anti-malware program. Similarly, if you're running VMware Fusion 2 or later, it includes a free copy of McAfee's VirusScan Plus, which makes it the obvious choice and the path of least resistance.

If you're using Boot Camp or VirtualBox, consider one of these options:

- **avast! Professional Edition.** This anti-malware product (`www.avast.com`) is free for home use; for business use, a one-year subscription costs $39.95.

- **ClamAV.** The Windows companion of ClamXav, this free, open-source software (`www.clamav.net`) is likely to be better at wiping out Windows malware than Mac malware.

- **Norton AntiVirus.** Symantec's anti-malware product also comes in a Windows version, and you can buy a bundle called Norton AntiVirus Dual Protection for Mac (`www.symantec.com/norton/macintosh/antivirus-dual-protection`, $69.99) that includes a copy for each platform. If you're planning to buy the Mac software anyway, buying the bundle can save you a bit of money.

- **VirusBarrier DP.** Much like Norton AntiVirus, Intego's VirusBarrier software, the Mac version of which was covered earlier in this chapter, comes in a DP (Dual Protection) bundle (`www.intego.com/virusbarrierDP/`, $79.95), which includes BitDefender Antivirus for Windows. Also available is Internet Security Barrier DP (`www.intego.com/isbDP/`, $99.95), which includes NetBarrier, VirusBarrier, and Personal Antispam for Mac and BitDefender Internet Security for Windows.

Summary

Malware, or malicious software — and how to prevent it from harming your Mac — was the topic of this chapter. I began by describing viruses, worms, Trojan horses, and several other common kinds of malware. I explained how your Mac can transmit malware to other computers without becoming infected itself and showed how to determine your level of risk for infection or transmission. Because most malware damage results from poor user decisions, I showed you how to use common sense to avoid the vast majority of malware. For times when common sense isn't good enough, though, I also described several popular Mac applications for stopping malware in its many forms. I introduced you to outbound firewalls — programs that watch for potentially illicit network connections — and explained some things no anti-malware software can do for you. For Mac users running Windows using Boot Camp or virtualization software, I finished the chapter with a discussion of extra steps needed to keep your computer malware-free.

Securing Your Wired Network

The infrastructure of the Internet largely comprises a physical network of fiber optic and copper cables spread across the globe. With a few exceptions (such as long-range Wi-Fi and satellite access), most homes and businesses with Internet access connect to the outside world via physical cables of some kind. For reasons of performance and security, most businesses rely primarily on wired networks, typically using Ethernet cabling to connect computers to each other and to the Internet by way of one or more switches, hubs, routers, or gateways. But even people who use Wi-Fi to access the Internet usually have a partially wired network — for example, the cabling going from an AirPort base station to a DSL, cable, fiber, or satellite modem and then to the Internet.

The information sent over the Internet is exactly the same regardless of whether it's carried by radio waves or Ethernet cables. But in terms of security, wired and wireless networks face somewhat different types of threats. The biggest risk in using wireless networks is direct snooping by someone in your proximity. But any portion of your wired network directly exposed to the public Internet without an intervening router, firewall, NAT gateway, or other mediating device is especially vulnerable to outside attack, which can come as easily from around the world as from a nearby source.

Whether or not your network is partially wireless, you should take steps to protect it from the malefactors who troll the wired Internet. This involves understanding a bit about the operation of devices such as routers, gateways, and modems and configuring them to prevent the Macs and other Internet-capable devices on your network from gaining inappropriate outside access — while giving yourself, family members, employees, and other trusted individuals the access to your network they need when they're in another location.

IN THIS CHAPTER

Grasping the fundamentals of common networking hardware

Learning how NAT and DHCP work

Giving outside computers access to part of your network

Directing outside services to particular computers on your network

Channeling Internet access through a local proxy server

Using 802.1X for network authentication

Understanding Gateways, Modems, and Routers

Gateways. Modems. Routers. Hubs. Switches. Access points. Firewalls. Base stations. All these terms and many more like them have been thrown around so carelessly for so long — especially by the companies that make Internet devices — that their meanings have become confused nearly to the point of irrelevancy. If you have a cable modem with a built-in Ethernet switch, does that make it a gateway? If it also has a Wi-Fi radio, does that mean it's an access point? If I have a router, do I also need a firewall? Questions like these can frustrate even the experts, partly because each company uses these terms in a slightly different way and partly because devices that combine multiple functions further blur the already fuzzy distinctions.

What I can do, however, is lay out a few basic concepts — and tell you how I use some of these terms in this book. I can't guarantee that this matches up with what's written on the box of the next gadget you buy, but it should at least give you a bit of direction.

Gateways

If the world were blanketed with Ethernet cabling the way it is with AC power lines (along with the switches, routers, and other doohickeys needed to make it all work), you could have a network connection run to your house or building and plug directly into it in much the same way that you plug in your toaster. But things don't work like that. For the most part, individuals who want to connect to the global Internet must do so by way of an intermediate network (such as a telephone or cable network) that may use any of several different protocols and delivery mechanisms. Even if your business leases a dedicated data line for Internet access, it almost certainly carries data in a somewhat different way than Ethernet does. As a result, at the point where that external infrastructure connects to your building, you need some sort of device to translate the data between the format used on the outside and the format used on your local network. Whatever device serves that purpose can be called a *gateway*.

So, in my usage at least, all DSL and cable modems are examples of gateways by virtue of the fact that they connect a local area network, or LAN (even if it has just one computer), with a wide area network, or WAN (specifically, for the purposes of this book, the Internet). If you use a different technology to connect your LAN to the Internet, some other type of device may function as a gateway, but almost without exception, some piece of equipment in every Internet-connected home or business serves this purpose.

Some manufacturers reserve the term *gateway* only for devices with built-in routers. For example, a device with a single Ethernet port that provides Internet access via DSL over your phone line would simply be called a DSL modem, but a DSL modem with three or four Ethernet ports and routing capabilities would be called a DSL gateway. Other manufacturers might call the same device a DSL router. As far as I'm concerned, all the above are also properly termed gateways.

Modems

A decade ago, the majority of people who connected to the Internet from home or while traveling did so using dial-up connections. The device that served as their gateway was a *modem*, which modulated and demodulated signals — turning them from digital (ones and zeros) to analog (screeches and bleeps) and back again. Although dial-up certainly still exists (and is, in fact, still the only way to connect to the Internet in some rural areas), it's been eclipsed by broadband Internet service of various kinds, all of which offer far more bandwidth and faster connections.

Most kinds of broadband services, whether based on telephone lines (DSL), coaxial cable, fiber optic cable, or satellite access, also use a device — frequently called a modem — to mediate access between the local computer or network and the Internet. Semantic purists sometimes complain that this is an incorrect usage, in that these devices don't translate data between digital and analog formats but merely from one digital format into another. Whether it's etymologically justifiable or not, though, this is the usage we're stuck with.

So, am I saying that all gateways are modems, and all modems are gateways? Not quite — although it can seem that way. Most residential and small-business broadband gateways today happen to be some sort of modem (using the broad definition), but the gateways used for dedicated lines (such as T1, T3, and DS3) would never be referred to as modems. Meanwhile, a modem is a gateway if it connects you to another network (in particular, the Internet); but two computers could use modems to connect directly to each other, without any other network being involved on either end, and in that case, I wouldn't call either modem a gateway.

Hubs, switches, and routers

In networking terms, hubs, switches, and routers are all devices that let multiple computers (or other networkable products) communicate with each other. You could easily find a router, a hub, and a switch with nearly identical outward appearance: a few Ethernet ports, some lights, and a power connector. But inside, they work differently and serve different purposes.

Hubs

Of all the ways to connect multiple Ethernet-capable devices together, a hub is the simplest and cheapest. A *hub* takes all the incoming data on any one of its ports and sends it out to all the other ports. This all-data-to-all-ports approach is usually effective for networks with just a few devices, but it has a few downsides. For one thing, it increases your overall network traffic dramatically, which can slow down access for all your devices. It also means the hub's total bandwidth is divided among all the ports. For example, if you have a five-port, 100 Mbps Ethernet hub, and four computers connected to it are sending out data at the same time, each one can have, at best, an effective throughput of 25 Mbps. So, on networks with more than a few computers, where large quantities of data are being transferred or where speed is extremely important, hubs may yield less-than-satisfactory performance.

Switches

Switches, like hubs, let you connect two or more Ethernet devices together. But unlike hubs, switches include some intelligence. They look at the incoming data on any port, determine which port the destination device is connected to, and send the data directly — and only — to that port. Because switches make a direct connection between the source port and the destination port, you don't have the problem of excess network traffic that you do with a hub, and each port gets the full bandwidth the switch supports; heavy access by one device won't drag down the rest. Because switches are so much speedier and more efficient than hubs but cost only a little bit more, they're a much better choice for just about every application.

Routers

If switches are smarter than hubs, routers are much smarter still. *Routers* look at each packet of incoming data, determine the most efficient route for it to get to its destination, and send it to the next point in its journey (which may be the final destination or another router). Whereas a switch is adequate for directing traffic within a network, a router is needed to pass traffic from one network (or subnet) to another. So, whenever you interconnect two networks — and that includes connecting your local network with the Internet — you use the services of at least one router.

A router on your ISP's side connects your local gateway to the Internet. But you may also have a router built into your DSL or cable modem or as a separate device (perhaps with other functions too) in order to let multiple devices share a single Internet connection. In some cases — depending on your ISP, your subscription type, and your gateway hardware — you may be able to connect multiple computers to the

Internet with nothing more than a switch attached to your cable or DSL modem. More commonly, though, a router of some kind on your end is required because routers can perform fancy tricks such as distributing private IP addresses to all the computers on a network and letting them all use a single public IP address. This is known as NAT and is covered later in this chapter.

Note

A device can be both a switch and a router; it can provide routing functions between your network and a remote network while offering an Ethernet switch for computers on your local network. For example, AirPort Extreme base stations and Time Capsules fall into this category. ■

Access points

The term *access point* is more or less synonymous with "wireless router." It's a device that lets multiple Wi-Fi devices connect to the Internet (or another network) wirelessly, performing routing functions for those devices as needed. Some DSL and cable modems have built-in access points, meaning you could also refer to the device as a gateway or router. It's also quite common for access points to include multi-port Ethernet switches.

Apple calls all their Wi-Fi access points *base stations*. So, for example, the AirPort Extreme and AirPort Express base stations — as well as the Time Capsule — are all access points. Except for the AirPort Express, all of Apple's current base stations also include Ethernet switches and can be used as wired or wireless routers.

Physical Network Breaches

For the most part, this book assumes that the risks your wired network faces are external — someone connecting over the Internet and trying to break into your computers in some fashion. Wireless networks face additional risks, as discussed in Chapter 16, but someone could also gain access to your wired network simply by plugging a computer, access point, or another device directly into it and then using that device to tunnel or relay data to an outside location.

When I say "simply," that of course implies that the person has physical access to your network and can install a device in a location where it wouldn't be noticed (such as a closet or hidden in a hard-to-reach corner). But keep in mind that this capability is well within reach of your company's employees, contractors, cleaning staff, and just about anyone else who can be inside the building — especially at times when few other people are there.

Physical network breaches are significant because they bypass any security that stands between your network and the outside world — gateways, routers, firewalls, and even VPNs — giving the attacker direct access to the computers and data on your internal network. If the attacker uses Wi-Fi to transmit data back to the outside world, even an Information Leak Detection System (discussed in Chapter 22) installed between your network and the outside world would be unlikely to detect it.

To reduce the risk of damage due to a physical network breach, do the following:

- Make sure the spots where your network is most vulnerable (such as server rooms and places where routers and other networking hardware are installed) are kept locked.

- Don't assume the Macs and any other servers on your local network are inherently secure; require usernames and strong passwords for all network access.

- If possible, configure your network to use 802.1X authentication (described later in this chapter) to block all network access by users who haven't provided valid credentials — and change users' network passwords regularly.

- Use Information Leak Detection software running on the individual computers on your network (in addition to any that monitor your network as a whole) to watch for sensitive data being sent across the network.

Understanding NAT, DHCP, and IPv6

The current version of the Internet Protocol (IP), version 4, has been in use since 1981. Among other things, IPv4 specifies how devices (or hosts) on the Internet are addressed and how data passes between them. But there's a problem, which is that the format used for creating IPv4 addresses — a dotted quad such as 123.45.67.89, with each segment having possible values from 0 to 255 — can produce, at most, about 4.3 billion unique addresses. That may sound like a lot, but every host on the Internet needs its own address — not only computers but also devices such as mobile phones, printers, DVRs, and even some light switches. When you add up all those devices, that pool of addresses starts shrinking in a hurry. Various estimates put the date of IPv4 address exhaustion somewhere between 2009 and 2011.

Fortunately, a solution to this problem has already been invented and (partially) deployed: IPv6, which uses a new addressing format with more than 340 undecillion possible addresses (that's 340 followed by 36 zeroes). But even though current versions of Mac OS X, Windows, and Linux support IPv6, a lot of the routers and other Internet infrastructure haven't yet been upgraded to work natively with IPv6, and the same goes for quite a few common Internet programs. As a result, an interim solution was needed.

NAT

In a few years, IPv6 will inevitably reach the level of mainstream usage that IPv4 has today. In the meantime, most of us have been using a temporary workaround to the problem of too few IP addresses (perhaps without even knowing it): *NAT*, or network address translation. Although NAT itself has a number of capabilities, the most common use to which it's put is enabling a single IP address to be used for multiple devices or even an entire network. Because many devices can thereby share a single IP address, the problem of a limited address pool becomes much less severe.

To oversimplify slightly, a NAT-capable router usually starts with a single public, routable IP address (one of the 4.3 billion possible IPv4 addresses). Then, it generates a series of private addresses (such as 10.0.0.1) and assigns them, as needed, to each device that wants to connect to the Internet through that router. Whenever a device makes an outgoing request for data, the router keeps track of which device asked for data from which outside IP address. That way, when the reply comes in, the router knows which device to channel it to. All this happens transparently, in the background, and usually with sufficient speed that users don't perceive any decrease in network performance.

Note

Although, in principle, a NAT router could assign just about any IP address to one of its clients, in practice, most of them hand out addresses in one of the following ranges, which are never used for public IP addresses: 10.0.0.0 through 10.255.255.255, 172.16.0.0 through 172.31.255.255, and 192.168.0.0 through 192.168.255.255. ∎

In addition to preventing each device from needing its own public IP address, NAT has an interesting side effect: It dramatically increases the network security of devices that use it! A NAT router accepts all outbound traffic from your local network, but it sends inbound traffic to your computers only in response to specific requests; everything else simply evaporates. So, if you type a URL into your web browser, the NAT router lets the web page through to your Mac; but if an outside computer tries to connect to your Mac, it gets only as far as your router because the customary configuration of NAT prevents outside computers from seeing past the router to the individual computers on your network.

In that sense, a NAT router functions much like a firewall, except that it blocks incoming traffic only passively — more or less as an accident of its design — instead of actively examining each packet and taking action prescribed by rules you've set up. Although a NAT setup, by itself, keeps a great deal of unwanted traffic from reaching your computers, you may still need a firewall for any of several reasons:

- A NAT doesn't block traffic to DMZ hosts (which I explain later in this chapter).
- If you use port forwarding (also described later in this chapter), data to those ports isn't filtered by a NAT.
- Firewalls are highly adaptable and can be tailored to your exact needs — which may be much more elaborate than what NAT provides.
- There are some tricky scanning techniques that can, in some situations, enable a hacker to get around NAT.

Those warnings aside, NAT is an excellent idea for most situations in which outside computers don't need direct inbound access to a computer on your network. Except in cases where some software or service refuses to function over NAT, it's a good way to improve your security without requiring a lot of extra effort. However, it's important, if at all possible, to avoid a double NAT configuration, in which a gateway or router itself obtains a private IP address via NAT and then creates a second NAT network, forcing all network traffic to and from your computer to go through two sets of NAT translations. Double NAT can wreak havoc with Back to My Mac, port forwarding, and other similar services — and can lead to slowdowns and errors. So, make sure at most one device on your network is functioning as a NAT router, and don't turn on NAT at all if your ISP already uses NAT on their end to supply a private (`10.x.x.x`, `172.16.x.x` through `172.31.x.x`, or `192.168.x.x`) IP address to your gateway.

You may already be using NAT on your network. If not and you want to activate it, consult the documentation that came with your gateway or router. AirPort base stations and Time Capsules can also function as NAT routers for both wired and wireless clients. To configure one of these devices to use NAT, follow these steps:

1. Open AirPort Utility, which is located in `/Applications/Utilities`.
2. Select your AirPort base station in the list on the left and then click Manual Setup. If you see a password prompt, type the base station's password and then click OK.
3. Click the Internet button on the toolbar.
4. From the Connection Sharing pop-up menu, choose Share a public IP address if it's not already selected.
5. Click Update and then wait for your base station to restart. The NAT router immediately begins distributing private IP addresses to any Mac on your wired or wireless network that's configured to use DHCP (discussed just ahead).

DHCP

Every computer connected to the Internet needs its own IP address, even if it's a private IP address used only by other computers on the local network and a NAT router, which redirects incoming and outgoing traffic using a separate, public IP address. Once upon a time, a network administrator would determine which IP address was to be used by each computer and then manually type it (along with several other pieces of information, such as the address of the router and DNS servers, and the subnet mask, which identifies the portion of the network to which the computer belongs) on the machines one by one. But that's tedious and error-prone work, so several automated systems were developed whereby a router or central computer could automatically configure a bunch of other computers with their IP addresses and other essential networking details. The most commonly used of these systems is called DHCP (Dynamic Host Configuration Protocol).

DHCP is marvelous because it saves individual computer users almost all the effort of network configuration. In most cases, if you simply leave your network settings at their defaults, they'll look for a DHCP server on the network, ask the server for the information they need, and fill it in automatically. Most home Internet users and many businesses, schools, and other organizations use DHCP as a convenience to users and administrators alike. Your home DSL or cable modem likely gets its public IP address from your ISP's DHCP server, and your Mac likely gets its private IP address from a DHCP server built into your gateway or router.

Note

The D in DHCP stands for dynamic, and in most DHCP configurations, that means (among other things) that any particular device's IP address can change from time to time. Normally, this process is transparent to users, but it can cause problems for computers with domain names, which work only when associated with known IP addresses. Dynamic DNS services, which track a computer's IP address as it changes and then update DNS records accordingly, were designed to address this problem, making computers with dynamic IP addresses locatable on the Internet by domain name. ■

The reason I mention DHCP here is that it commonly goes hand in hand with NAT. When the two services are paired, DHCP hands out private addresses to each device on your local network, and NAT ensures that packets traveling to and from those addresses get to the right places. You can set up NAT without relying on DHCP, but that's a more complicated process because it requires you to manually choose and type IP addresses and other information on each computer — and make sure you don't accidentally give the same address to two machines. So, unless you have a compelling need to give your computers static IP addresses, using DHCP along with NAT makes life much easier.

Note

Although DHCP is usually used to distribute private IP addresses, it can also be used with publicly routable addresses and even to set up clients automatically with static IP addresses (tied to machines' MAC addresses or unique identifiers called DHCP Client IDs). ■

Assuming a DHCP server is running on your network, you can configure your Mac to use DHCP by following these steps:

1. Choose ⇨ System Preferences and then click Network to open the Network pane.
2. If the lock icon in the lower-left corner of the window is in the locked state, click it, type an administrator's username and password, and then click OK.

3. Select your current network interface in the list on the left.

4. For Ethernet networks, choose Using DHCP from the Configure (in Leopard) or Configure IPv4 (in Snow Leopard) pop-up menu if it's not already selected. For AirPort networks, click Advanced to show additional configuration settings, click the TCP/IP tab, choose Using DHCP from the Configure or Configure IPv4 pop-up menu, and then click OK. Finally, click Apply. Your Mac immediately tries to contact the first available DHCP server on your network to obtain an IP address and related data.

IPv6 network security

As I mentioned earlier in this chapter, most of this book assumes the use of IPv4, the version of the Internet Protocol that's been in use since the early 1980s. But a new version, IPv6, which offers vastly more addresses, is on its way to becoming the new standard. From a security standpoint, this is both good news and bad news.

One good thing about IPv6 is that it builds in support for IPsec end-to-end encryption. Because so many security problems currently arise from an eavesdropper being able to watch unencrypted data flow over the Internet, this capability eliminates several whole categories of risk. Another good thing is that because there are so many possible addresses, it becomes harder for a hacker to randomly find any particular address in order to initiate an attack.

But IPv6 has some security issues too. One concern is that until the majority of the routers and other infrastructure of the Internet are upgraded (or replaced) to offer full IPv6 support, a great deal of IPv6 traffic can flow right past the very devices meant to intercept, block, or filter unwanted access. In addition to direct access over hardware that already supports IPv6, several different mechanisms exist to tunnel IPv6 traffic through the existing IPv4 network, and some of these methods are difficult to detect or block using existing security products. The upshot of all this is that if your Mac has IPv6 enabled (as it might, without your even realizing it), an intruder or malware program could potentially sneak right past your router or firewall and directly access your Mac.

Some firewalls let you configure rules to process IPv6 packets just as you can IPv4 packets, and others at least offer the capability of blocking incoming or outgoing packets that use IPv4 protocol 41, which is one of the most common means by which IPv6 traffic is tunneled through IPv4. In Leopard and Snow Leopard, you can regulate IPv6 traffic with the included IP6FW (an IPv6 version of IPFW) or with some third-party firewalls, such as DoorStop X.

Cross-Ref

For more on Mac OS X firewalls, see Chapter 17. ■

Broadly speaking, there are two approaches you could consider that would enable you to avoid IPv6-related security issues.

First, you could make sure all your network hardware and software is fully IPv6-compatible (which would mean checking with each product's developer or manufacturer and, where necessary, upgrading or buying replacements). Then, explicitly configure your routers, firewalls, and security software to block unwanted IPv6 traffic in the same ways they currently do for IPv4.

Alternatively, you could disable IPv6 on all your Macs (and also, if you want, on at least some of your other devices) to force all your hardware and software to use only IPv4 for the time being. To prevent a Mac from using IPv6, follow these steps:

1. Choose  ➚ System Preferences and then click Network to open the Network pane.

2. If the lock icon in the lower-left corner of the window is in the locked state, click it, type an administrator's username and password, and then click OK.

3. Choose your current network interface in the list on the left, click the Advanced button on the right side of the window, and then click the TCP/IP tab.

4. Choose Off from the Configure IPv6 pop-up menu.

5. Click OK and then click Apply.

6. Close System Preferences.

To configure an AirPort base station to block IPv6 traffic, follow these steps:

1. **Open AirPort Utility, which is located in** `/Applications/Utilities`.

2. **Choose your AirPort base station in the list on the left and then click Manual Setup.** If you see a password prompt, type the base station's password and then click OK.

3. **Click the Advanced button on the toolbar and then click IPv6.**

4. **To prevent devices outside your network from contacting computers that connect to the Internet via the AirPort base station using IPv6, click the Block incoming IPv6 connections check box.**

5. **To prevent IPv6 traffic on your local network from traveling beyond your AirPort base station to the Internet, choose Link-local only from the IPv6 Mode pop-up menu.**

6. **Click Update and then wait for your base station to restart.** The changes you made apply immediately.

Using Port Forwarding

Suppose you want to use one of the Macs on your local network as a web server. No problem: Just turn on Web Sharing. But if your Mac is behind a router that uses NAT (as is the case for most home and small-business networks), you might have a problem. Other Macs on your network can see your web server, but Macs on the outside can't! That's fine for an intranet server but not what you want if you were hoping to share your site with the world. This problem is a consequence of the way NAT hides all the computers on your local network and prevents incoming requests from reaching them. A computer outside your network can contact only your router — that's the only IP address exposed to the public. Although someone might try to contact that IP address and request a web page, the router isn't the device running the server, so it wouldn't be able to reply.

If your ISP offers static IP addresses, you can assign such an address to one of your Macs, thus removing the Mac from the NAT-based private network. However, this isn't always feasible or desirable. Perhaps you don't want the expense of a static IP address or perhaps you enjoy the security that NAT provides — and yet, you still want one of your Macs to be reachable, at least in a limited way, from the outside. A better solution is port forwarding. *Port forwarding* means that your router takes all incoming requests on a certain port (such as port 80, used by the web) and redirects those requests to the port of your choice (the same one or a different one) on one specific device that's otherwise using NAT to connect to the Internet with a private IP address.

For example, suppose your router's IP address is `111.222.333.444`, your iMac's private IP address is `10.0.1.2`, and you've configured port forwarding for port 80. Now, someone outside your network opens a web browser and tries to visit http://111.222.333.444. Your router accepts that request, notices that it's coming in on port 80, and redirects it to your iMac. As long as your iMac has Web Sharing turned on, it replies to the request, returning its default home page. The page goes back to the router, which reverses the previous procedure and relays the information to the computer that requested it.

Port forwarding can be used for any type of service for which you want some particular Mac on your network — but only one — to be visible to the outside world. If you want to run a public FTP server, forward port 21. To make a Mac with AFP file sharing visible to the public, forward port 548. And so on. You can find a list of common ports and their standard uses at http://en.wikipedia.org/wiki/List_of_ TCP_and_UDP_port_numbers. A router can forward many different ports to many different devices, but any given port can go to only one device. So, although you could have one Mac functioning as a chat server and a different Mac functioning as an FTP server, you can't use port forwarding to make two different FTP servers available on the same public IP address.

Note

Some services can run on more than one port, providing a potential loophole to this rule. For example, one Mac could run a web server on the standard port, 80, while another one used port 8080. Although this would work, it would require that incoming requests bound for the second Mac included the nonstandard port number — for example, http://111.222.333.444:8080. ■

Because of this limitation of one destination per port per IP address, port forwarding is appropriate only for small networks. And because you must configure it one port at a time, it's less than ideal for situations where you want one Mac to provide a large number of public network services (or expose an ever-changing selection of ports). In these cases, you're better off using a DMZ, NAT-PMP, or UPnP (all described later in this chapter) or getting a static IP address for that Mac.

Although port forwarding can be a fabulous solution to otherwise intractable problems, it also carries with it a risk. Each port you expose to the outside world provides another potential path for the bad guys (or their software) to access your computers and their data. Therefore, before setting up port forwarding, be sure you have other security measures (such as a well-configured firewall) in place on the target computer, and consider whether there might be some other way to get a similar end result without opening up one of your computers to outside access. For example, instead of letting outside users share files on your Mac directly via FTP or AFP, you could copy them to an outside server — a MobileMe iDisk, perhaps, or a shared folder using a service such as SugarSync or Dropbox.

Cross-Ref

For more on firewalls, see Chapter 17. ■

Setting up port forwarding is conceptually quite simple. You need just three pieces of information: the private IP address of the computer that will be sharing resources with the outside world, the port used by outside clients for the service you're running, and (optionally) the port you want your Mac to receive the data on. For example, a web server running on your Mac could be configured to accept incoming requests from your local network on port 80 but from the outside world on port 8080; but in general, the same port is used both externally and internally. Given these numbers, you log in to your router (often using a web browser) and then type them into a form.

Because every router is a bit different, I can't provide detailed directions for setting up port forwarding. However, you can find instructions for hundreds of models at `http://portforward.com`.

Cross-Ref

For more on configuring port forwarding (which Apple calls port mapping) for an AirPort base station or Time Capsule, see Chapter 16. ∎

Using a DMZ

In the real world, the term *demilitarized zone* (DMZ) refers to an area with no military presence — typically one that stands between two territories that were previously at war. It's a buffer zone designed to keep both sides out of trouble. In its metaphorical networking sense, a DMZ is a portion of a network that stands between the safe and comfy local network and the big, scary public network. Outside users can easily access computers in your DMZ but are prevented from going beyond it to reach the rest of your network; incoming network access from the DMZ is blocked. Meanwhile, other computers on your network can access machines in the DMZ or on the outside with equal ease. Another way to describe a DMZ is to say that it's a portion of your network outside the firewall (or between the NAT router and the gateway).

If you must run publicly accessible servers of one kind or another on your network, using a DMZ is a good way to make sure the rest of your computers are afforded the protection of a firewall or NAT router. Putting such servers behind the firewall would require more effort (carefully fine-tuning and monitoring the firewall such that it allows legitimate users while blocking hacking attempts) and still result in lower security. Web servers, FTP servers, and local proxy servers (described ahead in this chapter) are examples of computers that might fit well in a DMZ. Whereas port forwarding essentially punches holes through a NAT configuration for traffic on individual ports, a DMZ leaves your NAT intact, providing better security; it also enables you to freely use all the ports of each computer, assuming your outward-facing servers all have public IP addresses (which would typically be the case on a business network).

Using a DMZ is one way a business can share resources with the public without compromising security. However, this configuration is overkill for most home and small office networks. As a general guiding principle, you should consider externally hosted servers first; if those don't meet your needs, think about whether port forwarding would; and if neither is appropriate, a DMZ may be what you need.

Genuine DMZs

What I've described so far is a genuine DMZ, one that's separate from both local and public networks and prevents outside users with access to the computers on the DMZ from getting through to the local network. (Read on to learn about a different, somewhat misleading sense of the term.) There are a few different ways of setting these up, each with various pros and cons. Because this isn't a book on network design, I can't offer extensive advice for setting up this sort of DMZ. I can tell you, however, that suggestions are readily found on the web. For example, you can find advice for creating a basic DMZ for a home network that runs a public web server at `http://www.boutell.com/newfaq/creating/dmz.html` and some alternative advice at `http://en.wikipedia.org/wiki/Demilitarized_zone_(computing)`. One way or another, though, the key is to isolate your DMZ and your local network from each other (with an intervening router or firewall and using different subnets) and from the outside world.

DMZ hosts

For better or worse, the term DMZ has come to have an even more metaphorical meaning. Many routers let you designate a single computer on your network for which all ports are exposed to the public — that is, all requests from the outside that are directed to the router and not already destined for another computer are automatically sent to the so-called DMZ host. In other words, it's as though you set up port forwarding for every single port and designated the DMZ host as the one to receive all that traffic.

A DMZ host set up in this fashion has one of the attributes of a real DMZ: Incoming network traffic can get to it unimpeded. However, it's missing the crucial component that makes a DMZ a DMZ — it lacks a firewall or router between the so-called DMZ and the rest of your network, so nothing prevents a request from the DMZ from being sent on to your other computers. So, it offers little in the way of additional security but may provide convenience; it's easier to designate a computer as a DMZ host than to forward a large number of ports to it.

If you need to access one of your Macs remotely and your networking hardware doesn't support Back to My Mac, designating that Mac as a DMZ host can solve your problem. However, because this also undoes all the protection that NAT ordinarily provides, be sure to compensate by using a firewall, turning on all appropriate security features, and monitoring your Mac for unauthorized network access.

Cross-Ref

For more on Back to My Mac, see Chapter 4. For more on firewalls, see Chapter 17. For more on network monitoring, see Chapter 22. ■

Configuring a DMZ host is very much like configuring port forwarding — only easier because you need just one piece of information: the private IP address of the Mac that will serve as your DMZ. As with port forwarding, each router that offers this feature has a slightly different way of configuring it, and the router's documentation should be able to explain how to do it.

Cross-Ref

For more on configuring an AirPort base station or Time Capsule to use a default host (Apple's terminology for a DMZ host), see Chapter 16. ■

Using NAT-PMP or UPnP

So far in this chapter, I've explained two methods by which a computer outside your network can directly contact a computer inside the network, even when using NAT: port forwarding and a DMZ host. One problem with these two methods is that they require manual configuration of your router or gateway, which decreases your network's security in the process. Another problem is that they each make only one computer available for any given service. What if you want to (or have to) use NAT, but you also want to be able to reach more than one of your Macs from outside your network?

A number of methods exist to make this possible, at least in limited situations. Of these, the most popular are NAT-PMP (NAT Port Mapping Protocol), which was designed by Apple, and UPnP (Universal Plug and Play).

If your gateway (the device that connects your network to the Internet and functions as a NAT router — which may also be a switch, modem, and/or wireless access point) supports one of these two protocols, you can usually enable it by clicking a check box. Thereafter, the gateway performs what amounts to an automated version of port forwarding whenever your Mac runs software that supports NAT traversal. Examples include BitTorrent and other file-sharing clients, some chat software, and Back to My Mac, a MobileMe feature that lets you do file and screen sharing with a Mac on a remote network. NAT-PMP and UPnP don't expose all your devices or every port on a given device to the outside world but only those applications that have explicitly made their locations (public IP address and port) publicly known.

All current AirPort base stations and Time Capsules support NAT-PMP. To see if it's activated (and to turn it on if not), follow these steps:

1. **Open AirPort Utility, which is located in** `/Applications/Utilities`.

2. **Select your AirPort base station in the list on the left and then click Manual Setup.** If you see a password prompt, type the base station's password and then click OK.

3. **Click the Internet button on the toolbar and then click NAT.** The NAT tab is available only if your base station is configured to share a public IP address, meaning it distributes private addresses to connected clients.

4. **If the Enable NAT Port Mapping Protocol check box isn't already selected, click it, click Update, and then wait for your base station to restart.** The change takes effect immediately.

Using Proxy Servers

A *proxy server* is a device or a program that makes requests for information from the Internet on behalf of a client computer and then directs the response back to the client. Proxy servers can serve a wide variety of purposes, depending on how they're configured and where they're installed. For example, one popular use of a proxy server — a caching proxy server — is storing temporary copies of all files and web pages requested from the Internet. If a second computer later asks for the same file or web page, the proxy server can deliver it directly over the local network without having to download it again from scratch. This makes web browsing and downloading faster and reduces congestion on one's Internet connection.

Cross-Ref
For more on using proxy servers (outside your local network) to provide anonymous web-browsing capabilities, see Chapter 10. ∎

If you set up a proxy server between your local network and your gateway and then direct all Internet traffic (or all traffic of a particular type, such as web or FTP) through it, the proxy can do other things too. For one thing, you can configure it to filter incoming and/or outgoing data — for example, preventing employees on your network from visiting certain websites or from sending out certain types of information. It can also provide some security (and a small measure of anonymity) by making all outbound requests appear to have originated from a single computer and by blocking some incoming requests directed to particular devices on your local network.

Although in some sense they serve a function similar to that of NAT routers, proxy servers are less effective at hiding your internal network from the outside world. A NAT router operates at a fairly low level, redirecting Internet traffic on all ports from clients out to the Internet by rewriting portions of the individual packet headers, and blocking any inbound data that isn't in direct response to an outbound request. Proxy servers, on the other hand, operate at a higher level, channeling only certain types of data and resending each request rather than simply altering an existing request and passing it on.

Most home and small-business networks have little need for a local proxy server. One situation in which it might be useful, however, is when you have a low-bandwidth Internet connection and several people on your network frequently access the same web pages and download the same files — such as Apple software updates, which routinely run into the hundreds of megabytes. A caching proxy server can eliminate duplicate downloads and enable every user except the first one who retrieves any given piece of data to receive it much more quickly. In larger business settings, the primary use of a proxy server is to block users from accessing certain Internet resources or at least monitor what they do.

Proxy servers are sometimes integrated into routers or gateways, and when they are, their operation is usually invisible to users — that is, no client-side configuration is required, and it appears to users as though their requests are going directly to a server on the Internet. However, caching proxy servers and other types of proxy servers running on stand-alone computers on your network typically requires each client to be manually configured to use the proxy for whichever sorts of traffic it handles. Examples of proxy servers that can be installed on Mac OS X are Squid (`www.squid-cache.org`), a flexible, free, open-source proxy server, easily configured using another free program, SquidMan (`http://web.me.com/adg/squidman/`); DansGuardian (`http://dansguardian.org/`), whose primary function is content filtering (free for non-commercial use; commercial licenses start at $89 for up to 99 users and one server); and Privoxy (`www.privoxy.org`), a free, filtering web proxy.

To configure a Mac as a client to a software-based local proxy server, follow these steps:

1. Choose ⇨ System Preferences and then click Network to open the Network pane.

2. If the lock icon in the lower-left corner of the window is in the locked state, click it, type an administrator's username and password, and then click OK.

3. Choose your current network interface in the list on the left, click the Advanced button on the right side of the window, and then click the Proxies tab, shown in Figure 15.1.

4. In Leopard, choose Manually from the Configure Proxies pop-up menu.

5. Click the check box next to the protocol for which you want to configure a proxy.

6. Type the proxy server's domain name or IP address in the *Server Type* Proxy Server field and then type the port it uses (provided by the server operator) in the field to its right. If the server requires a username and password, click the Proxy server requires password check box and then type your username and password into the fields provided.

7. Repeat steps 5 and 6 for each additional protocol for which a proxy server is used.

8. Click OK to close the configuration dialog box and then close System Preferences. Internet traffic of the types you configured now flows through the selected proxy server(s) until you go back to the Network pane and deselect the check boxes for those protocols.

FIGURE 15.1

To configure your Mac to connect to a proxy server on your local network for one or more services, type the necessary settings in this window. In Snow Leopard, this dialog box looks slightly different (the Configure Proxies pop-up menu is missing).

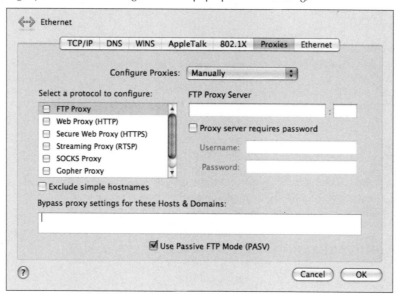

Using 802.1X

Ordinarily, when you connect a computer to a network (via Ethernet, Wi-Fi, or some other means), that computer automatically has network access. The user may need to provide credentials to log in to specific servers or resources, but access to the local network itself (and, usually, to the Internet) is open. A networking protocol known as 802.1X aims to increase network security by requiring each device to authenticate (typically, with a username and password, although other means of authentication, such as smart cards and biometrics, are also supported) before any network access is granted — other than to the authentication mechanism itself.

A typical implementation of 802.1X involves a central *authentication server* — usually a RADIUS server — that maintains a database of each user's credentials. A device that wants to connect to the network is called a *supplicant*; it sends a request for authentication to a device called an *authenticator*, which functions as a network switch. As long as the switch is off, supplicants can communicate only with the authenticator. But once the authenticator has validated the user's credentials against the information on the authentication server, it flips the switch, and the supplicant's traffic travels freely through the authenticator to the rest of the network.

Cross-Ref

For more on configuring Mac OS X Server's RADIUS server, see Chapter 31. ■

802.1X is used more frequently for wireless networks than for wired networks because its design provides considerably more security than conventional WEP, WPA, or WPA2 encryption that relies on a single encryption key (a password that's set globally for all clients and is typically a hassle to change). However, because it's a generic authentication mechanism, it can be used to provide security for any type of network, and implementing 802.1X makes sense whenever network devices contain highly sensitive information or where access to the network must be tightly controlled for legal reasons or because of corporate policy.

Cross-Ref

For more on the applications of 802.1X to wireless networks, see Chapter 16. ■

Because the design and setup of a complete 802.1X system for a network is complex and subject to a long list of variables, it's beyond what I can cover here. As usual, the web has many sources of information on this topic. However, I want to lay out the basics here — in particular, explaining how to configure your Mac to authenticate on a network that uses 802.1X.

Note

An Apple AirPort base station can function as an 802.1X authenticator for wireless (although not wired) networks. I cover this usage in Chapter 16. And as a reminder, I describe how to set up Mac OS X Server to function as a RADIUS authentication server in Chapter 31. ■

The authentication server

The first thing you need to implement 802.1X is an authentication server. This server's purpose is mainly to keep a list of who can log in and with what credentials, but you can configure an authentication server to require new passwords at certain intervals, to impose restrictions on password length and complexity, and to perform a variety of other authentication-related functions. If you're running Leopard Server or Snow Leopard Server, you have the necessary software built in. You can also install a number of third-party authentication server packages (including several versions of RADIUS) — which range in price from free to outlandishly expensive and in complexity from simple to painful.

The authenticator

The authenticator — the device that mediates network access for each client by using the authentication server to provide the details as to who's authorized — can be a wireless access point, a router, or even a fairly simple Ethernet switch. All that's required is that it have at least minimal configurability: You must be able to tell it to act as an authenticator and where to find the RADIUS database or other authentication server. This device must be installed between the protected portion of the network and any hosts for which you want to limit network access.

The supplicant

For the purposes of this book, your Mac is the supplicant — the device that wants to obtain network access. To configure your Mac to authenticate using 802.1X, follow these steps:

1. **Choose ⇨ System Preferences and then click Network to open the Network pane.**
2. **If the lock icon in the lower-left corner of the window is in the locked state, click it, type an administrator's username and password, and then click OK.**
3. **In the list on the left, select the network interface for which you want to configure 802.1X authentication.**

4. Click the Advanced button.

5. In the dialog box that opens, click the 802.1X tab (as shown in Figure 15.2).

FIGURE 15.2

If you're using an 802.1X authentication system on your network, you can configure your Mac to connect to it in this pane.

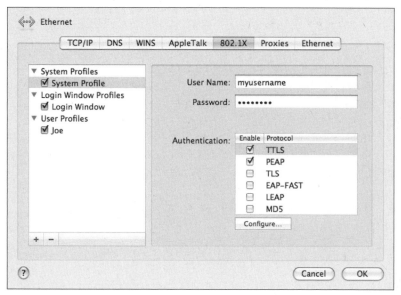

6. Click the Add (+) button in the lower-left corner of the window, and from the pop-up menu that appears, choose one of the following:

   - **Add User Profile.** For authentication specific to your user account

   - **Add Login Window Profile.** For simultaneous 802.1X authentication and login to a network directory service

   - **Add System Profile.** For authentication even when no user is logged in

   If in doubt, the choice most likely to work is Add User Profile.

7. Type your username and password in the fields provided.

8. In the Authentication portion of the window, click the check box next to each authentication protocol you want to enable. Your network administrator can tell you which option(s) you need to use. Some protocols require or optionally permit additional parameters; select a protocol and then click Configure to provide that information, if desired.

9. Click OK and then click Apply. Your changes take effect immediately. To set up 802.1X authentication for additional network interfaces, repeat steps 3 through 9.

10. Close System Preferences.

Summary

This chapter covered ways to keep a small Ethernet network secure from most outside attacks while giving users on the network access to the services they need. I began by explaining the basic operation of common networking hardware, such as routers, gateways, and DSL and cable modems. I then covered NAT and DHCP, two common methods (often used together) for giving computers Internet access using private IP addresses that aren't visible to the outside world. I explained in broad strokes how to configure a setup known as a DMZ (or demilitarized zone), both in the sense of an isolated network segment outside your firewall and in the sense of using a router or gateway to direct all outside Internet access to a particular IP address.

For more fine-grained access control, I then discussed port forwarding, in which requests for particular kinds of data are routed individually to selected computers on your network. I returned to the topic of proxy servers (discussed earlier in this book) to cover specific security uses on your local network and ended the chapter with a discussion of the 802.1X authentication protocol and how to use it on your wired network.

Securing Your Wireless Network

Wireless networks offer convenience and flexibility, but they also introduce new security risks. Whereas it may be difficult and dangerous for an attacker to physically tap into your local wired network, wireless traffic can extend well beyond your home or office. Anyone with the right equipment and know-how can *sniff* (or monitor) that traffic — easily, anonymously, and undetectably — and in many cases, with only slightly more effort, connect to your network themselves. Regardless of what safeguards you may have in place to protect your wired network, once you go wireless, all bets are off. The danger is especially high for people in densely populated urban areas or who use a Wi-Fi–equipped laptop in a public place.

Several methods exist to protect your wireless network. You can't prevent someone else from seeing the data your computer transmits and receives via Wi-Fi, but you can encrypt it so that it's useless to anyone who lacks the necessary password or other credentials. However, some various means of wireless encryption are trivially easy to break, and others provide much stronger security but with a corresponding increase in complexity.

This chapter discusses the major ways of protecting your wireless network, the pros and cons of each, and how to set them up both on the wireless access point that connects directly to the Internet and on your Mac. It also covers how to use wireless networks over which you have no personal control (such as those provided by public hotspots) and how to discover Wi-Fi networks in your vicinity and determine how secure they are — the very techniques an attacker might use against you.

Understanding wireless network security

Setting up the security features of an AirPort base station

Using the security features of third-party wireless access points

Configuring your Mac's security settings appropriately for your wireless network

Safely connecting to the Internet via a public Wi-Fi connection

Finding nearby wireless networks and assessing their security

Tip

This chapter covers the fundamentals of keeping a wireless network secure, but the topic is complex enough that it deserves its own book. And I can recommend just such a title: the ebook *Take Control of Your Wi-Fi Security* by Adam Engst and Glenn Fleishman (www.takecontrolbooks.com/wifi-security). ∎

Wireless Security Basics

In terms of security, the difference between communicating over a wired Ethernet connection and communicating over a wireless Ethernet connection is somewhat like the difference between talking to someone over the telephone and talking to someone in a crowded public place. Sure, there are ways someone can eavesdrop on a telephone call, but they take some doing, and for all practical purposes, most of us assume, with reasonable justification, that our telephone conversations are private. But if you're talking to someone in a restaurant, at a park, or in some other public place, there's always the possibility that someone nearby can overhear you — accidentally or otherwise. Similarly, although it's possible (with some difficulty) to tap into someone's wired Internet traffic, it's extraordinarily easy to listen in on wireless traffic and to do so even from a distance, without your having the slightest clue that your communication isn't private.

This fact should scare you — but just enough to stir you to do something about it. Although the threat of wireless eavesdropping is real, it's not difficult to protect yourself. As long as you understand the dangers and the remedies, you can take appropriate steps, and once you do, your wireless Internet usage will be just as private as it would be if you were using a wired connection (and maybe even more so).

At the same time, you should be aware of some so-called wireless security measures that turn out to be nothing of the kind. Along with procedures you can employ to gain genuine security, there are several oft-recommended steps that require effort and inconvenience but in return give only the appearance of increased security. These are things you're better off avoiding.

In this section, I look at some of the major steps you should and shouldn't consider taking to protect your wireless network. They fall into four broad categories: protecting your access point, controlling visibility, controlling access, and encrypting your connection (with considerable overlap between the last two).

Protecting your access point

Every access point has a variety of settings you can change, from changing the name of the wireless network to enabling encryption. In some cases (notably Apple base stations), you do this with a desktop utility, and in others, you connect to the access point over a wired or wireless network and then use a web browser to change its settings. Either way, once you modify the settings of the access point itself, you can remove or change any security features to suit your needs. It should go without saying that this is a capability you want to avoid giving to hackers and random passersby! The way you do this is to assign a password (and, in some cases, also a username) to your access point's administrative interface. This can and should be different from the password that clients use to gain wireless access.

Out of the box, most access points either have no password at all or have a simple, obvious password, such as admin or password. So, changing this as soon as you turn on your access point for the first time should be a top priority. As with any high-security password, it's important to choose something that neither a human nor a computer could guess. Ideally, make your administrative password a combination of lowercase and capital letters, numbers, and punctuation, with at least ten characters in all.

Controlling wireless network visibility

If you look at the contents of the wedge-shaped AirPort menu in your Mac's menu bar, you're likely to see the names of one or more (and possibly a great many) Wi-Fi networks in your vicinity. If that menu isn't there, open the Network pane of System Preferences, select your AirPort interface on the left, and then click the Show AirPort status in menu bar check box. I generally see at least a dozen when I'm at home in my Paris apartment, which isn't at all surprising because there are probably 50 or more other apartments and businesses within Wi-Fi range (about 300 feet) of my desk. Each of those names in the AirPort menu is an

SSID, or service set identifier. The SSID does nothing but announce the existence of a wireless network in a convenient, human-readable fashion.

Although every access point needs an SSID — even if it's one that's preset at the factory, such as "linksys" — operators of wireless access points (including AirPort base stations and Time Capsules) can choose whether to broadcast those names. Doing so makes the networks easier to find and therefore more convenient to connect to. Choosing not to broadcast the SSID means the network's name won't show up in the AirPort menu or in comparable lists of networks on other devices. Anyone in the vicinity can still connect to the network if (and only if) he or she knows its SSID. So, conventional wisdom says that by hiding the SSID, you're effectively hiding the network, preventing anyone from joining it unless you've personally shared with him or her the secret network name.

However, in this instance, conventional wisdom is wrong. Even if you turn off SSID broadcasting, it's easy for anyone to discover the name of your network merely by watching the wireless traffic, as you can do with scanning utilities, such as KisMAC, mentioned near the end of this chapter. Turning off the SSID broadcast doesn't hide your network at all; it only makes it a teensy bit harder to find. And because doing so makes it harder for legitimate users to join the network, it's worse than useless — it's creating an unnecessary inconvenience.

On the other hand, I do recommend customizing your access point's SSID to something that's easy for you to remember and is also unique so that you won't confuse it with your neighbors' access points. I explain how to do this for Apple base stations later in this chapter.

Controlling wireless network access

Once someone knows your wireless network's SSID, he or she can attempt to join it. On a Mac, this means selecting the SSID from the AirPort menu. What happens next — whether the access point grants access or not — depends on several factors. Some of them are worth worrying about, and others aren't.

Authentication

If your access point is set up to require authentication, that means users must provide a password (with or without a username) in order to connect to your network. If you use any sort of wireless encryption (including WEP and WPA, described ahead), authentication is necessary to join the network; in most cases, the password you type also serves as the key to encrypt the data sent over the network.

However, it's possible to require authentication without encrypting anything. One way to do this is to set up a configuration called a *captive portal*. This means anyone can connect to your wireless network, but initially, the only service anyone has access to on the network is a single web server (perhaps one embedded in a router or gateway); no matter what website someone tries to visit, the gateway page is all they see. That's the portal, and because it prevents all other network access, it keeps a connection captive, in a manner of speaking. Once a user has typed the necessary credentials on the site (which may also involve paying a fee), the portal releases the client, allowing packets to flow through to other sites and on other ports. If you've ever connected to a Wi-Fi hotspot in a restaurant, airport, or another public place, you've probably used a captive portal.

MAC address filtering

Almost all access points can selectively grant or block access to any wireless client based on its MAC address — not to be confused with Mac, the computer brand! Unlike IP addresses, MAC addresses have the form xx:xx:xx:xx:xx:xx, where each x is a hexadecimal digit (a number from 0 to 9 or a letter from A to F). Each network interface on your Mac has its own MAC address — for example, your built-in Ethernet card has one MAC address, whereas your AirPort card has a different one. When it comes to connecting to a Wi-Fi network, your AirPort card's MAC address is the one you need to be concerned with. What makes this filtering possible is that every network card's MAC address is unique.

In theory, this sounds like a great idea. If I allow only MAC addresses on a short list to connect to my base station and I know that all MAC addresses are unique, that should keep everyone else off my network, right? Well, there are two big flaws in this plan. The first is that every Wi-Fi device broadcasts its own MAC address in cleartext, easily viewable with a Wi-Fi scanning utility. And the second is that it's equally easy to spoof, or forge, a MAC address — to make it appear to an access point that your computer's MAC address is something other than what's coded into the hardware. So, if I can scan for the MAC address of a device that's allowed to be on your wireless network and then change my MAC address to match, I've tidily circumvented your clever filtering.

In other words, MAC address filtering is in the same category as SSID hiding. It seems like it should be effective, but in reality, it isn't; it only creates more work and inconvenience for you. In fairness, it keeps folks who are not technologically proficient off your network, so it may be useful for avoiding random hop-ons, but it provides no real security benefit.

DHCP restrictions

Most access points, especially those (the vast majority) that use NAT to share a single public IP address with multiple wireless clients, use DHCP to hand out IP addresses and other network settings to each client device. However, depending on which access point you use and how you have it set up, DHCP may be optional. You can perhaps turn it off or at least impose some restrictions on its use, such as limiting it to distributing only a very small number of IP addresses. The logic behind such a move is that if a would-be wireless client can't get an IP address, it can't do any harm on the network.

Cross-Ref
For more on DHCP, see Chapter 15. ■

Alas, once again, this logic doesn't hold up in real life. Even if a client doesn't get addressing information from a DHCP server, anyone with basic knowledge of networking could manually type the necessary information on a client computer. It may take a few tries, but the range of choices is sufficiently narrow that it wouldn't be difficult to come up with workable settings that would entirely circumvent the need for DHCP. In short, restricting DHCP is yet another pseudo-security measure that's not worth the effort.

Encrypting your wireless connection

So far, I've told you that most of the measures you can employ to keep ne'er-do-wells off your network are useless. Apart from choosing a good administrative password, the only steps worth taking are requiring authentication and encrypting your connection. These two things usually go hand in hand because encryption requires a key, and in most cases, the password you use to authenticate on a wireless network also serves as the encryption key. Authentication keeps unauthorized people from joining your wireless network, whereas encryption keeps people who haven't joined your network from making any sense of the wireless traffic they can detect and record using scanning or sniffing software. Unless you're setting up a public network with no pretense of security whatsoever, you should always turn on encryption on your wireless access point.

Wi-Fi encryption currently comes in two major flavors: WEP and WPA (with some further variations, especially for WPA). Both of these types of encryption secure the data as it travels between the access point and the client. Because that's often not enough to guarantee privacy, another sort of encryption — a VPN — can also be used with Wi-Fi connections (instead of, or in addition to, WEP or WPA). I discuss VPNs later in this chapter in the context of using public Wi-Fi hotspots.

Cross-Ref

For more on VPNs, see Chapter 12. ■

WEP

When the first version of the 802.11 wireless networking protocol was developed, it was obvious to the designers that there were some security concerns with sending data over radio waves that anyone with the proper equipment could intercept. To address this concern, the IEEE (Institute of Electrical and Electronics Engineers) developed WEP (Wired Equivalent Privacy), an encryption algorithm whose purpose — as the name suggests — was to make wireless access just as secure as wired access.

For the first few years of Wi-Fi's existence, WEP did indeed seem secure, and experts recommended that most people enable it, while cautioning that WEP does slow down wireless network access even as it increases security. WEP comes in two varieties: one that uses a 40-bit key and one that uses a 104-bit key. Ostensibly, the longer key should provide more security, and anyone who wanted to err on the paranoid side simply selected a longer key.

But then, researchers and hackers began discovering holes and weaknesses in WEP. To make a long story short, a series of attacks was developed that could enable anyone with a laptop and certain freely available software to watch traffic on a Wi-Fi network for a little while, capture all the packets that were transmitted, and analyze them to discover the encryption key — enabling them to freely read all data sent over the wireless network. At first, such attacks took anywhere from minutes to hours; nowadays, in certain situations, a WEP key can be broken in as little as 3 seconds. Furthermore, 104-bit WEP keys aren't significantly more difficult to break than the shorter keys.

Note

An example of software that runs on a Mac and that can crack WEP passwords with just a few clicks is KisMAC, described later in this chapter. Needless to say, I don't recommend doing this, except to prove to yourself how insecure your own wireless network is if it uses WEP! ■

Another shortcoming of WEP was that every client on a given wireless network had to use the same encryption key (that is, the same password), and although the key could be changed, doing so wasn't especially convenient. The result was that if someone happened to learn or guess the password for a wireless network, all the traffic for all its users was compromised thereafter — indefinitely (or until someone figured it out and changed the password).

There's a WEP implementation (sometimes called 802.1X WEP) in which a central server manages passwords and lets each user have a different one. Although this is more secure in the sense that someone who learns one user's password can't automatically decrypt other users' traffic, it's easy enough for an attacker to learn multiple passwords in a short period of time that the additional security offers very little benefit.

For the past several years, WEP has been widely regarded as so fundamentally flawed that almost no one recommends using it, especially given that highly secure alternatives (WPA and WPA2, described next) are available. One of the newest varieties of Wi-Fi, 802.11n, doesn't allow for the use of WEP at all.

The one situation in which you might consider using WEP is if you have old Wi-Fi equipment that doesn't support WPA. In the Mac world, that would mean the first-generation (graphite) or second-generation (snow) AirPort base stations or Macs with built-in AirPort cards running operating systems older than Mac OS X 10.3. Even the oldest Wi-Fi-capable Macs support WPA, as long as they're running a relatively modern version of Mac OS X. Arguably, WEP provides better protection than no encryption at all because even though it's easy to crack, doing so requires a modicum of technical knowledge, and the presence of WEP encryption discourages casual users from connecting to your network. But it's merely the digital equivalent of a Keep Off the Lawn sign — it provides no real barrier and doesn't reliably protect the data on your network. Therefore, if at all possible, consider getting rid of your old equipment and replacing it with newer, WPA-capable equipment.

WPA

WPA, or Wi-Fi Protected Access, is the wireless security protocol that replaces WEP. Its goal is to overcome all of WEP's weaknesses and provide even better security than WEP had initially promised.

Technically speaking, the security standard intended as the successor to WEP is called 802.11i, a specification of the IEEE (*WPA* is a term used by the Wi-Fi Alliance for products that meet its certification tests). The 802.11i standard took some time to evolve, however, and in the meantime, it was clear that something better than WEP had to be rolled out. WPA, introduced in 2003, was based on an early version of 802.11i, and its security comes from a protocol called TKIP (Temporal Key Integrity Protocol). TKIP enabled administrators to choose passwords up to 63 characters in length — much longer than those possible with WEP and inherently less vulnerable to certain kinds of attacks, because the length of the key wasn't fixed. In practice, TKIP has been quite secure. There's a known exploit that could enable an attacker to inject a small number of new data packets into a TKIP-protected network, which could potentially cause network problems but not reveal the wireless network's encrypted data.

Along with TKIP, WPA introduced support for two different ways of using passwords. The first way is the pre-shared key, or PSK. A PSK is simply a single password used (for both authentication and encryption) by all clients of a given access point, much like the passwords WEP uses. WPA based on a PSK is called WPA Personal; but using a single key limits security because everyone who connects to the network must know the key, and if someone learns that key, the encryption of the entire wireless network can be broken. In addition, WPA using a PSK is vulnerable to dictionary and brute-force attacks. That is, someone could rapidly try many thousands of words in an attempt to guess the network's password. However, because the time and effort required to guess a password increases with the password's complexity, a network using WPA Personal is effectively safe against such attacks as long as it uses a random password (including capital and lowercase letters, numbers, and punctuation) with at least 10 characters or a simple phrase or sentence containing at least 28 characters.

Even so, because a single, global password is never as secure as per-user passwords, WPA offered another password mechanism that uses the 802.1X authentication protocol. In this version of WPA, called WPA Enterprise, a central RADIUS authentication server keeps track of usernames and passwords for as many users as necessary; and not only does each user get an individual password, but thanks to a multi-step handshaking process, WPA Enterprise can create a customized encryption key for each user each time he or she connects — a key that's different from the password and that the user never even sees. The result is that learning a user's password doesn't permit an attacker to decrypt that user's data, and even if the attacker learned one encryption key, it would be useful only for decrypting the traffic for a single user, for a limited period of time, leaving the rest of the network safe.

Cross-Ref

For more on 802.1X, see Chapter 15. ■

WPA2

Eventually, the final 802.11i standard was ratified, and when it was, the Wi-Fi Alliance adopted it under the name WPA2. For all practical purposes, you can use WPA2 and 802.11i interchangeably, although WPA2 is the more common term by far. Like the first version of WPA, WPA2 comes in Personal and Enterprise varieties. The most significant change between WPA and WPA2 is that the latter offered a new security option: AES-CCMP (Advanced Encryption Standard-Counter Mode with Cipher Block Chaining Message Authentication Code Protocol). This brand of AES is (as of late 2009, at least) invulnerable to any of the exploits that have been found for WEP or WPA/TKIP and is generally considered completely secure as long as good passwords are used.

The only downside to WPA2 is that it requires even newer equipment than WPA does, and some older products that support WPA can't be upgraded to use WPA2. In the Apple world, any base station made before 2003 won't work with WPA2, and any Mac with the first-generation AirPort card, regardless of which version of Mac OS X it's running, can't use WPA2 either (although it can use WPA with Mac OS X 10.3 or later). Although the practical difference in security between WPA and WPA2 is slight, if you want the absolute latest and greatest in wireless security, make sure all your devices are new enough to support WPA2.

Note

Some access points, including all of Apple's base stations, have a mode that mixes WPA Personal and WPA2 Personal and a mode that mixes WPA Enterprise and WPA2 Enterprise. In one of these modes, WPA2 (with AES-CCMP) is used for clients that support it, while TKIP is used for those that don't. This is a fine compromise, with the only downside being a teensy amount of reduced security for those older clients. ■

Configuring an AirPort Base Station

Of the dozens of brands of wireless access points, the one most likely to be in a home or office populated by Macs is Apple. Apple's access points — AirPort base stations and Time Capsule backup appliances — have solid reputations for being reliable and easy to use, not to mention stylish. And unlike most third-party access points, which require logging in via a web browser to change their settings, you can configure Apple's wireless devices using a well-designed program called AirPort Utility that's included with Mac OS X. For all these reasons, the pages that follow focus on wireless security settings for Apple's products. Later, however, I do cover some of the basics of setting up third-party access points, even though it's impossible to provide complete instructions for all of them.

Most of the instructions in this section apply to any recent AirPort Extreme or AirPort Express base station or Time Capsule device (all of which I refer to generically as base stations), although certain models have features unavailable on others, and models manufactured before late 2002 lack WPA encryption. If you have any equipment too old to work with WPA, I strongly suggest replacing it with more modern products as soon as possible.

To oversimplify slightly, most AirPort base station settings fall into one of three broad categories: those that specify how the base station connects to the Internet (not covered here), those that affect how you can connect to the base station in order to perform administrative functions (described next), and those involving how the base station interacts with wired and wireless clients (discussed a bit later).

Note

Your AirPort base station or Time Capsule may offer any of numerous other features too, such as printer sharing and disk sharing, which I don't cover in this book. However, you can learn everything you might need to know about base station configuration in Glenn Fleishman's ebook *Take Control of your 802.11n AirPort Network* (www.takecontrolbooks.com/airport.html). **The ebook also goes into complete detail about options for connecting your base station to the Internet and creating networks that use more than one base station.** ■

Setting the base station security options

As I said earlier in this chapter, one of the first things you should do with any wireless access point is to assign a good, strong password to its administrative interface so no one else can change the device's settings and gain access to your network. In addition to setting a password for your base station, you can configure several other options that affect the security of the base station itself.

To set or change your base station's password, follow these steps:

1. **Open AirPort Utility, which is located in** /Applications/Utilities.

2. **Select your AirPort base station in the list on the left and then click Manual Setup.** If you see a password prompt, type the base station's password and then click OK.

3. **Click the AirPort button on the toolbar.** If you have AirPort Extreme or AirPort Express, click the Base Station tab. If you have Time Capsule, click the Time Capsule tab, shown in Figure 16.1.

FIGURE 16.1

The Time Capsule pane

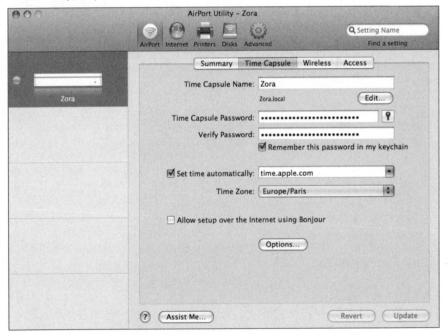

4. **In the Base Station Name or Time Capsule Name field (depending on your model), type a name for your device; this is the name by which it appears in AirPort Utility.** This can be the same as the SSID, but it need not be.

5. **In the Base Station Password (or Time Capsule Password) and Verify Password fields, type and confirm the password you want to use for configuring the base station.** Be sure to choose a strong password and preferably one different from the password used for wireless access.

6. **Optionally, to store the base station's administrative password in the keychain on your Mac, click the Remember this password in my keychain check box.** I recommend doing this, because it makes it easier for you to modify your base station in the future, as long as you connect from the same Mac using AirPort Utility.

7. **Click Update and then wait for your base station to restart.** The new name and/or password becomes effective immediately.

Ordinarily, you can make changes to your base station's configuration only if you're on the same local network (connected wirelessly or via Ethernet). However, it's possible to set up your base station so that you can change its configuration from another network. One way to do this is using Back to My Mac, a part of MobileMe. That's a fairly secure option (assuming, as always, that you use a good password and keep it safe), and it enables you to remotely access files stored on your Time Capsule or on an external disk attached to an AirPort Extreme base station (an AirPort Disk).

To set up AirPort Extreme or Time Capsule to use MobileMe, follow these steps:

1. **Open AirPort Utility, which is located in** `/Applications/Utilities`.

2. **Select your AirPort base station in the list on the left and then click Manual Setup.** If you see a password prompt, type the base station's password and then click OK.

3. **Click the Advanced button on the toolbar and then click MobileMe.**

4. **Type your MobileMe username and password in the fields provided.**

5. **Click Update and then wait for your base station to restart.** Your base station or Time Capsule should then show up in the sidebar of Finder windows when you're connected to a remote network — assuming your Mac has Back to My Mac enabled and any intervening routers, gateways, or firewalls support it.

Cross-Ref

For more on Back to My Mac, see Chapters 4 and 7. ∎

Another way to configure your base station remotely — if you're not a MobileMe member or if your setup doesn't support Back to My Mac — is to make it available directly on the Internet (either by IP address alone or by a domain name). This option is much less secure because it means anyone on the Internet could potentially get access to your base station, change its security settings, and see any files on an attached disk, if he or she knows (or can guess) your password. Therefore, I recommend setting this up only if you have a particular reason to want to change your base station's settings when you're not on the same network.

To set up remote configuration without MobileMe, follow these steps:

1. **Open AirPort Utility, which is located in** `/Applications/Utilities`.

2. **Select your AirPort base station in the list on the left and then click Manual Setup.** If you see a password prompt, type the base station's password and then click OK.

3. **Click the AirPort button on the toolbar.** If you have AirPort Extreme or AirPort Express, click the Base Station tab. If you have Time Capsule, click the Time Capsule tab.

4. **Click the Allow setup over the Internet using Bonjour check box.**

5. **Optionally, to make your base station available using a domain name (rather than only an IP address — useful in situations where your IP address may change from time to time), do the following:**

   1. Sign up for a domain name with a dynamic DNS service, such as those provided by easyDNS (`www.easydns.com`) or DynDNS.com (`www.dyndns.com`).

   2. Back in the Base Station (or Time Capsule) pane of AirPort Utility, click the Edit button beneath the base station's name.

   3. Click the Use dynamic global hostname check box.

   4. In the Hostname, User, and Password fields, type the domain name you set up in sub-step 1 and then type the username and password for your dynamic DNS account.

   5. Click Done.

6. **Click Update and then wait for your base station to restart.** Your base station can now be reached over the Internet — assuming all the intervening routers, gateways, and firewalls permit access.

To connect to your base station from another network, open AirPort utility, choose File ➪ Configure Other, type the IP address or domain name of your base station and its administrative password, and then click OK.

Setting wireless options

The next and much larger category of settings involves the ways in which the base station interacts with computers that connect to it in order to gain access to the local network, the Internet, or both. Except for settings that explicitly refer to Wi-Fi features (such as SSID broadcast and wireless client monitoring), these capabilities apply to wired clients too. That is, if you connect a Mac to your AirPort base station or Time Capsule using an Ethernet cable instead of wirelessly, you can still make use of the base station's NAT and DHCP server and related features.

Wireless security and password settings

If you read the first part of this chapter, you know that WEP security is so badly broken that you should never use it if you can avoid it. The only situations in which it's genuinely necessary are when you want to provide wireless service to older devices that don't support any variety of WPA. But in such cases, it's much better, if possible, to upgrade the Wi-Fi cards in those devices or to use a newer add-on (USB or PCMCIA) Wi-Fi adapter. And between WPA and WPA2, the latter is the better choice — again, except for those relatively few devices that work with WPA but not WPA2 — although even the first version of WPA is secure enough for most situations as long as you use a good password. In enterprise settings, WPA/WPA2 Enterprise is an even better choice because it gives each client a different password, creates encryption keys individually for each user on the fly, and lets you manage user credentials from a central location. But because of the additional expense and bother of setting up the additional infrastructure, it's not worth it for home and small office setups.

If you're using WPA or WPA2, be sure to choose a good password. In this context, good means completely random — including lowercase and capital letters, numbers, and punctuation — and at least 10 characters in length. But because passwords can be as long as 63 characters and because users need to type them only once (after which they can be stored in their keychains), choosing a 20- or 30- or 63-character password is even better.

To configure the wireless security and password settings for your base station, follow these steps:

1. **Open AirPort Utility, which is located in** `/Applications/Utilities`.

2. **Select your AirPort base station in the list on the left and then click Manual Setup.** If you see a password prompt, type the base station's password and then click OK.

3. **Click the AirPort button on the toolbar and then click the Wireless tab, shown in Figure 16.2.**

FIGURE 16.2

The Wireless pane

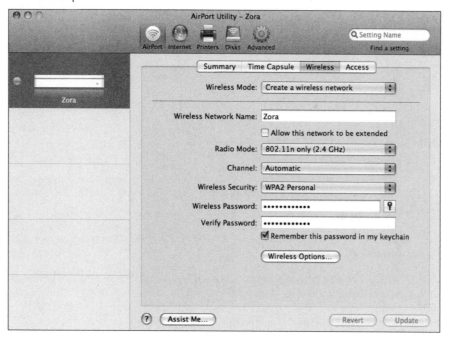

4. **From the Wireless Security pop-up menu, choose the type of encryption you want to use.** Your choices depend on the setting shown in the Radio Mode pop-up menu (see the AirPort Utility Help menu for assistance in choosing a radio mode). The options are:

   - **None.** No encryption. Use this only for public networks for which you intend to provide no security — or when you can guarantee that all clients will use another form of encryption, such as a VPN.

   - **WEP (Transitional Security Network).** This option appears only when the radio mode is 802.11n (802.11b/g compatible) or 802.11n (802.11a compatible). Avoid WEP if at all possible.

   - **WPA/WPA2 Personal.** This option appears only when the radio mode is 802.11n (802.11b/g compatible) or 802.11n (802.11a compatible). This setting means the base station offers WPA2 (with AES encryption) for clients that support it and WPA (with TKIP encryption) for those that don't using a pre-shared key for authentication.

   - **WPA2 Personal.** This is WPA2, with only AES encryption, using a pre-shared key.

- **WPA/WPA2 Enterprise.** This option appears only when the radio mode is 802.11n (802.11b/g compatible) or 802.11n (802.11a compatible). This setting means the base station offers WPA2 (with AES encryption) for clients that support it and WPA (with TKIP encryption) for those that don't by using a RADIUS server for authentication.
- **WPA2 Enterprise.** This is WPA2, with only AES encryption, using a RADIUS authentication server.

Note

When your AirPort base station is set to use the Enterprise version of WPA or WPA2, it functions as an authenticator on the network. ■

5. **If you chose WEP (Transitional Security Network), WPA/WPA2 Personal, or WPA2 Personal in step 4, type a password into the Wireless Password field and then type it again in the Verify Password field.** If the Remember this password in my keychain check box isn't already selected, click it. This setting lets you reconnect to the base station in the future without having to type your password again. But keep in mind that it's only as secure as your keychain, so take appropriate steps to prevent unauthorized keychain access.

Cross-Ref

For more on using Keychain, see Chapter 5. ■

6. **If you chose WPA/WPA2 Enterprise or WPA2 Enterprise in step 4, click the Configure RADIUS button to open the Access tab, shown in Figure 16.3, and then, using information supplied by the administrator who manages your RADIUS server, fill in the fields in this pane.**

Note

If you use either of the Enterprise varieties of WPA, each device that connects to your wireless network must also have 802.1X enabled and configured. ■

7. **Click Update and then wait for your base station to restart.** The new security settings take effect immediately.

Setting SSID options

When you first turn on your AirPort base station or Time Capsule, its network name, or SSID, is set to Apple Network, followed by the final six digits of the device's MAC address. You can and should change this to something friendlier. As discussed earlier in this chapter, an openly broadcast SSID makes it easier for users to find and join your network, and preventing the SSID broadcast has such an insignificant effect on security that it's effectively a waste of time — you force everyone who connects to your network to expend more effort, but it doesn't protect you in any way. Therefore, I recommend letting your base station continue broadcasting its SSID, but you can stop these broadcasts, which Apple somewhat misleadingly refers to as creating a closed network, if you prefer.

FIGURE 16.3

The Access pane

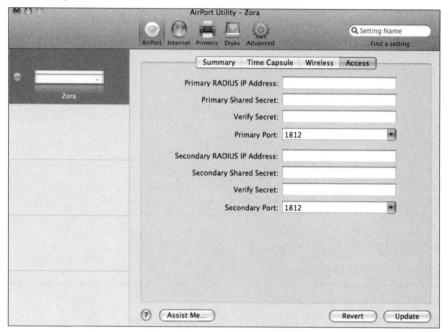

Wi-Fi Protected Setup (WPS)

A network that uses WPA Personal or WPA2 Personal should also use a long, complex password for maximum security. But such passwords are cumbersome to remember and type, so the newest WPA/WPA2-capable hardware offers a way to securely associate wireless clients with the network without their ever having to type the password manually. This mechanism is called Wi-Fi Protected Setup (WPS). Apple base stations manufactured since 2007 support WPS, as do numerous access points made by other manufacturers. However, because not all companies implement WPS the same way, your Mac may not be able to use WPS offered by a third-party access point, and any PCs you have won't be able to use WPS with an AirPort base station or Time Capsule.

To use WPS with Macs on your network (which must be running Leopard or higher), first configure your base station to use WPA Personal or WPA2 Personal, as described previously. Then, follow these steps:

1. **Open AirPort Utility, which is located in** /Applications/Utilities.

2. **Select your AirPort base station in the list on the left and then click Manual Setup.** If you see a password prompt, type the base station's password and then click OK.

continued

continued

3. **Choose Base Station ⇨ Add Wireless Clients.** The Wireless Client Setup Assistant window opens.

4. **Click one of these two radio buttons :**
   - **PIN.** With this option, each Mac that attempts to connect to your network generates a unique eight-digit number, which you then (see step 7) type in AirPort Utility.
   - **First attempt.** With this option, the first Mac that tries to connect to the wireless network after you've used this assistant is given access. This is slightly less secure, although slightly more convenient.

5. **Optionally, to restrict the next client that joins the network to using it for only 24 hours, click the Limit client's access to 24 hours check box.**

6. **Click Continue.**

7. **On the Mac you want to connect to your network, go to the AirPort menu and choose the name of your wireless network (which should appear in bold) and then:**
   - If you selected PIN in step 4, your Mac generates and displays a PIN on its screen. Type this number in the PIN field in AirPort Utility's Wireless Client Setup Assistant window and then click Continue.
   - If you selected First attempt in step 4, the Mac joins the network immediately.

No other steps are necessary; the newly associated Mac now has full network access.

To configure your base station's SSID options, follow these steps:

1. Open AirPort Utility, which is located in `/Applications/Utilities`.

2. Select your AirPort base station in the list on the left and then click **Manual Setup**. If you see a password prompt, type the base station's password and then click OK.

3. Click the AirPort button on the toolbar and then click the **Wireless** tab.

4. In the Wireless Network Name field, type the SSID you want to use for your wireless network.

5. Click the **Wireless Options** button. The dialog box shown in Figure 16.4 opens.

6. If you want to prevent the SSID from being broadcast, click the **Create a closed network** check box.

7. Click Done, click Update, and then wait for your base station to restart. The base station adopts its new SSID settings immediately.

Configuring MAC address access control

Another ostensible security measure that increases aggravation while offering practically no protection is allowing your base station to accept as clients only devices for which it knows the MAC address. Although this deters casual or unsophisticated users from joining your network, anyone with moderate technical skills can bypass this protection in under a minute, so I suggest not restricting access in this way.

FIGURE 16.4

The Wireless Options dialog box

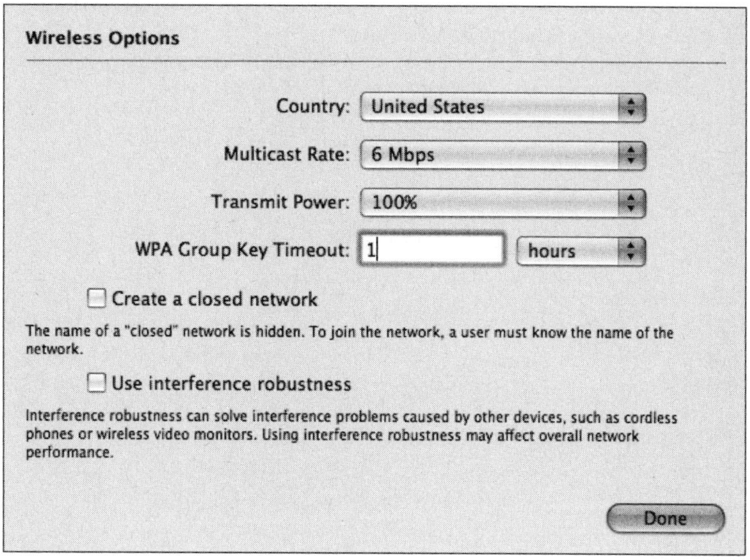

Wireless Options

Country: United States

Multicast Rate: 6 Mbps

Transmit Power: 100%

WPA Group Key Timeout: 1   hours

☐ Create a closed network

The name of a "closed" network is hidden. To join the network, a user must know the name of the network.

☐ Use interference robustness

Interference robustness can solve interference problems caused by other devices, such as cordless phones or wireless video monitors. Using interference robustness may affect overall network performance.

Done

Note

You can manually white-list MAC addresses only if your base station is set up to use WEP, WPA Personal, or WPA2 Personal. However, if you use an Enterprise version of WPA, you can use the same RADIUS server that handles authentication for your clients to check their MAC addresses, as described ahead. ■

To restrict access to devices with particular MAC addresses, follow these steps:

1. **Open AirPort Utility, which is located in** /Applications/Utilities.

2. **Select your AirPort base station in the list on the left and then click Manual Setup.** If you see a password prompt, type the base station's password and then click OK.

3. **Click the AirPort button on the toolbar and then click the Access tab.**

4. **For manual MAC address filtering (the usual case), do the following:**

   1. **Choose Timed Access from the MAC Address Access Control pop-up menu.**

   2. **Click the Add (+) button.** The dialog box shown in Figure 16.5 opens.

   3. **In the MAC Address field, type or paste the MAC address of the first device to which you want to grant access.** To type the address of the Mac you're using to run AirPort Utility, click This Computer. Optionally, type a description (such as the computer's name) in the Description field.

FIGURE 16.5

The Timed Access Control Setup Assistant dialog box

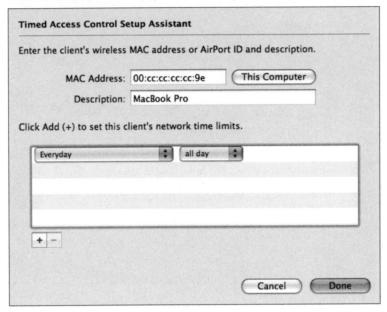

Note

For the purposes of this setting, the one you want is your AirPort card's MAC address. If you're uncertain as to the MAC address of a given Mac, open System Profiler (in `/Applications/Utilities`), select Network in the list on the left, select Airport at the top under Active Services, and then scroll down in the bottom pane until you see MAC Address, which is listed under the Ethernet heading. ∎

    4. **If you want to limit this particular device to accessing your Wi-Fi network only at certain times, choose a day or day range from the Everyday pop-up menu and either all day or between from the next menu; if you choose between, type the hours during which access is permitted.** To add more time ranges during which access is allowed for this client, click the Add (+) button and then repeat this step.

    5. **Click Done.**

  5. **To use a RADIUS server to determine which MAC addresses may join your AirPort network, do the following:**

    1. **Choose RADIUS from the MAC Address Access Control pop-up menu.** The window should then look like Figure 16.6.

    2. **Fill in the remaining fields using information supplied by the administrator who manages your RADIUS server.**

FIGURE 16.6

To use a RADIUS server to manage MAC address filtering for the clients on your network, type its details in this pane.

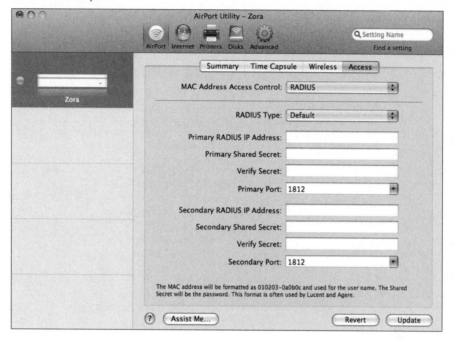

6. **If you ever want to disable MAC address filtering, choose Not Enabled from the MAC Address Access Control pop-up menu.**

7. **Click Update and then wait for your base station to restart.** The MAC address restrictions you set take effect immediately.

Configuring NAT

The most common configuration of AirPort base stations and other wireless routers is to use NAT to share one public IP address among all the clients, each of which then receives a private IP address for use within the local network. Because of the convenience and security this arrangement provides, you should use NAT unless one of the following is true:

- Your ISP has provided you with a range of publicly routable IP addresses and you want each computer that connects to your base station to use one of these. In this case, you can tell AirPort Utility which range of addresses to distribute to wireless clients.

- You want another router or gateway on your network — or your ISP's router — to perform NAT functions or you want to manually assign a static IP address to each computer. In this case, you can configure your AirPort base station to act as a bridge, passing on the network connection to wireless clients but not taking any responsibility for addressing.

Cross-Ref

For more on NAT, see Chapter 15. ■

To configure NAT for your AirPort base station's wireless clients, follow these steps:

1. **Open AirPort Utility, which is located in** /Applications/Utilities.

2. **Select your AirPort base station in the list on the left and then click Manual Setup.** If you see a password prompt, type the base station's password and then click OK.

3. **Click the Internet button on the toolbar.** The window should look something like Figure 16.7.

FIGURE 16.7

When you choose Share a public IP address from the pop-up menu at the bottom of this pane, you enable NAT for your wireless network.

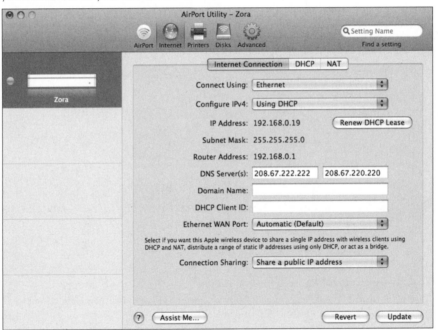

4. **To use NAT, choose Share a public IP address from the Connection Sharing pop-up menu.** If, instead, you want to distribute a range of fixed addresses to wireless clients, choose Distribute a range of IP addresses; if you do, be sure to read the instructions just ahead for configuring the DHCP server, because they explain how to adjust the range of IP addresses assigned to wireless

clients. Or to rely on another NAT router, such as your cable or DSL gateway, to supply IP addresses (or if you want to use manual addressing), choose Off (Bridge Mode).

5. **Click Update and then wait for your base station to restart.** The NAT router begins sharing addresses as soon as devices try to connect to the base station.

Note

Although NAT requires no further configuration, you can choose which range of private IP addresses it uses. Read the instructions on configuring the DHCP server for details. ■

Configuring the DHCP server

DHCP saves network users and administrators effort and confusion by distributing IP addresses, DNS and router locations, and other key network setup information from a central location rather than requiring it to be typed manually on each computer. AirPort base stations have built-in DHCP servers, and most AirPort configurations employ DHCP to make setup as simple as possible. DHCP is enabled automatically when NAT is turned on, but you can adjust some of its settings (only a couple of which I cover here), and you can also optionally use DHCP when distributing public IP addresses to AirPort clients.

As I mentioned earlier in this chapter, although some people recommend turning off DHCP on the grounds that it could supply an IP address to an unauthorized user, it's trivially easy for a network intruder to assign a valid IP address manually (bypassing DHCP altogether). And because Apple doesn't permit you to disable DHCP entirely on an AirPort base station when using NAT or distributing a range of public addresses, it's not worth worrying about.

To change the range of IP addresses your AirPort base station distributes using DHCP, follow these steps:

1. **Open AirPort Utility, which is located in** `/Applications/Utilities`.

2. **Select your AirPort base station in the list on the left and then click Manual Setup.** If you see a password prompt, type the base station's password and then click OK.

3. **Click the Internet button on the toolbar and then click the DHCP tab.** The DHCP tab is available only if your base station is configured to share a public IP address or distribute a range of addresses. If you're using NAT (Share a public IP address), the window should look approximately like Figure 16.8. Now do the following:

   1. **From the DHCP Beginning Address pop-up menu, choose the first portion of the address range you want to use** (`10.0`, `172.16`, or `192.168`).

   2. **In the two fields that follow, type the second portion of the first address you want to use.** For example, if you want the range of private addresses you distribute to be `172.16.1.100` through `172.16.1.255`, choose `172.16` from the pop-up menu and then type 1 and 100, respectively, into the two fields.

   3. **In the DHCP Ending Address field, type the last IP address in the range you want to distribute (for example,** `172.16.1.255`). Because performance decreases when a large number of clients are connected to a single base station, you may want to keep the range fairly small to limit the number of DHCP clients at any time.

If you're distributing a range of public IP addresses, the window should resemble Figure 16.9. Now do the following:

1. **In the DHCP Beginning Address field, type the starting IP address in the range you want to distribute.** Your ISP or network administrator should be able to tell you what range of addresses you can use.

2. **In the DHCP Ending Address field, type the last IP address in the range you want to distribute.**

4. **Click Update and then wait for your base station to restart.** The DHCP server begins distributing configuration details as soon as devices try to connect to the base station.

FIGURE 16.8

In this pane, you can optionally change the range of private addresses your base station's NAT router distributes.

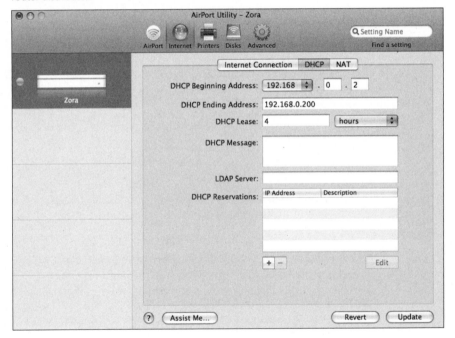

Configuring port mapping

If your base station has NAT enabled (that is, the Connection Sharing pop-up menu is set to Share a public IP address), you can optionally use port mapping — which the rest of the world refers to as port forwarding — to let particular client computers receive inbound Internet traffic on particular ports.

Cross-Ref

For more on port forwarding, see Chapter 15. ■

FIGURE 16.9

When using DHCP without NAT, this pane lets you specify the range of public IP addresses to distribute to your network.

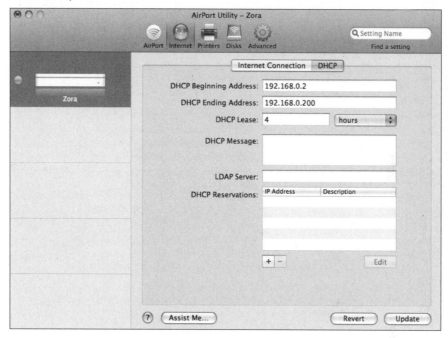

To set up port forwarding on your AirPort base station, follow these steps (note that your base station must have a public IP address; if it's behind another NAT router, this won't work):

1. **Open AirPort Utility, which is located in** /Applications/Utilities.

2. **Select your AirPort base station in the list on the left and then click Manual Setup.** If you see a password prompt, type the base station's password and then click OK.

3. **Click the Internet button on the toolbar and then click NAT.** The NAT tab is available only if your base station is configured to share a public IP address, meaning it distributes private addresses to connected clients.

4. **Click Configure Port Mappings to open a list of mapped ports (which is initially empty).**

5. **Click the Add (+) button.** The dialog box shown in Figure 16.10 opens.

6. **Choose a service (such as Personal File Sharing or Personal Web Sharing) from the Service pop-up menu to fill in the various Port fields automatically.** If the service you want to share isn't in this list, fill in the ports manually. If in doubt, keep in mind that most common services use only TCP ports, not UDP ports.

7. **In the Private IP Address field, type or paste the private IP address of the Mac that will be providing the service.** If you're uncertain what this is, go to that Mac, choose ⇨ System Preferences, and then click the Network icon. The private IP address is shown on the right side of the window.

FIGURE 16.10

Configure port forwarding (called port mapping in AirPort parlance) in this dialog box.

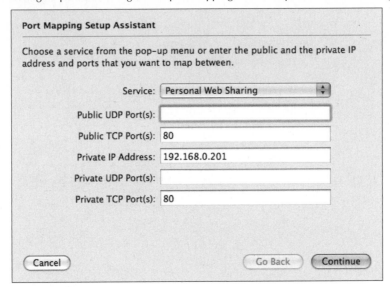

Port Mapping Setup Assistant

Choose a service from the pop-up menu or enter the public and the private IP address and ports that you want to map between.

Service:	Personal Web Sharing
Public UDP Port(s):	
Public TCP Port(s):	80
Private IP Address:	192.168.0.201
Private UDP Port(s):	
Private TCP Port(s):	80

Cancel   Go Back   Continue

8. **To forward additional ports, repeat steps 6 through 8 as needed.**

9. **Click Continue, click Update, and then wait for your base station to restart.** The port(s) you selected are then immediately forwarded to the Mac(s) you specified.

Configuring a default host

A default host — what most other access points refer to as a DMZ host — lets all Internet traffic from the outside that wasn't explicitly requested by some other client flow directly to a particular computer on your wireless network.

Cross-Ref
For more on DMZ, see Chapter 15. ■

To set up a DMZ host using an AirPort Extreme base station that has a publicly routable IP address, follow these steps:

1. **Open AirPort Utility, which is located in** /Applications/Utilities.

2. **Select your AirPort base station in the list on the left and then click Manual Setup.** If you see a password prompt, type the base station's password and then click OK.

3. **Click the Internet button on the toolbar and then click NAT.** The NAT tab is available only if your base station is configured to share a public IP address, meaning it distributes private addresses to connected clients.

4. **Click the Enable default host at check box, shown in Figure 16.11.**

5. **Type the private IP address of your desired DMZ host in the field provided.**

6. **Click Update and then wait for your base station to restart.** All inbound Internet traffic that wasn't requested by another computer is immediately redirected to the IP address you typed.

An AirPort base station's default host setting is what many routers and gateways refer to as a DMZ or a DMZ host.

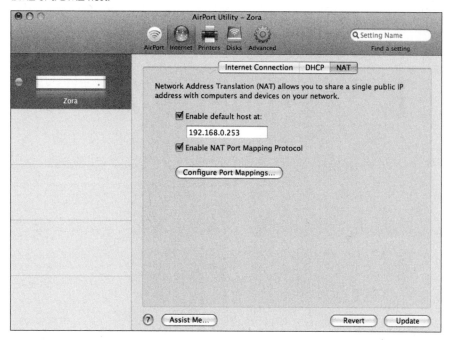

Configuring logging and SNMP

AirPort base stations can store and report a variety of details about their operation, which may be useful in tracking down problems or attempted security breaches. Logs, of course, simply store a list of entries about events that occurred, such as users connecting and settings being changed. SNMP (Simple Network Monitoring Protocol), on the other hand, provides live information over the network about statistics such as bandwidth usage and how many clients are connected. Unfortunately, Apple provides precious little information about how these features work, so if your needs for information about your base station's operation go beyond the fairly superficial, it may take some trial and error to get just the details you're looking for.

Logs

Base stations store limited logs internally and can also (with some fiddling) be made to send log information automatically to another computer that's running a program called `syslogd` (system log daemon) and is configured to listen for the base station's messages.

To view a base station's internal logs, follow these steps:

1. **Open AirPort Utility, which is located in** /Applications/Utilities.

2. **Select your AirPort base station in the list on the left and then click Manual Setup.** If you see a password prompt, type the base station's password and then click OK.

3. **Click the Advanced button on the toolbar and then click the Statistics tab.**

4. **Click the Logs and Statistics button.** The window changes to show new tabs (Logs, Wireless Clients, and, in some cases, DHCP Clients), as shown in Figure 16.12.

FIGURE 16.12

Your base station's log contains details that can help you diagnose problems or detect unauthorized access.

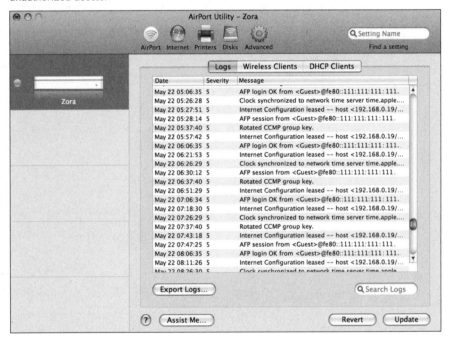

5. **To search within the log, you can either type in the search field or save the current log on your Mac, click Export Logs, select a location, and then click Save.** You can then open the log file with TextEdit or any other text editor.

You can also direct log output directly to a computer running syslogd. To do this, follow these steps:

1. **Open AirPort Utility, which is located in** /Applications/Utilities.

2. **Select your AirPort base station in the list on the left and then click Manual Setup.** If you see a password prompt, type the base station's password and then click OK.

3. **Click the Advanced button on the toolbar and then click the Statistics tab, shown in Figure 16.13.**

4. **In the Syslog Destination Address field, type the private IP address of the computer that will receive the base station log information.**

5. **From the Syslog Level pop-up menu, choose the level of log detail you want to store.** Lower levels provide less detail. However, Apple doesn't specify exactly which details are included at each level, so you may need to experiment to get the type of data you want. If in doubt, choose the most detailed level, 7 - Debug.

6. **Click Update and then wait for your base station to restart.**

7. **On the computer whose IP address you typed in step 4, make sure `syslogd` is configured to receive and store log messages from the base station.** Apple doesn't provide instructions for doing this, but if the computer in question is a Mac running Leopard or Snow Leopard, the directions at `http://meinit.nl/enable-apple-mac-os-x-machine-syslog-server` should get you started.

FIGURE 16.13

The Statistics pane

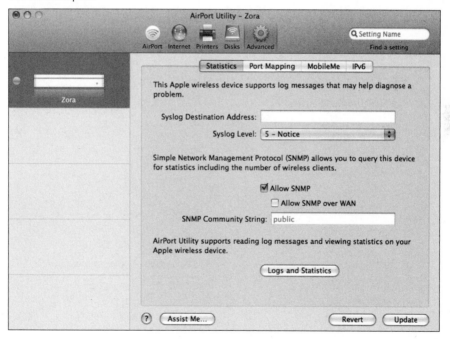

Wireless clients

Another part of the statistics AirPort Utility can deliver, without any other software required, is a list of all currently connected wireless clients, along with a live graph of the signal strength for each one. To display wireless client statistics, follow these steps:

1. **Open AirPort Utility, which is located in** `/Applications/Utilities`.
2. **Select your AirPort base station in the list on the left and then click Manual Setup.** If you see a password prompt, type the base station's password and then click OK.
3. **Click the Advanced button on the toolbar and then click the Statistics tab.**
4. **Click the Logs and Statistics button and then click the Wireless Clients tab.** The window should look similar to Figure 16.14.

FIGURE 16.14

See a graph showing the signal strength of each connected wireless client in this pane.

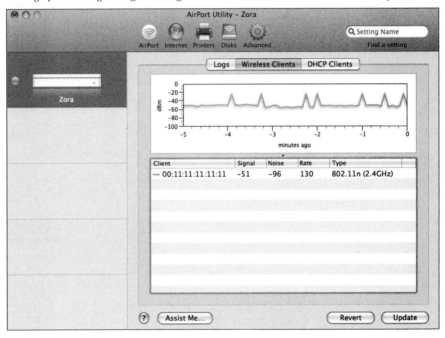

SNMP

To configure your base station to deliver real-time information about usage using SNMP, follow these steps:

1. **Open AirPort Utility, which is located in** `/Applications/Utilities`.
2. **Select your AirPort base station in the list on the left and then click Manual Setup.** If you see a password prompt, type the base station's password and then click OK.
3. **Click the Advanced button on the toolbar and then click the Statistics tab.**
4. **If the Allow SNMP check box isn't already selected, click it.** Optionally, type a name in the SNMP Community String field, which functions somewhat like a password. The default string, public, lets anyone see your base station's SNMP information.
5. **To enable computers beyond your local network to receive SNMP data from your base station, click the Allow SNMP over WAN check box (if this check box appears).**

6. **If you've made any changes, click Update and then wait for your base station to restart.** The base station begins broadcasting information immediately; use your favorite SNMP client (such as NetMonitorX, `www.sustworks.com/site/prod_ipmx_overview.html`) to view the data.

Setting up a guest network

AirPort Extreme base stations and Time Capsules released beginning in March 2009 (dual-band models) have a useful feature not available on earlier models: guest networking. If you turn on this feature, you create two separate wireless networks with the same device — one that's protected with a strong password (or 802.1X) for your personal or internal business use, and a separate network with little or no security that you can make available to guests so they can get Internet access without knowing your regular password or getting any access to your local network.

To activate guest networking, follow these steps:

1. **Open AirPort Utility, which is located in** `/Applications/Utilities`.

2. **Select your AirPort base station in the list on the left and then click Manual Setup.** If you see a password prompt, type the base station's password and then click OK.

3. **Click the AirPort button on the toolbar and then click Guest Network.** The Guest Network tab isn't available if your base station is set to Bridge Mode, as described earlier in this chapter.

4. **Click the Enable Guest Network check box.**

5. **Type a name for your guest network, which can be different from the one your main AirPort network uses.**

6. **Optionally, to allow any connected guests to communicate with each other (although not with devices on your local network) and to discover devices on the guest network using Bonjour, click the Allow Guest Network Clients check box.**

7. **To turn on WPA encryption and require a password for the guest network, choose either WPA/WPA2 Personal or WPA2 Personal from the Wireless Security pop-up menu and then type and verify a password.** For more information, see the instructions presented earlier in this chapter on setting up WPA on your base station.

8. **Click Update and then wait for your base station to restart.** The guest network becomes available immediately.

Configuring Third-Party Access Points

The previous section covered a wide variety of wireless security settings for Apple AirPort base stations and Time Capsules. But Apple is just one of many manufacturers of Wi-Fi access points, and because Macs work just fine with other brands too, you may have Wi-Fi equipment from another company.

The sheer number of products available and the varieties of features and interfaces they offer make it impossible for me to provide detailed instructions for configuring all of them. However, I can offer some general information that applies to the majority of third-party access points and go into slightly more detail for a few of the most popular brands. For brands not mentioned here or to learn how to configure additional settings, consult the documentation that came with your access point or the manufacturer's website.

Access point configuration basics

Although Apple includes AirPort Utility with every AirPort base station and Time Capsule (as well as with Mac OS X itself), such desktop configuration software is extremely uncommon. Instead, most access points include a simple built-in web server. You connect to the access point by pointing your browser to a special private IP address, type your administrative credentials to get access to the device's settings, and then use web-based forms to configure it. Depending on the device and what settings you change, you may need to restart the access point after making changes — which could involve clicking a button in the web interface, flipping a switch, or even unplugging and replugging the power cord.

What follows is a list of default URLs and login credentials for configuring several popular brands of access points, along with additional tips for learning about their security settings.

Note

If your access point still uses its default credentials, the very first thing you should do is change them! Select a strong password, apply it, log out, and log back in with the new password before doing anything else. Access points that keep their default credentials are a huge security risk because this enables anyone to disable or bypass any other security settings. ■

2Wire

Wireless access points made by 2Wire have WEP encryption enabled by default, using a ten-digit encryption key printed on a label on the bottom of the device. Be sure not to confuse the encryption key with the device's serial number. If you're connecting to the device wirelessly instead of over Ethernet, you need to type that encryption key after selecting the device from your AirPort menu. You can then configure the device by browsing to either `http://gateway.2wire.net` or `http://192.168.1.254`. To learn more about configuring 2Wire access points, visit `http://support.2wire.com/index.php?page=view&article=60`.

Belkin

Belkin access points can be configured by pointing your browser to `http://192.168.2.1`. After the page loads, click the Login link to open the Login window. By default, the administrative password is blank; click Submit to modify the device's settings. Belkin offers a series of videos on configuring security settings for their products — including how to enable WPA2. To see these videos, visit `www.belkin.com/support/?lid=en`, go to the bottom of the page, and then click the icon for the video you want to watch.

D-Link

The default URL for configuring most D-Link access points is `http://192.168.0.1`, but the last number varies on certain models (one might be `http://192.168.0.30`, another `http://192.168.0.50`, and so on), so consult your user manual for the URL your model uses. In any case, after connecting, you're prompted for a username and password; the default username is admin, and the default password is blank (none). To learn more, search for your model number on D-Link's support website at `http://support.dlink.com/faq`.

Linksys

Linksys distinguishes between products called wireless access points (which can be configured by browsing to either `http://192.168.1.251` or `http://192.168.1.245`) and wireless routers (whose default URL is `http://192.168.1.1`). Either way, you're prompted for your credentials. The username isn't set by default; until you've manually set one, leave it blank. The default password is admin. For more details on configuring the security settings of Linksys access points, see `www.linksysbycisco.com/US/en/learningcenter/HowtoSecureYourNetwork`.

Netgear

Netgear products use either of two URLs to access their configuration screens: `http://192.168.0.1` or `http://192.168.1.1`. Once you connect, the first thing you should see is a pop-up window asking for your credentials. By default, the username is admin and the password is password. For more details on configuring the Netgear access points, see `http://kb.netgear.com/app/answers/detail/a_id/112`.

Wireless Security Settings on Your Mac

Thus far, this chapter has discussed the types of security a Wi-Fi network may offer and how to configure the access points that provide wireless Internet access. However, you must also take some steps on your Mac to use wireless encryption. Often, it's just a matter of typing a password, but you may also have to choose an encryption method and make a few other decisions.

Cross-Ref

For more on configuring your Mac to connect to an authentication server using 802.1X (whether using Ethernet or Wi-Fi), see Chapter 15. ■

To connect to a wireless network, follow these steps:

1. **Look for the wedge-shaped AirPort menu in your menu bar.** If it isn't there, follow these steps:

   1. **Choose ⬦ System Preferences and then click Network.**
   2. **If the lock icon in the lower-left corner of the window is in the locked state, click it, type an administrator's username and password, and then click OK.**
   3. **Select your AirPort interface in the list on the left and then click the Show AirPort status in menu bar check box.**

2. **If the name (SSID) of the network to which you want to connect appears in the AirPort menu, follow these steps:**

   1. **Choose the network name from the menu.** If the network has no encryption (as shown by the absence of a lock icon next to the network name), you connect immediately; you can skip the remaining steps. If the network does use encryption, a dialog box opens, one version of which is shown in Figure 16.15 (the wording and options vary according to the type of encryption used).

FIGURE 16.15

When you connect to a WEP or WPA Personal wireless network, a dialog box opens, prompting you for your password. WPA Enterprise networks ask for more information.

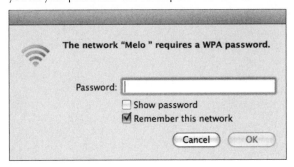

2. Type the wireless network password and any other requested information.

3. To store the credentials for this network in your keychain (so you won't have to type them again when joining the network with this computer), leave the Remember this network check box selected; otherwise, click it to deselect it.

4. Click OK to join.

3. If the network name (SSID) doesn't appear in the AirPort menu (meaning it's set not to broadcast its SSID), follow these steps:

1. Choose Join Other Network from the AirPort menu. The dialog box shown in Figure 16.16 opens.

FIGURE 16.16

When connecting to a network that doesn't broadcast its SSID, you must supply not only the network name but the type of encryption it uses.

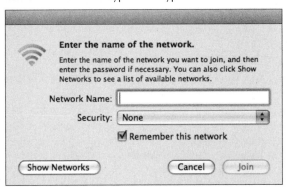

2. Type the SSID into the Network Name field.

3. **Choose the type of security the network uses from the Security pop-up menu.** If you don't know, you can either check with the network's administrator or simply try each setting in turn. If you see no error message and are able to connect to the Internet, you chose the right one.

4. **Depending on which security type you choose, one or more additional fields appear — a Password field, in some cases a User Name field, and, for WPA Enterprise security, additional pop-up menus for specifying 802.1X behavior and TLS Certificate — so fill in all these fields using information supplied by the network's administrator.**

5. **To store the credentials for this network in your keychain (so you won't have to type them again when joining the network with this computer), leave the Remember this network check box selected; otherwise, click it to deselect it.**

Note

Storing your password in your keychain makes connecting much easier, but as with all cases of using your keychain, the password (and thus the security of your wireless network) is only as safe as your keychain itself. If you have your keychain configured to unlock automatically, for example, or if you've chosen a simple password for your keychain, it may be imprudent to store your network password there. ■

6. **Click Join.** Assuming your credentials were correct, your Mac joins the network immediately.

Using Public Wi-Fi Hotspots

I've already discussed the dangers of using public Wi-Fi hotspots a few times in this book, but the warning bears repeating. When you use a public Wi-Fi connection, anyone with a computer within about 300 feet of you (sometimes even farther) can easily watch and record all the data you send and receive over the Internet. The process is trivially easy — all anyone need do is download and run some free software, and a couple of clicks later, your data (possibly including important passwords) is in their hands. Because the eavesdropper could be in another room, in another building, in a car, or around the corner, you may have no idea that someone is monitoring you. This is not a remote, hypothetical possibility; Wi-Fi eavesdropping is extremely common in public places, and the only safe assumption to make is that someone else is sniffing all your wireless data.

The danger still exists even if you are required to pay for network access (using a captive portal, as discussed earlier in this chapter), and even if the data is encrypted using a WEP, WPA, or WPA2 password. Most public Wi-Fi networks aren't encrypted, but of those that are, the vast majority use the same password for every client. Therefore, even if your data is being sent over the airwaves encrypted, anyone else who has access to the network also, ipso facto, knows the network password and could therefore use it to decrypt your data. So, don't let any claims of password protection or encryption on public hotspots lull you into a false sense of security.

Also bear in mind that even if you hop on the web quickly to check movie times or do something similarly innocent, your email program, online backup or syncing software, or any number of other background programs could make connections during that brief time without your ever realizing it, potentially sending various passwords and other private information across the network and into the hands of a hacker somewhere. And although I've used the word *public* to describe hazardous hotspots, in reality, this problem applies to any hotspot over which you have no control — it applies equally to your friend's AirPort base station and the internal network of a business client you're visiting, even though those aren't exactly public.

To put it as plainly as possible: Unless you're connecting to your own (or your company's) wireless access point using WPA/WPA2 (and assuming, for PSK versions of WPA, a strong password that's scrupulously kept secret), you must take additional steps to preserve the privacy of your data when you use Wi-Fi.

At present, there's only one good solution to the threat of eavesdropping while using someone else's Wi-Fi connection: a VPN. Fortunately, it's a highly effective solution (with a caveat or two), and it need not be expensive either; at least one VPN provider (Hotspot Shield, http://hotspotshield.com) is free (ad-supported), and numerous others offer their services for less than $10 per month. So, whether you use a VPN provided by your company, a VPN server or appliance on your home network, or a commercial VPN service, get in the habit of connecting to the VPN immediately when you connect to any Wi-Fi hotspot except your own.

Cross-Ref

For more on VPNs, see Chapter 12. ■

As for the caveats, there are really just two. First, if you have a choice, avoid PPTP VPNs. Although modern versions of PPTP are reasonably secure and probably not worth the effort for most would-be attackers to hack, they're less secure than L2TP-over-IPsec, Cisco IPsec, SSL/TLS, and OpenVPN systems. Second, if you control your own VPN, be sure to choose an excellent password. As with all forms of encryption, your security is only as good as your password, and if you choose a short, simple word that someone else can guess (or discover with a dictionary or brute-force attack), your encryption could become worthless.

If you must connect to a public Wi-Fi hotspot and find yourself unable to use a VPN for any reason, you can take a few steps to minimize your risks. Although you won't get all the security of a VPN, you can significantly improve your odds of thwarting eavesdroppers by doing the following:

- Use an SSH tunnel. You have to set up a separate tunnel for each service you use, but this provides excellent security.

Cross-Ref

For more on SSH tunnels, see Chapter 11. ■

- Use SSL for both incoming and outgoing email.

Cross-Ref

For more on email security, including SSL, see Chapter 9. ■

- When possible, stick to web pages encrypted with SSL — especially when using Gmail or other webmail interfaces.

Cross-Ref

For more on securely accessing websites, see Chapter 10. ■

- If SSL is unavailable for email or web access, be extremely careful not to send any personal or confidential data.
- Quit any programs you aren't actively using that may access the Internet.
- Limit the amount of time you're connected to the bare minimum. The longer you stay connected, the greater the chances someone could sniff private information.

Using Wi-Fi Scanning Software

The AirPort menu in your menu bar automatically lists all nearby Wi-Fi networks that broadcast their SSIDs; it even indicates which ones are encrypted by displaying a small padlock icon. In Snow Leopard, you can get additional details about the network to which you're currently connected (including the type of encryption it uses and the current signal strength) by holding down Option while clicking on the menu; for other networks, the information appears in a pop-up tool tip when you hover over the network name.

However, if you're running Leopard, or if you want to gather additional facts about the wireless networks in your vicinity or display the data in a more flexible form, you can use any of several readily available Wi-Fi scanning programs, which are often called *stumblers*.

Some stumblers exist only to help you gather information. One example is Koingo Software's AirRadar (`www.koingosw.com/products/airradar.php`, $9.95), shown in Figure 16.17. In addition to the information shown here, you can turn on numerous other columns, displaying information such as the manufacturer of each access point and whether it's an ad hoc network (created by a computer rather than a stand-alone access point). You can also graph the signal of each network over time. A similar program is iStumbler (`www.istumbler.net`, free). Although iStumbler lacks some of the polish of AirRadar, it offers additional features, such as the capability to monitor not only Wi-Fi networks but also Bluetooth.

However, there's another sort of stumbler that goes way beyond supplying information about local wireless networks. This other class of utility can also display networks that don't broadcast their SSIDs and capture all the wireless data from any network, enabling you to analyze it and even try to break into the network by using any of several common methods of attack. The most prominent example of this type of software for Mac OS X is the free, open-source KisMAC (`http://trac.kismac-ng.org`), a utility based on another open-source project called Kismet (`www.kismetwireless.net`). KisMAC is shown in Figure 16.18.

FIGURE 16.17

AirRadar shows numerous details for all the Wi-Fi networks in your vicinity.

Name	Enc Type	MAC Address	Channel	Signal	Signal Avg	Signal Max	Last Seen
Melo	WPA2, WPA	00:11:22:22:AA:22	6	49%	47%	51%	5/24/09 4:39:49 PM
Nora	WPA	00:11:11:11:11:11	6	68%	66%	68%	5/24/09 4:39:49 PM
Melo _media	WPA2, WPA	00:11:22:22:AA:22	36	34%	32%	34%	5/24/09 4:39:49 PM
rezorv	WPA	00:11:22:33:11:22	4	34%	31%	36%	5/24/09 4:39:49 PM
Zora	WPA2	00:11:22:22:AA:22	1	60%	59%	63%	5/24/09 4:39:49 PM
Livebox-9768	WPA	00:11:22:33:11:22	1	36%	33%	36%	5/24/09 4:39:49 PM
Croquette	WPA	00:11:22:22:AA:22	11	26%	6%	26%	5/24/09 4:39:49 PM
freephonie	WPA	96:11:22:33:11:22	4	29%	22%	32%	5/24/09 4:39:49 PM
James	WEP	00:11:22:22:AA:22	4	29%	18%	31%	5/24/09 4:39:49 PM
bma	WPA	8A:FF:22:FF:22:EC	11	0%	0%	0%	5/24/09 4:39:29 PM
inalambrico	WPA	3A:EE:EE:44:44:BC	11	0%	0%	0%	5/24/09 4:39:39 PM
freephonie	WPA	6A:11:22:33:11:22	11	26%	2%	27%	5/24/09 4:39:49 PM
Livebox-6b26	WEP	00:11:22:22:AA:22	10	25%	2%	26%	5/24/09 4:39:49 PM

KisMAC reveals many of the hidden secrets of any wireless network within range of your Mac.

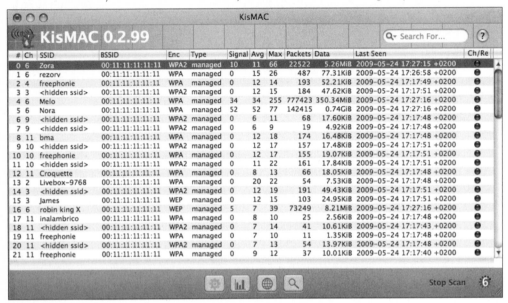

Caution

Using KisMAC or a similar utility for any purpose other than testing your own wireless network is ethically dubious at best, and in some jurisdictions (including Germany), it's illegal. Be sure to check local laws before using it — and use your power only for good! ∎

Although I would naturally never recommend using KisMAC to break into someone else's network, I think it's an excellent idea to use it to try to break into your own network. For example, if you aren't convinced that WEP is insecure, you can use KisMAC to watch your WEP-protected network for a while and then use one of its built-in attacks to figure out your WEP password. You'll be shocked, as I was, at how easy it is, and that should eliminate any lingering faith you may have in using WEP! Likewise, if you use WPA Personal or WPA2 Personal, you may recall from earlier in this chapter that your network is vulnerable to a dictionary attack and that therefore you should choose a long, complex password. So, try just such an attack on your own network using KisMAC's built-in tools and your own word list. If a few hours go by and KisMAC hasn't come up with the password, that suggests no one else will have better luck; but if your password is found, you'll know someone else could do the same thing just as easily and that you need to change it to something much more secure.

Although complete instructions on using KisMAC could fill an entire book, here are the basic steps you can take to get started:

1. Open the KisMAC application (from wherever you installed it).
2. Choose KisMAC ⇨ Preferences and then click Driver on the toolbar.

3. From the pop-up menu, choose Apple Airport Extreme card, passive mode, and then click the Add (+) button.

4. Close the Preferences window.

5. In the main KisMAC window, click Start Scan at the bottom.

6. When the authentication window opens, type your username and password and then click OK. KisMAC begins scanning for Wi-Fi networks.

7. By default, KisMAC hops around from channel to channel, but to focus on just one channel (namely, the one your base station is using) in order to collect more data from it, choose the channel you want from the Channel menu.

8. After collecting packets for a while (the rate at which KisMAC accumulates packets depends on many variables, including how active each network is), you can use the commands on the Crack submenu of the Network menu to try to determine any given network's password. Consult KisMAC's documentation for details on each method.

The only method that works against WPA-protected networks is choosing Network ⇨ Crack ⇨ Wordlist Attack ⇨ against WPA Key. Assuming you've collected enough packets, choosing this command results in a prompt to select a text file containing a list of words to check. Select a file and then click Open. KisMAC then tries every word in the list and alerts you if it finds the network's password.

Summary

This chapter explored the ways in which wireless networks are more prone to security issues than their wired counterparts and how to eliminate or mitigate the most common areas of risk. I began with an overview of the main technologies used to encrypt Wi-Fi traffic, including WEP, WPA, and 802.1X, outlining the benefits and limitations of each one.

Next, I walked you through the nuts and bolts of configuring the various security settings of Apple AirPort base stations and provided a brief overview of how to accomplish similar things with several common third-party brands of wireless access points. Because the access point is only half the equation, I then described how to set up your Mac to take advantage of the security features of your wireless network.

A discussion of the perils of public Wi-Fi hotspots followed, along with tips for keeping your network traffic safe when working in unfamiliar wireless territory. Finally, I described several common tools for locating Wi-Fi networks in your vicinity and determining their security features.

Using Firewalls

Firewalls serve as gatekeepers between your Mac's software and the Internet — monitoring the traffic that passes back and forth and selectively allowing or blocking information with particular sources, destinations, or characteristics. You can think of them as something like burglar bars on windows, which allow light and air in and don't hinder conversations with someone on the other side but prevent the bad guys from climbing in to harm you or steal your stuff. A firewall can't protect you against every possible outside threat, and its efficacy depends almost entirely on how prudently you've configured it. But it's a common-sense measure that can greatly reduce your risks of outside attacks without interfering with your everyday use of the Internet.

Mac OS X includes two different built-in firewalls (or three, depending on how you count), and this chapter explains how they work, how best to configure them, and which one(s) you should use. If you want even more power or more control, you can choose any of several third-party firewalls for Mac OS X, which I also cover here.

Note

You can purchase stand-alone firewall devices or configure a server to function solely as a firewall that protects the rest of your network, but this chapter focuses mainly on firewall applications intended to protect the individual Mac on which they're installed. If you're running Mac OS X Server, you can also use its built-in firewall, which is described in Chapter 31, to protect your network. ■

Understanding How Firewalls Work

Firewalls are a bit like chess: easy to learn but difficult to master. Simply by clicking a few buttons, you can activate a firewall with basic default settings and thereby increase your Mac's network security dramatically. On the other hand, you could invest hundreds of hours learning all the complexities of network

---

IN THIS CHAPTER

Learning firewall basics

Making the most of Mac OS X's built-in application firewall

Configuring IPFW, a Unix-based firewall included with Mac OS X

Setting up and using several major third-party firewalls

protocols and firewall configuration and still barely scratch the surface of everything your firewall has to offer. I make no attempt in this chapter to turn you into a firewall expert, but I hope to provide you with enough information so you can make informed decisions about whether to use a firewall on your Mac, what sort of firewall to use, and how to configure it to keep you reasonably safe without making your life unnecessarily complicated.

Firewall terminology

By way of background, you should first be familiar with some terms that are helpful to understanding firewalls:

- **Port.** Many kinds of data can be sent over a network, and each application or service on your Mac is designed to deal with only particular kinds. For example, your email client doesn't know about file sharing, and your web browser doesn't know about voice over IP. The way computers keep track of which sort of data needs to go where is by dividing it into *ports*, which you can think of as something like TV channels or radio stations. Tens of thousands of ports are available, of which some have standardized uses and others are available for individual programs to use as they see fit. A web browser normally listens for incoming data on port 80, for example, and an email client normally sends mail on port 25. An online backup program might choose an arbitrary port number, such as 4242, but allow you to change that in the event that some other program wanted to use the same port. A port is said to be open when an application or process responds to incoming messages on that port.

- **Protocol.** The vast majority of data sent over the Internet uses one of two *protocols*, or communication standards: TCP (Transmission Control Protocol) or UDP (User Datagram Protocol). You don't need to worry about the details of these two protocols, but you should be aware that each is appropriate for certain networking tasks and that firewalls treat traffic separately for each protocol. In addition, either or both of the protocols can use a particular port at any given time.

- **Packet.** A packet is a small, self-contained unit of data that includes, among other pieces of information, the address from which it was sent and its destination address. Data that travels over the Internet is broken into packets before being sent and is then reassembled on the other end. Most firewalls operate at the packet level, examining each one for its attributes before deciding whether to let it through. Such firewalls are sometimes called *packet-filtering firewalls*, and the process they use is known as *stateful packet inspection*.

- **Socket.** Each program that wants to communicate with a device elsewhere on the network creates a special sort of file called a *socket*, which specifies the protocol being used, the local IP address and port, and, in some cases, also the remote IP address and port. One way or another, all incoming and outgoing traffic goes through a socket. Some firewalls, instead of examining packets and allowing or blocking traffic at that level, regulate whether applications can create sockets to accept incoming Internet data. These are called *socket-filter firewalls* or *application firewalls*.

Why firewalls exist

The main problem that firewalls attempt to solve is unwanted network access behind the user's back. If you're running a web server on your Mac, then, by definition, port 80 is open because web servers normally listen on port 80. But all sorts of programs are running on your Mac all the time, and many of them listen for Internet access of one kind or another. This includes not only components of Mac OS X but also third-party software and, potentially, malware that's found its way onto your Mac. So, although network access by known processes trying to do useful things is perfectly fine, the biggest reason for firewalls is to prevent access on some port you didn't even know was open.

However, the fact that a port is open and responds to a request from the outside doesn't in itself indicate a problem, even if the source of the access is malicious. If an outside party sends a request to some random port, such as 12345, and a program listening on that port merely says "hello" in reply, no harm is done. But if the program with the open port has a bug or a hidden back door or if it's malware, your Mac could conceivably respond by giving the outside party access to your files, blocking your Internet connection, or doing all sorts of other unpleasant things.

Basic firewall operation

The usual way a firewall works is to begin by blocking all incoming traffic. Some firewalls also regulate outgoing traffic, but it's simpler to focus on just one direction for the present. Then, the firewall lets you selectively open access for just those specific kinds of data you want to permit — usually by port, protocol, source, or a combination of these. For example, if I want to run a web server on my Mac, I probably want my firewall to permit all incoming TCP traffic on port 80 (unless I choose a nonstandard port for my web server). If I know that I want only a particular computer to be able to access my web server, I could permit only incoming traffic from a certain IP address or even — if I want to be extremely restrictive — only incoming TCP traffic on port 80 from that single address.

Cross-Ref

For more on firewalls that filter outgoing traffic, see Chapter 14. ■

By creating a series of these openings or exceptions, you can enable other computers to have the access to your Mac they need, while blocking traffic from other sources or on other ports, which could potentially do you harm. This process of creating exceptions is often called "punching holes" in the firewall. In general, the more specific your exceptions are, the greater your security. On the other hand, creating more-restrictive exceptions requires more work and increases the chances you'll block some service you genuinely need. So, the trick in setting up a firewall — as with most things in this book — is to strike the best possible balance between security and convenience.

One of the things that makes firewall configuration intimidating for people without significant technical experience is that in order to do much of anything, you must know what port(s) and protocol(s) any particular service uses. For example, you may know that you want to provide remote login and file-sharing capabilities for your Mac but not have any idea that the former uses SSH (TCP on port 22) and the latter uses AFP (TCP on port 548). Apple attempted to address this problem with the application firewall introduced in Leopard (and discussed in more detail just ahead). It lets you ignore ports altogether, instead specifying which applications should be able to receive incoming data. Some third-party firewall programs offer varying degrees of assistance in figuring out which ports do what, although ultimately, it's up to each user to determine what sort of access to permit.

Do you need a firewall?

Given all the foregoing, do you need a firewall on your Mac? Some experts say absolutely yes; others say most likely not. The reality is that it depends on your situation.

If you have a Mac with a publicly routable IP address — especially one that functions as a server, gateway, or router — the answer is unequivocally yes. Because your Mac is directly accessible from the outside world, it's vulnerable to any holes or weaknesses that could be discovered and exploited in Mac OS X itself or any third-party Internet software you may have installed. Running a firewall of some sort is a no-brainer. Read the remainder of this chapter to decide what type(s) of firewall best suits your needs.

If, like most home and small-office users, you use NAT to provide private IP addresses for your Macs, you have a certain amount of automatic protection from outside access without doing anything. With a few exceptions, computers outside your network can't directly access any device on your local network, so a firewall becomes somewhat less crucial. However, NAT isn't entirely bulletproof — and, unlike firewalls, which actively monitor network traffic, NAT provides, at best, only passive blocking. In addition, if you use port forwarding, you open one or more ports on local computers to the outside world, and if you set up your router to use a DMZ host, that one computer loses all the protection NAT would otherwise offer.

Cross-Ref

For more on NAT, port forwarding, and DMZ hosts, see Chapter 15. ∎

In short: When in doubt, use a firewall. It may or may not help, but it won't hurt — the worst that could happen is that some useful service may be blocked, but then, after seeing an error message, you could simply punch a hole in your firewall for that particular service.

Of course, "use a firewall" is rather inadequate advice because there are so many different firewalls and so many ways of using them. In the remainder of this chapter, I discuss Mac OS X's two built-in firewalls, along with a number of third-party Mac firewalls, with some suggestions as to what you should use — and how — in various situations.

Using Mac OS X's Application Firewall

Mac OS X has had some kind of built-in firewall for a number of years. Up until Mac OS X 10.4 Tiger, the sole firewall included was IPFW (IP Firewall), a popular Unix firewall. System Preferences provided a graphical interface for setting up IPFW, but it was quite limited in the range of settings you could change; and despite offering only a simplified glimpse into IPFW, the preference pane was confusing for inexperienced users. Those who wanted more control over IPFW could use any of several third-party configuration tools or, if they were of a suitably geeky disposition, manually edit the text file that contained all the rules IPFW uses.

Leopard and Snow Leopard contain two firewalls. IPFW is still there, but it's turned off by default and accessible only from the command line or by using a specialized tool. I discuss both approaches later in this chapter. The new default firewall — and the one you can now configure in System Preferences — is an application firewall. That is, instead of allowing or blocking network access to individual packets based on the IP address or port of the incoming data, it allows or blocks incoming access to particular applications on your Mac.

Note

The very first release of Mac OS X 10.5 had significant problems with its application firewall; these were corrected in version 10.5.1 and later releases. ∎

The big advantage of Mac OS X's application firewall is that it's far simpler to understand and use than IPFW was in Tiger and earlier. You need not know anything about firewalls, ports, or other network arcana. Simply select an application and tell the firewall to allow or deny access.

In one limited sense, the application firewall offers greater granularity than a packet-filtering firewall. A conventional firewall could allow or block all incoming traffic on port 80, for example, but it couldn't block incoming traffic on port 80 for Safari while permitting it for Firefox. Mac OS X's application firewall can do that. Of course, the reverse also applies: The application firewall is unable to block all traffic on port 80, regardless of which application is used, while permitting traffic on port 8080. So, in most cases, the application firewall trades off flexibility for ease of use.

How the application firewall works

The application firewall offers three modes:

- **Allow all incoming connections (in Leopard) or, to use Snow Leopard's advanced terminology, "Off."** Either way, with this setting (the default), no blocking occurs.

- **Allow only essential services (Leopard) or Block all incoming connections (Snow Leopard).** This is the most restrictive setting. It means all incoming traffic is blocked except Bonjour (which allows devices on your local network to see each other automatically), DHCP (necessary to get an IP address and other network settings), and Internet Key Exchange (IKE), used by the IPsec security protocol. Use this setting only when you need maximum security and don't care about having any incoming access at all.

- **Set access for specific services and applications.** This mode (which doesn't have any particular name or label in Snow Leopard and is more of a side effect of turning the firewall on) is by far the best and most flexible of the three. It automatically permits access for any service you've turned on in the Sharing pane of System Preferences, such as File Sharing, Remote Login, and Screen Sharing; it also lets you add applications to its list and, for each one, specify whether you want to allow all incoming connections or block all incoming connections. In most cases, the logical tactic is to add to the list the applications for which you want to allow access and simply let the firewall block everything else.

However, in the last mode, which I recommend for most users, there's more going on than meets the eye.

When you add an application to the list, Mac OS X signs it — that is, it computes a unique value based on the current state of the program and stores that in a digital signature file inside the application itself. This file enables Mac OS X to detect if the application changes in any way, which could be a sign of tampering. You wouldn't want an application that's been tampered with to be able to receive network connections, so the next time the application requests network access, Mac OS X prompts you to confirm that you still allow it. This lets you re-accept applications that have been updated — or that modify themselves even when they run normally — with a single click while also alerting you to potential mischief by applications that shouldn't have changed.

For any application already signed by an authorized certificate authority — that includes all Apple applications and any third-party application for which the developer has gone to the extra trouble of obtaining a signature — the application firewall in Leopard allows incoming connections automatically, even if the application isn't in the list! (In Snow Leopard, you get to decide whether to enable this behavior by clicking a check box.) Therefore, it would be more accurate to say that Leopard's application firewall, when configured to Set access for specific services and applications, allows incoming network access for all services activated in the Sharing pane and all signed applications, unless otherwise specified. Either way, you can indeed specify that a signed application should have its incoming access blocked, as I explain in a moment.

Note

Little Snitch, covered in Chapter 14, is also a type of application firewall; it gives you more control over the behavior of individual applications than Mac OS X's built-in application firewall does — although it's not quite as easy to use and is more intrusive. ■

When to use the application firewall

The application firewall may not be as flexible as other firewalls, but it does provide reasonably good protection with very little effort. Even if you're behind a NAT router, there's always the chance that some unwanted traffic will sneak through, and having some firewall protection is a good idea. In almost all cases, setting the firewall to Set access for specific services and applications (in Leopard) or simply On (in Snow Leopard) is the right choice.

In addition, the application firewall is completely compatible with IPFW, so even if you need capabilities that only IPFW can provide, there's no harm in using both. IPFW filters incoming traffic at the packet level (looking for protocols, ports, and addresses you've specified), and the application firewall manages connections at the socket level.

The only situation in which I wouldn't recommend using Mac OS X's built-in application firewall is if you're also using a third-party firewall that doesn't rely on IPFW because the two firewalls may interact in undesirable ways, and debugging connection problems could be quite difficult.

Configuring the application firewall

To configure the application firewall, follow these steps:

1. **Choose ⇨ System Preferences and then click Security to open the Security pane.**
2. **If the lock icon in the lower-left corner of the window is in the locked state, click it, type an administrator's username and password, and then click OK.**
3. **Click the Firewall tab, shown in Figure 17.1 for Leopard and Figure 17.2 for Snow Leopard.**

FIGURE 17.1

The application firewall built into Leopard lets you specify which applications (rather than which ports or IP addresses) can receive inbound Internet connections.

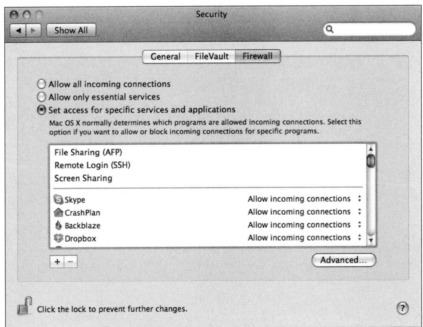

4. **In Snow Leopard, if the firewall isn't already on, click the Start button to activate it. In Leopard, click the radio button corresponding to the mode you want to use (as described earlier).** In virtually every case, the right choice is Set access for specific services and applications, so that's what I assume in the remaining steps.

5. **To specify access for a given application, remain in the same place in Leopard; in Snow Leopard, click the Advanced button to open the dialog box shown in Figure 17.3. Then, do one or more of the following:**

   - To add an application manually, click the Add (+) button, navigate to the application, select it, and then click Add. By default, newly added applications are set to Allow incoming connections. If instead you want to deny them, choose Block incoming connections from the pop-up menu next to the application's name. To remove an application, select it and then click the Remove (–) button.

   - In Snow Leopard only, to permit all signed applications to receive inbound traffic (as described earlier in this chapter), click the Automatically allow signed software to receive incoming connections check box. Either way, make sure the Block all incoming connections check box isn't selected.

   - To add an application on the fly, simply go about your business normally. When an application you've launched wants to enable incoming network access, a dialog box like the one shown in Figure 17.4 opens. Regardless of whether you click Allow or Deny, Mac OS X adds this application to the firewall list; but if you click Allow, it's set to Allow incoming connections, and if you click Deny, it's set to Block incoming connections. You can change this setting manually at any time.

FIGURE 17.2

Snow Leopard presents a simpler initial layout for the application firewall.

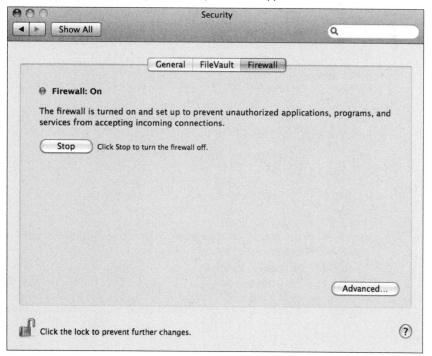

FIGURE 17.3

Snow Leopard puts its application-specific settings (and a few other controls) in this dialog box.

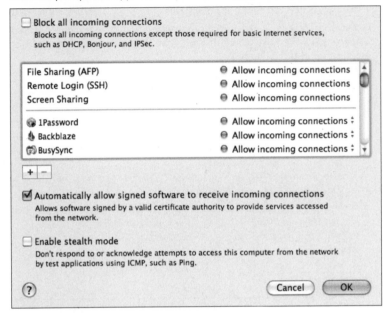

FIGURE 17.4

Ordinarily, you need never add an application to Mac OS X's firewall manually. Click Allow or Deny in this alert to add it to the list, with the appropriate status.

6. **In Snow Leopard, remain in the same place; in Leopard, click Advanced to open the dialog box shown in Figure 17.5.**

7. **To turn on stealth mode (optional but recommended), click the Enable Stealth Mode check box.** Stealth mode prevents Mac OS X from sending any reply whatsoever to traffic directed to a blocked application. With this check box deselected, Mac OS X doesn't allow traffic through, but it does enable the outside computer to tell that it has reached a valid destination, which could prompt an attacker to try harder to break into your system.

8. **In Leopard only, optionally click the Enable Firewall Logging check box.** (This feature is enabled automatically in Snow Leopard.) Doing so makes the firewall store information about activities, such as blocked attempts, in a log file, so you can later determine whether anyone has been trying to access blocked applications on your computer over the network.

9. **Click OK and then close System Preferences.**

FIGURE 17.5

In this dialog box, which opens when you click the Advanced button in the Firewall tab in Leopard, you can optionally activate logging and stealth mode — both of which are a good idea.

Using IPFW

The Unix program `ipfirewall`, version 2 (which I'll call by its more common name, IPFW — often seen in all-lowercase as `ipfw` or `ipfw2`), is included with Leopard and Snow Leopard even though it's disabled by default. It's a powerful, flexible, and well-liked firewall utility. It's found on most Unix and Unix-like computers and can provide enough protection for nearly any Mac. The only problem is that in the best tradition of Unix command-line software, it has an obscure, confusing user interface. That, compounded by its inherent complexity and wealth of options, makes it a formidable program to wrap one's head around.

Note

Mac OS X Server comes with a very nice user interface for managing its version of IPFW; I describe this in Chapter 31. ■

Nevertheless, if Mac OS X's built-in application firewall doesn't provide the level of protection or sophistication you require, IPFW is a fine choice — and you can't beat the price. This section gets you started with some of the basics and also gives you some advice as to where you can find more information.

IPFW is strictly for IPv4 traffic, but if you're also using IPv6 on your Mac, you'll be happy to know that Leopard and Snow Leopard also include an IPv6-capable version of IPFW called IP6FW! IPFW and IP6FW use similar syntax, but IP6FW has fewer options, and, of course, its rules must be specified using IPv6 addresses. As a result, if you want to set up your firewall to filter both IPv4 and IPv6 traffic, you need to duplicate most of your rules and then make a few tweaks so that both firewalls act correctly. I say a bit more about this as the chapter proceeds, although I don't provide detailed instructions for setting up an IPv6 firewall with IP6FW.

Cross-Ref

For more on IPv6 generally, see Chapter 15. ■

The IPFW process

The first thing you should understand about IPFW is the outline of how to configure and run it, including how to make it run automatically on startup. The program is located at `/sbin/ipfw` (IP6FW, likewise, is located at `/sbin/ip6fw`), but you can't simply run it by typing **sudo /sbin/ipfw** on the command line as you might expect. Instead, you must jump through a few hoops. The process I explain ahead involves the following:

- First, you need to understand a bit about the syntax IPFW uses to create the rules for each type of network traffic you want to block or allow.
- Second, you put the rules of your choice in a plain text configuration file.
- Third, you put commands to run IPFW using the rules you created, along with some other essential commands, in a shell script.
- Finally, you must create a `launchd` script (also a text file, stored in a special location) in order to tell Mac OS X to run your shell script at startup.

However, I should point out right up front that you need not necessarily do all this by hand. Any of several third-party utilities, described later in this section, can do all the complex stuff for you in the background, letting you concentrate solely on which rules you want to use.

IPFW syntax

IPFW relies on a series of rules that are processed in order. Each incoming packet is compared to the first rule in the list, and if it matches, the firewall takes whatever action is specified in the rule. If it doesn't match, IPFW moves on to the second rule, and then the next, and so on. If IPFW gets to the very end of its rules and not one of them has matched a given packet, it uses a default rule (which, in the case of Mac OS X, simply says to let any remaining packets through). If you want a different default action — such as to block any packet that hasn't been explicitly allowed by a previous rule —you must add that rule prior to the last one. In any case, each packet is ultimately acted upon by only one rule (the first rule it matches), so order is important.

So, to use a plain-English representation of what a simplistic ruleset might look like, consider the following:

```
1. Allow all TCP packets from any source destined for port 80.
2. Deny packets of any kind that didn't match the previous rule.
3. Let any remaining packets through.
```

The first rule enables your web server to receive incoming traffic. The second one blocks everything else. The third — the default rule that's built into the firewall and can't be changed — is effectively overridden by your second rule, which intercepts all remaining packets before they get there.

Note

If you end your rules with a "deny everything else" directive, technically you don't need any other deny rules — you can stick strictly with rules that allow traffic. However, it never hurts to add deny rules anyway, and you may want to have a less draconian default rule (or log packets that are denied), in which case, explicitly denying traffic of various kinds is exactly what you want. ∎

Now look at the same rules as they might exist in IPFW syntax:

```
100 allow tcp from any to any dst-port 80
65534 deny ip from any to any
65535 allow ip from any to any
```

Note

In this section, I describe the syntax for IPFW — that is, the IPv4 version of the firewall. Rules you create for IP6FW are in some cases different; see the IP6FW documentation, referenced ahead, for details. ■

IPFW commands are normally all lowercase. Here's how the first one breaks down:

- 100. Each rule begins with a number — it doesn't matter what the number is, only that the numbers go from smaller to larger and each one is unique.

- allow. Next is a command — in these examples, either allow or deny — which tells IPFW what action it will take with matching packets.

- tcp. After the command is the protocol, which is most often tcp, udp, icmp (Internet Control Message Protocol, used for pinging another computer), or ip (which means any protocol).

- from any to any dst-port 80. This portion of the rule always takes the form from *source* to *destination*. In this case, the source is any (any IP address), and the destination is also any (any IP address — for computers with more than one or that are acting as routers), on dst-port 80 (port 80). Instead of the second any, the rule could specify dst-ip, followed by a particular IP address, among other things.

In other words, this rule matches any TCP packet, from any source, heading for port 80 on this machine and allows it to pass.

The second rule (65534 — numbered that way so it's necessarily the next-to-last one) denies packets instead of allowing them (deny) and matches packets of any protocol (ip) and destined for any IP address (the second any). And the final rule (65535, the maximum number allowed) is just like the second, except that it allows packets through instead of denying them.

Here are some examples of the syntax used for other common rule types:

```
110 allow tcp from any to any dst-port 80 in
```

This rule is similar to rule 100 earlier, except that it adds the word in at the end. This specifies that it matches only incoming packets; out would match only outgoing packets, and a rule with neither word would match both incoming and outgoing packets.

```
120 allow tcp from 10.1.1.0/24 to any dst-port 548
```

In this rule, the source address is given explicitly instead of allowing traffic to port 548 from anywhere. But in this case, it's not allowing only traffic from a single address (10.1.1.0) but from a whole range of addresses. The /24 is an example of CIDR (Classless Inter-Domain Routing) notation, where the number after the slash represents the number of 1 (on) bits in the subnet mask. So, 10.1.1.0/24 is a shorthand (although somewhat obtuse) way of saying anything in the range of 10.1.1.0 through 10.1.1.255.

Tip

You can read more about CIDR notation at http://en.wikipedia.org/wiki/Classless_Inter-Domain_Routing. ■

```
130 allow tcp from 10.1.1.0/24, 127.0.0.1/8 to any dst-port 548
```

You can include more than one IP address, or address range, in the source or destination; simply type additional addresses, separated by commas.

```
140 allow tcp from any to any out keep-state
150 allow udp from any to any out keep-state
```

This pair of rules (one each for TCP and UDP) would ensure that all outgoing requests made by your computer can be answered (thanks to the `keep-state` option).

```
160 allow icmp from any to any icmptypes 8 out
170 allow icmp from any to any icmptypes 0 in
```

The Unix `ping` command, which uses the ICMP protocol, lets you check to see if another computer is alive and responsive. This pair of commands ensures that outgoing pings get through your firewall (the first one) and responses to those pings get back in (the second one).

```
65534 deny log logamount 1000 ip from any to any in
```

This rule is similar to the earlier version of rule 65534, except that it includes `log logamount 1000` after `deny`. The `log` command makes IPFW log any packet that matches this rule. Specifying `logamount` followed by a number means that a maximum of that number of packets is logged; if more packets than that come in that match this particular rule, they're blocked but not logged. It also adds the word `in` at the end, which means it blocks all incoming packets that haven't matched another rule but freely allows outgoing packets.

All this barely scratches the surface of IPFW syntax, even though it covers the majority of cases you're likely to encounter. To read the full list of options for IPFW, visit `http://developer.apple.com/documentation/Darwin/Reference/Manpages/man8/ipfw.8.html` or open a Terminal window and then type **man ipfw**. Likewise, the (similar but not identical) syntax for IP6FW can be seen by typing **man ip6fw** in a Terminal window or by visiting `http://developer.apple.com/documentation/Darwin/Reference/Manpages/man8/ip6fw.8.html`.

Creating an IPFW ruleset

Now it's time to specify the list of rules you want IPFW to use. You store these in a plain text file, and in the next phase of the instructions, you reference this file in the shell script that runs IPFW itself. Although you could build these rules directly into the shell script, keeping them separate makes them easier to read and modify.

Because of the curious way IPFW is designed, you can't merely hand it a list of rules; you must type a sequence of commands telling it to add each rule individually. In practical terms, this means that in your rule list, each rule must be preceded by the word `add` and a space. Any line beginning with # is a comment and is ignored by IPFW. I've included some comments in the following example to help you identify what each rule does.

Caution

These instructions assume you're setting up the firewall on a local Mac. If you're doing this over a network, you must be extremely careful that you don't inadvertently set a rule that will lock you out! In particular, be sure you allow SSH (port 22) access. ■

To create your ruleset file, follow these steps:

1. **Open Terminal, which is located in** `/Applications/Utilities`.
2. **Type** sudo nano /etc/firewall.conf **to create a new file in the** nano **text editor and then type the rules you want to use.** The following rules represent an example of a starting point. You may

prefer more or fewer rules, and please note that some of them won't work unless you customize them with the private IP address range of your local network.

```
# Permit loopback, which lets you access some services on
# your own Mac at the localhost or 127.0.0.1 address
add 100 allow ip from any to any via lo*
# Permit a response to most outgoing TCP and UDP packets
add 110 allow tcp from any to any out keep-state
add 111 allow udp from any to any out keep-state
# Permit responses from a DHCP server
# Unfortunately, the previous rules don't work with DHCP
add 120 allow udp from any 67 to any 68 in
# Permit outgoing pings and incoming ping responses.
add 130 allow icmp from any to any icmptypes 8 out
add 131 allow icmp from any to any icmptypes 0 in
# Permit Bonjour and Back to My Mac
add 140 allow udp from any to any 5353
add 141 allow udp from any 5353 to any 1024-65535 in
# Permit SSH (remote login)
add 150 allow tcp from any to any dst-port 22
# Permit iTunes music sharing on your local network
# IMPORTANT: Replace 10.0.0.1/24 with the actual private IP
# address range of your local network!
add 160 allow tcp from 10.0.0.1/24 to any dst-port 3689
# Permit AFP file sharing on your local network
# IMPORTANT: Replace 10.0.0.1/24 with the actual private IP
# address range of your local network!
add 170 allow tcp from 10.0.0.1/24 to any dst-port 548
# Permit Web sharing on port 80 (HTTP) and 443 (HTTPS)
add 180 allow tcp from any to any dst-port 80
add 181 allow tcp from any to any dst-port 443
# Block any incoming packets not already allowed
add 65534 deny log logamount 1000 ip from any to any in
```

Note

Many of these rules were suggested by blog entries on the security site Securosis. You can find additional suggestions at http://securosis.com/blog/comments/ipfw-rules-v20071212/. ∎

3. Press Control+X to exit nano, press Y to confirm that you want to save the file, and then press Return to confirm the file name.

If at any time you want to modify the rules later, simply repeat these steps to edit the file. However, simply editing the file doesn't activate your new rules. You must either restart your Mac or unload and reload the launchd item, as explained ahead.

Creating an IPFW shell script

Now that your IPFW rules are in place, the next step is to create a shell script that runs IPFW itself and loads the rules. This script could do a great many other things too, but for our purposes, we need only three elements: flush any previous rules, load the new rules, and enable logging.

To create your IPFW shell script, follow these steps:

1. **Open Terminal, which is located in** /Applications/Utilities.

2. **Type** cd /usr/local/sbin. If you see a message that says "No such file or directory," type **sudo mkdir -p /usr/local/sbin**, followed by **cd /usr/local/sbin**.

3. **Type** sudo nano firewall.sh **to create a new file in the** nano **text editor and then type the following exactly as shown:**

```
#!/bin/sh
# Flush any existing rules
/sbin/ipfw -q flush
# Run IPFW and load custom ruleset
/sbin/ipfw -q /etc/firewall.conf
# Enable detailed logging to /var/log/system.log
/usr/sbin/sysctl -w net.inet.ip.fw.verbose=1
```

4. **Press Control+X to exit** nano, **press Y to confirm that you want to save the file, and then press Return to confirm the file name.**

5. **To give your script the proper ownership and permissions, type the following two commands:**

```
sudo chown root:admin firewall.sh
sudo chmod 544 firewall.sh
```

In order to run the script, I use launchd, as described next.

Creating an IPFW launchd item

In Leopard and Snow Leopard, Apple's recommended way to run a program automatically when you start your computer (or in various other circumstances) is to use a utility called launchd, which reads specially formatted files from certain designated folders and follows their instructions. For the purposes of running IPFW on startup, you must create such a file, store it in /Library/LaunchDaemons, and then give it the necessary ownership and permissions.

To configure IPFW to run at startup, follow these steps:

1. **Open Terminal, which is located in** /Applications/Utilities.

2. **Type** cd /Library/LaunchDaemons. If you see a message that says "No such file or directory," type **sudo mkdir /Library/LaunchDaemons**, followed by **cd /Library/LaunchDaemons**.

3. **Type** sudo nano com.apple.firewall.plist **to create a new file in the** nano **text editor and then type the following exactly as shown:**

```
<?xml version="1.0" encoding="UTF-8"?>
<!DOCTYPE plist PUBLIC "-//Apple//DTD PLIST 1.0//EN"
    "http://www.apple.com/DTDs/PropertyList-1.0.dtd">
<plist version="1.0">
<dict>
    <key>Label</key>
    <string>com.apple.firewall</string>
    <key>ProgramArguments</key>
    <array>
        <string>/usr/local/sbin/firewall.sh</string>
```

```
    </array>
    <key>RunAtLoad</key>
    <true/>
 </dict>
 </plist>
```

4. Press Control+X to exit nano, press Y to confirm that you want to save the file, and then press Return to confirm the file name.

5. Type sudo chown root:admin com.apple.firewall.plist to set the ownership correctly for your new launchd item.

6. To load the launchd item and thereby run the firewall without having to restart first, type the following:

```
sudo launchctl load /Library/LaunchDaemons/com.apple.firewall.plist
```

7. To confirm that the firewall is running with your custom rules, type sudo ipfw show. You should see output similar to the following:

```
00100    332     502 allow ip from any to any via lo*
00110   1065    1158 allow tcp from any to any out keep-state
00111      0       0 allow udp from any to any out keep-state
00120      0       0 allow udp from any 67 to any dst-port 68 in
00130      0       0 allow icmp from any to any icmptypes 8 out
00131      0       0 allow icmp from any to any icmptypes 0 in
00140      0       0 allow udp from any to any dst-port 5353
00141      0       0 allow udp from any 5353 to any dst-port 1024-65535
   in
00150      0       0 allow tcp from any to any dst-port 22
00160      0       0 allow tcp from 10.0.0.0/24 to any dst-port 3689
00170      0       0 allow tcp from 10.0.0.0/24 to any dst-port 548
00180      0       0 allow tcp from any to any dst-port 80
00181      0       0 allow tcp from any to any dst-port 443
65534      6     405 deny log logamount 1000 ip from any to any in
65535 975503 516241802 allow ip from any to any
```

If you want to change any of your rules at any time, follow the instructions presented earlier for editing the firewall.conf file. Then, type the following two commands to unload the launchd items with your existing rules and reload the new rules:

```
sudo launchctl unload /Library/LaunchDaemons/com.apple.firewall.plist

sudo launchctl load /Library/LaunchDaemons/com.apple.firewall.plist
```

Configuring IPFW rules with third-party utilities

I know what you're thinking: What could possibly be easier than editing and managing a bunch of finicky, obscurely formatted text files on the command line? Well, if you want to use IPFW but you don't wear a propeller beanie to work and you'd rather avoid all the mess of the preceding few sections, you have another option. You can use any of several graphical utilities that serve as front ends to IPFW, creating files much like the ones you can make manually but in a friendlier, more elegant way.

Caution

Each of these utilities uses its own format for storing IPFW rules and running the program, and they aren't necessarily compatible with each other or with the files I previously described. Therefore, I urge you to use only one method of running IPFW — my manual method or one of these programs but not a combination of two or more. If you're already using my manual method, unload the launchctl item, remove it from `/Library/ LaunchDaemons`, and then type sudo ipfw -q flush before using one of these programs. ■

DoorStop X Firewall and Who's There? Firewall Advisor

The DoorStop X Firewall from Open Door Networks (www.opendoor.com, $49), shown in Figure 17.6, doesn't advertise the fact that it's a GUI for IPFW, but that's exactly what it is. On the plus side, it's unquestionably the simplest and clearest way to use IPFW under Leopard or Snow Leopard, and it offers one unusual and extremely useful feature: the capability to switch between sets of firewall rules based on your location (for example, a basic set for when you're at home and a stricter set for when you're on the road). On the minus side, it's the most expensive of the graphical IPFW front ends listed here — and it lacks many of the features of free alternatives, such as WaterRoof and Firewall Builder.

FIGURE 17.6

DoorStop X is one of the most user-friendly firewalls for Mac OS X — certainly the most pleasant-looking of the IPFW front ends.

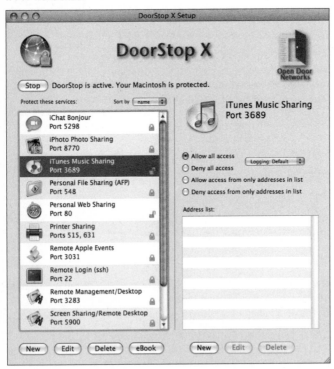

When you launch DoorStop X for the first time, an easy-to-understand assistant helps you to decide on the settings to start with, configures the underlying rules, and runs the firewall. Afterward, you can tweak the rules as you see fit — changing ports, allow/deny behavior, and the addresses from which access is permitted. A check box in DoorStop X's Preferences window lets you disable IPv6 for your entire computer, but you can't create IPv6-specific rules — it's all or nothing. Although you can specify allowed or blocked services by port and IP address and adjust the level of logging, that's pretty much it; support for UDP rules is limited, other protocols (besides TCP) aren't supported at all, and much of the power of IPFW remains inaccessible.

A companion product called Who's There? Firewall Advisor ($39 alone or $79 in a bundle with DoorStop X) helps make sense of IPFW logs — whether created by DoorStop X or not. In addition to displaying logs in a human-readable form (as shown in Figure 17.7), Who's There? offers an assessment of the level of risk of each attempted access, provides details on each listed service, features automatic domain name lookup of IP addresses, and features a button that lets you send email messages to a domain's administrators if illicit behavior is detected.

If you find yourself examining IPFW logs regularly, Who's There? could make the job quite a bit easier. However, I'm less enthusiastic about DoorStop X. Unless you urgently need the location awareness feature, you can get much greater capabilities (even at no cost) from some of the other programs on this list.

FIGURE 17.7

Who's There? Firewall Advisor gives you a more helpful way to examine IPFW log files and even report unwanted behavior to the ISP in charge of the offending IP address.

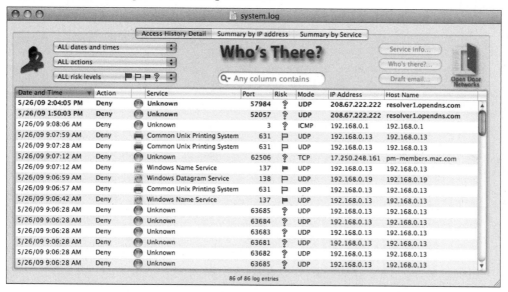

NoobProof

Compared to DoorStop X, the next step up in features (and the next step down in usability — although not by much) is NoobProof (www.hanynet.com/noobproof/, free), shown in Figure 17.8. For anyone without a great deal of technical know-how who wants more than the application firewall, it's a fine choice.

FIGURE 17.8

NoobProof is a simple, straightforward interface for configuring the IPFW firewall without having to learn any complicated syntax.

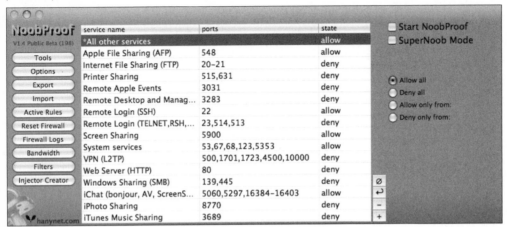

Although NoobProof doesn't provide access to all of IPFW's features, it makes the basics easy to use. The best way to get started with NoobProof is to choose Tools⇨ Start NoobProof Wizard. The wizard asks you a series of straightforward questions about the capabilities you want, including suggested choices for most settings. On the next-to-last screen of the wizard, if you click the Load firewall rules at system boot radio button, click Next, and then click Save and Activate this configuration, NoobProof saves your IPFW configuration file to disk in the proper format and configures Mac OS X to run it automatically at startup. With a couple of clicks, you can also turn the firewall off and/or remove the launchd item that runs it at startup.

WaterRoof

WaterRoof (www.hanynet.com/waterroof/, free), shown in Figure 17.9, is made by the same developer as NoobProof. Like NoobProof, it's a front end to IPFW, but it has vastly more features. If you need capabilities that NoobProof lacks or simply feel you can do without the training wheels, WaterRoof gives you access to the full power of IPFW.

Of special note, WaterRoof supports not only IPv4 but also IPv6, making it the only graphical interface to IP6FW I'm aware of for Mac OS X. It also provides reasonably straightforward to advanced IPFW features, such as routing, NAT support, and bandwidth management; and even though the interface is more complex than that of NoobProof, it's still only a matter of filling in forms (rather than trying to create text files and get them just right). WaterRoof also includes a firewall configuration wizard to walk you through a basic setup.

FIGURE 17.9

WaterRoof has one or more windows for each of its numerous activities, all available from the palette of buttons shown on the left.

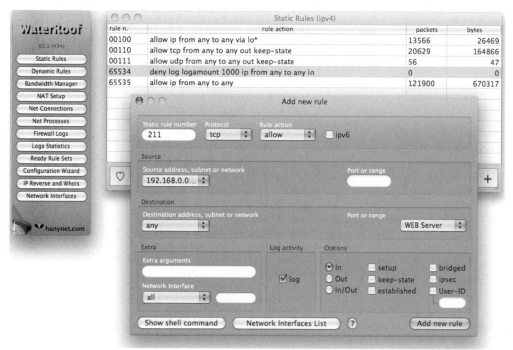

Firewall Builder

Firewall Builder (www.fwbuilder.org), shown in Figure 17.10, is a free, open-source, multi-platform firewall configuration utility available not only for Mac OS X but also for Windows and Linux. It enables you to manage several different firewall programs, including IPFW (but not IP6FW).

Firewall Builder can import existing firewall configurations or you can start from scratch and create your own. The process isn't nearly as simple as in NoobProof, but once you get the hang of the program's conventions, making quick changes to your rules is intuitive and straightforward.

You begin by defining a series of building blocks called objects, such as addresses and address ranges, hosts, networks, and services. Then, to create a rule, you can simply fill in the blanks (manually or using drag and drop) for fields such as Source, Destination, and Service with your predefined objects and then make a few other selections, such as whether to allow or deny service and whether the rule applies to incoming packets, outgoing packets, or both.

FIGURE 17.10

Firewall Builder lets you set up objects, shown on the left, such as addresses and services, and then drag them into the appropriate slots in rules, shown in the upper right.

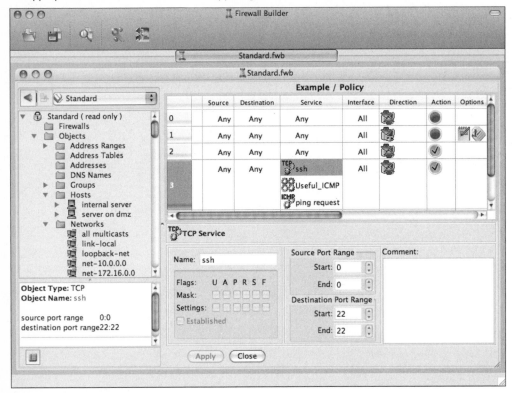

Once you have the set of rules you want, you can compile them in the form IPFW needs and then save them as a shell script. Unfortunately, Firewall Builder's automatic installation procedure doesn't work reliably, at least for local machines, under Mac OS X. Moreover, even if it did, if you wanted the script to run automatically at startup, you'd have to go through a manual procedure, and the details given in Firewall Builder's documentation are incorrect for Mac OS X.

Therefore, after creating a firewall in Firewall Builder, follow these steps to compile and install it:

1. **In Firewall Builder, select your firewall and then choose File ⇨ Save As.**

2. **Type a name for the firewall file (in this example, I call it `Firewall.fwb`), select a location (in this example, I stick with the default location of `~/Documents`), and then click Save.**

3. **Choose Rules ⇨ Compile.**

4. **In the window that opens, click the check box next to the firewall name and then click Next.**

5. **When you see a "Success" message, click Finish.** By doing this, you instruct Firewall Builder to save another copy of your firewall — this time with the extension .fb — in the same location as the original. This copy is in the form of the shell script IPFW expects.

6. **Open Terminal, which is located in** /Applications/Utilities.

7. **Type the following, substituting the name and path of your firewall file if different from what I suggested:**

   ```
   sudo cp ~/Documents/Firewall.fw /usr/local/sbin
   ```

8. **To give your script the proper ownership and permissions, type the following two commands (again, substituting the name of your file if different):**

   ```
   sudo chown root:admin /usr/local/sbin/Firewall.fw
   sudo chmod 544 /usr/local/sbin/Firewall.fw
   ```

9. **Type** cd /Library/LaunchDaemons. If you see a message that says "No such file or directory," type **sudo mkdir /Library/LaunchDaemons**, followed by **cd /Library/LaunchDaemons.**

10. **Type** sudo nano com.firewallbuilder.fw.plist **to create a new file in the** nano **text editor and then type the following exactly as shown:**

    ```
    <?xml version="1.0" encoding="UTF-8"?>
    <!DOCTYPE plist PUBLIC "-//Apple//DTD PLIST 1.0//EN"
        "http://www.apple.com/DTDs/PropertyList-1.0.dtd">
    <plist version="1.0">
    <dict>
    <key>Label</key>
    <string>com.firewallbuilder.fw</string>
    <key>ProgramArguments</key>
    <array>
    <string>/usr/local/sbin/Firewall.fw</string>
    </array>
    <key>RunAtLoad</key>
    <true/>
    </dict>
    </plist>
    ```

11. **Press Control+X to exit** nano, **press Y to confirm that you want to save the file, and then press Return to confirm the file name.**

12. **Type** sudo chown root:admin com.firewallbuilder.firewall.plist **to set the ownership correctly for your new** launchd **item.**

13. **To load the** launchd **item and thereby run the firewall without having to restart first, type the following:**

    ```
    sudo launchctl load /Library/LaunchDaemons/com.firewallbuilder.fw.plist
    ```

MacTuneUp

A relatively new product called MacTuneUp (www.macwareinc.com/products/MacTuneUp/overview.html, $34.99) includes a number of maintenance features, including the capability to make a bootable backup, system optimization routines, and a front end to IPFW. However, if you don't need the other features, a less-expensive program such as NoobProof or Firewall Builder gives you all the IPFW customization you need.

Using Other Third-Party Firewall Software

The combination of Mac OS X's application firewall and IPFW (configured in any of the ways described previously) should be more than adequate to serve the firewall needs of virtually any Mac user. Nevertheless, several other third-party firewalls are available that aren't based on IPFW, and they're worth looking into for two reasons. First, some of them offer novel features that you can't get with IPFW no matter how clever your rules are. And second, some of them offer clearer, more user-friendly interfaces than the IPFW front ends discussed previously. Unfortunately, the two attributes don't necessarily go together. For example, IPNetSentryX, described just ahead, is perhaps the most advanced Mac firewall in existence, but it's quite a challenge to understand. Intego NetBarrier, on the other hand, offers easily accessible firewall features but doesn't go nearly as far in its capabilities as the others listed here.

Intego NetBarrier

NetBarrier (www.intego.com/netbarrier/, $49.95), which I've mentioned on quite a few other occasions, includes a firewall (shown in Figure 17.11) among its long list of modules. Its range of capabilities is roughly similar to that of IPFW, and its rules function in more or less the same way — allowing or blocking packets, inbound or outbound, based on IP address, port, and protocol. You can also filter traffic by interface — for example, you can treat incoming or outgoing data transferred using your Mac's Ethernet interface differently than data transferred over its AirPort interface. IPFW can do this too, but NetBarrier makes that capability readily accessible. NetBarrier even lets you filter traffic by MAC address.

FIGURE 17.11

NetBarrier's Firewall module includes the usual list of blocked or allowed services, but you can also assign a schedule to each rule so it applies only at certain times.

Note

By virtue of its wide range of features, NetBarrier wins the award for being the security program that shows up in the most chapters of this book. I discuss its web privacy features in several parts of Chapter 10, its anti-malware features in Chapter 14, and its network monitoring capabilities in Chapter 22. ■

NetBarrier's firewall offers a couple of unique features. First, it lets you set a schedule for each rule. For example, if you run an Intranet web server on your Mac only during business hours, you could set up a rule to permit incoming traffic on port 80 only while your office is open. NetBarrier also includes a Trojans screen (part of the firewall but separate from the rules list) that lets you quickly block the incoming TCP or UDP ports used by a long list of Trojan horses.

The program has a preset list of applications and services for which you can permit access with a single click and a longer list of services you can add to a rule manually without having to know ahead of time which port(s) they use. However, although you can also manually specify protocols (TCP, UDP, ICMP, IGMP — Internet Group Management Protocol — or all the above) and ports or port ranges, doing so requires a considerable amount of digging through nested dialog boxes; it's not as obvious or straightforward as in most firewalls.

Although NetBarrier includes a perfectly capable firewall, I find it slightly more awkward to use than some of the IPFW front ends, and its extra features, while interesting, aren't compelling. So, if you have NetBarrier or plan to purchase it to make use of its other modules, by all means take advantage of its firewall too. But I wouldn't recommend buying the package solely for this feature.

IPNetSentryX and IPNetRouterX

If you need serious, high-octane, geek-worthy firewall capabilities, look no further than Sustainable Softworks (www.sustworks.com), developer of IPNetSentryX ($60) and IPNetRouterX ($100). The two programs share the same firewall engine; IPNetRouterX adds a full range of routing capabilities, including NAT, DHCP, DNS, load balancing, and much more. Among other things, this makes IPNetRouterX ideal to use as a firewall that regulates traffic not just for the Mac it's installed on but for an entire network (assuming the Mac you've installed it on has at least two independent Ethernet interfaces). As impressive as all those features are, though, for the purposes of this chapter, I'm concerned only with the local firewall aspect of the two programs. So, what I say here about IPNetSentryX also applies to IPNetRouterX.

Although IPNetSentryX lets you configure a conventional, static "allow/deny" firewall, that would be like using a MacBook as a doorstop — it would get the job done, but it's missing the point. What makes IPNetSentryX interesting and unusual is that it can dynamically adapt to network conditions on the fly. In its default configuration, for example, shown in Figure 17.12, the program watches for telltale signs of malicious network access, and when it detects one, it automatically blocks the IP address in question. Among the behaviors it knows how to watch for (and which you can configure to your liking) are access on ports Mac OS X doesn't normally use, port scanning, and denial-of-service (DoS) attacks.

The way it achieves all this is by using hierarchical rules, each of which examines one or more of 26 attributes a packet might have, including not only obvious things such as source IP address, protocol, and destination port but also TCP flags and options, the time, day, and date on which the packet was sent, and even the data contents of the packet itself — among other properties. When a packet matches, the rule can then take any of 23 different actions. Not only can it allow, block, and log, it can also send the packet on to the next rule in the hierarchy (or an entirely different group of rules) for evaluation, add the IP address to a trigger ("naughty") list, send an email message to an administrator, run an AppleScript, and just about anything else you can come up with. By constructing nested chains of these rules, which can use information (such as the trigger list) gathered by previous rules, a firewall administrator can create nearly any sort of behavior.

Unfortunately, all this power comes at the expense of brain-twisting complexity. Even if you feel entirely comfortable writing IPFW rules from scratch, IPNetSentryX is a whole new game, and it requires you to think about network traffic in a new way. Instead of simply "allow packets that are like X," you have to figure out how to express things like "if a packet has a dash of A and a sprinkle of B, but no C, and if a previous rule took action D, and the packet was sent on a Tuesday along with at least 20 but no more than 100 other similar packets, and contains the number 32,768, direct it to program E and send me a note about it when I get to work." In other words: If you're deeply familiar with the intricacies of IP networking, have some programming experience, enjoy solving complex puzzles, and revel in unlimited packet-filtering power, this is the firewall for you. But bear in mind that even such a person will have to expend some trial and effort to figure out how the program works — the documentation leaves a great deal to be desired.

One other complaint: Although IPNetSentryX has a check box that lets you block all IPv6 packets, that's the extent of its IPv6 awareness. Despite all its clever capabilities, it can't currently perform its automatic filtering magic on IPv6 traffic.

The bottom line? IPNetSentryX (or IPNetRouterX) is fantastic if you need it and are willing to devote the necessary effort to understanding it, but it's far beyond what most people need, even for a large, complex network. If your time is more valuable to you than the ultimate firewall, stick with something less fancy.

FIGURE 17.12

IPNetSentryX comes with default rules (a portion of which appear here) that look for many common kinds of improper behavior and block the offending IP addresses without requiring explicit rules for each case.

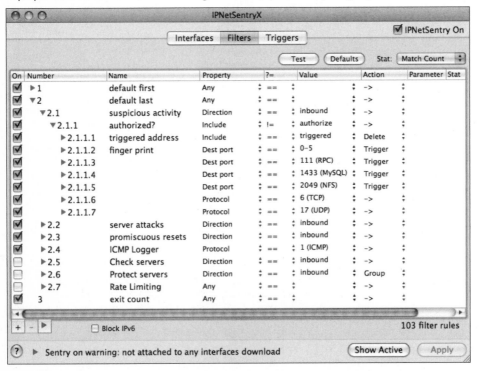

Norton Firewall for Mac

Last but not least is Norton Firewall for Mac, a component of Symantec's Norton Internet Security for Mac (www.symantec.com/norton/macintosh/internet-security, $79.99). Previous versions of Norton Firewall were front ends for IPFW, but the current version is a complete, stand-alone firewall. Norton Firewall has an outstanding mix of features (including some rather unusual ones) and a clear, uncomplicated interface.

Norton Firewall combines packet filtering with an application-based outbound firewall. Because the latter feature may not work correctly with Mac OS X's application firewall, Symantec recommends that you not use both at the same time. In its main firewall settings window, shown in Figure 17.13, you can turn either type of firewall on or off with a single click and then click the corresponding Configure button for more detailed modifications.

FIGURE 17.13

The two main firewall features in Norton Firewall for Mac can be activated or deactivated in this window with just one click each.

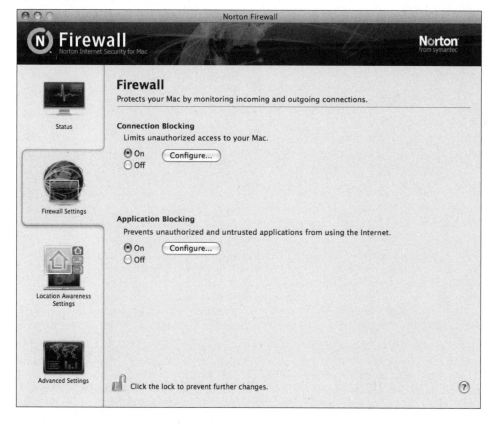

Cross-Ref

For more on the use of Norton Firewall for filtering outbound traffic, see Chapter 14. ∎

Connection Blocking is Norton Firewall's term for packet filtering, and it operates on the usual model of blocking or allowing packets bound for certain ports, as shown in Figure 17.14. It can filter incoming and outgoing traffic separately and offers both manual and assisted configuration.

FIGURE 17.14

The Connection Blocking portion of Norton Firewall lets you selectively block or allow access for various Internet services, as in most firewalls.

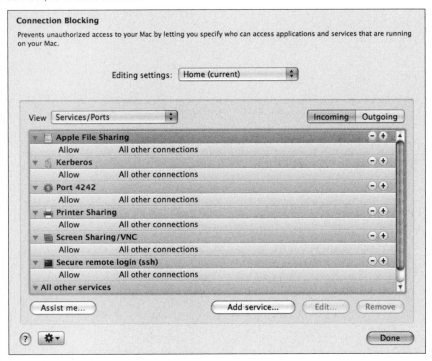

Like DoorStop X, Norton Firewall lets you set up different configurations for different locations, so your firewall can adapt to changing conditions as you move between home, work, and travel environments. However, what's especially good about Norton Firewall's design is that it makes use of the locations you've already set up in the Network pane of System Preferences. Instead of switching your network settings there and then manually changing your firewall, you can simply tell your firewall to change its settings automatically when you select a new network. This sort of convenience should be a mandatory part of every firewall.

Norton Firewall also includes something called DeepSight Community Download. If you activate this feature, the firewall takes note of any IP addresses it blocks due to improper behavior, sends those to a central server, and then shares that list with other Norton Firewall users. That way, you can automatically block access by any IP address that any Norton Firewall user has found to be problematic. I'm slightly dubious about the value of this feature because most of these connections should already be blocked by the firewall's other settings, and there's a nontrivial chance of false positives, which could prevent legitimate users from contacting your computer; but the feature can easily be disabled if you prefer.

Finally, like the other products in the Norton Internet Security suite, the firewall includes Vulnerability Protection, which automatically adds to your firewall the IP addresses of computers whose behavior matches a "signature" corresponding to an attempt to exploit holes or weaknesses in Mac OS X or your software.

My only significant complaint about Norton Firewall, except for the cost (keeping in mind that it's just one component of a larger package), is that the default settings are highly intrusive, with irritating alerts popping up constantly — giving the false impression that one's Mac is up to all sorts of illicit shenanigans. This is largely due to the Application Blocking feature, and thankfully, the alerts can be easily silenced (or the corresponding filtering behavior modified) so the firewall functions effectively without getting in your way.

Summary

Although I touched on firewalls several times earlier in this book, in this chapter, I went into detail about how they work, the various forms in which they appear, and how to put them to best use on your Mac. After giving an introduction to basic firewall concepts, I described the application firewall included with Leopard and Snow Leopard, explained how to configure it optimally, and also outlined some of its shortcomings. I next moved on to IPFW, a powerful Unix-based firewall that's been part of Mac OS X for years but which is normally hidden in Leopard and Snow Leopard.

For situations too complex for even IPFW, a third-party firewall may be a better choice, and Mac users have numerous options. So, I rounded out the chapter with descriptions of some of the most popular firewall applications that can run on your Mac.

Web Server Security

A pache, the world's most popular web server software, is built into every copy of Mac OS X. What's more, it takes just a few clicks to turn it on, making your Mac a web server you can use to run a personal or business website that the world can see. However, running a web server exposes your Mac to a number of additional risks and makes it much more of a target than it would otherwise be. In this chapter, I cover the fundamentals of protecting your Mac and its data while it's being used as a web server. Apart from configuring Apache and other parts of Mac OS X securely, you learn how to password-protect portions of your site, encrypt web pages with SSL, avoid common exploits and attacks, and, if applicable, keep any web-connected databases secure.

This chapter covers the sorts of things you should be concerned with when using the version of Apache in the standard version of Leopard or Snow Leopard and activated using the Sharing pane of System Preferences. Although most of the same general principles apply to other web servers, to custom builds of Apache, or to the version of Apache included with Mac OS X Server, I don't specifically address these other configurations in this chapter.

Cross-Ref

For more additional security considerations you need to be aware of when using the Mac OS X Server version of Apache, see Chapter 30. ∎

The Basics of Running a Secure Web Server

I want to begin this section with a few words of reassurance. If you're running a simple website (or several) on your Mac, with only static content, such as text, pictures, and movies — and if you take a few simple, commonsense steps to protect your Mac — you're quite safe. With such a setup, your risk of suffering at

IN THIS CHAPTER

Understanding and preventing security issues that affect Macs running web servers

Requiring authentication to view portions of a website

Encrypting transmissions of web pages with SSL

Preventing attackers from installing malicious software using web forms

Protecting databases used to deliver web content

the hands of web-trolling evildoers is barely higher than if you weren't running a web server at all. Fortunately, that's exactly what many home and small-office Mac users want to do.

The security risks involved in running a web server begin to creep in when you do any of the following:

- Use Server Side Includes (SSI) or Common Gateway Interface (CGI) programs to put dynamic content on your pages
- Use scripting languages, such as PHP, Perl, or Python, to process forms or perform other behind-the-scenes functions
- Use databases, such as MySQL, to store data for your websites

Note
Database programs with built-in web servers, such as FileMaker Pro and Panorama, are largely resistant to the sorts of dangers that affect common Unix-based database engines. ■

- Turn on software features without understanding what they do
- Paste code into your web pages that you don't understand

If you're doing none of these — for example, merely sharing a blog or photo gallery you created in iWeb with your friends and family — you can skim over this chapter, double-check a few essential settings, and leave it at that. But if you're engaging in any of those potentially risky behaviors, you should read everything here carefully and take every possible step to protect your Mac and its data.

General considerations

As with most security matters, the principle of least privilege applies in its own way to a Mac-based web server. You should start with settings as restrictive as possible and only relax them, selectively, to the point necessary to give others — especially those who'll access your web server from outside your local network — the capabilities they absolutely need. For example, someone accessing your website from the outside needs port 80 (or another port you designate) to be open in your firewall; an open port is a non-negotiable part of running a web server. But that's the exception; most if not all other ports should be closed unless or until they're actively needed for something.

Cross-Ref
For more on the principle of least privilege, see Chapter 3. For more on firewalls, see Chapter 17. ■

This concept reappears on many levels in the suggestions that follow, from the services you share on your Mac, to the Apache modules you activate, to the permissions you give to the files that make up your websites. In each case, the same rule applies: Keep a tight rein on the privileges you grant others, extending them only when a genuine need arises.

Sharing settings

When you turn on your Mac's web server, you invite access from the outside. Inevitably, people (or computers) with too much time on their hands begin to notice the existence of your web server and might begin probing it, looking for other services it might be offering (perhaps unwittingly), with the goal of exploiting some security hole to install malware, steal data, vandalize your website, or do any number of other unpleasant things. Therefore, it pays to have as few services as possible listening for outside access because having more than you need only increases the ways in which your Mac could be compromised.

The sharing services built into Mac OS X can all be turned on or off in the same place. To activate your web server and, at the same time, deactivate any unneeded services, follow these steps:

1. Choose ⇨ System Preferences and then click Sharing to open the Sharing pane.
2. **If the lock icon in the lower-left corner of the window is in the locked state, click it, type an administrator's username and password, and then click OK.**
3. **If the check box next to Web Sharing isn't already selected, click it, as shown in Figure 18.1.** This activates Apache, making your Mac's system-wide website immediately available at the IP address on the right under Your computer's website and your personal, user-specific website available at the address that appears beneath that. Each user on your Mac can have an individual website.

FIGURE 18.1

When you turn on Web Sharing in System Preferences, the window tells you what address others on your local network can use to contact your Mac's web server. This figure shows the pane as it appears in Leopard; Snow Leopard is slightly different.

4. **To turn off other settings for which the On check box is selected, click the relevant check box again.** Share only the services you're positive you need to be able to use from other Macs (on your local network or remotely). If in doubt, leave it off — you can always turn it back on later.

5. **Close System Preferences.**

Note

Unless your Mac has a publicly routable IP address — uncommon in home and small-office environments — the URLs shown in the Sharing pane work only on your local network. To make your web server available to the outside world by IP address, you must generally use port forwarding, as explained in Chapter 15. To go a step further and enable others to reach your Mac by domain name in addition to a numeric address, you must use a dynamic DNS service, such as DynDNS, which is discussed in Chapters 7 and 16. ∎

Once you've turned on Web Sharing, you can create web pages using the method of your choice and then put them in either `/Library/WebServer/Documents` (for your Mac's main site) or `~/Library/Sites` (for user-specific personal sites).

Firewall settings

Even if you've turned off most of your Mac's non-web-sharing services, a firewall running on your Mac can provide extra protection by preventing applications and processes you aren't even aware of from receiving incoming Internet traffic. And if you use a packet-filtering firewall such as IPFW (built into Mac OS X but disabled by default), you can increase the security for your web server by selectively blocking access from any IP address or address range that you discover to be problematic.

Cross-Ref

For more on firewalls, see Chapter 17. ∎

At minimum, you should turn on the default application firewall in Mac OS X by following these steps:

1. **Choose ⬤ ➪ System Preferences and then click Security to open the Security pane.**
2. **If the lock icon in the lower-left corner of the window is in the locked state, click it, type an administrator's username and password, and then click OK.**
3. **Click the Firewall tab, the Leopard version of which is shown in Figure 18.2.**
4. **In Leopard, click the Set access for specific services and applications radio button. In Snow Leopard, make sure the tab says "Firewall: On," and if not, click the Start button to turn it on.**
5. **Close System Preferences.**

If you use IPFW or any other packet-filtering firewall, be sure to open port 80 for incoming packets, and if you use SSL (discussed later in this chapter), also open port 443.

Network and routing setup

Although it's not always possible (especially if you have only one Mac or if your budget is limited), the safest practice is to separate your web server from the rest of your network. Ideally, your web server should contain no personal data at all — only data that you're comfortable sharing with the public — and should be connected to your network between your gateway and a router, which would then be configured to prevent any outside traffic coming through your web server from reaching the rest of your network. This type of configuration is known as a DMZ.

FIGURE 18.2

When Web Sharing is turned on, it's automatically added to the list of services that accept incoming connections.

Cross-Ref

For more on using a DMZ, see Chapter 15. ■

Keep in mind that the DMZ host setting offered by many routers and gateways isn't a true DMZ — it merely passes all incoming requests from the Internet through to a particular device on your network, without affording any protection to the rest of your computers.

Apache settings

The Sharing pane of System Preferences lets you turn Apache on and off with a single click. Unfortunately, that's as far as Mac OS X's graphical interface for Apache goes. If you want to do anything else — change its parameters, add or disable modules, or modify its behavior in any way — you must in most cases fiddle with one or more text files.

Note

Many of Apache's capabilities come not from the core Apache program but from a series of modules called Dynamic Shared Objects (DSOs). Apache is preconfigured with quite a few DSOs (although Mac OS X turns a few off by default), and you can add others to gain more features. ■

On the bright side, Apache's default settings under Leopard and Snow Leopard are quite good in terms of security and provide most of the features you might need. In most cases, you need to make changes only if you want to do things such as adding support for CGI applications, PHP, or other means of delivering dynamic content; changing the port Apache uses or its default directory; or customizing the ways in which Apache allows or blocks access to certain directories. And therein lies the danger: Any change you make to Apache's default settings could — if you're not careful — weaken your web server's security.

Almost any change you may need to make to Apache's configuration can be done by editing a single file — `/etc/apache2/httpd.conf`. Because this file is owned by root, you must use `sudo` to edit it; for example, by typing the following in Terminal:

```
sudo nano /etc/apache2/httpd.conf
```

You can find complete documentation for Apache at `http://httpd.apache.org/docs/2.2/` and details about most of the commands in `httpd.conf` at `http://httpd.apache.org/docs/2.2/mod/core.html`. Because the list of capabilities you can add or change in Apache is immensely long, I can only offer a couple of general words of advice. First, if at all possible, make only one change at a time. If something goes wrong, it'll be much easier to find and solve the problem if you don't have to consider many variables at once. And, second, remember the principle of least privilege: Don't turn on modules you don't need or grant access beyond what is necessary for your site.

I should note in passing that there are at least two graphical interfaces that let you configure Apache without dealing with text files. One is called iTools (`www.tenon.com/products/itools-osx/`, $349) — it's extremely full-featured but pricey for individuals. The other is a preference pane called Mapache (`www.khaitu.com/software/view/8`, $15), shown in Figure 18.3. Although Mapache is inexpensive, it offers access to only a few common features — not nearly everything you might need to modify in `httpd.conf`.

Note

The Server Admin application included with Mac OS X Server provides a graphical interface for adjusting most of Apache's features — but it doesn't work with the version of Apache included in the standard version of Mac OS X. I discuss this use of Server Admin in Chapter 30. ∎

File permissions

The files that make up your website — HTML files, cascading style sheet (CSS) files, graphics, and all the rest — have, like all files on your Mac, a designated owner, group, and permissions. In order to be able to modify the files yourself, you must have read and write access and, in general, also be the files' owner. So, for a typical HTML file, the permissions might look something like this:

```
-rw-r--r--   1 joe  staff  2628 Apr  7 16:18 index.html
```

Cross-Ref

For more on file ownership and permissions, see Chapter 3. ∎

That is, the owner, Joe, who's a non-administrative user and thus a member of the staff group, has read and write access; the group and everyone else have read-only access.

FIGURE 18.3

Mapache is a preference pane with a simplified interface for modifying some of Apache's most commonly used features.

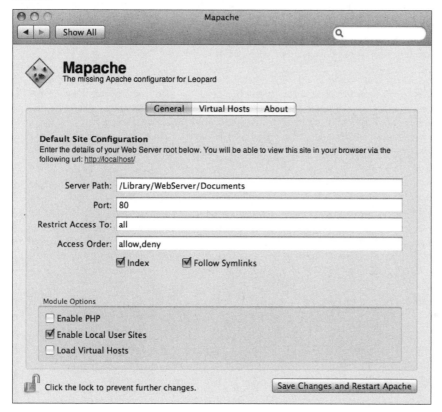

The folder in which the files are stored (that is, ~/Library/Sites or a subfolder inside it for individual users) also requires the x (executable) attribute in order for users to be able to list their contents, so it might look like this:

```
drwxr-xr-x   5 joe   staff   170 Apr  7 16:18 Sites
```

Your main Library/WebServer/Documents folder, because it's inside your main Library folder and therefore owned by root, normally looks like this:

```
drwxrwxr-x  35 root  admin  1190 May 15 16:39 Documents
```

All these permissions are perfectly fine, in that they share a few important attributes:

- They all permit the web server itself — a special user called www — to read the file by virtue of being world-readable (the last r in the permissions).

- None of them enable the web server to make changes to the file or its enclosing folder because the permissions for "other" lack a w.
- In the case of files, which could be programs, they're not executable (no x).

Note

Script files used by Apache modules, such as PHP, need not be executable in order to work because they're not running independently; they're being interpreted by another program. ■

The problem, though, is that in the course of creating, downloading, and modifying files for your website — potentially by various people who are using various pieces of software — permissions can sometimes get thrown out of whack. If permissions are too restrictive (for example, a file isn't world-readable), that file may not show up at all on your website. But a more serious problem is when a file — or, worse, a folder — is world-writable. That means anyone can make changes to it or delete it, and because the www user is part of everyone, the door is open for any of numerous possible hacks and exploits to modify your website from the outside.

For maximum security, then, check your sites periodically (by typing **ls -l** in Terminal) to make sure all their files and folders, up to and including the immediate enclosing folder, are not world-writable and, in the case of files, not world-executable. That generally means files should have a mode of 644 (-rw-r--r--) and folders should have a mode of 755 (drwxr-xr-x). If you need to enable files to be modified by the web server (for example, using a blogging package's built-in theme editor), you can change the theme files to 646 (-rw-r--rw), but realize that in so doing, you run a slight risk that someone from the outside could find a way to modify those particular files.

Dynamic website content

Nearly every discussion of web security mentions SSI (a method of embedding one page within another) and CGI as two technologies you should be careful with because of the fact that when implemented carelessly, they can result in all sorts of holes that an attacker could exploit to gain access to your computer. But honestly, I don't know if I've ever met anyone who used server-side includes, and CGI went out of vogue a decade ago.

All right, I'm exaggerating — but only a little. Most ordinary web developers in this day and age would never give a second's thought to using SSI or CGI. If you need dynamic content or live processing of data in some form, the usual way of getting that here in the twenty-first century is to use a web-friendly server-side scripting language, of which there's no shortage of options: PHP, Perl, Python, and Ruby are prominent examples. So, consider yourself duly warned, but because you probably weren't going to use SSI or CGI anyway, I'm not going to go into detail about their problems and how to avoid them. The information is readily available on the web if you're curious.

Note

Another approach is to use JavaScript embedded in web pages to send requests for data, often to a database, from the browser and display results dynamically — a technique known by the acronym AJAX, for Asynchronous JavaScript and XML. ■

However, having steered you toward scripting languages, I'm now obliged to warn you about all the dangers they can involve! All the languages mentioned can do far more than put information on a web page. They can interact with your file system (reading and writing files), send out email (including spam!), and even potentially run stand-alone programs on your Mac itself.

A discussion of all the ways you can get into trouble with scripting languages would be rather involved, in much the same way as a discussion about all the ways you can get into trouble with English! Therefore, I want to hit just a few highlights:

- **Know what you're doing.** A large percentage of security problems involving server-side scripting languages comes from people inexperienced in programming copying some code from a website and deploying it on their own without understanding how it works or, more generally, not knowing how to code defensively. I don't want to say that no one should ever use PHP without having a degree in computer science, but it's certainly true that a little knowledge can be dangerous. Avoid dabbling in scripting if you aren't willing to invest the effort to understand it at a reasonably thorough level.

- **Keep file permissions under control.** A rogue script that also happens to have write access can do untold damage. Refer to the previous discussion on permissions, and make sure your files and folders are properly locked down.

- **Keep an eye on your server.** Watch for spikes in access, examine your logs periodically, and, in general, be alert to any changes that could mean someone has found a way to take advantage of your code to do damage. If a problem does occur, the sooner you can catch it, the better.

- **Watch out for code injection attacks.** I discuss this particular danger, which is among the most common genres of exploit for websites, later in this chapter. But the short version is: Don't assume anything. Validate all user input, and watch out for files with greater privileges than they need.

Using HTTP Authentication

In addition to keeping your web server itself secure, another dimension of security you may need to consider is how to restrict access to your web server — or at least certain parts of it — to particular people. For example, if you run a personal website, you may want to have a section of the site with information that only family members should see; or for a business site, there may be a portion intended for public consumption and other pages to which only employees should have access. When the problem is regulating who can see certain pages and who can't, the solution is to use some form of authentication. In most cases, this means nothing more than asking users to type a username and password and then checking that they're valid before delivering web pages.

There are many ways of authenticating web access, and each has its pros and cons. Almost all of them involve some sort of programming — writing code that accepts input from a form on a web page and then takes the appropriate action. But another option exists, which requires no programming at all and is completely platform-neutral. Because this approach, called HTTP authentication, relies on features built into browsers rather than server-side logic, it lets you restrict access to certain files with very little effort.

HTTP authentication works like this: A visitor types the URL for a protected portion of your site and his or her browser displays a login window over a blank page. Each browser uses a different style, format, and wording in its login window; Safari's is shown in Figure 18.4. The visitor then types a username and password and clicks Log In (or a similar button), and the browser sends the credentials to the server. The server checks the information against its records (stored either in a special text file or in a database), and if the information matches, the server sends the requested page to the visitor. Each page in a protected area must be authenticated separately, but virtually all browsers store the user's credentials for the duration of the session, authenticating in the background with each request, so that the login window appears only once. After you type your credentials, Safari also gives you the option of saving them so they can be used automatically in future sessions too.

FIGURE 18.4

When a web browser displays a dialog box like this one, it means you're trying to connect to a site that uses HTTP authentication. The `:80` at the end of the address indicates an unencrypted site (meaning your login won't be encrypted either); if it ends in `:443`, the site uses SSL, so your login is encrypted.

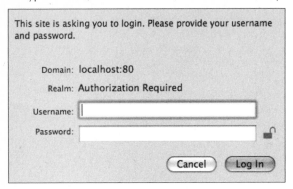

Note

HTTP authentication applies to all files in a designated folder (or any of its subfolders). For example, if you protect the folder `/secure`, **authentication would be required for** `http://your-site-address/secure/index.html` **as well as** `http://your-site-address/secure/subfolder/index.html`. **You can't use HTTP authentication to protect an individual file without also affecting all the other files in the directory.** ■

Although HTTP authentication is straightforward to implement, it's not without its downsides. For starters, you should understand that it provides only authentication, not encryption. Once someone knows a valid username and password combination, all web pages are sent in the clear (unless you also use SSL). So, it's not adequate, by itself, to protect highly sensitive data. In addition, HTTP authentication comes in two flavors: basic and digest. Basic is slightly easier to implement and supported by virtually every version of every browser in existence — but it sends passwords in the clear, and they could easily be sniffed in transit. Therefore, basic authentication should be used only in conjunction with SSL (described later in this chapter), which encrypts the entire authentication transaction as well as the contents of the pages themselves. Digest encrypts passwords in transit and is therefore a more secure method of authentication, even without the use of SSL, but some older browsers don't support it (although you're safe with Safari, Firefox, and most other modern browsers). And, finally, with either version, your security is only as good as your passwords, so be sure to pick good ones!

Cross-Ref

For more on passwords, see Chapter 6. ■

To set up a directory to use HTTP authentication, follow these steps:

1. **In the Finder, create the folder in which you want to store HTML files requiring authentication.** In this example, I assume you want a folder called `secure` at the top level of your Mac's main site, so that folder would be located at `/Library/WebServer/Documents/secure`.

2. **For testing purposes, put a valid HTML file in your newly created folder — even a simple copy of your main `index.html` file would be fine.** Don't put the actual files you want to protect here yet because protection isn't yet available. That comes later.

3. Open Terminal, which is located in `/Applications/Utilities`.

4. Type `sudo nano /etc/apache2/other/realms.conf` to open a new text file called `realms.conf`. This will be stored in `/etc/apache2/other` and will hold the instructions for telling Apache which folder to protect and where to find the credentials of those authorized to use it.

5. Type your administrator password when prompted and then press Return.

Note

The directives you're placing in this file could instead be put in various other places, such as a `.htaccess` file at the top level of your website or `/etc/apache2/httpd.conf`. However, keeping them in a separate, non-hidden file makes them more convenient to edit. Mac OS X's configuration of Apache automatically reads any configuration files placed in the `/etc/apache2/other` directory. ∎

6. Type one of the following blocks of text into the file:

   - To use basic authentication, type the following:

   ```
   <Location /secure>
     AuthType Basic
     AuthName "For authorized users only"
     AuthUserFile /etc/apache2/passwords
     Require valid-user
   </Location>
   ```

   If you want your protected folder to be named something other than `secure`, adjust the location name in the first (`Location`) line. Likewise, replace the text in the `AuthName` line with whatever message you want to appear in the login window.

   - To use digest authentication, type the following:

   ```
   <Location /secure>
     AuthType Digest
     AuthName "For authorized users only"
     AuthDigestDomain /secure/
     AuthUserFile /etc/apache2/digest
     Require valid-user
   </Location>
   ```

   If you want your protected folder to be named something other than `secure`, adjust the location name in the first (`Location`) line as well as in the fourth (`AuthDigestDomain`) line. Likewise, replace the text in the `AuthName` line with whatever message you want to appear in the login window.

7. Press Control+X to exit `nano`, press Y to confirm saving the file, and then press Return to confirm the file name.

8. Now create usernames and passwords for each person who can access the protected files. You can give the same credentials to more than one person, but it's less secure.

Note

This procedure stores passwords on disk in an encrypted form, so it's not possible to see a person's password by looking at the `passwords` file. By the way, it's possible to use a database rather than a plaintext file to store passwords, but that procedure is more complex, and I don't cover it here. ∎

If you chose basic authentication in step 6, follow these steps:

1. **Type** sudo htpasswd -c /etc/apache2/passwords *username*. Replace *username* with the first username you want to use — no spaces permitted.

2. **At the New password prompt, type a password and then press Return.**

3. **At the Re-type new password prompt, type the password again and then press Return.**

4. **To add passwords for additional users, type** sudo htpasswd /etc/apache2/passwords *username* (that is, omitting the -c from the original command) and then repeat substeps 2 and 3.

If you chose digest authentication in step 6, follow these steps:

1. **Type** sudo htdigest -c /etc/apache2/digest *"For authorized users only" username*. Replace *For authorized users only* with whatever you used in the AuthName line earlier in step 6, and replace *username* with the first username you want to use — no spaces permitted.

Note

Apache's documentation for htdigest **says that the command should include the name of the realm (the folder being protected), but by this it means the contents of the** AuthName **line (as odd as that may look), not the folder name itself or the contents of the** AuthDigestDomain **line, which may seem the more obvious interpretation.** ■

2. **At the New password prompt, type a password.**

3. **At the Re-type new password prompt, type the password again.**

4. **To add passwords for additional users, type** sudo htdigest /etc/apache2/digest *username* (that is, omitting the -c from the original command) and then repeat substeps 2 and 3.

9. **Restart the web server.** You can do this by opening the Sharing pane of System Preferences and then deselecting and then reselecting Web Sharing, but a far easier way, because you're already in Terminal, is to type **sudo apachectl graceful**.

10. **Test your secure realm by opening a web browser and navigating to** http://127.0.0.1/ secure/index.html. Substitute the name of your protected folder for secure, if applicable, and the name of the HTML file you copied there in step 2, if different). If everything is working correctly, you should see a login prompt.

11. **Type one of the username and password combinations you specified in step 8 and then click Log In.** Your page should then appear.

12. **After you're satisfied that authentication is working correctly, move the pages for which you want to require authentication into the protected folder.**

Securing a Site with SSL

HTTP Authentication can ensure that no one has access to sensitive content on your website without your permission. However, once someone has access — whether authentication was required or not — all data that goes back and forth between your server and the client's browser is ordinarily sent in the clear. So, if any of those exchanges were to be intercepted along the way (a particular danger if the client is connected to an unencrypted Wi-Fi network but still possible even with a completely wired connection), an eavesdropper could see any data the browser sends or receives.

If your website exists only to provide information to the public or to show off pictures of your family or recount your personal experiences in a blog, it's fine for the data to be sent in the clear because an eavesdropper could see only things intended for the general public. However, if your website collects any personal data using a web form or displays confidential information such as passwords, private addresses, or medical or legal records, authentication alone isn't enough — you should encrypt your site by using SSL.

Cross-Ref

For more on SSL, see Chapter 10. ■

SSL-encrypted web pages have URLs that begin with `https` rather than the usual `http`. With SSL enabled, the browser and the server negotiate with each other and establish a key pair for public-key encryption. The padlock icon in your browser confirms that you're viewing an encrypted page.

Protecting a site with SSL requires the server to have a valid SSL certificate and an accompanying private key and to know where to find them. In the case of Apache, it also requires that a built-in SSL module be activated (as it is by default). Obtaining and installing a certificate and key and setting up Apache to use them involve a number of steps but are ultimately quite easy.

Cross-Ref

For more on using SSL certificates for users of Mac OS X Server, see Chapter 27. For more on certificates in general, including an overview of Mac OS X's Certificate Assistant utility, see Chapter 5. ■

If you're creating a website intended for people outside your home or small business — the general public, business clients, or customers — you should get a certificate duly signed by a certificate authority so each user's browser can automatically recognize it as valid. This requires a bit of effort (and expense, because you must pay the certificate authority).

On the other hand, if you want to encrypt a site for your personal or family use or for the use of employees in a small company, you can use a simpler approach, which is to create a self-signed certificate. When a user connects to a site that employs a self-signed SSL certificate, a warning appears in the browser. However, the user can usually dismiss the warning with a single click (and, often, can set up the browser to trust this unsigned certificate permanently), and because this simple process is something that family members and employees probably wouldn't mind doing once, it might be a better approach in such situations. Regardless of whether a certificate is self-signed or signed by a certificate authority, it offers the same level of encryption.

Creating a certificate and activating SSL

To protect your website with SSL, follow these steps:

1. **Open Terminal, which is located in** `/Applications/Utilities`.
2. **To generate some pseudo-random data that will be used in a moment to help generate your private key, type the following commands:**

   ```
   sudo gzip -c --best /var/log/system.log > /usr/local/share/random.dat
   sudo openssl rand -rand file:/usr/local/share/random.dat 0
   sudo rm /usr/local/share/random.dat
   ```

3. **Using the information provided previously, decide whether to use a self-signed certificate or to have a certificate signed by a certificate authority and then follow the appropriate substeps.**

Note

The steps I provide here aren't the only ways of creating certificates and don't provide the strongest possible security, but they're adequate for home and most small-business use. ■

- For a self-signed certificate:

1. Type the following:

```
sudo openssl req -keyout /etc/apache2/server.key -newkey rsa:1024
  -nodes -x509 -days 3650 -out /etc/apache2/server.crt
```

2. **Respond to each query that appears and then press Return after each response.** All the information requested (your country, city, email address, and a few other details) is self-explanatory, except for one piece — the most important one — which is misleadingly labeled. When you see the prompt `Common Name (eg, YOUR name) []`, what it's really asking for is your web server's domain name! So, type the exact domain name at which users will access your site (for example, `www.mydomain.com`) or its IP address (for example, `123.234.012.123`). If you're only trying this out on your own Mac, and won't need to access your server from another computer, type **127.0.0.1**.

- For a certificate signed by a certificate authority:

1. Type the following:

```
sudo openssl req -keyout /etc/apache2/server.key -newkey rsa:1024
  -nodes -out server.pem
```

2. **Respond to each query that appears and then press Return after each response.** But note that when you see the prompt `Common Name (eg, YOUR name) []`, you must type your web server's domain name (for example, `www.mydomain.com`), not your personal name. Be careful with this step because your SSL certificate is valid only for the exact domain name you type here. At the end of this process, your Certificate Signing Request (CSR) file is located at `/etc/apache2/server.pem`.

3. **Sign up for an SSL certificate with the certificate authority of your choice, such as Thawte** (`www.thawte.com`) **or Instant SSL** (`www.instantssl.com`). During the process of purchasing a certificate, you're asked to supply your CSR, which you can do (depending on the provider) either by uploading or emailing the file `/etc/apache2/server.pem` or by pasting its contents into a web form.

4. **When the certificate authority supplies your certificate, save it as a plain text file at** `/etc/apache2/server.crt`. To ensure that this file has proper permissions, type the following two commands:

```
sudo chown root /etc/apache2/server.crt
sudo chmod 600 /etc/apache2/server.crt
```

4. **To edit your Apache configuration so that it supports SSL, type the following:**

```
sudo nano /etc/apache2/httpd.conf
```

5. **Scroll until you see this line:**

```
LoadModule ssl_module libexec/apache2/mod_ssl.so
```

It should appear exactly like that, but if it has a # before it (a comment symbol, which deactivates the line), remove the # to uncomment it.

6. **Continue scrolling until you get near the end of the file, where you should see this line:**

```
#Include /private/etc/apache2/extra/httpd-ssl.conf
```

Remove the # to uncomment it.

7. **Press Control+X to exit** nano, **press Y to confirm saving the file, and then press Return to confirm the file name.**

8. **Restart Apache by typing** sudo apachectl graceful.

Your web server is now running with SSL support. To test it, try visiting any page on your site, replacing the usual http with https, and verify that it loads correctly, with the padlock icon showing in your browser.

Note

Web pages served via SSL use port 443 by default. So, if you're using a firewall on your server (as you should be!), make sure port 443 is open. ■

If you used a self-signed certificate in step 3 in the previous set of steps, you see a warning like the one shown in Figure 18.5 when you first connect. To dismiss the warning for this session only, click Continue. Or assuming you're using Safari, store your approval of this certificate permanently in your keychain by clicking Show Certificate, clicking the check box labeled Always trust "*server-name*" when connecting to "*server-name*," and then clicking Continue. Type your username and password when prompted to do so and then click OK.

FIGURE 18.5

This warning appears when you connect to a site that uses SSL but without a certificate signed by a certificate authority.

Redirecting HTTP traffic to HTTPS

With this configuration in place, you can access any page on your site in either a secure form (by using an https URL) or an insecure form (by using http). However, in some situations, you may want to automatically redirect insecure requests to secure URLs. There are many ways to do this, but the approach that I prefer is to make a modification to one of Apache's configuration files (preferably the same one that contains the other settings for SSL) to redirect all requests beginning with http to the corresponding https URL. To do this, follow these steps:

1. **Open Terminal, which is located in** /Applications/Utilities.
2. **To edit the SSL configuration file using the** nano **text editor, type the following:**

   ```
   sudo nano /etc/apache2/extra/httpd-ssl.conf
   ```
3. **Scroll down to the very end of the file, after the line that reads** </VirtualHost>, **and type the following:**

   ```
   RewriteEngine On
   RewriteCond %{SERVER_PORT} !^443$
   RewriteRule ^/(.*) https://%{SERVER_NAME}/$1 [L,R]
   ```

Note

This procedure assumes that Apache's rewrite_module **is enabled, as it is by default in Mac OS X. ■**

4. Press Control+X to exit `nano`, press Y to confirm saving the file, and then press Return to confirm the file name.

5. Restart the web server by typing `sudo apachectl graceful`.

To test that the change is working, type any valid URL on your site into a web browser, starting with `http`, and then confirm that it's automatically replaced with `https`.

Avoiding Injection Attacks

A number of years ago, shortly after I began running websites on my own Xserve, I sat down at my computer one day to find my inbox full of complaints that my server had been sending out spam. I thought that I ran a pretty tight ship, so I was shocked and appalled to learn that someone had indeed found a way to hijack my server (a Mac, no less!) to send tons of junk mail. Of the 10,000 messages this hacker had attempted to send, about 3,000 got through before I discovered what was happening and blocked it.

When I investigated what had gone wrong, I found that I'd been the victim of a type of exploit known as an *injection attack*. An injection attack occurs when someone feeds a program a type of data that it wasn't expecting, and because of bugs, quirks, or unwise assumptions in the underlying code, it treats that unexpected data in an undesirable (but predictable) way. Although injection attacks take many forms, the variety I encountered that day — which is extremely common — involved a form on my site that let visitors send me feedback by email. What was supposed to happen was that the form took the information, such as the sender's email address and the message content, and then fed it to a simple PHP script, which in turn mailed it to me. But the attacker found a way to insert huge amounts of specially formatted data (including hundreds of email addresses) in those fields, and because my script made the naïve assumption that all input would be exactly what it was expecting, it simply passed all that data along to the outgoing mail routine, which interpreted it as a long series of messages to go to many people rather than a single message delivered only to me.

In fact, the attack was even trickier than that because it didn't require anyone to load my form manually and paste in data. Instead, the attacker's computer simply figured out the URL for the PHP script that sent out the mail and sent that script a `POST` request directly. The whole thing had been automated. Because my site used a mail-sending routine just like that of many other sites, all the attacker had to do was tell it to try the same procedure on one IP address after another until it found one with this vulnerability. In other words, even if I hadn't had a visible form on my website, the fact that a PHP file with the right (that is, wrong) code in it was sitting in a predictable place enabled someone to compromise my machine.

The moral of this story is that if your website contains anything beyond static files — that is, scripts or programs of any kind, including databases — you could be vulnerable to an injection attack, and you should take steps to minimize your risk. Although specific weaknesses depend on which scripting language you're using and the details of the code you use, these general principles can help to keep you out of trouble:

- **Stay up to date.** Newer versions of scripting languages often fix common security problems in older versions, in many cases without requiring changes to your code. Make sure you keep up with the latest stable releases.

- **Remove any unused scripts.** Scripts that aren't actively being used on your site should be deleted or moved to a part of your Mac not accessible from the outside world. Anything that just happens to be hanging around on your website could potentially be exploited.

- **Validate all input.** If you have code that accepts input from a form (or direct input in the form of queries built into URLs), validate it before you put it to use. For example, if you expect a certain field to contain an email address, check to make sure that it contains exactly one valid email address — and no other data — before passing it on to the next step in your script. Some other things you should check for in any code that processes or sends email messages include the following:

- **Forged From addresses.** For example, make sure that if a message claims to be from your domain that it's from a legitimate address.

- **Large numbers of URLs.** If a message contains more than a few URLs, it's unlikely to be a legitimate comment or query.

- **MIME content.** Look for MIME (Multipurpose Internet Mail Extensions) strings, such as `Content-Type`, `MIME-Version`, and `Message-Id`, which are dead giveaways that someone's trying to send out spam. These may appear in any field, including Name, From, To, Subject, and the message contents.

- **Excessive length.** If your script sees a name or email address with 100 characters, it's pretty clearly not legitimate. Check for unreasonable length in every field.

- **Bad HTTP referrer.** Assuming you're processing data for forms on your own site, your domain or IP address (or localhost, or 127.0.0.1) should be the referrer for any `GET` or `POST` requests allegedly from that form. If the referrer is anything else, it's a sign of danger.

Tip

Instead of coding all this validation by hand, you can make use of an Apache module called `mod_security` that automatically does a great deal of this work for you. David Di Gioia wrote a helpful article about using this module; you can read it at `www.pathf.com/blogs/2006/05/php_spam_inject/`. ∎

- **Watch for old PHP gotchas.** If you're using a version of PHP older than 6.0 — and especially if you're using version 4.x or earlier — your Mac may have some PHP features enabled that present attractive targets for exploitation. Without going into all the details, you should edit your `php.ini` file to disable `allow_url_fopen`, `magic_quotes_gpc`, `magic_quotes_runtime`, and `register_globals`. Consult the PHP documentation if you need explicit instructions.

- **Check file permissions.** As I mentioned earlier in this chapter, you should be sure that the files that make up your website — especially script files — have no more permission than is absolutely necessary. In particular, unless you have an extremely good reason to do so, avoid giving world write access to any script file.

- **Check your logs.** Skim through your web server access logs from time to time, and look for any `GET` or `POST` requests that appear to have unusual content or formatting. Your logs should tell you what data someone tried to send with each request, and if that data includes lots of email addresses, URLs, MIME commands, or other common components of a junk email message, you should consider blocking the IP address that sent those requests in your firewall.

- **Guard against SQL injection attacks.** If you use MySQL or another SQL database on your website (perhaps to run a blog based on WordPress or MovableType, for example), you run an additional risk. Even if your scripting code itself is flawless, someone could construct a specially formatted database query that includes commands to show all records, delete records, or cause other damage — an SQL injection attack. Because one method of attack involves the clever misuse of special characters, such as quotation marks, you can guard against it by making sure all such characters are *escaped* (or prepended with backslashes) before storing them in the database. Most scripting languages and database engines have built-in ways of doing this. For example, MySQL has a function called `mysql_real_escape_string`, and if you're accessing your database using PHP, you can call an identically named PHP function that sends any string through MySQL's escaping routine.

Tip

For much more advice on avoiding SQL injection attacks when using MySQL with PHP, read Chapter 3 of php | architect's Guide to PHP Security by Ilia Alshanetsky, available in free PDF form at `http://dev.mysql.com/tech-resources/articles/guide-to-php-security-ch3.pdf`. The advice is slightly dated (in that it mentions the now-deprecated `magic_quotes_gpc` function) but is extremely valuable nonetheless. ■

Database Security

The previous section covered injection attacks, one of the ways in which database servers are often compromised. But SQL servers are designed to operate over a network, and there's usually no expectation at all that a database resides on the same computer as a web server that uses it to store data or a client that connects for administrative purposes. Therefore, if you plan to administer your SQL server from a computer other than the one it's running on or use its data to feed a web server on another computer, you should take a few additional steps to prevent unauthorized users from getting administrative access to your database:

- **Customize firewall rules.** Although you can administer an SQL database from the command line using Terminal (either locally or over SSH), many people prefer a friendlier, fill-in-the-blanks interface. Some of the tools that offer this capability are conventional Mac OS X GUI programs — for example, MJ Media's free Sequel Pro (`www.sequelpro.com`) or Araelium Group's $25 Querious (`www.araelium.com/querious/`). For such applications, which communicate directly over the Internet, make sure the firewall on the Mac running your SQL server has the necessary port(s) open to enable you to access it from another computer. Or, for better security, configure the firewall to restrict incoming access on the designated ports to only those IP addresses that need it. By default, MySQL uses port 3306, whereas PostgreSQL uses port 5432. If you use a different database, consult its documentation to learn what port or ports it uses. On the other hand, if you use a single Mac to run the database and web server and to administer them both, there's no need for the database to communicate directly with the outside world, and you can (and should) have your firewall block both incoming and outgoing packets on that port.

Cross-Ref

For more on firewalls, see Chapter 17. ■

- **Manage access to web administration tools.** Another popular way of managing SQL databases is to use a web-based interface. On a web server (which may or may not be the same computer running your database), you install software such as Webmin (`www.webmin.com`) or phpMyAdmin (`www.phpmyadmin.net`), which communicates directly with your database and then permits you to interact with your database using a web browser. In other words, anyone with a web browser who knows the password to your web-based SQL administration interface could potentially gain access to your data. Luckily, both Webmin and phpMyAdmin let you restrict access to users with IP addresses you designate, which offers another layer of protection. Consult the software's documentation for instructions on managing access by IP address.

- **Use good passwords.** At the risk of sounding like a broken record, I want to reiterate that the passwords you choose for your SQL users (especially the root user, which has the greatest range of privileges) should be long and random. If someone on the outside can guess the password of a database user with the privileges to modify or delete data, your system could be compromised quickly.

Cross-Ref

For more on choosing good passwords, see Chapter 6. ∎

Summary

Any Mac (whether or not it's running Mac OS X Server) can be used as a web server, and by using built-in or freely available open-source software, your Mac can serve sophisticated, dynamic, database-driven sites. Along with this great power comes risk because running a web server opens your Mac to several potential avenues of attack. This chapter described ways of reducing that risk. I started by covering some of the basic settings you can use to improve your web server's security. I then described the use of HTTP authentication to create realms, which are portions of websites that require users to type credentials before viewing them.

I briefly outlined how to use SSL to encrypt data sent and received from your Mac's web server, and I provided some advice about preventing injection attacks, in which someone uses a web form to install executable software on your Mac. I ended the chapter with a look at securing some of the common database engines frequently used to supply the data for dynamic websites.

Using Logs

A s you use your Mac, Mac OS X itself and many third-party programs silently keep records about nearly everything that happens — especially errors and other unexpected behavior. All this information is stored in log files, which at first glance may appear to be hopelessly boring lists of numbers and technical minutiae. But when you're trying to figure out why some problem has occurred, logs can be your best friend. They may tell you who's been accessing your computer, which program was used when, which Internet servers have been contacted recently, and all sorts of other facts that can help you discover when and why your Mac was misused (whether by a program or a person). Needless to say, logs are useful for many other reasons too, such as tracking down crashes and misbehaving software, but in this chapter, I concentrate on exploring what logs can tell you about your Mac's security.

Log Basics

In computer programming generally — but especially in the Unix world — it's considered good form to make your software keep records of what it does. Although a typical user may not care that a MobileMe sync occurred at 3:15 p.m. on March 4, that Bob logged in at 3:30, or that Safari had trouble loading a web page at 3:45, this sort of information can be useful to developers who want to debug incorrect application behavior, system administrators who want to know what their users have been up to, and anyone with a need to make sure his or her computer is safe from intruders, eavesdroppers, and other bad guys. So, although you never see it happening, most of the programs on your Mac constantly record little snippets of information — each one time- and date-stamped — to text files called logs, stored in a quiet corner of your hard disk.

Millions of Mac users have never seen a log file and never will. In ordinary circumstances, you can do everything you need to do with your Mac on a daily basis without ever running into a log. But for security-conscious people, logs provide a way to find out what's been going on behind the scenes without your

IN THIS CHAPTER

Understanding the security information that logs can reveal

Making sure your logs contain the right data

Locating logs on your disk

Understanding the special console and system logs

Viewing logs' contents

Figuring out what to look for in logs

knowledge — giving you a chance to plug holes and correct security problems before they become serious. And in the event that your Mac does fall victim to a serious attack of some kind, careful review of your logs can tell you what went wrong so you can prevent it from happening again in the future.

What logs can tell you about security

Of the many uses to which the data in logs can be put, several of them have a direct bearing on security. Logs can let you see whether a person or computer may have tried (or even succeeded) to get access to something it shouldn't. To offer just a few of many examples, logs can tell you about the following:

- **Local login attempts.** When someone with physical access to your Mac logs in (or tries but fails), that information goes in a log file. For more on user accounts and how they relate to logging, see Chapter 3.

- **Remote login attempts.** Similarly, if you have Remote Login (SSH) enabled, any remote login attempts are logged. For more on SSH, see Chapters 7 and 11.

- **Firewall activity.** If you use Mac OS X's application firewall, IPFW, or a third-party firewall, you can configure the firewall to log blocked attempts (and, sometimes, successful attempts) by other computers to communicate with your Mac. For more on firewalls, see Chapter 17.

- **Use of the `sudo` command.** All administrative users on your Mac have access to the Unix `sudo` command, which lets them temporarily take on the privileges of the root user. By default, all uses of `sudo` are logged, allowing you to see which user executed which command and when. For more on `sudo`, see Chapter 3.

- **File sharing.** When you share files on your Mac using AFP, FTP, or SMB, all connections are logged. For more on File Sharing, see Chapters 7 and 11.

- **Web access.** If you use Web Sharing to run the Apache web server on your Mac, every request for a web page is logged with the requester's IP address and numerous other details. Errors (such as requests for nonexistent pages) are also logged. For more on web server security, see Chapter 18.

- **DNS lookups.** Every time your Mac connects to another computer on the Internet by its domain name (rather than by IP address), a record of the DNS information is cached — albeit briefly — in a file that functions somewhat like a log. For more on DNS, see Chapter 10.

- **Security software errors.** If you've installed security software of any kind, including backup software, antivirus software, or network monitoring tools, they almost certainly keep logs, and if they malfunction in any way, the information in those logs can help you to fix the problem.

What information is logged?

The specifics of what information any given application stores in log files — and in what format — are up to the software's developer. Some are more verbose; some less so. Some make a point of recording log messages in human-readable form, whereas others don't. So, the only real answer to the question of what information gets logged is "It depends."

Most programs adhere to a standard model of priority, also known as log severity. That is, each event that could potentially be logged is assigned one of several levels, ranging from "just saying hi" to "Danger, Will Robinson!" (or something like that). The idea is that not all log entries are equally important, and it's useful for anyone looking at logs to be able to identify, at a glance, whether a message was merely reporting on a normal state, recording an urgent problem, or something in between. There are seven customary log levels, ranging from most severe to least severe, with definitions adapted from the man page for `syslog(3)`:

- **Emergency (level 0).** An emergency or panic condition
- **Alert (level 1).** A condition that should be corrected immediately
- **Critical (level 2).** A critical condition
- **Error (level 3).** An error
- **Warning (level 4).** A warning message
- **Notice (level 5).** A condition that isn't an error but may need special handling
- **Info (level 6).** An informational message
- **Debug (level 7).** A debugging message

So, an Emergency log entry is something dreadful that requires immediate attention, an Alert entry is slightly less worrying, and so on, down to Info, which is merely an FYI. The Debug level includes extra information that's normally even less important than Info but which could be useful to a programmer trying to track down the source of an obscure bug.

Some applications let you choose what level of logging to use. In such programs, whichever level you choose, log messages from there on up to the greatest level of priority (that is, level 0) are recorded. For example, if you set an application to the Error level of logging, it also records Critical, Alert, and Emergency entries. Mac OS X's syslogd tool, described later in this chapter, lets you specify for each type of data it manages what happens at various levels of priority — for example, you can store entries of different severities in different places or alert an administrator if a particular service produces a log entry of a certain priority.

Unfortunately, although the seven priority levels are standard, what they mean isn't, because their definitions are rather imprecise. Does a certain sort of event count as a Warning or an Error? What level must I choose if I want to see log entries of a particular kind? There's usually no way to know, other than trial and error. You can set an application to a verbose level of logging (say, Notice or Info) in order to be sure you capture more potentially useful information, but the chattier your logs are, the more space they take up on disk and the harder they make it to find information of interest to you. If in doubt, choosing Warning or Error is usually adequate. Or set a lower level and then examine the logs to see what levels are assigned to the events you care about — and then adjust the logging level accordingly.

Storing logs safely

Because logs can contain such valuable information, it's essential that you be able to access them when you need them. But what if you're trying to track down the source of a malware program — and the program took the liberty of erasing the logs documenting its own existence? Or suppose you need to find the source of a remote login that resulted in your entire disk being erased. Once again, the logs are gone — and with them the evidence you need to figure out what happened. In short, you should take the same precautions with logs that you take with all your other data. To protect them from theft, fire, accidental or intentional deletion, and other disasters, you should be sure you have a copy on another computer — preferably one in another building.

One way to make this happen is simply to include logs in your regular backups, being sure to store a copy offsite (either by physically moving a disk to another location or by using an online backup service).

Cross-Ref

For more on backups, including offsite storage, see Chapter 8. ■

Another option is to store logs directly on another computer, bypassing your local hard disk altogether. Not all programs offer this capability, but some (including `syslogd`, discussed just ahead) do. If you choose this option, keep in mind that proper log recording is dependent on the network connection between your Mac and the computer that stores the logs.

Log rotation

Some logs, such as Apache logs on a busy web server, can grow by dozens of entries per second. Over time, active logs can swell to an unmanageable size, taking up valuable disk space and making analysis more difficult. To address this problem, Mac OS X automatically rotates certain logs that tend to be especially large. That is, it allows a log to grow only for a limited period of time and then it renames the old one (adding a number on the end and sometimes compressing it) and starts a new log. Once the number of archived logs has reached a predetermined point, Mac OS X purges the oldest log.

For logs stored in `/var/log` that are part of Mac OS X's rotation system, the current log for any program simply ends in the `.log` extension. The next-most-recent version of the log is compressed and gets the extension `.0.bz2` (for example, `secure.log.0.bz2`), with higher numbers indicating older logs. For logs stored in `/Library/Log` that are rotated automatically, the immediate predecessor of the current log gets an extension of `.1`, and the number increases with each older version.

Tip

You can change the interval of log rotation (and several other settings) for a number of system logs by editing the file `/etc/newsyslog.conf`. For details on the options available, type man newsyslog.conf in a Terminal window. ■

Adjusting syslogd Behavior

Most applications store their own log files in their own ways. For such applications, if you want to make any changes to the way they treat logs, consult the documentation provided by the developer. However, critical Mac OS X components take advantage of a system-wide logging message in Leopard and Snow Leopard called `syslogd` (system log daemon). This utility can store log messages locally or on a remote server and lets you choose exactly what behavior should occur for log entries from various sources and with various priority levels.

The `syslogd` process runs automatically in the background; to change its behavior, all you need to do is edit a single text file: `/etc/syslog.conf`. The default contents of the file are as follows (lines beginning with a # are commented out):

```
*.err;kern.*;auth.notice;authpriv,remoteauth,install.none;mail.crit
    /dev/console
*.notice;authpriv,remoteauth,ftp,install.none;kern.debug;mail.crit
    /var/log/system.log
# Send messages normally sent to the console also to the serial port.
# To stop messages from being sent out the serial port, comment out
    this line.
#*.err;kern.*;auth.notice;authpriv,remoteauth.none;mail.crit
    /dev/tty.serial
# The authpriv log file should be restricted access; these
```

```
# messages shouldn't go to terminals or publically-readable
# files.
auth.info;authpriv.*;remoteauth.crit          /var/log/secure.log
lpr.info                                       /var/log/lpr.log
mail.*                                         /var/log/mail.log
ftp.*                                          /var/log/ftp.log
install.*                                      /var/log/install.log
install.*                                      @127.0.0.1:32376
local0.*                                       /var/log/appfirewall.log
local1.*                                       /var/log/ipfw.log
*.emerg                                        *
```

Each entry in this configuration file consists of three components: the facility (the program or process recording a log); after a period separator, the priority (severity level); and, after one or more tabs, the action (usually a file in which the log entry is stored or the address of a remote server). The asterisk (*) is a wild card that can substitute for any facility or any priority, and a priority of none means that the item shouldn't be logged (unless overridden by a later directive). A given entry can have more than one facility or priority (separated by commas) and more than one facility/priority combination (separated by semicolons).

For example, this line logs all FTP entries, of any priority, to /var/log/ftp.log:

```
ftp.*                                          /var/log/ftp.log
```

This line, on the other hand, logs all auth messages with the priority of Info or higher, all authpriv messages, and all remoteauth messages with the priority Critical or higher to /var/log/secure.log (see just ahead for definitions of these terms):

```
auth.info;authpriv.*;remoteauth.crit          /var/log/secure.log
```

Examples of facilities you might want to concern yourself with are:

- auth. The system authorization system, which includes login attempts and the use of sudo
- authpriv. The same log messages as auth but stored in a file with limited access permissions
- remoteauth. Remote authorization — for example, login attempts via SSH
- ftp. File sharing via FTP
- install. The Apple installer, used for all Apple software and many third-party programs

To learn about other facilities — and additional details about altering syslog.conf — visit http://developer.apple.com/documentation/Darwin/Reference/ManPages/man5/syslog.conf.5.html or open Terminal and type **man syslog.conf**.

To edit syslog.conf, follow these steps:

1. **Open Terminal, which is located in** /Applications/Utilities.
2. **Type** sudo nano /etc/syslog.conf, **type your administrator password when prompted, and then press Return.**
3. **Using the previous information and the man page for** syslog.conf, **make any desired changes or additions to the file.** For example, you might want to reduce the priority level for remoteauth logged to /var/log/secure.log and from remoteauth.crit to remote-auth.info, giving you the same level of detail you get for local authorization requests. To log any item remotely, its action should be an @ sign followed by the IP address of the remote computer (which must be configured to accept inbound logs from another machine).

4. **Press Control +X to exit** nano, **press Y to confirm saving the file, and then press Return to confirm the file name.**

5. **Force** syslogd **to reload the configuration file by typing** sudo killall –HUP syslogd. Your changes take effect immediately.

Finding Logs

Almost all logs are stored in one of three places, so if you want to locate them manually, back them up, copy them, or do anything else with them, those are the spots where you should look. However, if you simply want to read the logs, you need not access them directly in the Finder — instead, use Console, as described next. Here's where you can find logs:

- /var/log. This folder, normally hidden in the Finder, contains logs for most of Mac OS X's system processes as well as for some third-party software that operates at a relatively low level — security-related software often falls into this category. To view the contents of this folder, type **cd /var/log** in Terminal. Or in the Finder, choose Go ➪ Go to Folder, type **/var/log**, as shown in Figure 19.1, and then click Go.

To view logs stored in the hidden /var/log folder, use the Finder's Go to Folder command.

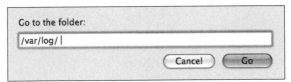

- /Library/Logs. This folder contains logs for a relatively small number of applications and processes that affect all user accounts. Backup programs and software update utilities often use this folder.

- ~/Library/Logs. Each user has a Logs folder in his or her individual Library folder. These Log folders contain most of the logs for third-party applications, noting the behavior of those applications when used by each particular user account.

Understanding the Console and System Logs

In addition to all the application- and process-specific log files Mac OS X stores, there are two special (and especially important) logs that don't fit the mold of the others: the console log and the system log.

The word *console* has several different meanings when applied to computers. Sometimes, for example, it refers to a terminal emulator program, but sometimes, it refers more generally to a command-line environment. These meanings, in turn, are metaphorical extensions of an earlier sense of console as a physical device (a keyboard paired with a display or printer) one used to interact with a multi-user computer system. In any case, whether you're talking about an old-fashioned mainframe or Mac OS X's command-line interface, the notion of sending output to the console refers to a program delivering some sort of textual message to whatever it considers the default location, where the operator can see it and take whatever action is required.

The Unix processes and GUI programs that make up Mac OS X send messages to the console constantly, but unless you're using Terminal to run a command-line program interactively, you normally never see these messages. In Mac OS X, they go into a special database called `asl.db`, whose contents can be displayed in real time by a utility included with Mac OS X that's called — you guessed it — Console. I discuss Console just ahead. So, one use of the Console utility is to display console messages.

However, to confuse matters further, the console messages stored in `asl.db` (which Mac OS X refers to as the Log Database) and displayed in Console fall into two categories. One category is system-wide messages (those sent by components of Mac OS X itself and by processes that affect all users), and the other is user-specific messages (those sent by applications being run by the current user). In Mac OS X, the user-specific messages are called *console messages*, a frustrating example of overloading a term with far too many meanings! Meanwhile, the remaining (system-wide) messages collectively constitute what's known as the system log, and in addition to being stored in `asl.db`, they're kept in a slightly different format in a file called `system.log`. In Leopard and Snow Leopard, there's no such thing as a file called `console.log`; rather, the console log is what you get if you use Console to view just the so-called console messages from the `asl.db` database.

To summarize, if you want the most comprehensive overview of all messages being sent to the console, you can use Console to view All Messages. If you want to see just console messages sent by applications run by the current user, you can use Console to view Console Messages. And, finally, if you want to see only system-wide messages, without the user-specific content, use Console to view `system.log`.

Note

Applications may send certain log entries (especially ones of greater priority) to the console — thus logging them in `system.log` — in addition to storing them in their own, application-specific log. ∎

Viewing logs in Console

Logs are plain text files, so you can read them using nearly any application — TextEdit, Word, a web browser, or a command-line program such as `cat` or `less`. However, a far better way to read logs is to use the Console utility included with Mac OS X. In addition to displaying the logs' content, Console provides a built-in directory of all the logs on your computer (assuming they're stored in any of several standard locations), lets you filter logs to display only the lines of interest to you, and provides other means of customizing what you see.

Note

Over the years, other log-reading utilities have come and gone, but because Console does such a good job, there's very little left for a third-party tool to offer. One notable exception, covered in Chapter 17, is Who's There? Firewall Adviser from Open Door Networks (`www.opendoor.com`, $39), which is designed specifically for viewing IPFW firewall logs and provides more ways of interacting with that data than Console does. ∎

Console basics

When you open Console for the very first time, you see a window that looks something like the one shown in Figure 19.2. By default, it displays Console Messages, which as previously explained are the status messages sent out by applications the current user is running. However, this is probably the least interesting information you can see in Console, but you must dig a bit to find the good stuff.

FIGURE 19.2

The initial view of Console provides a somewhat confusing, unhelpful view of the so-called Console Messages.

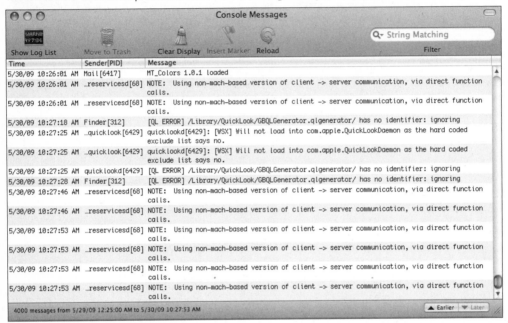

The first thing I suggest you do is to click the Show Log List button on the toolbar (or choose View ⇨ Show Log List). When you do this, the window changes to appear as in Figure 19.3, with a list of logs in the sidebar on the left. You can navigate through the hierarchical list of logs by clicking the disclosure triangles next to folder names, just as in the Finder's list view.

Note

You can also use Console to view logs that don't appear in this list (such as logs copied from other computers). To do so, choose File ⇨ Open, select a log, and then click Open. ∎

When viewing All Messages or Console Messages, Console displays entries in a table. You can change which columns appear by choosing commands from the Columns submenu of the View menu — for example, choose View ⇨ Columns ⇨ Level to display a column showing the priority of each item. As in all similar table views in Mac OS X, you can resize or rearrange the columns to your liking by dragging and dropping, and you can also resize the entire window to show more of each log entry on a single line, as shown in Figure 19.4.

If you select any other log (such as `system.log`) in the list on the left, Console displays it as a straight text list, as in Figure 19.5, instead of dividing it into a multi-column table. However, you can still resize the window as needed and drag the right edge of the sidebar to make it larger or smaller.

FIGURE 19.3

The most useful change you can make to Console's interface is to display the Log List in the sidebar.

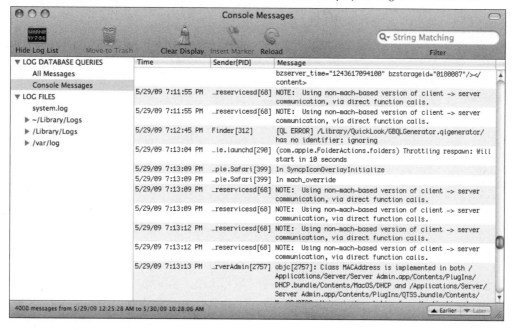

FIGURE 19.4

Add new columns, such as Level, to display extra information in Console — and resize the window to fit as much information as you want to see at once.

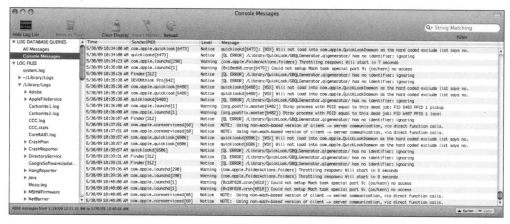

FIGURE 19.5

Unlike the Console Messages and All Messages views, Console's standard view of logs is a text list only — no columns.

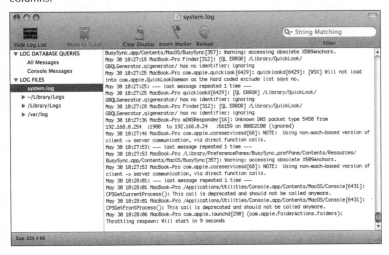

Useful Console features

A few features in Console are particularly useful and should be enormously helpful in making sense of log files:

- **Filter.** One of the handiest features in Console is its Filter field, located in the upper-right corner of the window. With any log selected, type a string into this field, and Console immediately filters the display to show only lines containing that string. For example, to display only the entries in system.log pertaining to backupd (the background process Time Machine uses), type **backupd** in the Filter field, as shown in Figure 19.6.

- **Clear.** If your window is cluttered with log entries and you want a clean slate, as it were (for example, to test a command in some application and see what entries appear in the log without having to worry that they'll blend in with the older entries), click Clear Display on the toolbar. Console clears the window but doesn't erase any entries in the log file itself.

- **Insert Marker.** To insert a time and date stamp at the end of the entries currently appearing in a given log, click Insert Marker on the toolbar. This marker isn't saved in the log file itself, but it can help you keep track of when certain log entries appeared when you're actively investigating something.

- **Log Database Queries.** For the log database only (that is, the contents of the asl.db database, which includes user-specific and system-wide console messages but not necessarily log entries from specific programs), you can construct and save special dynamic searches that act much like smart folders in the Finder or smart playlists in iTunes: You specify criteria and then when you select the query, all and only log entries matching those criteria appear. To create a log database query, follow these steps:

  1. Choose File ⇨ New Log Database Query. The window shown in Figure 19.7 opens.

FIGURE 19.6

When you type any text in the Filter field, Console displays only lines containing that text.

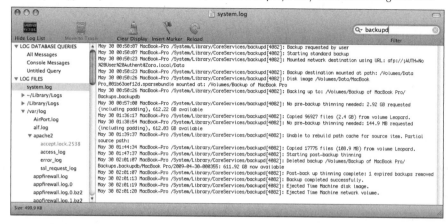

FIGURE 19.7

Construct a log database query to dynamically display log entries matching custom criteria.

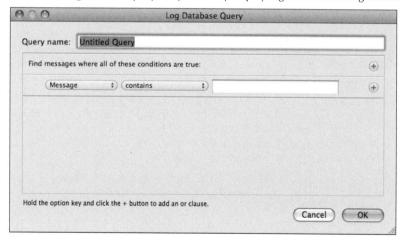

2. **Type a name for your query and then use the pop-up menus to describe a condition to match (such as Message contains auth).**

3. **To add another condition, click the Add (+) button and then once again use the pop-up menus to describe the condition you want to match.** Figure 19.8 shows an example of a query with two conditions.

4. **Click OK and then select your query in Console's sidebar under Log Database Queries to display only log entries matching your query.**

FIGURE 19.8

A completed log database query with two conditions resembles a smart folder or smart playlist.

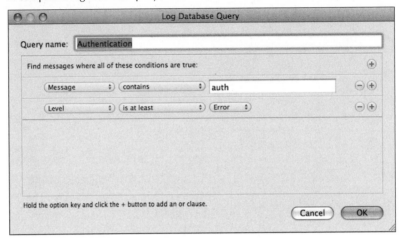

Looking for Useful Information

The first thing I should mention about Mac OS X's logs is that although they contain tons of useful information, that's nothing to the amount of useless information (under ordinary circumstances, at least). Many a user has peered into Console for the first time only to be thrown into a panic by the sheer number of messages (many of them labeled as errors or warnings). In fact, most log messages, even those that look slightly scary at first glance, are simply reporting normal events.

That said, although logs can also tell you (or an application's developer) a great deal about what might be causing crashes or other misbehavior, what this chapter is concerned with is information applicable to security rather than general-purpose debugging. Therefore, what I provide here isn't a complete tutorial on understanding logs but rather some guidelines as to how to find information that may be relevant to diagnosing and solving security problems.

For better or worse, Console offers no way to search all your logs at once nor does it group related entries from multiple logs in any way. As a result, in order to discover anything useful, you must at least have an idea of where to look; you can't simply go to a view of security problems or something of that sort. Therefore, what I present here is a list of the logs most commonly associated with security concerns — what the logs store and what to look for in terms of potential problems they may list.

Note
In some cases, you may have to look at both the current version of the log and previous versions (labeled with extensions .1, .2, .0.bz2, .1.bz2, and so on). ∎

System log

The first place you should look for log entries is system.log (or, if you prefer, the All Messages display) because it usually contains the most interesting and useful log entries from a wide variety of processes. Console helpfully lists it separately, at the top of the Log Files list in its sidebar.

Because your system log contains such a wide variety of information, I can't tell you precisely what to look for. I can, however, give you a few pointers:

- Try filtering on the name of the application or service for which you suspect problems. For concerns involving logins or authorization, filter on auth or a short username.

- Another way to identify trouble areas quickly is to filter for the words error or warning — but keep in mind that not all errors and warnings represent genuine problems.

- Repeated messages may be significant. If you see (in All Messages) the same message many times in a row or (in system.log) a message that says something like "last message repeated 10 times," it's worth checking into what keeps causing the same problem over and over.

- If you see something suspicious in your log, try looking it up on your favorite search engine. For example, suppose you see a number of messages that end in "Warning: accessing obsolete X509Anchors." To learn whether other people are experiencing something similar and whether anyone has posted ideas about solving it, search for that entire phrase in quotation marks. (By the way, that particular warning is generally harmless.)

Apache logs

If you're running a web server on your Mac, your Apache logs serve as a rich source of information — much of it potentially scary because so many automated programs are constantly scouring the web looking for trouble. The Apache logs are kept in /var/log/apache2.

Cross-Ref

For more on web server logs in terms of what information a web server may store about you, see Chapter 10. ■

The log access_log contains records of every request your web server responded to, even if the response was "No such file here."

A log entry indicating a successful response might look like this:

```
12.34.56.78 - - [29/Mar/2009:18:46:38 +0200] "GET /index.html
    HTTP/1.1" 200 1286 "http://someplace.com/file.html" "Mozilla/5.0
    (Macintosh; U; Intel Mac OS X 10.6; en-US; rv:1.9.0.8) Gecko/20$
```

The way you know it was successful is the number 200 after the GET request — that's HTTP for "the request was successful." If a request failed because the file simply wasn't there, you see a code of 404 in the same position, such as:

```
98.76.54.3 - - [30/May/2009:14:58:24 -0700] "GET /jkrobots.txt
    HTTP/1.1" 404 4187 "-" "msnbot/1.1 (+http://search.msn.com/msnbot.
    htm)"
```

For a list of all the other possible codes, which amount to numerous variations of "successful" and "unsuccessful," see www.w3.org/Protocols/rfc2616/rfc2616-sec10.html.

A second log, error_log, records only errors. It contains a great deal of overlap with access_log — for example, whenever someone gets a 404 response because a file isn't there, your error_log also lists that file as missing. However, the error_log lists other kinds of errors too, such as errors in database searches and invalid URLs in incoming requests.

Finally, if you've enabled SSL on your website, yet another log, `ssl_request_log`, lists all requests sent using HTTPS.

Cross-Ref

For more on securing a website using SSL, see Chapter 18. ■

Web server access and error logs almost invariably fill up with bad requests of various sorts. You could go crazy trying to block every robot and script that floods your site with irrelevant requests, and, in general, there's little point in trying — unless your Mac is being so overwhelmed with bogus web access that it's slowing down performance for legitimate users. In such cases, consider blocking the IP addresses of the most frequent troublemakers in your firewall.

Application firewall log

If you use Mac OS X's built-in application firewall and have enabled logging (optional in Leopard; always on in Snow Leopard), the firewall logs data about both allowed and blocked attempts to access applications on your Mac. The log is stored at `/var/log/appfirewall.log`.

Cross-Ref

For more on the application firewall, including how to enable logging, see Chapter 18. ■

If you've designated an application as explicitly allowed to receive incoming packets, you should see corresponding log entries like this:

```
May 26 09:32:16 MacBook-Pro Firewall[52]: JungleDiskMonito is
    listening from 127.0.0.1:10891 uid = 0 proto=6
```

Likewise, applications for which you've explicitly denied incoming access appear in the log like so:

```
May 26 09:40:31 MacBook-Pro Firewall[52]: Deny Skype data in from
    192.168.0.1:1901 uid = 0 proto=17
```

If a computer tries to connect to any port on your Mac that's not explicitly permitted or denied, you see a message resembling this one; interpret this as meaning an attempted connection was blocked. Filter on the word `attempt` to see other such entries. If you didn't activate Stealth Mode, the words "Stealth Mode" won't appear in log entries.

```
May 26 10:45:11 MacBook-Pro Firewall[52]: Stealth Mode connection
    attempt to TCP 192.168.0.15:49819 from 208.69.34.231:80
```

FTP log

If you share files on your Mac using FTP (not that I recommend doing so, because FTP is extremely insecure), a log of FTP activity is kept in `/var/ftp.log`. Most FTP transactions appear in the log in pairs.

A valid login looks something like this:

```
May 30 11:33:49 iMac ftpd[7018]: connection from 10.0.0.4 to 10.0.0.2
May 30 11:33:49 iMac ftpd[7018]: FTP LOGIN FROM localhost as sam
    (class: real, type: REAL)
```

If someone attempts to log in and fails (because of an incorrect username and/or password), you see a pair of messages along these lines — filter for `failed` to find these quickly:

```
May 30 11:34:39 iMac ftpd[7048]: connection from 10.0.0.6 to 10.0.0.2
May 30 11:34:39 iMac ftpd[7048]: FTP LOGIN FAILED FROM 10.0.0.6
```

A great many failed attempts in a short period of time is often a signal that someone is repeatedly guessing at passwords and trying to gain access without authorization.

Some FTP servers — although not the one built into the standard version of Mac OS X — support anonymous FTP, in which anyone can log in by typing the username `anonymous` and any password. If someone tries to connect to your Mac that way, you see error messages like these — filter for `refused` to see them easily:

```
May 30 11:33:50 iMac ftpd[7023]: connection from 10.0.0.5 to 10.0.0.2
May 30 11:33:50 iMac ftpd[7023]: ANONYMOUS FTP LOGIN REFUSED FROM
   10.0.0.5
```

Even though these requests aren't harmful because your FTP server doesn't allow anonymous connections in the first place, they could signal that someone is trolling for access to your files.

Finally, a successful file transfer might look like this:

```
May 30 11:34:28 iMac ftpd[7018]: Data traffic: 638283 bytes in 1 file
May 30 11:34:28 iMac ftpd[7018]: Total traffic: 650983 bytes in 4
   transfers
```

Installer log

The installer log, located at `/var/log/install.log`, records everything installed using Apple's installer utility — that includes Mac OS X itself (along with any system updates, including those installed by Software Update) and any other Apple software (iLife, iWork, Safari, and so on) as well as many, although not all, third-party programs. It also mentions for each installation whether administrator authorization was granted (which gives the installer the capability of putting files anywhere on your disk and granting them root permissions).

If you discover software running on your Mac that you aren't aware of having installed, check the installer log. The program may or may not be listed, because there are other ways of installing software, but if you do find a match, you can tell which installer was responsible for the program in question. Checking this log may help you to identify Trojan horses (as well as legitimate but hidden programs) installed as part of a larger package.

Samba logs

Samba refers to SMB (Server Message Block), which is one of Mac OS X's three built-in file-sharing methods — the one most commonly used for sharing files with Windows PCs. In the `/var/log/samba` folder, you should find `log.nmbd` (which lists overall SMB-related events, such as turning sharing on and off) and `log.smbd` (which lists both successful and failed SMB login attempts). The latter is the more interesting one for security purposes.

A successful SMB login would look something like this:

```
[2009/05/30 11:42:35, 1, pid=7171] /SourceCache/samba/samba-187.8/
   samba/source/smbd/service.c:make_connection_snum(1087)
```

```
snow-leopard (192.168.0.24) connect to service joe initially as user
    joe (uid=501, gid=20) (pid 7171)
```

And a logout would resemble the following:

```
[2009/05/30 11:46:29, 1, pid=7171] /SourceCache/samba/samba-187.8/
    samba/source/smbd/service.c:close_cnum(1284)
snow-leopard (192.168.0.24) closed connection to service joe
```

But what you're most likely concerned with is login failures. If you filter for the string eDSAuthFailed, you may see entries like these:

```
[2009/05/30 11:41:04, 0, pid=7161] /SourceCache/samba/samba-187.8/
    samba/source/auth/auth_odsam.c:opendirectory_ntlmv2_auth_user(330)
    dsDoNodeAuth gave -14090 [eDSAuthFailed]
[2009/05/30 11:41:04, 0, pid=7161] /SourceCache/samba/samba-187.8/
    samba/source/auth/auth_odsam.c:opendirectory_smb_pwd_check_
    ntlmv2(446)
    opendirectory_ntlmv2_auth_user gave -14090 [eDSAuthFailed]
[2009/05/30 11:41:04, 0, pid=7161] /SourceCache/samba/samba-187.8/
    samba/source/auth/auth_odsam.c:opendirectory_opendirectory_ntlm_
    password_check(522)
opendirectory_smb_pwd_check_ntlmv2 gave -14090 [eDSAuthFailed]
```

Each time you see a sequence like this, it means someone tried unsuccessfully to log in to your Mac using SMB. As with all failures, a few mistakes here and there should be expected, but if your log is full of failures, that could indicate an attempted security breach. You should consider turning off SMB, if possible, or blocking the offending IP address in your firewall.

Secure log

The secure log, located at /var/secure.log, contains records of events related to authorization — logging in (locally or remotely), using sudo, installing software, and most other cases where someone must type a password for a user account.

Note

Although the secure log makes a note of each usage of sudo, it doesn't tell you which command it was used to execute. For that information, consult the system log. ∎

Under ordinary circumstances, this log contains many messages along the following lines:

```
May 30 14:21:06 MacBook-Pro com.apple.SecurityServer[21]: uid 501
    succeeded authenticating as user joe (uid 501) for right com.
    apple.desktopservices.
May 30 14:21:06 MacBook-Pro com.apple.SecurityServer[21]: Succeeded
    authorizing right com.apple.desktopservices by client /System/
    Library/PrivateFrameworks/DesktopServicesPriv.framework/
    Versions/A/Resources/Locum for authorization created by /System/
    Library/CoreServices/Finder.app.
```

When you see the word "succeeded," you know that a password was typed correctly and that authorization worked. Depending on the nature of the message, a log entry may or may not include the name and/or user

ID (UID) of the person who logged in — in this pair of entries, which were part of the same authorization event, the first one has this information, whereas the second one doesn't.

Conversely, the word "failed" indicates that something went wrong — most often, a mistyped password:

```
May 30 14:28:37 MacBook-Pro com.apple.SecurityServer[21]: checkpw()
    returned -2; failed to authenticate user joe (uid 501).
May 30 14:28:37 MacBook-Pro com.apple.SecurityServer[21]: Failed to
    authorize right system.login.tty by client /usr/sbin/sshd for
    authorization created by /usr/sbin/sshd.
```

Because anyone can mistype a password occasionally, a few failure messages should cause no alarm. However, if you see dozens or hundreds of failure messages in rapid succession, that's a likely sign that someone (or, more likely, a program) is trying to break in by using a dictionary attack or brute-force attack to guess passwords. If you see something like this, a good course of action (after checking to make sure you've chosen an excellent password) is to block the offending IP address in your firewall.

Other logs

Depending on your Mac's configuration, you may also need to check out any number of other logs. Other logs you might want to check include these:

- **AirPort base station.** AirPort base stations and Time Capsule devices store logs internally unless you've activated remote logging.

Cross-Ref

For more on configuring and reading AirPort logs, see Chapter 16. ∎

- **Parental controls.** If you've set up any user accounts on your Mac as managed accounts, using parental controls to put limits on how and when the accounts can be used, you can view logs of those accounts' activities in the Parental Controls pane of System Preferences.

Cross-Ref

For more on parental controls, including how to view the associated logs, see Chapter 3. ∎

- **Backup programs.** Most backup programs store their logs in `/Library/Logs` or, less frequently, in `/var/log`. If you need to confirm when a backup session ran or what files were copied, look for a backup log.
- **Antivirus utilities.** Likewise, antivirus programs generally keep records of their scans somewhere in `/Library/Logs` or `/var/log`.
- **Other third-party security programs.** Assorted other security programs, such as NetBarrier and PGP, also maintain logs of their activities. Some of these may be in `~/Library/Logs`.
- **Directory Services cache.** Although it's not a full-blown log, the Directory Services cache stores information about recent DNS lookups. To display this information in a Terminal window, type **dscacheutil -cachedump -entries host**.

Cross-Ref

For more on the Directory Services cache, see Chapter 10. ∎

Summary

The logs generated automatically by Mac OS X itself and by numerous other applications store crucial information about errors, network and file access, and other activities that could indicate security breaches of various kinds. This chapter discussed the kinds of information that can be stored in logs — where to find them, how to understand them, and how you can use them to increase your security. Apple's Console utility, included with Mac OS X, is usually the easiest way to examine log files.

Part IV

Advanced Security Measures

Network Scanning

If you've read the previous few chapters and taken the advice about securing your wired and wireless networks as well as configuring a firewall on each of your Macs, you've made great strides in protecting your computers from network-based threats. But how can you be sure you're safe? How can you test your network to make sure it's as secure from hackers and other external threats as you hope it is?

This chapter contains the answer: You put yourself in the shoes of an attacker who wants to break into your network to run a series of tests to find out just what someone else can learn about your network and, in particular, the Macs connected to it. Once you've identified areas of weakness, you can go back and tweak your hardware and software settings to close security holes.

To perform this analysis, you can undertake a process known as *network scanning*. This general term refers to any system whereby one can collect data about the hosts on a network by sending a variety of inquiries across the network and analyzing the replies (if any). Of the hundreds of ways one could scan a network, in this chapter, I focus on just a couple of the most common ones — those you can employ without having an extensive understanding of network protocols. However, I want to make clear that this chapter is far from exhaustive, and a hacker could well use any of numerous other techniques to obtain information about your network.

Tip

If you want to get into more detail about network scanning and learn how to harden your network against more esoteric threats, read a good book on network scanning, such as Nmap Network Scanning by Gordon "Fyodor" Lyon (http://nmap.org/book). A large part of that book's content is available free at http://nmap.org/book/toc.html. ∎

What Can Network Scanning Reveal?

The extent of the information a hacker can learn about your network depends on several factors, including how many devices, of what types, and using which operating systems, are on the network; whether you use a NAT router; whether your computers are running firewall software and, if so, how the firewalls are configured; and whether the scan is being performed from inside your network or from the outside. However, in general, the following pieces of data about each device on your network — computers, routers, printers, iPhones, and so on — are potentially up for grabs:

- The device's (private and/or public) IP address
- The MAC address and manufacturer of the device
- Whether the device supports IPv4, IPv6, or both
- The date and time the device was last restarted
- The device's operating system (type and version)
- Which ports are open on the device and which are being filtered or blocked
- Which application is listening on each open port

For example, as I type this paragraph, I'm sitting in a library, using its Wi-Fi network, and a few moments ago, I performed a network scan as I describe ahead. I can see a half-dozen other patrons with laptops open, and I can tell just by looking which models some of them are. By cross-referencing what my eyes tell me with what my network scan tells me, I know that the guy over there with the beard and the headphones, with a white MacBook in front of him, has SMB file sharing turned on and is still using last week's version of iTunes — he hasn't upgraded to the new version yet. But, good for him, he's running CrashPlan on port 4242, for (encrypted) online backups. In fact, I now know a great deal more than that, not just about him but about numerous other people on the Wi-Fi network as well as some of the library's workstations and servers.

Being the responsible person that I am, I'm not going to misuse this information. But the fact that I can learn this sort of thing with just a few clicks should give you a bit of a chill. It means any two-bit hacker can likely learn the same — and much more — about the devices on your network. You may not think it particularly matters that someone knows your computer is running Mac OS X 10.5.7 and has a certain open port, but it's just a short step from knowing this information to being able to exploit it. By consulting readily available public sources, a hacker can learn about specific weaknesses that affect particular combinations of operating system, port, and application and then construct attacks that take advantage of these holes to take over someone's computer, steal his or her data, cause crashes, or instigate other mischief.

Note
The fact that a computer appears potentially open to a certain threat doesn't guarantee that the threat works. In Chapter 22, I provide an introduction to the art of confirming specific vulnerabilities on a network. ■

In short, network scanning can reveal an enormous amount of information that could facilitate attacks of various sorts — unless you take steps (as described later in this chapter and elsewhere in this book) to protect your Macs.

How Fingerprinting Works

In my previous description of a network scan, I gave several examples of information I learned about another computer on the network. By nature, network scans can reveal some information (such as IP and MAC addresses) explicitly because most computers politely reply to various network messages with exactly the information that was requested. However, a great deal of information that isn't sent directly (such as operating system version and the names of applications using certain ports) can be inferred by comparing a list of network characteristics with a database of known computers, operating systems, and applications. The process is much like comparing a digitized fingerprint with a fingerprint database and looking for matching patterns — hence, the name *fingerprinting*.

Fingerprinting can work at several levels. For example, when mapping a network, the software I use can analyze the types of responses that are sent to various kinds of packets and their TTL, or time to live, values (which vary from one operating system to the next), among other characteristics. By looking up the values received in a table, my software can determine, with high accuracy, the operating system used by each host.

Once I know what operating system a computer's running and which ports are open, I can apply fingerprinting techniques at a lower level to determine which application (and, sometimes, which version of an application) is listening on a given port. I can make a first, rough guess simply by looking up which applications commonly use given ports — but ports can be changed. To confirm my guess, I can use scanning software that makes use of the same general principle: Different applications respond in different, idiosyncratic ways to certain kinds of requests.

By way of introducing you to the topic of network scanning, I cover two basic techniques in this chapter: network mapping, which provides high-level information about network devices, and port scanning, which indicates what ports are open on each device (and sometimes more specific information about the applications using those ports). These are among the most common and easily executed procedures for learning how to gain access to a network, so if you perform them on your own equipment, you should be able to get a good sense of where you might be most vulnerable.

Network scanning encompasses a broad range of techniques, many of which go by more than one name. In addition, some names mean different things to different people or in different contexts. For example, you may hear the term *network enumeration*, which sounds like it should mean enumerating (listing) the devices on a network, but that's the one thing it's almost never used to mean. In some contexts, network enumeration is used as a synonym for port mapping or fingerprinting, particularly a variety of fingerprinting that attempts to determine which users, groups, shared volumes, and other resources exist on a given computer. Some utilities that perform network mapping or vulnerability testing (including nmap) can also do this sort of enumeration. In other contexts, the term refers to the general process of determining the attributes of a network (for example, by consulting a whois database) in order to obtain information that could be useful in network mapping, port scanning, or *firewalking* (a somewhat esoteric procedure, not covered in this book, for discovering weaknesses in a firewall).

Network Mapping

The first piece of information anyone needs to know in order to mount a successful attack on a computer is where to find it on the network. In other words, the attacker needs to discover a computer's IP address. On most networks, only a subset of the possible IP addresses are in use, so the trick is to narrow down all the possible addresses (which may be a handful or many thousands) to just those that are active. The process of examining a network (either the local network to which a computer is directly connected or a remote network) to find all the IP addresses in use is called *network mapping*. You may also hear this called by any number of other names, including *host discovery*, *host scanning*, and *network device location scanning* — or by terms referring to a particular type of scanning, such as *ICMP probing* or *ping sweeps*.

If a program did nothing other than produce a list of valid IP addresses on a network, that would count as network mapping and could, in and of itself, be useful. However, because an attacker ultimately needs considerably more to go on than an IP address, network mapping usually entails other tasks too, including at least basic sorts of fingerprinting (mentioned earlier) and port scanning (discussed later in this chapter). Most of the software you can use for network mapping optionally does these other tasks too.

Examining the network to which one is currently connected is fast and convenient, and assuming the computer doing the scanning has a valid (static or dynamic) IP address and an accompanying subnet mask, it's trivially easy to figure out the overall range of addresses to examine. For example, if your computer has an IP address of 192.168.0.19 and a subnet mask of 255.255.255.0, then you know that the possible range of IP addresses on your local network ranges from 192.168.0.0 to 192.168.0.255.

However, in order to find all the IP addresses on a remote network, you need to know, at minimum, the public IP address of one computer on the network — and preferably several — in order to infer the total number of addresses to scan. Command-line tools such as dig and nslookup or the Lookup tab of Network Utility (found in /Applications/Utilities) can tell you the public IP address of any computer with a domain name. Figuring out the possible range of IP addresses for networks without associated domain names (or, at least, not easily discoverable ones) may require more detective work, but that's beyond the scope of this chapter.

With a range of potential IP addresses in hand, you can begin scanning the network. The best-known network-mapping tool (available on most platforms) is nmap, which I discuss next. I also show how to accomplish some of the same tasks using a Mac OS X–only program called IPNetMonitorX.

Using nmap for network mapping

A free, open-source program called nmap (short for network mapper) contains an immense list of features for discovering just about anything one can imagine about any network. You can obtain a pre-built Mac OS X installer for nmap from http://nmap.org/. The package contains not only the command-line nmap tool itself, which you access using Terminal (found in /Applications/Utilities), but also several other programs, one of which is a graphical front end to nmap called Zenmap (covered ahead in the discussion of port scanning).

The basic syntax for nmap is pretty simple:

```
nmap [options] address(es)
```

The list of options from which you can choose is quite long; I detail a few of the more interesting ones in a moment. The address(es) can be a single IP address (which you might use if you're using nmap for port scanning, for example) or a range — expressed either in CIDR notation (for example, 192.168.0.0/24) or as a more-readable numeric range (for example, 192.168.0.0-255).

So, to get very basic information about your current local network, you could use a command such as the following, where -sP is an option that means *ping scan* — that is, send an ICMP (Internet Control Message Protocol) packet to port 80 on each device in the range and see if it responds:

```
nmap -sP 192.168.0.0-255
```

After nmap scans the address range provided, it delivers a list of results, which might look something like this:

```
Starting Nmap 4.85BETA9 ( http://nmap.org ) at 2009-06-05 12:16 CEST
Host 192.168.0.1 is up (0.00083s latency).
Host 192.168.0.4 is up (0.00043s latency).
Host 192.168.0.5 is up (0.00077s latency).
Host 192.168.0.7 is up (0.00072s latency).
Host 192.168.0.8 is up (0.00091s latency).
Nmap done: 256 IP addresses (5 hosts up) scanned in 5.37 seconds
```

If you execute the same command for a local network as the root user, nmap uses a different type of scanning (using ARP, or Address Resolution Protocol), which provides the MAC address and manufacturer of each host and also avoids certain kinds of firewalls and other security measures that may be in place to block ordinary pings — meaning you may see many more hosts. For example:

```
sudo nmap -sP 192.168.0.0-255
```

The result of such a scan might resemble this:

```
Starting Nmap 4.85BETA9 ( http://nmap.org ) at 2009-06-05 12:24 CEST
Host 192.168.0.4 is up.
Host 192.168.0.5 is up (1.1s latency).
MAC Address: 00:21:E9:96:E5:42 (Apple)
Host 192.168.0.8 is up (0.87s latency).
MAC Address: 00:21:9B:88:C5:86 (Dell)
Host 192.168.0.12 is up (0.87s latency).
MAC Address: 00:23:E6:72:95:99 (Unknown)
Host 192.168.0.15 is up (0.87s latency).
MAC Address: 00:11:11:6E:D5:13 (Intel)
Host 192.168.0.16 is up (1.1s latency).
MAC Address: 00:15:58:5C:75:21 (Foxconn)
Host 192.168.0.18 is up (1.1s latency).
MAC Address: 00:00:E8:43:95:16 (Accton Technology)
Host 192.168.0.19 is up (1.1s latency).
MAC Address: 00:21:9B:3F:85:44 (Dell)
Host 192.168.0.20 is up (0.69s latency).
MAC Address: 00:60:97:29:45:00 (3com)
Host 192.168.0.22 is up (0.69s latency).
MAC Address: 00:50:FC:1C:95:77 (Edimax Technology CO.)
Host 192.168.0.23 is up (0.69s latency).
MAC Address: 00:00:E8:0A:C5:43 (Accton Technology)
Host 192.168.0.39 is up (0.52s latency).
MAC Address: 00:11:11:FC:15:25 (Intel Corporate)
Host 192.168.0.201 is up (0.036s latency).
MAC Address: 00:50:AA:E5:65:12 (Konica Minolta Holdings)
Nmap done: 256 IP addresses (13 hosts up) scanned in 16.03 seconds
```

The MAC address is unique to each network card, and because each manufacturer is assigned one or more specific ranges of MAC addresses (the first three pairs of hex digits, such as 00:21:E9 for Apple), nmap can tell usually just by the MAC address who manufactured the network card (which, in most cases, is the same as the manufacturer of the overall device). Thus, even a very simple nmap scan like this one can provide basic fingerprinting information.

A few of the other nmap options you might find useful for basic discovery of IP addresses are the following:

- -n. Scans without attempting to look up the domain name of each host, which is usually much faster than the default setting, which does look up the domain name.

- -PO. (That's P followed by the letter O, not the digit 0.) This option, which requires root access, scans the network by sending out IP packets of the following types: ICMP, IGMP, and IP-in-IP. It can often identify hosts that don't respond to ordinary pings.

- -PR. Performs a scan of the local network using ARP (Address Resolution Protocol) rather than the slower but standard IP (Internet Protocol). When scanning a local Ethernet network, nmap uses this option by default. This is another method of identifying hosts for which ping access is blocked or disabled.

- -PS. Sends ping packets with the SYN flag set. Because this results in incomplete connections to the hosts, it often enables the scan to avoid detection. This procedure is often referred to as a half-open scan.

Note

Ordinarily, when two computers want to establish a TCP connection, they go through a three-step handshaking process. Computer 1 sends a SYN (synchronization) request to Computer 2. Computer 2 replies with a SYN-ACK (synchronization acknowledgement) message. Then, Computer 1 responds with an ACK (acknowledgement) message. Only after all three steps have occurred is a connection established. Some firewalls and network monitoring programs take notice only of established connections, so if a network-scanning tool can manage to skip one or two of the handshake steps, it may be able to get enough information to tell if the host is alive or if a port is open without exposing the fact that a scan is taking place. This process is sometimes called stealth scanning. ■

- -PA. Similar to -PS but sends packets with the ACK flag set instead. This accomplishes much the same thing but enables scans of some hosts and networks in which SYN packets are blocked.

- -PU. Sends UDP (User Datagram Protocol) pings rather than the more usual ICMP pings.

- -sL. Lists all hosts on the network, along with their domain names (unless -n is used), regardless of whether they're active.

To learn more about these options and the many others nmap provides, type **man nmap** in a Terminal window.

Note

I've been using the term network mapping figuratively, in that what you're getting with a network map is little more than a list of IP addresses. However, Zenmap, the graphical interface for nmap described later in this section, can create graphical diagrams that show the ways in which devices and networks are connected. These are logical maps rather than geographical maps, but in any case, they represent a much more map-like view of a network than a mere list. ■

Using IPNetMonitorX for network mapping

If you want a network-mapping tool that's a bit more user-friendly than nmap (even with the Zenmap interface) and designed expressly for Mac OS X, you might find Sustainable Softworks' IPNetMonitorX (www.sustworks.com/site/prod_ipmx_overview.html, $60) to be what you're looking for. Although it has far fewer features overall than nmap, it also offers a few capabilities that nmap lacks (such as showing AirPort signal strength and testing DHCP servers). It's more of a diagnostic and troubleshooting tool than a hacker's tool, but in terms of network mapping, it contains all the necessary basics.

To use IPNetMonitorX for network mapping, follow these steps:

1. **Download and install IPNetMonitorX and then open the application.**

2. **Choose Tool⇨Address Scan or click Address Scan in the Launcher palette.** The Address Scan window opens.

3. **In the Target field, type the address range you want to scan — using either CIDR notation or a numerical range, just as in** nmap. Alternatively, click the arrow control at the right of the Target field and then choose a preset network range from the pop-up menu.

4. **From the Using pop-up menu, choose which protocol to use: ping (the default — ICMP — is a good starting point), UDP, or TCP.**

5. **Click Scan.** As shown in Figure 20.1, IPNetMonitorX displays a list of IP addresses in the range you specified that respond to the protocol you selected — along with the MAC address, manufacturer, and (if available via Bonjour) name of each device.

FIGURE 20.1

IPNetMonitorX offers simple but effective scans that list all the active IP addresses on a network.

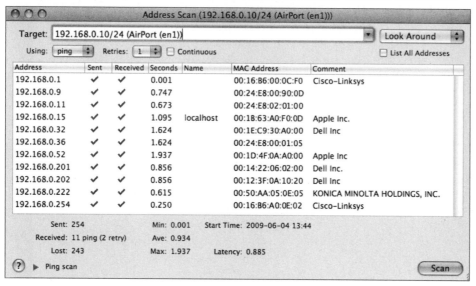

If the scan didn't return the addresses of devices you expect to find, repeat it with a different selection (such as UDP or TCP) from the Using pop-up menu. To list the domain name (if any) for each host along with its IP address, choose Domain Name from the pop-up menu in the upper-right corner of the window and then scan again.

Tip

Yet another tool Mac users can employ to perform network scanning is InterMapper (www.intermapper.com**). Prices range from $495 to $3,385, depending on the number of devices to be monitored. ■**

Port Scanning

As you may recall from earlier chapters in this book, a port is like a channel that's used for a particular sort of Internet data by one application at a time. When a program or service is listening on a given port — meaning it accepts incoming connections — that port is said to be open. Your Mac may use one port to send out data that's then received by a different port on another computer and vice versa. Most Internet traffic uses TCP, but some of it uses UDP, and a given port number can be used simultaneously by both protocols on a given computer.

Cross-Ref

For more on ports, see Chapters 15 and 17. ■

The total number of ports available is 65,536 (numbered from 0 to 65535). Of these, the first 1,024 (numbered from 0 to 1023) are referred to as the Well-Known Ports, and for most of them, their official uses are registered with the Internet Assigned Numbers Authority (IANA) — meaning they're seldom used for anything other than a single designated purpose. Ports ranging from 1024 to 49151 are called Registered Ports. A large number of these also have official usage designations per the IANA, although there are still thousands that can be freely used by any application. Finally, the ports in the range 49152 to 65535 are referred to as dynamic or private. They can be used but aren't eligible for registration with the IANA.

Tip

You can find an excellent list of common TCP and UDP ports at http://en.wikipedia.org/wiki/List_of_ TCP_and_UDP_port_numbers. **Apple provides its own list of the most common ports on Mac OS X at** http:// support.apple.com/kb/TS1629. ■

The fact that a particular port is open strongly suggests that its official (or unofficial but common) application is in use. For example, the backup application Retrospect is registered to use port 497, so if a computer has that port open, it's all but certain that Retrospect is the application listening on that port. Ultimately, the only thing a hacker cares about is what application is listening on a port, not which number the port is using. However, in the vast majority of cases, it's possible to override standard ports if there's some worthwhile reason to do so (such as trying to avoid network attacks or trying to work around uncooperative firewalls). So, although the existence of an open port (particularly one of the officially registered ones) provides strong prima facie evidence of the application that's listening on it, it's not a guarantee, and an attacker may need to perform additional tests or fingerprinting techniques to confirm which application is using which port.

With all that in mind, the next step beyond finding out which IP addresses on a network belong to functional, responsive computers is to determine which ports are open on each one (or on particular computers in which someone is interested). To do this, a program sends a message to each port on a computer in turn and takes note of the response, if any, it receives. The response can indicate whether the port is open, closed (the computer acknowledges that the port exists but no service is listening), blocked or filtered (a firewall or router is preventing access to the port, so its openness can't be determined), or unfiltered (not blocked but providing ambiguous information as to whether it's open or closed). Of these states, of course, the open, unblocked ports are most interesting and useful to an attacker. Thus, in order to keep your Mac secure, you want to minimize the number of open ports as well as minimize the amount of information your Mac gives out about ports that may or may not be open.

Many techniques can be used to scan for open TCP and UDP ports — on a single computer or on all the computers on a network — with varying degrees of sophistication and cleverness (which are often necessary to avoid the increasing number of roadblocks system administrators erect to stop such scans)! The nmap utility alone offers at least nine different port-scanning methods. What follows is an introduction to some of the easiest methods of port scanning using a few popular utilities.

Using Network Utility for port scanning

The quickest and most convenient way for most people to do a basic port scan is to use Apple's Network Utility, part of Mac OS X. Network Utility's port-scanning feature offers only standard TCP port scanning (not UDP or any of the more esoteric varieties designed to circumvent firewalls), but you can't beat it for ease of use.

To perform a port scan with Network Utility, follow these steps:

1. **Open Network Utility, which is located in** /Applications/Utilities.
2. **Click the Port Scan tab.**
3. **Type the IP address or domain name of the host you want to scan.** To scan for open ports on the Mac you're currently using, type **localhost** in the field.
4. **To restrict the range of ports scanned, click the Only test ports between check box and then type a starting and ending range.** In most cases, testing only ports 0 through 1023 is sufficient. If you don't restrict the range, Network Utility tests all 65,536 ports — which can take an extremely long time and which carries a high probability of setting off any detection systems that look for port-scanning behavior.
5. **Click Scan.** Network Utility scans the ports specified on the host you selected, displaying the open ports at the bottom of the window, as shown in Figure 20.2.

FIGURE 20.2

This pane in Network Utility lets you perform a basic TCP port scan.

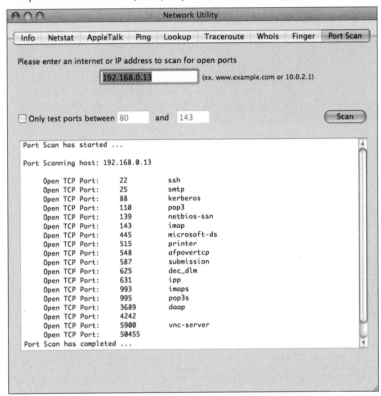

Using nmap for port scanning

The nmap utility, introduced earlier in this chapter in the context of network mapping, also contains extensive port-scanning capabilities (among other talents). Performing a port scan is as simple as adding an option or two to an existing network-mapping scan. For example, to perform a basic TCP scan to find open ports on the computer at 192.168.0.1, you could use this command:

```
nmap -sT 192.168.0.1
```

The output nmap produces looks something like this:

```
Interesting ports on 192.168.0.1:
Not shown: 993 closed ports
PORT    STATE SERVICE
25/tcp  open  smtp
80/tcp  open  http
110/tcp open  pop3
143/tcp open  imap
587/tcp open  submission
993/tcp open  imaps
995/tcp open  pop3s
Nmap done: 1 IP address (1 host up) scanned in 1.25 seconds
```

To be slightly sneakier and use SYN (or half-open) scanning to reduce the risk of detection, you change the flag from -sT to -sS. However, the -sS flag requires root access, and by default, it scans only port 80. To scan all ports with SYN packet, use this command:

```
sudo nmap -sS -P0 192.168.0.1
```

The output returned is similar (although it also includes the MAC address for computers on your local network).

However, a much better way to do port scanning with nmap is to forgo the command line altogether and instead use the Zenmap program, which is included with the Mac OS X installation of nmap and which not only makes it easier to type complex scanning commands but also displays the results in a graphical format.

Tip

Zenmap relies on X11, an optional component of Mac OS X, to provide its graphical interface. If X11 isn't in your /Applications folder, you see an incomprehensible error message when you try to run Zenmap. If you didn't install X11 along with Leopard or Snow Leopard, insert your Mac OS X Install DVD, open the Optional Installs folder, double-click the Optional Installs installer, and then follow the prompts to install X11. ■

To perform a port scan with Zenmap, follow these steps:

1. **After downloading and installing the nmap package (from http://nmap.org/), open Zenmap, which is located in /Applications.**

2. **In the Target field at the top, type the IP address of the host or network you want to scan.** As usual, you can type a single address or an address range using either CIDR notation or a numeric range.

3. **From the Profile pop-up menu, choose the kind of scan you want to perform.** Zenmap offers ten profiles (pre-built combinations of nmap settings) or you can create your own. The default choice, Intense scan, is a good place to start. Consult the program's documentation for information on what all the options mean.

4. **Click Scan.** Zenmap begins scanning the host or network, displaying the text results of the scan in the Nmap Output tab.

5. **When the scan has completed, you can view the results in several different ways.** For example:

   • Select a host in the list on the left and then click the Ports/Hosts tab to see a list of all ports whose statuses could be determined, as shown in Figure 20.3.

For any selected host, Zenmap tells you exactly which ports are open.

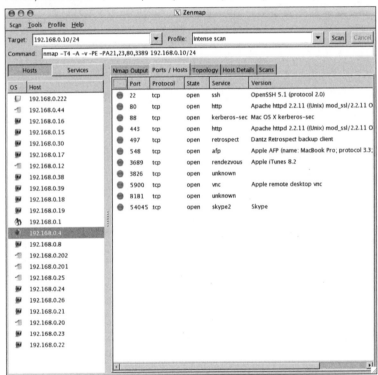

- Select a host in the list on the left and then click the Host Details tab to show information about that host, such as operating system, number of open ports, and time since the last boot, as shown in Figure 20.4.

FIGURE 20.4

Zenmap can list information about a selected host, including the operating system and the time since the last boot.

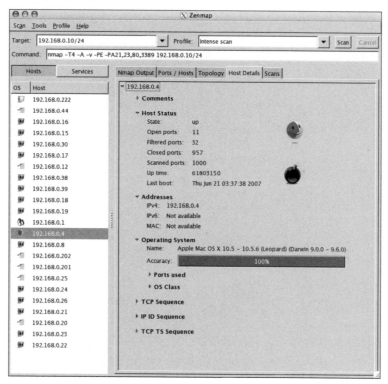

- Click the Services button to see a list of all services (such as FTP and HTTP) for which one or more hosts on the network has an open port. Then select that service to view the list of hosts on which that port is open.

- Click the Topology tab to view a graphical map of the network you've scanned, which you can zoom, rotate, and otherwise manipulate as you please. Figure 20.5 shows the map of a simple local network, and Figure 20.6 shows a map demonstrating how a local network connects to a remote network.

FIGURE 20.5

A simple local network or subnet, in which all the computers connect through the same router, appears as a ring in Zenmap. You can get more information on any host in the graph.

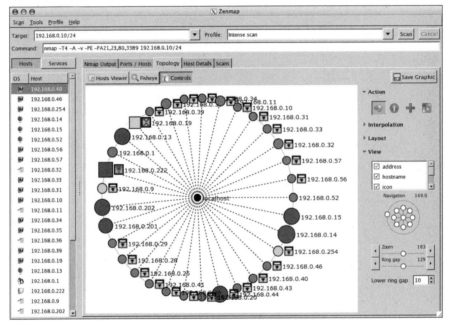

FIGURE 20.6

This map shows not only the hosts on the local network but how they connect with another network.

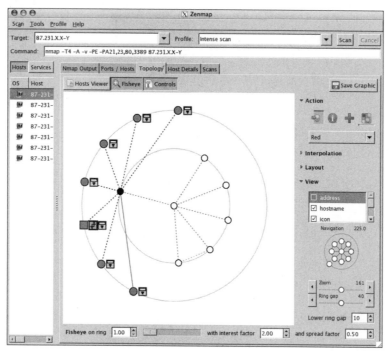

Using IPNetMonitorX for port scanning

IPNetMonitorX, mentioned earlier in the context of network mapping, also contains port-scanning capabilities. They're considerably more flexible than those offered by Network Utility while being more user-friendly than those of nmap (or even Zenmap).

To perform a basic port scan using IPNetMonitorX, follow these steps:

1. **Open IPNetMonitorX from wherever you installed the application.**

2. **Choose Tool ⇨ Port Scan or click Port Scan in the Launcher palette.** The Port Scan window opens.

3. **In the Target field, type the IP address or domain name of the computer you want to scan.**

4. **Type the first and last port numbers you want to scan in the Starting Port and Ending Port fields, respectively.** Scanning more ports takes longer but may also reveal more useful information.

5. **From the pop-up menu in the upper-right corner of the window, choose which protocol to use for the port scan.** The default, TCP, is usually a good choice to start with. To perform a half-open scan as described earlier, choose SYN from this menu and then choose an interface to use from the pop-up menu at the bottom of the window. Other choices are documented in the IPNetMonitorX help menu.

6. **Click Scan.** IPNetMonitorX uses the method you selected to scan the range of ports you specified, listing open ports it finds, along with the protocol accepted on that port and its description (if known), as shown in Figure 20.7.

FIGURE 20.7

IPNetMonitorX offers quite a few more options for port scanning than Network Utility (if not as many as Zenmap).

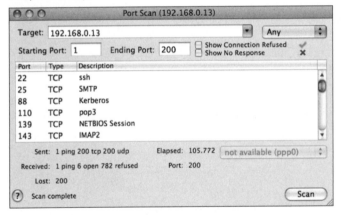

Tip

If you've already performed an address scan, you can also double-click any address in the Address Scan list to perform an immediate port scan on it. ■

Protecting Your Macs from Network Scanning

All right, you've mapped your network and found a list of IP addresses — and then you've scanned the ports on each of those IP addresses and found a bunch of open ports. What does it all mean, and should you worry that other people can get that same information? If so, what can you do about it?

The first thing to remember is that more information is available about a network when scanned from the inside than from the outside. So, if you performed your scans while on your local network, it pays to try them again from outside your network. Depending on what sort of router, gateway, and/or firewall you have between your network and the outside world, you may have little or nothing to worry about. For example, if you use a NAT router, such that none of your Macs have a publicly routable IP address, network mapping is extremely difficult (although not necessarily impossible) to perform from outside your network. Even if an attacker were able to determine a Mac's private IP address, port scanning would almost certainly fail — unless the Mac were configured in your gateway as a DMZ host or you've configured port forwarding to provide access to particular ports on that Mac from the outside.

Second, even the fact that someone has found an open port on a valid IP address with a known operating system, version, and application doesn't necessarily mean you're in danger. It only means there's a potential path by which an exploit could be delivered if one were found. If no exploits for that particular path exist, the fact that the port is open is not, in itself, a problem. After all, network scanning itself isn't harmful (unless someone overloads your network, or a particular computer, with packets — a form of denial-of-service [DoS] attack). It's the potential consequences of network scanning you want to avoid.

Nevertheless, because you have no way of knowing exhaustively what security holes exist now or may be found in the future, you should take as many of the following steps as possible to reduce your Macs' risk of network scans:

- **Use NAT if possible.** If most of your Macs have no need for publicly routable IP addresses, put them behind a NAT router. That step alone thwarts many forms of network scanning. If some of your Macs, but not all, need public addresses, put them in a (proper) DMZ.

- **Avoid DMZ hosts and port forwarding.** Sometimes, these mechanisms to give outside computers access to particular hosts on your network are truly necessary, but they do introduce greater risk, and it's better to avoid them if you can.

Cross-Ref

For more on NAT, port forwarding, DMZs, and DMZ host configurations, see Chapter 15. ■

- **Turn on your firewall.** Mac OS X's application firewall provides some protection against port scanning; using IPFW or a heavy-duty third-party firewall can provide even more. Be sure to block all unused ports, and if your firewall offers a stealth mode or explicit protection from port scans, turn it on.

Tip

For serious firewall protection against virtually any possible type of scanning, IPNetSentryX (or its relative, IPNetRouterX) is the best tool going on Mac OS X. It's overkill for most people, but it's better able to deal with scanning than conventional static firewalls. ■

Cross-Ref

For more on firewalls, including IPNetSentryX, see Chapter 17. ■

- **Consider a hardware firewall.** Firewall software running on your Mac typically protects only that one computer. A good stand-alone firewall (or a firewall built into a router or gateway) can provide scanning protection for your entire network.

- **Turn off unused services.** If a port isn't open in the first place, it can't be used as an avenue of attack. Be sure to turn off any sharing services you aren't actively using.

Cross-Ref

For more on sharing system resources, see Chapter 7. ■

- **Be careful about wireless security.** Even if your network is tricked out with a NAT router and a high-powered firewall, lax Wi-Fi security (such as using WEP encryption) can provide an attacker a direct path to your system.

Cross-Ref

For more on improving your wireless security, see Chapter 16. ■

- **Take the next step — vulnerability scanning.** To find out for sure whether any of the ports on your Macs that truly need to be open represent an actual security threat, perform tests to see if they contain any exploitable holes.

Cross-Ref

For more on vulnerability scanning, see Chapter 21. ■

Summary

One of the best ways to determine the security of your network is to employ the very techniques an attacker may use to probe all the devices on the network and their capabilities. Accordingly, this chapter covered the diagnostic use of network scanning, which can reveal hidden security flaws and holes in your setup. After describing network scanning generally, I provided details about two particular techniques. First was network mapping, in which one tries to compile a list of all the devices on a network and their IP addresses. And second was port scanning, which goes deeper by determining which ports on each network device are open. Finally, I reviewed methods for protecting your own network from these techniques.

Vulnerability Scanning and Testing

N etwork scanning, covered in Chapter 20, lets you determine what someone could learn about the Macs on your network at a relatively high level — such as their IP addresses and what ports are open. That's extremely useful information and can provide important clues to blocking security risks. However, there's another side of the equation, which is what software is running on a particular Mac, at a particular IP address, and listening on a particular port.

For example, the fact that a device with IP address 12.34.56.78 is listening on port 9100 doesn't, by itself, tell you whether it's at any risk. What matters is whether the software that's listening for incoming traffic on that port is subject to any specific attacks. It so happens that port 9100, my randomly chosen example, is mainly used by certain kinds of printers, so the biggest risk one might face with having that port open to the outside world is that someone outside your network may try to print something on your printer — potentially annoying but hardly a big deal. On the other hand, if the device in question is a Mac and if the software listening on a particular open port is outdated or faulty, it could open your Mac to all sorts of trouble, including being taken over remotely and having all its data stolen!

Accordingly, this chapter discusses a more specific and detailed type of scanning. Vulnerability scanning uses data about actual exploits that can be used against certain types of software running on certain hosts to determine exactly what risks each Mac may face. It can tell you, for example, that on some port you want to leave open to provide a useful network service, there's a potential risk from a common exploit — but that you can solve the problem simply by upgrading a piece of software. Because closing every network port is incompatible with basic Internet access, vulnerability scanning lets you find and address areas of weakness that may not be obvious or fixable at the network level.

Two of the programs discussed here, Nessus and SAINT, are designed only to discover whether vulnerabilities may exist and report that information — but not try to exploit the security holes. On the other hand, SAINTexploit and Metasploit can go one step further to implement the known attacks against vulnerable ports, which is the only way to be certain that your computers truly are at risk.

IN THIS CHAPTER

Finding security holes on your network with Nessus

Locating potential vulnerabilities with Saint

Testing known exploits on your network with Metasploit

Using Nessus

Nessus, widely regarded as the most comprehensive network vulnerability scanner currently available, is a commercial program distributed by Tenable Network Security (www.nessus.org). Earlier versions of Nessus were open source, and while the current version isn't, it's available at no charge for personal use. Commercial use requires a ProfessionalFeed Subscription, which costs $1,200 per year. The software is available for Mac OS X as well as Windows and several flavors of Linux. And unlike the other software described in this chapter, Nessus includes a full Mac OS X graphical interface rather than relying on the command line, a web browser, or X11 for user interaction.

Nessus overview

The overall design of Nessus takes a bit of getting used to, and it requires users to jump through a few hoops in order to get started. However, once you've done that, day-to-day operation of the software is quite simple, with all results provided in clear English.

The software consists of two modules: the Nessus Server and the Nessus Client. The server module performs the scanning, while the client module lets you interact with the server — sending it instructions and displaying the results it delivers. You can run the server and the client on the same computer or on different ones. If you're doing extensive testing on a large number of computers, you might want to install the client on some machine other than your regular Mac because it could adversely affect your Mac's performance. For less intense scans, installing both modules on the same computer is easier, and that's the arrangement I assume in the instructions that follow. But even if the client and server are running on the same computer, you must still go through an explicit process to connect the client to the server on each use.

Nessus can scan for vulnerabilities on a single computer, an IP address range, or an arbitrary list of addresses. It includes its own network-mapping and port-scanning capabilities, and it typically does such scans first, followed by further examination of open ports on active IP addresses in the range you've selected.

Cross-Ref
For more on network mapping and port scanning, see Chapter 20. ■

The list of data Nessus can collect is quite long, and you can choose any combination of problems to check for (each one described by an individual file called a plug-in) and options to use when scanning. A collection of such settings is known as a *policy*, and you can create as many different policies as you need. For example, you might have one policy that just scans quickly for the most obvious security holes, which you use on a regular basis, and another policy that exhaustively scans for every conceivable problem but which, because of the long time it takes to run, you use only occasionally.

Installing and configuring Nessus

Getting started with Nessus is only slightly more complicated than using other Mac OS X applications. After the initial setup, day-to-day operation is simpler.

To install Nessus and prepare it for use, follow these steps:

1. **Download the Nessus package for Mac OS X from** http://nessus.org/download **and then run the installer.**

2. **Open Nessus Server Manager, which by default is installed in** `/Applications/Nessus`. If prompted to do so, type your administrator username and password and then click OK. The Nessus Server Configuration window, shown in Figure 21.1, opens.

FIGURE 21.1

The Nessus Server Configuration window

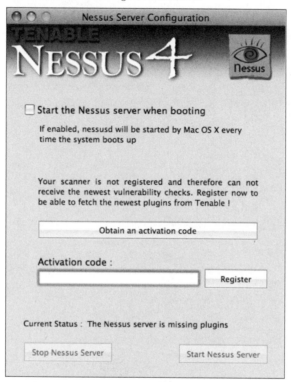

3. **If you don't already have an activation code, click Obtain an activation code to register on the Nessus website.** After you register, Nessus sends you an activation code by email. Type or paste that code into the Activation code field and then click Register. Nessus Server Manager then downloads the latest plug-ins, and the window changes to look like Figure 21.2.

4. **Optionally, you can click any of the following check boxes to select them:**
   - **Start the Nessus server when booting.** Runs the server automatically when you start your Mac. If you select this, you need not open Nessus Server Manager and start the server manually each time you want to use Nessus Client.
   - **Perform a daily plugin update.** Updates plug-ins automatically. If you don't select this, you can update the plug-ins manually at any time by clicking Update plugins.

- **Allow remote users to connect to this server.** You can leave this deselected if you're running the server and the client on the same computer. If this computer will run the server and you want to be able to connect to it from a client running on another computer, this check box should be selected. Then, click Manage Users to configure usernames and passwords for each remote user for whom access is permitted.

5. **Click Start Nessus Server.** The server runs in the background; you can quit the Nessus Server Manager application without stopping the server itself.

FIGURE 21.2

After typing your activation code, you can select additional settings and then run Nessus Server.

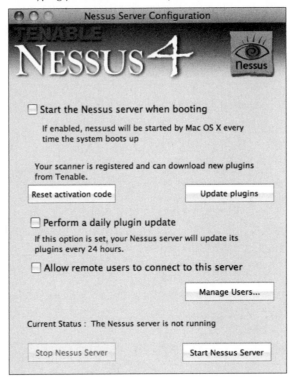

6. **Open Nessus Client, which by default is installed in** /Applications/Nessus. The window initially appears as shown in Figure 21.3.

FIGURE 21.3

Nessus Client enables you to interact with a Nessus Server, sending it instructions to perform scans on designated computers or networks according to a selected policy.

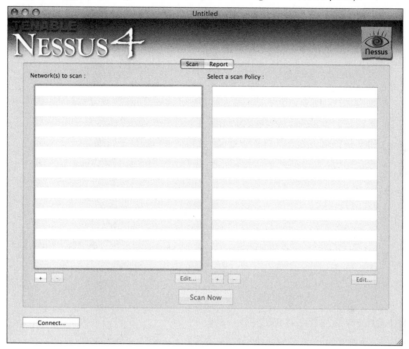

7. **Click Connect, and in the window that opens, as shown in Figure 21.4, select the Nessus server you want to use.** This is called Local server if it's running on the same Mac as the client. If the server doesn't appear in the list, click the Add (+) button to add it and then click Connect. Nessus Client then connects to the server you selected, making it ready to specify and perform scans.

Note

The first time you connect to a particular host, you may see a New Certificate alert, prompting you to accept that host's certificate. Click Yes when you see this window. ■

FIGURE 21.4

If you're running both client and server modules of Nessus on the same computer, select Local server in this window.

Select a Nessus Server :

Local server

| + | - | Edit... | | Close | Connect |

Selecting scan targets

With Nessus installed and connected, your next step is to specify which computer(s) to scan.

To select one or more scan targets, follow these steps:

1. **In Nessus Client, click the Scan tab and then click the Add (+) button below the Network(s) to scan list.** A Target window, as shown in Figure 21.5, opens.

2. **At the top of the window, click the radio button corresponding to which type of scan you want to perform.** In most cases, choose either Single host (to scan just one computer) or IP range (to scan a contiguous range of IP addresses).

3. **If you chose Single host in step 2, type that host's IP address in the Host name field; if you selected IP range, type the starting and ending addresses of the range in the Start address and End address fields, respectively; and then click Save.**

4. **Optionally, to define additional targets, repeat steps 1–3.**

5. **For each target you want to scan in this particular session, make sure its check box (in the Network(s) to scan list, in the main Nessus Client window) is selected (as it is by default).**

FIGURE 21.5

Although Nessus lets you specify targets in several different ways, the choices you're most likely to use are Single host and IP range.

Creating a scanning policy

The scanning policy specifies what sorts of checks to perform and with which options during any particular scan. You have thousands of choices here, but for basic scans, you can safely ignore most of them.

To configure a basic scanning policy, follow these steps:

1. **In Nessus Client, click the Scan tab and then click the Add (+) button below the Select a scan Policy list.** An Edit Policy window, as shown in Figure 21.6, opens.

2. **In the Policy pane, type a name for the policy.**

FIGURE 21.6

The Edit Policy window is where you lay out the details of what sorts of scans to undertake and how.

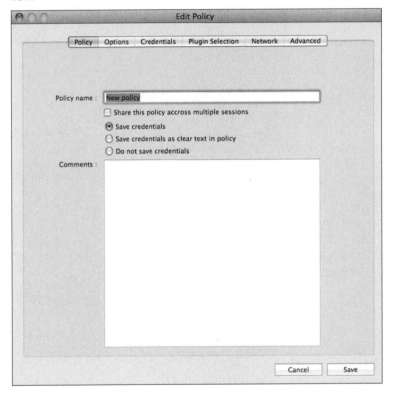

3. **Click the Options tab, shown in Figure 21.7, to show policy-wide options.** Most of these settings can stay at their defaults, but I want to call your attention to four items you might want to adjust:

   - **Number of hosts in parallel.** In this field, type the number of computers you want Nessus to scan simultaneously. The larger the number, the less time the scan takes — but the more overloaded your network (and the remote network, if any) will be.

   - **Number checks in parallel.** Likewise, in this field, type the number of tests you want Nessus to perform simultaneously on each computer it scans. A higher number may yield faster results, but it may also slow down the computer being scanned (not to mention the one running Nessus Server).

   - **Port scanner range.** By default, Nessus's built-in port scanner scans ports 1–15000. To use a different range, type it in this field.

   - **Safe checks.** Although Nessus was designed to be nonintrusive — and not to actively exploit security holes, as does Metasploit, described later in this chapter — some of the scans it performs can have side effects, such as crashing programs on the target computer or rendering network printers inoperable without a hardware reset. When the Safe checks check box is selected, as it is by default, Nessus skips any checks known to have dangerous side effects. In general, you should leave this selected unless you're checking only computers over which you have complete control and in a situation where the benefit of finding potential security holes outweighs the possibility of causing a crash or other disruption to the computer. To read more about safe checks, go to `http://blog.tenablesecurity.com/2006/09/understanding_t.html`.

FIGURE 21.7

In the Options pane, you can adjust how many scans Nessus performs at once and whether it skips scans that could crash computers and cause other problems.

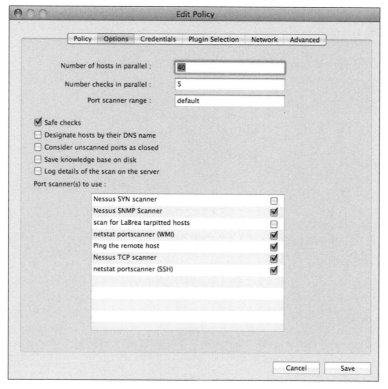

4. **Click the Credentials tab, shown in Figure 21.8, to show options that let you type user-names and passwords for various kinds of hosts and services.** In general, you shouldn't make changes in this pane, but if you want to show vulnerabilities as they would appear for someone who knows any of the credentials for devices on your network, you can type those credentials in this pane. First, choose the category from the pop-up menu at the top (such as SSH settings or Windows credentials) and then type the requested information (or as much of it as you know) in the fields provided.

5. **Click the Plugin Selection tab, shown in Figure 21.9, to show a list of the thousands of specific vulnerabilities Nessus can check for.** To show individual checks, click the disclosure triangle next to any category (such as MacOS X Local Security Checks).

FIGURE 21.8

If you want to test vulnerabilities that require user credentials, type those credentials in this pane.

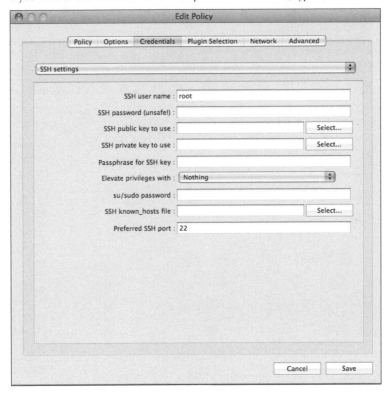

6. **Click a check box on the right side of the window to enable or disable either an individual check or an entire category** — or click Disable all or Enable all at the bottom of the window.

Tip

If you're checking a network with only Macs, it makes sense to disable all the categories representing other operating systems (such as Gentoo and HP-UX), although you should still enable checks that apply to many operating systems, such as firewalls and FTP. However, other than taking a bit longer, it never hurts to have too many checks — better safe than sorry. ■

Note

Feel free to explore the Network and Advanced tabs too, but you can skip them for the time being — the options they contain aren't crucial for setting up a basic scan. ■

7. **Click Save.** Nessus Client saves your policy in the list. If you want to create additional policies, repeat these steps.

FIGURE 21.9

The Plugin Selection pane is where all the magic happens — here, you can select any or all of over 11,000 plug-ins to test for an ever-growing number of vulnerabilities on many platforms.

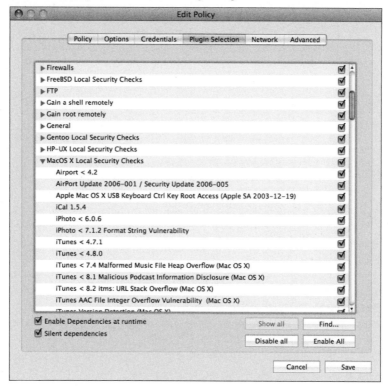

Running a customized scan

With your server connected and your target(s) and policy(ies) specified, running a scan itself is as easy as it gets.

To run a scan using the parameters you set up previously, follow these steps:

1. **In Nessus Client, make sure you've selected the check box(es) for the desired target(s).**
2. **Click a scan policy, as shown in Figure 21.10.**
3. **Click Scan Now.** Nessus begins the scan, which can take anywhere from seconds to hours, depending on how many checks you're performing, with which options, on how many hosts.

As the scan progresses, IP addresses appear in the Report pane in the list on the left. IP addresses that have been discovered to be active are gray until specific open ports are found, at which point they turn black or take on another color, as described next.

FIGURE 21.10

With your configuration completed, performing a scan simply requires selecting one or more targets, selecting a policy, and then clicking a button.

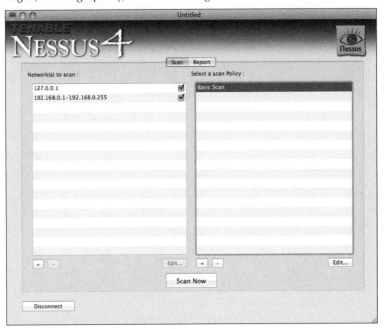

Interpreting scan results

When the scan has finished, the Report pane of the main Nessus window may look something like Figure 21.11. Each scanned IP address is listed; click the disclosure triangle next to any of them to see individual services provided on that address. The results are color-coded:

- **Black.** No vulnerabilities or only low-risk vulnerabilities found
- **Yellow.** Medium-risk vulnerabilities found
- **Red.** High-risk vulnerabilities found

These colors apply both to individual services and to the host. So, if you see that an IP address is red, that means at least one service provided by that IP address is also red.

Select an IP address to see a summary of its risk factors or select a service to show information about its associated vulnerabilities. A given service may have more than one vulnerability and each one may have a different risk level. The text provided for each vulnerability describes the nature of the problem, how serious the risk is, and what steps can be taken to solve it (such as blocking or filtering a port using a firewall or applying a software update).

As new vulnerabilities are discovered, software updated, and devices on the network removed or added, your risks change, so it pays to repeat this check from time to time. I suggest running Nessus at least once a month — being sure to update its list of plug-ins each time.

FIGURE 21.11

Details of each potential vulnerability and how to fix it, if applicable, are spelled out in plain English.

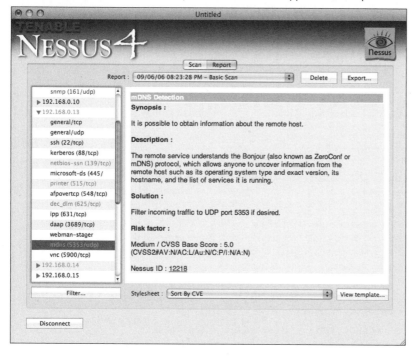

Using SAINT and SAINTexploit

SAINT, for Security Administrator's Integrated Network Tool (www.saintcorporation.com), is another multi-platform vulnerability scanner. Like Nessus, it was previously open source and is now a commercial application. Prices range from $425 (for a 10-host license) to $1,885 (for a 250-host license) if you're purchasing a one-year subscription and from $730 to $2,892 for a perpetual license. A 15-day trial version, which scans only two IP addresses, is also available (http://download.saintcorporation.com/downloads/freetrial/saint-install-7.1.5.gz).

By itself, SAINT only reports possible vulnerabilities — just like Nessus. But an add-on program called SAINTexploit (licenses for which cost the same as for SAINT itself) can perform *penetration testing* — that is, trying to exploit the vulnerabilities that may exist (which can cause significant harm and therefore should only be done to computers you control) for the purpose of security validation.

Apart from the high cost, SAINTexploit has very few Mac-specific exploits, although it does include a number of Linux or cross-platform exploits that could theoretically affect a Mac. Nevertheless, as it's quite a powerful tool, I want to provide a quick overview of how to install and use SAINT on Mac OS X.

To get started with SAINT, follow these steps:

1. **Download the Mac OS X version of SAINT from** `www.saintcorporation.com/my_account/download.html`. If you're using the trial version rather than purchasing the full product, you must fill out a form that includes, among other things, the two IP addresses you want to scan during your evaluation. Be sure to specify the IP addresses as they appear to other computers on your network — for example, if you're behind a NAT router, use the private IP addresses rather than your network's public IP address, and don't use `127.0.0.1` as one of your choices.

2. **Double-click the SAINT tar file (such as** `saint-install-7.0.x.tar`**) to expand its contents.** An installer file (such as `SAINT 7.0.x Installer`) appears in the same folder.

3. **Double-click the SAINT installer and follow the prompts to complete the installation.** They're self-explanatory (ranging from your agreement to the software license to whether you want a shortcut to SAINT put on your desktop), and you can safely accept all defaults.

4. **Locate your** `saint.key` **license file, drag it to the SAINT folder (which may have a name like** `saint-7.0.x`**) inside** `/Applications`**, and, if prompted to do so, authenticate with your administrator username and password.** You most likely received the license file as an email enclosure after purchasing SAINT or signing up for a free trial.

5. **If the Mac on which you're about to run SAINT doesn't have a reverse DNS entry (and if you have to ask what that means, it most likely doesn't), you must perform some additional steps to make sure SAINT's built-in web server works:**

    1. **In a Terminal window, edit the** `saint.cf` **file as the root user:**

        ```
        sudo nano /Applications/saint-7.0.x/config/saint.cf
        ```

    2. **Modify the path name as necessary to reflect where SAINT is installed on your Mac.** Find this line:

        ```
        $my_address = "";
        ```

    3. **Modify this line so that it reflects your Mac's private IP address — for example:**

        ```
        $my_address = "192.168.0.15";
        ```

    4. **Press Control+X to save the file, press Y to confirm, and then press Return to confirm the location.**

6. **Double-click the SAINT application (for example,** `SAINT 7.0.x`**).** If prompted for an administrator's password, type it and then press Return. Then, your default web browser opens to reveal the SAINT interface, as shown in Figure 21.12.

Once you finally get SAINT installed, you configure and run it using a web-based interface.

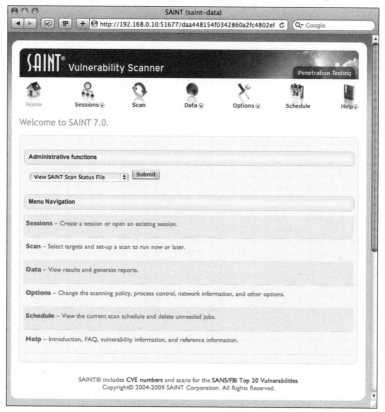

7. **Click the Scan icon to show the Scan Setup options, shown in Figure 21.13, and then configure at least the following settings:**
   - **Primary Targets.** Click the Primary Targets tab. Then, from the Add target(s) pop-up menu, choose By Single IP, by IP Range, By Subnet, or By Host Name, depending on what you want to scan. In the field(s) provided, type either a single IP address, an address range, a subnet, or a hostname and then click the corresponding Add button. The target(s) you typed appear in the Selected Targets list.

FIGURE 21.13

Determine which hosts you want to scan in this pane.

- **Firewall Support.** If the host you're scanning is behind a firewall, click the Firewall Support tab and then click either the Firewall Support or Extensive Firewall Support radio button.

8. **Click Scan Now.** SAINT begins the scan, reporting its current checks as it goes.

9. **To see the results of a completed scan, hover over the Data icon and then click the SAINTwriter link that appears beneath it. Click the Full Scan radio button under Default Reports, and then click Continue.** SAINT displays a page, as shown in Figure 21.14, that details all the problems found, including severity level and other details.

FIGURE 21.14

SAINT's reports provide both a graphical overview of results and details about all vulnerabilities found during a scan.

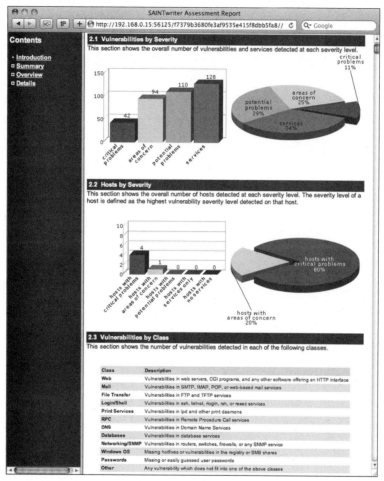

If you purchased the optional SAINTexploit add-on, it uses the same interface — it merely enables options on an additional set of tabs. SAINTexploit can function in two ways:

- **Automated penetration testing.** To have SAINTexploit test all relevant exploits, click the Penetration Testing tab, followed by the Pen Test icon, as shown in Figure 21.15. Fill in the options as you would for a regular scan and then click Run Pen Test Now.

● **Manual exploit testing.** To test a single particular exploit, click the Penetration Testing tab, hover over the Exploits icon, and then click the Exploits link that appears beneath it to show the page shown in Figure 21.16. Locate an exploit you want to test in the list and then click the Run Now button next to it.

FIGURE 21.15

Run automated penetration testing (using all relevant exploits) in the Pen Test pane.

FIGURE 21.16

List and run specific exploits in the Exploits pane.

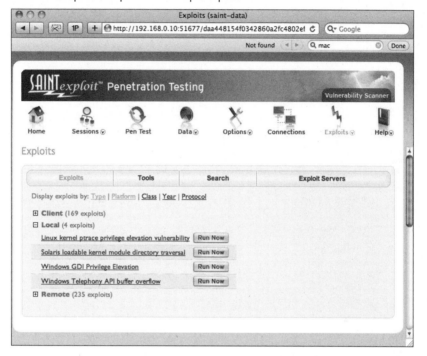

Using Metasploit

Whereas Nessus and SAINT can scan for potential vulnerabilities but not test them to see if they're actual vulnerabilities, a free, open-source tool called the Metasploit Framework (http://metasploit.com/), or Metasploit for short, offers (as does SAINTexploit) the remaining piece of the puzzle: It can exploit known vulnerabilities — enabling you to know for sure whether your computers are at risk.

Metasploit itself doesn't know how to exploit vulnerabilities; rather, it's a development and delivery mechanism. Researchers who discover security holes can use the Metasploit Framework to create instructions for carrying out exploits, which can then be shared with other users and tested on a variety of systems.

So, in Metasploit's usage, an *exploit* is a procedure, described in a module (a specially designed Ruby file), that attacks a known weakness in a particular program or service on one or more platforms. It's the code that Metasploit uses to break in. The Metasploit Framework ships with hundreds of exploits, and more are being developed all the time.

But once you're in, then what? Picking a lock may open the door, but the reason for doing so is to get at what's on the other side. So, the other key component of Metasploit is the *payload*, which is the set of instructions for taking some action on the target computer once the exploit has been successfully executed. Typical payloads include procedures to give the user shell access to the remote computer, execute a shell command, or gain screen-sharing access via VNC. For the most part, you can mix and match exploits with payloads as you see fit, although many payloads work only on certain platforms (and in particular, the range of payloads available for Mac OS X targets is pretty limited).

Metasploit interfaces

Metasploit comes with not one, not two, but four user interfaces. Although the underlying functionality is the same, you can get at Metasploit's features in any of the following ways:

- **Console.** The console is an interactive text-based interface. You type commands that list the options available in any given context, set the options to your liking, and then perform the exploits. Although the console is interactive, its usage is far from obvious because it's not always clear what actions are possible, required, or prohibited at any point in the process.

- **Command line.** For people who want to create shell scripts or other external programs to automate Metasploit, the program also comes with a noninteractive command-line interface in which all options for a given exploit must be listed in a special, abbreviated format in a single command.

- **Web interface.** Yet another way of using Metasploit is via its web interface. In this mode, Metasploit runs its own local web server on port 55555. Once you connect to that server, you can view and operate most of Metasploit's features, in a semigraphical way, in a series of movable, resizable windows that appear within a web page. This is an improvement over the console in the sense of making some of the ranges of choices clearer and more explicit, but it's a somewhat clunky implementation — and using some features requires you to open a console window within the web page.

- **GUI.** Finally, Metasploit comes with its own X11-based graphical user interface (GUI). In addition to showing all the appropriate options using standard controls, such as hierarchical lists and pop-up menus, the GUI includes a wizard that walks you through the steps of specifying the payload and options for each exploit, making it considerably easier to use, especially for beginners, than the other interfaces. The only downside is that installing all the necessary components to run the GUI interface on Mac OS X takes some doing.

Of these, the console is considered the main, or default, interface, and you can also access the console (as indeed you must, for certain tasks) from the web and GUI interfaces. Because the console and GUI interfaces offer, in my opinion, the best compromises between convenience and usability on Mac OS X, I provide instructions for those two interfaces in this section.

Installing Metasploit

Depending on your preferences and objectives, installing Metasploit can be trivially easy or an afternoon's work. The reason for this variation is that although Metasploit is based on Ruby — software that's built into Mac OS X — Leopard and Snow Leopard are missing certain pieces and have less-than-optimal versions of others to enable some of the Metasploit interfaces to work correctly. In some cases, you can download Metasploit and run it directly, with no alterations, and in other cases, you may need to jump through quite a few more hoops.

To install Metasploit, follow these steps (or as many of them as apply to your situation):

1. Download the Unix version of the Metasploit Framework from `http://metasploit.com/ framework`. The gzipped file should decompress automatically, leaving you with a `.tar` archive.

2. Double-click the `.tar` archive (a file with a name like `framework-3.2.tar`) to expand it into a folder (with a name like `framework-3.2`). Feel free to rename the folder to something more obvious, such as `Metasploit`, if you want.

3. Move the `Metasploit` folder (or whatever it's named) into your `/Applications` folder or another location of your choice. If you want to use the console, command-line, or web interface and you don't mind putting up with the occasional error message, you can stop here. To run Metasploit, double-click `msfcli` for the command-line version; `msfconsole` for the console version; or `msfweb` for the web version from within the `Metasploit` folder — and with the web version, point your browser at `http://127.0.0.1:55555`. If you want to install a newer version of Ruby (and supporting files) to get rid of those annoying error messages or if you aspire to run the GUI version, continue with the next series of steps. Although there are numerous ways of installing Ruby, the method I suggest here has the advantage of putting all the new software in a separate location — leaving your existing installation of Ruby and its supporting files untouched — while not requiring any manual compilation or other technically demanding steps.

4. Download MacPorts from `www.macports.org` (be sure to get the version appropriate for your version of Mac OS X) and then run the installer.

5. Open Terminal, which is located in `/Applications/Utilities`.

6. Type sudo port install ruby **to install Ruby using MacPorts.**

7. Type your administrator password when prompted, press Return, and then wait until all the status messages disappear and your command prompt returns.

8. Download RubyGems, a packaging system that can facilitate installing additional files Metasploit requires, from `http://rubyforge.org/frs/?group_id=126`. The gzipped file should decompress automatically, leaving you with a `.tar` archive.

9. Double-click the `.tar` archive (a file with a name like `rubygems-1.3.5.tar`) to expand it into a folder (with a name like `rubygems-1.3.5`).

10. Back in Terminal, switch to the RubyGems folder. If it's still in your `~/Downloads` folder and has the name shown in step 9, type **cd ~/Downloads/rubygems-1.3.5**.

11. To install RubyGems, type sudo ruby setup.rb install.

12. Type your administrator password when prompted, press Return, and then wait until all the status messages disappear and your command prompt returns.

13. To use RubyGems to install Rails, a web application development framework that Metasploit's web interface uses, type sudo gem install rails.

14. Type your administrator password when prompted, press Return, and then wait until all the status messages disappear and your command prompt returns. If you want to use the GUI version of Metasploit, continue with the remaining steps.

15. Check to see if X11 is in your `/Applications` folder; if not, insert your Mac OS X Install DVD, open the `Optional Installs` folder, double-click the Optional Installs installer, and then follow the prompts to install X11.

16. To install the Ruby-Gnome package, which contains a large number of files on which the GUI version of Metasploit depends, type sudo port install rb-gnome.

17. Type your administrator password when prompted, press Return, and then wait until all the status messages disappear and your command prompt returns.

Note

Installation of the Ruby-Gnome package takes a long time — multiple hours, even on a fast Mac, shouldn't be any surprise. ■

Having gone through all that, you can now double-click the file `msfgui` in the `Metasploit` folder to open the GUI version of Metasploit. Terminal opens a new window (which you should keep open as long as Metasploit is running) and then X11 opens, with a new Metasploit window, as shown in Figure 21.17.

FIGURE 21.17

It takes some doing, but you can get Metasploit to run in a fully graphical, X11-based interface on Mac OS X.

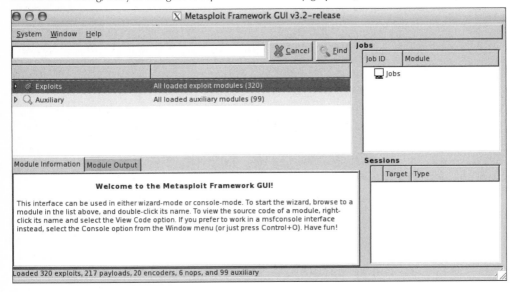

Basic Metasploit procedures

Regardless of which interface you choose, the process of using Metasploit follows the same general outline:

- **Choose an exploit.** Exploits are designed for specific versions of certain programs and services, so you must select one that works with the combination of operating system, software, and open ports on the target computer. Metasploit lists exploits grouped by category (such as operating system name) and also offers the capability to search for an exploit matching a keyword. For Mac OS X–specific exploits, use the search keyword "osx."

- **Pick a target.** Metasploit uses the term *target* to refer to the specific service being attacked — for example, a certain version of a particular browser on a particular operating system. Some exploits work only with a single target (and, therefore, there's nothing to set), some can set targets automatically, and some require you to set a target explicitly.

- **Select a payload.** Metasploit currently offers only a small number of payloads that work on Mac OS X targets, of which most produce an interactive shell session with the target computer. Experiment to find the payload that yields the best results for you.

- **Set options.** Each exploit and each payload typically have one or more options you can configure. Often, the default settings are fine, but sometimes, you must explicitly configure one or more settings. Among the most common options you'll encounter are these:
  - **RHOST.** Remote host, an exploit option. This is the IP address or domain name of the target host.
  - **RPORT.** Remote port, an exploit option. This is the port on the target host that you want to address.
  - **LHOST.** Local host, a payload option. This is normally the IP address of the computer running Metasploit — the address to which the results of the exploit are directed. A value of 0.0.0.0, often used as a default, means any IP address. In some cases, an attacker may want to specify a different LHOST — for example, to direct incoming data from an external network through a router that uses port forwarding.
  - **LPORT.** Local port, a payload option. This specifies the port on the attacking computer that will receive the incoming data. In most cases, the default setting should be correct.
- **Run the exploit.** Once all the options are selected, running the exploit is usually a matter of clicking a button or typing the word **exploit**. If the payload creates an interactive shell session, you can then type commands on the remote computer in a console window.

Running an exploit in the Metasploit console

Although the range of activities you can perform in Metasploit is almost endless, I want to provide just a brief example of how to go about performing an exploit using the console interface. In the next section, I describe the same process using the GUI interface.

Follow these steps:

1. **Double-click** msfconsole, **located in the** Metasploit **folder (wherever you installed it).** A Terminal window opens, showing the Metasploit console program, which looks something like this:

```
< metasploit >
 -----------
        \   ,__,
         \  (oo)____
            (__)    )\
               ||--|| *

      =[ msf v3.2-release
+ -- --=[ 320 exploits - 217 payloads
+ -- --=[ 20 encoders - 6 nops
      =[ 99 aux
msf >
```

2. **To show available exploits, type** show exploits. A list appears. Or to search for exploits (and payloads) by keyword, type **search** *keyword*.

3. **To choose an exploit, type** use *exploit*, **where** *exploit* **is the complete path of the exploit.** For example: **use osx/browser/safari_metadata_archive.** The prompt changes to reflect the name of the exploit.

4. **To show available targets, type** show targets. A list appears.

5. **To pick a target, type** set target *number*, **where** *number* **is replaced with the target number.** For example: **set target 0**. If there's only one item in the list, you need not explicitly select it.

6. **To show payloads that are compatible with the selected exploit, type** show payloads. A list appears.

7. **To select a payload, type** set payload *name*, **where** *name* **is replaced with the complete path of the payload.** For example: **set payload cmd/unix/reverse_perl**.

8. **To see which options are available, type** show options. A list similar to this appears:

```
Module options:
    Name        Current Setting   Required   Description
    ----        ---------------   --------   -----------
    SRVHOST     0.0.0.0           yes        The local host to listen on.
    SRVPORT     8080              yes        The local port to listen on.
    SSL         false             no         Use SSL
    URIPATH                       no         The URI to use for this
    exploit (default is random)

Payload options (cmd/unix/reverse_perl):
    Name     Current Setting   Required   Description
    ----     ---------------   --------   -----------
    LHOST                      yes        The local address
    LPORT    4444              yes        The local port
```

   If an option has yes in the Required column but nothing in the Current Setting column (or a setting you don't want), you can change it.

9. **To change an option, type** set *option value*, **where** *option* **is the name of the option, as shown in step 8 and** *value* **is the value you want it to have.** For example: **set LHOST 192.168.0.10**.

10. **To run the exploit, type** exploit. Metasploit runs the exploit and displays details about the results (including the output of a command you executed, if any). Not all exploits that fail tell you so in so many words. However, if an exploit is successful and the payload is an interactive shell, you should now be able to type commands on the remote computer.

Running an exploit in the Metasploit GUI

You can do exactly the same thing in the GUI version of Metasploit, only with fewer steps required — and more help along the way. Follow these steps:

1. **Double-click** msfgui, **located in the** Metasploit **folder (wherever you installed it).** A Terminal window opens, which you should leave open while Metasploit is running. Then, an X11 window opens with the Metasploit GUI itself, as shown in Figure 21.18.

2. **To find an exploit, look through the list in the upper left.** If you want to search by keyword, type the search term in the search field (no need to press Return or click a button). When you select an exploit, information about it appears at the bottom of the window, as shown in Figure 21.19.

3. **To choose an exploit, double-click it.** A wizard opens in order to walk you through the remaining steps.

FIGURE 21.18

Metasploit is a bit friendlier in its GUI incarnation.

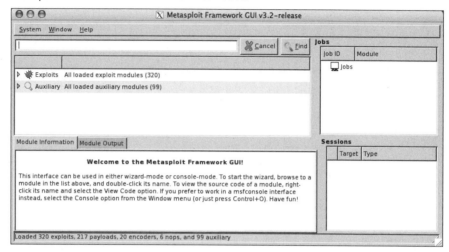

FIGURE 21.19

Select an exploit to show information about it.

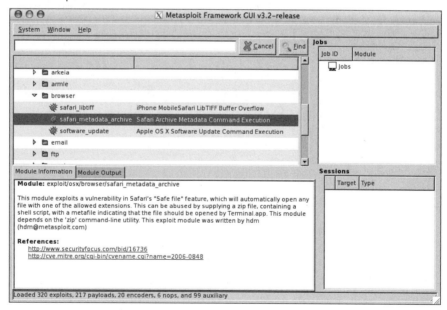

4. On the Select your target screen of the wizard, as shown in Figure 21.20, choose a target from the pop-up menu and then click Forward.

FIGURE 21.20

Choose your target here or keep the default setting if it says Automatic.

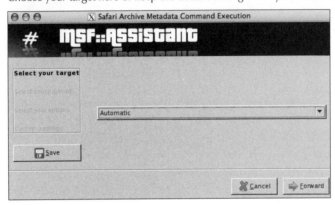

5. On the Select your payload screen, as shown in Figure 21.21, choose one of the compatible payloads from the pop-up menu to show a description of the payload at the bottom of the window and then click Forward.

FIGURE 21.21

Choose a payload from this pop-up menu.

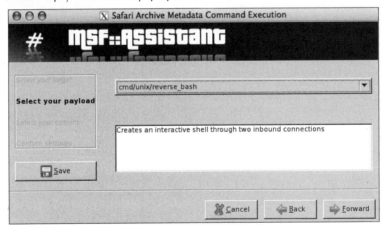

6. **On the Select your options screen, as shown in Figure 21.22, fill in any options you want to change and then click Forward.** The selections vary by exploit and payload.

FIGURE 21.22

In the Metasploit GUI, you can change options by filling in fields and using check boxes and other standard controls.

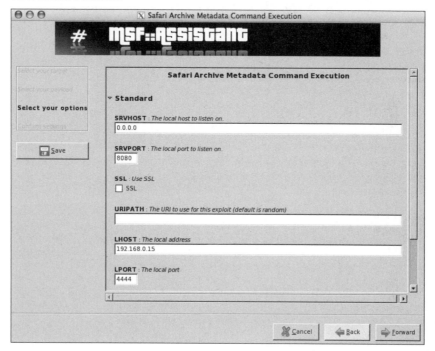

7. **To run the exploit, review your settings in the Confirm settings screen, as shown in Figure 21.23, and then click Apply.**

   Output, if any, appears in the Module Output pane of the main window, as shown in Figure 21.24. In cases where an exploit successfully opens a shell session, the session is listed in the lower-right corner of the main window; double-click a session name to open a separate console window for interacting with the remote computer.

To stop an exploit, Control+click an item in the Jobs list and then choose Kill Job from the pop-up menu.

FIGURE 21.23

Click Apply to run your exploit.

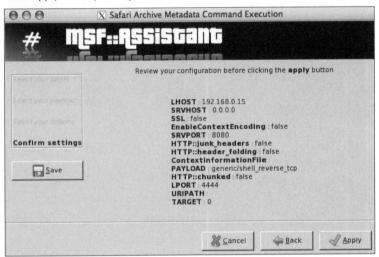

FIGURE 21.24

Output from your exploits and a list of open sessions appear in the main window when an exploit is running.

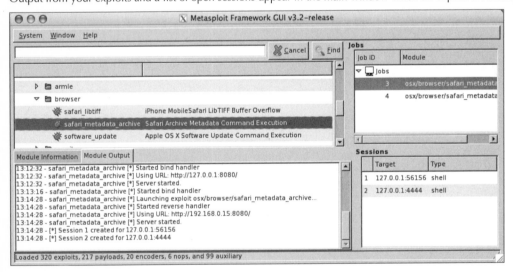

Summary

Whereas Chapter 20 discussed ways to determine a network's vulnerability to attack at a fairly high level, this chapter looked at how to determine specific risks of individual Macs on your network to exploits that can take advantage of open ports (including those you may want to leave open for one reason or another). I described two major tools for checking a Mac network for vulnerability to exploits: Nessus and SAINT (along with its optional SAINTexploit tool). I then introduced you to Metasploit, a tool that lets you try known exploits on your network in order to confirm potential weaknesses.

Network Monitoring

N etwork security isn't something you can assure with a one-time audit or configuration. The Internet is constantly evolving, as are the devices you may connect to it. Operating systems and applications undergo frequent updates, new methods of attack are invented, and new exploits are discovered. As a result, you can improve your security by regularly monitoring your network for any new breaches that may have slipped past your defenses.

This chapter covers several different sorts of network monitoring, including methods that simply watch for potential threats and alert you, methods that actively work to block new threats, and methods that help to ensure that no proprietary or confidential data is sent from your network to other locations on the Internet. It also briefly discusses ways of luring attackers away from your most important Macs by using a mechanism known as a honeypot.

The Varieties of Network Monitoring

The expression *network monitoring* often refers to the process of watching the servers, workstations, routers, and other devices on your network for signs of breakdowns, overloads, or other conditions that could cause them to fail. As important as that is, what I'm discussing here in this chapter is a different sense of the term: monitoring the data passed over your network (as opposed to network hardware itself) to detect unwanted incoming or outgoing information and, in some cases, to take action to prevent such occurrences.

Note

An example of software that monitors a network for equipment failures, performance issues, bandwidth usage, and such is InterMapper (www.intermapper. com), which also — as the name suggests — performs network-mapping functions. Licenses range from free (for up to five computers) to many thousands of dollars, depending on the extent of your monitoring needs. ■

IN THIS CHAPTER
Learning what information network monitoring can provide
Using systems that monitor a network for unauthorized access
Intelligently and dynamically blocking network intruders
Preventing unauthorized information from leaving your network
Learning about attempted attacks with honeypot decoys

Specifically, this chapter introduces you to the following types of monitoring:

- **Network intrusion detection system (NIDS).** A NIDS watches traffic on your network for tell-tale signs of intrusions by port scanners, robots and malware probing for holes, denial-of-service (DoS) attacks, unauthorized users trying to guess passwords, and other behavior you may want to be aware of as soon as possible. A NIDS is a subcategory of an IDS (intrusion detection system). When potentially dangerous activity appears, a NIDS can log it, alert an administrator, or both. A related term, *host-based intrusion detection system* (HIDS), can mean either software that looks for network-based intrusions directed only at the single computer it's running on (in other words, a NIDS that protects just one computer) or software that monitors files on the computer for potentially malicious changes (what I refer to as file integrity monitoring).

Cross-Ref

For more on file integrity monitoring, see Chapter 23. ■

- **Network intrusion prevention system (NIPS).** Whereas a NIDS exists only to watch for bad traffic and alert a human being who can then intervene, a NIPS takes matters into its own hands. Drawing on exactly the same data that a NIDS collects, a NIPS automatically blocks traffic from sources that it deems to be dangerous. In other words, a NIPS is essentially a dynamic firewall — one that doesn't block a specific IP address or traffic type until there's a good reason to do so. Once again, you can install software of this sort that protects only a single computer; that would make it a host-based intrusion prevention system — or HIPS!

- **Information leak detection system (ILDS).** A NIDS and a NIPS are concerned primarily with incoming connections — unwanted connections from outside your network. But a different sort of network monitoring watches outgoing data, specifically to discover whether anyone on your network is sending confidential or unauthorized information to the outside. To take a simple example, an ILDS could watch for social security numbers or credit card numbers being sent unencrypted over the web or in email and then alert the user or block the connection. But this concept can extend to any sort of data an individual or company wants to keep under control. This type of system also goes by names such as information leak prevention (ILP) and data loss prevention (DLP) — but in this context, the notion of prevention is implied even when the term used is *detection*.

- **Honeypots.** A honeypot is a decoy — a computer with no valuable data or resources on it — set up specifically to attract malicious traffic. Why would you want to do this? For one thing, a honeypot can give you valuable data about who's trying to attack your network and how so you can take that knowledge and use it to harden your other computers. In some cases, honeypots can also slow down attackers by making it harder for them to find legitimate computers on your network and by delaying responses; this can buy you time to plug holes and prevent more serious problems.

These aren't by any means the only varieties of network monitoring that can affect your network's security, but they're among the most common and useful.

Network Intrusion Detection Systems

The first type of network monitoring in this chapter's parade of acronyms is the network intrusion detection system, or NIDS. *Intrusion* refers to any sort of unauthorized access — but, in particular, a NIDS may look for evidence of things such as network mapping, port scanning (even of the stealth variety that specifically seeks to evade detection), fingerprinting, repeated unsuccessful login attempts, floods of data intended as a denial-of-service (DoS) attack, services commonly associated with malware of various sorts, and other behaviors that might rightly worry a network administrator.

Note

I discuss network mapping, port scanning, and fingerprinting in Chapter 20. They're useful techniques for you to try on your own network, but your goal should be to use techniques such as a NIDS to improve your network's defenses to the point where even you can't successfully execute a network map or port scan on your Macs from another computer on your network! A perfect port scanner could defeat any NIDS, and a perfect NIDS could detect any port scanner — but perfect tools of either sort don't exist. ■

At first glance, a NIDS may seem to accomplish the same thing as a firewall. Both aim to help you keep out unwanted traffic, so to that extent, they're in the same general category. However, firewalls are generally static and dumb. They do what you tell them to do, such as blocking all incoming access from a certain IP address or to a certain port, but they usually don't learn or adapt on their own; you must manually add or change rules to get them to behave differently. In addition, because firewalls work at a low level, they know very little about the nature of the traffic they're transmitting or blocking. For example, a firewall may let through all traffic to port 22 — a good thing if you're running an SSH server on one of your computers. But port 22 could also be used as an avenue of attack, and a firewall has no way to distinguish good traffic on port 22 from bad traffic. A NIDS can do just that because it inspects the contents of each packet and can go even further by detecting patterns over time in a sequence of packets. So, a NIDS provides a much richer set of data that can tell you how to adjust your firewall or make other changes to improve the security on your network.

The core feature of a NIDS is data collection. The NIDS sniffs all the traffic on your network looking for certain kinds of unwanted data. It knows what counts as unwanted either because the traffic matches a signature — known bad behavior that you or someone else described in a pattern-matching rule — or because the NIDS has built a picture over time of what normal network traffic looks like, and it notices something anomalous (even if it doesn't match a specific signature).

Once it discovers suspicious traffic, the NIDS does something with it — at minimum, it displays it on-screen, writes it to a log file, or stores it in a database. In addition, a NIDS may pop up an alert, send an email message or SMS to a system administrator, run a shell script, or take some other action to alert the person in charge to examine the data it discovered and take any appropriate action. Sometimes, however, these extra actions require custom programming or third-party add-on software to implement.

Note

A NIDS that takes matters into its own hands and blocks or refuses unwanted traffic is a NIPS — a network intrusion prevention service — which I discuss later in this chapter. ■

Although most network intrusions come from outside your network, a NIDS can sniff all network traffic, regardless of its origin, enabling it to detect attacks originating within your network. This could be anything from a malware program sending out private data or running an illicit chat server to a spy computer hidden by a disgruntled employee in a corner of the server closet.

A NIDS may take the form of a stand-alone appliance, but more often, it's software running on a computer that's dedicated to collecting and analyzing data. NIDS software can also run on a production computer that's used for other things, but if it's required to analyze a large quantity of network data, it can adversely affect the computer's performance for other tasks. Ideally, a NIDS should be installed in a logical position on the network where it's able to see all the traffic that reaches the computers you're trying to protect — in other words, behind your firewall, if you use a stand-alone firewall. If you have a DMZ, you may opt to install a NIDS there instead (or in addition), where it can provide advance warning of potential attacks before they ever reach your production network.

Using Snort as a NIDS

If a NIDS sounds useful to you and if you want to use your Mac to run NIDS software, the best choice is probably Sourcefire's Snort (www.snort.org), a free, open-source NIDS/NIPS tool that's extremely popular and well-supported on many different platforms. It's not the only Mac-compatible NIDS program (I mention others later in this section), but it's the one about which you can find the most extensive documentation and help.

Snort relies on rules to describe the signatures it looks for. You can write your own rules, but it makes more sense to rely primarily on the thousands of rules created and maintained by Snort's developers — and updated constantly, as new threats are discovered. The ruleset package isn't included with Snort; you must download it separately and move the rules manually to the right location. Before you can download the Snort ruleset, you must be a registered Snort user. Registration is free, but the ruleset you can download as a free user is always at least 30 days out of date. In order to stay on top of the very latest rules, you must be a paid subscriber. Subscriptions cost $29.99 per year for personal use or $499.00 for business use.

Setting up Snort is a nontrivial exercise. Although you can get a basic installation up and running in less than half an hour, you may want to add several more pieces in order to make it truly useful. Because of a chain of dependencies in these various pieces, setup can be a bit of a chore.

Note

Once upon a time, there was a program called HenWen, which not only provided a complete, Mac OS X–native GUI for Snort but even bundled Snort itself right in the application and included helpful add-on tools, such as Guardian (described later in this chapter). Alas, HenWen hasn't been updated in several years, and the most recent version isn't fully compatible with Leopard or Snow Leopard. Therefore, unfortunately, modern Mac OS X users wanting to run Snort must spend some quality time on the command line. ■

Installing and configuring Snort

Before you begin the process of setting up Snort, understand that it requires considerable mucking around in Terminal — and perhaps some trial and error to get everything working just the way you want. Although you can certainly download and compile the Snort source code from scratch, that process requires even more steps because of a number of obscure settings that must be changed and extra software that must be installed to work on Mac OS X. Therefore, I recommend using MacPorts to install Snort, which takes care of some of those dependencies and extra steps for you automatically.

To install Snort and configure it for basic operation, follow these steps:

1. **If you haven't already done so at some point in the past, download MacPorts from** www.macports.org **(be sure to get the version appropriate for your version of Mac OS X) and then run the installer.**

2. **Open Terminal, which is located in** /Applications/Utilities.

3. **To install Snort, type** sudo port install snort +server. The +server flag configures Snort to run automatically at startup — a setup that would otherwise require extra effort. However, if you don't want Snort to run at startup, you can leave off the +server part of the command.

4. **To register as a Snort user (required to download rules), go to** www.snort.org/signup, **fill out the form, and then click Sign Up.** The Snort site sends you an email message. Click the activation link in this message to verify your address and activate your account.

5. **To download the rules, go to** www.snort.org, **click the Sign In button, sign in using your newly created credentials, click the Get Rules button, and then download the version of the rules listed under "Sourcefire VRT Certified Rules — The Official Snort Ruleset (registered-user release)" that corresponds to your version of Snort.** That should be a version number, such as 2.8, rather than Current. The gzipped .tar file should unzip automatically. Double-click the .tar file to decompress the ruleset archive, which should be a folder with a name similar to snortrules-snapshot-2.8_s.

Note

The Snort ruleset is quite large — nearly 100MB compressed and nearly 500MB when expanded. ∎

6. **Back in Terminal, move into the folder in which the Snort ruleset is located.** For example: cd ~/Downloads/snortrules-snapshot-2.8_s. Modify the command as necessary to go to the appropriate folder.

7. **Copy the rules folder to the proper location by typing** sudo cp -R rules /opt/local/ etc/snort.

8. **Move a few other important files into their proper locations by typing** sudo cp etc/*. config /opt/local/etc/snort.

9. **Modify the Snort configuration file by following these steps:**

    1. Copy the sample file and then open it in nano:

        ```
        cd /opt/local/etc/snort
        sudo cp snort.conf.dist snort.conf
        sudo nano snort.conf
        ```

    2. Locate this section:

        ```
        # Path to your rules files (this can be a relative path)
        # Note for Windows users:  You are advised to make this an
          absolute path,
        # such as:  c:\snort\rules
        var RULE_PATH ../rules
        ```

    3. Change the last line so that it reads as follows:

        ```
        var RULE_PATH /opt/local/etc/snort/rules
        ```

10. **Press Control+X to exit** nano, **press Y to confirm you want to save changes, and then press Return to confirm the file name.**

11. **Create a directory to hold Snort log files by typing** sudo mkdir /var/log/snort.

You're now ready to run Snort — although you may have to return to the snort.conf file to make a few more modifications depending on what happens.

Running Snort from Terminal

Before you do anything else, you should run Snort in its simplest mode (which simply displays packet headers on the screen) just to confirm that it works. Type **sudo snort -v** to do this.

If Snort is working correctly, your screen should fill with network data that Snort has sniffed. To stop Snort, press Control+C.

Some other basic options are worth knowing:

- `-i`. By default, Snort listens on port en0 (normally your built-in Ethernet connection). To listen on a different interface, use the `-i` flag. For example, to listen on en1, normally used for AirPort, type **sudo snort -i en1 -v**.

- `-d` and `-e`. To capture more data, you can add one or both of the following flags: `-d` (which adds application data in transit) and `-e` (which adds data link layer headers). You can combine them with `-v` in any order — for example `-vde` or `-dev`.

- `-l`. To save data to a log file in addition to displaying it on-screen, use the `-l` flag, followed by the log location. In the configuration I've recommended, that's `/var/log/snort`, so the entire command might look like **sudo snort -vde -l /var/log/snort**.

- `-D`. Run Snort as a daemon (in the background). Once you've got Snort configured the way you want it to be and have confirmed that it runs correctly in the foreground, use this flag to run it in the background so you need not keep a Terminal window open.

So far, though, Snort has ignored the ruleset we installed earlier. To use the ruleset, which puts Snort in what it calls IDS mode, you must use the `-c` flag, followed by the location of `snort.conf`. For example, this command runs Snort in IDS mode, capturing several different kinds of data and storing them in a log file:

```
sudo snort -vde -l /var/log/snort/ -c /opt/local/etc/snort/snort.conf
```

In this mode, Snort captures only the data specified by the rules in the ruleset, which is to say much less than it does otherwise! This is a good thing because with a more focused set of data, there's less to look at and analyze, and interesting bits are thus more evident.

When you type the previous command for the first time, you may get a scary-sounding `Fatal Error, Quitting` message. Depending on a large number of variables, including which version of Snort and the ruleset you're using, your Mac's configuration, and which other changes you may have made manually to `snort.conf` or individual rule files, some things might not work quite right, leading to error messages. To solve the problem, look at the line immediately above the `Fatal Error` line. For example, suppose you see this error message:

```
ERROR: /opt/local/etc/snort/rules/exploit.rules(143) => Invalid port:
    [8008,8028]
```

This means Snort can't understand the port specification on line 143 of the file `rules/exploit.rules`. You could edit the file in question, go to that line, and either correct the problem (if you can tell what it is) or comment out the line (if you can't) or you could edit `snort.conf` by commenting out the line that loads this file — for example:

```
#include $RULE_PATH/exploit.rules
```

It may require some trial and error to identify and correct or comment out all the lines (or files) that produce error messages, but working your way through them can help you learn Snort syntax — and the limitations of your system. Don't forget to consult the Snort Users Manual, included with Snort, for background information and advice.

As an experiment, run Snort using the previous command for a few minutes to collect a bit of data and then press Control+C to stop it; then, find the name of the file you want to examine:

```
ls /var/log/snort
```

This should produce a list of file names in that directory, such as the following:

```
drwxr-xr-x    5 root   wheel    170 Jun 10 16:20 .
drwxr-xr-x   75 root   wheel   2550 Jun 10 15:00 ..
-rw-------    1 root   wheel   1724 Jun 10 16:20 alert
-rw-------    1 root   wheel   3948 Jun 10 16:09 snort.log.1244642967
-rw-------    1 root   wheel    240 Jun 10 16:20 snort.log.1244643634
```

The `alert` file is perhaps the most important one, because it contains records of only those events Snort thinks are worth alerting an administrator about. It's a plain text file, which you can view with `cat`, `less`, or any text editor.

The other Snort logs are stored in a binary format; to view them, you must use Snort with the `-r` flag. To examine the last log in the list, for example, you would then type this command:

```
sudo snort -r /var/log/snort/snort.log.1244643634
```

The output, which may go on for many screens, should look just like what you saw while Snort was running. For example, you may see a lot of blocks like these:

```
06/10-15:44:27.809129 192.168.0.47:55317 -> 192.168.0.255:5353
UDP TTL:128 TOS:0x0 ID:10755 IpLen:20 DgmLen:99 Len: 71
00 00 00 00 00 02 00 00 00 00 00 00 0C 5F 68 6F  .............._ho
73 74 2D 63 6F 6E 66 69 67 04 5F 75 64 70 05 6C  st-config._udp.l
6F 63 61 6C 00 00 21 00 01 0D 5F 6E 65 74 77 6F  ocal..!..._netwo
72 6B 2D 73 63 61 6E 04 5F 74 63 70 05 6C 6F 63  rk-scan._tcp.loc
61 6C 00 00 21 00 01                             al..!..
=+=+=+=+=+=+=+=+=+=+=+=+=+=+=+=+=+=+=+=+=+=+=+=+=+=+=+=+=+=+=+=+=+=+=+=
    +=+=+
06/10-15:44:28.504451 209.85.227.157:80 -> 192.168.0.54:2336
TCP TTL:54 TOS:0x0 ID:65224 IpLen:20 DgmLen:183
***AP*** Seq: 0x958C6683  Ack: 0x8A505E81  Win: 0x2358  TcpLen: 20
64 69 76 20 69 64 3D 61 75 73 5C 78 33 65 5C 78  div id=aus\x3e\x
33 63 64 69 76 20 69 64 3D 61 75 62 67 5C 78 33  3cdiv id=aubg\x3
65 5C 78 33 63 2F 64 69 76 5C 78 33 65 5C 78 33  e\x3c/div\x3e\x3
63 64 69 76 20 69 64 3D 61 64 73 5C 78 33 65 5C  cdiv id=ads\x3e\
78 33 63 75 6C 20 69 64 3D 6C 6F 61 64 20 73 74  x3cul id=load st
79 6C 65 3D 5C 22 64 69 73 70 6C 61 79 3A 6E 6F  yle=\"display:no
6E 65 5C 22 5C 78 33 65 5C 78 33 63 6C 69 20 73  ne\"\x3e\x3cli s
74 79 6C 65 3D 5C 22 77 69 64 74 68 3A 31 30 30  tyle=\"width:100
25 5C 22 5C 78 33 65 5C 78 33 63 74 61 0D 0A     %\"\x3e\x3cta..
=+=+=+=+=+=+=+=+=+=+=+=+=+=+=+=+=+=+=+=+=+=+=+=+=+=+=+=+=+=+=+=+=+=+=+=
    +=+=+
```

```
06/10-15:44:28.606001 89.2.0.1:53 -> 192.168.0.54:1025
UDP TTL:61 TOS:0x0 ID:0 IpLen:20 DgmLen:169 DF Len: 141
4A FF 81 80 00 01 00 05 00 00 00 00 07 70 61 67   J...........pag
65 61 64 32 11 67 6F 6F 67 6C 65 73 79 6E 64 69   ead2.googlesyndi
63 61 74 69 6F 6E 03 63 6F 6D 00 00 01 00 01 C0   cation.com......
0C 00 05 00 01 00 00 26 B2 00 12 06 70 61 67 65   .......&....page
61 64 01 6C 06 67 6F 6F 67 6C 65 C0 26 C0 3B 00   ad.l.google.&.;.
01 00 01 00 00 00 AA 00 04 D1 55 E3 A5 C0 3B 00   ..........U...;.
01 00 01 00 00 00 AA 00 04 D1 55 E3 A7 C0 3B 00   ..........U...;.
01 00 01 00 00 00 AA 00 04 D1 55 E3 A4 C0 3B 00   ..........U...;.
01 00 01 00 00 00 AA 00 04 D1 55 E3 A6            ..........U..
```

Very exciting, isn't it? Unless you enjoy decoding long strings of hexadecimal data on the fly, probably not so much. So, although this raw format might be great for people writing their own analysis software, what most people find more useful is a nicely formatted version of the data. Or, better yet, a nicely formatted version of only the interesting data, which is to say the alerts produced by improper access, not all the random packets that fly across the network. You can get this (after a fashion) by using a Snort plug-in called BASE.

Using Snort with BASE

If you want a more user-friendly way to look at Snort data, try Basic Analysis and Security Engine, or BASE — an add-on to Snort that lets you view nicely formatted data in a web browser (http://sourceforge. net/projects/secureideas). The end results you get with BASE are vastly more helpful than what the raw log files show you, but there's a catch. Setting up BASE is a bit complicated because it depends on a database (which Snort can optionally use to store its data), and that in turn requires that you make modifications to Snort's configuration. So, a number of steps lie ahead, but they're all worth it given the improvements they make in Snort's data reporting.

Assuming you've already set up Snort according to the directions offered earlier, follow these additional steps to get it working with BASE:

Note

These instructions are loosely based on Mark Duling's excellent article on Snort configuration, located at http://homepage.mac.com/duling/halfdozen/Snort-Howto.html. ∎

1. **To install the necessary software packages using MacPorts, type the following commands.** If you've already installed Snort, you must deactivate it and then run the install command again because in this case, it's being configured with a different option. Some of these commands take a while to complete; wait until the command prompt returns.

    ```
    sudo port deactivate snort
    sudo port install snort +mysql5 +server
    sudo port install mysql5-server
    sudo port install base
    ```

2. **To set up the files and folders BASE needs, type the following commands:**

    ```
    cd /Library/WebServer/Documents
    sudo ln -s /opt/local/share/adodb5 adodb
    sudo ln -s /opt/local/share/base base
    cd /opt/local/share/base
    sudo cp base_conf.php.dist base_conf.php
    ```

3. **You must also edit the BASE configuration file by typing** sudo nano /opt/local/share/base/ base_conf.php. Look for the lines in the file beginning with the variables shown and then modify them so they look like this, substituting *MySQLsnortpassword* both places it appears with a password of your choosing, which will be used for the Snort user to access the MySQL database:

```
$BASE_urlpath      = '/base';
$DBlib_path        = '/Library/WebServer/Documents/adodb';
$alert_dbname      = 'snort';
$alert_host        = '127.0.0.1';
$alert_password    = 'MySQLsnortpassword';
$archive_dbname    = 'snort';
$archive_host      = '127.0.0.1';
$archive_password  = 'MySQLsnortpassword';
```

4. **Press Control+X to exit** nano, **press Y to confirm you want to save changes, and then press Return to confirm the file name.**

5. **To adjust your Snort configuration to work with a MySQL database, open it in** nano **by typing** sudo nano /opt/local/etc/snort/snort.conf.

6. **Locate the section beginning with this label:**

```
# database: log to a variety of databases
# -------------------------------------
```

7. **Add a line at the bottom of the section, substituting** *MySQLsnortpassword* **with the one you selected earlier and adjusting the** dbname:

```
output database: alert, mysql, user=snort password=MySQLsnortpassword
    dbname=snort host=localhost
```

8. **Press Control+X to exit** nano, **press Y to confirm you want to save changes, and then press Return to confirm the file name.**

9. **Perform a first-time MySQL setup by typing** sudo -u mysql mysql_install_db5.

10. **To run MySQL as well as make sure it loads when you start your Mac, type** sudo launchctl load -w /Library/LaunchDaemons/org.macports.mysql5-server.plist.

11. **To set the password for the MySQL root user, type** sudo mysqladmin5 -u root password *MySQLrootpassword*, **substituting** *MySQLrootpassword* **with a password of your choosing, which will be used for the MySQL root user.**

12. **To add a Snort user to MySQL, type** mysql5 -u root -p **to run MySQL interactively.**

13. **When prompted, type the password you selected in step 11 and then press Return.**

14. **When the** mysql> **prompt appears, type each of the following commands in sequence, substituting** *MySQLsnortpassword* **with the password you selected earlier.** Be sure to include the semicolon after each line before pressing Return:

```
create database snort;
grant INSERT,SELECT on root.* to snort@localhost;
grant CREATE,INSERT,SELECT,DELETE,UPDATE on snort.* to
    snort@localhost;
grant CREATE,INSERT,SELECT,DELETE,UPDATE on snort.* to snort;
SET PASSWORD FOR snort@localhost =
    OLD_PASSWORD('MySQLsnortpassword');
exit
```

15. To add the tables to MySQL that Snort and BASE need, type the following two commands, typing your root password (from step 11) each time as prompted:

```
cat /opt/local/share/snort/schemas/create_mysql | mysql5 -u root -p
    snort
cat /opt/local/share/base/sql/create_base_tbls_mysql.sql | mysql5 -u
    root -p snort
```

16. To modify Apache's configuration file so that it uses PHP (included with Leopard and Snow Leopard), follow these steps:

   1. Type sudo nano /etc/apache2/httpd.conf.

   2. Locate this line:

   ```
   #LoadModule php5_module         libexec/apache2/libphp5.so
   ```

   3. Uncomment it by removing the # at the beginning:

   ```
   LoadModule php5_module          libexec/apache2/libphp5.so
   ```

   4. Locate this section:

   ```
   <IfModule dir_module>
       DirectoryIndex index.html
   </IfModule>
   ```

   5. Add index.php to the end of the middle line:

   ```
   <IfModule dir_module>
       DirectoryIndex index.html index.php
   </IfModule>
   ```

   6. Press Control+X to exit nano, press Y to confirm you want to save changes, and then press Return to confirm the file name.

17. **If Web Sharing is already turned on, restart it by typing** sudo apachectl graceful. If it's not already running, type **sudo apachectl start**.

18. **To run Snort in the background (and without saving its data in a local file, because it's now using a MySQL database), type** sudo snort -D -vde -c /opt/local/etc/snort/snort.conf.

19. **Configure Snort to run automatically at startup by using the following command:**

```
sudo launchctl load -w /Library/LaunchDaemons/org.macports.snort.
    plist
```

20. **To see your lovely web-formatted Snort data, point your browser at** http://localhost/base/. If all goes well, you should see something similar to Figure 22.1.

FIGURE 22.1

It took a lot of steps to get here, but this image shows how BASE might look in your web browser once you have it configured to analyze and report on Snort's findings.

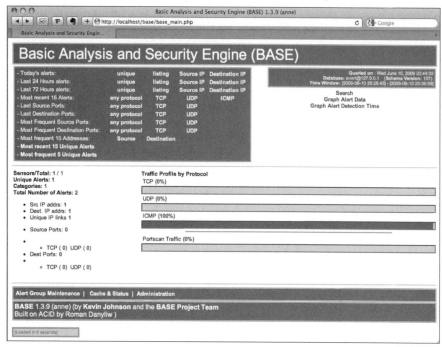

The BASE display should look pretty boring unless or until attacks or network probes begin appearing on the network that match Snort's rules, in which case more data appears in the window and you can click any of the numerous links to get more detail on any event. For example, if you click the ICMP link in the Most recent 15 Alerts row, you might see something similar to Figure 22.2.

BASE's display updates itself automatically every so often; you need not reload the page manually. Unfortunately, BASE doesn't email alerts automatically, but after alerts have appeared, you can use the Administration link at the bottom of the page to email alerts manually to a system administrator. To learn more about BASE, consult the documentation located in /opt/local/share/base/docs.

Note

To learn about other Snort add-ons, visit www.snort.org/downloads/additional-downloads. ■

FIGURE 22.2

BASE lets you drill down in any number of ways to get more information about the events that interest you.

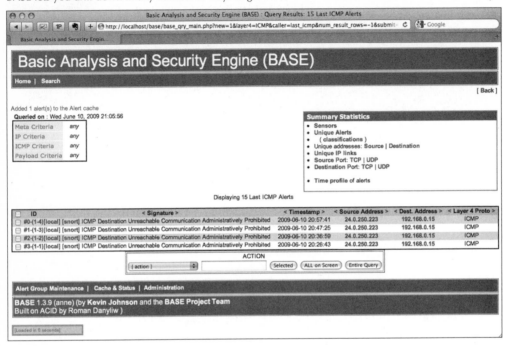

Other third-party NIDS tools

Although BASE provides a capable and user-friendly view of your Snort data, you can also use any number of other tools to analyze it, report on it, or take any other appropriate action. The following tools are all free, open-source packages that can look for interesting patterns in logs generated by Snort or other NIDS software — but that don't perform the data collection tasks themselves:

- **Logsurfer:** www.crypt.gen.nz/logsurfer
- **PreludeIDS Universal SIM (Security Information Management):** www.prelude-ids.com
- **SEC (Simple Event Correlator):** http://kodu.neti.ee/~risto/sec

In terms of monitoring and collecting raw data, I'm aware of only one other Mac-compatible NIDS program in the same category as Snort: Bro Intrusion Detection System (www.bro-ids.org). Like Snort, Bro is free and open source; it also has a reasonably large community of supporters, although Bro is still much less well-known than Snort. In addition to reporting on unwanted network access, Bro can take actions such as running shell scripts — which could enable it to work with firewalls or other mechanisms to block access, turning it into a NIPS of sorts.

Network Intrusion Prevention Systems

Finding possible intrusions is helpful to a system administrator who wants to learn what the bad guys are up to and take action, manually, to improve the network's defenses. However, even the best administrator can't react instantly or be available to respond to new threats 24 hours a day. Moreover, by the time a NIDS has noticed a problem, some damage may already be done. As a result, there's an even more powerful tool, a network intrusion prevention system, or NIPS. A NIPS relies on the same infrastructure as a NIDS but adds a component: a hook that ties into a system that can cut off an attacker's access, such as a firewall or router. An administrator can typically configure a NIPS such that whenever malicious traffic matching a certain description or level of severity appears, a new firewall rule is added or other appropriate action is taken to protect the network automatically.

Unlike a NIDS, which can sniff network traffic from anywhere on the network, a NIPS — or at least the component that does the blocking of network traffic — must reside in a device that's logically between the outside world and the local network. So, for example, a Mac that uses software to act as a NIPS could be connected between the gateway or firewall and a router that mediates Internet access for the rest of the network, or it can be the same Mac that functions as a network firewall; but one way or another, the NIPS can't block network traffic unless the data is forced to go through it.

Using Snort as a NIPS

Because Snort is so good at detecting network intrusions, wouldn't it be great if you could plug it directly into a firewall so that malicious access is automatically blocked? Couldn't the NIDS go just one step further and become a NIPS?

This notion hasn't escaped the attention of Snort's designers, and as a matter of fact, they've built just such a capability into the program. By operating Snort in what's known as inline mode, it no longer merely sniffs network traffic passively but interacts directly with a firewall called `iptables`, automatically updating the firewall's rules to block access by any host that's shown itself to be acting badly. So, the combination of Snort and `iptables` amounts to a dynamic firewall — one that adjusts itself to new threats — even previously unknown ones — in real time.

However, when it comes to making use of that capability, I have some good news and some bad news.

The bad news is that `iptables` doesn't run on a Mac. Even though it's Unix software, `iptables` is designed specifically for Linux and depends on components of the Linux kernel that don't exist in Mac OS X. Therefore, for want of the necessary infrastructure, Snort can't run in inline mode on a Mac.

But here's some good news: You can work around this limitation with a little clever trickery in the form of a free Perl script by Roland Gafner called Guardian (`www.chaotic.org/guardian/`). Guardian watches your Snort log, and every time a new attack appears there, it sends a one-line command to the IPFW firewall, adding the attacker's IP address to its list of blocked hosts. By default, the host remains blocked for 24 hours, but you can adjust that to your liking. It's not true integration, and the Guardian script doesn't have every feature you might want, but it makes for a quick-and-dirty (and free!) solution.

Before you attempt to implement this setup, be aware of the following:

- You must already have IPFW up and running properly.

Cross-Ref

For more on IPFW and the third-party tools for configuring it, see Chapter 17. ∎

- You must already have Snort up and running properly — and be saving its logs to a file (whether or not you also store logs in a database).

- Assuming a reasonably standard configuration of IPFW, this arrangement protects only the Mac it's running on, not your entire network. Unless you have a Mac (with two Ethernet interfaces) configured to filter all your network traffic through its IPFW firewall, this solution is for one computer only.

- Setting this up requires a bit of technical acumen — I provide only the basic steps here, not every last detail needed to configure, test, and maintain the system.

- Because Guardian doesn't pay attention to the severity or nature of a suspected attack, the possibility of false positives exists, which could lead to blocking legitimate computers from accessing your Mac. You can, however, configure Guardian to ignore certain IP addresses altogether.

If you're content with these disclaimers, follow these steps — again, presented only at a high level — to use Snort as a NIPS:

1. **Download Guardian from** `www.chaotic.org/guardian/` **and then decompress it.**

2. **Edit the** `guardian.conf` **file.** It contains comments explaining each setting, but in particular, note the following:

   - The interface should be set to whichever interface your Mac uses to connect to the Internet, such as en0 (typically your built-in Ethernet interface) or en1 (typically your AirPort card).

   - To ignore one or more IP addresses, put them in the file /etc/guardian.ignore.

   - To adjust how long a host is blocked, change the TimeLimit setting. The default, 86400 (seconds), is equivalent to 24 hours.

3. **Copy the guardian script itself,** `guardian.pl`, **to the** `/usr/local/bin` **directory and then copy the edited** `guardian.conf` **file to** `/etc`.

4. **In the scripts folder inside the guardian folder, find the scripts** `freebsd_block.sh` **and** `freebsd_unblock.sh`, **rename these** `block.sh` **and** `unblock.sh`, **respectively, and then copy them to a folder in your path.** I recommend /usr/local/bin — the same directory as the guardian script itself — to make them easy to find.

5. **To run Guardian manually, type** sudo guardian.pl -c /etc/guardian.conf.

6. **To run Guardian automatically, use** `cron`, `launchd`, **or another scheduling mechanism of your choice.**

I recommend closely monitoring your Snort log and your IPFW ruleset after turning on Guardian to make sure it's not overreacting to harmless network activity.

Using IPNetSentryX or IPNetRouterX as a NIPS

Two products from Sustainable Softworks (`www.sustworks.com`) — IPNetSentryX ($60) and IPNetRouterX ($100) — include what amounts to dynamic firewalls, which is to say they can react to changing network conditions and automatically block access as needed. That sounds very much indeed like a NIPS, and although one could quibble that they're less powerful or flexible than a true stand-alone NIPS, they can more than get the job done for the typical Mac user (or server).

Cross-Ref

For more on using IPNetSentryX and IPNetRouterX as firewalls, see Chapter 17. ∎

The dynamic firewall itself is the same between the two programs, but IPNetRouterX includes a boatload of other routing features. As such, it can be used to provide NIPS protection to an entire network — as long as it's implemented at an appropriate place in the chain of network devices, and on a Mac with two Ethernet interfaces — whereas IPNetSentryX provides protection only for the Mac it's running on.

In fact, either program could also behave as a NIDS; although they're designed to block unwanted traffic by default, the programs can take almost any sort of action in response to unwanted traffic, including sending an email alert or running an AppleScript.

IPNetSentryX, shown in Figure 22.3, and IPNetRouterX each come preconfigured with a set of hierarchical rules that can identify and keep out many kinds of malicious traffic. These aren't static pattern-matching rules, however, so they're not like the kinds of signatures Snort uses to identify specific threats. Rather, they identify behavior matching broad (and flexible) categories of threats. On the downside, the built-in rules are neither exhaustive nor perfect, and they're not updated on a regular schedule, so if they turn out to be insufficient for your needs, you have to figure out how to create your own — not the simplest process.

FIGURE 22.3

The default rules built into IPNetSentryX and IPNetRouterX can dynamically watch for — and block — many kinds of illicit network activity.

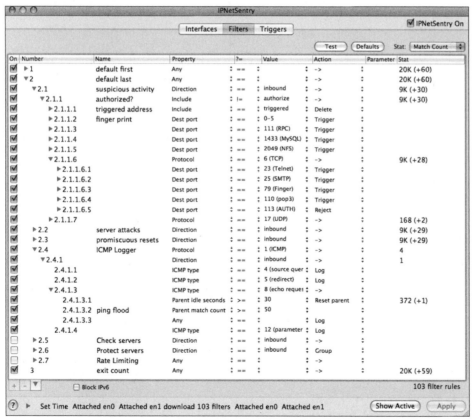

In addition, although IPNetSentryX and IPNetRouterX have a Traffic Discovery feature (discussed ahead) that enables an administrator to determine certain long-term usage patterns, this doesn't lead to automatic identification of anomalous traffic, as Snort can provide.

Basic usage

IPNetSentryX and IPNetRouterX are configured by default to watch for and block a number of types of probes, scans, and fingerprinting attempts. To turn on either program and enjoy immediate protection, follow these steps:

1. **Install the software per the developer's instructions and then double-click the application.**

2. **In the main window, of which IPNetRouterX's is shown in Figure 22.4, click the Defaults button and then click Apply.** This configures the program's preferences to their factory presets.

FIGURE 22.4

IPNetRouterX's main window looks like this in its original, default state.

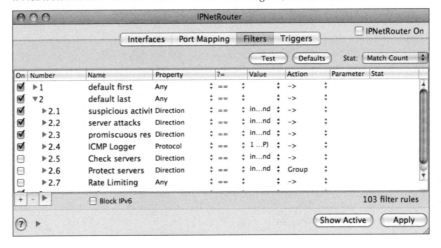

---

3. **Click the check box for IPNetRouter On or IPNetSentry On, depending on which program you're using.** The firewall immediately becomes active.

How triggers work

These two products' NIPS capabilities come largely from their use of *triggers*, which identify troublesome hosts. Although a single rule can block or drop individual matching packets, triggers are much more interesting because they persist over time and provide information that another rule can use.

Here's a basic idea of how they work. A rule specifies a certain condition and says that the action to take when that condition is met is "Trigger." For example, notice in Figure 22.5 that rule 2.1.1.2, with the name "finger print," has Trigger in the Action column. This rule says that if the destination port of any packet is 0–5, the host that sent it belongs on the naughty list (under the assumption that legitimate hosts would never try to contact any of those ports).

FIGURE 22.5

This portion of the default rules in IPNetSentryX and IPNetRouterX shows how a rule can result in an IP address being added to the Triggers list and how future rules can then use that information to influence their behavior.

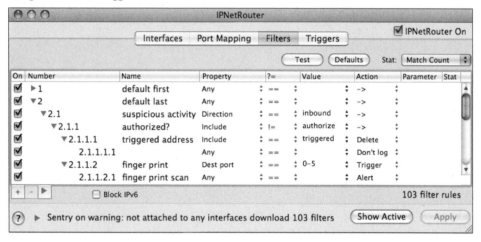

Now, suppose an incoming packet does in fact match a rule with an action of Trigger. The originating IP address appears in the Triggers pane, as shown in Figure 22.6. By default, hosts added to this list remain there for an hour, but you can change the default time by using the Default Duration pop-up menu at the bottom of the window or change the time for any particular host by clicking the pop-up menu in the Duration column. Be sure to click Apply after making any changes in this pane.

FIGURE 22.6

The Triggers pane displays the "naughty" list — the IP addresses of the hosts that matched a rule indicating severe misbehavior.

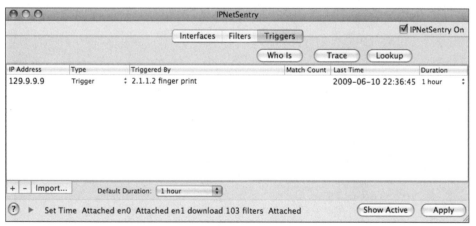

Then, referring back to Figure 22.5, notice rule 2.1.1.1. Its value is "triggered," and its action is "Delete." That means the next time an incoming packet comes in whose address is on the Triggers list, that packet is deleted — end of story. You could change the action to something else, if you prefer — such as Reject, Drop Connection, or Delay — but, essentially, that one rule keeps out all future access from any IP address that another rule adds to the Triggers list, for as long as the default setting specifies (which can be anywhere from a minute to forever).

Therefore, the main challenge confronting you as a firewall administrator (apart from learning the unusual syntax of these programs) is how to identify problematic network behavior that isn't already handled by an existing rule. Once you've discovered a new type of attack or malicious behavior, you can settle down in a comfy chair with the programs' documentation and determine how to adjust their settings to deal with them. One way to do this is to use the programs' Traffic Discovery feature. It's not automatic, but it does provide very useful information.

Using Traffic Discovery

To use Traffic Discovery, choose Tool ⇨ Traffic Discovery in either application. In the window that appears, click the Traffic Discovery On check box. You'll then see something similar to Figure 22.7. By default, the window displays a list of all services the computer is using, along with details about the interface, last time used, number of bytes in and out, and other information. If you see large numbers in one of the Bytes columns or an unusual item in the Name or Service column, you can investigate it further.

FIGURE 22.7

The Traffic Discovery window in IPNetSentryX and IPNetRouterX gives you an easily readable view of which processes on your Mac are sending data where.

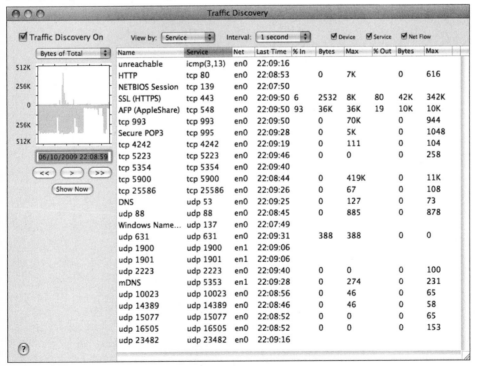

One useful way to get additional information on your computer's network usage is to choose Net Flow from the View by pop-up menu. The display changes as shown in Figure 22.8. For each open connection, the window shows the IP address and port for both the source and destination as well as the quantity of data transferred and the last time that combination was in use.

Unfortunately, Traffic Discovery is resource-intensive and chews up a lot of disk space, so it's not a good idea to have it on all the time — except perhaps on a dedicated Mac that's just running one of these programs.

FIGURE 22.8

The Net Flow view lets you see both the source and destination (by IP address and port) of all active network connections on your Mac.

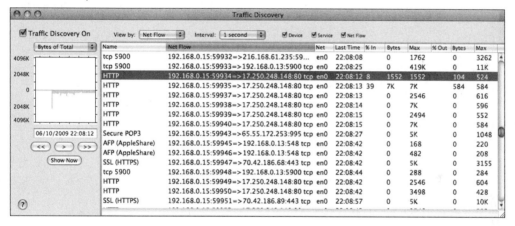

Using Intego NetBarrier

It doesn't approach the level of sophistication offered by Snort, IPNetSentryX, or IPNetRouterX, but Intego's NetBarrier software (www.intego.com/netbarrier/, $49.95), about which much has been said elsewhere in this book, includes a few NIPS features that far surpass the other options in ease of use.

Cross-Ref

For more on NetBarrier, see Chapter 10 (web privacy features), Chapter 14 (anti-malware features), and Chapter 17 (firewall features). ■

You configure NetBarrier's NIPS capabilities primarily in the Policy window (choose View ➪ Policy). NetBarrier offers six anti-intrusion features — all of which, naturally, apply only to the Mac on which the software is installed (making them, according to some definitions at least, HIPS features). To enable one of the features, click its check box (if it's not already selected); all are enabled by default except Ping Broadcasts:

- **Buffer Overflow Attacks.** These exploits take advantage of programming errors that enable software to store data in parts of memory that the software isn't supposed to be using.

- **Intrusion Attempts.** NetBarrier uses this term narrowly to refer to repeated unsuccessful login attempts — whether via file sharing, web sharing, or email.

- **Ping Attacks.** One form of a denial-of-service (DoS) attack involves sending ping packets with such great frequency that your computer is unable to keep up with them, which can cause it to slow down or crash.

- **Ping Broadcasts.** This is a technique used to discover active IP addresses on a network, in which a computer pings a special address that rebroadcasts the ping to all the other computers on the same subnet.

- **Port Scans.** A port scan is a procedure (which can be used for good or evil) to discover which ports on a computer have software actively listening on them.

- **SYN Flooding.** Similar to ping attacks, this procedure sends only the SYN (synchronize) portion of each network handshake — but does so repeatedly in an effort to bring down the target system.

For each option you enable, you can configure a number of other options, which appear when an item is selected in the list on the left. For example, if you select Port Scans, as shown in Figure 22.9, you can choose whether to be alerted in one or more ways (NIDS behavior) or whether the offending IP address should be put in NetBarrier's Stop List — and, if so, for how long (NIPS behavior, reminiscent of the triggers in IPNetSentryX and IPNetRouterX). In addition, if you click the Advanced tab, you can adjust the sensitivity — that is, how frequent pings must be to trigger an alert. Each other anti-intrusion feature has its own set of configurable options.

FIGURE 22.9

NetBarrier's Policy window lets you activate any of a half-dozen NIPS features, all of which (like Port Scans, shown here) offer a variety of configurable options.

In addition, if you click Options at the bottom of the list of intrusion types, as shown in Figure 22.10, you can adjust several global settings, including using Stealth Mode, in which no replies are sent to pings.

Although NetBarrier's NIPS features are specific to a single Mac and have only limited configurability, their superior ease of use makes them an excellent choice for individual users and small networks.

FIGURE 22.10

The Options view of NetBarrier's Policy window displays settings that apply globally to all the NIPS features in the program.

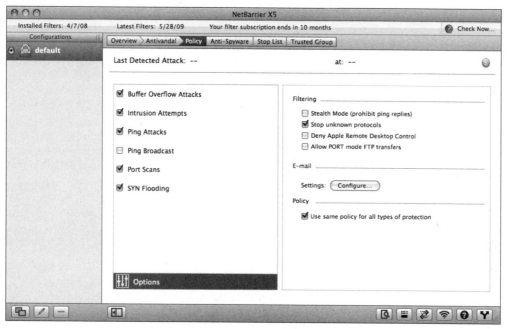

Information Leak Detection Systems

Now we come to the other side of the network monitoring equation: keeping an eye on data that leaves (or attempts to leave) your local network. Software or hardware that does this is known as (among other things) an *information leak detection system*, or ILDS. Even though the term refers to detection, ILDS products usually offer protection too — blocking outgoing data that should remain within the network.

To take a basic example, suppose you're setting up a Mac for family members — some of whom lack technical savvy or are a bit absentminded. You may want to make sure they don't accidentally send information such as credit card numbers, bank account information, or even your home address over the Internet insecurely (through email, for example, or using a non-SSL-protected web page). An ILDS can do this by watching data going over the network, looking for matches to keywords or other patterns you've designated, and blocking traffic that contains it — perhaps displaying an alert so the user knows what happened. Of course, a full-blown ILDS is overkill for an individual Mac, and software such as NetBarrier (discussed ahead) can competently keep tabs on the outgoing data for single computers.

However, if you're protecting sensitive data on a corporate network, the situation is a bit different. It may be impractical to install and maintain monitoring software on each computer, and some central authority may want to determine what data should be blocked. For example, you may want to prevent employees from mentioning a top-secret product under development, divulging personal information about clients or patients, or sending information relevant to a pending lawsuit to someone not authorized to see it. In cases such as these, installing a network-wide ILDS appliance (such as the GTB Inspector, `www.gtbtechnologies.com`) between your network and your gateway may be just what you need.

Unfortunately, I'm not aware of any ready-to-use network ILDS packages designed to run natively on Mac OS X. Short of buying a stand-alone box or looking for software that runs on another platform, you may be able to hack something together using Snort or rely on host-specific products even though they lack centralized management and protect just one Mac at a time.

Using Snort for ILDS

Because Snort, discussed at length earlier in this chapter, can monitor all the traffic on your local network, it can detect patterns of outgoing data as easily as patterns of incoming data. You have but to define one or more rules describing the patterns you want it to search for. Writing Snort rules requires more of an explanation than I can provide in this book — see the Snort documentation for details.

However, lacking a good set of pre-built ILDS rules, this could be a labor-intensive undertaking. In addition, Snort, by itself, is powerless to stop transmission of data. Even when coupled with a firewall, the best it can do is block all access to or from a particular IP address or port; it can't selectively filter out just certain email messages, chat sessions, or posts to web forms, for example.

Other ILDS options

Several other programs, already discussed in other contexts in this book, have ILDS-like capabilities, albeit ones that apply only to the Mac they're running on and match only exact strings (not regular expressions or wildcard patterns). Here are a few examples:

- **Internet Cleanup.** Network SpyAlert, one of the components of Internet Cleanup (`http://my.smithmicro.com/mac/cleanup/index.html`, $29.99), includes a feature called Personal Info Protector. Turn on this feature and supply any information you want to protect, and Internet Cleanup prevents your computer from sending it in an unencrypted form.

- **NetBarrier.** Yet another module of the ubiquitous NetBarrier is Data, shown in Figure 22.11. With the Protect my Data check box selected, the program watches for any information you've typed on this screen and then takes whatever action you specify in the Options view (such as displaying an alert or playing a sound) when you try to send it over the Internet. You can specify trusted services (such as an email program) that are allowed to send the information without intervention.

- **Norton Internet Security for Mac.** Norton Confidential, a constituent of Norton Internet Security for Mac (www.symantec.com/norton/macintosh, $79.95), includes a feature called Information Guard. As shown in Figure 22.12, if you enable Information Guard and type information (such as a credit card number), Norton Confidential can block the information from being sent over the Internet and optionally notify you when this happens.

FIGURE 22.11

NetBarrier's Data window lets you specify particular pieces of information that shouldn't be permitted to leave your computer over the network without express permission.

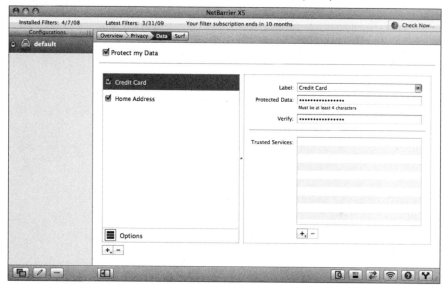

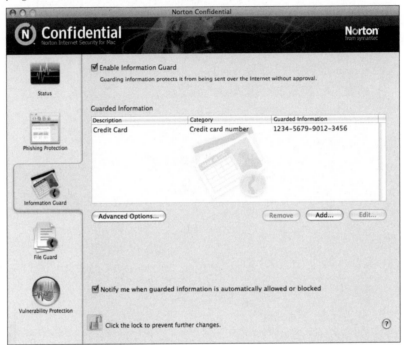

FIGURE 22.12

Norton Confidential takes much the same approach to protecting private information as Internet Cleanup and NetBarrier. List the data you want to protect, and the software alerts you if a program tries to send it unencrypted over the Internet.

Honeypot Monitoring

The final concept I want to mention in this chapter is that of a *honeypot*, a computer configured specifically to attract all the unsavory characters you normally try so hard to keep away from your Macs! Setting up a honeypot is something no one should undertake lightly — if you manage a small home or office network, especially one with few or no public servers, it's not worth your time or effort. However, honeypots can have value on large networks, especially those with high-value data or resources or those frequently the target of break-ins.

Because the design and administration of honeypots is a long and complex topic and this book is primarily geared toward those whose networks are too small to benefit from them, I've chosen not to provide detailed instructions here on setting them up. Nevertheless, honeypots are intriguing and useful enough that those interested in Mac security should have at least a passing acquaintance with how they work.

The main reason for honeypots is to provide a source of information — to help you, as a network administrator, discover exactly what the bad guys are up to without endangering your data. Based on what you see happening on the honeypot, you can take steps to protect your production computers and perhaps even predict imminent attacks.

Ordinarily, a honeypot's existence isn't advertised at all. It's just a computer sitting on your network, without any links or pointers to it whatsoever — but also with few or no security measures in place. The honeypot attracts hackers simply because it responds to network mapping, port scans, and other discovery techniques — it's visible and available in ways that most of your computers should not be. So, it should be among the first computers targeted when, during one of the innumerable random scans that are always taking place, someone stumbles upon your network.

Honeypots can take a number of forms, but they always have two common characteristics. First, the honeypot computer contains no useful data itself. It's not part of your production network, has no interesting files on it at all, and is in fact walled off from your active network by a reliable firewall. Thus, the honeypot can only, by definition, receive illegitimate traffic (unless it comes from you, of course). That in turn means that all the data you collect from it represents hacking activity. And second, a honeypot captures every piece of network data it receives (using Snort, for example, or another similar tool). In fact, if you installed a plain vanilla version of Mac OS X on an otherwise unused Mac, put it outside your firewall, and used Snort to monitor everything that came its way, that by itself could qualify it as a honeypot.

What I've just described is sometimes known as a high-interaction honeypot. If anyone were to try to connect to it from the outside, it would behave exactly as a Mac should because that's what it is! So, attackers can freely go about probing, scanning, and generally poking around — perhaps believing they've got access to a system with valuable data — and all the while, you're actually learning more about their behavior than they are about yours.

Of course, because a hacker could do some damage to that computer — installing malware, for example, or disabling it in some way — you couldn't allow it to serve as a public playground indefinitely. Sooner or later, you would want to restore it to a pristine state (preserving the logs that were generated, of course). Doing so repeatedly can take a lot of time and effort; meanwhile, you run a certain risk that an attacker might do more harm than you'd prepared for.

So, another option is a low-interaction honeypot, which limits the range of activities an attacker can engage in — but also gives you, the computer's operator, more control. In a low-interaction honeypot, specially designed software masquerades as real services. For example, you might have a program that pretends to be an FTP server or one that emulates Mac OS X's bash shell. The point of these impostors is to trick attackers into spending as much time as possible interacting with the computer as though it were the real thing, the better to collect information about what they're trying to accomplish and how — and to steal their time away from trying to hack your real computers.

One popular way of setting up low-interaction honeypots is to use a free, open-source software package called Honeyd (www.honeyd.org). Honeyd can emulate not just one program but thousands of distinct computers, each with its own IP address, even though it's running on a single CPU. You can use it to intercept data directed at any otherwise unused IP address on your network and, in so doing, make it harder for attackers to find legitimate machines. In addition, Honeyd can emulate a wide variety of operating systems and programs, so one of the fake IP addresses could appear to be a Windows XP computer running an FTP server and another could appear to be a Linux box running servers for SSH and Telnet.

Note
Honeyd can be made to run on Mac OS X, but it takes some doing and isn't for the faint of heart. There was once a Mac OS X GUI for Honeyd, called HoneyPotX, but it hasn't been updated since 2003 and doesn't work reliably on Leopard or Snow Leopard. ■

Summary

No matter how carefully you've configured and tested your firewall and no matter how thoroughly you've plugged known security holes, an attacker could potentially find another way in. Instead of setting up your network and assuming it'll always remain safe, you can actively monitor your network for attempted breaches, as described in this chapter. I looked at network monitoring from several angles. First, I described a network intrusion detection system (NIDS), designed to alert you to unauthorized access of various kinds. Next, I turned to a network intrusion prevention system (NIPS), which builds on the capabilities of a NIDS to dynamically block attackers. Looking at network monitoring from the inside out, I covered an information leak detection system (ILDS), which prevents users on your network from sending sensitive information of one kind or another to the outside world. Finally, I looked at the use of honeypots to lure potential attackers away from your computers and gather data that can be used to protect them.

Monitoring File Integrity

Certain files on your computer — word-processing documents, spreadsheets, logs, caches, preference files, and so on — change pretty much every time you use them, and that's completely normal. However, some files should never change unless you explicitly install an update. That includes most of the components of Mac OS X itself, along with the majority of third-party applications. If these important, low-level files are changing without your active involvement, it may be a sign that malware is at work or that a network intruder is modifying your system behind your back.

File integrity monitoring (sometimes referred to as *host integrity monitoring*) simply means watching for unexpected file changes. If you watch the right files using the right tools, you can receive an appropriate warning when suspicious file modifications take place, enabling you to take immediate corrective action. As a bonus, these same techniques enable you to know with complete certainty exactly what components are copied to your hard disk when you install new software. If you've ever wondered where some mysterious file came from or worried that a program might have installed spyware or other nasty stuff behind your back, you can use the information in this chapter to create before and after views of your disk so you can keep a much closer eye on new installations in the future.

Understanding File Integrity Monitoring

The term *file integrity monitoring* may sound very high-tech and complicated, but it's a very simple notion: letting you know when files change. Changes to files can range from obvious (deleting a file or adding a new one) to minor (adding data to an existing file) to subtle (changing ownership, permissions, or other metadata without affecting the file's contents). As someone who's concerned about the security of Macs on your network, you should be concerned with things like these:

- Modifications to the components of Mac OS X itself (particularly anything in the /System folder) — by an installer, user action, or malware — without your permission or knowledge

- Installation of server applications or other programs that aren't permitted or appropriate for your situation

- Modification of system-wide preferences, firewall rules, and other vital security settings

- Deletion of important data (which could mean that a person or a program is trying to cover up misbehavior)

- Addition of user accounts without your express approval

With file integrity monitoring software, you take a snapshot of your disk as it appears in a known good state (such as right after a clean installation of Mac OS X) and then take additional snapshots on a regular basis, comparing them to the original (or to the previous one, as the case may be). Doing so gives you a clear, complete list of all the files that were different on your Mac between one time and the next. If you see anything that looks suspicious, you can then investigate further and take any necessary steps to remove unwanted files, change permissions, or do whatever else is required to improve the computer's security.

Most programs that monitor file integrity let you either include or exempt certain folders — for example, you may care very much about /System but not at all about ~/Documents, whose contents change regularly without ever being problematic. Some alert you to metadata changes too, and some don't; some perform scans and deliver reports automatically, whereas others require manual operation or a home-grown script for automation.

In this chapter, I discuss a few common tools that can monitor file integrity under Mac OS X. This isn't an exhaustive list, and I don't provide detailed usage instructions, but this should be enough information to get you started.

Tripwire

One of the most popular (and most commonly recommended) file integrity monitors is the free, open-source Tripwire, which can be compiled to work on most platforms, including Mac OS X. It's a command-line-only program and somewhat odd to set up, but once you have it configured, you can run it quickly as often as you like to check for and report on file changes since the last run.

Because Tripwire wasn't designed expressly for Mac OS X, it doesn't notice most metadata changes (including changes to file permissions). However, it can effectively report on any content changes, additions, or deletions to any of the files on your disk.

Note

To learn more about what you can do with Tripwire after you've installed it, type man tripwire **in Terminal.** ■

To install Tripwire, follow these steps:

1. **Download the Tripwire source code from** http://sourceforge.net/projects/tripwire/files. On that page, look for a file with a name similar to tripwire-2.4.1.2-src.tar.bz2 (the version number may vary). Put this file in a location where it's convenient to work with it — for the purpose of these instructions, put it in your home folder.

2. **Open Terminal, located in** /Applications/Utilities. Because the shell automatically puts you in your home folder, you need not change directories unless you put the downloaded file somewhere else, in which case type **cd** to go to that location.

3. **To unarchive the Tripwire source, type** tar -xvf tripwire-2.4.1.2-src.tar.bz2 **(changing the file name to match yours, if necessary).**

4. **Move into the Tripwire directory by typing** cd tripwire-2.4.1.2-src — **again, changing the name if necessary.**

5. **To prepare a configuration file for your Mac, type** ./configure. The configuration script runs and should return you to the command prompt in a few seconds.

6. **Compile Tripwire by typing** make. Compilation takes a few minutes, during which time lots of text scrolls by. When the command prompt reappears, compilation is done.

7. **Install Tripwire by typing** sudo make install. Follow the prompts to accept the license agreement and install the software. Most of the questions should be self-explanatory. You're asked to type both site-wide and local passphrases a few times to confirm various parts of the installation. At the end, you should see the message "The installation succeeded."

Configuring Tripwire's policy

Most of the settings you might want to adjust in order to make Tripwire behave the way you want it to on a Mac are found in a single text file that holds its policy: /usr/local/etc/twpol.txt. You can view this file's contents by typing **sudo cat /usr/local/etc/twpol.txt** in a Terminal window. The bulk of the file contains lines like these, which specify directories Tripwire should monitor and with what parameters (lines beginning with # are commented out — those directories aren't monitored):

```
/bin                 -> $(SEC_READONLY) ;
/sbin                -> $(SEC_READONLY) ;
/usr/bin             -> $(SEC_READONLY) ;
/usr/lib             -> $(SEC_READONLY) ;
/usr/libexec         -> $(SEC_READONLY) ;
/usr/sbin            -> $(SEC_READONLY) ;
#/usr/X11R6          -> $(SEC_READONLY)(recurse=2) ; # May not be
    present
#/usr/X11R6/man      -> $(SEC_DYNAMIC)-i(recurse=1) ; # May not be
    present
/usr/share           -> $(SEC_READONLY) ;
/usr/share/man       -> $(SEC_DYNAMIC)-i(recurse=1) ;
```

Although you can use the file as is, it may not produce quite the results you're expecting because the version of the Mac OS X policy file included with Tripwire as of late 2009 is 6 years out of date — it lists directories that no longer exist and omits some that do. Therefore, before doing anything else, you should take a spin through the entire file (comparing it to your Mac's actual file system) and update it as necessary — deleting or commenting out directories that don't exist, adding new ones you want to watch, and changing any other preferences that don't suit you. For complete details, read Tripwire's documentation at /usr/local/doc/tripwire/policyguide.txt.

However, merely changing this file by hand isn't enough. Because Tripwire's whole purpose is to detect changes — which naturally include the components of Tripwire itself — the policy file is digitally signed. So, after making any changes, you must re-sign the file in order for Tripwire to recognize it as valid.

To configure Tripwire's policy (assuming you're still in the same Terminal window you used when installing it), follow these steps:

1. To assume root access necessary to perform some of the following commands, type sudo -s.

Note

Because of the special permissions the Tripwire installer assigns to some of its components, this is one of the rare cases in which sudo alone won't suffice to execute the commands — you must use sudo -s to temporarily log in as root. ∎

2. To edit the policy file in the nano text editor, type nano /usr/local/etc/twpol.txt. Make any desired changes, as previously described.

3. Press Control⇨+X to exit nano, press Y to confirm saving the file, and then press Return to confirm the file name.

4. To sign the changed policy file, type /usr/local/sbin/twadmin -m p > /usr/local/etc/twpol.txt.

5. You can (and should) now stop masquerading as the root user by typing exit.

Running Tripwire

Now that Tripwire is installed and configured, your next step is to initialize the database in which Tripwire stores digital signatures of your files, enabling the program to tell when something has changed. Then, you can monitor file changes easily. Follow these steps:

1. To initialize the Tripwire database, type sudo /usr/local/sbin/tripwire --init. When prompted, type the local passphrase you created when installing Tripwire earlier. Tripwire now scans all the directories on your disk that were specified in your policy file and adds file details to the database. This process can be quite time-consuming.

2. To have Tripwire scan your system and report any changes since it was initialized (or the database was updated manually, as described in the next step), type sudo /usr/local/sbin/tripwire --check. Once again, be prepared for the scan to take quite a while because it must check all the designated folders on your disk. When the process completes, Tripwire displays a report showing any changed files. The report can go on for many pages; it begins with a table summarizing how many files of which types have changed (along with a severity level for each change) and then lists individual changes using the same headings and organization as in the twpol.txt file.

3. After making deliberate changes to your system (such as installing new software in a location Tripwire watches), update your Tripwire database — so that it doesn't flag all those changes the next time you check it — by typing the following, replacing *date* with the current date:

```
sudo /usr/local/sbin/tripwire --update -a -r /usr/local/sbin/report/
    date.twr
```

Tip

If you run Tripwire only manually, on occasion, you're unlikely to detect important changes until it's much too late — and you'll also have trouble separating legitimate changes from problematic ones in the Tripwire reports. Therefore, I suggest creating a shell script, Automator workflow, or some other automated routine that performs the previous steps 2 and 3 daily, either saving the output of step 2 to a dated log file, emailing it to yourself, or both. ∎

Radmind

Radmind (Remote Administration Daemon), created by the University of Michigan Research Systems Unix Group (`http://rsug.itd.umich.edu/software/radmind/`), is a free, open-source system available for most popular computer platforms. Unlike Tripwire, which merely monitors files for changes, Radmind's file integrity monitoring is more of a side effect of its main function, which is to distribute entire system installations to multiple computers, keep them all updated, and enable an administrator to revert them to a predetermined state if necessary. That is, its mission isn't just to report changes but rather to reverse them.

Tip

If you decide to download Radmind, start with the Radmind Assistant, available at `http://rsug.itd.umich.edu/software/radmind/download.html`. **Install that first. It includes a copy of the Radmind Tools package itself, but because the included version may be older than what's built in to the Radmind Assistant installer, you should then also download and install the latest Radmind Tools package separately. ∎**

Another crucial difference between Tripwire and Radmind is that the latter requires both client and server components. Radmind doesn't simply take a snapshot of the way files look at a particular moment and compare it to another snapshot; instead, it asks you to create a special set of files on the server that will function as a base (you can do this by having Radmind use any existing client as a model). The base includes not only the files you want to have on each Mac (*positive loadsets*) but also *negative loadsets*, which specify which files or folders should be left alone (for example, you might want Radmind to completely ignore the `/Users` folder).

In typical usage, the server checks selected clients to make sure their installations match the base, and if they don't, Radmind copies or deletes any files necessary to make them identical (not counting any items included in negative loadsets). You can do this manually or set it to happen automatically on a schedule — for example, every night to update a lab full of Macs. You can also reconfigure a client (for example, install new software) and then use that client to update the base on the server so that the new configuration can be pushed down to all the other Macs on the network that are managed with Radmind.

Although Radmind is extremely powerful, its client-server design means it's not an appropriate choice for individual Macs.

Samhain

Samhain (`www.la-samhna.de/samhain/`), which is another free, open-source file integrity monitor, can be used either as a stand-alone program on individual computers (like Tripwire) or as a client-server monitoring and management system (like Radmind). It monitors most file metadata (including ownership, permissions, modification dates, and ACLs) and lets you exclude folders or files you want to ignore. Unlike Tripwire, Samhain has built-in scheduling, although you can also run it manually if you prefer.

Samhain isn't available in binary form for Mac OS X like Radmind and Baseline (described next) are; as with Tripwire, you must compile it from source code, install it, and configure it manually before use. Unfortunately, just as Samhain has a great many more features than Tripwire, it's also significantly more complicated to use. If you're interested in delving into its many options, consult the documentation at `www.la-samhna.de/samhain/manual/` for guidance.

Baseline

This next program is quite different from all the others discussed in this chapter. Baseline, from MildMannered Industries (www.mildmanneredindustries.com/baseline/), isn't open source or free (it costs $20), but it was designed from the ground up exclusively for Mac OS X. As a result, it has a lovely, easy-to-understand user interface, requires no compilation or other command-line procedures, and requires no installation. It doesn't offer (or require) client-server operation or built-in scheduling, but it can be automated with AppleScript if you want. For individual users — particularly those without advanced technical skills — Baseline offers the most accessible way to track file integrity.

When you launch Baseline, your local volumes appear in a list on the left. Before you can do anything else, you must perform a complete scan on a volume in order to establish the eponymous baseline. To do this, click the Scan or Rescan button on the toolbar. Baseline scans your disk and then displays a graphical TreeMap view, as shown in Figure 23.1, with larger files taking up larger blocks. Hover over any block with your mouse, and Baseline displays the name and size of that file. You can then store this baseline to use for future comparisons.

Note
Baseline works only with entire volumes; you can't search only selected folders or exclude folders. ■

When you do a future scan (for example, on a daily basis or after installing new software), Baseline's TreeMap view highlights changes from the previously selected baseline in colors representing positive or negative size changes (red and blue, respectively) and the amount of change (darker shades of red and blue indicating larger changes).

FIGURE 23.1

In Baseline's default TreeMap view, all the files on your disk are shown in blocks corresponding to their sizes. Hover over any block with your pointer, and a pop-up indicator tells you the name and size of the selected file.

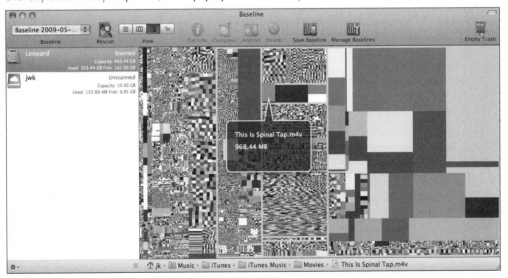

However, to get a quick overview of exactly what's different between one baseline and the next, you can display a List view (choose View⇨As List) or a column view (choose View⇨As Columns) and then optionally filter the display so it shows only changed folders and files (choose View⇨Show Changes Only). The resulting display, which may look something like Figure 23.2, gives you an easy-to-read list of what's changed and by how much.

Because one of Baseline's intended purposes is to help you find files that are taking up lots of space on your disk, it has built-in controls to let you delete files or folders, compress files (with Gzip), and archive folders (compressing them into gzipped tar (.tgz) archives and moving the originals to the Trash). Baseline can also scan your entire disk for duplicated files, enabling you to save space by deleting redundant copies. It also supports Time Machine, meaning that if you use it to scan a disk that was used for Time Machine backups, it treats only the original instance of each file as one that occupies space, not the additional hard links created during each run for folders and files that haven't changed since the last time.

Cross-Ref

For more on Time Machine, see Chapter 8. ■

FIGURE 23.2

To get an at-a-glance overview of which items on your disk have changed, in which direction, and by how much since the last baseline, use Baseline's List view.

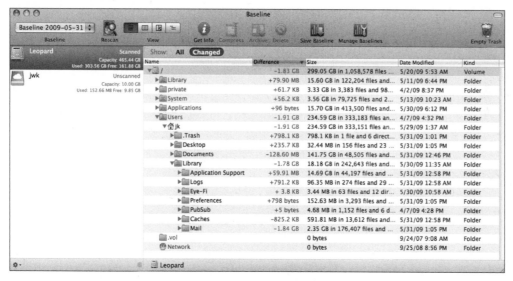

Sonar

The final file integrity monitoring program I want to mention is called Sonar (www.matterform.com/mac_software/file_security/, $17.95). Like Baseline, it's a friendly, Mac OS X–native application that requires no special skill to use. What sets it apart from the other software in this list is that Sonar watches your file system for changes in real time. It can inform you instantly when a file has changed, instead of waiting for you to perform a time-consuming (manual or scheduled) scan. A related program from the same developer called Yank (www.matterform.com/mac_software/uninstaller, $19.95) can create custom uninstallers to thoroughly remove any software installed on your system, even if it doesn't include its own uninstaller or if its uninstaller misses certain files.

Summary

This chapter discussed the importance of knowing when files on your Mac may have changed without your knowledge because this could mean that malware is at work or that a network-based attack of some sort has taken place. I described the process of monitoring file integrity using an open-source tool called Tripwire in some detail, briefly discussed Radmind and Samhain — two other open-source tools — and ended with a description of the somewhat less sophisticated but much friendlier utilities Baseline and Sonar.

Forensics: Discovering What Went Wrong

T he word *forensics* has a number of meanings and can conjure up images of everything from high school speech competitions to medical examiners performing autopsies. In the computer world, forensics refers to an examination of a computer's data that, ideally, prevents any of that data from changing in the course of the investigation. For example, if a computer is suspected of having been used in a crime or if an employer believes that an employee has misused company equipment, investigators or law enforcement personnel might undertake a forensic examination of a computer to look for evidence of wrongdoing. In such cases, it's important that the integrity of the data be preserved during the investigation so potential evidence doesn't disappear while it's being examined and so investigators can't be accused of planting false evidence.

As interesting and important as that aspect of forensics may be, however, the main focus of this chapter isn't on tracking down incriminating files to be used in legal proceedings. This being a book on Mac security, my primary concern here is helping you discover the source of a digital security breach (such as a malware infestation or a network intrusion) so you can take measures to prevent such problems from occurring in the future. In this chapter, the main goal is to track down and correct a problem, whether or not you've preserved evidence of it.

Nevertheless, I do include some information about the stricter, more legally constrained sense of computer forensics in this chapter, partly for those who need to perform such an investigation and partly to demonstrate how easy it would be for someone with the right equipment and software to learn a vast amount of information about your Mac usage that you may prefer to keep private. Knowing what someone else can find out about you with considerable ease may give you some much-needed perspective on your own security measures — from password choice and keychain use to the ways you clean up your web-browsing records.

IN THIS CHAPTER

Understanding the basics of computer forensics

Finding software that shouldn't be running on your Mac

Discovering what network connections are in progress

Examining a compromised Mac with MacForensicsLab

Using other forensics utilities

Overview of Computer Forensics

Investigating the manner in which a Mac may have been compromised and how it came to be that way can be a lengthy and tedious process. Whether you choose to undertake it at all and the extent to which you delve into a computer's secrets depend on the severity and impact of the problem, the amount of time you have available, and what's at stake. For example, if a random malware program has started displaying advertising messages or running a chat service on a single Mac, that's an annoyance, for sure — but not serious enough to spend days of detailed work tracking down. On the other hand, if someone has broken into your Mac over the network and stolen company secrets, if an employee has been sending confidential information to your competitors, or if files on a Mac may contain evidence of a crime, it's clearly worth pulling out all the stops to investigate.

The very first decision you must make when you discover or suspect that a Mac has a serious security issue is what to do next — and it's an extremely important decision, with potentially long-term consequences. Specifically, doing anything at all, including turning off the computer, could potentially alter its data in ways that make it harder to analyze later or even destroy the very evidence you're looking for. To decide what you should do next, consider the following factors.

Live versus deferred analysis

When a Mac is running — even if it's actively doing something bad, such as sending out spam — you have an opportunity to observe what's happening in real time, and that information can be extremely useful. For example, you can check to see which processes on your Mac are communicating with which computers elsewhere on the Internet (as explained later in this chapter), enabling you to get a much more direct understanding of certain problems than you can get by trying to reconstruct — from looking at files on the disk — what may have been happening. For that matter, a clever hacker could design software in such a way that it deletes itself on shutdown or startup, making it more difficult to find out afterward what has happened.

In addition, if a Mac is running, chances are extremely good that the current user's keychain is unlocked. (As I've cautioned elsewhere in this book, security-conscious users should make sure that their keychains are locked when not in use, that their keychains have passwords different from the ones for their user accounts, and that they aren't unlocked automatically on login.) This fact enables certain tools (such as MacLockPick II, described later in this chapter) to extract all the passwords for that user, which can in turn be used to decrypt files, log in to secure websites, and reveal lots of other private information. Similarly, whole-disk encryption products leave all your data in a vulnerable state until the computer is shut down or the drive removed, and even programs that encrypt disk images (including FileVault) offer free access to files as long as the image is mounted. Although all this is troubling from a privacy perspective, it can be extremely useful to someone trying to uncover data that would be locked and unreachable after the computer is turned off.

Cross-Ref
For more on general security settings (such as disabling automatic login), see Chapter 4. For more on Keychain, see Chapter 5. For more on choosing good passwords, see Chapter 6. For more on encryption, see Chapter 13. ■

On the other hand, it's also true that as long as a Mac is running, changes to its disk are occurring. If nothing else, background processes remain active and record log entries. But other software may also be running and changing the files on disk — Mail, FTP or file-sharing programs, databases, and many others, not to mention malware! A running Mac could be sending confidential information over the Internet, and it could even be actively deleting crucial data. And the more the data on disk changes, the more any potential evidence could be contaminated. So, in some situations, it's important to swiftly stop a Mac from doing whatever bad thing it's doing.

When deciding whether to examine a Mac in place or defer analysis, your best options are these:

- **Do nothing.** That is, leave the Mac in whatever state you find it in — on or off — and don't touch it. This is the right thing to do in case of a crime or a suspected crime; leave all decisions to the police or other investigators.

- **Take a snapshot, but leave the computer running.** If you need to determine what your Mac is currently doing on the network, if you know or suspect that it contains encrypted data that will lock when you shut it down, or if you want to attempt getting at the contents of a user's unlocked keychain, use one of the programs described later in this chapter to save an image of the entire disk and optionally use MacLockPick II to extract keychain and other private data. If the Mac appears to be actively causing trouble on the network, such as sending out spam, disconnect the Ethernet cable and/or turn off the AirPort card and then proceed with your live analysis — but keep in mind that some misbehavior can be detected most readily when an active network connection is in progress. This approach gives you static data that you can work with later, even if you accidentally change something, while giving you the advantages of watching the computer in action.

- **Turn it off.** If you have any reason to suspect that leaving the Mac on will result in greater liability or exposure of confidential data or if you want to be absolutely certain you preserve it in its current state without allowing any further files to change, turn it off and unplug it — then, later on, examine the computer's hard disk in a way that prevents any data on it from changing (as I explain ahead).

Note

If you don't have a spare Mac handy and can't afford any downtime, you might consider this variation of "turn it off." Take a snapshot of the disk and then erase the disk and restore a known good copy of the entire disk from a recent bootable duplicate. You won't be able to do as much in the way of investigation, but your Mac will be up and running again much more quickly. ■

Choosing whether to save a disk image

Regardless of whether you choose to turn off the Mac or disconnect it from the network before proceeding, you can opt to make a complete copy of its disk(s), storing them on another volume as read-only images that you can later investigate without needing the original disk(s) and without having to worry that you'll accidentally change something on the disk(s) as you examine it (them).

Although the notion of cloning a disk (whether to another disk or to a disk image file) should be familiar to anyone who read the portion of this book about backups, the process needed to create a disk image for forensic analysis is somewhat different in that it must copy not only the files on your disk but all the data — including the disk catalog and the contents of all the free space, which may contain deleted files. In other words, for forensic purposes, you want a bit-by-bit image rather than a file-by-file image. Several of the programs mentioned later in this chapter can produce just such a file, which is sometimes called a *golden master*.

Cross-Ref

For more on backups, including exact duplicates, see Chapter 8. ■

If you're creating an image from the startup disk of a Mac that's currently running or any disk mounted with write access, changes to the disk can occur while the image is being made, with the result that the image doesn't perfectly represent the state of the disk at any given point in time. Such an image is known as a *smeared* image, which may still be forensically valuable but which is less reliable from a legal standpoint than an image created from a disk that can't be changed.

Images are mandatory when evidence must be preserved for later examination; but in cases where you simply want to get your Mac back into working order as soon as possible and you're under no legal or policy constraints to collect evidence, you can skip this step and simply work with the live data.

Preventing disk changes

On a normal Mac, the mere fact of mounting a disk makes changes both to that disk and to the startup volume (if different). If you've chosen to pursue your investigation on a Mac while it's still running, you must also accept the possibility of changes to the disk. However, if the Mac has been shut down, you can ensure that its disk doesn't change when you examine it. This leads to the question of how you get access to the disk in the first place.

One option is to start up the Mac from a specially designed CD or DVD that contains a bootable system, forensics software, and settings that prevent any new data from being written to the disk. (MacForensicsLab, described later, can be used this way.) In this setup, you need a place to store the information you extract from the disk — that could be an external hard drive, a flash drive, or possibly even a network volume, depending on the amount of data involved.

A second option is to start the Mac from a second (internal or external) hard drive — again, with forensics software installed. The problem with this approach is that Mac OS X still tries to mount the computer's regular startup disk as soon as it's finished booting, which can change it. You can prevent this from happening by deleting the file `/System/Library/LaunchDaemons/com.apple.diskarbitrationd.plist` on the disk you'll use to start the Mac, although this isn't ideal because under ordinary circumstances, Mac OS X doesn't work properly without that file — and messing with the contents of `/System` is generally unwise.

A third option is to physically remove the disk from the Mac you're examining and install it as a secondary disk inside another Mac — or put it in an external case and attach it via USB, FireWire, or eSATA. If both Macs include FireWire ports, you can accomplish essentially the same thing, with less effort, by using FireWire target disk mode. Start the good Mac normally and connect a FireWire cable between the two Macs. Turn on the Mac whose disk you want to investigate while holding down the T key. That Mac's internal drive appears as an external volume on the other Mac. However, as with the second option, you run into the problem of the target disk being changed as it's mounted.

You can disable Mac OS X's mechanism for automatically mounting disks (because automatic mounting implies write access) by typing **sudo launchctl unload /System/Library/LaunchDaemons/com.apple.diskarbitrationd.plist** in a Terminal window, attaching a disk, and then using a command such as **mkdir /Volumes/temp; sudo mount -t hfs -o rdonly /dev/*disk1s1* /Volumes/temp**, where *disk1s1* is replaced with the proper number for the disk in question. This works in Snow Leopard, but unfortunately, the `mount` command in Leopard often fails when the `rdonly` (read only) option is used. However, if you're unwilling to turn off automatic mounting, if the command just described doesn't work for you, or if you simply want an easier and more foolproof way to mount disks without any possibility of writing data to them, another option is available.

This alternative way to prevent data from changing when examining a disk on another Mac or starting from a secondary hard disk is to use a device called a *write blocker*. Like an ordinary hard drive interface, a write blocker (sometimes called a forensic bridge) lets you connect a bare IDE, SATA, or SCSI drive to a computer (usually via USB, FireWire, or eSATA) — but without any possibility of data being written to the drive. For the privilege of having what amounts to a connector that's missing a standard feature, you might pay anywhere from sub-$100 to well over $1,000, depending on what capabilities and extras you want. In other words, this isn't the sort of thing an individual or a small office would keep lying around just in case, but a large business or a law-enforcement agency may well have several.

Write blockers are available from companies such as the following:

- Digital Intelligence (`www.digitalintelligence.com/forensicwriteblockers.php`)
- MyKey Technology (`www.mykeytech.com`)
- SubRosaSoft (`http://www.macforensicslab.com/ProductsAndServices/index.php?main_page=product_info&cPath=12&products_id=107`)
- WiebeTech (`www.wiebetech.com/home.php?home=5`)

Looking for Rogue Processes

When you're examining a live Mac that may have unwanted software running, your ultimate goal may be to delete the software, but you have to find it first. This isn't as simple as it sounds because malware and hacks rarely appear as ordinary applications in the `/Applications` folder. Surprisingly enough, though, it may be easier to find software that's actively running than software that merely exists as a file on your disk — it (usually) has nowhere to hide.

Tip

Manually looking for unwanted software can provide lots of useful information, but it also involves a certain amount of guesswork and is rather time-consuming. In the vast majority of cases, simply running a good anti-malware program (see Chapter 14) is a faster and more direct solution. ■

The Activity Monitor utility is a good place to start because it's easy to use and helps you to narrow down the possible range of culprits quickly, as I describe next. However, to find a program based on its network activity, a more direct approach is to use a program called `lsof` (discussed just afterward).

Caution

When deleting troublesome files, the possibility also exists that you'll delete something you need (but didn't realize you need). Therefore, before doing anything, I strongly suggest that you create a backup of your entire disk. If you created a forensic image, as discussed earlier, that can serve as a backup. ■

Using Activity Monitor

Rogue processes are more likely than not to be running invisibly in the background. Therefore, before you do anything else, you should quit all software running visibly in the foreground —that can help you zero in on what might be the problem — and then look for suspicious programs. Follow these steps:

1. **Quit all applications shown as running in your Dock (with a glowing dot).**

2. **Look at the right side of your menu bar — it may contain status menus for one or more third-party programs.** Examples include Dropbox, QuickKeys, PGP, MenuMeters, and Eye-Fi Manager, among countless others. Some of these menus may contain Quit or Stop commands — if they do, use them. If not, open the associated preference pane or manager application to see if you can find a command to quit the process.

3. **Open Activity Monitor, which is located in** `/Applications/Utilities`.

4. **Choose My Processes from the pop-up menu at the top of the window to show only processes owned by your user account and then click the Process Name column to sort by process name, as shown in Figure 24.1.**

5. **Find any processes that you recognize — that is, software you know you installed but which doesn't have a visible interface at the moment.** Examples may include BusySync (calendar synchronization), Microsoft AU Daemon (automatic updating for Microsoft software), backup and maintenance software, and other utilities. For each one, select it, click Quit Process, and then click Quit. Repeat this for all remaining processes with your username. You should now be down to processes you don't recognize (although there may be dozens of these).

6. **Work your way methodically through the list that remains, making sure you know what each item is.** If you don't immediately recognize it as a component of Mac OS X or a program you installed, you can find out what it is by trying one of the following:

   - Type **man** *process-name* (e.g., **man krb5kdc**) in a Terminal window.

   - Do a quick web search on the process name in question.

   - Consult a web page that lists many standard processes in Mac OS X, such as `http://theprimepixel.com/list-of-mac-osx-common-processes`.

   If none of these suggestions yield any information on a process, chances are good that it's either the malware you're looking for or some other harmless but nonessential program. Make a note of its name and Process ID; in the next step, you can locate and delete it.

7. **Open Terminal, which is located in** `/Applications/Utilities`.

FIGURE 24.1

In Activity Monitor, you can see processes that are normally invisible and optionally quit them.

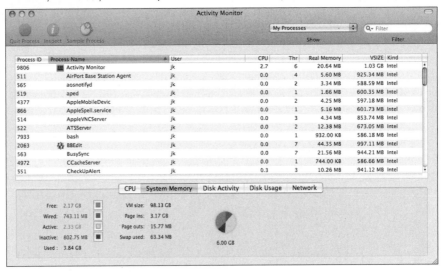

8. **Type** ps *PID*, **where** *PID* **is replaced with the Process ID of the process you're looking for.** The output should look something like this:

```
PID   TT  STAT      TIME COMMAND
123   ??  S      1:40.05 /usr/sbin/abcde
```

By looking at the Command column, you can see the location of the program in question: `/usr/sbin/abcde`. To delete it, type **sudo rm** *pathname*, where *pathname* is the complete path to the file in question. Type your administrator password when prompted and then press Return.

Caution

If you incautiously delete a crucial component of Mac OS X, you could crash your Mac and/or prevent it from starting correctly — in which case the remedy is to restore the file (or better yet, the entire operating system) from a backup. You do have a backup, right? ∎

Using lsof

If you know something about what a rogue program is doing — for example, sending out spam on port 25, communicating with a particular IP address on the Internet, or listening on port 56789 — you may be able to locate it directly and easily, without any guessing at all, using a handy utility called `lsof` (list open files) built into Mac OS X.

If you're a networking pro — particularly if you're accustomed to debugging network issues under Windows — you might have expected me to mention a different program here: `netstat` (as in network status), which does indeed display a detailed list of all the open network connections on one's computer and which is also included with Mac OS X (both as a command-line program and as a feature in Network Utility, located in the `/Applications/Utilities` folder). The problem with the Mac OS X version of `netstat` is that it lacks the option to provide one piece of information crucial to learning where any given piece of software is — the PID (process ID) associated with each open port. Although `lsof` presents its data in a slightly less elegant and less detailed format, it does include the PID, which makes a world of difference when tracking down unauthorized software.

To track down what software is communicating with which computers on the Internet, follow these steps:

1. **Open Terminal, which is located in** `/Applications/Utilities`.

2. **Type** sudo lsof -i –P.

3. **Type your administrator password when prompted and then press Return.** `lsof` displays a list (which may be quite long) of all files (including, significantly, sockets) involved in network access.

A typical excerpt from this listing may resemble the following:

```
COMMAND    PID          USER  FD   TYPE    DEVICE SIZE/OFF NODE NAME
Skype      542          joe   30u  IPv4 0x16d71e64     0t0  TCP *:54045 (LISTEN)
Skype      542          joe   33u  IPv4 0x16d7966c     0t0  TCP
   10.124.5.238:54330->173-27-56-155.client.mchsi.com:10701 (ESTABLISHED)
Skype      542          joe   36u  IPv4 0x16d9466c     0t0  TCP
   10.124.5.238:54331->173-28-69-204.client.mchsi.com:13825 (ESTABLISHED)
```

In this listing, the columns you're most interested in are the first three (`Command`, `PID`, and `User`) and the last one (`Name`). What this says is that the Skype application, with a PID of 542, owned by the user joe, is currently listening for incoming connections on port 54045 (the first line), and it's established two connections (the next two lines) with a local IP address of `10.124.5.238`. The first of these uses port 54330 locally and is connected to port 10701 on the computer with IP address `173.27.56.155` (you can figure out the other on your own).

Now, it so happens that I know exactly where the Skype application is (as you probably do too) — in my `/Applications` folder — but if you don't recognize the command or know where the executable file is located, use the `ps` command (as explained earlier in this chapter): type **ps** *PID*, where *PID* is the PID of the process you're looking for. As before, once you've identified a rogue program, you can delete it, but remember that if you delete something that's actually a legitimate file, you could destabilize the Mac.

If you identify the process that's carrying on unsavory conversations over the Internet as a shell script interpreter (such as `sh` or `bash`), that doesn't tell you much. What you really want to know is what script is being run. The next section can help you figure that out.

Looking for Rogue Software

If you know that malware or other unauthorized software is installed on a Mac but it's not actively running, finding it can be challenging. By nature, malware usually hides in obscure locations, uses innocent-looking or misleading names, and may use other tricks to avoid detection.

As before, the easiest way to find such programs is to run a commercial anti-malware utility. Such programs contain extensive databases of the characteristics of known malware programs — as well as heuristics that enable them to identify much as-yet-unknown malware — and can find them wherever they may lurk on your disk by scanning every file.

Cross-Ref
For more on anti-malware software, see Chapter 14. ■

If you can't use anti-malware software for some reason, if you don't trust its results, or if it fails to locate malicious software that you're sure is there, you can use a few tricks to track it down.

Tip
One popular hiding place for malware is the `/var/tmp` **directory because it's world-writable.** ■

The first thing to keep in mind is that a program can't do any good (or any damage) when it's simply sitting idle on your hard disk. Only when the software is actively running can it accomplish anything. Therefore, it stands to reason that the program's designer would include some mechanism to make sure it runs — either at startup, on a recurring schedule, or in response to a frequent user action (such as launching a program you're likely to use every day).

Leopard and Snow Leopard can use any of four main mechanisms to open programs automatically:

- **Launchd.** A component of Mac OS X called Launch Services provides management for processes that must run on demand, at startup, or on a fixed schedule. A daemon called `launchd` runs in the background all the time and takes action based on specially formatted configuration files found in the `LaunchAgents` or `LaunchDaemons` folders located in `/System`, `/Library`, and ~/Library. You can look through all those folders manually, opening each file to see what program it runs — or save yourself some effort and download Peter Borg's free, open-source utility, Lingon (http://tuppis.com/lingon/), shown in Figure 24.2, which gives you a convenient way to view and manage all the launchd items on your Mac. Most launchd items are perfectly legitimate, but if you find one you don't recognize and discover that it points to a program you've never heard of, it's worth investigating in more detail.

Note

Among the programs launchd can run are shell scripts, and although the launchd item and the shell script may both be entirely valid components of Mac OS X, a hacker or malware program may have added commands to an existing shell script that's run automatically (such as /usr/sbin/periodic or any of the scripts it uses in the various /etc/periodic subdirectories) in order to hide their execution. If you want to make absolutely certain nothing's hiding in any of these or many other scripts, the only reliable way is to compare them with the versions in a clean copy of (the same version of) Mac OS X. ■

FIGURE 24.2

Lingon provides a convenient graphical interface for viewing and editing launchd items — wherever they may be on your Mac.

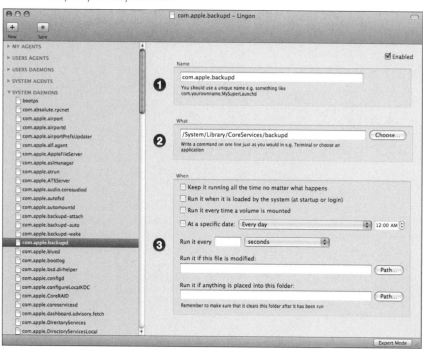

- **Cron.** Prior to the introduction of Launch Services in Tiger, Mac OS X relied primarily on cron, a scheduling utility found in almost every version of Unix, for running programs on fixed schedules. Even though Apple now recommends using launchd instead, cron is still present and could still be used to run unwanted programs. The text files `cron` uses to store its parameters are called *crontabs*. The system-wide crontab, if any, is stored at `/etc/crontab`; user-specific crontabs, which bear the names of the user accounts, are stored in `/var/at/tabs`. Using `sudo`, you can examine these files with `nano` or the text editor of your choice to see what they do. Or opt for a conventional Mac OS X application that gives you an easier way to do the same thing: Abstracture's free Cronnix (`http://h775982.serverkompetenz.net:9080/abstracture_public/projects-en/cronnix`), shown in Figure 24.3. By default, Cronnix displays the crontab for the current user; choose File ⇨ Open System Crontab to show the contents of `/etc/crontab`. But also check the crontab for each other user on the Mac, including root, by choosing File ⇨ Open for User, typing the username, and then clicking Open.

FIGURE 24.3

Instead of delving into the Unix `crontab` command, you can display and edit crontab items for all users in Cronnix.

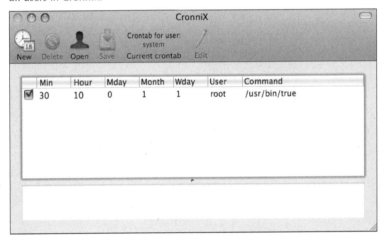

- **Startup Items.** Whereas `cron` was the standard pre-Leopard way to run programs on a schedule, the corresponding mechanism for running programs when the Mac starts up was to put folders containing specially formatted files in `/Library/StartupItems` or `/System/Library/StartupItems`. Although Apple now deprecates this practice too (because Launch Services can accomplish the same thing more easily and elegantly), Leopard and Snow Leopard still support the old mechanism, and therefore, a number of common programs (such as some backup, virtualization, and anti-piracy programs) continue to make use of it. Therefore, check both of the folders to see what they contain, and take special note of anything you don't recognize, which may require more scrutiny.

Note

In a standard installation of Leopard or Snow Leopard, the folder `/System/Library/StartupItems` **is normally empty, and I'm unaware of any Apple software that uses it. However, at least one well-known Trojan horse uses this folder to store a startup item called** `iWorkServices`**, which often goes unnoticed because it looks like something that might belong there. The moral is: Be highly suspicious of anything in that folder.** ■

- **Login Items.** The final standard mechanism Leopard and Snow Leopard contain for running programs automatically is the list of Login Items found in the Accounts pane of System Preferences for each user. Anything in this list (which can include not only applications but also folders, files, or volumes) opens automatically when the user logs in; and if the Mac is configured to log in a user automatically on startup, that means these items run whenever the Mac is turned on or restarted. You can add items to this list manually, but most of its contents are placed there by installers or by applications with a preference check box something along the lines of Load at startup. To determine the location of any item in this list, hover over it with your pointer for a moment; the entire path shows up in a yellow tooltip, as shown in Figure 24.4. To remove an item, select it and then click the minus (–) button.

FIGURE 24.4

The Login Items list contains files, folders, volumes, and applications that open automatically when you log in to your user account.

Of course, a program need not be launched automatically; if the developer can count on users to launch it manually, that's nearly as good. So, another way of hiding malware is to package it inside existing applications. Apart from scripts and command-line programs, all Mac OS X applications are distributed as special folders (called packages or bundles) that appear to be single files. To see what's inside an application, Control+click its icon in the Finder and then choose Show Package Contents from the pop-up menu. In some situations, malicious code placed inside an existing application can be made to run when the user double-clicks the application to open it.

Because you may not know what's supposed to be inside any given application bundle, finding malicious software there may involve comparing applications' contents to a known good copy on another computer — an admittedly tedious task. All Apple applications as well as any application you've added to Mac OS X's application firewall and some (but not all) other third-party applications are code-signed, meaning Mac OS X can detect any changes and alert you accordingly. However, you (or another user on the Mac) may have dismissed such an alert without realizing what it meant, and an attacker could even have gone to the bother of altering an application and then adding it to the firewall to sign it, making it appear to be legitimate.

Cross-Ref

For more on how the application firewall works, see Chapter 17. ■

Therefore, if you notice any suspicious behavior immediately after opening an application, the best way to be sure that it hasn't been compromised is to install a fresh copy from scratch. If you also keep a copy of the previous version and compare the two, you should be able to tell what, if any, changes were made to its contents.

Using MacForensicsLab

SubRosaSoft's MacForensicsLab (www.macforensicslab.com/ProductsAndServices/index.php?main_page=product_info&cPath=1&products_id=1, $1,195, with a $200 discount for law enforcement) is the best-known full-featured forensics suite for Mac OS X. In contrast to the programs and procedures described earlier in this chapter, MacForensicsLab isn't geared toward finding malware or security leaks. Rather, it's designed to look for data on a hard disk that can be used as evidence that the computer was involved in some type of wrongdoing or to provide leads for law enforcement or corporate officials investigating a crime or policy violation. If you watch movies or TV shows in which agents swoop into the bad guy's lair, confiscate a bunch of computers, and shortly thereafter turn up the name of Mr. Big, the location of the missing canisters, or pictures of previous victims, MacForensicsLab is exactly the kind of software they would have used to figure that out.

MacForensicsLab takes the strict notion of forensics quite seriously. The program is designed from top to bottom to preserve data in the state in which it was found, to validate the integrity of that data (to prove it wasn't tampered with after the fact), and to log every action an investigator takes so that any search or discovery can be re-created by a third party. The program can provide a detailed data trail of everything that happened with a disk to serve as evidence in legal proceedings.

Some of the program's major features are the following:

- Uses a single program to acquire and analyze disk images (unlike some of the other packages described later in this chapter, which require the use of different programs for each activity)
- Acquires bit-for-bit disk images (often, even from damaged or corrupted disks) so deleted files can be recovered even from the disk image, virtual memory swap files can be investigated, and other normally hidden files read
- Works with disks using a variety of formats and originating on a variety of platforms
- Contains sophisticated pattern-matching tools — for example, one that searches photos for skin tones and another that looks for patterns of digits that could be credit card or social security numbers

- Displays reports of web-browsing activity, system preferences, Address Book contents, email accounts, iChat transcripts, and other common data

- Comes in Windows and Linux versions that contain most of the same features (although not the acquisition of Mac OS X images or the analysis of live Mac OS X volumes)

- Enables accounts to be created for each examiner and files for each case so each person's activity in analyzing each image can be tracked separately and evidence from multiple sources doesn't get intermingled

Note

MacForensicsLab uses a USB dongle to enforce its license (preventing more than one copy from running at a time). ■

Installing and configuring MacForensicsLab

You can run MacForensicsLab in either of two ways: by starting up from its included DVD, which can boot both Intel- and PowerPC-based Macs, or by installing the software on your hard drive.

If you have only one installation of Mac OS X and it's on the Mac you're examining, then the best choice is to boot from the DVD and run the software from there, storing an image of the target disk (and all the records of your investigation) on an external hard drive.

Alternatively, if you have more than one Mac, a safer and more convenient procedure is to install MacForensicsLab on one of them, which you'll use for analysis, remove the hard drive from the target Mac, and connect it to the analysis Mac using a write blocker (described earlier in this chapter). Yet another option is to put a bootable copy of Mac OS X on an external drive, install MacForensicsLab on that drive, and then use that drive to start up the Mac under investigation. The possibility of data change on the target drive still exists in this setup, unless you've removed the drive and re-attached it by using a write blocker.

Installation

To install MacForensicsLab on a hard disk, follow these steps:

1. **Connect the HASP license dongle to a USB port on your Mac.**
2. **Download the latest version of MacForensicsLab from** www.macforensicslab.com.
3. **If the downloaded ZIP file doesn't decompress automatically, double-click it to decompress it.**
4. **Drag the MacForensicsLab icon to the** /Applications **folder.**
5. **Double-click the MacForensicsLab icon in** /Applications. After the splash screen disappears, a dialog box opens, containing a single large Install button.
6. **Click Install, type an administrator's username and password, and then click OK.**

Or to run MacForensicsLab from the DVD, follow these steps:

1. **Connect the HASP license dongle to a USB port on your Mac.**
2. **Insert the DVD in your Mac's optical drive.**
3. **Turn on (or restart) the computer, holding down the C key until the Apple logo appears.** The Mac boots, and MacForensicsLab runs automatically.

Regardless of the way in which you run MacForensicsLab, after launching the program, it prompts you to disable disk arbitration, as shown in Figure 24.5, which prevents connected drives from being mounted automatically. Unless you have a good reason to choose otherwise, click Disable to confirm that you want to disable it. After you've done this, you can connect the target drive (again, preferably by way of a write blocker).

Disabling disk arbitration prevents Mac OS X from automatically mounting (and thereby altering the data on) newly connected drives.

Starting an investigation

With the software running and the disk attached, you're almost — but not quite — ready to acquire an image. First, you have to go through a few extra preliminary procedures to set up the database or file in which MacForensicsLab will store its data, designate at least one investigator, and open a case. To do all this, follow these steps:

1. **In the Preferences window, which appears automatically when MacForensicsLab runs, click the Database icon on the toolbar.**

2. **Choose a data storage mechanism:**
   - If you want to use an existing MySQL or REAL SQL server to hold the data from your investigation (so examiners working on multiple computers can access the same data easily), click either the MySQL or REAL SQL Server tab, type the information requested, and optionally test it by clicking Connect.
   - To store all the data in a file on disk (a more convenient option, especially when only one person is examining the data), click the Local File tab, as shown in Figure 24.6. Click Create, type a file name and choose a location, and then click Save. Be sure not to choose a location on the disk you're examining.

3. **To set up an examiner, click Examiners on the toolbar, as shown in Figure 24.7.** Click the plus (+) button, type a name (and optionally other information) for the examiner, and then click Save. Repeat this step as necessary to set up additional examiners.

FIGURE 24.6

Storing MacForensicsLab data in a local file, as opposed to a database, is easier to configure and ideal for an individual investigator.

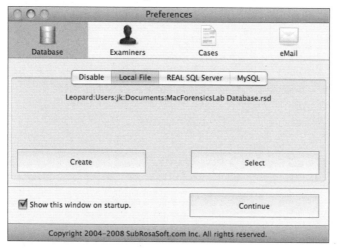

FIGURE 24.7

You must configure at least one examiner before starting an investigation in MacForensicsLab.

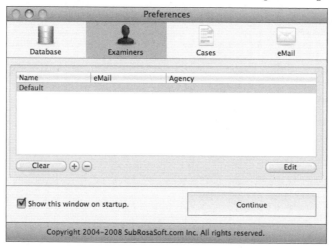

4. **To set up a case, click Cases on the toolbar, as shown in Figure 24.8.** Click the plus (+) button, type a reference (a name or ID number) and optionally a description for the case, and then click Save.

FIGURE 24.8

The case lets you keep all data for a certain investigation together and separate from other investigations (even if they involve the same underlying data).

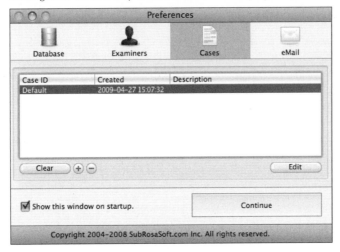

5. When you're finished with this initial setup, click Continue to show the main window, shown in Figure 24.9, in which you can perform the investigation.

FIGURE 24.9

MacForensicsLab's main window shows all the devices and volumes available for analysis and provides buttons to initiate the most common commands.

Acquiring an image

Although it's possible to use MacForensicsLab to examine live data on a disk, for the sake of preserving evidence, the preferred approach is to begin by creating a replica of the disk under investigation in the form of a disk image file and then perform all your analysis on that image. To acquire an image, follow these steps:

1. **In the main window, select a volume and then click Acquire.** The Acquire window, shown in Figure 24.10, opens.

2. **Select any desired options (consult the MacForensicsLab documentation for details) or leave all the default settings and then click Start.** A Save dialog box opens.

3. **Navigate to a location where the image will be stored (ideally on a separate hard drive — never on the same drive you're making a copy of) and then click Save.** MacForensicsLab creates the image, which can take a considerable period of time (longer if the drive is larger, damaged, or both).

FIGURE 24.10

In the Acquire window, select the options you want to use when acquiring a disk image.

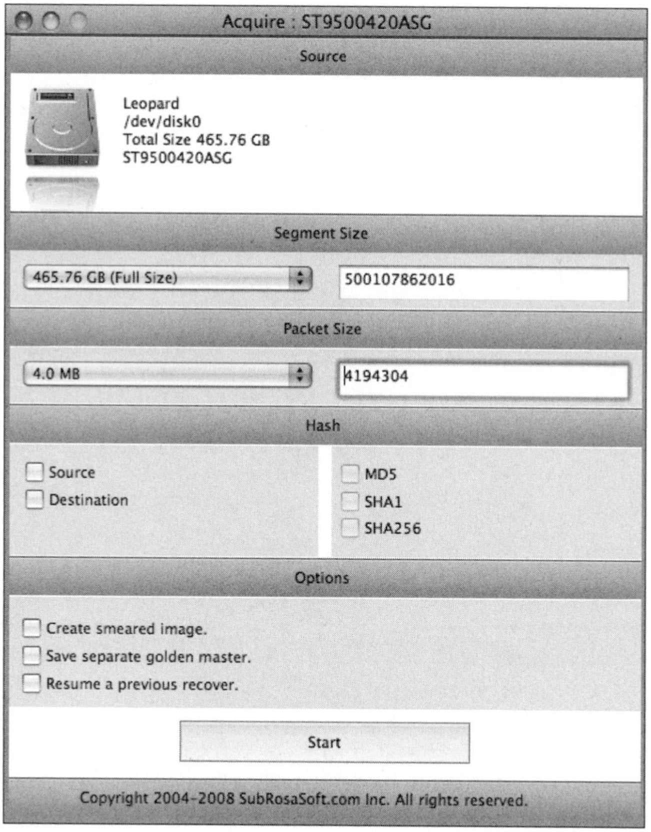

Working with an image

With the image safely acquired, you can unmount the original target hard disk or even continue your investigation on another computer. MacForensicsLab has a long list of analysis features, and I couldn't hope to cover them all here. However, I can give you a high-level overview of the steps you might take to examine a disk image. This information applies to the disk as a whole; for user-specific data, see the next section.

Assuming you're on a Mac with MacForensicsLab running and the image available on a local or network volume, follow these steps to work with it:

1. **In MacForensicsLab's main window, choose File ➪ Attach Disk Image, select the image file, and then click Open.** MacForensicsLab mounts the image, which is locked to prevent writing data to it.

2. **To search the image for text keywords, click the Search button at the bottom of the main window.** The Search window, shown in Figure 24.11, opens.

The Search window enables you to search a disk image for text keywords.

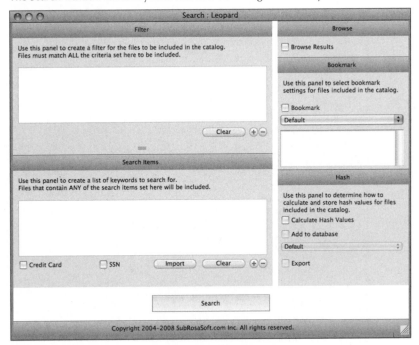

3. **To search for keywords, click the plus (+) button in the Search Items pane, type the information you want to find (or to search for credit card and/or social security numbers, click the Credit Card and/or SSN check boxes to select them), and then click Search.** MacForensicsLab searches the image and displays a list of matching results.

Note

MacForensicsLab provides extensive search capabilities that go far beyond this sort of simple keyword search; consult the included documentation for details. ■

4. To find graphics on the disk image, select a volume or folder in the main window and then click **Browse**. The Browse window, shown in Figure 24.12, opens.

5. Select the options you want (for example, the minimum and maximum file size and dimensions in pixels and whether or not to search for skin tones) and then click **Browse**. MacForensicsLab searches the image for matching files and displays a list of results.

6. To search for files that may have been erased or damaged, select the disk image in the main window and then click **Salvage**. The Salvage window, shown in Figure 24.13, opens.

7. To narrow down what's searched for, click Supported File Formats, select one or more file formats to search for, and then click Continue.

8. To search for files embedded within other files, click the Search for embedded files check box and then click the Start a new scan button.

MacForensicsLab searches the image for files matching your criteria. In the list that appears, you can display a preview of the files that are found and, if desired, restore them to another location.

FIGURE 24.12

Although not perhaps what you might expect with a name like Browse, this window lets you search for files (particularly graphics files) with certain sizes and other characteristics.

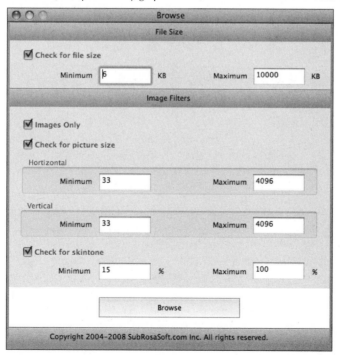

FIGURE 24.13

Use the Salvage window to search for data that's hidden, deleted, or corrupted.

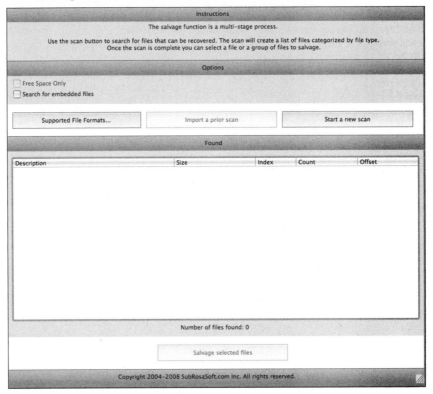

Auditing user data

In addition to the tools described here for searching an entire disk image, MacForensicsLab has a set of features designed to extract and display common types of user-specific data from each account represented on the image. MacForensicsLab uses the term *auditing* to describe these features.

To audit user data, follow these steps:

1. **With the image selected in the main window, click Audit.** The Audit window opens.
2. **From the Please Select a User pop-up menu at the top of the window, choose a username and then click Audit.** The window fills with user-specific data, as shown in Figure 24.14.
3. **Click a tab (Folder, Preferences, Address Book, Cookies, Safari, iChat, eMail, or System) to show the corresponding type of information.**

Once again, this overview barely scratches the surface of what MacForensicsLab can do, but the software includes an extensive 123-page PDF manual with complete details on the program's other capabilities.

The various tabs of the Audit window display user-specific data extracted from the selected user's account.

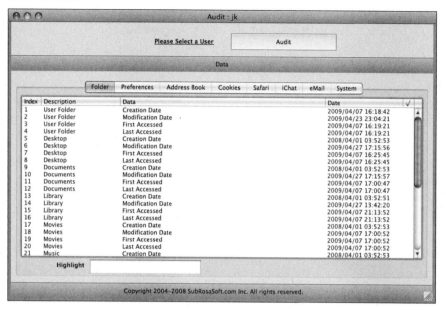

Other Forensics Tools

Although I happen to think MacForensicsLab is a pretty thorough and well-designed forensics package, it's not the only game in town. Other tools offer different ranges of features that may be more appropriate for your needs.

MacLockPick II

Of all the forensics software I've tried for Mac OS X, MacLockPick II, from the makers of MacForensicsLab (www.MacForensicsLab.com, $499.95), is the scariest by far. (Whether that's a good thing or a bad thing depends on your point of view.) The purpose of this application is to extract as much information as possible from the current user's account on a running Mac, without leaving behind any trace that it was even used. The software comes on a tiny, specially designed USB flash drive. After configuring the software beforehand (on either a Mac or a PC) to collect the pieces of data you want, you insert the key in the target computer, launch the MacLockPick program, and wait for a few minutes while it searches for interesting information (which it then copies to the flash drive itself or to another external volume you've connected). You can then remove the flash drive and examine the data at your leisure, on your own computer, using the MacLockPick Reader application, shown in Figure 24.15.

FIGURE 24.15

The MacLockPick Reader application displays all the information captured using MacLockPick II. This example shows just a tiny portion of the user's Firefox browsing history.

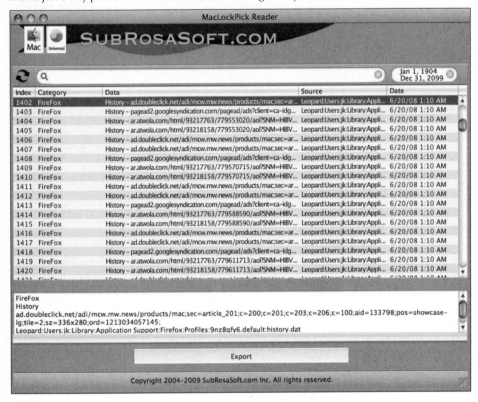

Here's a partial list of the details MacLockPick II can rapidly extract from a disk:

- Browsing history, bookmarks, cookies, and download lists from Safari and Firefox plus form autofill values for Firefox only
- The entire contents of the user's Address Book
- Transcripts of saved iChat conversations, records of all Skype calls and chats, and buddy lists for both applications
- Information about all computers to which the Mac is currently connected (including IP address and port)
- The contents of the Mac's Clipboard
- The bash history file, which lists commands typed in Terminal
- A list of all processes currently running on the Mac
- A screenshot of the Mac's screen as it appears when the program runs

- Most of the data from the user's iPhone, including records of all incoming and outgoing calls and SMS messages (with time, date, number, and call duration), notes, and your wallpaper (background photo)

- The contents of the user's keychain, assuming it's unlocked when MacLockPick II is used (this feature is included only in the version available exclusively to law enforcement)

That last item is particularly significant. I tried out the law enforcement version of MacLockPick II on one of my own Macs that I'd thought was reasonably secure, and within a few minutes, it told me — in addition to all the listed information — that Mac's login password! On my test Mac, I'd reused a password — I used the same password for my Mac OS X user account as I'd used for another resource and stored in my keychain. So, after extracting all the passwords from my keychain, MacLockPick II used them to perform a quick dictionary attack on my user account, and that was all it took. Needless to say, I changed that password right away!

I do know better than to intentionally reuse passwords, and I also know better than to leave my keychain unlocked when I'm not at my computer. Had I not done those two things on my test Mac, MacLockPick II would have been foiled in a couple of its data collection procedures, but as long as I was logged in (assuming I hadn't put the computer to sleep or activated the screen saver, with the Mac set to require a password to bring it back to life), it still would have collected a great deal of other, unprotected information.

That's why this program is so scary — it illustrates how easy it would be for someone with physical access to your Mac to learn an enormous amount of personal information about you, your computer, and your iPhone and potentially gather the passwords he or she needs to decrypt files, read all your email, and gather even more data; and all it takes for this to happen is for you to leave your Mac unattended for 5 minutes. The vast majority of Mac users don't employ any of the security techniques that I recommend that could thwart a tool like this, and that fact is what makes it so effective.

Note

My recommendations for securing your Mac in a way that would protect it against most (or all) of the checks MacLockPick II performs are scattered throughout this book. But in particular, see my suggestions for securing logins in Chapter 4, locking your keychain in Chapter 5, covering your web-browsing tracks in Chapter 10, and encrypting files in Chapter 13. ∎

But the flip side, of course, is that if you're a police officer investigating a crime or an IT manager looking for evidence of corporate espionage, this tool can be incredibly useful for forensic analysis (not to mention being easy enough for anyone to use — even without a technical background).

MacQuisition

BlackBag's MacQuisition CF (http://blackbagtech.com/store/software/blackbag_macquisition_cf.html, $599) is a tool for acquiring a complete image of a hard disk. It's distributed in the form of a flash RAM card that plugs into included adapters for USB, FireWire 400, and FireWire 800. Based on that description, MacQuisition may sound superficially similar to MacLockPick II, but in fact, it works in an entirely different way. Instead of pulling live data from a running Mac, MacQuisition is designed to safely (without writing any data to the disk being investigated) copy all the data from a computer that's been shut down.

To use MacQuisition, you plug in the MacQuisition CF device, turn on the Mac while holding down the Option key, and select MacQuisition as the startup volume for your Mac. Once it's booted from the flash drive, you can run the software and store an image of the target disk on another external drive or a network volume.

MacQuisition CF itself merely copies the data in a secure fashion; it doesn't include any analysis capabilities. To analyze the data collected with MacQuisition, you must use a different set of tools, such as BlackBag's Forensic Suite.

BlackBag Forensic Suite

BlackBag Forensic Suite (http://blackbagtech.com/store/software/blackbag_macintosh_forensic_suite.html, $799) is a set of software tools for analyzing data on a hard disk (or, ideally, a read-only image of a disk) in order to find specific pieces of information with particular forensic value. That puts it in the same general category as MacForensicsLab, described earlier in this chapter. However, unlike MacForensicsLab, which is a single, integrated package, BlackBag Forensic Suite comes as a large collection of individual, task-specific programs. An included ToolBar application provides buttons to launch many of the other programs with just one click, as shown in Figure 24.16.

FIGURE 24.16

BlackBag Forensic Suite consists of a large number of individual tools, most of which can be accessed using the toolbar (which appears on the left). A few other sample tools are shown.

The BlackBag website claims the suite contains 19 tools. However, the ToolBar (not a tool itself) lists 25 programs — and the package contains 7 programs not listed on the toolbar, not counting 6 others listed in an Older Applications folder. So, I count somewhere between 32 and 38 tools, but in any case, it's quite a few. Of these, some of the most interesting are FileSpy, which shows the text contents of any file; GraphicView, which does something similar for the graphical portions of files; ImageBuster, which searches raw disk image files for keywords; and Phantom Search, which locates all the invisible files in a folder or volume. It can also analyze Safari caches, bookmarks, history, and cookies, among many other things.

BlackBag Forensic Suite's lack of integration and its old-school, minimalist interface make it much less user-friendly than MacForensicsLab. It also lacks the capability to analyze several types of data that have become more common in recent years — for example, GraphicView can't open PDF files. Unless you have a particular need for one of BlackBag Forensic Suite's tools that you can't find anywhere else, you may find MacForensicsLab to hold more appeal.

Mac Marshal

Cyber Security Technologies' Mac Marshal (`www.cyberstc.com/products_mac.asp`, $995 but free to law enforcement), a relative newcomer in Mac forensics software, is also designed to analyze previously acquired disk images. However, unlike BlackBag Forensic Suite, Mac Marshal is highly automated, providing a wealth of data without a great deal of effort (and without the need for extensive technical knowledge).

Mac Marshal can locate and display common information types such as Address Book contents, iChat transcripts, Safari history and other browsing details, and much of the data stored on an iPhone. It can also detect and analyze Boot Camp partitions and virtual machines created by Parallels Desktop, VirtualBox, and VMware Fusion — making it easier to discover files that may have been hidden in a secondary operating system on a Mac. The software includes built-in tools for performing dictionary or brute-force attacks on encrypted disk images.

The Sleuth Kit

All the programs mentioned so far have been commercial Mac OS X applications. A free, open-source option also exists: the Sleuth Kit (`www.sleuthkit.org/sleuthkit/desc.php`), a set of command-line programs for performing various sorts of forensic analysis. However, although the tools run on Mac OS X, they weren't designed specifically for Mac OS X, and as a result, they lack direct support for HFS (the usual Mac file system) and much of the Mac-specific data types all the other programs listed in this section can analyze.

Summary

If, despite all your efforts at prevention, your Mac has been the victim of some sort of attack — malware, unauthorized network access, data theft, or whatever — learning exactly what happened and why can help you to prevent similar problems in the future (and, in some cases, identify the source of the attack, which may be especially crucial information if a crime has been committed). This chapter provided a brief overview of computer forensics, including a discussion of how to identify illicit processes and applications, how to tell what programs are communicating with whom over the Internet, and analyzing a potentially compromised Mac using MacForensicsLab or other tools.

Part V

Securing
Mac OS X Server

Mac OS X Server Security Overview

The standard version of Mac OS X offers a long list of ways to share files and other resources, making it easy for users to exchange information with other devices on their local network or around the world. However, Apple also offers a version of their operating system called Mac OS X Server, which includes many additional server capabilities and is also an ideal tool for organizations of any size to manage their internal network as well as provide services to users on the Internet without tremendous technical challenges.

Nearly everything discussed so far in this book applies equally to Mac OS X and Mac OS X Server. However, because the server version has extra features — and ones that make it more likely to be visible to the outside world — those managing a Mac OS X Server installation should know some additional facts to keep their server and the rest of their network secure.

The remainder of this book discusses issues specific to Mac OS X Server, and this chapter provides background information to explain some of the most important Mac OS X Server concepts.

Comparing Mac OS X and Mac OS X Server

If you're already running Mac OS X Server, you may be intimately familiar with its design and what makes it different from the standard version of Mac OS X. But if you're considering whether to purchase it for your business or have been tasked with managing a Mac OS X Server installation someone else has set up, you may find it helpful to understand what you're getting yourself into. What makes Mac OS X Server different from plain old Mac OS X?

The first thing I want to clarify is that the standard version of Mac OS X — the one most people run — is not "Mac OS X Client." That is, the fact that there's a version of the operating system with "Server" in the name doesn't somehow imply that the other version is a client. Any operating system can act as either a client or a server (or both at the same time) for various activities, and that's certainly true of Mac OS X and Mac OS X Server. So, if I need to say something about the normal, non-server version of Mac OS X to distinguish it from Mac OS X Server, I use expressions such as "the standard version" or "regular" or "ordinary" Mac OS X. Apart from such uses, the statements that I make generally apply to both versions of the operating system.

In fact, it can hardly be otherwise because Mac OS X and Mac OS X Server are mostly identical. The multitude of Unix pieces that make up the core of the operating system — the Finder, the menu bar, the Dock, applications such as Mail and Address Book, and utilities such as Terminal and Disk Utility — are exactly the same between the two operating systems. Any application that can run on Mac OS X can also run on Mac OS X Server, and that includes everything from Photo Booth to InDesign. If you wanted to, you could use a Mac running Mac OS X Server as your everyday computer, and you would be able to do everything with it that you could on any other Mac. The only significant exception is that Mac OS X Server isn't supported on laptops, such as the MacBook Pro, although even there, you can run it without difficulty if you use virtualization software such as VMware Fusion or Parallels Desktop.

The best way to think of Mac OS X Server is as a superset of Mac OS X. It's the same Mac OS X you know and love — plus a bunch of other stuff that gives it powerful new capabilities. And as the name suggests, all those additional capabilities are geared toward providing services to other devices. Dozens of server features are built into Mac OS X Server (you can see a complete list at www.apple.com/server/macosx/ specs.html). Some of the most important ones, particularly in terms of their security features, are the following:

- **Calendar server.** Enable shared calendars for an entire organization using iCal Server.
- **Chat server.** Mac OS X Server includes iChat Server for intra-network instant messaging.
- **Directory services.** As I discuss later in this chapter, Mac OS X Server uses Open Directory to provide centralized management of users, groups, and authentication for an entire network.
- **File serving.** You can serve files from Mac OS X Server using such protocols as AFP, SMB, FTP, NFS, and WebDAV.
- **Firewall.** Although every Mac includes built-in firewall software, Mac OS X Server offers much more extensive customization in a handy graphical UI — and assuming the Mac it's running on has more than one Ethernet port, it can also provide firewall services to an entire network.
- **Mail server.** Along with built-in POP, IMAP, and SMTP servers, Mac OS X Server can serve mailing lists, filter out spam and viruses, provide web-based access to email, and encrypt mail transfers using SSL.
- **VPN.** You can use Mac OS X Server to set up a VPN, allowing remote users to securely connect to a single computer or your entire network.
- **Web server.** Mac OS X Server includes Apache 2, along with many programs and services that work together with it, such as Perl, PHP, Python, Ruby, MySQL, and WebDAV.

Some server features, such as iCal Server and Podcast Producer, are unique to Mac OS X Server (although comparable third-party products may exist). Others, such as Apache and the Postfix SMTP server, also come with the regular version of Mac OS X, but Mac OS X Server includes a series of administrative tools that provide an outstanding, straightforward user interface for configuring and managing websites, a mail server, and other services that would otherwise require much more effort to run.

These administrative tools are your window into all the activities going on behind the scenes on your server, and as the administrator of a Mac OS X Server installation, you'll be using them often. You may still have to pop in to Terminal on occasion, but for the most part, everything you need to do in order to administer

Mac OS X Server can be done in a convenient and friendly graphical interface. Because the remaining chapters in this book refer frequently to these programs, a quick overview is in order:

- **Server Admin.** This application, shown in Figure 25.1, is the central control panel for activating and configuring most of the services Mac OS X Server offers, such as AFP, DNS, iChat, Mail, Open Directory, VPN, and the web server. When in doubt, this is the first place you should look for any server management functions.

- **Server Preferences.** With a visual appearance similar to System Preferences, Server Preferences, shown in Figure 25.2, offers a simplified interface for managing a subset of the services you would otherwise configure with Server Admin and Workgroup Manager. If you're comfortable using those other tools, you need never touch Server Preferences, but it's a quicker and friendlier way to access many common server features.

- **System Preferences.** Like the regular version of Mac OS X, Mac OS X Server has a System Preferences application for configuring settings such as Dock and Spotlight behavior, displays, network connections, and Software Update. However, the Mac OS X Server version has fewer features because many of the features normally managed in System Preferences (such as file and web sharing) are handled by other administrative tools.

- **Workgroup Manager.** Although the Server Preferences application provides basic configuration of network users and groups, Workgroup Manager, shown in Figure 25.3, offers a far more detailed view of the data, giving you more control over the capabilities and restrictions associated with each account.

FIGURE 25.1

Server Admin is your one-stop destination for managing almost every service Mac OS X Server offers.

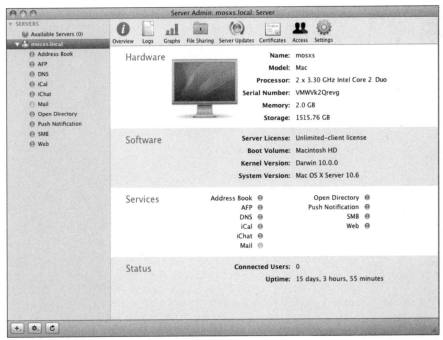

FIGURE 25.2

For a quicker and simpler way to adjust a few of the most commonly used server settings, use the Server Preferences application.

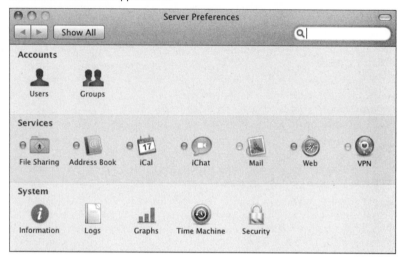

FIGURE 25.3

To gain fine-grained control over every configurable user and group setting — much more than Server Admin offers — open Workgroup Manager.

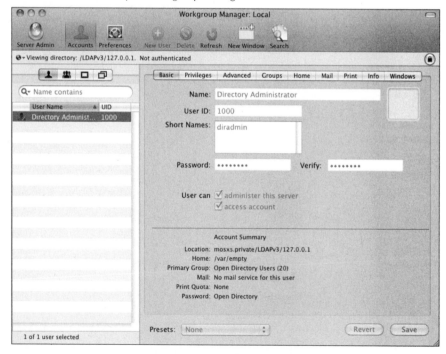

- **Xgrid Admin.** Apple's Xgrid technology is a way to group multiple Macs together to increase the amount of computing power available for certain CPU-intensive tasks. The Xgrid Admin utility lets you manage these special networks.

Note
Mac OS X Server also includes several administrative tools not covered in this book, such as Podcast Composer, RAID Admin, Server Assistant, Server Monitor, and System Image Utility. ■

Although most of the server features and user interface are the same between Leopard Server and Snow Leopard Server, the latter includes several interesting changes:

- **Address Book Server.** An easy-to-use, flexible alternative to LDAP for sharing basic contact information among network users

- **iCal Server 2.** A new version of iCal Server that includes push notifications, broader client compatibility, and a web client

- **Mail Server.** An improved email facility in which Apple replaced the Cyrus POP/IMAP server with Dovecot, added push email support, and included several other new features

- **Mobile Access Server.** A new reverse proxy server that enables remote users to connect securely to services running on Mac OS X Server without using a VPN

- **Podcast Producer 2.** An enhanced and updated version of the tool for encoding and publishing audio or video podcasts, along with a graphical editor for podcast workflows called Podcast Composer

- **Wiki Server 2.** A significant overhaul to the Wiki server, which lets users collaborate freely on websites, even from an iPhone

Mac OS X Server Security Fundamentals

As I said earlier in this chapter, virtually everything that's true of the regular version of Mac OS X is also true of Mac OS X Server. The underlying operating system is the same, so everything you've already learned about physical security, the Keychain, file encryption, network security, and all the rest is equally applicable here. Especially if you happen to be using a Mac running Mac OS X Server as a normal workstation (in addition to functioning as a server), be sure to review the rest of this book for important security tips.

Apart from the fact that all services are off unless you explicitly turn them on (whether during installation or later), Mac OS X Server has default settings for most services that are fairly permissive in terms of security. Although the operating system has the capability to be quite secure, it's up to you, as the administrator, to know which settings must be configured in which way and to take the appropriate steps to make your setup secure. Activating a bunch of services without first thinking through your security needs and carefully examining each setting is extremely unwise and can lead to an insecure server and network.

A good place to start in familiarizing yourself with the security issues of Mac OS X Server is Apple's *Security Configuration Guide*. You can download this free PDF for whichever version of Mac OS X Server you're using from `www.apple.com/support/security/guides`. The Leopard version, for example, runs to 476 pages and goes into excruciating detail about each setting that has any sort of security consideration. It's a long and dense read, for sure, but it provides far more information than I can offer in this book.

I would like to call your attention, though, to a few areas of particular concern. The first is administrator access. On a Mac OS X Server computer, as on any Mac, you can set up local user accounts with administrative privileges — enabling those users to change virtually anything on the server. I discuss the configuration of local user accounts later in this chapter.

If you're using Mac OS X Server to manage the accounts and permissions of an entire network (which could be tens of thousands of people), the practical implication is that the administrator has extensive control over not just one computer but many. That, in turn, makes it crucial for you to treat administrator accounts with the utmost care. For example, be sure to choose long, complex, random passwords, and keep them private. Limit the number of administrators, and make sure each one understands the importance of guarding his or her account information. After all, if an administrator account were hacked, it could have disastrous consequences for every user on your network.

Cross-Ref

For more on choosing good passwords, see Chapter 6. ■

Second, think long and hard about keeping the server hardware itself safe. There's little chance that someone will swipe an Xserve from your server room when no one's looking, but theft isn't the only consideration. As with all Macs, anyone with physical access to a computer running Mac OS X Server can access private data and make modifications to the machine that bypass otherwise reliable safeguards. Therefore, I strongly recommend keeping any computer running Mac OS X Server in a locked room with limited access — and employing additional measures such as video surveillance, an alarm system, or a biometric door lock might be appropriate in large installations or in any organization where a great deal of confidential information is generated.

Finally, consider that with Mac OS X Server, you can set up policies that apply to every user on your network. For example, you can enforce the use of passwords with at least a given length, prevent users from accessing certain types of data or visiting particular websites, and even log all the activities of each user. Some administrators, excited about the level of control they have and eager to plug every possible security hole, set up highly restrictive policies that make everyday computer use a chore and an aggravation, whereas others go to the opposite extreme, at which every user is implicitly trusted to make wise decisions and respect the organization's rules. Ideally, you should strike a balance somewhere in the middle.

In any case, my advice is not to make such decisions unilaterally and to avoid restricting user behavior without a good, specific reason — and "because you can" isn't a reason! Before configuring your server, I suggest sitting down with a few key decision-makers in your organization (and perhaps a few representative users too) to discuss the ins and outs of network security and assemble a cogent written security policy. Once all your users understand exactly what they can and can't do — and why — you can implement appropriate settings at the server level.

Understanding Open Directory

A single Mac can have an account for just one user — or a handful of accounts or dozens. Each user, in turn, can have an address book that provides names and email addresses for any number of people, and that address book data is stored on a part of the disk dedicated to that user's account. This arrangement works perfectly well in situations where a person has just one Mac and even in environments where several Macs are in use.

However, there comes a point at which maintaining individual user accounts on each computer and individual address books for each user is more effort than it's worth. For example, suppose you're the administrator of a company with 50 employees, each with his or her own Mac. In order to set up everyone's user accounts, passwords, permissions, network configurations, and other details, you must go through a similar series of steps on each of those 50 computers — and when something changes, you must again carry out your updating tasks 50 times. And what if someone needs to switch computers for some reason? Ah, too bad: The new computer doesn't know who he or she is and must have all his or her account information added again by hand!

Meanwhile, every employee wants his or her address book to contain the names and email addresses of all the others, so that means a tremendous duplication of effort to keep them all accurate, up to date, and in sync. Now, imagine that it's not a company of 50 people but a university of 50,000, and you can see the need for a centralized way to manage user information — a single location from which one or more administrators can enter and update names, addresses, passwords, and other important details, which then become available anywhere on the network (subject to whatever restrictions the administrator implements). All this and more can be done by a *directory service*, of which there are many varieties.

On Mac OS X Server, the directory service is called Open Directory. Although it's possible to use Mac OS X Server without employing Open Directory at all, the concept is integral to many of the shared resources you're likely to provide with your server. And because so many of those resources have security implications involving passwords, authentication, and authorization, you need at least a basic understanding of Open Directory to make good security decisions.

The problem, however, is defining what Open Directory actually is. It isn't a program, a protocol, or a specification — not exactly. Rather, it's the expression Apple uses to refer to its own implementation of several interrelated services — all having to do with identifying users on a network and determining how they can go about accessing various resources. You may end up using some Open Directory elements but not others, and you may even use Open Directory as a sort of conduit to access directory services provided by other systems, such as Microsoft Active Directory.

To oversimplify somewhat, Open Directory on Mac OS X Server involves the following main components:

- **An LDAP server.** LDAP (Lightweight Directory Access Protocol) is a protocol for storing hierarchical directory information and accessing it over a network. Large organizations often use LDAP to provide a central address book for all their users, although LDAP's capabilities go well beyond that. Open Directory's LDAP server is based on OpenLDAP, which (as the name suggests) is an open-source implementation of the protocol.

- **A password server.** Mac OS X Server has a feature creatively named Password Server (discussed later in this chapter) that provides authentication (verifying a user's credentials, such as username and password). This information is stored separately from the LDAP directory data.

- **A Kerberos key distribution center (KDC).** Also described later in this chapter, Kerberos is a secure, bi-directional authentication protocol that can enable a person to sign in just once and gain access to a wide range of services (instead of typing credentials separately for each one). Mac OS X Server has a built-in KDC, but Open Directory can also connect to a KDC running on another computer. Kerberos can be used instead of Password Server for many (but not all) kinds of authentication.

The key thing to notice is that Open Directory isn't a single monolithic service but rather a framework that can integrate a variety of components (even ones from different manufacturers, computers, and platforms), each designed for a specific task.

Note

In the context of Open Directory (or any other directory service), a domain is a storage container for directory data — which could mean a database or any of various file formats. A computer running Mac OS X Server is referred to as an Open Directory master if it hosts one or more Open Directory domains. If you have more than one computer running Mac OS X Server, you can also designate one or more Open Directory replicas, which contain automatically synchronized copies of the directory data on the master. These extra servers can reduce the load on the master and can take over in case the master fails. ■

One helpful way to look at Open Directory is from the point of view of an individual user. If Alisha has a Mac that doesn't use an Open Directory server, all the information about her account — her name, passwords, permissions, and so on — resides in files on her computer. So, when she types her username and password to log in, Mac OS X checks them against locally stored data. On the other hand, suppose Bernard has a Mac that does connect to an Open Directory server. When he types his credentials in a login window, his Mac first checks its local records to see if his account information is there. If not, it automatically connects to the Open Directory server (which he previously configured in the Accounts pane of System Preferences). Assuming the server is online, Mac OS X checks it for Bernard's account, and if it's there, it uses the information on the server to determine whether he can log in and what resources he can access.

In fact, the interactions among computers can be much more complex than this. With Open Directory, you might have several different servers (or several services running on a single computer), each of which manages a different sort of account information. You can specify a search policy specifying the order in which various databases and files are checked to validate credentials, and what happens behind the scenes for one user accessing one resource may be entirely different from what happens to another. But from the user's viewpoint, it's all transparent. As long as Open Directory is set up properly, Bernard should have exactly the same experience of logging in as Alisha does but with greatly improved flexibility and administrative convenience.

Cross-Ref

For more on Open Directory, see Chapter 26. ■

Understanding Password Server and Kerberos

Previously, I explained that Open Directory includes an LDAP server, which stores and distributes information about users' identities. However, LDAP isn't ideal for managing passwords. Instead, Open Directory uses either of two mechanisms to authenticate users (confirm their identities) and *authorize* them (give them access to whichever resources they're approved to use). Either way, password data is stored in a secure database separate from the LDAP data.

Note

This section assumes that your server is configured to serve as an Open Directory master — that it's designated as the central repository for directory information. It's also possible for Mac OS X Server to function as a replica of another Open Directory server, to connect to another server (such as Microsoft Active Directory) for directory data, or to have Open Directory turned off altogether, in which case only local accounts are available. ■

The first mechanism is called Password Server. It's not a separate program or even a separately configurable service but rather a feature of Open Directory that stores and validates passwords. Password Server is flexible in that it uses the SASL (Simple Authentication and Security Layer) framework to support all the different authentication methods that may be used by the various server and client software users might run — for example, CRAM-MD5 for IMAP, Digest-MD5 for the login window, and NTLM for SMB. When you create a new network user account and choose Open Directory as the password type, Password Server is automatically used to manage the password.

Note

In lieu of Open Directory, you can choose Crypt Password as a network user's password type. This password type is much less secure and should be used only when needed for compatibility with Macs running Mac OS X 10.1 or earlier. Meanwhile, passwords for local accounts (described later in this chapter) as opposed to network accounts can have a type of either Open Directory or Shadow Password, the latter of which is available only on the server itself and can't be shared. ■

Cross-Ref

For more on configuring user accounts, including password types and authentication methods, see Chapter 26. ■

The second authentication mechanism is called Kerberos; like Password Server, it's built into Open Directory and doesn't appear as an independent program or service. Kerberos is an industry-standard protocol that does more than merely confirm a user's password. It also securely identifies the client to the server as well as the server to the client — each side can be sure they know the true identity of the other. More interestingly, Kerberos lets a user authenticate just once and thereafter access any number of services on any number of computers, as long as they all use the same Kerberos KDC and are all "Kerberized" — that is, designed or modified to support Kerberos. An administrator can control how long this single sign-in permission lasts.

The practical upshot is that if you're using a Mac running Mac OS X that connects to a properly configured Open Directory server running on Mac OS X Server, typing your username and password at the login prompt also lets you use all the following services (assuming they're activated) on the server without providing your credentials again:

- AFP, FTP, and NFS file sharing (plus SMB — but only if the server also connects to a separate Microsoft Active Directory server)
- Email (POP, IMAP, and SMTP)
- iChat server
- LDAP directory service
- Print server
- VPN
- Web server
- Xgrid

If other services (running on the Mac OS X Server computer or another that's connected to the same KDC) have been Kerberized, the user can access those too.

Note

There's one minor "gotcha" to this login process. In Mac OS X, the login window can either show a list of users (the default) — in which case a user can simply click a name and then type a password — or blanks to type both a username and a password. In the former case, users must click Other in the list and then type their username and password the first time they connect to an Open Directory server. ■

Fortunately, you don't have to choose between Password Server and Kerberos. As long as Open Directory is active and you use the Open Directory password type when creating user accounts, Mac OS X Server stores password information in both databases and even keeps the two systems' password policies (for all users or for individual users) in sync automatically. When a user attempts to log in, Mac OS X Server uses Kerberos if applicable (that is, if it's configured properly and the service in question has been Kerberized), and if not, it defaults to Password Server. So, for the most part, the operation of these two authentication mechanisms is transparent to users and administrators alike.

However, Kerberos is rather picky about the way it's initially set up. For example, your server must have active, matching forward and reverse DNS entries when you turn on Open Directory the first time in order for the Kerberos KDC to configure itself correctly.

To learn about all the ins and outs of Open Directory in general and Kerberos and Password Server in particular — including setup, migration, and troubleshooting instructions — consult Apple's free PDF *Open Directory Administration*, available at `www.apple.com/server/macosx/resources/documentation.html`.

Choosing Which Services to Run

As I explained earlier in this chapter, the list of services you can offer on a computer running Mac OS X Server is quite long. During your initial setup of Mac OS X Server, the Server Assistant program asks you what services you want to provide and activates those automatically. Afterward, you can change your mind — adding or deactivating services as you want — using Server Admin. But the question is which of the many services you should use.

The trivial answer is that you should run all and only the services you need. If your organization installed an Xserve to function as a web server, for example, then clearly you need to have the web server turned on. But my advice is to avoid turning on anything you're not sure you need. Because every running service provides another possible avenue of attack, another way someone could potentially exploit a bug or security hole to gain control of your server or steal your data, the safest practice is to leave any service you're not actively using turned off and to turn it on only when the specific need arises. If you're not certain that you need a service running, you probably don't.

Cross-Ref

For more on securing Mac OS X Server's web server, see Chapter 30. ■

One area in which this decision is especially important is file sharing. If you know you need to share files from a computer running Mac OS X Server, you can use any or all of four services: AFP, FTP, NFS, and SMB. Of these, NFS is technically the most secure in that it can be configured to encrypt all traffic; on the other hand, AFP (which encrypts the authentication process but not other data transfer) is generally the best choice for an all-Mac network. FTP is the least secure by far and should be used only if you must offer files to clients outside your network that can use no other protocol for some reason. SMB can be reasonably secure and may be an appropriate choice if you must share files with Windows computers. However, because many operating systems — especially more recent versions — support a wide range of file-sharing protocols, it's best to start with just one and turn on additional protocols only if there's a demonstrated need (namely, you encounter a client that can't connect).

Cross-Ref

For more on configuring security for all the file-sharing protocols that Mac OS X Server supports, see Chapter 29. ■

Remember that even though a single Mac running Mac OS X Server can provide many services and potentially meet all the server needs of a small organization, the design of the operating system supports and encourages the use of multiple physical servers. By using more than one server computer, you can distribute the computing load to increase performance, create redundancy that can keep services running if any one server goes down, or both. Another benefit of using multiple servers is keeping services isolated from each other. For example, you could have one Mac running Mac OS X Server with only AFP turned on, another with Open Directory running, and a third functioning solely as a web server. By doing this, you greatly reduce your vulnerability because even if someone were able to hack into one of your servers, the attacker would be able to access only the data and services specific to that one machine — the rest of your network would be unaffected.

Once you've decided which services to use, turning them on (or others off) is simple. Although you can start and stop some services using Server Preferences, Server Admin gives you the entire list of possible services, so at least until you've settled on a final list of services and are sure they're all available in Server Preferences, I recommend making your changes in Server Admin so you can see the whole picture.

The sidebar on the left of the Server Admin window lists all the servers you've added (Server Admin can be used to manage installations of Mac OS X Server on more than one Mac) and, for each one, the services that are available. Because the list of potential services is so long, Server Admin lets you customize the list so that only the services you may at some point want to run are shown in the list. A service that appears in the list can be running or stopped (as shown by a green or clear dot, respectively), but you can't run a service unless it appears in the list (and, conversely, you can't remove a service from the list while it's running).

To determine which services are listed in Server Admin, follow these steps:

1. **Open Server Admin, which is located in** `/Applications/Server`.
2. **In the sidebar on the left, select your server.**
3. **If no services are listed under the server name, click the disclosure triangle next to the server name to reveal them.**
4. **If the service names are dimmed, choose Server ⇨ Connect, type your username and password if they're not already filled in, and then click Connect.** The list of services refreshes, and those currently running appear with a green dot next to them.
5. **Click the Settings button on the toolbar and then click the Services tab.** A list of services appears, as shown in Figure 25.4.
6. **For each service you want to add to the list, click the check box to its left.**
7. **To remove a service, first make sure it's not running, as indicated by a clear dot next to its name, and then click its check box to deselect it.** If it is running, you must stop it first, per the directions that follow, and then repeat steps 2 through 5.
8. **Click Save.** In a few moments, the list refreshes to reflect your changes.

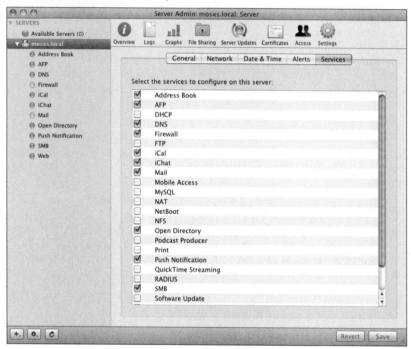

FIGURE 25.4

The sidebar on the left of the Server Admin window lists all the services you can currently configure (running or not); to change the contents of this list, go to the Services pane and select or deselect the check boxes for any of the services shown.

With the list of services modified to show just those you expect to run at some point, you can turn individual services on or off with just a few clicks. To activate or deactivate a service shown in Server Admin, follow these steps:

1. Open Server Admin, which is located in `/Applications/Server`.

2. In the sidebar on the left, select your server.

3. If no services are listed under the server name, click the disclosure triangle next to the server name to reveal them.

4. If the service names are dimmed, choose Server ➪ Connect, type your username and password if they're not already filled in, and then click Connect. The list of services refreshes, and those that are currently running appear with a green dot next to them.

5. Select a service in the list on the left. For example, Figure 25.5 shows the window as it appears with SMB selected.

6. As appropriate, click either the Start *Service* or Stop *Service* button (where *Service* is the name of the service you've selected) located beneath the sidebar. The service starts up or shuts down.

FIGURE 25.5

Activating or deactivating any service listed in Server Admin's sidebar is as simple as selecting it and then clicking the Start or Stop button at the bottom.

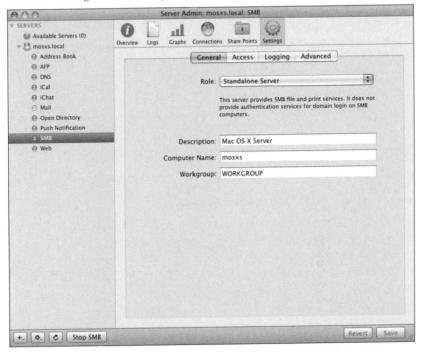

Configuring Local User Accounts

One of the uses to which you'll most likely put Mac OS X Server is creating network-wide accounts using Open Directory so user data can be managed in a single location and all users have access to the same resources and account data no matter which computer they use to log in.

Cross-Ref

For more on creating and managing Open Directory network accounts, see Chapter 26. ■

However, entirely separate from these network user accounts are the local accounts, which apply to users accessing the server directly. These accounts can fall into three categories:

- **Administrators.** When you initially set up Mac OS X Server, you created an administrator account. As usual, this administrator can modify nearly anything on the server itself, which includes adding, deleting, and changing local users, turning network services on and off, and modifying other server settings. You can create one or more additional administrators too, each of which has the same set of privileges. I describe how to do this just ahead.

- **Directory administrators.** At the same time Mac OS X Server created an initial administrator account, it may have also created a second account, for a directory administrator; in any case, you can create more manually. An initial directory administrator account is created during setup if you opted to make your computer an Open Directory master. By default, this account's name is Directory Administrator, its short name is diradmin, and its password is the same as that of the original administrator. A directory administrator has all the privileges of a regular administrator plus the ability to modify directory entries (such as user and group accounts). You must use Workgroup Manager to create new directory administrator accounts, as I explain shortly.

- **Other users.** Although administrators are the people most likely to be using Mac OS X Server, you can use the Accounts pane of System Preferences to create other account types — including standard and managed accounts — just as you can on the regular version of Mac OS X. These accounts would grant users limited access only to the server computer itself. The most likely reason to create such accounts would be a setting in which the server computer must also function as a workstation and be used by people who should not have administrative privileges. However, I suggest avoiding such accounts if possible and restricting all access to the server to administrators.

Cross-Ref

For more on creating and managing all the types of user accounts that apply to individual Macs, see Chapter 3. ■

To add an administrator account, follow these steps:

1. Choose ➪ System Preferences and then click the Accounts icon.
2. If the lock icon in the lower-left corner of the window is in the locked state, click it, type an administrator's username and password, and then click OK.
3. Click the Add (+) button below the list of accounts.
4. From the New Account pop-up menu, shown in Figure 25.6, choose Administrator.
5. Fill in the Full Name and Account name fields.

FIGURE 25.6

In the New Account dialog box, you specify the type of account, short and long usernames, password, and an optional password hint for an additional administrator.

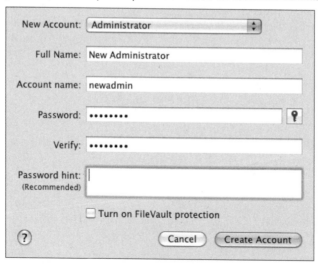

6. Type and verify a password and optionally type a password hint.

7. Click Create Account.

8. Close System Preferences.

Accounts for directory administrators, unlike regular administrator accounts, don't appear in the Accounts pane of System Preferences or in the Users pane of Server Preferences. Instead, you manage these accounts using Workgroup Manager.

To add a directory administrator account, follow these steps:

1. **Open Workgroup Manager, which is located in** `/Applications/Server`.

2. **In the Connect dialog box, type the username and password of the administrator account you created when you initially set up Mac OS X Server and then click Connect.**

3. **Look just below the toolbar on the left side, where a status bar shows your current directory domain. If it's anything other than LDAPv3 followed by the server's IP address, click the globe icon and then choose the appropriate LDAP domain from the pop-up menu that appears.**

4. **If the status bar says "Not authenticated," click the lock icon on the right side of the bar, type the username and password for an existing directory administrator (use diradmin and the password for the original administrator account, respectively, if you haven't created any other directory administrator accounts), and then click Authenticate.** The window should look something like Figure 25.7.

FIGURE 25.7

Workgroup Manager lets you add, delete, and modify user accounts — including accounts for directory administrators, as shown here.

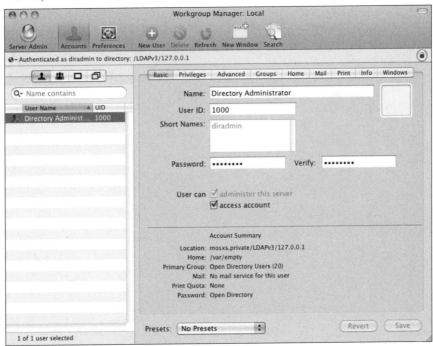

5. To add a directory administrator, click the New User button on the toolbar, and if an alert appears stating "New users may not have access to services," click OK.

6. At minimum, fill in the fields for Name, Short Names, Password, and Verify.

7. Click the Privileges tab and then choose Full from the Administration capabilities pop-up menu.

8. Click Save. The new directory administrator account becomes active immediately.

Summary

This chapter provided an overview of the security considerations in Mac OS X Server that go beyond those of the standard version of Mac OS X. After comparing the two operating systems briefly, I discussed the main security issues any Mac OS X Server administrator must take into account. I then explored Open Directory, which lets an organization store credentials for a large number of users in a centralized database — in particular, Password Server and Kerberos, two mechanisms Open Directory can use for authentication. I also discussed the important decision of which services to run and which to avoid on Mac OS X Server and how to configure the accounts of administrators and other local users on the server.

Using Directory Services

O pen Directory, Apple's suite of directory service technologies, provides network-wide authentication, authorization, contact information, and numerous other capabilities. In addition, Mac OS X Server can tie into an existing Microsoft Active Directory domain on your network. Either way, you get a flexible centralized mechanism for defining users, groups, and the resources they can access. Almost every service included in Mac OS X Server makes use of directory services in some fashion. Because so many of the security choices you make when setting up and running a server involve determining who can access what, it's important to understand the fundamentals of how Mac OS X Server's directory services function.

Cross-Ref

For more on Open Directory and some of the problems it solves, see Chapter 25. ■

In this chapter, I provide a quick introduction to configuring Open Directory (especially some of its key security settings), setting up users and groups, and connecting to Active Directory.

Configuring Open Directory

Like so many aspects of Mac OS X Server, Open Directory has a seemingly endless number of configurable options. If you know where to look and you dig deep enough, you can uncover a startling array of preferences and fiddly settings — the better to customize your server's behavior to your exact specifications. Apple's

---

IN THIS CHAPTER

Setting up Open Directory

Configuring network users and groups

Connecting client Macs to Open Directory

Combining Open Directory with Windows Active Directory

own documentation, the free PDF *Open Directory Administration* (available at www.apple.com/server/ macosx/resources/documentation.html), is about 300 pages long, and even at that, it may not address every single detail you care about — although some of Apple's other guides for Mac OS X Server administrators pick up part of the slack.

Needless to say, given the complexity of Open Directory, I can only scratch the surface in this book. So, I want to look at Open Directory from a relatively high level, concentrating on the basic steps you can take to use this service safely for authentication and directory services on your network. This involves a handful of settings that affect Open Directory's overall functioning as well as the crucial process of setting up users and groups.

Activating Open Directory

Depending on the choices you made when you installed Mac OS X Server, Open Directory may already be active — in fact, that's the most likely situation by far. Unlike most services, Open Directory can't simply be turned on or off by clicking a button. It's automatically active if you've chosen a role other than Standalone Server (as described in the next section) and if your server — particularly its DNS settings — is configured correctly.

To verify whether Open Directory is running, follow these steps:

1. **Open Server Admin, which is located in** /Applications/Server.
2. **In the sidebar on the left, select your server.**
3. **If no services are listed under the server name, click the disclosure triangle next to the server name to reveal them.**
4. **If the service names are dimmed, choose Server ⇨ Connect, type your username and password if they're not already filled in, and then click Connect.** The list of services refreshes, and those currently running appear with a green dot next to them.
5. **Look for Open Directory in the sidebar under your server name.** If it's there and if the dot next to it is green, Open Directory is running. If the dot is white — or if Open Directory doesn't appear in the list — it's not running. You can add Open Directory to the list, if necessary, by selecting your server name, clicking Settings, clicking Services, clicking the check box next to Open Directory, and then clicking Save.

Cross-Ref

For more on modifying the list of services, see Chapter 25. ∎

6. **To see details about Open Directory's current role and the state of each of its constituent services, select Open Directory in the sidebar list and then click the Overview button on the toolbar.** Your window should look something like Figure 26.1; the text shown will differ depending on the server's Open Directory configuration.

If Open Directory isn't running or if you want to change the way in which it's used, continue with the steps in the next section.

If Open Directory is running correctly, you see a green dot next to its name and Running next to one or more (usually all three) services on the right.

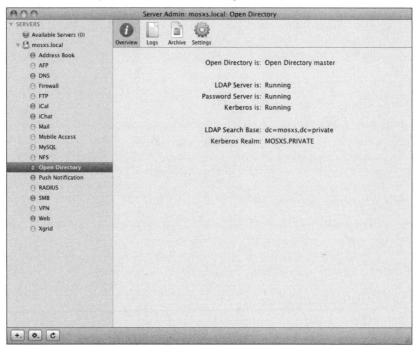

Choosing an Open Directory role

Mac OS X Server lets you operate Open Directory in any of four different roles. The role you choose determines how your server interacts with other computers on your network and what sorts of services you can make available on the network. Ordinarily, the role is chosen in the process of setting up Mac OS X Server for the first time, but if you decide later that you want Open Directory to function differently, you can change the role later. The four options are as follows:

- **Standalone Server.** Open Directory handles authentication and directory information for the server only. That is, an administrator or other user can connect directly to the server over the network, but the server can't be used to authenticate someone logging in to or using services on another computer on your network. If you have only one server and if you have no need to offer centralized authentication or address book services (for example, you use your server only for basic file and web serving), this is an appropriate setting. However, note that much of the rest of this chapter doesn't apply to servers with this setting because the primary value of Open Directory is in providing directory and authentication services across a network.

- **Open Directory master.** This is probably the most common setting and the one I assume you're using for most of the discussion in this chapter. When your server is functioning as an Open Directory master, it lets connected users authenticate for the purpose of logging in to or using services on other computers on your network (as well as, of course, the server on which Open Directory is running). With this setting, individual servers (and even client computers) need not store separate account records for each user. Even if you're running an Open Directory master, you need not necessarily have other servers on your network or require users to depend on your server when logging in. Therefore, if you're uncertain whether to use the Standalone Server or Open Directory master role, the latter provides more flexibility without imposing any significant constraints.

Note

If the current role is Open Directory master and yet the service isn't running, the most likely cause is an error in your DNS settings. Your server must have valid, matching forward and reverse DNS entries — that is, looking up your server's domain name must return its IP address (forward DNS) and looking up its IP address must return its domain name (reverse DNS). If not, contact the administrator of your DNS service to arrange to have those entries updated as necessary. Then, to repair your Open Directory configuration, follow the instructions found in Apple's *Open Directory Administration* PDF. ∎

- **Open Directory replica.** In this role, your server maintains a copy of the Open Directory data stored on another server. It can provide the same set of authorization and directory services to users that an Open Directory master can, but you can't modify records directly on the replica. One reason to set up a replica is redundancy; if your main server should go offline for any reason, users can still authenticate and obtain directory information. Another reason is distributing the load on busy networks. Replicas are overkill on small networks, and they require that you have at least two servers. However, with large networks (especially those spread out over a large geographical area, such as a college campus), setting up multiple servers as Open Directory replicas becomes important. I say little about Open Directory replicas in this book; for the full details, consult Apple's *Open Directory Administration* PDF.

- **Connect to another directory.** If you already have another directory server on your network, such as a Microsoft Active Directory server, Open Directory can use it for directory services, authentication, or both. For example, your network might use Active Directory to store contact information and login credentials for all your users (Mac and Windows), but use Mac OS X Server to offer services specific to Mac users, such as network home folders and managed preferences. By connecting to another directory, you avoid duplicating account information on multiple servers, while using each server for the activities it performs best. I provide more information on the use of Active Directory with Open Directory later in this chapter.

To change Open Directory on your server to function in a different role from its current one, follow these steps:

1. **Open Server Admin, which is located in** /Applications/Server.
2. **In the sidebar on the left, select your server.**
3. **If no services are listed under the server name, click the disclosure triangle next to the server name to reveal them.**
4. **If the service names are dimmed, choose Server ⇨ Connect, type your username and password if they're not already filled in, and then click Connect.** The list of services refreshes, and those currently running appear with a green dot next to them.

5. **Select Open Directory in the sidebar under your server name.** If Open Directory doesn't appear in the list, you must first add it by selecting your server name, clicking Settings, clicking Services, clicking the check box next to Open Directory, and then clicking Save.

6. **Click the Settings button on the toolbar.**

7. **Click the General tab and then click the Change button.** Open Directory Assistant, as shown in Figure 26.2, opens.

FIGURE 26.2

Open Directory Assistant lets you change your Open Directory role. The options shown here depend on the server's current role.

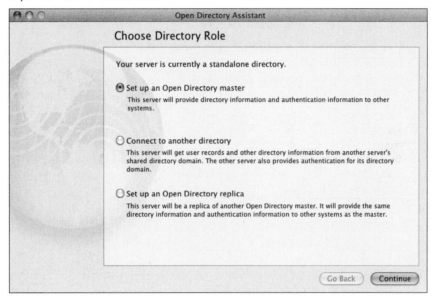

8. **Click the radio button corresponding to the role you want and then click Continue.** Follow the on-screen instructions, which vary according to the roles you're switching from and to but in general require clicking a few OK and Continue buttons to agree to informational messages.

9. **If you're switching to an Open Directory master, one of the screens you see, as shown in Figure 26.3, asks you to set up a directory administrator account.** You can keep the default long and short names (Directory Administrator and diradmin, respectively) or change them to your liking. Either way, type and verify a password for the directory administrator, which should be different from those of any existing administrator account, and then click Continue.

10. **At the final screen in Open Directory Assistant, click Done.** Open Directory is now configured to use the new role you chose.

Cross-Ref

For more on how the directory administrator account differs from ordinary administrator accounts, see Chapter 25. ■

The instructions that follow for configuring LDAP settings, policy settings, and user and group accounts assume that your server's role is Open Directory master.

Note

If you've configured Open Directory to connect to another directory, you must perform an additional step to tell the server which directory to connect to. I explain this process near the end of this chapter. ■

FIGURE 26.3

When switching your server's role to that of Open Directory master, you must create a directory administrator account as part of the process.

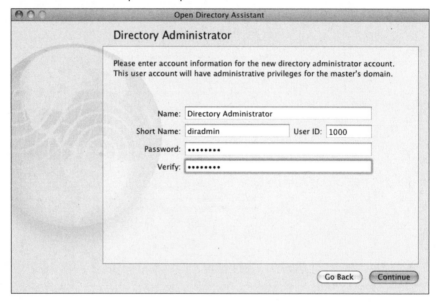

LDAP settings

Open Directory's built-in LDAP server ordinarily requires little configuration other than setting up individual user records (as covered later in this chapter). However, you may want to adjust one or two global settings.

To change Open Directory's LDAP settings, follow these steps:

1. **Open Server Admin, which is located in** `/Applications/Server`.
2. **In the sidebar on the left, select your server.**
3. **If no services are listed under the server name, click the disclosure triangle next to the server name to reveal them.**
4. **If the service names are dimmed, choose Server⇨ Connect, type your username and password if they're not already filled in, and then click Connect.** The list of services refreshes, and those currently running appear with a green dot next to them.

5. **Select Open Directory in the sidebar under your server name.** If Open Directory doesn't appear in the list, you must first add it by selecting your server name, clicking Settings, clicking Services, clicking the check box next to Open Directory, and then clicking Save.

6. **Click the Settings button on the toolbar.**

7. **Click the LDAP tab, shown in Figure 26.4.**

8. **To enable SSL for communication between your Open Directory LDAP server and LDAP clients on your network — which enables packets sent by the server to be digitally signed or encrypted — click the Enable SSL check box and then select an SSL certificate from the Certificate pop-up menu.** After selecting this option, you must also choose whether packets are signed, encrypted, or both, as described in the next section.

9. **Optionally, type a maximum number of search results (use a lower number to improve performance when your LDAP server contains many thousands of records), a different timeout value, or both.**

10. **Click Save.** The new settings become active immediately.

FIGURE 26.4

Although it's unnecessary for most installations, you can enable SSL for LDAP in this pane.

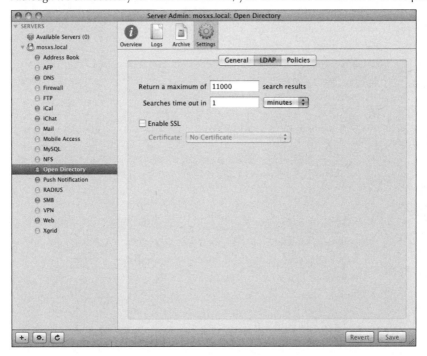

Policy settings

An Open Directory master can specify a number of policies regarding the ways client computers may, must, or must not use its services. These policies — some of which can be overridden for individual users —

include settings such as what length and complexity of password is required for users, whether authentication is used for client computers, and what types of authentication may be used by services that depend on Open Directory.

To configure global policies for your Open Directory master, follow these steps:

1. **Open Server Admin, which is located in** `/Applications/Server`.
2. **In the sidebar on the left, select your server.**
3. **If no services are listed under the server name, click the disclosure triangle next to the server name to reveal them.**
4. **If the service names are dimmed, choose Server⇨Connect, type your username and password if they're not already filled in, and then click Connect.** The list of services refreshes, and those currently running appear with a green dot next to them.
5. **Select Open Directory in the sidebar under your server name.** If Open Directory doesn't appear in the list, you must first add it by selecting your server name, clicking Settings, clicking Services, clicking the check box next to Open Directory, and then clicking Save.
6. **Click the Settings button on the toolbar.**
7. **Click the Policies tab (in Snow Leopard Server) or the Policy tab (in Leopard Server).**
8. **To configure password policies, click the Passwords tab, shown in Figure 26.5.** This pane contains numerous options you can adjust. Click the check box next to a policy to enable or disable it and, if appropriate, fill in other details. The settings are as follows:

Disable login:

- **on specific date.** Prevents any user from logging in after the date specified, unless overridden by that user's account settings
- **after using it for ___ days.** Prevents login after the specified number of days of access (starting with the user's first access of the account)
- **after inactive for ___ days.** Prevents login if the account hasn't been used in the number of days shown
- **after user makes ___ failed attempts.** Disables login if the password is typed incorrectly the number of times shown (useful for preventing dictionary and brute-force attacks to user accounts)

Passwords must:

- **differ from account name.** Requires passwords to be different from the user's username
- **contain at least one letter.** Requires every password to have at least one alphabetic character
- **contain both uppercase and lowercase letters.** Requires passwords to mix cases of letters
- **contain at least one numeric character.** Requires at least one digit in passwords
- **contain a character that isn't a letter or number.** Requires passwords to contain punctuation or other special characters
- **be reset on first user login.** Specifies that the password set up initially by the administrator is only for the user's first login, after which the user must change it to a password of his or her own choosing
- **contain at least ___ characters.** Requires a minimum length for passwords — this number should be no lower than 9

- **differ from last ___ passwords used.** Prevents users from reusing passwords they've recently chosen
- **be reset every ___ days/weeks/months.** Requires users to select a new password after the time period shown

FIGURE 26.5

In this pane, set global password policies, which apply to every user unless overridden by a particular user account.

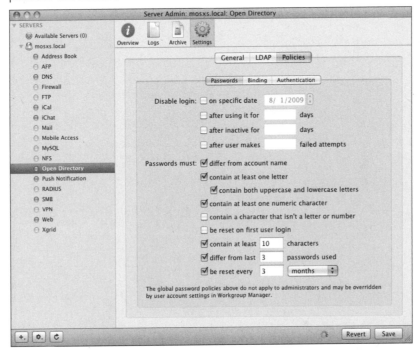

Note

As this pane states, password policies don't apply to **administrators**, and some of them can be overridden by user account settings (as described later in this chapter). ■

9. To configure binding and general security policies, click the Binding tab, shown in Figure 26.6, and then click the check box next to a policy to enable it or disable it:

- **Enable authenticated directory binding.** If this check box is selected, users can have the option of authenticating when connecting to the Open Directory server. This is a bi-directional authentication, in which client and server must prove their identity to each other. This option should always be enabled.

- **Require authenticated binding between directory and clients.** If authentication is enabled by the previous item, you can optionally require it by selecting this one.

FIGURE 26.6

In this pane, determine whether or how clients authenticate to the LDAP server as well as other security settings affecting communication between client and server.

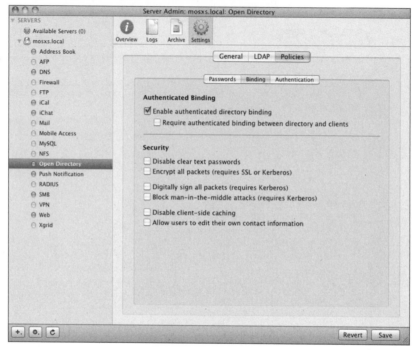

- **Disable clear text passwords.** If this is selected, authentication methods using cleartext (unencrypted) passwords are disallowed.

- **Encrypt all packets (requires SSL or Kerberos).** When using SSL, encrypts all directory data sent to clients. In most cases, this is unnecessary.

- **Digitally sign all packets (requires Kerberos).** Enables the client to confirm that directory data coming from the server is valid and hasn't been tampered with. In most cases, as with encrypting all packets, this setting is unnecessary.

- **Block man-in-the-middle attacks (requires Kerberos).** In conjunction with digital signing (previous item), this prevents another server from masquerading as your LDAP server.

- **Disable client-side caching.** When this is selected, LDAP clients can't cache any directory data locally, instead connecting to the server for fresh data each time.

- **Allow users to edit their own contact information.** This is a convenience for users and administrators alike and should be enabled unless you have a particular need to control all contact information centrally.

10. **To configure authentication settings, click the Authentication tab, shown in Figure 26.7.** All the authentication methods in this pane are less secure than what Kerberos offers and, as a result, should be disabled unless specifically required by a client on your network (as indicated next to each method). Click the check box next to a method to enable or disable it:

- NTLMv1 and NTLMv2 (clients using Windows NT/98 or later)
- LAN Manager (Windows 95 clients)
- MS-CHAPv2 (VPN service clients)
- WebDAV-Digest (web service clients)
- APOP (POP3 mail service clients)

11. **Click Save.** The new settings become active immediately.

FIGURE 26.7

Select allowable authentication methods for Open Directory clients in this pane.

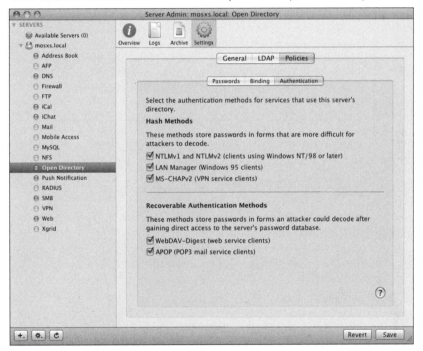

Configuring Open Directory users and groups

It probably goes without saying that none of the other Open Directory settings have any meaning without accounts for specific users and groups. User accounts can hold not only a username and password but also detailed contact information and information on which of numerous resources (such as an email account and access to a print server) are active for that user. After creating users and optionally organizing them by groups, you can easily enable or block access to various services on your network.

Note
As a reminder, the instructions in this section assume you're configuring a server whose role is Open Directory master. ■

Among many other settings, an Open Directory administrator can exercise detailed control over dozens of Mac OS X preferences for each user (to an even greater extent than ordinary parental controls). Because the possibilities for managing user accounts are so extensive, I recommend reading Apple's free PDF *User Management*, available as usual at `www.apple.com/server/macosx/resources/documentation.html`. In this section, I show you how to create user and group accounts as well as set up a few important account attributes.

Cross-Ref

For more on parental controls for individual Mac OS X computers, see Chapter 3. ■

Mac OS X Server provides two different interfaces for managing users and groups. The Server Preferences utility, found in `/Applications/Server` (and, likely, also in your Dock), is a simplified way to create accounts and adjust the most common settings. For example, if you click the Users icon and then the Services tab, as shown in Figure 26.8, you can turn on or off the user's access to any of seven common services with a single click in a check box. The other tabs (Account, Contact Info, and Groups) let you specify the user's name, password, address and phone numbers, group membership, and other characteristics, and the Groups pane of Server Preferences offers a similarly easy way to create and manage groups.

FIGURE 26.8

Server Preferences provides a way to adjust basic server settings, including basic user and group attributes, without all the clutter of Workgroup Manager.

If your needs are modest, Server Preferences offers a convenient and clutter-free way to control user and group settings. However, I prefer to use Workgroup Manager, which lets administrators manage every aspect of user and group accounts. It contains a superset of the features in Server Preferences, but it's not much more complicated to use. As a result, this section explains the use of Workgroup Manager for setting up users and groups.

Configuring users

To create and configure a user account, follow these steps:

1. Open Workgroup Manager, which is located in `/Applications/Server`.

2. In the Connect dialog box, type the username and password of the administrator account you created when you initially set up Mac OS X Server and then click Connect.

3. If anything other than LDAPv3 followed by the server's IP address is in the status bar on the left, click the globe icon and then choose the appropriate LDAP domain from the pop-up menu that appears.

4. If the status bar says "Not authenticated," click the lock icon on the right side of the bar, type the username and password for an existing directory administrator (use diradmin and the password for the original administrator account, respectively, if you haven't created any other directory administrator accounts), and then click Authenticate.

5. Click the Accounts icon on the toolbar and then click the User tab (the single silhouette icon) on the left side of the window.

6. To add a user, click the New User button on the toolbar, and if an alert appears stating "New users may not have access to services," click OK.

7. **At minimum, fill in the Name, Short Names, Password, and Verify fields.** The window should now look similar to Figure 26.9. To make the user an administrator of the server, also click the administer this server check box.

FIGURE 26.9

Fill in the user's name, short name, and password in this pane.

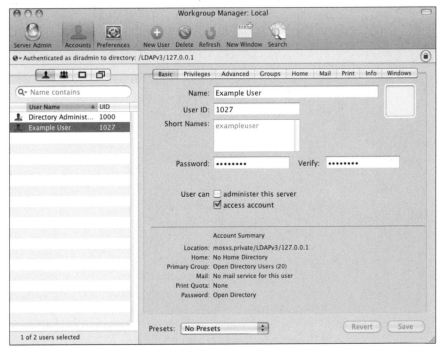

Note

Every user account must have at least one (primary) short name, but you can add extra short names for convenience. ■

8. Click the Privileges tab, shown in Figure 26.10, and then choose one of the following from the Administration capabilities pop-up menu:

- **None.** The user (even if an administrator for the server itself) can't make changes to settings in Workgroup Manager.

- **Limited.** The user can modify only certain user and group accounts. To add an account for which this user can make modifications, click the Add (+) button and then drag the account name from the list that appears. Then, for each selected user or group account, click one or more check boxes to specify what the current user can affect regarding that account: Manage user passwords, Edit managed preferences, Edit user information, or Edit group information.

- **Full.** The user is a directory administrator and can change any and all account settings in Workgroup Manager.

FIGURE 26.10

Determine whether the user can make modifications to other user and group accounts here.

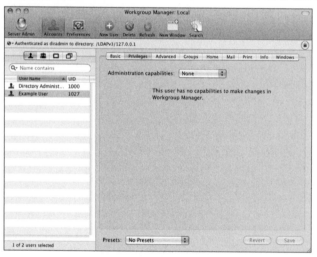

9. Click the Advanced tab, shown in Figure 26.11. To let the user log in simultaneously on more than one computer on your network, click the Allow simultaneous login on managed computers check box. To permit command-line logins via SSH, choose a shell (such as /bin/bash) from the Login Shell pop-up menu. Finally, check the User Password Type pop-up menu, which should say Open Directory. The other option, Crypt Password, is less secure, doesn't support single sign-on, and is necessary only when a computer running Mac OS X 10.1 or earlier connects to your server.

10. Click Options to open the dialog box shown in Figure 26.12. In this dialog box, you can set login and password policies that apply only to this user and override any global policies you may have set previously. Click the check box for each option you want to enable and then fill in any required fields.

FIGURE 26.11

In this pane, define how the user can log in and how the password is stored.

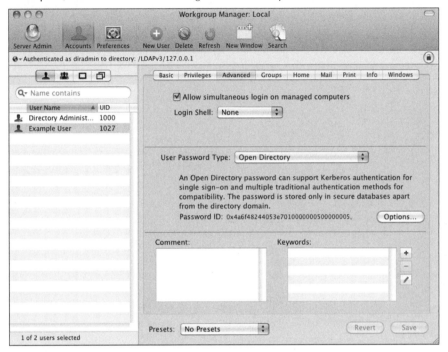

FIGURE 26.12

User-specific login and password policies, which override any global policies you created, are configured in this dialog box.

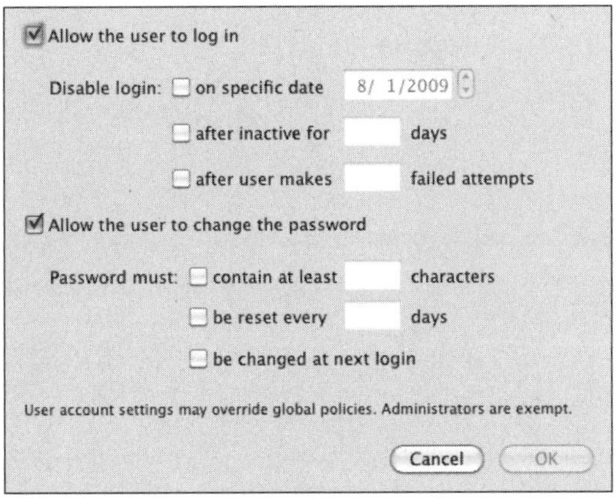

11. **To add the user to any existing groups, click the Groups tab.** You can create additional groups later and assign users to them, as discussed shortly.

12. **Click the Add (+) button to open a list of groups and then drag any group from the list into the Other Groups field, as shown in Figure 26.13.**

Note

For instructions on setting up additional user attributes not covered here, read Apple's *User Management* PDF guide. ■

13. **Click Save.** The new account becomes active immediately.

Note

If you want to be sure that all future users you create automatically have email access enabled, you can create a preset — a template used for new accounts. Consult Apple's documentation for instructions. ■

FIGURE 26.13

Drag a group to the Other Groups field to add a user to that group.

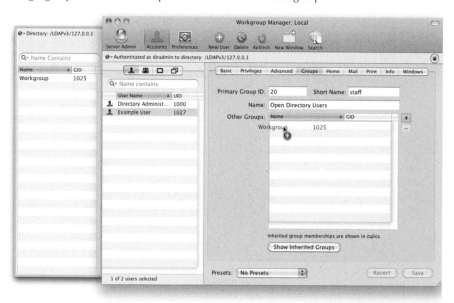

Configuring groups

To create and configure a group account, follow these steps:

1. **Open Workgroup Manager, which is located in** `/Applications/Server`.

2. **In the Connect dialog box, type the username and password of the administrator account you created when you initially set up Mac OS X Server and then click Connect.**

3. If anything other than LDAPv3 followed by the server's IP address is in the status bar on the left, click the globe icon and then choose the appropriate LDAP domain from the pop-up menu that appears.

4. If the status bar says "Not authenticated," click the lock icon on the right side of the bar, type the username and password for an existing directory administrator (use diradmin and the password for the original administrator account, respectively, if you haven't created any other directory administrator accounts), and then click Authenticate.

5. Click the Accounts icon on the toolbar and then click the Group tab (the icon with three silhouettes) on the left side of the window.

6. To add a group, click the New Group button on the toolbar.

7. **At minimum, fill in the Name and Short Name fields.** The window should now look similar to Figure 26.14.

FIGURE 26.14

Fill in the group's name and short name in this pane.

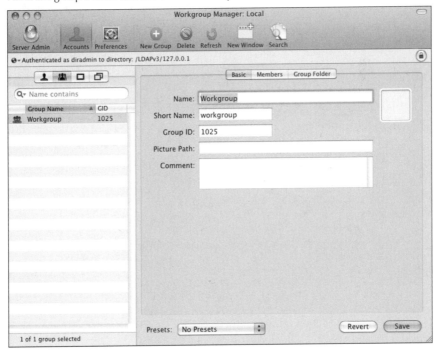

8. Click the Members tab.

9. To add users to the group, click the Add (+) button and then, from the list that appears on the side of the window, drag a user to the list, as shown in Figure 26.15. Repeat as necessary to add more users to the group.

10. **Click Save.** The new group becomes active immediately.

FIGURE 26.15

Add users to a group using drag and drop.

Setting up Open Directory clients

Once Open Directory itself, all the necessary users and groups, and any applicable services (as discussed in later chapters of this book) have been set up and turned on, the last piece of the puzzle is telling individual Macs on your network to connect to the Open Directory server for their authentication and directory needs.

Automatically configure a client

In certain situations, Mac OS X may prompt you to connect to an Open Directory server and then walk you through the process without having to do anything special. This occurs when there's an Open Directory server on the same subnet as the Mac in question, the server has an account whose short or long username matches one of those on the local Mac, and the server is running one or more services that support automatic configuration (including, among others, AFP, Mail, and iCal). If all this is true, a message may appear on the user's screen asking if he or she wants to join that Open Directory domain and then displays an assistant that helps the user perform each step of the process.

If that invitation doesn't appear, you can manually configure a Mac to connect to an Open Directory domain. The procedure to do so is different between Leopard and Snow Leopard.

Configure a Leopard client to connect to Open Directory

To configure a Mac running Mac OS X 10.5 Leopard to connect to an Open Directory server, follow these steps:

1. **Open Directory Utility, which is located in** `/Applications/Utilities`, **shown in Figure 26.16.** If the directory server to which you want to connect is already listed, no further action is required — you can quit Directory Utility.

2. **If the lock icon in the lower-left corner of the window is in the locked state, click it, type an administrator's username and password, and then click OK.**

FIGURE 26.16

In Leopard, Directory Utility lets you configure a Mac to connect to an Open Directory server.

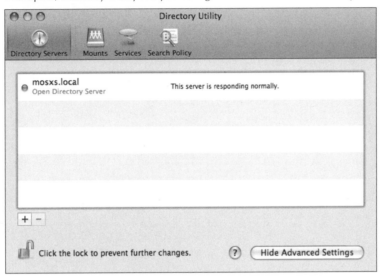

3. **Click the Add (+) button.** A dialog box opens.

4. **From the Add a new directory of type pop-up menu, choose Open Directory.**

5. **Click the arrow to the right of the Server Name or IP Address field and then look for your Open Directory server in the list that appears.** If it's there, select it. If not, type its domain name or IP address in the field.

6. **If the Open Directory server is configured to use SSL for LDAP (as described earlier in this chapter), click the Encrypt using SSL check box.** If you select this and the server isn't properly configured, the setup won't work.

7. **Click OK.** Your newly selected Open Directory server appears in Directory Utility's list and is ready to be used for authentication and directory services.

8. **Quit Directory Utility.**

Configure a Snow Leopard client to connect to Open Directory

To configure a Mac running Mac OS X 10.6 Snow Leopard to connect to an Open Directory server, follow these steps:

1. **Choose Apple ⇨ System Preferences and then click the Accounts icon.**

2. **If the lock icon in the lower-left corner of the window is in the locked state, click it, type an administrator's username and password, and then click OK.**

3. **Click Login Options at the bottom of the account list on the left, as shown in Figure 26.17.**

4. **Click the Join button next to Network Account Server.** A dialog box opens.

5. **Click the arrow to the right of the Server field and then look for your Open Directory server in the list that appears.** If it's there, select it. If not, type its domain name or IP address in the field.

6. **Click OK.** Mac OS X connects to the selected server. You should now see the name of the server next to Network Account Server (with a green dot if it's functioning normally), and the Join button becomes Edit.

FIGURE 26.17

In Snow Leopard, you can connect to an Open Directory server directly from the Accounts pane of System Preferences — that's what the inconspicuous Join button is for.

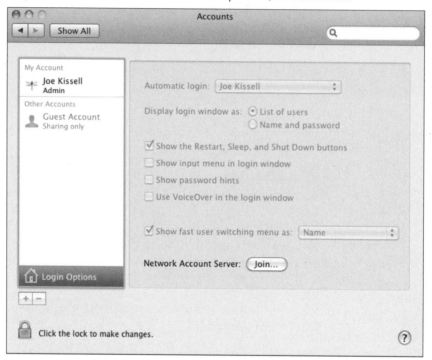

Using Windows Directory Services

Although the world would undoubtedly be a much happier place if everyone used Macs, there are still a few unenlightened souls here and there who use Windows. For better or worse, Windows is still the predominant operating system in corporate environments, and as such, many large organizations rely on Microsoft Active Directory servers to provide the same sorts of centralized authentication and directory services Open Directory offers. Like Open Directory, Active Directory offers Kerberos single sign-on capabilities, and either directory service can be used directly by both Mac and Windows clients (although each also offers certain platform-specific features).

If your network is Mac-only — or even if your servers are Mac-only — there's nothing for you to see here; move right along to the next chapter. However, if you're adding one or more servers running Mac OS X Server to a network that already uses Active Directory, you may want to know a few things about how Open Directory and Active Directory work together.

One thing to be aware of is that any given service can tie into only one Kerberos server for single sign-on authentication. An Active Directory server can provide single sign-on access to all the services running on that server or to external services joined to its Kerberos realm. Open Directory can do the same thing. But if a user signs in to Active Directory with Kerberos, that single sign-on won't be good for services for which Open Directory provides Kerberos authentication — and vice versa — because they're in two different realms. So, as a practical matter, it's best to have only one Kerberos realm. Depending on your needs and preferences, that can be supplied by either Open Directory or Active Directory. If you have more than one active Kerberos realm, it won't cause your network to implode, but it will mean single sign-on is restricted to a particular set of services, and users will have to authenticate separately to access another set of services.

Of the many ways in which Open Directory and Active Directory can co-exist on a network, allow me to give two common usage examples, with steps to configure each one.

Using Active Directory for directory services

In this scenario, Open Directory relies on Active Directory for user records and Kerberos authentication and, as a result, doesn't run its own LDAP or Kerberos services. However, Mac OS X Server still maintains separate local directory information and can provide authentication to users who connect directly to the server.

To set up Open Directory in this way, follow these steps:

1. **If necessary, follow steps presented earlier in this chapter to change the Open Directory role to Connect to another directory.**
2. **Click the Open Directory Utility button.** Directory Utility opens.
3. **Click the lock icon in the corner of the window, type your administrator username and password, and then click OK.**
4. **If the Enable check box next to Active Directory is deselected, click it and then click Apply.**
5. **Click the Search Policy button on the toolbar and then click the Authentication tab.** If the Active Directory domain already appears in the list, skip to the next step. If not, do the following:
   1. **Choose Apple ⇨ System Preferences and then click the Accounts icon.**
   2. **If the lock icon in the lower-left corner of the window is in the locked state, click it, type an administrator's username and password, and then click OK.**
   3. **Click Login Options at the bottom of the account list on the left.**
   4. **Click the button labeled Join or Edit.**
   5. **If one or more servers is already listed, click the Add (+) button.**
   6. **Click the arrow to the right of the Server Name or IP Address field and then look for your Active Directory server in the list that appears.** If it's there, select it. If not, type its domain name or IP address in the field.
   7. **Close System Preferences.**
6. **Confirm that the Active Directory server now appears in the Search Policy list in Directory Utility, quit Directory Utility, and then switch back to Server Admin.**
7. **Click the Settings button on the toolbar.**
8. **Click the General tab.**
9. **Click the Join Kerberos button.** A dialog box opens.
10. **From the pop-up menu, choose the Active Directory realm to which you want to connect.**
11. **Type the username and password of a Kerberos administrator (or a user to whom the administrator has delegated Kerberos authority).**

12. **Click OK.** Open Directory immediately begins using the selected Active Directory server to provide directory and authentication services.

Setting up a magic triangle

In another approach — a type of configuration called a *magic triangle* — Active Directory again provides both Kerberos authentication and directory services, but the Open Directory role is set to master, and Open Directory provides generic services (such as print and file sharing) to all clients on the network. In this setup, you can optionally augment user records from Active Directory, which means leave them as is on the Active Directory server but add supplemental information (such as managed preferences) in Open Directory, specifically to provide more services to Mac users on your network.

Note

Apple provides details on augmenting records in its *User Management* PDF guide. ∎

To set up Open Directory in this way, follow these steps:

1. **If necessary, follow steps presented earlier in this chapter to change the Open Directory role to Standalone Server.** Even though the role will later be changed to Open Directory master, it must start out as a stand-alone server for the process to work correctly.

2. **Choose Apple ⇨ System Preferences and then click the Accounts icon.**

3. **If the lock icon in the lower-left corner of the window is in the locked state, click it, type an administrator's username and password, and then click OK.**

4. **Click Login Options at the bottom of the account list on the left.**

5. **Click the button labeled Join or Edit.**

6. **If one or more servers is already listed, click the Add (+) button.**

7. **Click the arrow at the right of the Server Name or IP Address field and then look for your Active Directory server in the list that appears.** If it's there, select it. If not, type its domain name or IP address in the field.

8. **Close System Preferences.**

9. **Once again, follow steps presented earlier in this chapter, but this time, change the Open Directory role to Open Directory master.**

10. **To disable Kerberos, open Terminal, found in** `/Applications/Utilities`, **and then type** sudo sso_util remove -k -a *username* -p *password* -r *KERBEROSREALM*, **where the** *username*, *password*, **and** *KERBEROSREALM* **are replaced with a directory administrator's credentials and the name of your Kerberos realm.** Type your administrator password when prompted.

11. **Still in Terminal, to use Active Directory to Kerberize the services on your Mac OS X Server machine, type** sudo disconfigad -enablesso. Your magic triangle configuration should now be active.

Summary

This chapter covered basic configuration of Open Directory, the set of technologies Mac OS X Server uses to manage network user accounts. I explained the basics of configuring overall settings (particularly those with overt security implications) as well as creating users and groups. I also briefly discussed how to use Open Directory along with Microsoft Active Directory.

Working with SSL Certificates

Many of the services Mac OS X Server can run — including iCal, iChat, Mail (POP, IMAP, and SMTP), RADIUS, VPN, web, and, in Snow Leopard Server, Address Book — optionally support the use of SSL (Secure Sockets Layer) in order to encrypt all the data sent between client and server in either direction. SSL dramatically improves the security of network communications and, as such, should be used whenever possible. The only compelling reason not to use SSL is if you must offer a client a service that doesn't support SSL for some reason; those are increasingly few and far between.

Cross-Ref

For more on SSL and email, see Chapter 9. For more on SSL and web browsing, see Chapter 10. ∎

SSL uses a form of public-key encryption (or, more broadly, Public Key Infrastructure — PKI) to secure data. In PKI, to oversimplify slightly, encryption keys come in sets of two: a *public key* (used by others to encrypt data sent to you) and a *private key* (used by you to decrypt data you receive). On Mac OS X, you can store any of these keys in your keychain so applications such as Mail and Safari can automatically find and use them to encrypt or decrypt data as necessary.

Cross-Ref

For more on keychains, including how they manage encryption keys, see Chapter 5. ∎

In order for Mac OS X Server to encrypt its services using SSL, it must have one or more *certificates* installed. A certificate is a file that includes, among other things, a public key, identification details (such as the name of the entity using the certificate and the domain name of the server it goes with), and a digital signature certifying that the certificate's owner does in fact have the identity stated in the certificate. Once you have an SSL certificate, you can use it for as many different services as you need. You can also use different certificates for different purposes, if you prefer.

IN THIS CHAPTER

Understanding SSL certificates

Obtaining an official SSL certificate

Making your own SSL certificate

Serving as your own certificate authority

Installing and modifying certificates in Mac OS X Server

This chapter describes the process of obtaining, installing, and using SSL certificates. It covers both the conventional usage case — in which you obtain a certificate duly signed by a trusted certificate authority — and the process of creating your own self-signed certificates. It even describes how you can become a certificate authority yourself and why you might want to do that.

Certificate Overview

Working with certificates has historically been a cumbersome and confusing process, requiring the use of arcane command-line tools, potentially confusing email exchanges with certificate authorities, and a long list of steps to install and manage certificates, not to mention integrating them with various services your server may provide. (And, sad to say, if you're running a web server on the regular, non-server version of Mac OS X and want to set it up for SSL, you may still have to go through many of those steps, as I detail in Chapter 18.) In Leopard Server and Snow Leopard Server, however, most of that agony is a thing of the past. Using friendly, straightforward programs provided with Mac OS X Server, you can easily create and manage any sort of certificate you may need.

Most of the common activities you might need to perform involving certificates take place right in Server Admin, thanks to a built-in feature called Certificate Manager (which you may use without even realizing it). For some less-common activities, you can use a different tool: Certificate Assistant, which you can access from within the Keychain Access utility.

The first decision to make is whether to obtain a proper certificate, signed by a well-known certificate authority, or to create a self-signed certificate. Either type of certificate provides equally good encryption, but the two types vary in the amount of inconvenience they may entail for you (as the server's administrator) and for users who connect to your server.

Certificate authorities

The role of a certificate authority is to vouch for the identity of a person or organization. So, when a certificate authority signs your SSL certificate, that ordinarily means they've checked your (personal or business) credentials to verify that you are who you claim to be. Of course, anyone — including you — can set up shop as a certificate authority. In order for the trust of a certificate authority to mean something, users need to know they can trust the certificate authority itself!

To address this issue, certificates follow a chain of authority. That is, the credentials of any certificate authority can themselves be verified by a higher certificate authority, all the way up to any of several organizations designated as root certificate authorities.

Suppose certificate authority #1 signs your certificate, and its identity is verified by certificate authority #2. In turn, the identity of certificate authority #2 is verified by a root certificate authority. The authority of the root certificate authority trickles down, as it were, making your SSL certificate trusted by virtue of the chain that connects it to the top of the hierarchy.

Every copy of Mac OS X (as well as all other modern operating systems) contains a copy of the certificates for each current root certificate authority — as well as numerous intermediate certificate authorities — in a built-in keychain. When a program on your Mac encounters an SSL certificate, it looks at the certificate authority that signed it. If that certificate authority matches one of the root or intermediate certificate authorities for which you already have a certificate, the SSL certificate is considered valid. If there's no immediate match, your operating system begins following the chain of authority upward. As long as there's a direct series of links between the certificate authority that signed your certificate and one of the trusted certificates stored in your keychain, the SSL certificate is still valid.

If no valid chain can be found, the user receives a warning that the certificate isn't inherently trusted. If the user believes the party that issued the certificate is trustworthy, he or she can add the certificate to his or her keychain and then mark it as trusted so it can be used in the future without any further warnings.

Cross-Ref

For more on how to add certificates to your keychain and mark them as trusted, see Chapter 5. ■

Users can also add to their keychains certificates for new certificate authorities. For example, if your company decides to become a certificate authority and sign all the SSL certificates it issues, it might distribute its certificate authority certificate to all the computers inside the company so any SSL certificate that your company signs is automatically trusted.

All things being equal, using SSL certificates signed by either a root certificate authority or a well-known intermediate certificate authority that's in turn vouched for by a root certificate authority results in the best and most transparent experience for users. They'll never see any troubling warning messages; everything should just work.

If that's true, why should there be any other option?

In the first place, certificate authorities charge for their services. The amount you'll pay for a certificate depends on the certificate authority and on numerous other variables, such as the period of validity (all certificates expire eventually), the strength of encryption used, the amount of after-sales support offered, and the number of domain names for which the certificate is valid. Each certificate must specify either a single domain name or subdomain range, such as `*.example.com`, from which it can be used. Certificates that cover subdomains — also known as wildcard certificates — are more expensive. Depending on your budget and your needs, the cost of purchasing and renewing SSL certificates could be a barrier.

Second, getting a certificate signed by a certificate authority requires a few more steps than signing one yourself and, in some cases, can take several days or longer. (I describe both processes just ahead.) If you're only experimenting with SSL, if you must support many domain names, or if the hassle of installing certificates on your users' computers is less than the hassle of going through the process to get your certificates signed by a certificate authority, a self-signed certificate may be the way to go.

Self-signed certificates

Every SSL certificate must include a signature, but nothing prevents you from signing your own certificate — in effect, saying that you vouch for yourself! You can create and install a self-signed certificate in Mac OS X Server with just a few clicks.

Apart from the fact that self-signed certificates require each user to go through a few extra clicks to confirm to the operating system that the certificates are trusted, they work just as well as certificates signed by certificate authorities. Of course, when I say "work," I mean that they provide equally good encryption as other certificates; they can't, however, be counted on to provide accurate identification of the entity running the server, which is another important reason for using SSL certificates in the first place.

Note

Once you've created (or received) a certificate and installed it, following the instructions just ahead, you must also turn on SSL support for each service you want to encrypt and then select the proper certificate for each one from a pop-up menu. I explain how to do this for email in Chapter 28, the web server in Chapter 30, and a variety of other services in Chapter 31. ■

Creating a Self-Signed Certificate

If a self-signed SSL certificate is adequate for your needs, you can create and install one easily.

To create a self-signed certificate, follow these steps:

1. **Open Server Admin, which is located in** `/Applications/Server`.
2. **In the sidebar on the left, select your server.**
3. **If no services are listed under the server name, click the disclosure triangle next to the server name to reveal them.**
4. **If the service names are dimmed, choose Server⇨Connect, type your username and password if they're not already filled in, and then click Connect.** The list of services refreshes, and those currently running appear with a green dot next to them.
5. **Click the Certificates button on the toolbar.**
6. **Just below the list of certificates, click the Add (+) button and then choose Create a Certificate Identity from the pop-up menu, as shown in Figure 27.1.** Certificate Assistant opens.

FIGURE 27.1

To begin the process of creating a self-signed certificate, choose Create a Certificate Identity from this rather obscure pop-up menu.

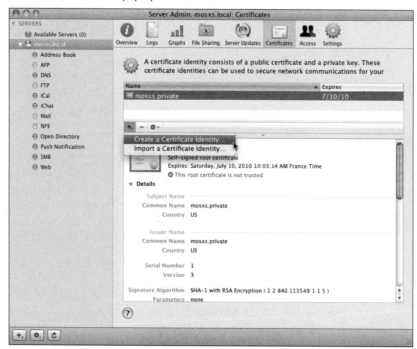

7. **On the first screen of Certificate Assistant, shown in Figure 27.2, type a name for your certificate (your choice), choose Self Signed Root from the Identity Type (or, in Leopard, Type) pop-up menu, and then choose SSL Server from the Certificate Type pop-up menu (in Leopard, this menu appears on the second screen of Certificate Assistant).** Also, click the Let me override defaults check box. Although this step results in an extra seven screens to complete, some of them contain information you'll likely want to change or at least verify.

FIGURE 27.2

The Certificate Assistant walks you through the steps of creating an SSL certificate, but you may need to override the default settings.

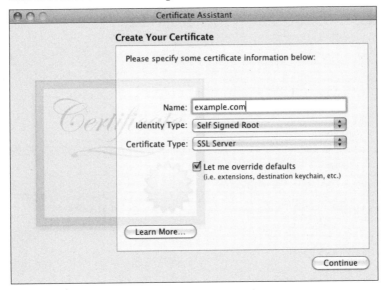

8. **Read the notice about creating a self-signed certificate and then click Continue.**

9. **Work your way through the next several screens, filling in the information requested and clicking the Continue button after each one.** In most cases, the defaults are fine — and you can always click the Learn More button to get details about that screen's options. However, I want to make a few specific recommendations:

   - **On the screen asking for address information, be certain that the field labeled "Name (Common Name)" contains the exact domain name of your server — the one specified in its Reverse DNS entry.** If this field isn't correct, the SSL certificate won't work.

   - **On the Key Usage Extension screen, select the uses to which you may want to put your certificate.** Under Capabilities, I suggest making sure to click the following check boxes: Signature, Key Encipherment, Data Encipherment, and Key Agreement. If you're uncertain what you need, click the Learn More button.

- **On the Extended Key Usage Extension screen, select the specific capabilities of your certificate.** At minimum, I suggest making sure to click the following check boxes: SSL Server Authentication, PKINIT Server Authentication, iChat Signing, iChat Encryption, and Email Protection.

- **You most likely don't need the Basic Constraints Extension and can therefore deselect the Include Basic Constraints Extension check box.**

After you click the final Continue button, Certificate Assistant creates your certificate, along with its public and private keys. The certificate appears in Server Admin's list (ready for use by any service that supports SSL), as shown in Figure 27.3, and the certificate and key PEM files are stored in /etc/certificates.

FIGURE 27.3

All installed SSL certificates (self-signed or certificate authority–signed) appear in this list in Server Admin.

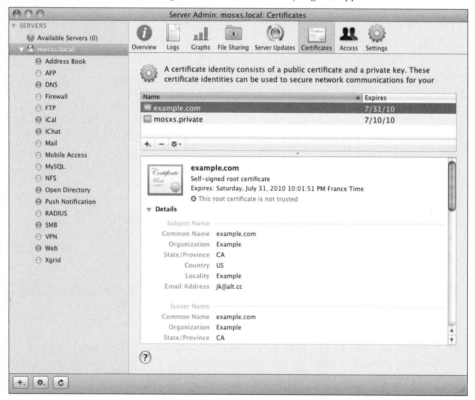

Requesting a Certificate from a Certificate Authority

If you've decided to go the route of getting a proper, official SSL certificate signed by a certificate authority, the recommended process is to create a self-signed certificate, generate a Certificate Signing Request (CSR) and submit it to a certificate authority, and then replace your self-signed certificate with the one signed by the certificate authority.

To obtain a signed certificate from a certificate authority, follow these steps:

1. **Follow all the steps earlier in this chapter to create a self-signed certificate.**

2. **Open Server Admin, which is located in** `/Applications/Server`.

3. **In the sidebar on the left, select your server.**

4. **If no services are listed under the server name, click the disclosure triangle next to the server name to reveal them.**

5. **If the service names are dimmed, choose Server⇨Connect, type your username and password if they're not already filled in, and then click Connect.** The list of services refreshes, and those currently running appear with a green dot next to them.

6. **Click the Certificates button on the toolbar.**

7. **Select the certificate that you want to have signed.**

8. **Click the Action pop-up menu (with the gear icon) below the list of certificates and then choose Generate Certificate Signing Request (CSR).** A dialog box opens, containing the text of the CSR (a long block of characters).

9. **Click the Save button, type a name for your CSR (or accept the default), select a location, and then click Save to save the file to disk.**

10. **Choose a certificate authority (of which many can be easily found on the web) and then follow its process for ordering a certificate.** As part of this process, the certificate authority will explain how to deliver the CSR to them — usually either by pasting the text into a web form or by emailing the contents of the CSR to a special address. Then, wait for the certificate authority to return your certificate — a process that can take anywhere from minutes to days, depending on the certificate authority and the options you've chosen.

11. **When the certificate authority returns your certificate, save it to your desktop.**

12. **Return to the Certificates pane of Server Admin, as in steps 1 through 6.**

13. **Select the certificate for which you now have the signed version.**

14. **Click the Action pop-up menu (with the gear icon) below the list of certificates and then choose Replace Certificate with Signed or Renewed Certificate.** The dialog box shown in Figure 27.4 opens.

FIGURE 27.4

To add your newly signed certificate to Server Admin, drop it (and your private key) in this dialog box.

15. Drag the certificate file your certificate authority provides to the dialog box, along with your private key (normally located in /etc/certificates), and then click the Replace Certificate button. Your signed certificate is now ready for use.

Creating and Using a Certificate Authority

In most cases, an SSL certificate signed by an existing certificate authority is the best solution, and when something simpler is needed, a self-signed certificate usually suffices. However, there may be situations in which you want to create your own certificate authority. For example, if your organization plans to issue a variety of different certificates (without having an external certificate authority sign them) but doesn't want to require its users to install multiple certificates and set their computers to trust them, it might designate itself as a certificate authority. By installing the certificate authority's root certificate on each user's device and marking it as trusted, the organization can ensure that all future certificates signed by that certificate authority are also trusted. You need not create these certificates yourself, but you — the administrator of the computer with the certificate authority certificate — must sign all requests generated by others.

To create a certificate authority, follow these steps:

1. Open Keychain Access, which is located in /Applications/Utilities.
2. Choose Keychain Access ⇨ Certificate Assistant ⇨ Create a Certificate Authority. Certificate Assistant opens, displaying the Create Your Certificate Authority screen shown in Figure 27.5.

FIGURE 27.5

Using Certificate Assistant, creating your own certificate authority is just as easy as creating a certificate.

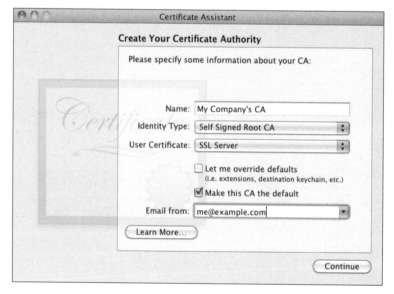

3. In the Name field, type your company's name, and in the Email from field, type the email address of the appropriate administrative contact (such as you) for this certificate authority.

4. Choose Self Signed Root CA from the Identity Type pop-up menu and SSL Server from the User Certificate pop-up menu.

5. Optionally, to ensure that your new certificate authority is used by default for signing all certificates from now on, click the Make this CA the default check box.

6. Click Continue. Certificate Assistant creates the certificate authority root certificate and installs it in your keychain. It also displays a window of other options, as shown in Figure 27.6, with which you can view your new certificate authority, mail invitations to your users to enable them to request certificates signed by your certificate authority, and more.

FIGURE 27.6

Once a certificate authority has been created, Certificate Assistant offers several options for putting it to use.

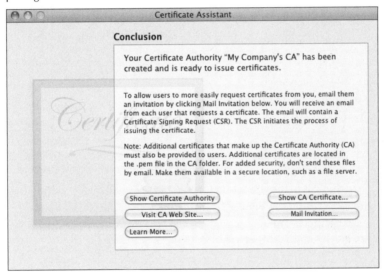

7. Click the Close button to close Certificate Assistant.

Cross-Ref

For more on installing a new certificate authority certificate on other Macs, see Chapter 5. ■

To sign a certificate with your own certificate authority, follow these steps:

1. **Obtain a CSR for the new certificate.** If you're creating the certificate yourself, you can generate your own CSR, following the instructions earlier in this chapter. Otherwise, you'll most likely receive a CSR in the form of a file sent by email. In either case, have the CSR file handy.

2. **Open Keychain Access, which is located in** `/Applications/Utilities`.

3. **Choose Keychain Access ⇨ Certificate Assistant ⇨ Create a Certificate For Someone Else as a Certificate Authority.** Certificate Assistant opens, displaying the window shown in Figure 27.7.

FIGURE 27.7

Now that you're a certificate authority, you get to sign other users' certificates. You do so by dragging the CSR to this window.

4. **Drag the CSR to the window per the instructions and then click Continue.**
5. **From the Issuing CA pop-up menu, choose your certificate authority.**
6. **Click Continue.** Certificate Assistant creates the signed certificate (in the form of a PEM file), opens a new email message in Mail, attaches the certificate, and addresses the message to the person who submitted the CSR.
7. **Click Send to send the email message, return to Certificate Assistant, and then click Done.**

Managing Certificates

Although the vast majority of activities you may need to perform with certificates under Mac OS X Server is encompassed in the instructions earlier in this chapter, you may need to carry out two potential management tasks from time to time: deleting certificates and importing certificates.

Note

As a reminder, after installing a certificate, you must turn on SSL support and select your preferred certificate for each service you want to encrypt. Find instructions for email in Chapter 28, for the web server in Chapter 30, and for several other services in Chapter 31. ∎

To delete a certificate, follow these steps:

1. **Open Server Admin, which is located in** `/Applications/Server`.

2. **In the sidebar on the left, select your server.**

3. **If no services are listed under the server name, click the disclosure triangle next to the server name to reveal them.**

4. **If the service names are dimmed, choose Server⇨ Connect, type your username and password if they're not already filled in, and then click Connect.** The list of services refreshes, and those currently running appear with a green dot next to them.

5. **Click the Certificates button on the toolbar.**

6. **Select a certificate, click the Remove (–) button, and then click Delete to confirm.** Server Admin deletes the certificate immediately.

To import a certificate, follow these steps:

1. **Open Server Admin, which is located in** `/Applications/Server`.

2. **In the sidebar on the left, select your server.**

3. **If no services are listed under the server name, click the disclosure triangle next to the server name to reveal them.**

4. **If the service names are dimmed, choose Server⇨ Connect, type your username and password if they're not already filled in, and then click Connect.** The list of services refreshes, and those currently running appear with a green dot next to them.

5. **Click the Certificates button on the toolbar.**

6. **Just below the list of certificates, click the Add (+) button and then choose Import a Certificate Identity from the pop-up menu.** A dialog box opens.

7. **Drag the PEM files for the certificate you want to import, along with its associated private key, to the window.**

8. **Click Import.** If requested to do so, type the passphrase for the certificate's private key and then click OK. Server Admin imports the selected certificate.

Summary

In this chapter, I explored the use of SSL certificates in Mac OS X Server, which provides additional certificate-related tools not found in the standard version of Mac OS X. I explained how to request a proper certificate from a certificate authority — or, if that's more than you need, how to create your own self-signed certificate or even your own certificate authority.

Securing Email Services

M ac OS X Server can provide a full range of email services for your organization: handling all incoming and outgoing mail (even from multiple
domains), offering users the option to check their mail from a web
browser, running mailing lists, filtering messages for viruses and spam, and even
(starting with Snow Leopard) delivering push email and letting users filter mail
on the server before it reaches their inboxes. And all these features can be configured using the easy-to-understand administrative tools included with Mac OS X
Server.

However, before you begin using the mail server, you should be aware of certain
security risks and the steps you can take to minimize them. With an optimal configuration, you can be confident that your users' passwords and messages won't
be intercepted in transit, that spammers won't be able to use your server to send
out junk mail, and that the majority of junk mail sent to your users from the outside is caught before it gets to them.

Mac OS X Mail Server Overview

Like nearly all mail servers, the one built into Mac OS X Server has two major
components: an SMTP server (Postfix) that handles communication with other
mail servers and a POP/IMAP server (Cyrus in Leopard; Dovecot in Snow
Leopard) that handles retrieval and management of your users' mail. Depending
on your needs, you might turn on only one or two of these protocols, but the
most common arrangement is to offer all three. For each one, you have a variety
of choices involving security.

Note
In addition to SMTP, POP, and IMAP services, Mac OS X Server offers a
webmail interface (SquirrelMail) and a mailing list server (Mailman),
neither of which I cover in this book. ∎

The first thing you should ponder is how you want to structure your mail services with respect to the other services you're providing with Mac OS X Server — and whether running your own mail server is the best solution for your organization.

My personal experience running mail services on Mac OS X Server has been that it's highly resource-intensive, which means that if your organization sends or receives a great deal of email — and especially if you employ server-based spam and virus filtering — it can slow down other processes running on the same computer (such as a web server). Your mileage may vary, of course, depending on such variables as the number and speed of your server's processors, the amount of RAM it has, the volume of mail transferred, and the variety of other processes running on it.

Regardless, the safest practice and the one that will yield best performance — if you can afford it — is to dedicate at least one server to running only email services and use additional copies of Mac OS X Server running on other computers for web, file sharing, and the like. For even greater granularity, you could designate one computer to handle only outgoing mail or use a different server for each email domain. You can also use a cluster of mail servers to evenly spread out the load.

Yet another possibility, odd though it may sound in a chapter about running a mail server, is to not run your own mail server at all! Even if you use Mac OS X Server to host your website, file sharing, and other services for your domain, you can easily configure your DNS records in such a way that your domain's email is handled by another provider, and the experience is seamless for your own users as well as for people sending you mail from the outside. For example, Google Apps (`www.google.com/a`) lets you use Gmail to send and receive mail using your organization's existing domain name; the Standard Edition is free, whereas the more advanced Premier Edition costs $50 per user per year for commercial use but is free to schools and nonprofit organizations. Many other email providers also offer POP, IMAP, and SMTP services for organizations at a modest cost.

Outsourcing your email services in this way has several advantages. You can let someone else worry about security settings, maintenance, upgrades, processor loads, backups, and other irritating details, and you can also enjoy the benefit of advanced spam filtering and other features that would be difficult to replicate on Mac OS X Server. And you need never worry that you'll lose email access because of a server crash or an outage on your end.

On the other hand, even major providers like Google have technical problems themselves from time to time, and by putting your email in someone else's hands, you give up a certain measure of control. So, while I don't want to discourage you from running your own mail server if that's what you feel is best, I do think it's worth giving at least a bit of thought as to whether you may save time and effort by not doing so. Just to provide a data point or two, I switched my own domain's email from Mac OS X Server to Google Apps, as did a company I work closely with, and we've both found that the move reduced our workload and stress.

If you're still certain you want to stick with Mac OS X Server for your email, you need to pay attention to several categories of security concerns:

- **Authentication.** Some form of authentication is required when users connect via POP or IMAP because it's essential for the server to know whose mail to display. However, not all authentication methods are secure. It's possible (depending on how the mail server's preferences are set) for users to send their passwords as cleartext, which someone sniffing network traffic could intercept — giving them access to that user's mail (and other account resources). Authentication is optional for SMTP but highly recommended. Again, sending passwords in the clear is possible unless the server settings are configured to disallow it.

- **SMTP relay.** You want people elsewhere on the Internet to be able to send messages to users in your domain, and you want your own users to be able to send outgoing mail. However, you almost certainly want to block computers from outside your network or users without accounts on your server from using it to send mail. If you permit your mail server to be used freely as an SMTP relay, you'll inevitably find it becomes a magnet for spammers. However, managing settings to selectively restrict SMTP access in just the right way can be somewhat tricky.

- **Spam and malware.** You can't prevent spammers from trying to send junk mail — including viruses and other malware — to users on your network. However, you can take steps to filter out at least the most obvious junk mail before it reaches your users' inboxes.

- **SSL.** Even if you use secure authentication for POP/IMAP and SMTP, that protects only the password while it's in transit, not the contents of email messages. However, you can enable SSL on your mail server so all messages are encrypted as they travel between your users' client software and the server, significantly reducing the possibility of confidential email being intercepted.

I discuss each of these security categories throughout the rest of this chapter.

Tip

This chapter covers only the barest basics of Mac OS X Server's mail server. For much more thorough information, consult Apple's free PDF *Mail Service Administration*, available at `www.apple.com/server/macosx/resources/documentation.html`. ∎

Configuring Authentication Options

Your first order of business when configuring your mail server is to ensure that when users connect with Mail, Entourage, or their favorite email client, their username and password are transmitted securely to the server. On both the server side and the client side, authentication methods must be set up separately for POP/IMAP and SMTP.

Mac OS X Server supports several different authentication methods; you can select just one or several each for incoming and outgoing mail. Selecting a method means the server will agree to use that method if a client requests it; the only way to require a particular method is to select just that one method. As tempting as it may be to enable all the options to ensure global compatibility, doing so puts your users at greater risk. The wisest course is to enable only secure methods and then to educate your users about setting up their email software to use those methods.

Note

Regardless of your authentication settings, if you enable SSL (as discussed later in this chapter), usernames and passwords are always sent securely. ∎

To determine which authentication methods your mail server will accept, follow these steps:

1. **Open Server Admin, which is located in** `/Applications/Server`.
2. **In the sidebar on the left, select your server.**
3. **If no services are listed under the server name, click the disclosure triangle next to the server name to reveal them.**

4. **If the service names are dimmed, choose Server⇨Connect, type your username and password if they're not already filled in, and then click Connect.** The list of services refreshes, and those currently running appear with a green dot next to them.

5. **In the sidebar, under your server name, select Mail.**

6. **Click the Settings button on the toolbar.**

7. **Click the Advanced tab and then click the Security tab.** The window should resemble Figure 28.1.

FIGURE 28.1

In this remote corner of Server Admin, you can select which authentication methods your mail server accepts as well as set up its SSL configuration.

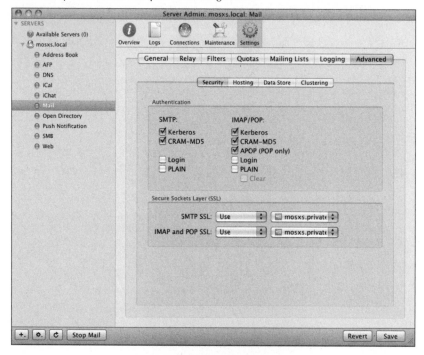

8. **In the Authentication section, click the check box next to each SMTP and POP/IMAP authentication method you want the server to accept.** Here are my recommendations:

   - Select both Kerberos and CRAM-MD5 for SMTP and IMAP/POP because both are secure methods.

   - If you enable POP access, select APOP, which is also a secure method.

   - Avoid using the Login, PLAIN, and Clear methods if at all possible because they send passwords in an insecure manner. The only reason to use these methods is if someone wants to connect using an old or poorly designed email client, and a better approach in that case is to encourage the user to use a modern program that can handle one of the other authentication methods.

9. **Click Save.** The new settings become available immediately (or as soon as you start the mail server).

Note

Users must normally configure their email clients to use one of the authentication methods you've enabled (a few may be able to figure out the right method automatically). To read about email client configuration, see Chapter 9. ■

Using SSL for Email

Encrypting mail sent between a client and a server using SSL is such a good idea, it should be the default on every mail server. And it probably would be, except for the detail that each server needs its own customized SSL certificate — preferably signed by a well-known certificate authority — and these can cost money and require a few extra steps to install and configure. Although you can use a self-signed certificate that you create yourself for free, this requires all your users to jump through extra hoops to convince their email clients to trust the certificate. But this minor inconvenience is well worth it for the security it provides for your users. With SSL in place, users can safely send and receive email without worrying that someone else could intercept their communication, even if they're using an open Wi-Fi hotspot.

As a reminder, using SSL encrypts messages only while they're in transit. They're still stored in cleartext on the server's hard drive as well as on the client device, unless users encrypt them separately using software such as PGP.

Cross-Ref

For more on the client side of using SSL as well as encrypting email end-to-end with PGP and other software, see Chapter 9. For more on how to obtain and install SSL certificates — a prerequisite to the steps that follow — see Chapter 27. ■

To configure the mail server to use SSL, follow these steps:

1. **Open Server Admin, which is located in** `/Applications/Server`.
2. **In the sidebar on the left, select your server.**
3. **If no services are listed under the server name, click the disclosure triangle next to the server name to reveal them.**
4. **If the service names are dimmed, choose Server ⇨ Connect, type your username and password if they're not already filled in, and then click Connect.** The list of services refreshes, and those currently running appear with a green dot next to them.
5. **In the sidebar, under your server name, select Mail.**
6. **Click the Settings button on the toolbar.**
7. **Click the Advanced tab and then click the Security tab.**
8. **In the Secure Sockets Layer (SSL) section, for both SMTP SSL and IMAP and POP SSL, choose either Use or Require from the left-hand pop-up menu and choose a certificate appropriate for email from the right-hand pop-up menu.** Choosing Use means SSL is available and will be used if a client requests it. Choosing Require means the server will accept connections from clients only if they use SSL.

Note

Although you could enable SSL for only incoming or outgoing mail, it takes only two extra clicks to do both, and the extra security makes that a smart choice. ■

> 9. **Click Save.** SSL connections become available immediately (or as soon as you start the mail server).

Tip

Even with SSL implemented as described here, communication between your mail server and other mail servers normally remains unencrypted, so in theory, a message could still be intercepted between your server and another server. But there's a technique you can use to encrypt connections between your server and another specific SMTP server that you know supports SSL. You can read about this method at www.macosxhints.com/ article.php?story=20081125140400323. ■

Configuring Relay Options

SMTP servers are usually described as being for outgoing mail, but that's an oversimplification. It's true that when your email client wants to send a message to someone else, it connects to an SMTP server. But what happens next is that your SMTP server connects to another SMTP server (either the one the recipient uses or an intermediate server that sends the message one step closer to it) in order to deliver the message to its destination. Conversely, when someone sends you a message, the other person's SMTP server talks to your SMTP server to exchange the data. So, in fact, SMTP servers both send and receive email. And then, once a message is on its destination server, POP or IMAP software takes over to handle delivering the message to the user's email client.

Whenever an SMTP server is being used to send a message to another server — whether that message originated from a local user, a remote email client, or an upstream SMTP server — it's said to be a *relay*. That means about half of what any SMTP server does is relaying; the other half is receiving email destined for a local user. Mac OS X Server's SMTP server can deliver messages directly to their destination server (the usual case) or it can be configured to relay all outgoing messages to some other SMTP server.

Relaying, then, is a proper and necessary part of any SMTP server's operation. However, the one thing you probably don't want is for just anyone to be able to send (relay) mail through your SMTP server. Your own users must be able to use your server as a relay, and if you run other mail servers, you may want to also give them permission to relay messages, regardless of which user originated them. But if your server freely accepts relay requests from any other client or server, it's said to be an *open relay*. This is something to be avoided because open relays are quickly found by spammers and are hijacked to send out junk mail in great quantities. If your server is an open relay, you not only become complicit in spam-sending sprees, but you also sacrifice your own server's performance to meet the whims of random miscreants. Even worse, your server may be put on blacklists, preventing your own users from sending out legitimate messages!

Note

You can configure Mac OS X Server to prevent any SMTP server known to be an open relay from sending messages to your users (even if they don't attempt to relay messages to other servers). Even though Server Admin puts this feature in the same area as relaying settings, it's actually an anti-spam feature, and for that reason, I discuss it separately later in this chapter. ■

One way to prevent your SMTP server from being an open relay is to require that everyone connecting to it in order to send mail (but not servers sending mail to your users) supply a valid username and password. Spammers won't know the credentials of any user on your server, so that prevents them from connecting. SMTP authentication may require an additional setup step or two on the client side, and some older clients don't offer the option, but in general, it's an effective and reasonable choice.

If you followed the steps earlier in this chapter to choose one or more SMTP authentication methods, you've already set up your mail service to require authentication. That is, as long as at least one check box under SMTP in the Security pane of the Advanced pane is selected, authentication of some sort is required, and your server isn't an open relay.

Another approach to closing an open relay is to maintain a white list of IP addresses from which relays are accepted — for example, the addresses of servers on your own network. If anyone connects from another IP address, the server ignores them. You can also create a blacklist of servers from which relays are explicitly blocked, but doing so doesn't prevent your server from being an open relay.

You can also combine the two approaches. With both restrictions active, your SMTP server accepts relays from any server on your white list (without requiring authentication) as well as from anyone who can supply proper credentials (even if that person's IP address isn't on your white list). Of the two approaches, authentication is the more powerful and flexible, but it doesn't hurt to use both if your network configuration warrants it.

To configure the SMTP relay white list or blacklist for Mac OS X Server's mail service, follow these steps:

1. **Open Server Admin, which is located in** `/Applications/Server`.

2. **In the sidebar on the left, select your server.**

3. **If no services are listed under the server name, click the disclosure triangle next to the server name to reveal them.**

4. **If the service names are dimmed, choose Server ⇨ Connect, type your username and password if they're not already filled in, and then click Connect.** The list of services refreshes, and those currently running appear with a green dot next to them.

5. **In the sidebar, under your server name, select Mail.**

6. **Click the Settings button on the toolbar.**

7. **Click the Relay tab.** The window should resemble Figure 28.2.

8. **To use a white list (specifying hosts that can relay messages without authenticating), click the Accept SMTP relays only from these hosts and networks check box.**

9. **Click the Add (+) button and then type a domain name, an IP address, or an address range (using CIDR notation).** Repeat as necessary to add more addresses.

Cross-Ref
For more on CIDR notation, see Chapter 17. ■

10. **To use a blacklist (specifying hosts that can't relay messages — and aren't even given the chance to authenticate), click the Refuse all messages from these hosts and networks check box.**

11. **Click the Add (+) button and then type a domain name, an IP address, or an address range (using CIDR notation).** Repeat as necessary to add more addresses.

12. **Click Save.** The new settings take effect immediately (or as soon as you start the mail server).

FIGURE 28.2

In the Relay pane, you can specify a white list (hosts that can relay mail without authenticating), a blacklist (hosts that can never relay mail), or both.

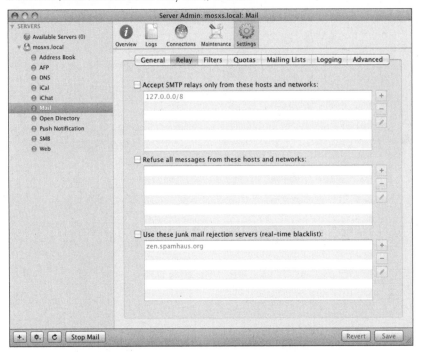

Configuring Spam and Virus Protection

Having secured authentication, encrypted message transfer, and protected your server from being used by spammers, you have just one other major security task to complete before turning on your mail server: doing your users a favor by filtering out as much junk mail as possible, including viruses that may have been sent by email. Of course, your users should also use spam filtering software that runs on their own computers, but with the proper settings, you can eliminate some of the most egregious junk mail before it's ever delivered — or at least mark it to help users identify it as likely spam.

Cross-Ref

For more on client-side spam filtering, see Chapter 9. ■

Mac OS X employs three main mechanisms for filtering junk mail. First, there's a Bayesian junk mail filter — one that, like the filter built into Mail, can learn about the characteristics of good and bad messages as you use it, becoming more accurate over time. You can adjust the sensitivity of this filter and configure several other attributes. Second, there's a separate virus filter, which matches the contents of attachments against the signatures of known viruses. Both of these filters are powered by open-source software included with Mac OS X Server (SpamAssassin for spam filtering and ClamAV for virus filtering).

The third filtering method is a bit different: blocking incoming SMTP traffic based on information supplied by Real-time Blacklist (RBL) servers, also known as black-hole servers. A number of organizations maintain lists of SMTP servers operating as open relays or which are known to have been used for sending out spam. These lists are dynamic: Servers are added to them as they're discovered and are deleted from them if the server's operator can demonstrate that the open relay has been closed or other misbehavior brought under control. When a computer tries to make an SMTP connection to your server in order to deliver mail to a local user, Mac OS X Server can cross-reference its IP address against one or more RBLs; if a match is found, the connection is rejected before any messages are received.

Although RBLs are a clever idea — and do indeed dramatically reduce spam — I've been unfortunate enough to have had my own mail server mistakenly added to these lists more than once, with the result that perfectly good mail was prevented from reaching entire domains. There can be many reasons for such mistakes — one example is users running software that reports spammers to an RBL and misidentifying legitimate email messages as spam. Getting removed from these lists often requires a lot of time and hassle. Because I've experienced firsthand the aggravation of being unable to send valid messages as a result of overzealous RBL behavior, I'm reluctant to recommend using them. But the capability is there if you want to use it.

To configure the junk and virus filters, follow these steps:

1. **Open Server Admin, which is located in** `/Applications/Server`.

2. **In the sidebar on the left, select your server.**

3. **If no services are listed under the server name, click the disclosure triangle next to the server name to reveal them.**

4. **If the service names are dimmed, choose Server ➪ Connect, type your username and password if they're not already filled in, and then click Connect.** The list of services refreshes, and those currently running appear with a green dot next to them.

5. **In the sidebar, under your server name, select Mail.**

6. **Click the Settings button on the toolbar.**

7. **Click the Filters tab.** The window should resemble Figure 28.3.

8. **Click the Enable junk mail filtering check box to activate the Bayesian filter and then adjust the following attributes to your liking:**

   - **Minimum junk mail score.** Drag this slider left or right to indicate how aggressive the filter should be. I recommend starting toward the left (Cautious) side of the scale, monitoring its performance, and gradually moving the slider to the right. When you notice more than a trivial number of false positives, back it off a notch.

   - **Accepted languages.** Most email messages have a header specifying the sender's text-encoding language, using a two-letter identifier. The spam filter can use this characteristic to identify likely spam. However, doing so can prevent legitimate messages that happen to have been composed by, for example, someone who happens to be in France from getting through. So, this list serves as a white list that overrides the junk mail filter: If a language's two-letter code is in the list, it won't be marked as spam, regardless of other characteristics. To modify the list, click the button with the pencil icon, select or deselect languages, and then click OK.

FIGURE 28.3

In this pane, you can enable junk and virus filtering as well as configure a variety of settings for each.

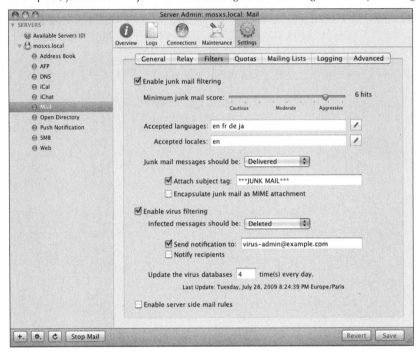

- **Accepted locales.** Similar to accepted languages, this field contains a white list of locales from which no message will be marked as spam. Modify it per the instructions presented earlier.

- **Junk mail messages should be.** From this pop-up menu, choose Bounced (to return the message to its sender), Deleted (to erase the message), Delivered (to send it to the recipient's inbox, even though it might be junk), or Redirected (to send it to someone else, such as a system administrator). Depending on which option you choose, you can fill in additional details. For example, if you choose Delivered, you can add a tag to the subject (as shown in Figure 28.3) to help the recipient identify it as likely spam. My advice is to initially choose Delivered, at least until you've adjusted the minimum junk mail score for maximum accuracy, and then move on to Deleted.

Note

The process of training the junk filter to recognize good and bad messages in order to improve its accuracy is more involved than I can explain in this book. Detailed instructions are found in Apple's PDF *Mail Service Administration*, referenced earlier in this chapter. ∎

9. Click the Enable virus filtering check box to activate the virus filter and then adjust the following attributes to your liking:

- **Infected messages should be.** From this pop-up menu, choose Bounced (to return the message to its sender), Deleted (to erase the message), or Quarantine (to send it to a special directory where an administrator can examine it). Depending on which option you choose, you can fill in additional details.

- **Notify recipients.** Click this check box if you want the mail server to send a notice to the would-be recipient of a message stating that a message was caught by the virus filter.

- **Update the virus databases.** Type a number to indicate how many times per day the virus database should be updated with the latest virus definitions.

10. **Click Save.** The new filtering settings take effect immediately (or as soon as you start the mail server).

To configure the mail server to use an RBL — if you're sure you want to do that — follow these steps:

1. **Open Server Admin, which is located in** `/Applications/Server`.

2. **In the sidebar on the left, select your server.**

3. **If no services are listed under the server name, click the disclosure triangle next to the server name to reveal them.**

4. **If the service names are dimmed, choose Server⇨Connect, type your username and password if they're not already filled in, and then click Connect.** The list of services refreshes, and those currently running appear with a green dot next to them.

5. **In the sidebar, under your server name, select Mail.**

6. **Click the Settings button on the toolbar.**

7. **Click the Relay tab.**

8. **Click the Use these junk mail rejection servers (real-time blacklist) check box.**

9. **Click the Add (+) button and then type the domain name or IP address of an RBL server.** To remove a server, select it and then click the Remove (–) button.

10. **Click Save.** The new settings take effect immediately (or as soon as you start the mail server).

Turning On the Mail Service

Once you have all the relevant security settings adjusted to your liking, you can activate the mail service. Depending on whether or how you've already configured user accounts, this may also require you to change settings for individual users.

Begin by following these steps to turn on the mail server:

1. **Open Server Admin, which is located in** `/Applications/Server`.

2. **In the sidebar on the left, select your server.**

3. **If no services are listed under the server name, click the disclosure triangle next to the server name to reveal them.**

4. **If the service names are dimmed, choose Server⇨Connect, type your username and password if they're not already filled in, and then click Connect.** The list of services refreshes, and those currently running appear with a green dot next to them.

5. In the sidebar, under your server name, select Mail.

6. Click the Settings button on the toolbar.

7. **Click the General tab.** The window should resemble Figure 28.4.

8. If you haven't already done so, type the server's domain name and hostname (likely to be the same) in the Domain name and Host name fields, respectively.

9. Optionally, to enable push notifications, click the Add button, choose a Mac OS X Server computer (which can be the current server), fill in administrator credentials as requested, and then click Connect.

10. **To enable the SMTP server, click the Enable SMTP check box and then click the Allow incoming mail check box.** All the other SMTP check boxes are optional and rarely used; consult Apple's documentation for details.

11. **To enable the IMAP server, click the Enable IMAP with maximum of ___ connections check box.** Optionally, change the number of connections to more or less than 1,000, depending on the number of clients that may connect at once.

12. To enable the POP server, click the Enable POP check box.

13. **Click Save.** The servers you selected start up immediately.

FIGURE 28.4

In this pane, determine basic mail server settings and turn on mail services.

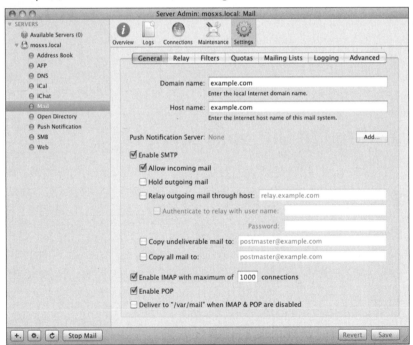

Note

Having selected which mail services you want to use, you can then deactivate or reactivate all of them at once by clicking Stop Mail or Start Mail at the bottom of the window. ■

Last but not least, make sure each user account for which you want to provide email access is configured correctly. Even if your server is running POP, IMAP, and SMTP servers, mail access for any or all of these doesn't exist for any given user until you enable it.

To adjust a user's email account settings, follow these steps:

1. Open Workgroup Manager, which is located in `/Applications/Server`.

2. In the Connect dialog box, type the username and password of the administrator account you created when you initially set up Mac OS X Server and then click Connect.

3. If anything other than LDAPv3 followed by the server's IP address is in the status bar on the left, click the globe icon and then choose the appropriate LDAP domain from the pop-up menu that appears.

4. If the status bar says "Not authenticated," click the lock icon on the right side of the bar, type the username and password for an existing directory administrator (use diradmin and the password for the original administrator account, respectively, if you haven't created any other directory administrator accounts), and then click Authenticate. The window should look similar to Figure 28.5.

FIGURE 28.5

Configure email access for an individual user in this pane.

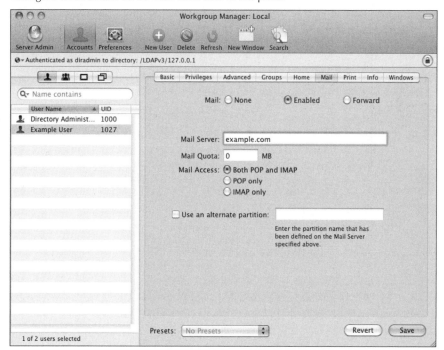

5. Select a user account in the list on the left.

6. Click the Mail tab.

7. Click the Enabled radio button.

8. In the Mail Server field, type the domain name of your mail server.

9. To enforce a mail storage quota (especially useful for IMAP accounts), type a number in the Mail Quota field. With the default setting of 0, no quota is imposed.

10. Click one of the following radio buttons: Both POP and IMAP (my recommendation), POP only, or IMAP only.

11. Click Save. The new email account becomes active immediately.

Note

If you want to be sure that all future users you create automatically have email access enabled, you can create a preset — a template used for new accounts. Consult Apple's documentation for instructions. ■

Summary

Mac OS X Server includes a powerful mail server with advanced administrative tools. This chapter discussed the security factors to consider when using the mail server and how to configure it to protect both the server itself and your users. In particular, I showed how to ensure that your users log in securely, how to use SSL to encrypt communication between the server and its clients, how to lock down the server's relaying feature, and how to make the most of its built-in spam and virus filters. Finally, I described the process of activating the mail server and setting up individual accounts to use the type(s) of email accounts you prefer.

Securing File Sharing

The standard version of Mac OS X lets any user share files over the network using any combination of AFP (Apple Filing Protocol), SMB (Server Message Block), and FTP (File Transfer Protocol). It also lets you modify the permissions of files and folders as well as define the ways in which users and groups can access certain resources. Mac OS X Server inherits all these capabilities but adds many additional features.

For one thing, Mac OS X Server also supports serving files using the NFS (Network File System) protocol. The standard version of Mac OS X can function as an NFS client but not as a server. In addition, for every supported protocol, Server Admin offers extensive control over settings and permissions, making it much easier to create ACLs, work with users and groups, choose authentication methods, limit resource usage, and tweak numerous other parameters.

As usual, the full details of how Mac OS X Server's file-sharing features operate and how to configure them optimally could fill a book — and they do: Apple's free PDF guide *File Server Administration* (for Snow Leopard; the Leopard version is called *File Services Administration*), available at www.apple.com/server/macosx/resources/documentation.html. In this chapter, I want to introduce you to the basics of Mac OS X Server's file-sharing capabilities, concentrating on security — which protocols offer which security features and how to configure some of the most common security settings.

About File-Sharing Protocols

In many cases, the differences between file-sharing protocols are nearly irrelevant as far as the end user is concerned. That is, using any of the available protocols, a user can browse files on a server somewhere, upload and download files, or even open them directly from a mounted network volume. Not only that, but nearly all recent versions of Mac OS X, Windows, and Unix-like operating systems (including Linux) let you connect to servers using SMB, FTP, or NFS, and all

Macs can connect via AFP. Because all the protocols let you achieve the same end result — moving files from one computer to another — the differences may seem subtle and unimportant at first glance.

Note
Technically, Mac OS X Server does offer another method of sharing files: WebDAV. Because that mechanism is handled separately from other file sharing — as part of the web server — I cover it in Chapter 30. ■

And yet, each protocol has certain pros and cons compared to the others. As an administrator, your goal should be to choose the most flexible and secure file-sharing methods that meet your users' needs while not running any service that isn't necessary. So, even if you could guarantee ultimate flexibility by running all four protocols, you also increase your security risks (to say nothing of your own administrative hassles). Thus, your first step is to choose the one or more file-sharing protocols that make the most sense for your network.

What follows is a brief overview of the capabilities and limitations of each choice.

Cross-Ref
For more on AFP, SMB, and FTP, see Chapter 7. For more on how to connect to remote servers using any protocol with the standard version of Mac OS X, see Chapter 11. ■

AFP

AFP, as the A suggests, is an Apple invention and is built into all versions of Mac OS X. When you access files over a network using AFP, you can be certain that all permissions (including ACLs) and other data are transferred properly, just as they would be when connecting to a local volume. Authentication can be encrypted using Kerberos, so you need not worry that passwords will be sent in the clear.

Years ago, Mac OS X provided an option to encrypt all AFP network traffic using OpenSSH, but that capability no longer exists. Therefore, apart from your user credentials, all file data sent and received via AFP is unencrypted and could in theory be sniffed in transit. This is unlikely to be a concern on a local Ethernet network or a wireless network that uses WPA or WPA2 encryption. However, if you're connecting to an AFP server from a remote network, the data you exchange could be vulnerable unless you use a VPN or some other method of encrypting your connection.

Cross-Ref
For more on VPN, see Chapters 12 and 31. ■

If you have only Macs on your network, AFP is the logical choice because it ensures the most seamless experience all around, and you need never worry that some important capability may not be fully supported by your file-sharing mechanism.

The only significant drawback to AFP is that Windows and Unix don't include AFP support, so if you have users that must connect from another operating system, you must use another protocol (either instead of or in addition to AFP).

SMB

Just as AFP is the standard file-sharing protocol on Macs, SMB is the standard on Windows. Like AFP, SMB as implemented by Mac OS X Server respects all file permissions and ACLs. SMB also offers the option of secure authentication using Kerberos or other methods. However, like AFP, it has no option to encrypt all data transfers — if you need them to be encrypted, you must use the NFS protocol, a VPN, or some other mechanism.

Although SMB can be finicky when dealing with Mac files that have resource forks or metadata such as extended attributes, Mac OS X Server's manner of handling SMB normally manages all these details with aplomb, making the process of dealing with complex Mac files completely transparent to both Windows and Mac users. One minor downside to using SMB on Mac OS X Server is that the protocol uses three ports (137, 138, and 139), whereas AFP uses only one (548), which could require a tiny bit of additional firewall configuration effort.

Whereas Windows lacks AFP support, Mac OS X supports both AFP and SMB. In other words, if you must offer file-sharing services to both Mac and Windows clients and want to use just one protocol, SMB is the right choice — it's the most universal. On the other hand, there's also little disadvantage to using AFP and SMB together, as long as both are configured to use secure authentication.

FTP

As I explained earlier in this book, FTP is an old and therefore virtually universal file-sharing protocol, but it's insecure. The data itself isn't encrypted during transfer, and although it's possible to authenticate securely to a Mac OS X Server-based FTP server using Kerberos, this requires the use of a Kerberized FTP client (a rare commodity — Fetch is the best-known example). In most cases, it's all too easy for someone to sniff someone's FTP password, which could give the attacker access to all sorts of other resources. FTP also has trouble with Mac metadata. It doesn't respect ACLs, and files with resource forks or other metadata may not transfer correctly. Because there are so many other excellent methods of transferring files, I recommend against even turning on the FTP server. If you absolutely must use it, however, I suggest setting up special user accounts exclusively for FTP access so if someone did discover an FTP password, the scope of damage they could cause would be limited.

NFS

NFS is a file-sharing protocol seen most often on Unix computers, although Mac OS X and Windows also support it. One of the unique features of NFS is that not only authentication can be encrypted (using Kerberos), but if you prefer, all data transfer can be encrypted. On the other hand, NFS doesn't natively support the ACLs or SACLs (service access control lists, discussed later in this chapter), potentially making it more complex to configure access permissions in the way you want. Worse, NFS lacks proper support for Mac OS X metadata, such as extended attributes, and it doesn't enable files to be searched over the network using Spotlight (as AFP and SMB can do).

The encryption capability of NFS notwithstanding, there are few situations in which the use of this protocol is compelling because almost every client that might connect to your server using NFS could also connect via SMB. Because of the more complex configuration and the lack of support for important features such as metadata and ACLs, I recommend skipping NFS unless your server is required to serve files to clients that can connect in no other way.

Configuring AFP

If you've decided to use AFP, you can turn it on and configure its basic security settings easily. Separately, you must determine which folders or volumes will be shared and which users or groups have permission to access them; I cover those matters near the end of this chapter.

To activate AFP and adjust its settings, follow these steps:

1. **Open Server Admin, which is located in** `/Applications/Server`.

2. **In the sidebar on the left, select your server.**

3. **If no services are listed under the server name, click the disclosure triangle next to the server name to reveal them.**

4. **If the service names are dimmed, choose Server⇨ Connect, type your username and password if they're not already filled in, and then click Connect.** The list of services refreshes, and those currently running appear with a green dot next to them.

5. **In the sidebar under your server name, select AFP.** If AFP doesn't appear in the list, you must first add it by selecting your server name, clicking Settings, clicking Services, clicking the check box next to AFP, and then clicking Save.

Cross-Ref

For more on modifying the list of services, see Chapter 25. ∎

6. **If AFP isn't already running (that is, the dot next to AFP in the list isn't green), click the Start AFP button at the bottom of the window.**

7. **Click the Settings button on the toolbar.**

8. **Click the Access tab, shown in Figure 29.1.**

FIGURE 29.1

Set authentication method and guest access for the AFP service in this pane.

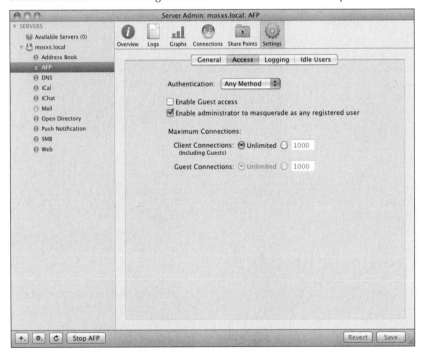

9. **From the Authentication pop-up menu, choose one of the following:**
   - **Any Method.** Uses either cleartext (unencrypted) passwords or Kerberos
   - **Kerberos.** Uses only Kerberos — the preferred choice
   - **Standard.** Uses only cleartext (unencrypted) passwords

10. **If the Enable Guest access check box is selected, click it to deselect it.**

11. **Optionally, to disconnect users after they've been idle for a period of time (reducing the possibility that someone might use an existing AFP connection on an unattended computer), click the Idle Users tab, shown in Figure 29.2, click the Disconnect idle users after ___ minutes check box, and then fill in a number of minutes.** To make exceptions for certain user types, make sure the appropriate check boxes are selected.

12. **Click Save.** The new settings become active immediately.

FIGURE 29.2

In this pane, configure whether or when to disconnect users who have been connected via AFP but have been idle for a period of time.

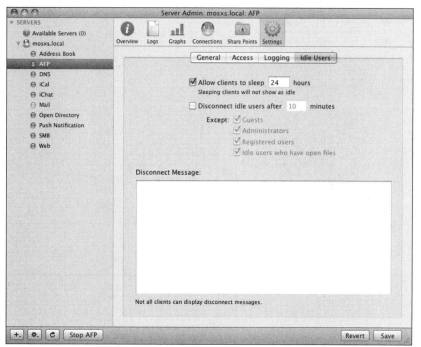

Configuring SMB

To share files using SMB, you follow a procedure similar to that for AFP. In addition to turning on and configuring the service itself, you must set up access to particular shared folders and volumes, as explained later in this chapter.

To activate SMB and adjust its settings, follow these steps:

1. **Open Server Admin, which is located in** `/Applications/Server`.

2. **In the sidebar on the left, select your server.**

3. **If no services are listed under the server name, click the disclosure triangle next to the server name to reveal them.**

4. **If the service names are dimmed, choose Server ⇨ Connect, type your username and password if they're not already filled in, and then click Connect.** The list of services refreshes, and those currently running appear with a green dot next to them.

5. **In the sidebar under your server name, select SMB.** If SMB doesn't appear in the list, you must first add it by selecting your server name, clicking Settings, clicking Services, clicking the check box next to SMB, and then clicking Save.

6. **If SMB isn't already running (that is, the dot next to SMB in the list isn't green), click the Start SMB button at the bottom of the window.**

7. **Click the Settings button on the toolbar.**

8. **Click the Access tab, shown in Figure 29.3.**

FIGURE 29.3

Set authentication method and guest access for the SMB service in this pane.

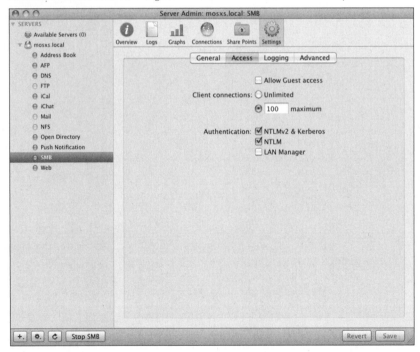

9. **Click the check box next to one or more authentication methods to select or deselect it, as appropriate:**

    - **NTLMv2 & Kerberos.** This secure authentication method can be used only by clients running Windows NT or Windows 98 or later.

    - **NTLM.** This somewhat less-secure authentication method may be required for clients that don't support the newer version of NTL.

    - **LAN Manager.** This cleartext authentication method is needed only for Windows 95 clients and should be disabled otherwise.

10. **If the Allow Guest access check box is selected, click it to deselect it.**

11. **Click Save.** The new settings become active immediately.

Configuring FTP

FTP is an insecure protocol that I suggest you avoid. If you must use it, though, be aware that it has a great many configuration options, which you can learn more about in Apple's documentation. Here, I cover only a few of the most basic parameters.

To activate FTP and adjust its settings, follow these steps:

1. **Open Server Admin, which is located in** `/Applications/Server`.

2. **In the sidebar on the left, select your server.**

3. **If no services are listed under the server name, click the disclosure triangle next to the server name to reveal them.**

4. **If the service names are dimmed, choose Server⇨ Connect, type your username and password if they're not already filled in, and then click Connect.** The list of services refreshes, and those currently running appear with a green dot next to them.

5. **In the sidebar under your server name, select FTP.** If FTP doesn't appear in the list, you must first add it by selecting your server name, clicking Settings, clicking Services, clicking the check box next to FTP, and then clicking Save.

6. **If FTP isn't already running (that is, the dot next to FTP in the list isn't green), click the Start FTP button at the bottom of the window.**

7. **Click the Settings button on the toolbar.**

8. **Click the General tab, shown in Figure 29.4.**

9. **From the Authentication pop-up menu, choose one of the following:**

    - **Any Method.** Uses either Kerberos or conventional cleartext authentication

    - **Kerberos.** Uses only Kerberos for encrypted authentication — this is by far the best choice, but it requires use of a Kerberized FTP client, such as Fetch.

    - **Standard.** Uses only the standard method to transmit your credentials in cleartext

10. **If the Enable anonymous access check box is selected, click it to deselect it.**

11. **Click Save.** The new settings become active immediately.

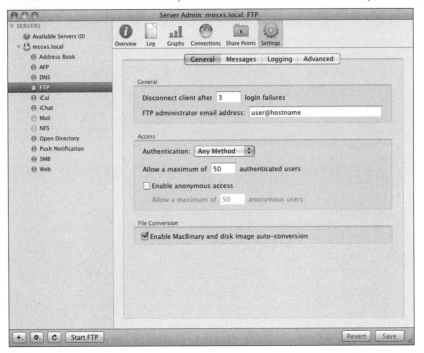

FIGURE 29.4

Set authentication method and anonymous access for the FTP service in this pane.

Configuring NFS

Most Mac OS X Server administrators never need to worry about NFS, but if you have a special need to support Unix clients that can't use another file-sharing protocol or if the extra security of encrypted connections outweighs the various limitations of NFS, you can complete basic setup in a few steps. As usual, you must also configure shared resources separately, as discussed in the next section.

To activate NFS and adjust its settings, follow these steps:

1. **Open Server Admin, which is located in** /Applications/Server.
2. **In the sidebar on the left, select your server.**
3. **If no services are listed under the server name, click the disclosure triangle next to the server name to reveal them.**
4. **If the service names are dimmed, choose Server⇨Connect, type your username and password if they're not already filled in, and then click Connect.** The list of services refreshes, and those currently running appear with a green dot next to them.

5. **In the sidebar under your server name, select NFS.** If NFS doesn't appear in the list, you must first add it by selecting your server name, clicking Settings, clicking Services, clicking the check box next to AFP, and then clicking Save.

6. **If NFS isn't already running (that is, the dot next to NFS in the list isn't green), click the Start NFS button at the bottom of the window.** Normally, no further adjustments are required. However, if you want to adjust the protocols used by NFS, click the Settings button on the tool-bar, shown in Figure 29.5, click the radio button next to your choice, and then click Save. The new settings become active immediately.

FIGURE 29.5

The minimalist Settings pane offers only a couple of options for NFS; others are found elsewhere in Server Admin, as described later in this chapter.

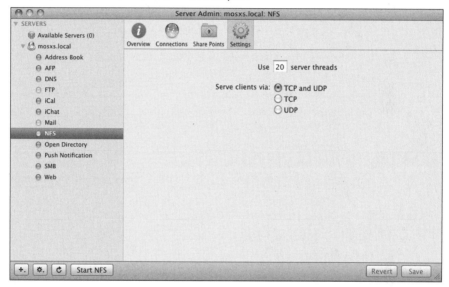

Note

To determine whether or to what extent NFS uses encryption, read the instructions that follow for setting protocol options. ∎

Configuring a Share Point

So far in this chapter, I've described only the file-sharing protocols available in Mac OS X Server — how they work, how to activate them, and how to set basic security features. However, in addition to turning on a file-sharing system, you must also determine which folders or volumes should be shared (meaning they become *share points*) and which users and groups should have access permissions of various kinds for each share point.

Creating a share point

To create a new share point, all you need to do is locate a folder or volume and then designate it as an item to be shared. Afterward, you can determine which protocols are used to share that item and what user and group permissions apply to it.

To create a new share point, follow these steps:

1. **Open Server Admin, which is located in** `/Applications/Server`.

2. **In the sidebar on the left, select your server.**

3. **If no services are listed under the server name, click the disclosure triangle next to the server name to reveal them.**

4. **If the service names are dimmed, choose Server ⇨ Connect, type your username and password if they're not already filled in, and then click Connect.** The list of services refreshes, and those currently running appear with a green dot next to them.

5. **Click the File Sharing button on the toolbar.** If AFP, FTP, NFS, or SMB is selected in the list on the left, the toolbar icon changes to say Share Points, but it has the same function.

6. **Click Volumes (just under the toolbar) and then click Browse (to its right).**

7. **Navigate to a folder or volume you want to share and then select it.**

8. **Click the Share button, which appears only when a valid share point candidate is selected.**

9. **Click Save at the bottom of the window.** Server Admin adds the selected folder or volume to the list of share points, which you can see by clicking Share Points (and then, optionally, List).

Setting protocol options

For each share point, you can determine which protocol(s) can be used to access it and, in most cases, adjust several other security settings.

To determine the protocol settings for a given share point, follow these steps:

1. **Open Server Admin, which is located in** `/Applications/Server`.

2. **In the sidebar on the left, select your server.**

3. **If no services are listed under the server name, click the disclosure triangle next to the server name to reveal them.**

4. **If the service names are dimmed, choose Server ⇨ Connect, type your username and password if they're not already filled in, and then click Connect.** The list of services refreshes, and those currently running appear with a green dot next to them.

5. **Click the File Sharing button on the toolbar.** If AFP, FTP, NFS, or SMB is selected in the list on the left, the toolbar icon changes to say Share Points, but it has the same function.

6. **Click Share Points (just under the toolbar) and then click List (to its right).**

7. **Select a share point in the list and then click the Share Point tab, shown in Figure 29.6.**

FIGURE 29.6

Select a share point in this list in Server Admin to configure, among other things, the options for which protocols can be used to access it — and with which features.

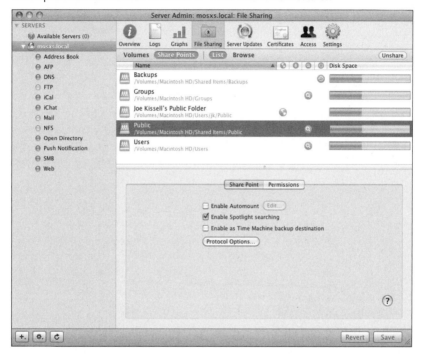

8. **Click the Protocol Options button to open a dialog box with options for each protocol.** In this dialog box, click a tab at the top and then adjust the settings to your liking:

   - **AFP.** In the AFP pane, shown in Figure 29.7, click the Share this item using AFP check box in order to make the share point available via AFP. Optionally, click the Allow AFP guest access check box — but I recommend leaving guest access disabled.

   - **SMB.** In the SMB pane, shown in Figure 29.8, click the Share this item using SMB check box in order to make the share point available via SMB. Optionally, click the Allow SMB guest access check box — but I recommend leaving guest access disabled. To learn about the other options in this pane, consult Apple's documentation.

   - **FTP.** In the FTP pane, shown in Figure 29.9, click the Share this item using FTP check box in order to make the share point available via FTP. Optionally, click the Allow FTP guest access check box — but I recommend leaving guest access disabled.

FIGURE 29.7

Turn AFP access to a share point on or off and determine guest access in this pane.

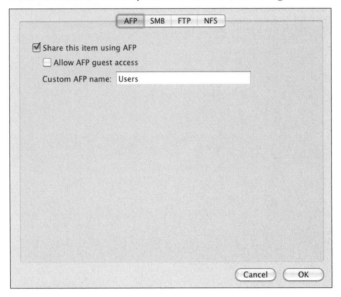

FIGURE 29.8

Turn SMB access to a share point on or off and determine guest access (among other options) in this pane.

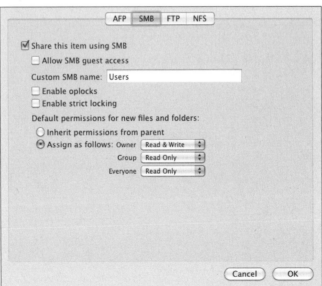

FIGURE 29.9

Turn FTP access to a share point on or off and determine guest access in this pane.

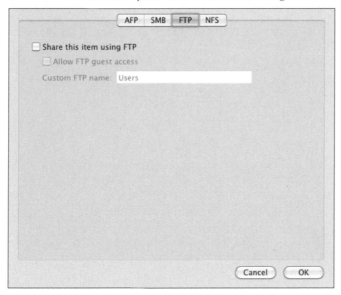

- **NFS.** In the NFS pane, shown in Figure 29.10, click the Export this item and its contents to check box in order to make the share point available via NFS. In NFS lingo, *export* means *share*. From the pop-up menu at the top, choose Client List to restrict access to only certain computers (in which case, click the Add (+) button and then type the domain name or IP address of a host or range of hosts using CIDR notation); Subnet to restrict access to all and only hosts on a particular subnet (in which case, type a subnet address and subnet mask into the fields that appear); or World to permit anyone to access the share point without authenticating. Needless to say, you should avoid World if possible.

  From the Mapping pop-up menu, choose a method for mapping privileges from the local system to the share point. Root to Root is usually the most appropriate choice, although Root to Nobody provides somewhat higher security; see Apple's documentation for further details.

  To adjust encryption settings for authentication and file transfer, choose an option from the Minimum Security pop-up menu. Any of the choices beginning with Kerberos results in secure authentication. If you choose Kerberos v5 with data integrity, NFS checks the data for errors during transmission. And if you choose Kerberos v5 with data integrity and privacy, NFS also encrypts all data transfers.

9. **Click OK to close the Protocol Options dialog box.**
10. **Click Save at the bottom of the window.** The new settings become active immediately.

FIGURE 29.10

In this pane, export (share) a folder or volume using NFS, specify who can connect to it, and choose other security options.

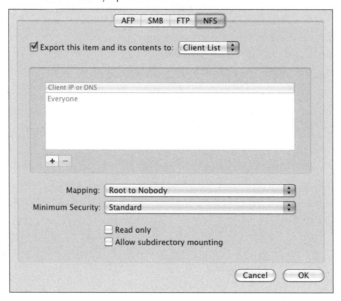

Restricting access to a share point

Having designated a folder or volume as a share point and set options specific to the protocol(s) you want to use, you must also specify which users and groups can access each share point and with what permissions. Permissions can include POSIX permissions (that is, read, write, and execute permissions for user, group, and other), the more fine-grained ACLs, or both. Fortunately, Server Admin lets you configure both types of permissions in a handy graphical interface instead of having to resort to arcane command-line programs in Terminal.

Cross-Ref

For more on POSIX permissions and ACLs, see Chapter 3. ■

To determine who can access a share point and to what extent, follow these steps:

1. Open Server Admin, which is located in /Applications/Server.
2. In the sidebar on the left, select your server.
3. If no services are listed under the server name, click the disclosure triangle next to the server name to reveal them.

4. **If the service names are dimmed, choose Server⇨Connect, type your username and password if they're not already filled in, and then click Connect.** The list of services refreshes, and those currently running appear with a green dot next to them.

5. **Click the File Sharing button on the toolbar.** If AFP, FTP, NFS, or SMB is selected in the list on the left, the toolbar icon changes to say Share Points, but it has the same function.

6. **Click Share Points (just under the toolbar) and then click List (to its right).**

7. **Select a share point in the list and then click the Permissions tab, shown in Figure 29.11.** Current permissions are shown at the bottom of the window, divided into ACL (at the top) and POSIX (at the bottom) categories.

The Permissions pane displays and lets you edit both POSIX and ACL permissions for a share point.

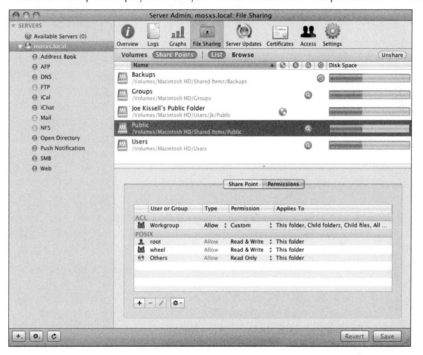

8. **To adjust POSIX permissions for root, group, or others, click the pop-up menu in the Permission column of the relevant row and make a new choice.** Alternatively, double-click any row to open a dialog box in which you can change the user or group name and selectively turn read, write, and execute permissions on or off.

9. To add permissions for another user or group, click the Add (+) button at the bottom to open the Users & Groups palette. In this palette, click either the Users button or the Groups button and then drag an entity to the ACL section of the Permissions list, shown in Figure 29.12.

FIGURE 29.12

Drag a user or group from this floating palette to the ACL list to add an entry for that entity.

10. To change the ACL permissions for an entity (one you added manually, as in step 9, or one already present), you can choose Deny or Allow from the Type pop-up menu or any of the prebuilt permission combinations from the Permission pop-up menu. For more control, double-click the row to open a dialog box like the one shown in Figure 29.13. Choose either Allow or Deny from the Permission Type pop-up menu at the top and then click check boxes to select them or deselect them, as appropriate, to reflect the combination of permissions you want to give this user or group for the selected share point. Click OK to close the dialog box box.

11. **Click Save at the bottom of the window.** The new settings become active immediately.

FIGURE 29.13

In this dialog box, you can select exactly which ACL options should apply to the selected entity for a certain share point.

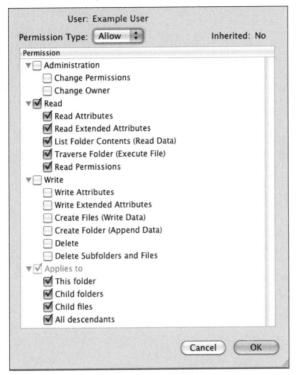

Restricting access to file-sharing services

In addition to restricting access to individual share points based on protocol, user, or group, you can also set or modify SACLs, which determine, at a much higher level, which users and groups can access what file-sharing services on the server. (SACLs apply only to AFP, FTP, and SMB — not to NFS.) For example, you could disallow a certain user from using AFP to access any share point on your server at the protocol level, even if that user has permission at the level of the share point itself.

Note
SACLs also apply to other services (such as Mail and iChat). ∎

To configure SACL settings, follow these steps:

1. Open Server Admin, which is located in /Applications/Server.

2. In the sidebar on the left, select your server.

3. If no services are listed under the server name, click the disclosure triangle next to the server name to reveal them.

4. If the service names are dimmed, choose Server⇨Connect, type your username and password if they're not already filled in, and then click Connect. The list of services refreshes, and those currently running appear with a green dot next to them.

5. Click the Access button on the toolbar.

6. Click the Services tab, shown in Figure 29.14.

FIGURE 29.14

In this pane, set up SACL options to exercise control over which users and groups can use what services.

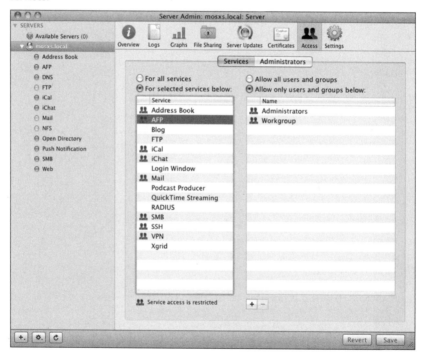

7. On the left side, click either the For all services radio button (to determine which users and groups can access any service) or the For selected services below radio button (to determine which users and groups can access particular services). In the latter case, select a service from the Service list on the left.

8. **On the right side, click either the Allow all users and groups radio button to let everyone access the service(s) selected in step 7, or the Allow only users and groups below radio button to restrict access more specifically.** In the latter case, click the Add (+) button at the bottom to open the Users & Groups palette. In this palette, click either the Users button or the Groups button and then drag an entity to the list of users and groups in the main window. To remove a user or group, select it and then click the Remove (–) button.

9. **Click Save at the bottom of the window.** The new settings become active immediately.

Summary

File sharing is one of the key uses of Mac OS X Server, and in this chapter, I explained how to share files securely on your network using a variety of protocols. After discussing the basics of secure file sharing, I covered each of the available protocols in turn: Apple Filing Protocol (AFP), Server Message Block (SMB), File Transfer Protocol (FTP), and Network File System (NFS). I wrapped up the chapter with a look at how to designate a folder or volume as a share point and how to configure it so only certain users and groups can share particular sets of files.

Securing the Web Server

Mac OS X Server can host any number of websites of any complexity, from the most basic to the most elaborate. Setting up a basic site is simple, yet Mac OS X Server provides detailed control over configuring every facet of your web server's overall behavior as well as the characteristics of individual sites.

In this chapter, I couldn't hope to tell you everything you may want to know about setting up websites, so I assume you already know the basics (or can learn about them elsewhere) and focus here solely on the settings that have the most interesting security implications. These include a few miscellaneous site-specific settings, using realms to limit access to portions of your site, encrypting your site using SSL, and setting up your server to function as a forward proxy server for the rest of your network.

Tip

For thorough instructions on all aspects of setting up and running websites using Mac OS X Server, read Apple's free PDF *Web Technologies Administration,* available at www.apple.com/server/macosx/ resources/documentation.html. ■

Configuring Web Options

For each site you run on your server, you can turn on or off any of five (in Snow Leopard Server) or six (in Leopard Server) different site-wide options, each of which increases the capabilities of your web server in some way but also has the potential to open security holes. As a result, you should stick with the general principle of leaving everything turned off unless you're certain that you need to have it turned on.

To adjust your per-site options, follow these steps:

1. Open Server Admin, which is located in `/Applications/Server`.

2. In the sidebar on the left, select your server.

3. If no services are listed under the server name, click the disclosure triangle next to the server name to reveal them.

4. If the service names are dimmed, choose Server⇨Connect, type your username and password if they're not already filled in, and then click Connect. The list of services refreshes, and those currently running appear with a green dot next to them.

5. In the sidebar under your server name, select Web. If Web doesn't appear in the list, you must first add it by selecting your server name, clicking Settings, clicking Services, clicking the check box next to Web, and then clicking Save.

Cross-Ref

For more on modifying the list of services, see Chapter 25. ■

6. If the web server isn't already running (that is, the dot next to Web in the list isn't green), click the Start Web button at the bottom of the window.

7. Click the Sites button on the toolbar.

8. In the list of sites at the top of the window, select a site for which you want to configure options.

9. Click the Options tab, shown in Figure 30.1.

10. Click any of the following check boxes to select or deselect them, as the case may be:

   - **Folder Listing.** When selected, this option enables users to list all the contents of a folder on your web server by browsing to the folder name without a specific file name. For example, going to `www.yoursite.com/stuff` would list the files in your `stuff` folder, unless you have your site configured to display a default file (such as `index.html`) and a file by that name is present in the folder. Because this feature can expose information about files on your server that you may not want the public to be aware of (not to mention make browsing more confusing), I suggest leaving it disabled.

   - **WebDAV.** WebDAV (Web-based Distributed Authoring and Versioning) is a mechanism that uses HTTP — the same protocol used for serving and viewing websites — to share files. Using WebDAV, you can enable a web designer (or even, in theory, anyone in the world) to modify pages on your website or upload new pages, in lieu of using FTP or another separate file-sharing mechanism. This can be useful in many situations, but unless or until you're sure you need it, leave it turned off. Once you do activate it, you must separately configure WebDAV access to all or part of your site for users and groups using realms; I explain how to do this later in this chapter.

   - **CGI Execution.** CGI (Common Gateway Interface) is a protocol that lets an external program process data on behalf of your web server. When a client sends a request for a certain CGI action, your web server passes it on to the CGI program, receives the results back, and returns them to the client. Although CGI programs can enable your server to do all kinds of interesting things, you shouldn't enable support for them unless you have a specific need to do so. Most sites work just fine without CGI support, and if CGI Execution is enabled, that's one more potential avenue by which an attacker could try to gain control of your server or cause other problems.

- **Server Side Includes (SSI).** The main reason for this technology is to enable one web page to display the contents of another page. It can also be used for displaying dynamic information such as times and dates. SSI is seldom used these days, in preference to languages such as PHP and Ruby for putting dynamic content on web pages. Because it could theoretically be exploited to grant external access to private resources, it's best to leave it turned off unless it's needed for a particular site feature.

- **Allow All Overrides.** A number of site-specific settings can be changed through the use of `.conf` files, special text files stored in `/etc/httpd/sites`, or through `.htaccess` files, which can be used for redirections and other on-the-fly configuration changes. Turning on this feature lets Apache read and process both kinds of files. In my experience, it's so common to use one or both of these techniques to modify site behavior that leaving this turned off could lead to frustration later on as you try to figure out why things don't work. However, turning it on also means giving anyone with access to the folders in which site content is stored the capability to break all sorts of things about the site's behavior.

- **Spotlight Searching.** This option (available only in Leopard Server) turns on Spotlight indexing for the site, enabling users to search its contents.

11. **Click Save.** The new settings become active immediately.

FIGURE 30.1

The check boxes in the Options pane let you turn several site-specific features on or off. This pane is slightly different in Leopard Server.

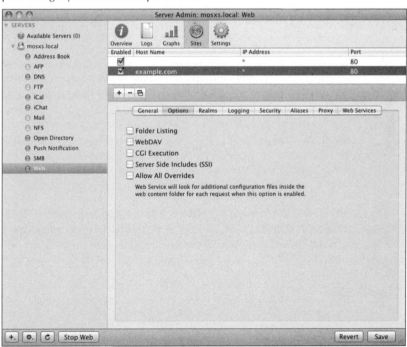

813

Configuring Web Services

Besides the content provided by the pages you or your users place on your websites, Mac OS X Server has several features you can optionally add to any hosted sites that rely on the web server, such as blogs and wikis. Although these extra features don't pose an intrinsic security risk, enabling them gives your users additional ways to publish information on your website, and you may want to avoid or restrict those capabilities.

To adjust the settings for these add-on web services, follow these steps:

1. Open Server Admin, which is located in `/Applications/Server`.

2. In the sidebar on the left, select your server.

3. If no services are listed under the server name, click the disclosure triangle next to the server name to reveal them.

4. If the service names are dimmed, choose Server⇨Connect, type your username and password if they're not already filled in, and then click Connect. The list of services refreshes, and those currently running appear with a green dot next to them.

5. In the sidebar under your server name, select Web. If Web doesn't appear in the list, you must first add it by selecting your server name, clicking Settings, clicking Services, clicking the check box next to Web, and then clicking Save.

6. If the web server isn't already running (that is, the dot next to Web in the list isn't green), click the Start Web button at the bottom of the window.

7. Click the Sites button on the toolbar.

8. In the list of sites at the top of the window, select a site for which you want to configure options.

9. Click the Web Services tab, shown in Figure 30.2.

10. Click any of the following check boxes to select or deselect them, as the case may be (names and locations vary depending on which version of Mac OS X Server you're using):

    - Wikis (Snow Leopard Server) or Wiki and blog (Leopard Server). Wikis are websites that users can edit directly in their web browsers and are ideal for collaborative writing and editing projects or sites with information requiring ever-changing details from many contributors.

    - Blogs (Snow Leopard Server) or Blog (Leopard Server). Blogs let authorized users or groups create dated entries detailing anything from personal diaries and opinions to product development news or corporate policy changes.

Note

Setting up a wiki or blog requires just one click, but Mac OS X Server offers much more control in how these services are managed. To learn about them, read Apple's free PDFs *Wiki Server Administration* and *Wiki Tools Deployment Guide* (which also covers blogs), available at `www.apple.com/server/macosx/resources/documentation.html`. ∎

    - Calendar (Snow Leopard Server) or Web calendar (Leopard Server). If you're running iCal Server on Mac OS X Server, you can offer your users an optional web-based interface to their calendars (instead of or in addition to using iCal or another desktop calendar application) by enabling this option.

Cross-Ref

For more on activating and configuring iCal Server, see Chapter 31. ■

- **Mail (Snow Leopard Server) or Webmail (Leopard Server).** If you've activated Mac OS X Server's mail server, you can select this box to give your users the option of checking their email via their web browsers. With this check box selected, Snow Leopard Server provides two additional options, both of which are available only if you've activated SSL for your site (as described later in this chapter): configure server-side mail rules — to sort and otherwise process messages before they reach the user's inbox — and the self-explanatory "change their password." Because both of these options are quite useful, I suggest selecting them if possible.

Note

Leopard Server has an additional check box: Mailing list web archive, which lets subscribers to Mailman mailing lists (not covered in this book) review and search previous list messages on the web. ■

11. **Click Save.** The new settings become active immediately.

FIGURE 30.2

In the Web Services pane, you can activate or deactivate web features, including blogs and wikis.

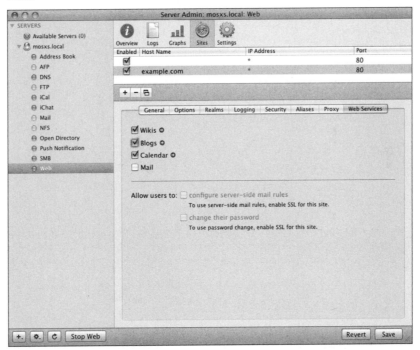

Controlling Site Access with Realms

In the context of websites, a *realm* is a portion of your site (typically a folder and all the files and folders within it) for which you have designated access restrictions. You protect realms with a username and password so whenever someone tries to access content in a realm, his or her browser displays an HTTP authentication dialog box, like the one shown in Figure 30.3. Once the user supplies a valid set of credentials, the server grants access to the page requested and to all other pages within the realm.

Realms aren't the sole way to restrict access to portions of your website. For example, you could use an ordinary web form that sends users' credentials to a PHP program to verify access permission. However, as long as your list of users isn't long, realms are easy to set up without any programming, are supported by virtually every web browser, and provide good security (at least as long as you use an encrypted authentication method, as I describe shortly).

The access restrictions you apply to realms in Mac OS X Server determine not only the way in which authentication is used when browsing the site in a web browser but also who can access the site's files and to what extent via WebDAV, a protocol for sharing files via HTTP. (I discuss WebDAV setup elsewhere in this chapter.)

FIGURE 30.3

When a user visits a URL corresponding to a protected realm in Safari, a dialog box like this one requests authentication.

Note

In Mac OS X Server, you can restrict access to realms only based on user and group accounts you've already set up. Therefore, you should decide which users and groups you may want to be able to access your realm before doing anything else. Instructions for setting up users and groups can be found in Chapter 26. ■

To use a realm to restrict who can access a portion of your website, follow these steps:

1. Open Server Admin, which is located in /Applications/Server.
2. In the sidebar on the left, select your server.

3. If no services are listed under the server name, click the disclosure triangle next to the server name to reveal them.

4. **If the service names are dimmed, choose Server ⇨ Connect, type your username and password if they're not already filled in, and then click Connect.** The list of services refreshes, and those currently running appear with a green dot next to them.

5. **In the sidebar under your server name, select Web.** If Web doesn't appear in the list, you must first add it by selecting your server name, clicking Settings, clicking Services, clicking the check box next to Web, and then clicking Save.

6. **If the web server isn't already running (that is, the dot next to Web in the list isn't green), click the Start Web button at the bottom of the window.**

7. **Click the Sites button on the toolbar.**

8. **In the list of sites at the top of the window, select a site for which you want to configure a realm.**

9. **Click the Realms tab, shown in Figure 30.4.**

10. **Click the Add (+) button below the Realms list.** The dialog box shown in Figure 30.5 opens.

FIGURE 30.4

In the Realms pane, you can specify portions of a site for which access — via a web browser or WebDAV — is restricted.

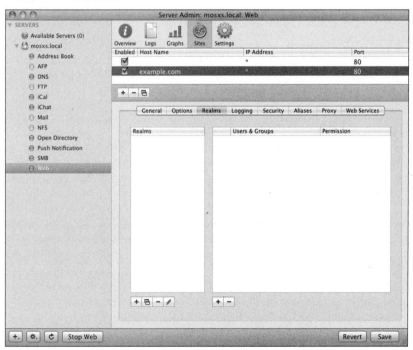

FIGURE 30.5

Realms offer only minimal security with Basic authentication. To be sure credentials are encrypted, choose one of the other options.

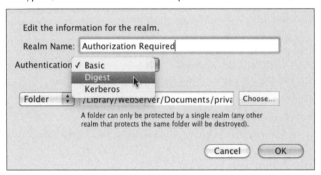

11. **In the Realm Name field, type the text you want to appear in the authorization dialog box.** This need not be the name of the realm; it can be a helpful message, such as "Authorization Required" or "Type your email address and password."

12. **From the Authentication pop-up menu, choose one of the following:**

    • **Basic.** The credentials are sent in clear, unencrypted text. I recommend not using this option.

    • **Digest.** The credentials are sent using an encrypted hash, which is moderately secure.

    • **Kerberos.** The credentials are sent securely using Kerberos. This is the best option to use as long as your server hosts or is connected to a Kerberos realm.

13. **To designate a folder within your site as a realm, choose Folder from the pop-up menu and then type the complete path to the folder (as it appears on the server's hard disk) in the field that follows or click Choose, navigate to the folder, and then select it.** Alternatively, to designate a logical portion of your site (which may not correspond to a physical folder) as a realm, choose Location from the pop-up menu and then type a URL. Every URL that begins with the string you typed is then considered part of the realm.

14. **Click OK to confirm creation of the realm.**

15. **In the list of realms in the main Server Admin window, select the realm you just created.** The field on the right contains the list of users and groups with access to the realm and what their permissions are. Initially, a placeholder user called Everyone is set up but without access permission.

16. **To add permissions for a user or group, click the Add (+) button beneath the list of users and groups to open the Users & Groups palette.** In this palette, click either the Users button or the Groups button and then drag an entity to the Users & Groups list, as shown in Figure 30.6.

17. **To change the permissions for an entity, click the Permissions area next to the entity's name and then choose one of the following from the pop-up menu that appears:**

    • **Browse Only.** Can browse web pages

    • **Browse and Read WebDAV.** Can browse web pages and read its files using WebDAV

    • **Browse and Read/Write WebDAV.** Can browse web pages and read or write its files using WebDAV

    • **None.** No access to the pages via a browser or WebDAV

18. **Click Save.** Your realm becomes active immediately.

FIGURE 30.6

Drag a user or group from this floating palette to the Users & Groups list to add an entry for that entity.

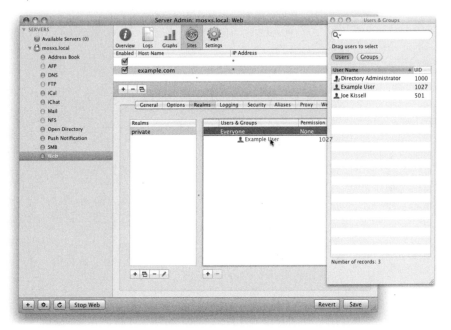

Enabling SSL

As discussed in several other places throughout this book, SSL (Secure Sockets Layer) enables all the communication between a web server and a browser to be encrypted. Anyone sniffing the network traffic at any point between the two would be unable to see the contents of web pages sent, the values of form values typed, or any other potentially confidential data. In addition, using SSL enables the person viewing your site to verify your credentials — to confirm that the site he or she connected to is the one he or she meant to be connected to.

Cross-Ref
For more on activating SSL for a website on the standard version of Mac OS X, see Chapter 18. For more on SSL from the point of view of a person browsing the web, see Chapter 10. ■

SSL is easy to implement in Mac OS X Server, and if you'll be serving websites that send or receive private information, it's a good idea to do so. You could, of course, use SSL by default for all your sites to keep every bit of data transferred secure on principle. However, doing so puts a slightly higher strain on your server's CPU because of the extra work required to encrypt and decrypt all the data. For sites with a modest number of visitors, this effect may not be noticeable, but if you have an extremely busy site, using SSL can decrease the number of visitors you can effectively serve at once.

Also keep in mind that SSL must be turned on individually for each domain, and SSL certificates are tied to specific domain names. So, even though you could have dozens of sites running on your server and could use SSL for each of them, that would mean obtaining a certificate (and, in general, paying a fee to a certificate authority) for each one.

The process of activating SSL for a site takes only a few clicks, but before you can perform them, you must already have a valid SSL certificate installed for the domain name in question.

Cross-Ref

For more on obtaining and installing an SSL certificate, see Chapter 27. ■

To activate SSL for a website hosted on your server, follow these steps:

1. **Open Server Admin, which is located in** `/Applications/Server`.
2. **In the sidebar on the left, select your server.**
3. **If no services are listed under the server name, click the disclosure triangle next to the server name to reveal them.**
4. **If the service names are dimmed, choose Server ⇨ Connect, type your username and password if they're not already filled in, and then click Connect.** The list of services refreshes, and those currently running appear with a green dot next to them.
5. **In the sidebar under your server name, select Web.** If Web doesn't appear in the list, you must first add it by selecting your server name, clicking Settings, clicking Services, clicking the check box next to Web, and then clicking Save.
6. **If the web server isn't already running (that is, the dot next to Web in the list isn't green), click the Start Web button at the bottom of the window.**
7. **Click the Sites button on the toolbar.**
8. **In the list of sites at the top of the window, select a site for which you want to activate SSL.**
9. **Click the Security tab, shown in Figure 30.7.**
10. **Click the Enable Secure Sockets Layer (SSL) check box.** A dialog box opens with a message informing you that the site's port has changed to 443.
11. **Click OK.**
12. **From the Certificate pop-up menu, choose an installed certificate with a domain name matching the name of your site.**
13. **Click Save.** Because the web server must restart in order for SSL to take effect, a dialog box opens, asking if you want to restart the web server now.
14. **Click Restart.** The web server restarts, and SSL becomes available on your site immediately.

Once SSL is active on a site, visitors can access it using the same domain name as previously but with a URL starting with `https` rather than `http`. However, visitors typing the `http` URL aren't automatically redirected to the secure version of your site; instead, by default, they just see an error message.

FIGURE 30.7

Turning on SSL for a site is as easy as clicking a check box and selecting a certificate from a pop-up menu.

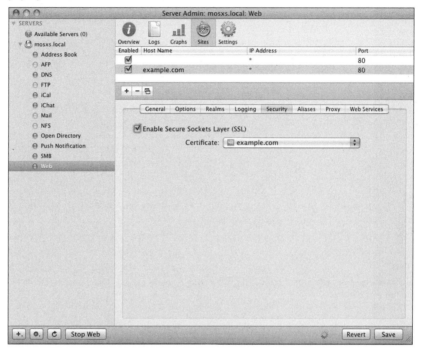

In Mac OS X Server, the easiest way to redirect visitors who use `http` URLs to their `https` equivalents is to follow these steps:

1. **With your SSL-enabled site still selected (as in steps 1 through 8 in the previous set of steps), click the Duplicate button (just to the right of the Remove [–] button).** Server Admin makes a copy of your site settings.

2. **In the Host Name field, type a name for your site, such as the existing site name followed by "nonsecure."**

3. **Click the Security tab.**

4. **Click the Enable Secure Sockets Layer (SSL) check box to deselect it.** A dialog box opens with a message informing you that the site's port has changed to 80. Click OK.

5. **Click the Aliases tab.**

6. **Near the bottom of the window, below the URL Aliases and Redirects list, click the Add (+) button.** A dialog box opens.

7. **From the Type pop-up menu, choose RedirectMatch.**

8. In the Pattern field, type /(.*).

9. In the Path field, type https://*your-domain-name*/$1, where *your-domain-name* is replaced with your site's domain name.

10. Click OK.

11. **Click Save.** The redirection becomes active immediately.

To test that the change is working, type any valid URL on your site, starting with http, and confirm that it's automatically replaced with https.

Configuring the Forward Proxy Server

Mac OS X Server has two built-in proxy servers. First is a forward proxy server, which offers both caching of frequently accessed web content (to improve network performance and reduce bandwidth consumption) and blocking of domains you don't want users on your network to be able to access. In either case, the proxy works only when other computers on your local network are configured to access the web through your server. To enforce this, you may need to configure your organization's firewall to prevent direct outgoing access to the web. The second proxy server is a reverse proxy server (not covered in this book), which can re-route incoming web traffic to various web servers — for example, balancing the load across several physical servers while appearing, to outside users, to be a single server.

Cross-Ref

For more on setting up Mac OS X as a client to connect to a proxy server, see Chapter 10. ■

Unlike the other services discussed in this chapter, the forward proxy server isn't restricted to a single site. Rather, it uses your web server's infrastructure to provide proxy services globally. To set up the forward proxy server, follow these steps:

1. **Open Server Admin, which is located in** /Applications/Server.

2. **In the sidebar on the left, select your server.**

3. **If no services are listed under the server name, click the disclosure triangle next to the server name to reveal them.**

4. **If the service names are dimmed, choose Server ➪ Connect, type your username and password if they're not already filled in, and then click Connect.** The list of services refreshes, and those currently running appear with a green dot next to them.

5. **In the sidebar under your server name, select Web.** If Web doesn't appear in the list, you must first add it by selecting your server name, clicking Settings, clicking Services, clicking the check box next to Web, and then clicking Save.

6. **If the web server isn't already running (that is, the dot next to Web in the list isn't green), click the Start Web button at the bottom of the window.**

7. **Click the Settings button on the toolbar.**

8. **Click the Proxy tab, shown in Figure 30.8.**

9. **Click the Enable Forward Proxy check box.**

10. **To restrict access to your proxy, click the Control Access To Proxy check box.** To restrict access only to computers in one domain (typically, the domain of your own network), type that domain in the Allowed Domain field.

FIGURE 30.8

Enable the forward proxy server in this pane, optionally adding sites for which access is blocked.

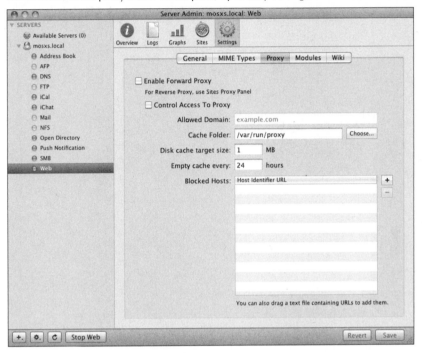

11. **To prevent users who connect to your proxy server from accessing certain domains, click the Add (+) button next to the Blocked Hosts list and then type a domain name or IP address.** Repeat this step as necessary to block more domains.

12. **Click Save.** The proxy server becomes active immediately.

Summary

Mac OS X Server includes Apache for serving complex websites. This chapter described the use of Mac OS X Server's administrative tools for securing the web server in ways that would require considerably more effort in the standard version of Mac OS X. I described recommended settings for basic server options and web services as well as secure realms using HTTP authentication, using SSL to encrypt web data as it travels between client and server. I also discussed setting up Mac OS X Server to function as a forward proxy server for other computers on your network.

Securing Other Network Services

A part from major server functions such as web, mail, and file sharing, Mac OS X Server offers a long list of other services that you can make available to users on your network. All of these are, as you might expect, covered in great detail in PDF documentation that you can download free from Apple at www.apple.com/server/macosx/resources/documentation.html.

In this final chapter, I offer some brief guidance on security settings for a potpourri of other Mac OS X Server features. I begin with the firewall, which can protect not only the server itself but other Macs on your network, and then move on to the VPN server, which enables you to offer remote users a way to connect securely to your network. I then provide a quick overview of several other server features, including iCal, iChat, and Address Book servers.

As with many Mac OS X Server features, most of the services discussed in this chapter can be configured using either the simplified interface of Server Preferences or the more advanced interface of Server Admin. Because Server Admin provides a comprehensive way to adjust the behavior of these services, this chapter provides only the version of the instructions that use Server Admin.

Configuring the Mac OS X Server Firewall

The firewall software built into Mac OS X Server is IPFW, which is also present (but hidden) in the standard version of Mac OS X. Mac OS X Server doesn't use the simpler application firewall found in the Security pane of System Preferences in Mac OS X. The main difference is that Mac OS X Server includes a complete graphical interface for configuring IPFW, making it easy to access the firewall's extensive capabilities without fiddling around on the command line or down-loading third-party configuration software.

IN THIS CHAPTER

Securing the built-in firewall in Mac OS X Server

Offering VPN services to your users

Offering secure Address Book access

Sharing iCal resources securely

Running a secure iChat server

Providing mobile users secure access to your server without using a VPN

Protecting your MySQL server

Securely using NetBoot

Using the RADIUS server to authorize AirPort users

Cross-Ref

For more on general firewall principles as well as how to set up the built-in firewalls in the standard version of Mac OS X, see Chapter 17. ■

The primary purpose of the firewall is to protect your server — which is likely to be exposed directly to the public Internet and offering numerous network services — from both random and targeted attacks. Unlike ordinary Macs, which often hide safely behind NAT routers, servers usually have no such intrinsic (if passive) protection and are easier targets. So, using a firewall and configuring it to be as restrictive as possible while enabling essential services are extremely important precautions to take.

It should come as no surprise that you can turn on the firewall, with basic settings, with just a few clicks. But for more complex firewall needs, Mac OS X Server also lets you dig deeply into firewall settings, tailoring them to your exact specifications.

Basic setup

Before doing anything else, you should turn on your firewall and become familiar with a few basics of its operation.

To turn on the firewall, follow these steps:

1. **Open Server Admin, which is located in** `/Applications/Server`**.**
2. **In the sidebar on the left, select your server.**
3. **If no services are listed under the server name, click the disclosure triangle next to the server name to reveal them.**
4. **If the service names are dimmed, choose Server ⇨ Connect, type your username and password if they're not already filled in, and then click Connect.** The list of services refreshes, and those currently running appear with a green dot next to them.
5. **In the sidebar under your server name, select Firewall.** If Firewall doesn't appear in the list, you must first add it by selecting your server name, clicking Settings, clicking Services, clicking the check box next to Firewall, and then clicking Save.

Cross-Ref

For more on modifying the list of services, see Chapter 25. ■

6. **If the firewall isn't already running (that is, the dot next to Firewall in the list isn't green), click the Start Firewall button at the bottom of the window.** The firewall starts up immediately.

The default firewall configuration is to block all incoming ports except a small handful of ports essential to Mac OS X Server's operation, including the ones used by SSH and Server Admin for remote administration. This means that if you want to make any additional services available to the outside world, you must explicitly open one or more additional ports to traffic.

Caution

If you're sitting in front of the Mac that's running Mac OS X Server, you can freely make whatever changes you need to the firewall, correcting any mistakes you make as you go. However, if you're connecting to the server remotely using some method other than Server Admin, turning on the firewall could block the ports used by whatever mechanism you're using to control the server. For example, using Timbuktu Pro for screen sharing would fall into this category. Therefore, before turning on the firewall over a remote connection, make sure you've added rules (as described shortly) to open the port(s) necessary for your own remote access. ■

Configuring standard services

In keeping with the theme of making frequently used features as easy to access as possible, Mac OS X Server provides a fairly extensive list of common services you may want to run on your server, conveniently labeled with plain-English names as well as the ports they use. To set up the firewall to allow traffic through for these services, you need do nothing more than click a check box and then click Save.

To open ports used for common services to incoming traffic, follow these steps:

1. **Follow the steps presented earlier to open Server Admin and select the firewall service.**

2. **Click the Settings button on the toolbar.**

3. **Click the Services tab, shown in Figure 31.1.**

FIGURE 31.1

In this pane, you can punch a hole in the firewall for commonly used services with just a couple of clicks.

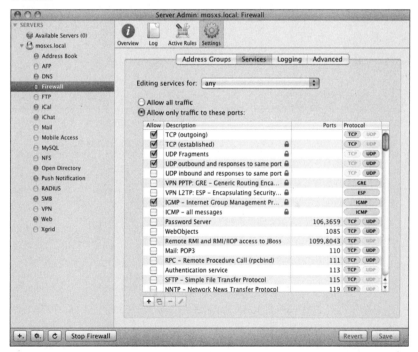

4. **Make sure the Editing services for pop-up menu is set to any, as it is by default, and that the Allow only traffic to these ports radio button is selected (also the default).**

5. **In the list, scroll down to find the service you want to expose to the Internet and then click the check box in its Allow column.** Repeat as necessary for additional services.

6. **Optionally, to add a service to the list that you may need to turn on and off regularly, click the Add (+) button at the bottom of the list, type the name of the service in the Name field,**

type its port in the Port field, and then choose either TCP, UDP, or TCP and UDP (as appropriate) from the Protocol pop-up menu.

7. **Click OK.** The service you added then appears in the list, and you can select it to open that port.

8. **Click Save.** The new settings are applied immediately.

Advanced settings

The list of ports on the Services tab provides enough configurability for many people all by itself, especially because you can modify the list yourself as needed. However, not all firewall rules you may need are as simple as "keep this port open." When you need greater specificity, you can create more elaborate rules in the Advanced pane.

But first, you should be aware that the Mac OS X Server firewall has a convenience feature called Address Groups. You can specify a list or range of IP addresses (such as those for your internal network, the network of another branch of your company, or a known circle of malicious computers). The rules you specify on the Advanced tab can use these preset groups of addresses. Address groups are entirely optional, but if you think you might want to use them when creating advanced rules, set them up by following these steps:

1. **Follow the steps presented earlier to open Server Admin and select the Firewall service.**

2. **Click the Settings button on the toolbar.**

3. **Click the Address Groups tab, shown in Figure 31.2.**

In the Address Groups pane, set up groups of addresses to which you can refer later in advanced rules.

4. **Click the Add (+) button at the bottom of the list, and in the dialog box that opens, type a group name, click the Add (+) button, and then type one or more IP addresses or address ranges (using CIDR notation).**

Cross-Ref

For more on CIDR notation, see Chapter 17. ■

5. **Click OK.** The new address group appears in the list.

6. **Click Save.** The newly defined groups can now be used in advanced rules.

To configure advanced firewall rules and settings, follow these steps:

1. **Follow the steps presented earlier to open Server Admin and select the Firewall service.**

2. **Click the Settings button on the toolbar.**

3. **Click the Advanced tab, shown in Figure 31.3.**

4. **To enable Stealth Mode, click the Enable for TCP check box, the Enable for UDP check box, or both.** Stealth Mode means the firewall doesn't send a failure message in response to a request to access a blocked port, so the computer making the request isn't clued in to the fact that a firewall is operational and that the service in question may be active but blocked.

5. **To add an advanced rule, click the Add (+) button at the bottom of the list.** The dialog box shown in Figure 31.4 opens.

FIGURE 31.3

In the Advanced pane, you can create much more detailed and specific rules than the basic rules found in the Services pane.

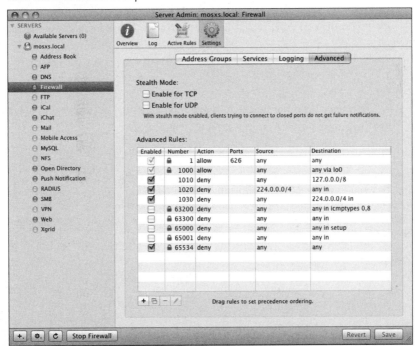

829

6. Choose the settings you want for your rule:

    ● **Action.** Choose Allow or Deny from the Action pop-up menu to specify whether matching packets are allowed or blocked. To use another action, such as log, choose Other and then type the name of the action into the field provided.

Note

Here and throughout the dialog box for creating advanced rules, the Other choice pops up repeatedly, allowing IPFW experts to manually type a variety of obscure settings. To learn more about what these additional options are, consult the IPFW documentation — for example, by typing man ipfw **in a Terminal window.** ■

    ● **Protocol.** Choose UDP or TCP from the Protocol pop-up menu. To use another protocol, choose Other and then type the name of the protocol in the field provided.

    ● **Service.** Choose the name of a commonly used service (the same options that appear in the Services pane) to pre-fill the port(s) used by that service in the dialog box. Or choose Other to fill in your own port details.

    ● **Log all packets matching this rule.** Click this check box to record matches to this rule in a log file.

    ● **Source Address.** From the Address pop-up menu under Source, choose any, the name of an address group you defined yourself, or Other to set the source address for matching packets. If you chose Other, type the source address or address range in the field to the right.

    ● **Source Port.** To match packets originating from a particular port, type the port number in the Port field under Source.

    ● **Destination Address.** From the Address pop-up menu under Destination, choose any, the name of an address group you defined yourself, or Other to set the destination address for matching packets. If you chose Other, type the destination address or address range in the field to the right.

    ● **Destination Port.** To match packets targeting a particular port, type the port number in the Port field under Destination.

    ● **Interface.** From this pop-up menu, choose In (for incoming packets), Out (for outgoing packets), or Other; if Other, type the interface in the field to the right.

7. Click OK.
8. **To change the order in which rules apply, drag rules up or down in the list.**
9. **Click Save.** The new settings are applied immediately.

Note

A built-in firewall feature that requires no configuration (and can't be turned off either, as long as the firewall is running) is one that counts the number of consecutive unsuccessful login attempts. If the number reaches 10, the firewall blocks the IP address from which the request originated for 15 minutes. This is a safety feature that prevents both automated break-in attempts (such as dictionary attacks) and people trying to guess another user's password repeatedly. ■

FIGURE 31.4

In this dialog box, you can specify exactly the sort of firewall rule you need.

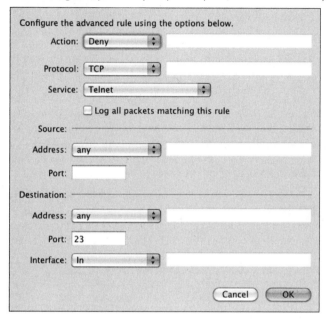

Protecting your network

Because Mac OS X Server is most commonly installed on Macs that have (or can be fitted with) multiple Ethernet interfaces, you can also use the server's firewall to protect other computers on your network. Doing so requires that your network cabling be physically routed in such a way that your Mac OS X Server computer is between your internal network and your outside connection — for example, plugging one Ethernet port into your upstream network interface and the other into a switch to which the rest of the devices on your network connect.

The simplest way to set this up is to use an automated program called Gateway Setup Assistant, which walks you through the setup of a number of services (among them NAT, DHCP, VPN, and firewall) so your server functions as a NAT router.

To use Gateway Setup Assistant, follow these steps:

1. **Open Server Admin, which is located in** `/Applications/Server`.
2. **In the sidebar on the left, select your server.**
3. **If no services are listed under the server name, click the disclosure triangle next to the server name to reveal them.**

4. **If the service names are dimmed, choose Server⇨Connect, type your username and password if they're not already filled in, and then click Connect.** The list of services refreshes, and those currently running appear with a green dot next to them.

5. **In the sidebar under your server name, select NAT.** If NAT doesn't appear in the list, you must first add it by selecting your server name, clicking Settings, clicking Services, clicking the check box next to NAT, and then clicking Save.

6. **Click the Overview button on the toolbar, shown in Figure 31.5.**

7. **Click the Gateway Setup Assistant button.** Gateway Setup Assistant launches.

8. **Step through the screens in the assistant, whose contents vary based on your server's configuration and the choices you make, and then click Continue to advance from one screen to the next.** When you're finished, your computer will be functioning as a gateway.

9. **Review your (now revised) firewall rules following the instructions presented earlier in this chapter, opening ports as necessary for essential services that are blocked by default or adding new advanced rules to suit your needs.**

FIGURE 31.5

You can launch Gateway Setup Assistant from the Overview pane of the NAT service in Server Admin.

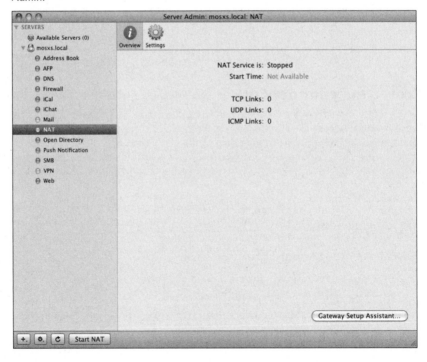

Using Mac OS X Server's VPN Services

VPNs have shown up in numerous spots in this book. Because they let a user encrypt all the network traffic traveling between a local computer and a remote computer or network, they provide excellent security (even in inherently insecure situations such as using open Wi-Fi hotspots). They also give the user access to resources that would otherwise be available only on the local network, making them ideal for employees who need to reach servers behind a corporate firewall when working from home or traveling.

Cross-Ref

For more on VPNs, see Chapter 7 (sharing files and other resources with other users), Chapter 11 (accessing other computers securely, even with unencrypted protocols such as FTP), Chapter 12 (VPNs from the client's viewpoint), and Chapter 16 (using wireless networks securely). ■

Of course, configuring a client computer for VPN access is only half the equation. You also need a VPN server to connect to on the other end — one that's already connected to the network you need access to (and, usually, also to the public Internet). You can sign up for commercial VPN services or buy stand-alone VPN appliances that do nothing but provide VPN services to your users. However, if you have Mac OS X Server, you already have everything you need to provide VPN access to your users. Mac OS X Server's VPN services let you turn on L2TP over IPsec, PPTP, or both and exercise complete control over who can connect to the VPN from the outside.

Choosing a transport protocol

Before you start setting anything up, you should decide which of the two protocols you want to use. Of the two, L2TP over IPsec is the more secure. It uses stronger encryption and can optionally use Kerberos for authentication, which is not only secure but also makes it possible for users to type their credentials just once and gain access to a wide range of network services. L2TP requires the use of either SSL certificates (which may be self-signed) or a shared secret — a string of characters, used as an identifier (rather than as a password or encryption key), that must be typed on both the server and all client computers. PPTP is an older and somewhat less secure protocol, but it works with PCs running older (pre-Windows XP) versions of Windows as well as Macs running Mac OS X 10.2 or earlier.

Cross-Ref

For more on creating and using SSL certificates, see Chapter 27. ■

My suggestion is to use L2TP over IPsec exclusively, as long as the users who will connect to your VPN have suitable operating system support. If you need to support older clients, turn on PPTP too. Even though PPTP is more universal and would work across all supported devices, its lower security and less-convenient authentication make it less desirable.

Configuring L2TP over IPsec

To enable VPN access using L2TP over IPsec, follow these steps:

1. **Open Server Admin, which is located in** `/Applications/Server`.
2. **In the sidebar on the left, select your server.**
3. **If no services are listed under the server name, click the disclosure triangle next to the server name to reveal them.**

4. **If the service names are dimmed, choose Server⇨Connect, type your username and password if they're not already filled in, and then click Connect.** The list of services refreshes, and those currently running appear with a green dot next to them.

5. **In the sidebar under your server name, select VPN.** If VPN doesn't appear in the list, you must first add it by selecting your server name, clicking Settings, clicking Services, clicking the check box next to VPN, and then clicking Save.

6. **Click the Settings button on the toolbar.**

7. **Click the L2TP tab, shown in Figure 31.6.**

8. **Click the Enable L2TP over IPsec check box.**

9. **In the Starting IP address field, type the first IP address in the range that will be assigned to VPN users.** Apple's suggested value is **192.168.0.128**.

10. **In the Ending IP address field, type the last IP address in the range that will be assigned to VPN users.** Apple's suggested value is **192.168.0.255**.

FIGURE 31.6

To use L2TP over IPsec for VPN services, configure the options in this pane.

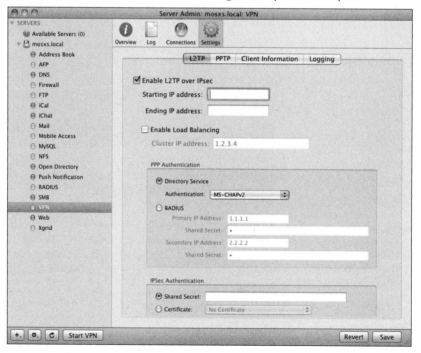

Note

If you use both L2TP over IPsec and PPTP, you must select different address ranges for each one in these two steps. ■

11. If you're using more than one VPN server and you want to balance the load between them, click the Enable Load Balancing check box and then type the IP address of the server cluster in the Cluster IP address field.

12. In the PPP Authentication area, click the radio button corresponding to the type of authentication to use: either Directory Service (in which case, choose either Kerberos, the recommended method, or MS-CHAPv2) or RADIUS (in which case, fill in the fields with information about your RADIUS servers).

13. In the IPSec Authentication area, click the radio button corresponding to the type of authentication to use: either Shared Secret (in which case, type a string that will be the shared secret for both server and clients) or Certificate (in which case, choose a certificate from the pop-up menu). Certificate is the better choice if possible.

14. Click Save.

15. To turn on L2TP over IPsec now that it's been configured, click the Start VPN button. If PPTP is already running, the VPN service is already active, so you can skip this step.

Note

If you haven't already done so, be sure to open the necessary ports in your firewall for your VPN service(s), as described earlier in this chapter. ■

Configuring PPTP

To enable VPN access using PPTP, follow these steps:

1. Open Server Admin, which is located in `/Applications/Server`.

2. In the sidebar on the left, select your server.

3. If no services are listed under the server name, click the disclosure triangle next to the server name to reveal them.

4. If the service names are dimmed, choose Server ⇨ Connect, type your username and password if they're not already filled in, and then click Connect. The list of services refreshes, and those currently running appear with a green dot next to them.

5. In the sidebar under your server name, select VPN. If VPN doesn't appear in the list, you must first add it by selecting your server name, clicking Settings, clicking Services, clicking the check box next to VPN, and then clicking Save.

6. Click the Settings button on the toolbar.

7. Click the PPTP tab, shown in Figure 31.7.

8. Click the Enable PPTP check box.

9. In the Starting IP address field, type the first IP address in the range that will be assigned to VPN users. Apple's suggested value is **192.168.0.128**.

10. In the Ending IP address field, type the last IP address in the range that will be assigned to VPN users. Apple's suggested value is **192.168.0.255**.

Note

If you use both L2TP over IPsec and PPTP, you must select different address ranges for each one in these two steps. ■

FIGURE 31.7

To use PPTP for VPN services, configure the options in this pane.

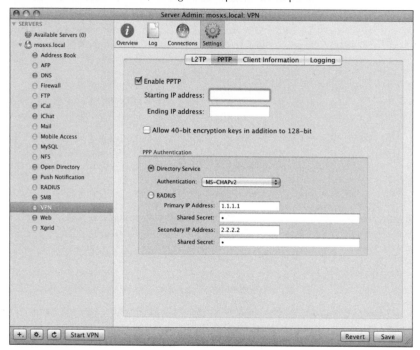

11. **Only if you have a client that requires it, click the Allow 40-bit encryption keys in addition to 128-bit check box.** This option dramatically reduces your security, so it should be avoided unless necessary.

12. **In the PPP Authentication area, click the radio button corresponding to the type of authentication to use: either Directory Service (in which case, choose either Kerberos, the recommended method, or MS-CHAPv2) or RADIUS (in which case, fill in the fields with information about your RADIUS servers).**

13. **Click Save.**

14. **To turn on PPTP now that it's been configured, click the Start VPN button.** If L2TP over IPsec is already running, the VPN service is already active, so you can skip this step.

Restricting VPN access

If you want only certain users or groups to be able to use VPN services, you can specify access using an SACL, just as you can for file sharing and other services.

To restrict VPN access using a SACL, follow these steps:

1. **Open Server Admin, which is located in** `/Applications/Server`.

2. **In the sidebar on the left, select your server.**

3. If no services are listed under the server name, click the disclosure triangle next to the server name to reveal them.

4. If the service names are dimmed, choose Server ➪ Connect, type your username and password if they're not already filled in, and then click Connect. The list of services refreshes, and those currently running appear with a green dot next to them.

5. Click the Access button on the toolbar.

6. Click the Services tab.

7. On the left side, click the For selected services below radio button.

8. Select VPN from the Service list on the left.

9. On the right side, click the Allow only users and groups below radio button.

10. Click the Add (+) button at the bottom to open the Users & Groups palette. In this palette, click either the Users button or the Groups button and then drag an entity to the list of users and groups in the main window. To remove a user or group, select it and then click the Remove (–) button.

11. Click Save at the bottom of the window. The new settings become active immediately.

Note

You can also block VPN access for users with certain IP addresses by creating a firewall rule, as discussed earlier in this chapter. ∎

Tip

To learn more about managing VPN services, read Apple's free PDF *Network Services Administration*, available at `www.apple.com/server/macosx/resources/documentation.html`. ∎

Securing Address Book Server

One of the new features Apple introduced in Snow Leopard Server was Address Book Server, which enables an organization to host individual and group address books on a server, making them available both to the Address Book application in Mac OS X and, optionally, via the web. Address Book Server can be used instead of or in addition to LDAP for contact information, although LDAP is still used for directory services.

The security features you can configure for Address Book Server are the authentication method(s) supported and whether to use SSL, resulting in encrypted transfer of all contact data across the network. In general, SSL is unnecessary if all your users are on the local network. For remote users, it adds a small amount of security, but because the types of data typically sent and received by this service aren't normally highly confidential, you may feel that the bother outweighs the benefit.

Before you can activate SSL for Address Book Server, you must already have a valid SSL certificate installed for the domain name in question.

To configure Address Book Server's security features, follow these steps:

1. Open Server Admin, which is located in `/Applications/Server`.

2. In the sidebar on the left, select your server.

3. If no services are listed under the server name, click the disclosure triangle next to the server name to reveal them.

4. **If the service names are dimmed, choose Server⇨Connect, type your username and password if they're not already filled in, and then click Connect.** The list of services refreshes, and those currently running appear with a green dot next to them.

5. **In the sidebar under your server name, select Address Book.** If Address Book doesn't appear in the list, you must first add it by selecting your server name, clicking Settings, clicking Services, clicking the check box next to Address Book, and then clicking Save.

6. **If the Address Book Server isn't already running (that is, the dot next to Address Book in the list isn't green), click the Start Address Book button at the bottom of the window.**

7. **Click the Settings button on the toolbar.**

8. **Click the Authentication tab, shown in Figure 31.8.**

9. **From the Type pop-up menu, choose one of the following authentication methods:**

   - **Digest.** Uses only the HTTP Digest method of authentication, which securely encrypts passwords

   - **Kerberos.** Uses only Kerberos for authentication (which, in turn, requires that Kerberos be set up correctly in Open Directory)

   - **Any Method.** Uses either Digest or Kerberos, as requested by the client. Because both available methods are secure, Any Method is a reasonable default choice; switch to Kerberos only if you're sure that all clients can use it.

FIGURE 31.8

In this pane, set up authentication and encryption options for Address Book Server.

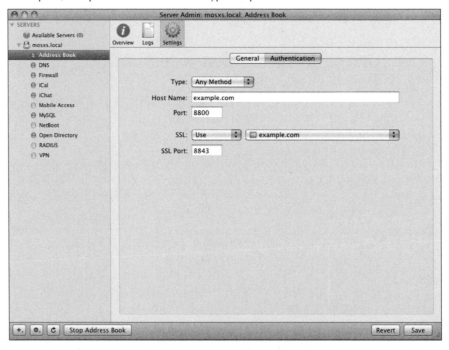

10. **In the Host Name field, type a fully qualified domain name for the Address Book Server, if different from the default name.** The hostname in this field must have valid, matching forward and reverse DNS entries.

11. **Optionally, in the Port field, type a new port number.** In most cases, the default value of 8800 is fine.

12. **From the SSL pop-up menu, choose one of the following options:**

    - **Use.** Requires users to connect via SSL

    - **Redirect.** Requires the use of SSL but automatically redirects users connecting to the standard port to the secure port used by SSL

    - **Don't Use.** Disables SSL

13. **From the pop-up menu to the right of the SSL menu, choose an SSL certificate.**

14. **Optionally, in the SSL Port field, type a new port number.** In most cases, the default value of 8843 is fine.

15. **Click Save.** A dialog box opens, asking if you want to restart Address Book Server now.

16. **Click Restart.** Address Book Server restarts, and the new settings become active immediately.

Securing iCal Server

iCal Server is Mac OS X Server's shared calendar and scheduling service, which lets users and groups access centrally stored calendar data — either using a desktop program such as iCal on Mac OS X, Mozilla Sunbird (www.mozilla.org/projects/calendar/sunbird) on almost any platform, or an optional web-based interface.

The security features you can configure for iCal Server are identical to those of Address Book Server: the authentication method(s) supported and whether to use SSL, resulting in encrypted transfer of all calendar data across the network. If you feel it's essential to protect your calendar data from the possibility of being sniffed by someone watching the Internet traffic between your server and (presumably remote) users, SSL provides an easy way to do that — but for most installations, it's not essential.

Before you can activate SSL for iCal Server, you must already have a valid SSL certificate installed for the domain name in question.

To configure iCal Server's security features, follow these steps:

1. **Open Server Admin, which is located in** /Applications/Server.

2. **In the sidebar on the left, select your server.**

3. **If no services are listed under the server name, click the disclosure triangle next to the server name to reveal them.**

4. **If the service names are dimmed, choose Server ➪ Connect, type your username and password if they're not already filled in, and then click Connect.** The list of services refreshes, and those currently running appear with a green dot next to them.

5. **In the sidebar under your server name, select iCal.** If iCal doesn't appear in the list, you must first add it by selecting your server name, clicking Settings, clicking Services, clicking the check box next to iCal, and then clicking Save.

6. **If iCal Server isn't already running (that is, the dot next to iCal in the list isn't green), click the Start iCal button at the bottom of the window.**

7. **Click the Settings button on the toolbar.**

8. **Click the Authentication tab, shown in Figure 31.9.**

9. **From the Type pop-up menu, choose one of the following authentication methods:**

   - **Digest.** Uses only the HTTP Digest method of authentication, which securely encrypts passwords

   - **Kerberos.** Uses only Kerberos for authentication (which, in turn, requires that Kerberos be set up correctly in Open Directory)

   - **Any Method.** Uses either Digest or Kerberos, as requested by the client. Because both available methods are secure, Any Method is a reasonable default choice; switch to Kerberos only if you're sure that all clients can use it.

FIGURE 31.9

In this pane, set up authentication and encryption options for iCal Server.

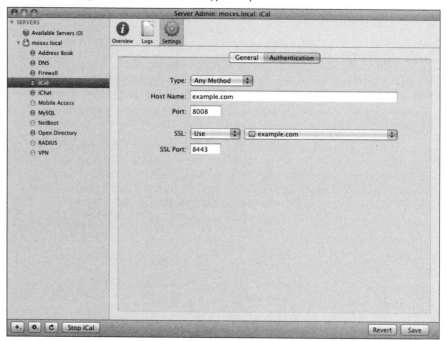

10. **In the Host Name field, type a fully qualified domain name for iCal Server, if different from the default name.** The hostname in this field must have valid, matching forward and reverse DNS entries.

11. **Optionally, in the Port field, type a new port number.** In most cases, the default value of 8008 is fine.

12. **From the SSL pop-up menu, choose one of the following options:**
    - **Use.** Requires users to connect via SSL
    - **Redirect.** Requires the use of SSL but automatically redirects users connecting to the standard port to the secure port used by SSL
    - **Don't Use.** Disables SSL

13. **From the pop-up menu to the right of the SSL menu, choose an SSL certificate.**

14. **Optionally, in the SSL Port field, type a new port number.** In most cases, the default value of 8843 is fine.

15. **Click Save.** A dialog box opens, asking if you want to restart iCal Server now.

16. **Click Restart.** iCal Server restarts, and the new settings become active immediately.

Securing iChat Server

iChat, Apple's instant messaging application built into every copy of Mac OS X, enables users to carry on private or group conversations using text, audio, or video; share files; and even show slide shows, videos, and Keynote presentations remotely. The communication is typically mediated by a server (although direct peer-to-peer connections are usually possible too), and iChat can connect to accounts on AIM (AOL Instant Messenger), MobileMe, Jabber, and Google Talk servers.

Mac OS X Server includes the Jabber-compliant iChat Server, letting an organization run its own service for managing instant messaging. Like MobileMe, iChat Server offers an option to securely encrypt all data transfer — but without requiring individual paid user accounts. It also gives administrators control over which users and groups can use the service and which features are available.

The security features you can configure for iChat Server are similar to those of Address Book Server and iCal Server in that they include the authentication method(s) supported and whether to use SSL (which is an excellent idea and significantly more important in the context of instant messaging than for calendar or contact data). In addition, you can choose whether to enable federation (joining your server to another one so your users can connect to others with accounts on either server) and, if so, whether to require that server-to-server communication be encrypted.

Before you can activate SSL for iChat Server, you must already have a valid SSL certificate installed for the domain name in question.

To configure iChat Server's security features, follow these steps:

1. **Open Server Admin, which is located in** `/Applications/Server`.

2. **In the sidebar on the left, select your server.**

3. **If no services are listed under the server name, click the disclosure triangle next to the server name to reveal them.**

4. **If the service names are dimmed, choose Server ⇨ Connect, type your username and password if they're not already filled in, and then click Connect.** The list of services refreshes, and those currently running appear with a green dot next to them.

5. **In the sidebar under your server name, select iChat.** If iChat doesn't appear in the list, you must first add it by selecting your server name, clicking Settings, clicking Services, clicking the check box next to iChat, and then clicking Save.

6. If the iChat server isn't already running (that is, the dot next to iChat in the list isn't green), click the Start iChat button at the bottom of the window.

7. Click the Settings button on the toolbar.

8. Click the General tab, shown in Figure 31.10.

9. **To add a domain name other than your server's default name, click the Add (+) button under the Host Domains field and then type a domain name.** All hostnames in this field must have valid, matching forward and reverse DNS entries.

FIGURE 31.10

In this pane, set up authentication and encryption options for iChat Server.

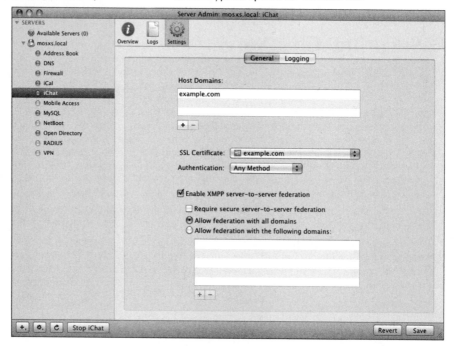

10. From the SSL Certificate pop-up menu, choose an SSL certificate to activate SSL.

11. From the Authentication pop-up menu, choose one of the following authentication methods:

- **Standard.** Uses only password authentication, which means passwords may be sent in the clear unless SSL is turned on

- **Kerberos.** Uses only Kerberos for secure authentication (which, in turn, requires that Kerberos be set up correctly in Open Directory)

- **Any Method.** Uses either password authentication or Kerberos, as requested by the client

12. **To enable your iChat Server to join with other instant messaging servers, click the Enable XMPP server-to-server federation check box if it's not already selected.** After doing so, you can optionally do the following:

    - Click the Require secure server-to-server federation check box if you want to permit connection to other servers only when they use SSL.
    - Click Allow federation with the following domains to limit iChat Server to connecting to specific instant messaging servers. Then, for each one you want to enable, click the Add (+) button and then type the server's domain name.

13. **Click Save.** A dialog box opens, asking if you want to restart iChat Server now.

14. **Click Restart.** iChat Server restarts, and the new settings become active immediately. Users must then configure iChat (or another Jabber client) on their computers to connect to your server for instant messaging services.

Securing the Mobile Access Server

New in Snow Leopard Server is Mobile Access Server, which gives remote users a way to securely access certain services (specifically, IMAP, SMTP, and any service that uses HTTP, such as the web server, iCal Server, and Address Book Server) by way of a reverse proxy server —without the need for a VPN. The Mobile Access server always uses SSL to encrypt data sent and received over the Internet.

To configure the Mobile Access Server, follow these steps:

1. **Open Server Admin, which is located in** `/Applications/Server`.
2. **In the sidebar on the left, select your server.**
3. **If no services are listed under the server name, click the disclosure triangle next to the server name to reveal them.**
4. **If the service names are dimmed, choose Server⇨Connect, type your username and password if they're not already filled in, and then click Connect.** The list of services refreshes, and those currently running appear with a green dot next to them.
5. **In the sidebar under your server name, select Mobile Access.** If Mobile Access doesn't appear in the list, you must first add it by selecting your server name, clicking Settings, clicking Services, clicking the check box next to Mobile Access, and then clicking Save.
6. **Click the Settings button on the toolbar, shown in Figure 31.11.**
7. **To use Mobile Access to forward Address Book requests, follow these steps:**
    1. **Click the Forward Address Book traffic to internal server check box.**
    2. **In the Forward Address Book traffic to internal server field, type the IP address or domain name of your Address Book Server.**
    3. **Click Advanced.** The dialog box shown in Figure 31.12 opens.
    4. **Choose a certificate from the SSL Certificate pop-up menu.**
    5. **If you want to change the default settings for Incoming Port, Address Book Host Name, or Address Book Host Port, type the desired values into the appropriate fields.**
    6. **If the Address Book Server uses SSL, click the Use SSL check box.**
    7. **Click OK.**

Configure which services are used with Mobile Access in this pane.

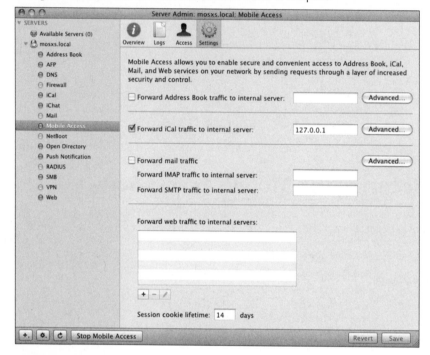

Set up advanced Mobile Access options for Address Book Server in this dialog box.

8. To use Mobile Access to forward iCal requests, follow these steps:

   1. Click the Forward iCal traffic to internal server check box.

2. In the Forward iCal traffic to internal server field, type the IP address or domain name of your iCal server.

3. **Click Advanced.** The dialog box shown in Figure 31.13 opens.

Set up advanced Mobile Access options for iCal Server in this dialog box.

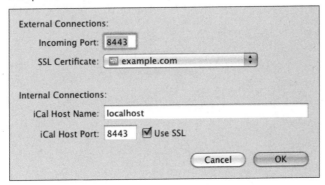

4. Choose a certificate from the SSL Certificate pop-up menu.

5. If you want to change the default settings for Incoming Port, iCal Host Name, or iCal Host Port, type the desired values into the appropriate fields.

6. If the iCal server uses SSL, click the Use SSL check box.

7. Click OK.

9. To use Mobile Access to forward Mail requests, follow these steps:

   1. Click the Forward mail traffic check box.

   2. In the Forward IMAP traffic to internal server field, type the IP address or domain name of your IMAP server.

   3. In the Forward SMTP traffic to internal server field, type the IP address or domain name of your SMTP server.

   4. **Click Advanced.** The dialog box shown in Figure 31.14 opens.

   5. Choose a certificate from both the IMAP SSL Certificate and SMTP SSL Certificate pop-up menus.

   6. If you want to change the default settings for Incoming IMAP Port, Incoming SMTP Port, IMAP Host Port, or SMTP Host Name, type the desired values into the appropriate fields.

   7. In the IMAP Host Name field, type the domain name of your IMAP server.

   8. If your IMAP server uses SSL, click the Use SSL check box.

   9. In the SMTP Host Name field, type the domain name of your SMTP server.

   10. Click OK.

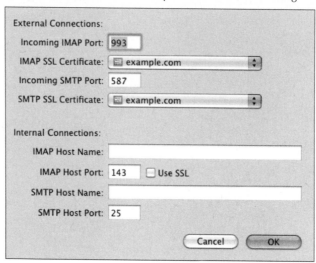

FIGURE 31.14

Set up advanced Mobile Access options for Mail in this dialog box.

10. To use Mobile Access to forward web requests, follow these steps:

   1. Click the Forward web traffic to internal servers check box.

   2. Click the Add (+) button.

   3. Type the IP address or domain name of your web server.

11. Click Save.

12. To determine which users and groups have access to Mobile Access, click the Access button on the toolbar and then follow these steps:

   1. **To let anyone access any of the reverse proxies, click the Allow access to Address Book, iCal, Mail and Web proxies for everyone radio button.** Or to restrict access to certain users or groups, click the Allow access to the selected proxies for these users and groups radio button.

   2. Click the Add (+) button to show the list of users and groups and then drag users or groups from the list to the main window, as shown in Figure 31.15.

   3. For each user or group, click the check box(es) corresponding to the service(s) to which you want to grant them access.

   4. Click Save.

13. **To start the Mobile Access service, click the Start Mobile Access button.** The service starts within a few seconds or so.

To determine who can use Mobile Access, drag users and groups to this list.

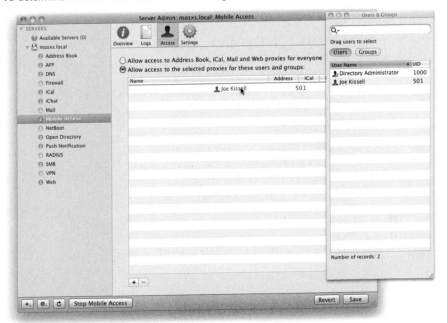

Securing MySQL

MySQL is a popular open-source database frequently used for blogs and other web-hosted content because it's easy to access using languages such as Perl and PHP. Administrators and users can work with MySQL databases either from the local command line (using Terminal), a remote command line (using SSH), a web browser (with the addition of management software such as phpMyAdmin or Webmin), or any of numerous third-party client programs that communicate directly to the server and offer a (semi-) graphical interface.

By default, Mac OS X Server's built-in MySQL server is turned off. Before you turn it on for the first time, you should set a root password for it, which provides unlimited administrative control. Afterward, you can use any of the aforementioned methods to add more user accounts and specify with great precision what operations each account may perform. You can also choose whether to permit direct network access to the MySQL server. This is usually desirable because remote administration is frequently necessary, but it entails a slightly increased security risk. The alternative is to allow only local users and programs running on the server itself to access the MySQL service.

To configure security settings for MySQL, follow these steps:

1. **Open Server Admin, which is located in** `/Applications/Server`.
2. **In the sidebar on the left, select your server.**
3. **If no services are listed under the server name, click the disclosure triangle next to the server name to reveal them.**

4. **If the service names are dimmed, choose Server⇨Connect, type your username and password if they're not already filled in, and then click Connect.** The list of services refreshes, and those currently running appear with a green dot next to them.

5. **In the sidebar under your server name, select MySQL.** If MySQL doesn't appear in the list, you must first add it by selecting your server name, clicking Settings, clicking Services, clicking the check box next to MySQL, and then clicking Save.

6. **If MySQL is already running (as signified by a green dot next to its name in the sidebar), click the Stop MySQL button to stop it.**

7. **Click the Settings button on the toolbar, shown in Figure 31.16.**

Configure basic MySQL security options in this pane.

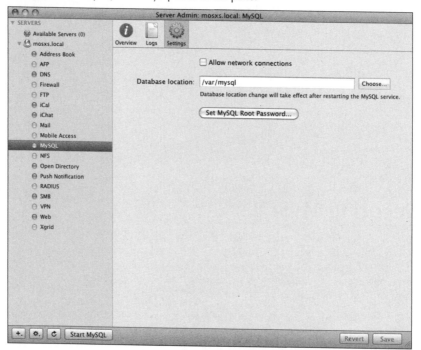

8. **To set the root password, click Set MySQL Root Password, and in the dialog box that opens, type and verify a password and then click OK.**

9. **Optionally, to enable direct, remote access to your MySQL server, click the Allow network connections check box.**

10. **Click Save to save your settings.**

11. **Click the Start MySQL button to activate the MySQL server.** You may see a message that says "Service port may be restricted." If so, click OK and then make sure your firewall is configured to permit access to port 3306. (Firewall configuration is discussed elsewhere in this chapter.)

Securing NetBoot

NetBoot allows a Mac OS X Server administrator to create special disk images that can then be used to boot other Macs over the network rather than from local hard disks. This can simplify the management of large installations of Macs by eliminating the need to install and update Mac OS X and other software individually on each one.

Note

To learn more about NetBoot, read Apple's free PDF guide *System Imaging and Software Update Administration,* **available at** `www.apple.com/server/macosx/resources/documentation.html.` ■

Because NetBoot is used only on local Ethernet networks — not over the public Internet or Wi-Fi — and because the disk images require administrator access to create and modify them, security concerns are minimal. The only specific security control offered is the capability to restrict client access to NetBoot using the MAC address of the clients' Ethernet cards. You can configure either a list of MAC addresses for which NetBoot access is permitted or a list of MAC addresses for which it's blocked.

To configure NetBoot filtering, follow these steps:

1. **Open Server Admin, which is located in** `/Applications/Server`.
2. **In the sidebar on the left, select your server.**
3. **If no services are listed under the server name, click the disclosure triangle next to the server name to reveal them.**
4. **If the service names are dimmed, choose Server ⇨ Connect, type your username and password if they're not already filled in, and then click Connect.** The list of services refreshes, and those currently running appear with a green dot next to them.
5. **In the sidebar under your server name, select NetBoot.** If NetBoot doesn't appear in the list, you must first add it by selecting your server name, clicking Settings, clicking Services, clicking the check box next to NetBoot, and then clicking Save.
6. **Click the Settings button on the toolbar.**
7. **Click the Filters tab, shown in Figure 31.17.**
8. **Click the Enable NetBoot/DHCP filtering check box.**
9. **To permit only specific computers to connect, click the Allow only clients listed below (deny others) radio button.** Or to permit any computer except specific ones to connect, click the Deny only clients listed below (allow others) radio button.
10. **To add computers to the list of those allowed or blocked, click the Add (+) button, and in the dialog box that opens, type or paste one or more MAC addresses and then click OK.** You can determine the MAC address of a Mac's Ethernet card in one of the following ways:
    - Type the domain name or IP address of the Mac in the Host Name field and then click Find.
    - On the Mac in question, open System Profiler, found in `/Applications/Utilities`. In the list on the left, select Network and then select Ethernet in the list of active services in the upper-right pane of the window. The lower pane displays the MAC address, among other details.
11. **Click Save.** The restrictions become active when NetBoot is activated.

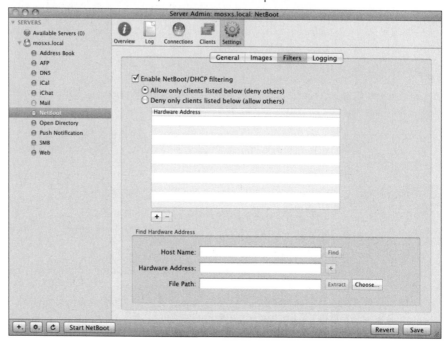

FIGURE 31.17

Filter client access to NetBoot by MAC address in this pane.

Before you can turn on NetBoot, you must configure and share at least one disk image and enable NetBoot on at least one network interface.

Configuring RADIUS

The term *RADIUS* (Remote Authentication Dial In User Service) is a bit of an anachronism in that its primary use these days has nothing to do with dial-in network access. Instead, it's now used mainly as an authorization mechanism for wireless networks. On Mac OS X Server, RADIUS lets you restrict access to your wireless network via AirPort base stations to those who have authenticated against an Open Directory database.

Cross-Ref

For more on RADIUS, see Chapter 16. ■

To set up Mac OS X Server's RADIUS service, follow these steps:

1. Open Server Admin, which is located in /Applications/Server.
2. In the sidebar on the left, select your server.

3. If no services are listed under the server name, click the disclosure triangle next to the server name to reveal them.

4. **If the service names are dimmed, choose Server ⇨ Connect, type your username and password if they're not already filled in, and then click Connect.** The list of services refreshes, and those currently running appear with a green dot next to them.

5. **In the sidebar under your server name, select RADIUS.** If RADIUS doesn't appear in the list, you must first add it by selecting your server name, clicking Settings, clicking Services, clicking the check box next to RADIUS, and then clicking Save.

6. **Click the Base Stations button on the toolbar, shown in Figure 31.18.**

FIGURE 31.18

In this pane, add AirPort base stations that will use RADIUS authorization.

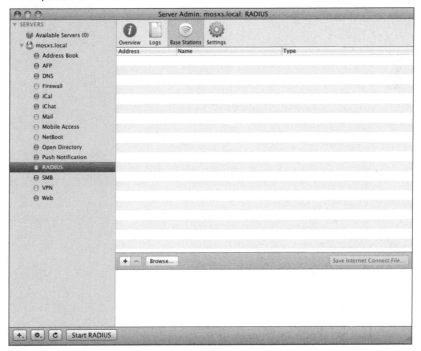

7. **Click Browse, and in the dialog box that opens, select an AirPort base station.**

8. **Type the base station's password and then click Add.** If the base station you want to add doesn't appear in the list, instead click the Add (+) button, fill in all the details requested, and then click Add. Server Admin then modifies the base station to use WPA2 Enterprise security with RADIUS authentication.

9. **Click the Settings button on the toolbar, shown in Figure 31.19.**

FIGURE 31.19

Set up RADIUS security options in this pane.

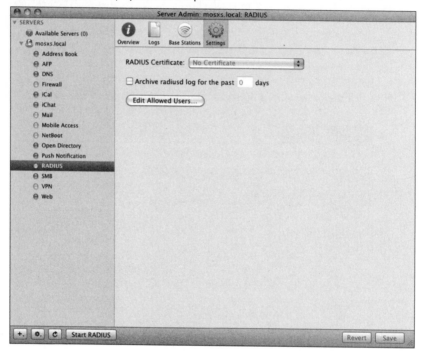

10. To configure RADIUS to use SSL for communicating with base stations, choose a certificate from the RADIUS Certificate pop-up menu.

11. Click Save.

12. **Click Start RADIUS to start the RADIUS service.** It begins running within a few seconds or so.

Summary

In this final chapter, I discussed security settings for the remaining network features of Mac OS X Server. I began with a look at the firewall, going into some detail about configuring it for common usages. I then described the process of setting up and using the VPN server to provide secure remote access to your users. Finally, I touched on the best ways to configure several other network services: Address Book Server, iCal Server, iChat Server, Mobile Access Server, NetBoot, and RADIUS.

Glossary

802.1X A networking protocol that requires each device to authenticate before any network access is granted

absolute mode A manner of using the Unix chmod command in which a complete set of permissions is specified with a single octal string

access control list (ACL) A list that specifies which users and groups can perform various actions with a given file, folder, or volume

access point A wireless router; a device that lets multiple Wi-Fi devices connect to the Internet (or another network) wirelessly

account A unique number or name associated with a certain user who has permission to access a computer or service

adware Software that displays advertising, often by using pop-up windows

algorithm A mathematical formula used to encrypt data (also known as a *cipher*)

application firewall A firewall that filters network requests based on the application sending or receiving data (also known as a *socket-filter firewall*)

asymmetric cipher A cipher that uses one key to encrypt data and a different key to decrypt it (also known as a *public-key cipher*)

authentication The process of identifying oneself to a computer system; for example, by typing a username and its associated password

authentication server A server program that maintains a central database of each user's credentials

authenticator In the 802.1X protocol, a device that confirms a user's credentials as stored on an authentication server and functions as a network switch

authorization The process of granting privileges or access rights for various resources to a user after authentication

bandwidth throttling A feature whereby an application artificially limits its usage of network bandwidth (particularly upstream bandwidth)

base station Apple's term for an access point

best practice A procedure that experts recommend following in order to achieve the highest possible security or another ideal condition

biometric Using measurements of bodily attributes (such as fingerprints or iris scans) to uniquely identify someone

bit mask A sequence of binary numbers that can filter or adjust the values of other sequences

block-level incremental update A feature whereby a backup program copies only the blocks of data (rather than entire files) that have changed since its last run

botnet A massive robotic network for sending out spam, sharing files illegally, running chat servers, or bombarding certain servers or networks with access requests to make them crash or prevent legitimate users from reaching them

bridged networking A networking method for virtual machines in which the guest operating system communicates directly to your router or gateway, getting its own IP address

Glossary

brute-force attack A method of discovering a password or encryption key in which a computer tries every possible combination of characters until the correct one is found

byte-level incremental update A feature whereby a backup program copies only the individual bytes of data (rather than entire files or blocks) that have changed since its last run

caching proxy server A server that stores temporary copies of all files and web pages requested from the Internet and delivers them to one or more client computers

captive portal A mechanism whereby a wireless access point blocks network access until a user has authenticated using a web page

certificate A digital file containing the public SSL key for a person or organization plus identification details and a digital signature certifying its authenticity

certificate authority An organization that vouches for (certifies) the identities of other people and organizations

CGI (Common Gateway Interface) A protocol used by a web server for processing data by way of external programs

cipher A mathematical formula used to encrypt data (also known as an *algorithm*)

ciphertext The encrypted contents of a file or message

cleartext The human-readable contents of a file or message before encryption or after decryption

cold boot attack A method of recovering encrypted data in which someone restarts your computer, immediately uses special software to copy all the as-yet unerased contents of your RAM to a file, and then scans that file for passwords that were temporarily stored in RAM

console Depending on the context, a terminal emulator program, a command-line environment, or the default output destination of a command-line environment

console message In Mac OS X, user-specific messages (those sent by applications being run by the current user) stored in the Log Database, `asl.db`

credentials Information that uniquely identifies a user to a computer system, such as the combination of a username and password

definition In anti-malware software, a technical description of a particular piece of known malware (also known as a *signature*)

degausser A very powerful electromagnet designed for erasing disks

DHCP (Dynamic Host Configuration Protocol) A system whereby a router or central computer can automatically configure other computers with their IP addresses and essential networking details

dictionary attack A method of discovering a password or encryption key in which a computer tries each string on a long list (typically derived from one or more dictionaries) until the correct one is found

digest An encrypted checksum of the text of a digitally signed email message

directory service A network resource that stores and provides access to information about users

disk image A file that functions as a disk when mounted (and can therefore contain other files and folders) but as an ordinary file when not mounted

DMZ (demilitarized zone) A portion of a network that stands between a local network and the public network, typically used to provide outside access to certain server resources without endangering the rest of the network

DNS (domain name system) A mechanism for associating human-readable computer names with their numeric IP addresses

entropy A mathematical measurement of the randomness of a password

escape To prepend a character with a backslash, indicating that it should be interpreted literally

exploit A procedure that attacks a known weakness in a particular program or service on one or more platforms

factor Any of three broad categories of information that can be used (singly or together) to prove one's identity: something you know (such as a password); something you have (such as a smart card); or something you are (a physical characteristic, such as a fingerprint)

false negative A spam message that your spam filter misses, mistaking it for a good message

false positive A legitimate message that your spam filter mistakenly thinks is junk

favicon A tiny icon that appears next to a URL in a browser's address bar

file integrity monitoring The process of detecting when files change compared to an initial state and notifying an administrator accordingly (also known as *host integrity monitoring*)

fingerprinting The process of inferring a computer's operating system version or the names of applications using certain ports by comparing a list of network characteristics with a database of known computers, operating systems, and applications

firewalking A network-scanning technique for determining weaknesses in a firewall and locating routers beyond it

firewall Hardware or software that selectively blocks network traffic

firmware Low-level software built into a computer or other electronic device that contains basic operating instructions

FTP (File Transfer Protocol) A common (but insecure) protocol for transferring files between computers

gateway A device that translates network data between the format used on an outside network and the format used on a local network

GID (group identifier) A number uniquely identifying a group of user accounts

golden master A disk image containing a bit-by-bit copy of an original disk

header Any of several lines of text at the beginning of an email message that provide information such as who sent the message, to whom, on what date, and with what subject

heuristics In the context of anti-malware software, a method of examining files and program behavior for signs of malicious activity

host discovery Any process for examining a network to find all the IP addresses in use (also known as *host scanning*, *network device location scanning*, and *network mapping*)

host integrity monitoring The process of detecting when files change compared to an initial state and notifying an administrator accordingly (also known as *file integrity monitoring*)

host-only networking A networking method for virtual machines in which the guest operating system has networking access to the host computer but can't see the network beyond

host scanning Any process for examining a network to find all the IP addresses in use (also known as *host discovery*, *network device location scanning*, and *network mapping*)

hosts file A text file containing a list of domain names and their associated IP addresses, used in lieu of (or as a step preliminary to) DNS lookups

hub A device for connecting multiple Ethernet devices together that takes all the incoming data on any one of its ports and sends it out to all the other ports

ICMP (Internet Control Message Protocol) An Internet protocol used mainly for sending short error or diagnostic messages, such as pings

ICMP probing The process of examining a network to find all the IP addresses in use by sending a series of ICMP ping messages (also known as a *ping sweep*)

Glossary

inheritance A specification as to whether an ACL entry should be carried over to any newly created files or folders inside it

injection attack An exploit in which someone feeds a program a type of data that it wasn't expecting, causing the program to react in an undesirable (but predictable) way

Kerberos A secure, bi-directional authentication protocol that can enable a user to sign in just once and get access to a wide range of services

key A piece of information, such as a password, that a cipher uses to encrypt or decrypt data

keystroke logger (or keylogger) A program that logs all the keystrokes typed on a computer

LDAP (Lightweight Directory Access Protocol) A protocol for storing hierarchical directory information and accessing it over a network

MAC (Media Access Control) address A string of characters programmed into a device's network interface that can uniquely identify the device on a network

macro A type of program that uses an application's features without relying on any outside framework

macro virus A virus written in an application's macro programming language and attached to a file like other macros

malware Malicious software, such as worms, Trojan horses, keystroke loggers, and root kits

man-in-the-middle attack A process by which an attacker inserts his or her computer between yours and the server to which you're connecting, retransmitting all the data from your computer to the server and vice versa

metadata Extra information about a file or folder beyond its actual content

mode The complete set of permissions for a file or directory

modem A device that converts data between analog and digital formats, enabling transmission of network data over telephone lines or another infrastructure

multi-factor authentication Authentication using two or more factors, such as a password plus a biometric measurement

NAT (network address translation) A method by which a router can use a single public IP address to provide Internet access to multiple devices, each of which receives a unique private IP address

negative loadset In Radmind, files or folders that shouldn't be changed when distributing a system installation from a central computer to client computers

network device location scanning Any process for examining a network to find all the IP addresses in use (also known as *host discovery*, *host scanning*, and *network mapping*)

network enumeration Depending on the context, a synonym for port mapping or fingerprinting or the general process of determining the attributes of a network in order to obtain information that could be useful in network mapping, port scanning, or firewalking

network mapping Any process for examining a network to find all the IP addresses in use (also known as *host discovery*, *host scanning*, and *network device location scanning*)

network monitoring The process of monitoring the data passed over a network to detect unwanted incoming or outgoing information

network scanning Any system whereby one can collect data about the hosts on a network by sending a variety of inquiries across the network and analyzing the replies (if any)

octal Base-8 notation

on-access scanning An operational mode of anti-malware programs in which the software looks for telltale signs of malware as you download or open files or when you mount a new volume

on-demand scanning An operational mode of anti-malware programs in which the software searches for malware only when you explicitly request it to do so

onion routing A method of network communication in which every request for a web page is encrypted and then sent through one or several intermediate nodes — each of which wraps it in an additional layer of encryption — before going to the server

Open Directory master A computer running Mac OS X Server that hosts one or more Open Directory domains

Open Directory replica A computer running Mac OS X Server that contains an automatically synchronized copy of the directory data on an Open Directory master

open relay An SMTP server that permits any host to connect to it, without authentication, in order to send outgoing email

opportunistic encryption A process used by PGP in which the software checks upon sending an email message if the recipient has a public key in your PGP keyring or on the PGP keyserver and, if so, automatically signs and encrypts the message

outbound firewall Software that can watch for outgoing connections and either block you or alert you

packet-filtering firewall Software or hardware that monitors network traffic, selectively blocking or allowing individual packets based on characteristics such as source and destination IP address and port

parental controls A collective term for several technologies Apple uses to let a computer's administrators restrict and monitor actions of individual users

parity In a RAID, blocks of data that enable the array to rebuild missing blocks from any member disk

passphrase A term given to passwords that implies they should be long, complex, or composed of multiple words

payload A set of instructions for taking some action on a successfully exploited target computer

penetration testing A procedure whereby a program attempts to exploit known or suspected security vulnerabilities

PGP (Pretty Good Privacy) A popular public-key encryption tool, which adheres to an open, public standard called OpenPGP

phishing The process of luring people into disclosing their passwords, account numbers, or other credentials by sending email messages directing them to fraudulent websites

ping sweep The process of examining a network to find all the IP addresses in use by sending a series of ICMP ping messages (also known as *ICMP probing*)

port A logical pathway for data communication, identified by a unique number

port forwarding A feature whereby a router takes all incoming requests on a certain port and redirects them to the port of one's choice on one specific device that's otherwise using NAT to connect to the Internet with a private IP address

positive loadset In Radmind, the files or folders to be included when distributing a system installation from a central computer to client computers

privacy A state in which other people can't get at personal or confidential information without your knowledge and permission

private key In public-key cryptography, the key used to decrypt incoming data

proxy server A computer or program that makes requests for information from the Internet on behalf of a client computer and then directs the response back to the client

public key In public-key cryptography, the key used to encrypt outgoing data

public-key cipher A cipher that uses one key to encrypt data and a different key to decrypt it (also known as an *asymmetric cipher*)

Glossary

public-key cryptography Any cryptographic system based on a public-key cipher

RAID (redundant array of independent [or inexpensive] disks) A set of two or more physical disks that are combined in any of numerous ways to behave as a single disk

realm A portion of a website (typically a folder and all the files and folders within it) for which access is restricted and controlled using HTTP authentication

relay An SMTP server used to send outgoing email messages (see also *open relay*)

rootkit A general term for any mechanism whereby malware can disguise itself to prevent detection — often, even by anti-malware programs

router A device for connecting computers or networks that looks at each packet of incoming data, determines the most efficient route for it to get to its destination, and then sends it to the next point on its journey

S/MIME (Secure/Multipurpose Internet Mail Extensions) A standard for digitally signing and encrypting email messages using public-key encryption

security The existence of effective barriers protecting you, your property, or your information in some way

server-side includes (SSI) A scripting language used to serve dynamic web pages

share point A folder or volume that has been shared over the network and which can therefore be mounted as a separate volume by client computers

shared networking A networking method for virtual machines in which the host computer functions as a NAT server, giving the guest operating system a private IP address

signature In anti-malware software, a technical description of a particular piece of known malware (also known as a *definition*)

smeared image A disk image created while files are open and changing, which may therefore not represent the exact state of a hard disk at any particular moment

sniffing Covertly observing network traffic

socket An endpoint for network data communication, identified by a combination of IP address and port

socket-filter firewall A firewall that filters network requests based on the application sending or receiving data (also known as an *application firewall*)

spoof To forge the identity of a computer, email sender, or other entity

spyware Any sort of computer program that collects information about you or your computer and then sends it to someone else without your knowledge and consent

SSID (Service Set Identifier) A string of characters that identifies a Wi-Fi access point

stateful packet inspection The process used by a packet-filtering firewall to identify and track the state of the packets forming a network connection

stealth scanning A method of network scanning in which the scanning tool skips one or more handshake steps in order to tell if a host is alive or a port is open without exposing the fact that a scan is taking place

stumbler A program that locates nearby wireless networks and provides information about their characteristics

supplicant In 802.1X authentication, a device that wants to connect to the network

switch A device for connecting two or more Ethernet devices together that examines the incoming data on any port, determines which port the destination device is connected to, and sends the data directly to that port

symbolic mode A manner of using the Unix chmod command in which individual permissions (such as read, write, and execute) are enabled or disabled for the user, group, and others

symmetric cipher A cipher that uses the same key to encrypt and decrypt data

TCP (Transmission Control Protocol) A protocol that handles data transmission between programs on computers connected to the Internet

tracking cookie A cookie that records data about visits to multiple sites, revealing to each one where a user has been previously

trigger As used by IPNetRouterX and IPNetSentryX, the IP address of a computer that was previously identified as making unwanted requests

Trojan horse A program that appears to be innocent or helpful but which conceals a dangerous payload

tunneling Using an SSH connection to encrypt another kind of network traffic

UDP (User Datagram Protocol) A protocol for sending data over the Internet without prior handshaking

UID (user identifier) A number that uniquely identifies a user account

umask A template that specifies how file permissions are to be set

virus A self-replicating, self-propagating program generally invisible and intended to cause mischief of some sort

voice over IP (VoIP) A method of conducting real-time audio conversations over an IP network; specifically, a system that uses the Internet to carry audio conversations to or from conventional telephone networks

Wake-on-LAN (WoL) A standard that enables one computer to send a signal to another over Ethernet to wake it from a low-power sleep mode

WebDAV Short for Web-based Distributed Authoring and Versioning; a mechanism by which one can manage files on another computer using HTTP

WEP (Wired Equivalent Privacy) An algorithm (now known to be insecure) used to encrypt data sent over a Wi-Fi network

worm A self-replicating program having the capability of spreading from one computer to another entirely on its own, without attaching itself to an application or waiting for a user to transfer an infected file to someone else

WPA (Wi-Fi Protected Access) The successor to WEP, a highly secure standard for encrypting wireless network traffic

WPS (Wi-Fi Protected Setup) A method for securely adding devices to a wireless network without requiring an explicit password

write blocker A hardware device that enables a computer to read data from a hard disk or other storage mechanism without any possibility of writing new data to the device

zombie software Software that turns your computer into a remote-controlled server without your knowledge

Where to Find More Information

T his book covers a wide range of topics, but given the broad and changing nature of computer security, no single reference can be entirely comprehensive. To learn more about computer security in general and Mac security in particular — and to keep up to date with the latest threats and solutions — consult the following resources.

Apple Publications

Apple has published a series of free PDF documents that cover the security features of Mac OS X:

- *Mac OS X Security Technical Brief* (Leopard version): `http://images.apple.com/macosx/pdf/MacOSX_Leopard_Security_TB.pdf`

- *Mac OS X Security Configuration* (Leopard version): `http://images.apple.com/server/macosx/docs/Leopard_Security_Config_20080530.pdf`

- *Mac OS X Server Security Configuration Guide* (Leopard version): `http://images.apple.com/server/macosx/docs/Leopard_Server_Security_Config_v10.5.pdf`

- *Smart Card Setup Guide*: `http://images.apple.com/server/macosx/docs/Smart_Card_Setup_Guide.pdf`

Note

With the release of Snow Leopard, Apple will likely add PDFs to address security features of the new platform. ∎

Take Control ebooks

The Take Control series of electronic books, to which I've contributed numerous titles, covers primarily Mac-related subjects. Most of these books are available as downloadable PDFs that cost between $10 and $15 or as spiral-bound, printed books for a somewhat higher price. The titles that expand on issues covered in this book include the following:

- *Take Control of Back to My Mac* by Glenn Fleishman:
  www.takecontrolbooks.com/back-to-my-mac
- *Take Control of Easy Backups in Leopard* by Joe Kissell:
  www.takecontrolbooks.com/leopard-easy-backup
- *Take Control of the Mac Command Line with Terminal* by Joe Kissell:
  www.takecontrolbooks.com/command-line
- *Take Control of Mac OS X Backups* by Joe Kissell:
  www.takecontrolbooks.com/backup-macosx
- *Take Control of Maintaining Your Mac* by Joe Kissell:
  www.takecontrolbooks.com/maintaining-mac
- *Take Control of Passwords in Mac OS X* by Joe Kissell:
  www.takecontrolbooks.com/passwords-macosx
- *Take Control of Permissions in Leopard* by Brian Tanaka:
  www.takecontrolbooks.com/leopard-permissions
- *Take Control of Screen Sharing in Leopard* by Glenn Fleishman:
  www.takecontrolbooks.com/leopard-screen-sharing
- *Take Control of Sharing Files in Leopard* by Glenn Fleishman:
  www.takecontrolbooks.com/leopard-sharing
- *Take Control of Spam with Apple Mail* by Joe Kissell:
  www.takecontrolbooks.com/spam-apple-mail
- *Take Control of Users and Accounts in Leopard* by Kirk McElhearn:
  www.takecontrolbooks.com/leopard-users
- *Take Control of Your 802.11n AirPort Network* by Glenn Fleishman:
  www.takecontrolbooks.com/airport-n
- *Take Control of Your Wi-Fi Security* by Glenn Fleishman and Adam C. Engst:
  www.takecontrolbooks.com/wifi-security

Other Books

Some other titles (both print and electronic) that cover issues discussed in this book are:

- *Apple Training Series: Mac OS X Security and Mobility v10.6* (Peachpit, 2009)
- *Foundations of Mac OS X Leopard Security* by Charles Edge, William Barker, and Zack Smith (Apress, 2008)
- *The Mac Hacker's Handbook* by Charlie Miller and Dino Dai Zovi (Wiley, 2009)
- *Mac Security Superguide* (Macworld, 2008). I contributed to this compilation of articles from *Macworld* magazine: www.macworld.com/superguide/macsecurity/
- *The Myths of Security* by John Viega (O'Reilly, 2009)
- *Schneier on Security* by Bruce Schneier (Wiley, 2008)
- "Securing Mac OS X Leopard (10.5)," a white paper by Daniel Cuthbert of Corsaire Research: http://research.corsaire.com/whitepapers/080818-securing-mac-os-x-leopard.pdf
- *Security Power Tools* by Bryan Burns, Jennifer Granick, Steve Manzuik, Paul Guersch, Dave Killion, Nicolas Beauchesne, Eric Moret, Julien Sobrier, Michael Lynn, Eric Markham, Chris Iezzoni, and Philippe Biondi (O'Reilly, 2007)
- *Snow Leopard Server (Developer Reference)* by Daniel Eran Dilger (Wiley, 2010)

Online Resources

Of the countless websites and other online resources that cover computer security, the following may be of particular interest to readers of this book:

- **AFP548.** This site (www.afp548.com) covers the use of Mac OS X Server. See especially their security section (www.afp548.com/index.php?topic=security).
- **Ars Technica.** This technology news and analysis site (http://arstechnica.com) includes sections devoted to Apple (http://arstechnica.com/apple.ars) and to security (http://arstechnica.com/security.ars).
- **Network Security Blog by Martin McKeay.** McKeay covers a variety of network security issues, many of which could affect Macs (www.mckeay.net).
- **Network Security Podcast by Martin McKeay and Rich Mogull.** McKeay and *TidBITS* Security Editor Rich Mogull discuss network security issues in this weekly podcast (http://netsecpodcast.com).
- *Macworld.* This magazine and website, to which I'm a senior contributor, covers Mac topics of all sorts (www.macworld.com), including security (www.macworld.com/topics/security.html).

Appendix: Where to Find More Information

- **Schneier.com.** The website of security expert Bruce Schneier (www.schneier.com) should be required reading for anyone interested in security. See especially his blog Schneier on Security (www.schneier.com/blog) and his Crypto-Gram Security Newsletter (www.schneier.com/crypto-gram.html).

- **SecureMac.** This Mac security website (www.securemac.com) also distributes MacScan, an anti-malware program discussed in Chapter 14.

- *TidBITS.* Since 1990, TidBITS (www.tidbits.com/), of which I currently serve as senior editor, has covered topics involving the Mac and the Internet. See in particular their Safe Computing topic (http://db.tidbits.com/section/security).

Index

Index

Index

Index

Index

Index

Index

Index

Index

Index

Index

Index

Index